CD-ROM included in book.

Rendering with Radiance

The Art and Science of Lighting Visualization

The Morgan Kaufmann Series in Computer Graphics and Geometric Modeling

Series Editor, Brian A. Barsky

Rendering with Radiance: The Art and Science of Lighting Visualization
Greg Ward Larson and Rob Shakespeare

Introduction to Implicit Surfaces
Edited by Jules Bloomenthal

Wavelets for Computer Graphics: Theory and Applications
Eric J. Stollniz, Tony D. DeRose, and David H. Salesin

Jim Blinn's Corner: A Trip Down the Graphics Pipeline
Jim Blinn

Interactive Curves and Surfaces: A Multimedia Tutorial of CAGD
Alyn Rockwood and Peter Chambers

Principles of Digital Image Synthesis
Andrew S. Glassner

Radiosity & Global Illumination
Francois X. Sillion and Claude Puech

Knotty: A B-Spline Visualization Program
Jonathan Yen

User Interface Management Systems: Models and Algorithms
Dan R. Olsen, Jr.

Making Them Move: Mechanics, Control, and Animation of Articulated Figures
Edited by Norman I. Badler, Brian A. Barsky, and David Zeltzer

Geometric and Solid Modeling: An Introduction
Christoph M. Hoffmann

An Introduction to Splines for Use in Computer Graphics and Geometric Modeling
Richard H. Bartels, John C. Beatty, and Brian A. Barsky

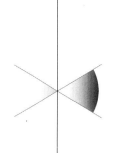

Rendering with Radiance

The Art and Science of Lighting Visualization

Greg Ward Larson & Rob Shakespeare

with additional material by

Charles Ehrlich
John Mardaljevic
Erich Phillips
Peter Apian-Bennewitz

MK®

MORGAN KAUFMANN PUBLISHERS
San Francisco, California

Sponsoring Editor	Diane D. Cerra
Director of Production and Manufacturing	Yonie Overton
Production Editor	Edward Wade
Production Assistant	Pamela Sullivan
Assistant Editor	Marilyn Uffner Alan
Cover Design	Ross Carron Design
Text Design, Color Insert Preparation	Mark Ong, Side By Side Studios
Illustration	Illustrious Interactive
Composition	Patty Rozycki
Copyeditor	Judith Abrahms
Proofreader	Ken DellaPenta
Indexer	Steve Rath
Printer	Courier Corporation

Morgan Kaufmann Publishers, Inc.
Editorial and Sales Office
340 Pine Street, Sixth Floor
San Francisco, CA 94104-3205
USA

Telephone	415-392-2665
Facsimile	415-982-2665
Email	mkp@mkp.com
Website	*www.mkp.com*
Order toll free	800-745-7323

02 01 00 99 98 5 4 3 2 1

Library of Congress Cataloging-in-Publication Data

Larson, Greg Ward.
Rendering with Radiance : the art and science of lighting visualization / Greg Ward Larson & Rob Shakespeare.
p. cm.
Includes bibliographical references and index.
ISBN-1-55860-499-5
1. Lighting, Architectural and decorative—Data processing.
2. Light—Computer simulation 3. Radiance (Computer program)
I. Shakespeare, Rob
TH7703.L284 1998
621.32'0285'5369--dc21 98-12223
CIP

To all who passionately practice the lighting art, especially Marie.

—Rob Shakespeare

To Nature, who gives us marvelous complexity, all the while making it look easy.

—Greg Ward Larson

Of dragons and unicorns this is said,
The one true path is the one that's tread.

A lighting designer may imagine visions in his head, but testing them out and, more importantly, describing and selling them are formidable tasks. I began my career 40 years ago as a lighting designer in the London theatre. At the time such a profession hardly existed there. To convince people to employ me, I built myself a half-inch-to-the-foot model, complete with tiny lights and 120 channels of dimming. It did its job and for several years every show was lit in miniature in my studio.

The ability to create lighting offline, away from the massive costs of the real-world stage or arena, is an astonishing advantage to the designer. The advent of moving "intelligent" lights in the theatre has made the visualization of them almost mandatory. Today the designer has not only brightness to manipulate, but also pan, tilt, focus, color, and so on for every moment of the production. Several lighting companies are exploring lighting simulation software.

Radiance offers a radical new departure for the lighting designer. It's not only photo-realistic rendering but full lighting visualization: visualization that looks good and is accurate photometrically. What limitless horizons open up for the professional theatre lighting designer! With this amazing software, design talent can develop their design and demonstrate to the most industrial and unimaginative of clients the potential that lies in light. This book brilliantly describes the process.

The future of stage lighting lies in three-dimensional computer modeling. I believe that lighting controls will all be built around such visualization engines in the not-too-distant future. The pioneer work described in this awesome book will have a profound impact upon the future of lighting design.

—Richard Pilbrow

The rust-colored shadow of an autumn leaf can move a child to tears. The harsh, sudden glare of a flashlight can make your heart skip a beat. Sunrises bring optimism and hope around the world.

People are visual creatures, and light profoundly affects us. Computer-generated images have the potential to transcend their technology and reach our emotions, if their technology is powerful enough. *Radiance* has that power. Ward Larson and Shakespeare have combined a user's manual, technical reference, and expert lighting advice from working professionals to create a volume of enduring value. With this software and book you can create images that speak with light.

—Andrew Glassner, Microsoft Research

Contents

PREFACE

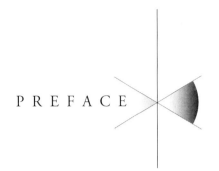

How to Use This Book

This book and its accompanying CD-ROM make up the definitive reference on the *Radiance Lighting Simulation and Rendering System*. This suite of UNIX programs was developed over the course of 10 years, under funding from the U.S. Department of Energy and the Swiss federal government, primarily by the first author, Greg Ward Larson. Although *Radiance* is now available commercially for other operating systems, the free version is still available with C source code only for UNIX, so this version is the one we focus on in this book (specifically, release 3.1). New releases will be made available from the *Radiance* Website for the foreseeable future, at *radsite.lbl.gov/radiance/*. There are currently no restrictions (or warranties) on the use of *Radiance* for any application, public or private, but the software itself may not be resold or distributed without a license from the Regents of the University of California, who hold the copyright. (See the notice at the end of the book for details.)

What Is *Radiance*?

Radiance is a collection of fifty-odd programs that do everything from object modeling to point calculation, rendering, image processing, and display. The system was originally developed as a research tool to explore advanced rendering techniques for lighting design. It has evolved over the years into a highly sophisticated lighting visualization system, which is both challenging and rewarding to learn. *Radiance* is unique in its ability to accurately simulate light behavior in complicated environments, which means two things: correct numerical results, and renderings that are indistinguishable from photographs. There is simply no other physically based rendering system, free or otherwise, with as much power and flexibility as *Radiance*.

There are a few core *Radiance* programs that everyone will use, several others that most will use, and many more that only a few will use. These programs will be introduced in the order of most frequently to least frequently needed in Part I (Chapters 1 through 4). The most advanced users may even combine programs to create new functionality specific to their needs, and we will offer some guidance for them in Chapter 4 as well.

Users typically fall into one of the following categories:

- Computer graphics enthusiasts
  People who want the most realistic rendering software available and/or are working with a relatively small budget.
- Researchers
  Graduate students and professors who want source-level access to advanced techniques in rendering and global illumination, or a basis for comparison to their own rendering algorithms.
- Designers
  Architects, illumination engineers, and other designers who need accurate tools for predicting light levels and visual appearance in novel situations and who have the time and energy to invest in a sophisticated rendering system.
- Students
  Computer graphics and design students using *Radiance* as part of their coursework in rendering or CAD modeling.
- Industry professionals
  Professionals working in the arts, entertainment, and litigation who need rendering tools with the latest in local and global illumination methods to obtain results of the highest quality and veracity.

Even if you do not fall into any of the above categories, if you are looking for something out of the ordinary, something that challenges your skills and your imagination, thumb through the pages of this book and glimpse some of the possibilities. The book is divided into three sections: tutorials, applications, and calculation methods. A glossary at the end of the book contains important terms and their definitions, and additional reference materials are provided on the CD-ROM.

Part I: Tutorials

The tutorial chapters were written by both authors. Greg Ward Larson wrote most of the introduction, and Rob Shakespeare, an expert in lighting design who is renowned in the worlds of stage and exterior lighting, created two scenes to introduce users to the concepts they will need for their own lighting studies in Chapters 2 and 3. In Chapter 4, Greg comes back with some simple examples and some advanced ones for users with a penchant for programming and data analysis.

Chapter 1, Introduction, provides a broad overview of lighting simulation and its relationship to rendering, and includes the general principles underlying the *Radiance* system and its design, plus a short tutorial to get the beginner started.

Chapter 2, Scene 1 Tutorial, steps through the construction of a simple cafe scene, introducing the basic concepts and programs needed for everyday rendering.

Chapter 3, Scene 2 Tutorial, demonstrates a more advanced scene, introducing physical light sources, sky simulation, indirect illumination, textures and patterns, complex surfaces, and object generators.

Chapter 4, *Radiance* Scripting Techniques, gives some examples of scripting, which can be used to manipulate scene input and simulation output.

Part II: Applications

The application chapters, 5 through 9, give specific examples and advice for lighting and daylighting analysis, roadway lighting, dramatic lighting, and animation. These chapters were solicited from and authored by experienced *Radiance* users who are experts in these areas. Readers may be interested in one or more of these chapters, depending on their specific needs.

Chapter 5, Lighting Analysis, by Charles Ehrlich, explains lighting analysis methods in detail, including data collection, luminaire modeling, computation, and visualization techniques. Ehrlich has worked with *Radiance* almost from the beginning and has extensive experience in consulting for daylight and lighting design. His tireless enthusiasm and fertile imagination have been responsible for countless new features and program improvements.

Chapter 6, Daylight Simulation, by John Mardaljevic, explains how to accurately calculate values and render with daylight using four progressive case studies: an unobstructed overcast sky, a simple windowed office space, an office with external obstructions, and the same office under a sunny sky. A brief example of the secondary source calculation is then followed by a final case study taken from a real-life design problem involving a large atrium building. Dr. Mardaljevic has worked extensively with *Radiance* and validating its daylight simulation capabilities, and has produced some of the most impressive models ever built with the system's scripting utilities.

Chapter 7, Roadway Lighting, by Erich Phillips, describes roadway lighting applications, standards for roadway lighting, photometric data, visualization techniques, and human perception metrics. Dr. Phillips is an expert in roadway lighting and accident reconstruction, and has used *Radiance* in his work for over six years.

Chapter 8, Dramatic Lighting, by Rob Shakespeare, features lighting applications for theater and exterior structures. Examples are taken from stage productions, nighttime lighting of high-rise buildings, and bridges.

Chapter 9, Animation, by Peter Apian-Bennewitz, looks specifically at animation, describing techniques for view path generation, network process farming, and file management. Dr. Apian-Bennewitz is also an expert in advanced daylighting systems, and has developed methods for measuring and simulating transparent insulation materials and redirecting windows. His experience with animation also includes other rendering tools, such as Rayshade, and he has produced a number of animations on single- and parallel-processor networks.

Part III: Calculation Methods

The calculation methods chapters, 10 through 15, provide details of how the local and global illumination calculations in *Radiance* work, and are recommended reading for researchers, for those who wish to gain a deeper understanding of the system, and for users who wish to obtain the best results. These chapters were written by Greg Ward Larson, who developed most of the algorithms described.

Chapter 10, Deterministic and Stochastic Ray Tracing, is a basic introduction to the calculation techniques and principles employed in *Radiance*.

Chapter 11, Direct Calculation, provides a detailed explanation of the methods used to calculate direct contributions from light sources, including virtual sources resulting from specular reflections.

Chapter 12, Indirect Calculation, describes the methods used to calculate specular, directional diffuse, and diffuse scattering and interreflection among surfaces.

Chapter 13, Secondary Light Sources, describes special methods used for handling very bright indirect sources of illumination, such as windows, skylights, and reflective light fixtures.

Chapter 14, Single-Scatter Participating Media (Mist), describes a new calculation of light-scattering participating media.

Chapter 15, Parallel Rendering Computations, describes methods for parallel computations on multiprocessor machines and workstation networks. Parallel processing may be used for large single-frame images or animated sequences.

Acknowledgments

During a collaborative research project involving the late Gary Gaiser and myself, we discovered the exciting visualization work of Peter Ngai, who, in turn, introduced me to Greg Ward Larson and *Radiance* in 1989. Those first *Radiance* pictures incited a vision that drives much of my work today. Though *Radiance* was being developed for illumination engineering audiences, there was clearly a place for this brilliant set of tools in all walks of the lighting art. With the gracious support of Indiana University, especially Prof. R. Keith Michael (then Chairperson of the Department of Theatre and Drama), Dean Mort Lowengrub from the College of Arts and Science, Assoc. Dean Jeff Alberts from the University Graduate School, and the staff of the Center for Innovative Computer Applications, the Theatre Computer Visualization Center (TCVC) was born in 1992 to advance lighting visualization in the arts. It is through the resources of TCVC that I learned to integrate *Radiance* into the core of my own theater and architectural lighting design process, which has resulted in my facilitating the use of photoaccurate visualization in the instruction and practice of all aspects of lighting design.

My major reason for joining Greg in the writing of this book was to entice and guide others to the wonderful benefits of using *Radiance*. Without the encouragement and editing skills of Marie Shakespeare, this task would have been far too arduous. As she progressed along the *Radiance* learning curve herself, she continually asked, "Why isn't there a book to help me out when you are not around to answer my questions?" Well here it is at last! Thanks to Cindy Larson for being the first to tackle the writing of a comprehensive *Radiance* tutorial. Her work provided excellent insights that helped me to structure Chapters 2 and 3. Thanks also to Ian Ashdown for his careful and detailed critiques of the manuscript and to our publisher for providing such excellent and friendly advice and support.

Rob Shakespeare

A comprehensive list of those who have helped in the development and exploration of *Radiance* would fill a chapter, so instead I'm going to offer general thanks and appreciation to everyone who has ever used the software and written to me about it. You were my inspiration these long years to continue my efforts. (Well, that and the neat pictures.) What started as a bootleg project under the guidance of Francis Rubinstein grew into a sizeable collection of tools I'd be lost without. Besides Francis, I would like to thank Bob Clear for always being there to answer my questions, Sam Berman and Rudy Verderber for supporting my initial work, and Jean-Louis Scartezzini and Steve Selkowitz for their more recent support. In addition to the U.S. Dept. of Energy, who funded the initial development, the Swiss government, the Dept. of Naval Research, and the Federal Aviation Administration have made important funding contributions to further *Radiance* development. For handling legal issues and *Radiance* licensing, I am grateful to Martha Luehrmann, Kristin Weissman, and Viviana Wolinksy.

I would like to offer special thanks to the people who have provided direct help in developing and testing this software and its author: Robert Amor, Harald Backert, Harold Borkin, Paul Bourke, Jean Brange, Tim Burr, Jim Callahan, Simon Crone, Jean-Jacques Delauney, John DeValpine, Michael Donn, Angus Dorbie, Jo Dubiel, Hans Erhorn, Kevin Gilson, Jon Hand, Greg Hauser, David Jones, Ann Kovach, Bob Lipman, Daniel Lucias, Kevin Matthews, Reuben McFarland, Don McLean, Georg Mischler, Richard Mistrick, Martin Moeck, Mojtaba Navvab, Eric Ost, Werner Osterhaus, Mark Roberts, Scott Routen, Martin Thomas, Philip Thompson, Steve Walker, Florian Wenz, and Tony Yuricich. Each of you has provided me with invaluable help at one time or another, and some of you provided it continuously.

A few names are conspicuously absent from the above list, and those are the people who have contributed as coauthors on this book. Since their names are on the title page, I will forgo listing them again here, but these individuals have been very active with *Radiance* for a long time, and that is why I invited them to share the pain of writing a book. You have each earned my undying respect and gratitude. For invaluable help on the Website and in preparing the CD-ROM, I would like to thank Rachel Chadwell, Danny Fuller, Patrick Sibenaler, and Veronika

Summeraur. Diane Cerra, our editor, and Mike Morgan have both played major roles in getting these pages to press, as have Edward Wade, our production editor, Judith Abrahms, our copyeditor, and Ken DellaPenta, our proofreader.

There are a great many kind and excellent people working in computer graphics and lighting research. I would like to thank some of these researchers, who have come to my aid on various occasions: Jim Arvo, Michael Cohen, Anthony Dekker, David DiLaura, Jim Ferwerda, Andrew Glassner, Don Greenberg, Pat Hanrahan, Erik Jansen, Jim Kajiya, Marc Levoy, Karol Myszkowski, Mecky Ne'eman, François Sillion, Michael Siminovitch, Seth Teller, Ken Torrance, and Jack Tumblin. In addition, I have had the great pleasure of working closely with other well-known computer graphics experts: Eric Chen, Paul Diefenbach, Julie Dorsey, Eric Haines, Paul Heckbert, Gary Meyer, Jeffry Nimeroff, Sumant Pattanaik, Christine Piatko, Christoph Schlick, Carlo Sequin, Peter Shirley, and Ken Turkowski. Perhaps less well-known in computer graphics but very big on my list are the individuals who have worked by my side over the years: Liliana Beltran, Raphaël Compagnon, Rosinda Duarte, Karl Grau, Anat Grynberg, Rob Hitchcock, Isaac Kwo, Eleanor Lee, Jennifer O'Conner, Kostantinos Papamichael, Saba Rofchaei, Lisa Sewart, and Brian Smith. Each of you has a special place in my heart.

My final thanks I give to the people who have most changed my life. First, thanks to my wife, Cindy Larson, for all her help and support, and for having the wisdom *not* to coauthor this book while trying to manage two lively girls and a work-weary husband in a small house. Second, thanks to Ian Ashdown for getting me into this mess in the first place, and for helping me out of it. Third, thanks to Bill Johnston for giving me a good start in computer graphics 14 years ago. Fourth, thanks to Dan Baum for giving me a new lease on life at SGI. And finally, thanks to Holly Rushmeier for being my friend and collaborator, through thick and through thin.

Greg Ward Larson

PART I

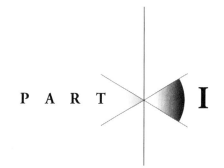

TUTORIALS

CHAPTER 1

Introduction

Radiance is a professional tool kit for visualizing lighting in virtual environments. It consists of over 50 tools, many of which cannot be found anywhere else and, because of their almost endless possibilities, may appear complex to the beginner. To make it easy to get started, this chapter is written as a complete introduction; at the end of it, you will be able to create and render scenes of your own. More advanced concepts are elaborated in the remaining tutorials in this section.

We start off by illustrating what distinguishes *Radiance* from other rendering tools, namely its ability to predict reality. Next, we introduce some of the important tools and concepts that will be needed to understand the material in this book. Finally, we offer a short tutorial, which is designed to give you some immediate hands-on experience with the software.

1.1 Photorealism and Lighting Visualization

Rendering is the process of taking a 3D geometric description and making a 2D image from a specific view. This term is taken from traditional practice in architectural and artistic drawing, whose rules of perspective were developed centuries ago. These rules have been elaborated, refined, and codified in modern computer-aided design (CAD) software. More recent advances in computer lighting models (called *local* and *global illumination models*) have developed further into the field known as *photorealistic* rendering. In most cases, we call an image photorealistic if it "looks as real as a photograph." Although this is a laudable goal, there is still a big difference between something that *looks* real and something that is a good reproduction of reality. We begin this book with a hypothetical example to illustrate this important difference.

Imagine yourself as a third-year design student in the architecture department of a large university. For your term project, you are charged with the design, modeling, and rendering of a three-story office complex. In addition to design drawings, you must produce full-color renderings of the inside and outside of your structure. You may produce the renderings by hand or using computer software. In addition, you must produce a daylight study of one room in your structure, using whatever means you have available. Most students are building scale models of their designs to photograph outdoors, but you want to use the computer both for renderings and for daylight analysis. (After all, the CAD program you are using, DesignWorkshop, has settings for the time of day and time of year and claims to do solar studies.)

The design and modeling phases of your project go well, and soon you have a complete set of drawings to hand in. You then turn your attention to rendering and daylighting analysis. You have some success rendering exterior views of your building, though you are a bit disappointed by the flat shading produced by the CAD software, which gives your renderings the sort of cheesy look so familiar in computer graphics. You do learn how to set the solar position, though, and you are emboldened to attempt rendering the interior for your daylight study.

Much to your dismay, you find that no matter how hard you try, you cannot get anything even remotely believable for your interior views. You finally decide that the CAD software is just not up to the task, and look into some of the other rendering programs at your disposal. You have heard good things about 3-D Studio, so you make use of the export and import options to get your model over to this package and start to play around with it. First, you struggle for some time to get the sun in a known position, since the coordinate system is different and there is no clear mechanism for getting the right kind of light source in the right place. Finally, you get yourself reoriented and generate a view of the interior. Although the results are an improvement over the CAD renderings, they still look very strange, and light is not bouncing around as you would expect. There is a sun patch on the floor, which you expected, but no light from this patch is reflected to the rest of the room. In fact, the rest of the room appears to have a constant illumination that is unrelated to the light coming in. (You try a number of sun positions to verify this hypothesis.)

After spending some time with the 3-D Studio manual, you decide that the only way to get the effects you are looking for is to create what are called "ambient lights," invisible sources of illumination that brighten up those parts of the room you expect to be bright. You experiment with these imaginary sources for a while until you get some results that you think are worth showing to your instructor. Your instructor looks at them, then asks you a very annoying question: "How do you know this is what it will look like?"

You think about this for a moment before realizing that all you have done is create a rendering that meets your expectations! In fact, you have learned nothing about daylight in the process, and you have no real confidence that the actual space will look anything like your rendering. Since the purpose of a daylight study is to determine how well a building lets light into its interior, this method of rendering is useless because it is not predictive. It may be photorealistic, since it looks as if it *could* be a real photograph, but it isn't *accurate,* because it has no physical basis in reality. Light does not interact in your rendering system the same way it would in a real environment, so the results are not true to reality. In fact, you had to introduce completely nonphysical, nonexistent sources into the model just to get it to look reasonable; you spent a lot of extra time and gained no new insights in the process.

Fortunately, you have another option. Using the *Radiance* export facility of DesignWorkshop, you can render your model with a valid lighting visualization program. Between the reference manual on the CD-ROM and the short tutorial at the end of this chapter, you can learn enough about the programs and material definitions to complete your exported model and generate some simple renderings. From Chapter 6, Daylight Simulation, you can learn the basics of accurate daylight calculation, and you will soon be generating some very nice renderings of your interior, renderings that not only look great but are predictive of the way the real space would appear. As a bonus, you can also determine accurate daylight factors at various points in the room, and your exterior renderings will look better as well.

This story illustrates the difference between *photorealistic rendering* and *lighting visualization.* The former is useful in situations where you only want to fool the audience into thinking it's real. The latter is what's needed when the appearance in the rendering must match actual physical conditions. An additional benefit of lighting visualizations is that they often look more realistic as well, since they do in fact correspond much better to reality.

1.1.1 Requirements for Lighting Visualization

The first requirement for a valid lighting visualization program is that it correctly solve the *global illumination* problem. Specifically, it must compute the ways light bounces among the various surfaces in the 3D model. If absolute quantities are desired from the simulation, it must further perform its computation in *physical units*, such as units of radiance or radiant exitance (radiosity).

The second requirement, which is equally important, is that the *local illumination* model also adhere to physical reality. This model describes the way light is emitted, reflected, and transmitted by each surface. Many lighting visualization programs are based on the *radiosity method* [Ash94] [SP94], which typically models surfaces as ideal Lambertian diffusers. This is at best a gross simplification, but it is a very convenient one to make, computationally speaking. The best methods include specular and directional-diffuse reflection as well, as in *Radiance*. (Note: Do not confuse the units with the methods named after them. See the Glossary for further explanations.) Most important, the local illumination model must include an accurate simulation of emission from light sources, because if this is not done correctly, nothing done afterward can save the result.

Past these basic requirements, there are some important practical issues to consider. Although opinions differ, we believe that the following goals must be met by any useful lighting visualization system, and that these capabilities are intrinsic to *Radiance:*

- **Accurately calculates luminance and radiance.** Luminance is the photometric unit that is best correlated with what the human eye actually sees. Radiance is the radiometric equivalent of luminance, and is expressed in SI (Standard International) units of watts/steradian/m^2. *Radiance* (the software) endeavors to produce accurate predictions of these values in modeled environments, and in so doing permits the calculation of other, derived metrics (for all metrics are derivable from this basic quantity) as well as synthetic images (renderings).
- **Models both electric light and daylight.** Since *Radiance* is designed for general lighting prediction, we wish to include all important sources of illumination. For architectural spaces, the two critical sources are electric light and daylight. Modeling electric light accurately means using measured and/or calculated output distribution data for light fixtures (luminaires). Modeling daylight accurately means following the initial intense radiation from the sun and redistributing it through its various reflections from other surfaces, and scattering from the sky. (Section 3.1 demonstrates the use of IES luminaire data and shows how to set up daylight simulations.)

- **Supports a variety of reflectance models**. The accuracy of a luminance or radiance calculation depends critically on the accuracy of the surface reflectance model, because that determines as much as the illumination how light will be returned to the eye. *Radiance* includes some 25 different surface material types, one of which is an arbitrary bidirectional reflectance-transmittance distribution function (BRTDF). Each material type has several tunable parameters that determine its behavior, and many have procedural and data inputs as well. In addition, these basic materials can be combined in all manners with 12 different pattern and texture types, and even with each other. Most important, every material type is based on reasonable approximations to the physics of light interaction with particular surfaces, rather than derived with the more prevalent motive of algorithmic convenience.
- **Supports complicated geometry.** Great efforts are made in *Radiance* to minimize the impact of complicated geometry on the memory and processing requirements. Storage complexity increases linearly with the number of surfaces, and computational complexity increases sublinearly, on the order of the cube root of the number of surfaces or less. To further reduce the memory overhead of complicated scenes, *Radiance* employs *instancing* to maintain a list of repeated objects and their occurrences in the scene. Using this technique, it is possible to model scenes (such as a forest) with millions of surface primitives in only a few megabytes of RAM.
- **Takes unmodified input from CAD systems**. One of the basic precepts of *Radiance* is that scene geometry can be taken from almost any source. We think it is unreasonable to restrict you to a rendering system for creating your geometry when CAD systems are available for just this purpose. We also think it is unreasonable to require you to condition your CAD models by orienting surface normals or meshing surfaces, since this is pointless drudgery and must be repeated if the model is regenerated. The one requirement in *Radiance* is that there be some way to associate materials with surfaces, and this is more a prerequisite for interesting renderings than it is a *Radiance*-specific requirement.

Now that we have outlined what *Radiance* does, let us look at how well it does it.

1.1.2 Examples of Lighting Visualization

Plate 1 shows a *Radiance* rendering of a conference room. The model for this room was derived by measuring the dimensions of the real space and furnishings shown in Plate 2. The similarity between the two images testifies to the accuracy of the luminance calculation, even if no numeric values are shown. Plate 3 shows the same image with superimposed isolux contours indicating lines of equal illumination on room surfaces. A lighting designer or architect could use this numerical information to assess the adequacy of the electric lights in simulation before installing them in reality.

Figure 1.1 shows a comparison between measured illuminance values under daylight conditions and *Radiance* predictions based on simultaneous measurements of the sun and sky components [Mar95]. This attests to the numeric accuracy of the daylight calculation in *Radiance.*

Plate 4 shows a *Radiance* rendering of a daylighted office space. Plate 5 shows a photo of the actual space, taken under similar conditions. The reflectance function of the table was measured with a gloss meter, and these measurements were used in assigning the reflectance properties in *Radiance.* Again, the similarity between the two images testifies to the accuracy of the calculation.

Plate 6 demonstrates some of the material properties that can be modeled in *Radiance.* The candleholders exhibit anisotropic reflection as though the metal had been brushed circumferentially. The table also shows anisotropic behavior because of the application of varnish over the woodgrain, which can be seen in the elongated highlights from two candles. The woodgrain pattern was taken from a scanned photograph and staggered with a user-defined coordinate mapping procedure. Finally, the silver box displays an anisotropic reflection pattern modeled with another procedure that simulates the effect of carving many S-shaped grooves in the surface. Plate 7 shows the same scene rendered with diffuse surfaces, such as one might obtain from a view-independent radiosity system.

Plate 8 shows the interior of a stadium, which was modeled with AutoCAD and then exported to *Radiance* for rendering. The scene contains tens of thousands of surfaces. Plate 9 shows the exterior of the same structure. The trees were included as instances, each one including many thousands of surfaces but requiring only a few bytes of additional memory.

1.2 *Radiance* Tools and Concepts

Radiance is a lighting simulation program that synthesizes images from 3D geometric models of physical spaces. The input model describes each surface's shape, size, location, and composition. A model often contains many thousands of surfaces, and is often produced by a separate CAD program. Besides arbitrary (planar) polygons, *Radiance* directly models spheres and cones. Generator programs are provided for the creation of more complex shapes from these basic surface primitives. Exam-

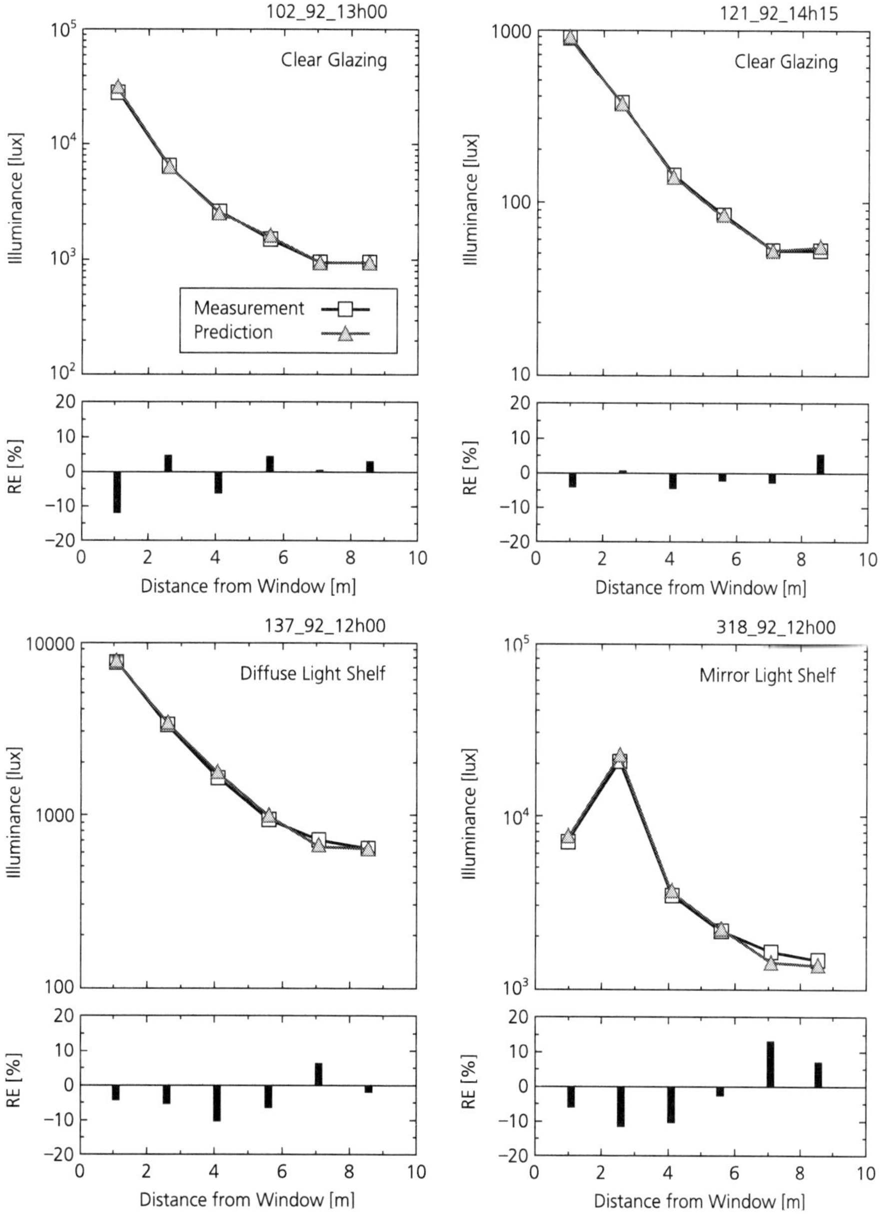

Figure 1.1 An experimental comparison between *Radiance* calculations and real measurements under daylight conditions [Mar95].

ples include boxes, prisms, and surfaces of revolution. A transformation utility permits the simple duplication of objects and the hierarchical construction of a scene.

To be more specific about what *Radiance* does, let's look at some of its features one at a time. We will start by breaking the calculation into segments for clearer discussion. These are

- *Scene geometry:* the model used to represent the shapes of objects in an environment, and the methods for entering and compiling this information
- *Surface materials:* the mathematical models used to characterize light interaction with surfaces
- *Lighting simulation and rendering:* the technique used to calculate light propagation in an environment and the nature of the values computed
- *Image manipulation and analysis:* image processing and conversion capabilities
- *Integration:* interconnection and automation of rendering and analysis processes, and links to other systems and computing environments

1.2.1 Scene Geometry

Scene geometry within the rendering programs is modeled using *boundary representation* (B-rep) of three basic surface classes, defined below.

- *Polygon:* An *n*-sided planar polygon, with no fewer than three sides. A polygon may be concave or convex as long as it is a well-defined surface (i.e., no two sides may intersect, though they may coincide). Surface orientation is determined by vertex ordering. Vertices read counterclockwise from the front. Holes in polygons are represented using *seams*. If the vertices are nonplanar, a warning is issued and the average plane is used, which may result in cracks in the rendering of adjacent surfaces.
- *Sphere:* Defined by a center and a radius. Its surface may point outward or inward.
- *Cone:* Includes the truncated right cone, the truncated right cylinder, and the ring (a disk with an inner and an outer radius).

Each surface primitive is independent in the sense that there is no sharing of vertices or other geometric information between primitives. Besides the above-mentioned local geometric types, there is one distant geometric type:

- *Source:* A direction and subtended angle indicating a solid angle of light entering the environment, such as light that might come from the sun or the sky.

From this short list of geometric entities, you might conclude that the geometric model of *Radiance* is very limited. If it were not for the object manipulators and generators, you might be right. Because generator commands are placed *inline*, their output is expanded as more input, effectively adding to the geometric entities supported by *Radiance*. Some of these commands are listed below:

- **xform**: Scales, rotates, and moves *Radiance* objects and scene descriptions. Combined with the inline command expansion feature, permits easy creation of a scene hierarchy for easy modification and manipulation of complex environments. Also provides an array feature for repeating objects.
- **genbox**: Creates a parallelepiped with sharp, beveled, or rounded corners.
- **genprism**: Creates a truncated prism, extruded from a specified polygon along a given vector. Optionally rounds corners.
- **genrev**: Generates a surface of revolution based on a user-defined function and a desired resolution. The resulting object is built out of stacked cones.
- **genworm**: Generates a variable-radius "worm" along a user-specified parametric curve in 3D space. The object is built out of cones joined by spheres.
- **gensurf**: Generates a general parametric surface patch from a user-defined function or data set. The object is created from optionally smoothed quadrilaterals and triangles.
- **gensky**: Generates a description of a clear, intermediate, overcast, or uniform sky, with or without a sun.
- **replmarks**: Replaces special "mark" polygons with object descriptions. Useful for separating light sources or detail geometry for manipulation in a CAD system.

Although it is possible to create highly sophisticated scene geometries using nothing more than a text editor and the primitives and programs included with *Radiance*, most people prefer to use a CAD program to create their scenes. Translator programs for a few different CAD formats are included with the main *Radiance* software. Others are available from the ftp site *(ftp://radsite.lbl.gov/; http://radsite.lbl.gov/radiance/)* or other sources. Listed below are some of the translators we can recommend.

- **archicad2rad**: converts from ArchiCAD RIB exports to *Radiance* (for Macintosh)
- **arch2rad**: converts from Architrion Text Format to *Radiance*
- **arris2rad**: converts ARRIS Integra files to *Radiance*
- **dem2rad**: converts from Digital Elevation Maps to gensurf input
- **ies2rad**: converts from the IES standard luminaire file format to *Radiance*
- **mgf2rad**: converts from the Materials and Geometry Format to *Radiance*
- **nff2rad**: converts from Eric Haines's Neutral File Format to *Radiance*

- **obj2rad**: converts from Wavefront's *.obj* format to *Radiance*
- **radout**: converts ACAD R12 to *Radiance* (ADS-C add-on utility)
- **rad2mgf**: converts from *Radiance* to the Materials and Geometry Format
- **stratastudio**: converts Macintosh StrataStudio files to *Radiance*
- **thf2rad**: converts from the GDS Things File format to *Radiance*
- **tmesh2rad**: converts a basic triangle-mesh to *Radiance*
- **torad**: converts from DXF to *Radiance* (AutoLISP routine must be loaded from within AutoCAD)

In addition to the listed surface primitive types, generators, manipulators, and translators, *Radiance* includes two additional features to make geometric modeling simpler and more efficient:

- *Antimatter.* Antimatter is a pseudomaterial that can be used to subtract portions of a surface, implementing a sort of crude constructive solid geometry (CSG). CSG normally provides all possible Boolean operations between two volumes, including union and intersection. However, subtraction is the most useful operation after union, and union is provided by default when two opaque surfaces intersect in *Radiance*. (This occurs by virtue of the fact that the inside is not visible from the outside.)[1]
- *Instance.* An instance is defined in terms of a *Radiance octree*, which contains any number of surfaces confined to a region of space. Multiple occurrences of the same octree in a given scene will use only as much memory as that required for a single instance, plus some small amount of additional memory to store the associated transformations for each instance's location. This mechanism is most frequently used for furnishings and the like, but can be applied to nearly anything, from building parts to a collection of furniture to trees in a forest. *Radiance* scenes including millions of surface primitives have been rendered using this technique.

When the geometry has been defined in one or more *scene files*, this information is compiled into an octree using the **oconv** command. The octree data structure is necessary for efficient rendering, and for including geometry with the instance primitive. The oconv program compiles one or more *Radiance* scene description files into an octree file, which the rendering programs require to accelerate the ray-tracing process. In this book, the *.oct* extension is added as a convention to identify octrees produced by oconv.

---

1. Note that there are many limitations associated with the implementation of antimatter. Most notably, two antimatter objects cannot intersect, or chaos will result. It is generally wiser, therefore, to express the desired object by conventional B-rep methods, such as collections of triangles.

The following example converts three scene description files into an octree input file:

```
% oconv materials.rad objects.rad lighting.rad > scent.oct
```

1.2.2 Surface Materials

Although the geometric model is very important, equally important to a rendering algorithm is its representation of materials, which determines how light interacts with the geometry. The most sophisticated geometric model in the world will look mundane when rendered with a simple diffuse-plus-Phong shading model. (Most radiosity programs are purely diffuse.)

For this reason, *Radiance* pays careful attention to materials, more perhaps than any other rendering system. Version 3.1 has 25 material types and 12 other modifier types. Many modifiers also accept data and/or procedures as part of their definitions. This adds up to unprecedented flexibility and generality, and to a little bit of confusion. It is sometimes difficult to choose from among so many possibilities the primitive that is appropriate for a particular material. Let's look at a few of the choices:

- *Light:* Light is used for an emitting surface, and it is by material type that *Radiance* determines which surfaces act as light sources. Lights are usually visible in a rendering, as opposed to many systems that employ non-physical sources, then hide the evidence. A pattern is usually associated with a light source to give it the appropriate directional distribution. Lights do not reflect.
- *Illum:* Illum is a special light type for secondary sources, sometimes called *impostors*. An example of a secondary source is a window where sky light enters a room. Since it is much more efficient for the calculation to search for light sources, marking the window as an illum can improve rendering quality without adding to the computation time.
- *Plastic:* Despite its artificial-sounding name, most materials fall into this category. A plastic surface has a color associated with diffusely reflected radiation, but the specular component is uncolored. This type is used for materials such as plastic, painted surfaces, wood, and nonmetalic rock.
- *Metal:* Metal is exactly the same as plastic, except that the specular component is modified by the material color.

- *Dielectric:* A dielectric surface refracts and reflects radiation and is transparent. Common dielectric materials include glass, water, and crystals. A thin glass surface is best represented using the glass type, which computes multiple internal reflections without tracing rays, thus saving significant rendering time without compromising accuracy.
- *Trans:* A trans material transmits and reflects light with both diffuse and specular components going in each direction. This type is appropriate for thin translucent materials.
- *BRTDfunc:* This is the most general programmable material, providing inputs for pure specular, directional diffuse, and diffuse reflection and transmission. Each component has an associated (programmable) color, and reflectances may be different when seen from each side of the surface. The disadvantages of using this type are its complexity and the fact that directional diffuse reflections are not computed with Monte Carlo sampling as they are for the built-in types.

Most other material types are variations on those listed above, some using data or functions to modify the directional-diffuse component. Other variations provide anisotropy (elongation) in the highlights for materials such as brushed aluminum and varnished wood. Finally, there are a few other light source materials for controlling this part of the calculation and materials for generating *virtual light sources* by specular reflection or redirection of radiation.

All material types also accept zero or more patterns or textures, which modify the local color or surface orientation according to user-definable procedures or data. This mechanism is very general and thus also serves as a source of confusion for the user, so we will spend some time on the subject in the tutorials.

1.2.3 Lighting Simulation and Rendering

Radiance employs a light-backwards ray-tracing method, extended from the original algorithm introduced to computer graphics by Whitted in 1980 [Whi80]. Light is followed along geometric rays from the point of measurement (the view point or virtual photometer) into the scene and back to the light sources. The result is mathematically equivalent to following light forward, but the process is generally more efficient because most of the light leaving a source never reaches the point of interest. To take a typical example, a 512-by-512-pixel rendering of a bare light bulb in a lightly colored room would take about a month on the world's fastest supercomputer using a naive forward ray-tracing method. The same rendering takes about three seconds using *Radiance*. (Mind you, we are talking about a very fast computer here.)

The chief difficulty of light-backwards ray tracing as practiced by most rendering software is that it is an incomplete model of light interaction. In particular, the original algorithm fails for diffuse interreflection between objects, which it usually approximates with a constant "ambient" term in the illumination equation. Without a complete computation of global illumination, a rendering method cannot produce accurate values and is therefore of limited use as a predictive tool. *Radiance* overcomes this shortcoming with an efficient algorithm for computing and caching *indirect irradiance* values over surfaces, while also providing more accurate and realistic light sources and surface materials.

Physically accurate rendering of realistic environments requires very careful treatment of light sources, since they are the starting points of all illumination. If the direct component is not computed properly, it does not matter what happens afterwards, since the calculation is garbage. Most rendering systems, since they do not care much about accuracy, pay little attention to direct lighting. In fact, the basic illumination equations frequently disobey simple physical laws for the sake of user convenience, allowing light to fall off linearly with distance from a point source, or even to remain constant.

The details of the local and global illumination algorithms in *Radiance* are described in Part III, Calculation Methods, Chapters 10 through 15. Here, we will only mention the main rendering programs and what they produce:

- **rview:** The interactive program for scene viewing. The displayed resolution is progressively refined until the user enters a command to change the view or other rendering parameters. This is meant primarily as a quick way to preview a scene, check for inconsistencies and light placement, and select views for final, high-quality rendering with rpict.

  The example below selects an initial camera location (-vp: vantage point) 10 feet along the negative *y*-axis, looking in the positive *y* direction (-vd: view direction) with up in the positive *z* direction (-vu: view up). An ambient light level (-av: ambient value) is added, enabling the shadowed areas to be illuminated in the *scene.oct* data set.

  ```
  % rview -vd 0 1 0 -vp 0 -10 0 -vu 0 0 1 -av .1 .1 .1 scene.oct
  ```

- **rpict:** This rendering program produces the highest-quality raw (unfiltered) pictures. A *Radiance* picture is a 2D collection of real color radiance values, which, unlike a conventional computer graphics image, is also valuable for lighting visualization and analysis. The picture is not generally viewed until the rendering calculation is complete and the output has been passed through pfilt for exposure adjustment and antialiasing.

The example below creates an image taken from a virtual camera located and oriented by the view file (-vf) *scene.vf.* This view was determined, then written into the *scene.vf* file, using functions built into rview. The image will be 512 pixels square, and the program will report the status of the rendering progress every 30 seconds. The output of rpict, namely the picture, is redirected (>) into the *scene.pic* file. In this book, the *.vf* extension is added to view files and *.pic* to pictures.

```
% rpict -vf scene.vf -x 512 -y 512 -t 30 scene.oct > scene.pic
```

- **rtrace:** This program computes individual radiance or irradiance values for lighting analysis or other custom applications. Input is a scene octree (as for rview and rpict) plus the positions of the desired point calculations. This program is often called as a subprocess by other *Radiance* programs or scripts.

As we have mentioned above, rtrace is also employed by other *Radiance* programs to evaluate radiance or irradiance for other types of analysis. For example, **mkillum** computes radiance entering through windows, skylights, and other "secondary sources" where concentrated illumination can be better represented in the calculation using the illum primitive. (Secondary sources are introduced in the tutorial at the end of this chapter and explored in detail in Chapters 6 and 13.) Another program that calls rtrace is **findglare**, which locates and quantifies glare sources in a scene. Here is a list of similar lighting analysis tools.

- **dayfact:** An interactive script to compute illuminance values and daylight factors on a specified work plane. Output is one or more contour line plots.
- **findglare:** An image and scene analysis program that takes a picture and/or octree and computes bright sources that would cause discomfort glare in a human observer.
- **glare:** An interactive script that simplifies the generation and interpretation of findglare results. Produces plots and values.
- **glarendx:** A back end to convert findglare output to one of the supported glare indices. Also called glare.
- **mkillum:** Converts specified scene surfaces into illum secondary sources for more efficient rendering.

The findglare program is particularly interesting because it will accept a *Radiance* picture as input as well as the original scene description for rtrace. Since a picture in *Radiance* contains physical radiance values, it is equivalent to a large collection of rtrace evaluations, and findglare takes advantage of this fact. In the next section, we look at some of the other *Radiance* tools tailored specifically for picture processing.

1.2.4 Image Manipulation and Analysis

As we mentioned in the preceding section, a *Radiance* picture is unlike any other computer graphics image you are likely to encounter. First and foremost, the pixel values are real numbers corresponding to the physical quantity of radiance (recorded in watts/steradian/m^2). These values are stored in a compact, 4-byte/pixel, run-length encoded format. (See the File Formats section of the CD-ROM for more details.) Second, the ASCII header contains pertinent information on the generating commands, view options, exposure adjustments, and color values that can be used to recover pixel ray parameters and other information needed for various types of image processing.

The most essential *Radiance* image manipulation program is pfilt, which adjusts the picture exposure and performs antialiasing by filtering the original image down to a lower resolution. (This is called *supersampling.*) More advanced features include the ability to adaptively filter overbright pixels caused by inadequate sampling [RW94] and add optional star patterns. Here is a list of the most important *Radiance* picture manipulators.

- **falsecolor:** Converts a picture to a false-color representation of luminance values with a corresponding legend for easy interpretation. (See Plate 3 for an example.) Options are included to compute contour lines and superimpose them on another (same-size) picture, change scales and interpretations, and print extrema. This program is actually implemented as a C-shell script, which calls other programs such as pcomb and pcompos.
- **macbethcal:** Calibrates color and contrast for scanned images based on a scan of the Macbeth Color Checker chart. May also be used to compute color and contrast correction for output devices such as film recorders. Output is a pixel-mapping function for pcomb or pcond.
- **pcomb:** Manipulates pixel values in arbitrary ways based on the functional programming language used throughout *Radiance.*
- **pcompos:** Composites pictures together in any desired montage.
- **pcond:** Conditions pictures for output to specific devices, compressing the dynamic range as necessary to fit within display capabilities [LRP97]. Also takes calibration files from macbethcal.
- **pextrem:** Finds and returns the minimum and maximum pixel values and locations.
- **pfilt:** Performs antialiasing and exposure adjustment. A picture is not really finished until it has passed through this filter.
- **pflip:** Flips pictures left-to-right and/or top-to-bottom.

- **pinterp:** Interpolates or extrapolates pictures with corresponding z-buffers as produced by rpict. Often used to compute in-between frames to speed up walk-through animations.
- **protate:** Rotates a picture 90 degrees clockwise.
- **pvalue:** Converts between *Radiance* picture format and various ASCII and raw-data formats for convenient manipulation.
- **ximage:** Displays one or more *Radiance* pictures on an X11 windows server. Provides functions to query individual and area pixel values and computes ray origins and directions for input to rtrace.

In addition, there are many programs to convert to and from foreign image formats, such as AVS, PICT, PPM, Sun rasterfile, PostScript, and Targa. These programs have names of the form **ra_*fmt***, where *fmt* is the commonly used abbreviation or filename extension for the foreign image format. For example, **ra_ppm** converts to and from Poskanzer Pixmap formats. In most cases, reverse conversions (importing into *Radiance*) are supported by the same program with a **-r** option. However, a few reverse conversions are too difficult or cumbersome and are not supported. This is the case for the Macintosh PICT and PostScript formats. In other cases, not all representations within the defined format are recognized, such as TIFF, which contains almost too many data tags to enumerate, including a raw FAX type—the data stream sent over a phone line!

1.2.5 Integration

Having all these individual tools provides great flexibility, but the number of commands and options can overwhelm the casual user. Even an experienced user who understands most of what is going on does not want to be bothered with constantly having to think about the details. We therefore introduce a few executive programs to simplify the rendering process. The most important of these tools are listed below.

- **rad:** This is probably the single most useful program in the entire *Radiance* system, since it controls scene compilation, rendering, and filtering from a single interface. Through the setting of intuitive control variables in a short ASCII file, rad sets calculation parameters and options for rview, rpict, and pfilt, and also automatically runs mkillum and updates the octree and output pictures with changes to the scene description files.
- **trad:** This is a graphical user interface (GUI) built on top of rad using the Tcl/Tk package [Ous94]. To the utility of rad it adds process tracking, help screens, and image file conversions.

- **ranimate:** This control program handles many of the administrative tasks associated with creating an animation. It coordinates one or more processes on one or more host machines, juggles files within limited disk space, and interpolates frames, even adding motion blur if desired.

In addition to these tools within the UNIX *Radiance* distribution, there are a few other systems that integrate *Radiance* in CAD or other environments, and we should mention them here.

- *ADELINE:* A collection of CAD, simulation, and visualization tools for MS-DOS systems, which includes a DOS version of *Radiance*. Integration between components is of variable quality, but it does include a good translator from DXF format CAD files, and it includes LBNL's SUPERLITE program in addition to *Radiance*. This package is available from LBNL and other contributors. See the Website *radsite.lbl.gov/adeline/index.html* for details.
- *ddrad:* A user interface based on AutoCAD, which includes the ability to export geometry and define *Radiance* materials interactively. It was written by Georg Mischler and friends and is available free from the Website *www.schorsch.com/autocad/radiance.html.*
- *GENESYS:* A lighting design package from the GENLYTE Group. It runs on MS-DOS computers. It includes an earlier DOS version of *Radiance* and has a nice user interface for designing simple layouts with a large catalog of luminaires.
- *SiView:* An advanced, integrated system featuring *Radiance* for MS-DOS and Windows platforms. It is available from Siemens Lighting in Traunreut, Germany. It requires the separate purchase of both AutoCAD and ADELINE.

Other integrated systems have been created with *Radiance*, but we are not aware of any that are publicly available at the time of this writing.

Next, we present a short tutorial, which demonstrates the essential commands and techniques of the system.

1.3 Scene 0 Tutorial

This tutorial is designed to give a quick introduction to the system. We do not go into much depth because our purpose is to touch on as many aspects of the system as possible in a short space. The tutorials in the chapters that follow will provide a more complete learning experience and are recommended to all readers who wish to use the system in a serious way. If you find the condensed style of the following tutorial too confusing you may wish to skip to Chapter 2 and return to this later.

We assume a certain amount of familiarity with the UNIX operating system and its text editing facilities. You will need the *Radiance* reference manual on the CD-ROM to understand the following examples of scene creation and program interaction. Text in *italics* is variable input.

1.3.1 Input of a Simple Room

In this example, we will use a text editor to create the input for a simple room containing a box, a ball, and a light source. In most applications, a CAD system would be used to describe a scene's geometry, which would then be combined with surface materials, light fixtures, and (optionally) furniture. To get a more intimate understanding of the input to *Radiance*, we will start without the advantages of a CAD program or an object library.

The scene we will be working toward is shown in Figure 1.2. It is usually helpful to start with a simple drawing showing the coordinate axes and the relative locations of major surfaces.

The minimum input required to get an image is a source of illumination and an object to reflect light to the "camera."[2] We will begin with two spheres, one emissive and the other reflective. First we define the materials, then the spheres themselves. Actually, the order is important only insofar as each modifier definition (i.e., material) must appear before its first reference. (Consult the *Radiance* manual for an explanation of the primitive types and their parameters.) Start your favorite text editor (vi in this example) to create the following file, called *room.rad*:

```
% vi room.rad
#
#  My first scene.
#

#
# The basic primitive format is:
#
# modifier TYPE identifier
# number_string_arguments [string arguments...]
# number_integer_arguments [integer arguments...]
# number_real_arguments [string real...]
#
```

2. In fact, a *Radiance* renderer can be thought of as an invisible camera in a simulated world.

```
# The special modifier "void" means no modifier.
# TYPE is one of a finite number of
# predefined types, and the meaning of
# the arguments following is determined by
# this type. (See Radiance Reference
# Manual on the CD-ROM for details).
# The identifier may be used as a modifier later
# in this file or in files following this one.
# All values are separated by white
# space (spaces, tabs, newlines).
#

# this is the material for my light source:


void light bright
0
0
3  100  100  100
#^ r_radiance g_radiance b_radiance

# this is the material for my test ball:

void plastic red_plastic
0
0
5  .7  .05  .05  .05  .05
#^  red  green  blue  specularity  roughness

# here is the light source:

bright sphere fixture
0
0
4  2  1  1.5  .125
#^  xcent  ycent  zcent  radius

# here is the ball:

red_plastic sphere ball
0
0
4  .7  1.125  .625  .125
```

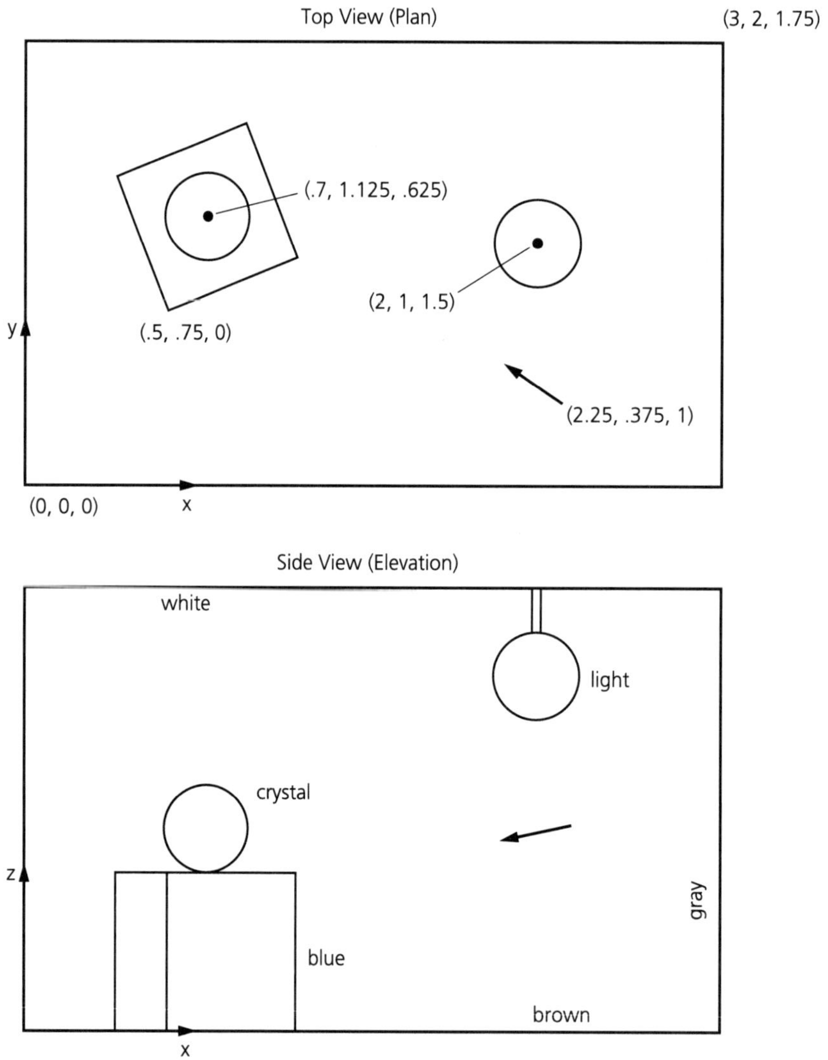

Figure 1.2 A simple room with a block, a ball, and a light source.

Now that we have a simple scene description, we may look at it with the interactive viewing program, rview. First, however, we must create the octree file that will be used to accelerate the rendering process. To do this, type the following command:

```
% oconv room.rad > test.oct
```

Note that the extension *.rad* and *.oct* are not enforced by the program, but are merely a convenience to aid the user in identifying files later. The command **getinfo** can be used to get information on the origin of binary (unviewable) files created by *Radiance* utilities. Try entering the command

```
% getinfo test.oct
```

The usefulness of such a function will be apparent when you find yourself with a dozen files called *test?.pic*.

To make an image of our scene, we must select a suitable set of view parameters telling *Radiance* where to point its camera. To simplify our example, we will use the same starting position for all our renderings and change views only once rview is started:

```
% rview -vp 2.25 .375 1 -vd -.25 .125 -.125 -av .5 .5 .5 test.oct
```

The **-vp** option gives the view point; the **-vd** option gives the view direction vector. The **-av** option specifies the amount of light globally present in the scene, permitting portions of the scene that are not illuminated directly to be visible. Rview has many more options, and their default values may be discovered using

```
% rview -defaults
```

You should start to see an image of a red ball forming on your screen. Take this opportunity to try each of the rview commands, as described in the manual. If you make a mistake in a view specification, use the **last** command to get back to where you were. It is probably a good idea to save your favorite view using the following command from within rview:

```
: view default.vf
```

You can create any number of viewfiles with this command, and retrieve them with

```
: last viewfile
```

If you look around enough, you may even be able to see the light source itself. Unlike those in many rendering programs, the light sources in *Radiance* are visible objects. This illustrates the basic principle that underlies the program, which is the simulation of physical spaces. Since it is not possible to create an invisible light source in reality, there is no reason to do it in simulation.

Still, there is no guarantee that the user will create physically meaningful descriptions. For example, we have just floated a red ball next to a light source somewhere in intergalactic space. In the interest of making this scene more realistic, let's enclose the light and ball in a room by adding the following text to *room.rad:*

```
% vi room.rad
# the wall material:

void plastic gray_paint
0
0
5  .5  .5  .5  0  0

# a box-shaped room:

!genbox gray_paint room 3 2 1.75 -i
```

The generator program **genbox** is just a command that produces a *Radiance* description; it is executed when the file is read. It is more convenient than specifying the coordinates of four vertices for each of six polygons, and can be changed later quite easily. (See the genbox manual page on the CD-ROM for further details.)

You can now look at the modified scene, but remember first to regenerate the octree:

```
% oconv room.rad > test.oct
% rview -vf default.vf -av .5 .5 .5 test.oct
```

This is better, but our ball and light source are still floating, which is an unrealistic condition for most rooms. Let's put in a box under the table and a rod to suspend the light from the ceiling:

```
# a shiny blue box:

void plastic blue_plastic
0
0
5 .1 .1 .6 .05 .1

!genbox blue_plastic box .5 .5 .5 \
       | xform -rz 15 -t  .5 .75 0

# a chrome rod to suspend
# the light from the ceiling:

void metal chrome
0
0
5  .8  .8  .8  .9  0
```

```
chrome cylinder fixture_support
0
0
7
        2       1       1.5
        2       1       1.75
        .05
```

Note that this time the output of genbox was "piped" into another program, **xform**. (The backslash merely continues the line.) Xform is used to move, scale, and rotate *Radiance* descriptions. Genbox always creates a box in the positive octant of 3D space, with one corner at the origin. This was what we wanted for the room, but here we wanted the box moved away from the wall and rotated slightly. First we rotated the box 15 degrees about the *z*-axis (pivoting on the origin), then we translated the corner from the origin to (.5, .75, 0). By no small coincidence, this position is directly under our original ball.

After viewing this new arrangement, you can try changing some of the materials—here are a few examples:

```
# solid crystal:

void dielectric crystal
0
0
5  .5  .5  .5  1.5  0

# dark brown:

void plastic brown
0
0
5  .2  .1  .1  0  0

# light gray:

void plastic white
0
0
5  .7  .7  .7  0  0
```

To change the ball from red plastic to the crystal defined above, simply replace `red_plastic sphere ball` with `crystal sphere ball`. Note once again that the definitions of the new materials must precede any references to them. Changing the materials for the floor and ceiling of the room is a little more difficult. Since genbox creates six rectangles, all using the same material, it is necessary to replace the command with its output before we can make the required changes. To do this, enter the command directly:

```
% genbox gray_paint room 3 2 1.75 -i >> room.rad
```

The double arrow >> causes the output to be appended to the end of the file, rather than overwriting its contents. Now edit the file and change the ceiling material to `white`, and the floor material to `brown`. (Hint: The ceiling is the polygon whose z coordinates are all high. And don't forget to remove the original genbox command from the file!)

Once you have chosen a nice view, you can generate a high-resolution image in batch mode using the rpict command:

```
% rpict -vf myview -av .5 .5 .5 test.oct > test.pic &
[PID]
```

The ampersand `&` causes the program to run in the background, so you can log out and go home while the computer continues to work on your picture. The bracketed number `[PID]` printed by the C-shell command interpreter is the process ID that can be used later to check the progress or kill the program. This number can also be determined by the `ps` command

```
% ps
```

The number preceding the rpict command is the process ID. If you want to kill the process, use the command

```
% kill PID
```

If you only want to get a progress report without killing the process, use this form:

```
% kill -CONT PID
```

This sends a continue signal to rpict, which causes it to print out the percentage of completion. Note that this is a special feature of rpict and will not work with most programs. Also note that this works only for the current login session. If you log on later on a different terminal (or window), rpict will not send the report to the correct place. It is usually a good idea, therefore, to give rpict an error file argument if it is running a long job:

```
% rpict -e errfile ...
```

Now sending a continue signal will cause rpict to report to the end of the specified error file. Alternatively, you may use the **-t** option to generate reports automatically at regular intervals. You can check the reports at any time by printing the file:

```
% cat errfile
```

This file will also contain a header and any errors that occurred.

1.3.2 Filtering and Displaying a Picture

If you are running *Radiance* under X11, you can use the **ximage** program to display a rendered picture. Try the following command:

```
% ximage -e auto test.pic &
```

The `-e auto` option tells ximage to perform a histogram exposure adjustment on the picture, to insure that all areas of the image are visible.

You may notice that the pixels are jagged in the original output from rpict. This is because the picture has not been *filtered*, and filtering is the principal means of antialiasing in *Radiance*. The program pfilt performs this task, as well as adjusting the exposure in a linear fashion, which does not disturb the physical meanings of the resultant pixels. Try the following command sequence:

```
% pfilt -x /2 -y /2 test.pic > testfilt.pic
% ximage testfilt.pic &
```

There is a space between the **-x** option and its argument, but there is no space between the / character and the 2. This sequence has the effect of reducing our original image size by one half and bringing it into the appropriate brightness range for direct display, without the `-e auto` option.

If you wish to print out a picture or convert it to another format, a number of conversion utilities are available. For example, the program **ra_ps** will convert a *Radiance* picture to a PostScript file, which may then be sent to a printer. Try the command

```
% ra_ps -c testfilt.pic | lpr
```

(You may have to substitute another command for **lpr** to send a PostScript job to your printer.) This will print out the filtered picture on a color PostScript printer. If your printer does not have color, simply leave off the -c option for grayscale output. If you wish to apply the same kind of dynamic range compression provided by the `-e auto` option of ximage, you may use the **pcond** program as follows:

```
% pcond testfilt.pic | ra_ps -c | lpr
```

The pcond program offers many advanced features for reproducing scene visibility, and we recommend that you consult the manual page on the CD-ROM for more details.

1.3.3 Addition of a Window

Adding a window to the room requires two basic steps. The first step is to cut a hole in the wall and put in a piece of glass. The second step is to put something outside to make the view worth having. Since there are no explicit holes allowed in *Radiance* polygons, we use the trick of coincident edges (making a seam) to give the appearance of a hole. The new polygon for the window wall is shown in Figure 1.3.

To create the window wall, change the appropriate polygon in the scene file (modified part in italics). If you haven't done so already, follow the instructions in the preceding section to change the genbox command in the file to its corresponding polygons so we can edit them.

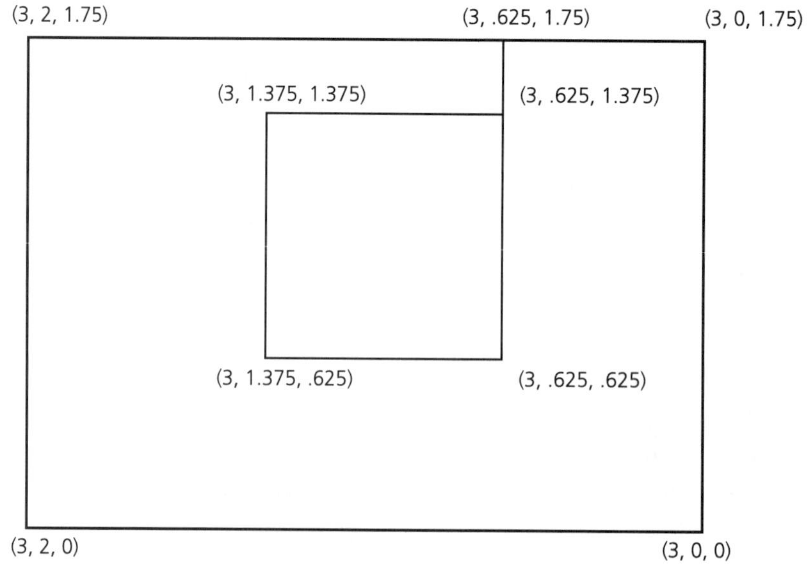

Figure 1.3 The window wall with a hole cut in it.

```
% vi room.rad
gray_paint polygon room.5137
0
0
30
        3      2       1.75
        3      2       0
        3      0       0
        3      0       1.75
        3       .625   1.75
        3       .625    .625
        3      1.375    .625
        3      1.375   1.375
        3       .625   1.375
        3       .625   1.75
```

Next, create a separate file for the window. (The use of separate files is desirable for parts of the scene that will be manipulated independently, as we will see in a moment.)

```
% vi window.rad
# an 88% transmittance glass window has
# a transmission of 96%:

void glass window_glass
0
0
3 .96 .96 .96

window_glass polygon window
0
0
12
        3       .625      1.375
        3      1.375      1.375
        3      1.375       .625
        3       .625       .625
```

The vertex order is very important, especially for polygons with holes. Normally, vertices are listed in counterclockwise order as seen from the front (the room interior in this case). However, the hole of a polygon has its vertices listed in the opposite order. This ensures that the seam does not cross itself. The front of the window should face into our room, since it will later act as a light source, and a light source emits only from its front side.

The next step is the description of the scene outside the window. A special-purpose generator, **gensky**, will create a description of the sun and sky, which will be stored in a separate file. The arguments to gensky are the month, day, and hour (local standard time). The following command produces a description for 10:00 AM standard time on March 20 at latitude 40 degrees, longitude 98 degrees:

```
% gensky 3 20 10 -a 40 -o 98 -m 105 > sky.rad
```

The file *sky.rad* contains only a description of the sun and the sky *distribution*. The actual sky and ground are still undefined, so we will create another short file containing a generic background:

```
% vi outside.rad
#
# A standard sky and ground to follow
# a gensky sun and sky distribution.
#

skyfunc glow sky_glow
0
0
4 .9 .9 1.15 0

sky_glow source sky
0
0
4 0 0 1 180

skyfunc glow ground_glow
0
0
4 1.4 .9 .6 0

ground_glow source ground
0
0
4 0 0 -1 180
```

We can now put these elements together in one octree file using oconv:

```
% oconv outside.rad sky.rad window.rad room.rad > test.oct
```

Note that the above command causes the following error message:

```
oconv: fatal - (outside.rad): undefined modifier "skyfunc"
```

The modifier is undefined because we put *outside.rad*, which uses skyfunc, before *sky.rad*, where skyfunc is defined. It is therefore necessary to change the order of the files so that skyfunc is defined *before* it is used:

```
% oconv sky.rad outside.rad window.rad room.rad > test.oct
```

Now let's look at our modified scene, using the same command as before:

```
% rview -vf default.vf -av .5 .5 .5 test.oct
```

As you look around the scene, you will need to adjust the exposure repeatedly to be able to see detail over the wide dynamic range now present. To do this, wait a few seconds after choosing each new view and enter the command

```
: exposure 1
```

or simply

```
: e 1
```

All commands in rview can be abbreviated by using one or two letters. Additional control over the exposure is possible by changing the multiplier factor to a value greater than 1 to lighten or less than 1 to darken. It is also possible to use absolute settings and spot normalization. (See the rview manual page on the CD-ROM for details.)

You may notice that, other than a patch of sun on the floor, the window does not seem to illuminate the room. In *Radiance*, certain surfaces act as light sources and others do not. Whether or not a surface is a light source is determined by its material type. Surfaces made from the material types light, illum, spotlight, and glow will act as light sources, whereas surfaces made from plastic, metal, glass, and other material types will not. In order for the window to directly illuminate the room, it is therefore necessary to change its material type. We will use the type illum because it is specially designed for "secondary" light sources, such as windows and other bright objects, which are not merely emitters but have other important visual properties. An illum will act as a light source for parts of the calculation, but when viewed directly will appear as if made from a different material (or disappear altogether).

Rather than modify the contents of *window.rad*, which is a perfectly valid description of a nonsource window, let's create a new file, which we can substitute during octree creation, called *srcwindow.rad:*

```
% vi srcwindow.rad
#
# An emissive window
#

# visible glass type for illum:

void glass window_glass
0
0
3 .96 .96 .96

# window distribution function,
# including angular transmittance:

skyfunc brightfunc window_dist
2 winxmit winxmit.cal
0
0

# illum for window, using 88% transmittance
# at normal incidence:

window_dist illum window_illum
1 window_glass
0
3 .88 .88 .88

# the source polygon:

window_illum polygon window
0
0
12
        3     .625    1.375
        3    1.375    1.375
        3    1.375     .625
        3     .625     .625
```

You should notice a couple of things in this file. The first definition is the normal glass type, `window_glass`, which is used for the alternate material for the illum `window_illum`. Next is the window distribution function, which is the sky distribution modified by angular transmittance of glass defined in *winxmit.cal*. Finally comes the illum itself, which is the secondary source material for the window.

To look at the scene, simply substitute *srcwindow.rad* for *window.rad* in the previous oconv command, thus:

```
% oconv sky.rad outside.rad srcwindow.rad room.rad > test.oct
```

You can look at the room at different times by changing the gensky command used to create *sky.rad* and regenerating the octree. (Although the octree does not strictly need to be recreated for *every* change to the input files, it is good to get into the habit until the exceptions are well understood.)

1.3.4 Automating the Rendering Process

Until now, we have been using the individual *Radiance* programs directly to create octrees and perform renderings. By creating a control file, we can leave the details of running the right commands with the right options in the right order to the *Radiance* executive program, rad. Similar to the UNIX `make` command, rad pays attention to file-modified times in deciding whether or not the octree needs to be rebuilt or other files need to be updated. Rad also has a lot of built-in "smarts" about *Radiance* rendering options, and improves rendering time and quality by optimizing parameter values based on qualitative information in the control file instead of relying on defaults. Finally, rad can quickly find reasonable views without forcing you to think too much in terms of *xyz* coordinate positions and directions.

A control file contains a list of variable assignments, generally one per line. Some variables can be assigned multiple values; these variables are given in lowercase. Variables that can have only a single value are given in uppercase. Here is a minimal control file, which we'll call *simple.rif*:

```
# My first "rad input file"
##############################
# First, we must specify the "ZONE" for this
# scene, which gives the x, y, and z dimensions
# of our space.  The "I" stands for
# "interior", since we are interested in
# the inside of this space:
```

```
ZONE= I  0 3  0 2  0 1.75
# xmin xmax ymin ymax zmin zmax

##############################
# Next, we need to tell rad what scene input
# files to use and in what order.  For this, we
# use the lowercase variable "scene", which
# allows multiple values.  Literally, all
# the values are concatenated by rad, in the
# order we give them, on the oconv command line:

scene= sky.rad outside.rad
scene= srcwindow.rad
scene= room.rad

##############################
# Technically, we could stop here and let
# rad figure out the rest, but it is very
# useful to also give an exposure value that
# is appropriate for this scene.  We can discover
# this value from within rview using the "e ="
# command once we have found the exposure level
# we like.  For the interior of our space
# under these particular lighting conditions,
# an exposure value of 0.5 works well:

EXPOSURE= 0.5
# This could as well have been "-1" (f-stops)
```

Once we have this simple input file, we can start using rad to run our commands for us, as in this example:

```
% rad -o x11 simple.rif
```

The **-o** option tells rad to run rview under X11 instead of creating pictures (the default action) using rpict. If you are using a different window system, then you should substitute the appropriate driver module for `x11`. To discover what modules are available with your version of rview, type

```
% rview -devices
```

Once started, rad shows us the commands as it executes them: first oconv, then rview.

Since we didn't specify a view in our control file, rad picks one for us, which it calls `X`. This is one of the standard views, and it means "from the maximum *x* position." As another example, the view `yZ` would mean "from the minimum *y* and maximum *z* position." The actual positions are determined from the `ZONE` specification, and are just inside the boundaries for an interior zone, and well outside the boundaries for an exterior zone. (Please take a few moments at this time to consult the rad manual page on the CD-ROM, under "view," to learn more about these standard identifiers.) We could have selected a different standard view on the command line using the -v option, as in this example:

```
% rad -o x11 -v Zl simple.rif
```

This specification gives us a parallel projection from `Z`, the maximum *z* position (i.e., a plan view). Rather than executing another rad command, we can get the same view functionality from within rview using the `L` command. (This is a single-letter command, corresponding roughly to the "last" command for retrieving views from files, explained earlier.) This command actually consults rad using the current control file to compute the desired view. The complementary `V` command appends the current view to the end of the control file for later access and batch rendering. For example, you can put the default viewpoint into your control file using the rview commands:

```
: last default.vf
```

followed by

```
: V def
```

(Shorter view names are better because they end up being part of the picture file name, which can get quite long.) Move around in rview to find a few different views you like, and save them (with sensible names) to the control file using the `V` command. If you make a mistake and save a view you later decide you dislike, you must edit the control file and manually remove the corresponding line.

Looking through the rad manual page, you will notice that there are many variables we have left unspecified in our simple control file. To discover what values these variables are given, we can use the -e option (together with -n and -s to avoid actually doing anything):

```
% rad -e -n -s simple.rif
```

Some of these default values do not make sense for our scene. In particular, the `VARIABILITY` is not `Low`, because there is sunlight entering our space. We should also change the `DETAIL` variable from `Medium` to `Low` because our space is really quite simple. Once we are satisfied with the geometry in our scene, we will probably want to raise the quality of output from the default value of Low. It is also a good idea to specify an ambient file name, so that renderings requiring an indirect calculation will be more efficient. We can add the following lines to *simple.rif* to correct these problems:

```
# We can abbreviate VARIABILITY with 3 letters
VAR= High
# Anything starting with upper or lower 'L' is LOW
DET= L
# Go for a medium-quality result
QUAL= Med
# The file in which to store indirect values
AMB= simple.amb
```

If we want to create picture files for the selected views in batch mode, we can run rad in the background, as follows:

```
% rad simple.rif &
```

This will, of course, echo the commands before they are executed, which may be undesirable for a background job. So we can use the "silent" mode instead:

```
% rad -s simple.rif &
```

Better still, we may want rad to record the commands executed, along with any error reports or other messages, to an error file:

```
% rad simple.rif >& errs &
```

The >& notation is recognized by the C-shell to mean "redirect both the standard output and the standard error to a file." Bourne shell users should use the following form instead:

```
% rad simple.rif > errs 2>&1 &
```

1.3.5 Outside Geometry

If the exterior of a space is not approximated well by an infinitely distant sky and ground, we can add a better description to calculate a more accurate window output distribution as well as a better view outside the window. Let's add a ground plane and a nearby building to the *outside.rad* file we created earlier and call this new file *outside2.rad:*

```
# Terra Firma:

void plastic ground_mat
0
0
5 .28 .18 .12 0 0

ground_mat ring groundplane
0
0
8
       0       0       -.01
       0       0       1
       0       30

# A big, ugly, mirrored-glass building:

void mirror reflect20
0
0
3 .15 .2 .2

!genbox reflect20 building 10 10 2 \
       | xform -t 10 5 0
```

Note that groundplane was given a slightly negative z value. This is very important so that the ground does not peek through the floor we have defined. The material type *mirror*, used to define the neighboring structure, is special in *Radiance*. Surfaces of this type as well as the types *prism1* and *prism2* participate in something called the virtual light source calculation. In short, this means that the surfaces of the building we have created will reflect sunlight and any other light source present in our scene. The virtual light source material types should be used sparingly, since they can result in substantial growth in the calculation. It would be a good idea, in the example given above, to remove the bottom surface of the building (which cannot be seen from the outside anyway) and to change the roof type to metal or some nonreflecting material. This can be done using the same manual process described earlier for changing the room surface materials.

Now that we have a better description of the outside, what do we do with it? If we simply substitute it into our scene without changing the description of the window illum, the distribution of light from the window will be slightly wrong because the skybright function describes only light from the sky and the ground, not from other structures. Using this approximation might be acceptable in some cases, but at other times it is necessary to consider outside geometry and/or shading systems to reach a reasonable level of accuracy. There are two ways to an accurate calculation of light from a window. The first is to treat the window as an ordinary window and rely on the default interreflection calculation of *Radiance*, and the second is to use the program mkillum to calculate the window distribution separately so that we can still treat it as an illum light source. Let's try them both.

Using the default interreflection calculation is probably easier, but, as we shall see, it takes a little longer to get a good result in this case. To use the interreflection calculation, we modify the scene specification and a few other variables in *simple.rif* to create a new control file, called *inter.rif*:

```
ZONE= I  0 3  0 2  0 1.75
# new exterior description
scene= sky.rad outside2.rad
# go back to simple window
scene= window.rad
scene= room.rad
EXP= 0.5
VAR= High
DET= L
QUAL= Med
# Be sure to use a unique name here
AMB= inter.amb
# One bounce now for illumination
INDIRECT= 1
view= def -vp 2.25 .375 1 -vd -.25 .125 -.125
```

To look at the scene with rview, simply run

```
% rad -o x11 inter.rif
```

Probably the first thing you notice after starting rview is that nothing happens. It takes the calculation a while to get going because it must trace many rays at the outset to determine the contribution at each point from the window area. Once rview has stored up some values, the progress rate improves, but it never really reaches blistering speed.

A more efficient alternative in this case is to use the program mkillum to create a modified window file that uses calculated data values to define its light output distribution. Applying mkillum is relatively straightforward in this case. Simply create a new control file from *inter.rif*, and name it *illum.rif*, making the following changes:

```
ZONE= I  0 3  0 2  0 1.75
scene= sky.rad outside2.rad
scene= room.rad
# window will be made into illum
illum= window.rad
EXP= 0.5
VAR= High
DET= L
QUAL= Med
# Be sure to use a unique name here
AMB= illum.amb
# No interreflections necessary with illum
INDIRECT= 0
# Options for mkillum
mkillum= -av 18 18 18 -ab 0
view= def -vp 2.25 .375 1 -vd -.25 .125 -.125
```

The -av value given to mkillum is appropriate for the outside, which is much brighter, as suggested by the output of the gensky command stored in *sky.rad*. The -ab option is set to 0 because outside the building we do not expect interreflections to play as important a role as they do in the interior (and we are also trying to save some time). To view the scene interactively, we again use rad:

```
% rad -o x11 illum.rif
```

You will notice that the calculation proceeds much more quickly and even produces a smoother-looking result. However, aside from waiting for mkillum to finish, there is an additional price for this speed advantage. The contribution from the sun patch on the floor is no longer being considered, since we are not performing an interreflection calculation inside our space. The light from the window is being taken care of by the mkillum output, but the solar patch is not. In most cases, we endeavor to prevent direct sun from entering the space, and in the morning hours this is true for our model, but otherwise it is necessary to use the diffuse interreflection calculation to correctly account for all contributions. Note that the interreflection calculation is turned on automatically when the `QUALITY` variable in the control file is changed to `High`.

1.4 Conclusion

By now, you should have a fair idea of what *Radiance* has to offer and should even have gained some insight into the way it all works together. If the Scene 0 tutorial left you with some unanswered questions, we recommend that you continue with the Scene 1 tutorial in Chapter 2. After that, the Scene 2 tutorial in Chapter 3 provides some very interesting surprises. Chapter 4 continues with examples of "scripting" in *Radiance.* Part II, Applications (Chapters 5 through 9), gives application-specific advice and case studies. Part III, Calculation Methods (Chapters 10 through 15), goes into graphic detail to describe what exactly is going on inside *Radiance;* this is important to the advanced user who wants greater understanding and control, as well as to the graphics researcher who wants to know.

Radiance has been used to visualize the lighting of homes, apartments, hotels, offices, libraries, churches, theaters, museums, stadiums, roads, tunnels, bridges, airports, jets, and space shuttles. It has answered questions about light levels, esthetics, daylight utilization, visual comfort and visibility, energy savings potential, solar panel coverage, computer vision, and circumstances surrounding accidents. If you can imagine it, and you want to know what it will *really* look like, *Radiance* is the tool that can show you.

CHAPTER 2

Scene 1 Tutorial

This tutorial provides a base from which to begin your own journey into physically based rendering. *Radiance* has no familiar-looking CAD interface. Instead, most of its resources are accessed through text files. At first this might appear to be a handicap in creating and manipulating dimensional objects. However, experience demonstrates that without menus, buttons, and layers, all the wealth of *Radiance* remains accessible. The program is so rich in modeling methods that no interface has harnessed these resources without limiting the user's options. Any object that can be seen or touched can likely be simulated in *Radiance.* That's why it has so much value to artists, engineers, scientists, architects, and anyone who wants to create a photo-accurate image. If the program doesn't have the built-in surface or geometry tool you need, but your analytical and math skills are sharp, you can add your own solution by writing a *Radiance* function.

Certainly there are conversion programs, called *filters,* which turn 3D model files from many CAD programs into *Radiance* text files. It is common practice to import some of these "CAD-sculpted" objects or to convert part of an architect's computer model directly into a *Radiance* file when pressed for time. However, it is likely that if you learn how to write a *Radiance* scene description file using a text editor, you will have greater control over objects, shorter rendering times, and, consequently, the ability to explore variations of your scene more rapidly.

The fastest route to making a picture with *Radiance* is to plunge right into the modeling process. Thus, instead of introducing the tutorial with a detailed overview of concepts and nomenclature, we present only the bare essentials. Once you have become familiar with the look and feel of *Radiance* by working through the annotated Scene 1 exercise, it will be easier for you to engage its full capabilities.

The Scene 2 exercise releases the power of *Radiance*. When you have the Scene 1 exercise under your belt, we will engage the details of mastering the resources of this program to efficiently model and visualize complex environments. We will include examples of physically based electric lighting and daylighting that demonstrate *Radiance*'s global illumination capabilities. If you have had some experience with *Radiance*, skim over Scene 1 and enjoy the second half of the tutorial. As in any rich language, there are many ways to convey the same idea with *Radiance*. Even an experienced user can be intrigued by and benefit from exploring the way someone else builds an object or constructs a scene.

Radiance is written for the UNIX operating system. Though some proprietary versions have been translated to other operating environments, we will assume that you are using UNIX. To help those who are new to this operating system, the first part of the tutorial includes brief descriptions of UNIX commands as they are encountered.

2.1 Essential Programs

Chapter 1 introduced the significant functions and programs within *Radiance*. With each release, new capabilities are added and older methods refined. But regardless of the version, four programs make up the critical path to producing a picture.

First, **oconv** converts scene descriptions into the octree format that the rendering programs use as input. The octree file is viewed interactively using **rview** or rendered into a higher-resolution picture using **rpict**. **Pfilt** can then be applied to the rendered picture to adjust the size and exposure.

Before these programs can be put into action, text files describing the materials, geometry, and lighting of the scene need to be produced. Of course, there are many other programs in the *Radiance* collection, but these will be introduced in context throughout the tutorials and application chapters.

2.2 Description of Scene 1

This Scene 1 tutorial constructs the corner of an upscale coffee shop. It includes a table, a few stools, a vase containing a flower, and a mirror. To keep the example uncomplicated, only segments of the floor, wall, and ceiling will be created.

The purpose of this simple scene is to provide a jump-start example of the image-making process. Only information critical to the construction of the scene is included, so that progress towards creating your first *Radiance* rendering is not slowed down. Remember that the manual on the CD-ROM is rich in details concerning every aspect of *Radiance* and should be used as a companion text while you work through the tutorial.

2.3 Creating the Scene 1 Project Directory

There are many methods of organizing the text files that make up a project. It can become most confusing if all these files are located in the same directory. Similarly, a plethora of subdirectories can also create chaos. In the Scene 2 tutorial, a project organizer called **rad** will be explained, but to expose the way *Radiance* handles files, we will construct and assemble our first image without the benefits of rad. With only a few exceptions, *Radiance* does not restrict the locations of data, provided that the path to a file is included. The directory structure and names that are described here are suggestions that can be modified or built on as you become more familiar with *Radiance* and establish your own methodologies.

To set up for the first exercise, create a directory called *scene1:*

```
% mkdir scene1  [to contain scene description, octree and viewing files]
```

Move to this directory and make two subdirectories, where images and library objects will be stored.

```
% cd scene1
% mkdir pics      [subdirectory for image files]
% mkdir lib       [subdirectory for object files]
```

This structure enables us to separate most of the individual object files from files that are used to assemble and render the scene. Since some complex projects require hundreds of individual files, incorporating a simple directory structure from the beginning will help reduce data nightmares later on.

2.4 Constructing Basic Objects

The complexity of the following examples and the approaches to building them are structured in a progressive manner. Later examples will demonstrate much more efficient modeling methods, but our first priority is to rapidly introduce modeling basics so you can view a *Radiance* image as quickly as possible. Begin by sketching the whole scene on graph paper, in plan view, so that the initial locations of objects and their sizes can be simply determined. An example is shown in Figure 2.1. Of course, the size and location of objects can be altered at any point in the process, but it is generally wise to start with an overview of the layout of the scene.

A few conventions are common to all surfaces described in *Radiance. Radiance* will work with almost any unit of measurement, provided that it is in either an integer or a floating-point numerical format. You can even include objects built with differing units in the same project by carefully applying scale conversions. For simplicity, the tutorial will use decimal feet as the scale for all objects.

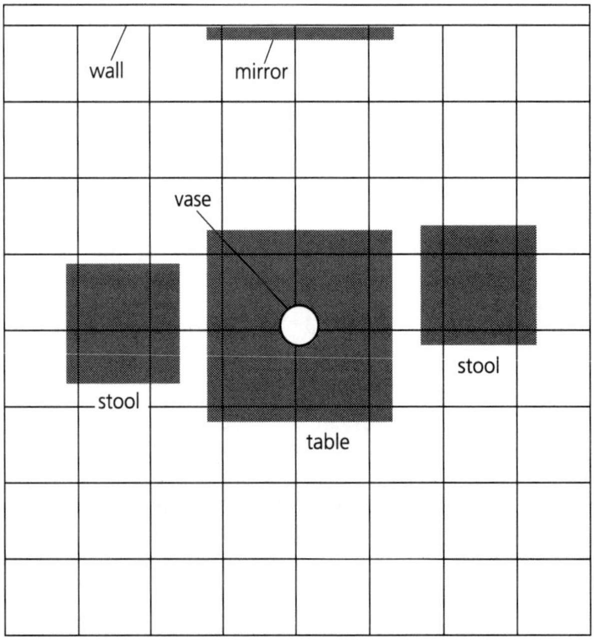

Figure 2.1 Sketch of the Scene 1 plan.

Coordinate System

Radiance requires that surface geometry be described in the familiar *x*-axis, *y*-axis, *z*-axis Cartesian coordinate system, as illustrated in Figure 2.2. Though an object can be created with any orientation in this 3D environment, some of the functions in *Radiance* use defaults, with +*z* for up, +*y* for north, and +*x* for east. An object can be explicitly constructed in its final scene location, but if it is necessary to move it later on, the process becomes very tedious. It is wise to build each object around the 0 0 0 vertex and aligned with the axis that will help you rotate, orient, or translate it to its destination. If you are experienced with CAD modeling programs, this is similar to establishing an insertion point for an object, then moving it into the scene. All rotations in *Radiance* spin around the primary axes.

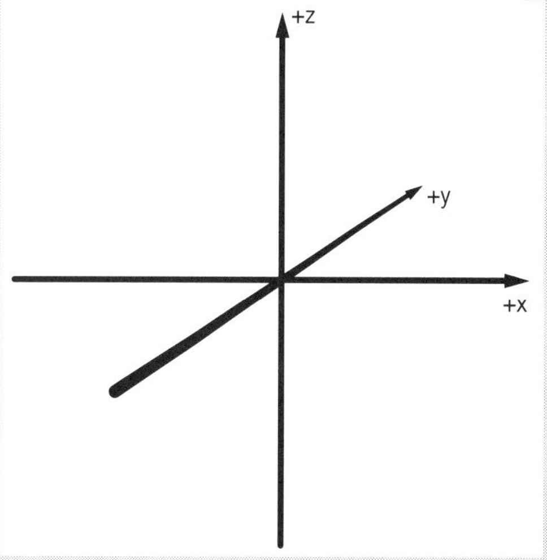

Figure 2.2 The Cartesian coordinate system.

Creating a simple stool begins to reveal these conventions and introduces methods for handling geometric objects. As in nature, each surface of the stool must have a material property that reflects/refracts light so that it can be seen. *Radiance* provides several methods for describing these surface properties. When you are constructing small scenes, it is possible to list the material property definition in the same file as its associated geometry, but in general, it is good practice to establish an independent material description file. This provides an efficient method for altering a material property without having to open and edit all the object files that use it. We will locate the material file in the scene directory.

2.4.1 Creating *material1.rad*

The stool is finished in a satin brown paint. To convey this information to *Radiance*, place the following seven lines in a file called *material1.rad* and save it in the *scene1* directory. Notice that the first lines are preceded by a pound sign (#). Information following a pound sign is skipped by the *Radiance* programs and is called a comment line.

```
# material1.rad
#
# Scene 1 material file
void  plastic  brown_satin_paint
0
0
5  0.4  0.25  0.05  0.05  0.03
```

As in any language, syntax is critical. As different material and geometry descriptions are deployed, pay attention to their formats. Though the descriptions appear strange at first, they all follow a similar pattern and you will eventually find them easy to remember. Our definition of `brown_satin_paint` is in a typical *Radiance* text format.

```
# plastic description:
#
# a material with no modifiers void, made of plastic, named
# brown_satin_paint.
# nothing on this line 0.
# nothing on this line 0.
# 5 variables follow, amount of red, green, blue, specularity, roughness
```

This example exposes the basic structure that will enable us to define surfaces, materials, textures, and patterns. In *Radiance*, these definitions are referred to as scene descriptions. The format for a scene description primitive is as follows:

```
modifier      type              identifier
n             S1 S2 S3 ..Sn     [S is a string or word]
0                               [reserved for future Integers]
m             R1 R2 R3 ..Rm     [R is a real or floating-point number]
```

Scene description primitives inherit properties through modifiers. If the primitive has no modifier, the word `void` is used as a placeholder. Our definition of `brown_satin_paint` has no modifiers. It is a self-contained description, but you cannot see it until it is combined with a surface! As you will see in the *stool_1.rad* file that follows, `brown_satin_paint` will be placed in the modifier location to link its *plastic* material property to the various surface descriptions of the stool.

Plastic is probably the most frequently used material in *Radiance*. Do not confuse this word with the limited applications of its real-world petroleum-based counterpart. Think of it as a basic opaque building material that is not made of metal. Of course there will be exceptions, but wood, concrete, skin, carpet, dirt, and porcelain would all be constructed from the plastic material type. Plastic differs from *metal* only in its reflected highlights. While plastic can reflect the color of a light source in its highlights, the same reflections in metal are filtered by the metal's color. Compare the reflections in a green Victorian gazing ball to those in a glazed green porcelain plate. In contrast to the full spectrum of reflection in the plate, the image in the gazing ball is filtered as though being seen through green sunglasses.

The amounts of red, green, and blue define the reflectivity of this plastic material. If these values are all 0, the material will absorb all light that strikes it and appear pitch-black. Conversely, if the values are 1 (100% reflective), any light that strikes the material will be reflected. These descriptions of white and black are extremes that do not exist in nature. No surface is a 100% reflector or a 100% absorber. To create our `brown_satin_paint`, the plastic material will reflect 40% of any red light that strikes it, 25% of any green, and 5% of any blue. Color values larger than 1 can cause the material to glow, so be careful to place any decimal points accurately!

The specularity and roughness parameters control the way light will be reflected off the material. If both are set to 0, the surface is perfectly diffuse and reflects light equally in all directions. By varying these values, many specular and spread reflection properties can be defined. You cannot see your face reflected in a wall painted with satin paint, but you might see a bare light bulb reflected as a fuzzy ball of light. If our value for specularity (.05) were followed with a roughness value of 0, the surface would appear to have the properties of a smooth porcelain plate, enabling you to see the faint reflection of your face. By adding a roughness factor (.03), a diffusing component is mixed in, producing the reflection patterns associated with a satin finish.

Right-Hand Rule

Though some *Radiance* materials have two identical sides, such as plastic, we need a method to specify the surface that will receive a single-sided material. The left polygon in Figure 2.3 illustrates the surface normal direction resulting from ordering the vertices in a counterclockwise direction. If the vertices order is reversed, as shown in the polygon on the right, the surface normal points in the opposite direction. The right-hand rule is a convenient method to remember the direction in which to order the vertices so that you know which way the surface faces. Imagine that you are grasping a surface normal in your right hand, with your thumb pointing away from the surface. The direction of your fingers indicate the order in which to list the vertices so that the surface will face in the direction of your thumb. In general, it is a good practice to follow the right-hand rule when creating any surface so complications do not arise if you change a surface from a two-sided to a single-sided material.

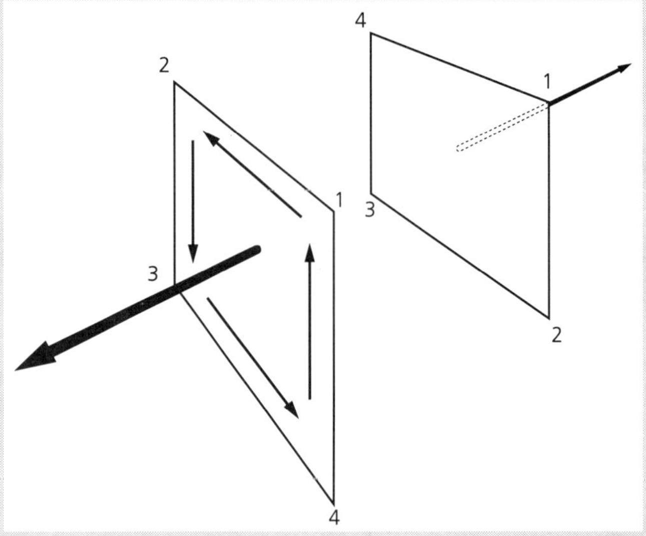

Figure 2.3 The direction of the surface is determined by the order in which the vertices are listed. By reversing the order of the left polygon's vertices, the right polygon faces in the opposite direction.

2.4.2 Creating *stool_1.rad*

Each surface of the stool will be created using polygons, which are among the basic building blocks in *Radiance*. These polygons can be created explicitly or by using one of the built-in polygon generator functions. The seat of the *stool_1.rad* will be made by describing explicit polygons.

Our first piece of geometry describes the top surface of the stool's seat. It is constructed following the right-hand-rule convention, with its surface normal pointing upward (see Figure 2.3). This means that the order in which the vertices or corners of the shape are listed has significance.

Each geometric shape requires a material surface in order to be seen, so the definition of every piece of geometry must have a material associated with it. We begin by using the plastic material that we have just described. In *Radiance*, plastic is a surface that has two sides (can be seen from the front or the back), but there are other materials that are only one-sided, such as *mirror*. How can you determine the side of a surface that will be mirrored? The mirror will appear on the surface normal side.

```
brown_satin_paint   polygon   stool_top
0
0
12      -0.75        -0.75       2.6
         0.75        -0.75       2.6
         0.75         0.75       2.6
        -0.75         0.75       2.6
```

This scene description primitive of the `stool_top` reads

```
# polygon description:
#
# using the modifier brown_satin_paint, create a polygon, named stool_top
# nothing on this line 0
# nothing on this line 0
# 12 values follow,       x1        y1        z1
#                         x2        y2        z2
#                         x3        y3        z3
#                         x4        y4        z4
```

Note that 12 values describe the four sets of 3D coordinates that form the corners of the `stool_top` (see Figure 2.4(a)). An unlimited variety of polygon shapes can be described using any number of coordinates as long as they lie on the same plane and the correct number of values is declared (Figure 2.4(b)). This is a difference between *Radiance* and many other modeling systems, which limit a polygon to a three- or four-sided description.

The edges of the seat are next. The directions of the compass have been used to provide each surface with a unique descriptive name. Though unique polygon names are not required in this example, they prove to be very useful identifiers when you are troubleshooting.

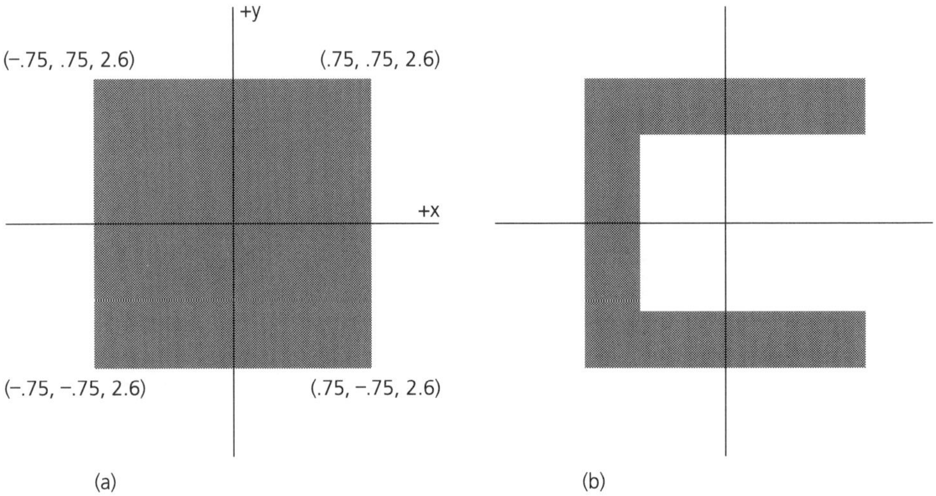

Figure 2.4 The `stool_top` polygon (a), and an eight-coordinate planar polygon (b).

```
brown_satin_paint    polygon    stool_side_n
0
0
12      -0.75        .75        2.45
        -0.75        .75        2.6
         0.75        .75        2.6
         0.75        .75        2.45

brown_satin_paint    polygon    stool_side_s
0
0
12      -0.75        -.75        2.45
         0.75        -.75        2.45
         0.75        -.75        2.6
        -0.75        -.75        2.6

brown_satin_paint    polygon    stool_side_e
0
0
12       0.75        -.75       2.45
         0.75         .75       2.45
         0.75         .75       2.6
         0.75        -.75       2.6
```

```
brown_satin_paint   polygon   stool_side_w
0
0
12      -0.75       -.75       2.45
        -0.75       -.75       2.6
        -0.75        .75       2.6
        -0.75        .75       2.45
```

It would become very tedious to have to construct each of the stool's polygons using the longhand method shown above. *Radiance* provides several functions that generate polygons based on simpler descriptions of 3D shapes. These polygon generators are invaluable to the modeling process. To form the four legs, the polygon generator called **genprism** could be used. In the following example, genprism is preceded by an exclamation mark (`!`). This indicates to the oconv program that the scene description line begins with a function instead of a modifier. If the `!` is omitted, an error message is issued, warning that an undefined modifier has been used. The backslash (`\`) followed by a carriage return (ENTER) is a continuation character used to extend the genprism command over successive lines.

```
!genprism brown_satin_paint   stool_leg_sw \
     4    -0.7 -0.7    -0.6 -0.7   -0.6 -0.6   -0.7 -0.6     -l  0 0 2.5
```

The description of this shape could be read as follows:

```
# genprism description:
#
# The ! tells the program that a function follows.
# Use genprism, and material brown_satin_paint, to create the leg
# polygons with the name stool_leg_sw
# 4 pairs of x y coordinates follow, x1 y1  x2 y2  x3 y3  x4 y4
# extruded along the length of vector -l which begins at 0 0 0 and
# ends at x y z

# genprism formal definition:
#
# genprism  mod  id   n   x1 y1  x2 y2... xn yn  [-l xl yl zl]
```

Polygons with Holes

Since there are no explicit holes allowed in *Radiance* polygons, we can create the appearance of a hole by using an invisible seam. In Figure 2.5, the arrow indicates the order of the vertices to create the open polygon on the left. The apparent hole in the polygon on the right is created by changing the vertices just above the gap so that they are coincident with the bottom edge. The dotted line indicates this invisible seam.

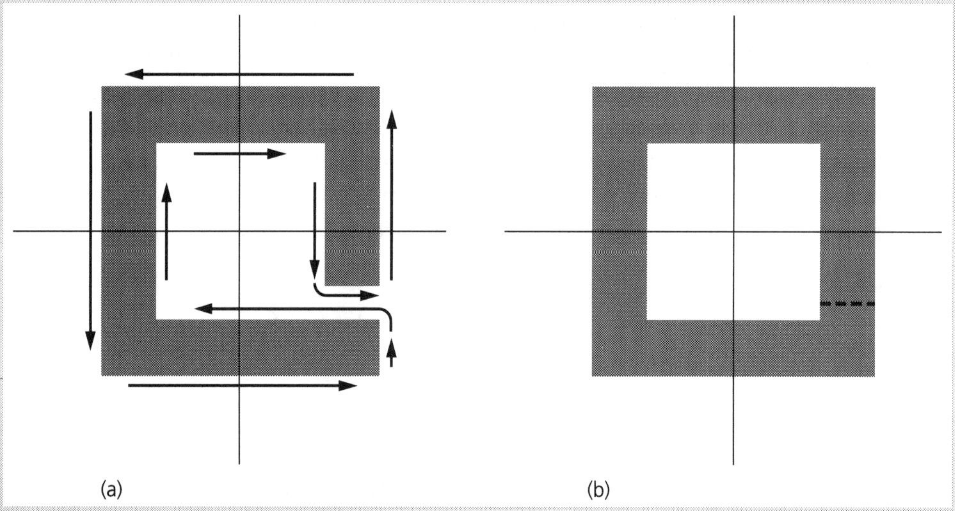

Figure 2.5 The gap in the left polygon (a) is closed to produce the effect of the hole in the right polygon (b).

To view the polygon data that genprism actually produces, redirect (>) the output into a text file and then read the scene description primitives that have been automatically generated. Enter the following on the command line:

```
% genprism brown_satin_paint stool_leg_sw 4 -0.7 -0.7 -0.6 -0.7 -0.6
  -0.6 -0.7 -0.6 -1 0 0 2.5    >    look.txt
```

Then view the output of the genprism function by listing the content of *look.txt* through the **more** function:

```
% more look.txt
```

```
# genprism brown_satin_paint stool_leg_sw \
    4  -0.7  -0.7  -0.6  -0.7  -0.6  -0.6  -0.7  -0.6  -l 0 0 2.5

brown_satin_paint polygon stool_leg_sw.b
0
0
12
        -0.7        -0.7        0
        -0.6        -0.7        0
        -0.6        -0.6        0
        -0.7        -0.6        0

brown_satin_paint polygon stool_leg_sw.e
0
0
12
        -0.7        -0.6        2.5
        -0.6        -0.6        2.5
        -0.6        -0.7        2.5
        -0.7        -0.7        2.5

brown_satin_paint polygon stool_leg_sw.1
0
0
12
        -0.7        -0.7        0
        -0.7        -0.7        2.5
        -0.6        -0.7        2.5
        -0.6        -0.7        0

brown_satin_paint polygon stool_leg_sw.2
0
0
12
        -0.6        -0.7        0
        -0.6        -0.7        2.5
        -0.6        -0.6        2.5
        -0.6        -0.6        0
```

```
brown_satin_paint polygon stool_leg_sw.3
0
0
12
        -0.6        -0.6        0
        -0.6        -0.6        2.5
        -0.7        -0.6        2.5
        -0.7        -0.6        0

brown_satin_paint polygon stool_leg_sw.4
0
0
12
        -0.7        -0.6        0
        -0.7        -0.6        2.5
        -0.7        -0.7        2.5
        -0.7        -0.7        0
```

Note that the generator has done the tedious work for you! Genprism has created the six polygons needed to form each leg and has automatically appended a unique number to each name. If there were a need to edit an object created by a generator, the output could be redirected to a file, edited, and then incorporated into the scene description as a unique file. You might use this technique to remove the top surface of a box. Of course, the original generator description, such as our genprism example, would need to be removed so that the geometry would not be duplicated.

The remaining three legs could be created in the same manner.

```
!genprism brown_satin_paint stool_leg_se \
    4   0.7  -0.7     0.7  -0.6     0.6  -0.6    0.6  -0.7   -1   0 0 2.5

!genprism brown_satin_paint stool_leg_ne \
   4    0.7  0.7      0.6  0.7      0.6  0.6     0.7  0.6    -1   0 0 2.5

!genprism brown_satin_paint stool_leg_nw \
   4     -0.7 0.7      -0.7 0.6      -0.6 0.6      -0.6 0.7    -1   0 0 2.5
```

Place the seat and leg descriptions of the stool in a text file called *stool_1.rad* and locate it in the *lib* directory.

2.4.3 Viewing *stool_1.rad*

To view the stool, you must first convert the materials and objects into an octree format. We will use the program oconv to merge and convert *materials1.rad* and *stool_1.rad* into the octree file *stool_1.oct*. The order of the input files is important. If oconv encounters the stool description before knowing about the `brown_satin_paint` material, an error message will be issued because it finds an undefined modifier and the program will stop. Always locate dependent files after files that contain their modifiers. The following example is executed in the *scene1* directory, where *materials1.rad* resides. To inform oconv where to find the *stool_1.rad* file, its path has been declared. The "." that begins the *./lib/stool_1.rad* path explicitly states that the subdirectory *lib* is a branch from the current directory. An alternative practice is to omit the ./ and use *lib/stool_1.rad.*

```
% oconv material1.rad  ./lib/stool_1.rad  > stool_1.oct
```

A simple unlighted impression of the stool can be viewed by calling the rview program. (See Figure 2.6.) The default view is from 0 0 0 looking in the +*y* direction. The view is oriented with +*z* as up. Taking a vantage point at floor level and peering between the stool legs toward a black void is not very useful, so we need to instruct rview to change our view location. Vector descriptions are used to establish the view up (-vu) and view direction (-vd). The base of the vector is located at 0 0 0, and you provide a coordinate that aims the view. This view direction is then moved to an *xyz* coordinate to establish the vantage point (-vp). To provide basic visibility, we will set the ambient light value (`-av r g b`) to 1 1 1. There is no significance to the order in which these parameters are listed, except that the octree file must be last.

```
% rview -vu 0 0 1 -vd 0 1 0 -vp 0 -10 2 -av 1 1 1 stool_1.oct
```

Once rview has opened the image, several commands enable you to change your vantage point, and so on. A complete listing is contained in *The Radiance Reference Manual* on the CD-ROM under rview. Here are a few examples of what you might enter in the rview command window. Replace the numbers used in these examples with your own values and note that you can simply enter the first letter of each command instead of typing the complete word.

`move 2`	moves you closer to an object (zoom in)
`move .5`	moves you away from an object (zoom out)
`pivot 45`	pivots you 45 degrees to the right (some CAD programs refer to this as "orbit")
`pivot 0 45`	pivots you 45 degrees upwards

`rotate 10`	rotates camera 10 degrees to the right
`rotate 0 10`	rotates camera up 10 degrees
`last`	restores the previous view
`view filename.vf`	writes a file named *filename.vf* that contains the current viewing information. Any filename and extension can be used.
`trace`	provides geometry and luminance data for the object under the cursor
`exposure`	adjusts the exposure based on the luminance of the surface under the cursor
`quit`	exit rview

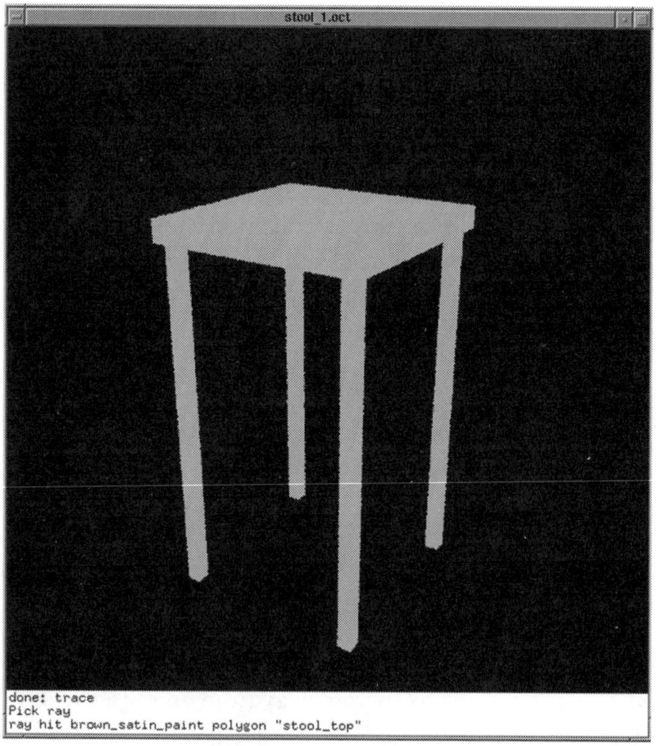

Figure 2.6 Rview generates an interactive view of a scene. Commands are entered in the text window at the bottom of the screen. The stool is flat shaded by setting the ambient light values (-av) to 1 1 1.

As the scene descriptions become complex, it will be more efficient to set up the rad program to handle files and control the rendering process. For now, the file-handling method described in Scene 1 will suffice.

A summary of the process of creating an object and viewing it includes

- Creating a material description file
- Creating an object description file
- Converting these descriptions into an octree file using oconv
- Viewing the object shape using rview

This completes our first task. What follows is an annotated description of the rest of the objects needed for Scene 1. Locate each file in the *lib* directory. Use oconv, then rview to check the shape and orientation of the objects you are making.

2.4.4 Creating *table_1.rad*

This stylish bar table will be constructed using the **genbox** polygon generator function. (See Figure 2.7.) The whole table can be created with five definitions. In a later example, you will discover that the table could actually be described in two definitions by using the array option to copy a single leg into four locations. Meanwhile, note how this generator function simplifies the creation of the table. We will use the center of the table at floor level for the insertion point $x = 0$, $y = 0$, $z = 0$, or (0 0 0). The 2.5-foot-square tabletop has a thickness of .15 foot and is supported by slender legs. (See Figure 2.8.)

Xform is a workhorse function that transforms scene descriptions. This means that it can relocate, rotate, scale, and mirror any object or group of objects, or even whole scenes. In the following example, xform is used to move the `table_top` from the location in which it was constructed on the *xy* plane to its final height of 3.3 feet, centered over 0 0 0.

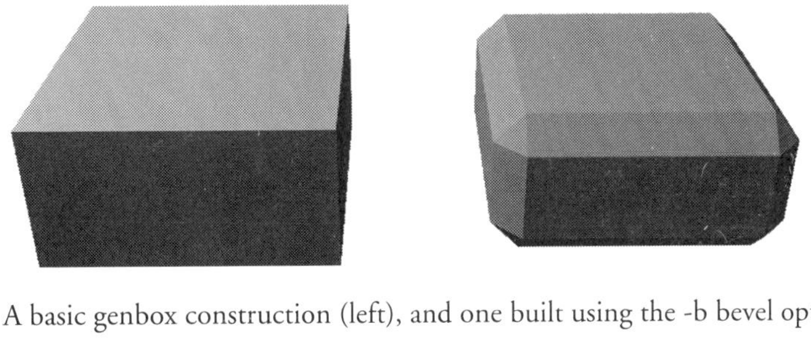

Figure 2.7 A basic genbox construction (left), and one built using the -b bevel option (right).

```
!genbox   brown_satin_paint   table_top \
          2.5    2.5    0.15   -r .05 \
          | xform  -t  -1.25  -1.25  3.15
```

This example could be read as follows:

```
# Use genbox, and modifier brown_satin_paint, to create
# the polygons for the object named table_top.
# One corner of the box begins at 0 0 0 with the extreme
# opposite corner at x y z.
# Round each box edge with a radius (-r) of n.
# Pipe(|) table_top through the xform function to translate (-t)
# the box's origin to x y z.

# genbox formal definition:
#
# genbox  mod   id   x y z  [-r n] [-b n]
```

Note the inclusion of -r in the genbox description. This option produce a series of cylinders and spheres that round all the edges of the box to the specified radius. If -b is used instead, all edges are beveled 45 degrees to the designated width. The -r option should only be used with opaque materials, because the spheres and cylinders that make up the rounded edges are fully exposed when the material is transparent.

The same `genbox | xform` procedure can be followed to create and locate the table base and legs.

Figure 2.8 Coffee bar table with beveled tabletop edges.

```
!genbox   brown_satin_paint   table_base \
          1.2    1.2   0.15 \
          | xform   -t  -.6  -.6   0

!genbox   brown_satin_paint   table_leg_sw    \
          .15    .15   3.15  | xform   -t   -.6  -.6  0

!genbox   brown_satin_paint   table_leg_se    \
          .15    .15   3.15  | xform   -t   .45  -.6  0

!genbox   brown_satin_paint   table_leg_ne    \
          .15    .15   3.15  | xform   -t   .45    .45  0

!genbox   brown_satin_paint   table_leg_nw    \
          .15    .15   3.15  | xform   -t   -.6    .45   0
```

2.4.5 Creating *vase1.rad*

Many 3D modeling programs rely solely on polygons to describe the geometry of surfaces. To produce the effect of a smooth spherical surface, thousands of tiny polygons are needed to reduce the faceted appearance. This can result in huge geometry files. To address this problem, *Radiance* defines certain shapes by using an equation instead of multitudes of polygons. When a ray intercepts one of these objects, the equation, not a polygon facet, determines the surface location and normal. This results in an efficiently defined, infinitely smooth surface. *Spheres* and *cones* are defined in this manner within *Radiance*. All other surface definitions result in *polygons*.

Vase1.rad will be constructed from the cone family, a *ring*, and a sphere (see Figure 2.9). To keep this first example simple, plastic will be used so that the overlapping of some surfaces within the vase will not be revealed. Because this vase will

Figure 2.9 Vase constructed from a variety of smooth curved surfaces.

never need to contain real water, the interior of an object such as this is inconsequential. This form of modeling is mostly concerned with outward appearances! If you want to see how the individual surfaces overlap, you might experiment with the transparent glass material that is included with the vase material descriptions.

Add these material descriptions to the *material1.rad* file:

```
void        plastic        red_porcelain
0
0
5       .7        .2        .1        .05        .02

void        plastic        cream_porcelain
0
0
5       .6        .4        .3        .05        .02

# substitute the following modifier for red_porcelain in the vase
# descriptions to view the internal structure.
void        glass          transparent_porcelain
0
0
3       .6        .4        .3
```

We will build the vase from the base up. Start with a cone that supports the sphere or bowl of the vase.

```
red_porcelain  cone vase_a
0
0
8           0       0       3.3
            0       0       3.4
            .20     .18

# cone description:
#
# Using the modifier red_porcelain, construct a cone named vase_a.
# nothing on this line (0)
# nothing on this line (0)
# 8 values follow. The first x1 y1 z1 coordinate determines the center
# of one cone end.
```

```
# The next x2 y2 z2 coordinate determines the center of the other end.
# The first cone end has a radius of r1; the other end has a radius of
# r2.

# cone formal definition:
#
# mod  cone  id
# 0
# 0
# 8   x1 y1 z1  x2 y2 z2  radius1  radius2

red_porcelain  sphere    vase_b
0
0
4    0 0 3.6  .3

# sphere description:
#
# using the modifier red_porcelain, construct a sphere named vase_b.
# nothing on this line 0
# nothing on this line 0
# 4 values follow. The center of the sphere is located at x1 y1 z1 and
# has radius r1.

# sphere formal definition:
#
# mod  sphere  id
# 0
# 0
# 4  x1 y1 z1  radius
```

The remaining neck and vase top are constructed from a *cylinder* and a cone. To provide thickness, a ring will form the rim and a cone will be used to model the upper inside surface.

```
red_porcelain  cylinder  vase_c
0
0
7    0 0 3.8
     0 0 4.6
     .05
```

```
# cylinder description:
#
# Using the modifier red_porcelain, construct a cylinder named vase_c.
# Nothing on this line 0.
# Nothing on this line 0.
# 7 values follow. The first x1 y1 z1 coordinate determines the center of
# one cylinder end.
# The second x2 y2 z2 coordinate determines the center of the other end.
# The cylinder has a radius of r1.

red_porcelain  cone vase_d
0
0
8    0 0 4.6
     0 0 4.625
     .05  .08

cream_porcelain     ring vase_e
0
0
8    0 0 4.625
     0 0 1
     .08  .06

# ring description:
#
# using the modifier cream_porcelain, construct a ring named vase_e.
# nothing on this line 0.
# nothing on this line 0.
# 8 values follow. The x1 y1 z1 coordinate determines the ring's center.
# The vector from 0 0 0 to xv yv zv defines the direction in which the
# ring faces.
# The outside radius is r1 and the inside radius is r2.

# ring formal definition:
#
# mod  ring  id
# 0
# 0
# 8  x1 y1 z1  xv yv zv  radius1  radius2
```

```
cream_porcelain    cone vase_f
0
0
8    0 0 4.625
     0 0 4.6
     .06 .03

cream_porcelain  cylinder  vase_g
0
0
7    0 0 3.8
     0 0 4.6
     .03
```

2.4.6 Creating *lamp_shade1.rad*

To begin the lighting exploration of Scene 1, let's experiment with the effect of pendant light fixtures located to the left and right of the table. Since the two luminaires are identical, we will construct one unit first (see Figure 2.10), then copy it to its final destinations in the *scene1.all* file using xform.

There is no need for us to be concerned about a way to suspend the luminaires until we have resolved their final locations and heights. After determining the placement that provides the desired effect, we could add the requisite length of cable from the ceiling to the luminaire (a narrow-radius cylinder!).

The outsides of the lamp shades are painted with green gloss enamel; the insides are matte white. Each will be lamped with a spherical 55-watt frosted light bulb, which is 6 inches in diameter. A catalog from a lamp manufacturer provides these data, along with lamp life and lumen output. An alternative source of generic lamp

Figure 2.10 Pendant lamp shade with a semispecular finish.

data is the reference section of the *IES Lighting Handbook*, published by the Illuminating Engineering Society of North America. Add the following material descriptions to *material1.rad:*

```
void  plastic  green_gloss
0
0
5       .1 .6 .2 .1 .02

void  plastic  white_matte
0
0
5       .8 .8 .8 0 0

void  light  55w_lamplight
0
0
3       26.956529 17.772748 6.815494

# light formal definition:
#
#  mod  light  id
#  0
#  0
#  3       red green blue
```

Finally we see a description that includes light! The simplest method of adding light to a scene is to modify a surface with a *Radiance* material called *light*. The surface, which might be a sphere (light bulb) or a cylinder (fluorescent tube) is transformed into a light source. If we know that we can represent the tungsten light bulb using a .25-foot-radius sphere, and that a 55-watt lamp emits approximately 800 lumens, a program called **lampcolor** can be used to determine light values so that the sphere will become a radiant lamp based on the light output and color of actual light sources. This process and the engineering behind these metrics will be covered in great detail in the technical chapters. For now, enjoy the fact that at last you have physically based light! This is how lampcolor is used:

```
% lampcolor
Enter lamp type [tungsten]: halogen
Enter length unit [meter]: feet
Enter lamp geometry [polygon]: sphere
```

```
Sphere radius [1]: .25
Enter total lamp lumens [0]: 800
Lamp color (RGB) = 26.956529 17.772748 6.815494
```

The resulting RGB values are then used in the `55w_lamplight` light description.

Now, in a file called *lamp_shade1.rad*, build the shade with its rim centered at 0 0 0. First begin with the outside surface.

```
green_gloss  cone  shade_out_1
0
0
8       0 0 0
        0 0 .2
        .75 .7

green_gloss  cone  shade_out_2
0
0
8       0 0 .2
        0 0 .4
        .7 .3

green_gloss  cone  shade_out_3
0
0
8       0 0 .4
        0 0 .7
        .3 .2

green_gloss  ring  shade_out_4
0
0
8       0 0 .7
        0 0  1
        .2  0
```

Now define the rim and inside surface.

```
white_matte  ring  shade_in_0
0
0
8       0 0 0
        0 0 -1
        .75 .725

white_matte  cone  shade_in_1
0
0
8       0 0 0
        0 0 .2
        .725 .675

white_matte  cone  shade_in_2
0
0
8       0 0 .2
        0 0 .4
        .675 .275

white_matte  cone  shade_in_3
0
0
8       0 0 .4
        0 0 .675
        .275 .175

white_matte  ring  shade_in_4
0
0
8       0 0 .675
        0 0  1
        .175  0
```

Complete the light fixture by placing the decorative spherical lamp in the center of the shade.

```
55w_lamplight sphere  55w_lightbulb
0
0
4        0 0 .3    .25
```

The bottom rim of the pendant luminaire is centered on the *xy* plane. It is good practice to include a comment line, at the top of the file, indicating this insertion point. If you want to use this luminaire again in future projects, you will not have to scrutinize the scene descriptions to discover where the object is located. Include the following comment at the head of the preceding luminaire descriptions:

```
# 18" diameter pendent luminaire. Rim centered at 0 0 0 on the xy plane.
```

2.4.7 Creating *tile_4.rad*

The table and stools need a floor beneath them. Our floor will be an 8-foot square with a checkered tile pattern. Rather than constructing 64 tiles using a longhand method, we use *tile_4.rad*, which contains descriptions of four tiles that are assembled into a 2-foot square of floor. This pattern will be copied several times into the final scene description. Applying this approach certainly simplifies the modeling process. As you will see when the whole floor is assembled, one additional description will generate the 1664 polygons that make up the tiled floor. Add the following materials to the *materials1.rad* file:

```
void  plastic  red_tile
0
0
5       .4  .01 .05 0 0

void  plastic  white_tile
0
0
5       .6  .5 .4 0 0
```

The tiles will have slightly beveled edges and will butt together. Recall that the -b, or bevel, parameter calculates and adds a sloped polygon to every edge. Each of the colored clay tiles is 1 foot square and .1 foot thick, with a bevel of .025 feet. Place the following descriptions in *tile_4.rad* in the *lib* directory.

```
!genbox red_tile    tile_sw  1 1 .1 -b .025  |  xform  -t 0 0  -.1
!genbox white_tile  tile_se  1 1 .1 -b .025  |  xform  -t 1 0  -.1
!genbox red_tile    tile_ne  1 1 .1 -b .025  |  xform  -t 1 1  -.1
!genbox white_tile  tile_nw  1 1 .1 -b .025  |  xform  -t 0 1  -.1
```

Xform is used to locate each tile in a checkerboard pattern (see Figure 2.11) and to lower them by −.1 feet so that their top surfaces are flush with the *xy* plane. We do not want the table and chair legs sunk into the tiles!

2.4.8 Creating *wall_ceiling.rad*

Now that the floor is constructed, a wall and a ceiling are needed. For the purposes of this tutorial, only an 8-foot segment of the wall and ceiling will be added to the scene, enabling you to view the setting easily from three sides. In the Scene 2 tutorial, we will explore ways to peer into rooms through walls, but in the spirit of this jump-start, simplicity will rule. The ceiling is located 8 feet above the floor.

These surfaces can be rapidly added to the scene description by again using genbox. First we need to decide on the wall and ceiling material descriptions. Until the color scheme is finalized, we will make them from the material called `white_matte`, which is already defined in *material1.rad*. All we need to do is create a file called *wall_ceiling.rad* and add it to the library of files in the *lib* directory.

```
!genbox white_matte wall     8 .2 8   |  xform  -t -4  4  0
!genbox white_matte ceiling  8 8  .2  |  xform  -t -4 -4  8
```

Notice that xform moves the ceiling and wall to their final locations.

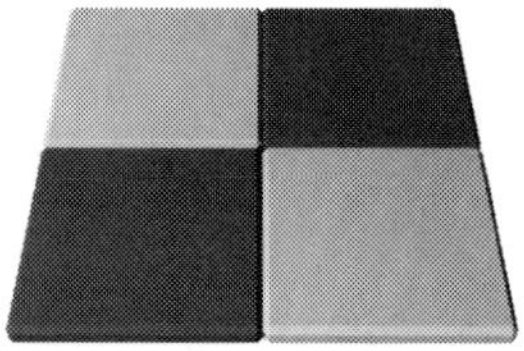

Figure 2.11 Xform is used to copy and move tiles into a checkerboard pattern.

2.4.9 Creating *mirror_1.rad*

To add interest to the scene, a circular mirror with an antique copper frame, as shown in Figure 2.12, will be hung on the wall behind the table. Though we might know where we want to locate the mirror on the wall, we will construct it around the 0 0 0 insertion point and locate it with xform when we assemble the whole scene. This will make it easier for us to modify its tilt and height.

Another of the basic materials in *Radiance* is called mirror. It requires three values, which represent the color and reflectivity of the surface. Mirror differs from specular plastic or metal in that it automatically behaves as a secondary light source. If a ray of light strikes the mirror surface, it is reflected into the scene and contributes to the illumination.

We might guess at the RGB values and specularity of an antique copper finish, but in this case, the *Radiance* distribution includes an example of oxidized copper that gives us a physically based starting point. This information is located in a list of material descriptions found in the *Radiance ..ray/lib* directory in the *material.rad* file. Though not comprehensive, the contents of this file can provide valuable insights into the descriptions of many construction materials and paint colors. The visual properties of these materials have been measured with devices such as reflectometers and spectrometers, and those data have been transcribed into *Radiance* scene descriptions. The fact that *Radiance* can import and use these physically based data separates it from most other rendering programs.

The `oxidized_copper` description, provided with *Radiance*, indicates that metal should be used along with a specularity of .3 and a roughness of .2. Any highlights reflecting off this metal material will be tinted by its copper color.

Figure 2.12 Circular wall mirror constructed using cylinders, tubes, and rings.

Add the following definitions to the *material1.rad* file:

```
void mirror mirror_glass
0
0
3  .8 .8 .8

void metal antique_copper
0
0
5  .136  .102  .083  .3  .2

# mirror formal definition:
#
#  mod  mirror  id
#  0
#  0
#  3  red green blue

# metal formal definition:
#
#  mod  metal  id
#  0
#  0
#  5  red green blue specularity  roughness
```

Now, in the file *mirror_1.rad*, let's create a 2.5-foot-diameter mirror and its copper frame. Construct the mirror with a vertical orientation centered at 0 0 0.

```
mirror_glass ring mirror
0
0
8  0 0 0
   0 -1 0
   1.25 0

# outside surface of frame
antique_copper cylinder f1
0
0
7  0 0 0
   0 -.1 0
   1.35
```

```
# inside surface of frame
antique_copper tube f2
0
0
7  0 0 0
   0 -.1 0
   1.25

# front surface of frame
antique_copper ring f3
0
0
8 0 -.1 0
  0 -1 0
  1.25 1.35
```

The frame's inner rim (`f2`) is constructed from the surface of a *tube*. The tube definition is the same as that for a cylinder, except that the normals are directed inward. If we defined the frame's inner rim as a cylinder instead, and made it from a single-sided material, it would have no visible surface attributes. There are three pairs of smooth curved surface types that are identical except for the direction of their surface normals:

Inward-pointing normals	Outward-pointing normals
bubble	*sphere*
cup	*cone*
tube	*cylinder*

2.4.10 Creating *leaf_1.rad*

The vase looks rather bleak, so let's add a flower on a leafy stem. Leaves do not lie in a single flat plane, nor do they have identical orientations. These organic shapes are not easily modeled, so we will create a strategy to guide us through the construction of the leaf system.

The files that follow will be inserted into the collector file called *flower_1.rad*. First we will make leaf segment *leaf_1.rad*, which will be multiplied into a file called *leaves_1.rad*. In turn, *leaves_1.rad* will be used to add a complete sprig of leaves to the file called *flower_1.rad*, where the stem and bud will be defined. This may seem a little confusing at first, but being able to create smaller components of an object in individual files actually provides great flexibility in manipulating the final assembly. In summary, we will build a nine-leaf cluster from a simple half leaf and then add a rosebud and stem.

The data for this "parent" half leaf are derived by sketching its shape on graph paper, as shown in Figure 2.13. The center of the leaf lies along the positive *y*-axis, with the shape defined to the left (negative *x* quadrant). Add the following material definition to the *material1.rad* file:

```
void plastic green1
0
0
5 .02 .9 .1 .04 .03
```

Create a file called *leaf_1.rad* in the *lib* directory, which contains the description of the half-leaf segment.

```
green1 polygon leaf1
0
0
27         0         0     0
           -.01       .1   0
           -.1        .2   0
           -.09       .2   0
           -.15       .33  0
           -.12       .32  0
           -.11       .52  0
           -.09       .51  0
           0          .62  0
```

2.4.11 Creating *leaves_1.rad*

Now we will compose a group of nine leaves to form a small branch. An important issue must be considered here. How much detail do we need in our image to convey the sense of the flower? Does every vein in a leaf need to be modeled? The purpose of the rose is to provide a focal point for the scene. It is not going to be studied in close-up, so fine detail can be omitted. In fact, we will omit the stem segments that would hold the leaves together, because it is unlikely that this detail will ever appear in our cafe pictures. Too often, when a scene is modeled, a great amount of fine detail is created that never sees the light of day. A very large proportion of the image-making process is often consumed by modeling, so review the purpose and size of each object before building it. Though experience is a great guide in matters

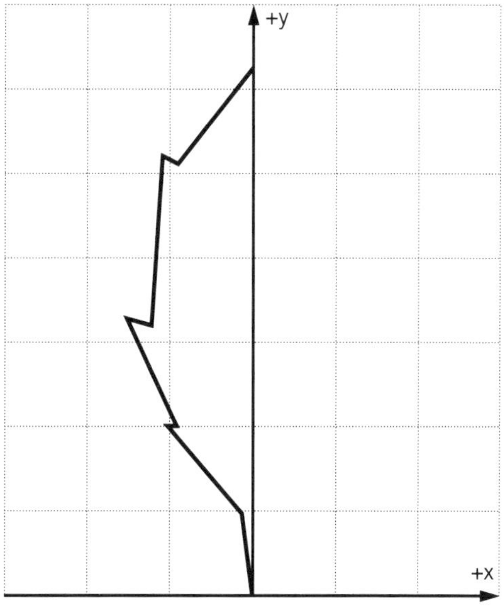

Figure 2.13 Coordinates for a half-leaf segment can be obtained by sketching the leaf's profile on graph paper.

of resolution, if the detail is likely to be smaller than an image pixel, leave it out! Spending the additional hours on an artifact whose detail will never be seen adds an extra burden to the size of the data set and results in a much longer rendering time. If in doubt, leave it out. It is always possible to add detail later, if a close-up is required.

Leaves_1.rad contains manipulations of the *leaf_1.rad* file and creates several variations of whole leaves. This is accomplished by using two additional xform transformations. First -s is used to scale the size of the *leaf_1.rad* segment. Then -rx, -ry, and -rz rotate the *leaf_1.rad* about the three primary axes. The right-hand rule comes into play again and is illustrated in Figure 2.14. A positive rotation around the *x*-axis would spin in the direction of your fingers if you held the axis with your right hand with your thumb pointing in the positive *x* direction. The same principle applies to rotating about the *y*- and *z*-axes.

Finally, the xform mirror options (-mx, -my, and -mz) are called to reflect the leaf segments into a whole branch. Do not confuse this xform translation argument with the material description of the same name. The mirror argument could be used to transform one half of a Rorschach image into a whole, while the mirror material would simply reflect your face peering at the page. (See Figure 2.15.)

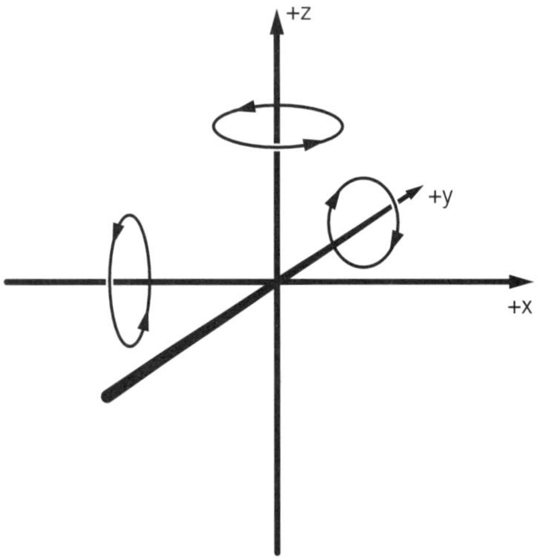

Figure 2.14 Positive rotations about the *x*-, *y*-, and *z*-axes are illustrated using the right-hand rule.

The first pair of xform commands in the *leaves_1.rad* file creates the bottom right leaf on the branch. To create a partially folded leaf, it is first tilted about the *y*-axis (-ry -10 degrees). The orientation is completed by additional rotations about the *x*- and *y*-axes, before the leaf is scaled to its appropriate size and moved to its final location.

The xform command `-n 1b` inserts a copy of *leaf_1.rad*, moves it to the location of `-n 1a`, then mirrors it around the *x*-axis. This creates the other half of the leaf. Because the ensuing transformations are identical, the leaf segments remain joined. Figure 2.16 illustrates this manipulation of the leaf segment into a half branch.

The full scene description in the *scene1* directory uses xform to include the *leaves_1.rad* file, located in the *./lib* subdirectory. Once xform follows the path to this scene description file, the default directory is temporarily updated to *scene1/lib*. If a scene description file references component files within this same directory, no path names are required. Therefore, the xform reference to *leaf_1.rad*, within *leaves_1.rad*, requires no path name. The advantage of this approach surfaces when you are building large scenes composed of complex scene descriptions, each referencing a family of component files. To help you keep track of the scene components, each of these families can be located in its own subdirectory. But do

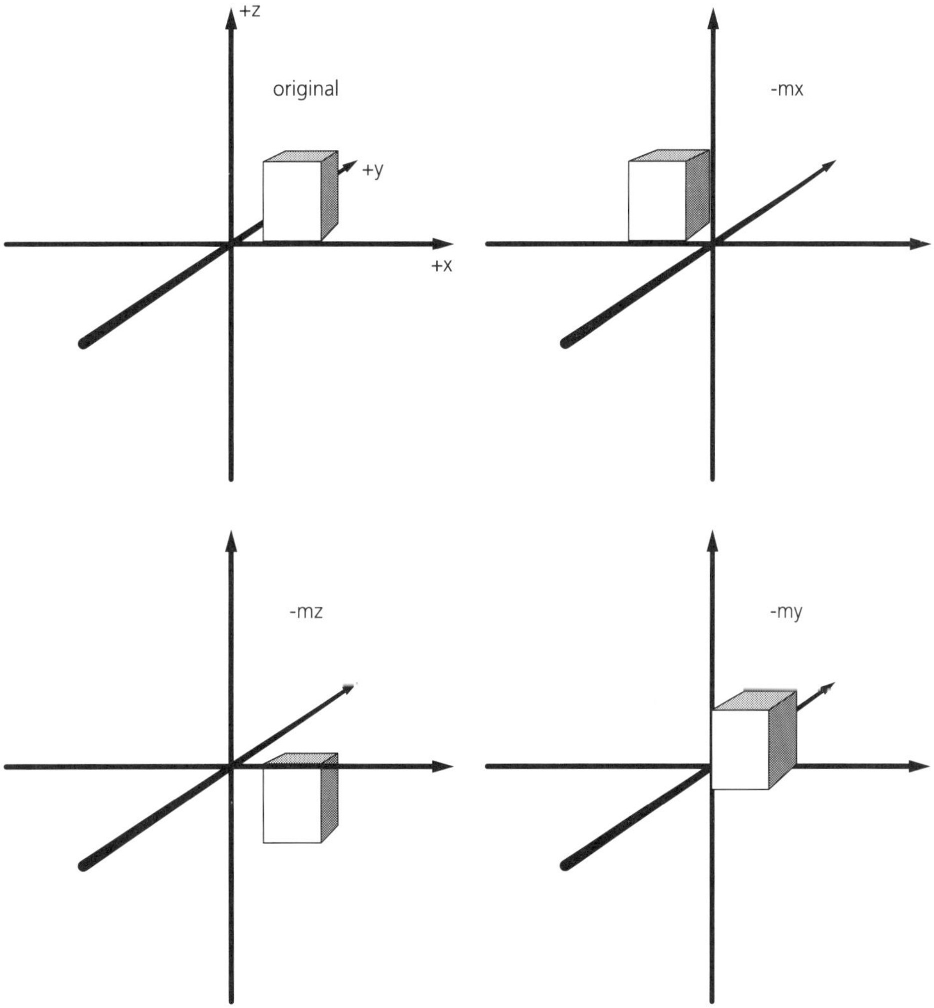

Figure 2.15 The original location of an object is shown in the upper left example. The other examples result from applying the mirror option in an xform transformation of the original object. Unlike some CAD modeling systems, objects are always mirrored about a principal axis.

not forget to provide the xform command in the full scene description file with the initial path to these complex scene descriptions, or you will receive a warning such as this:

```
oconv: cannot open scene file "leaves_1.rad": No such file or directory
```

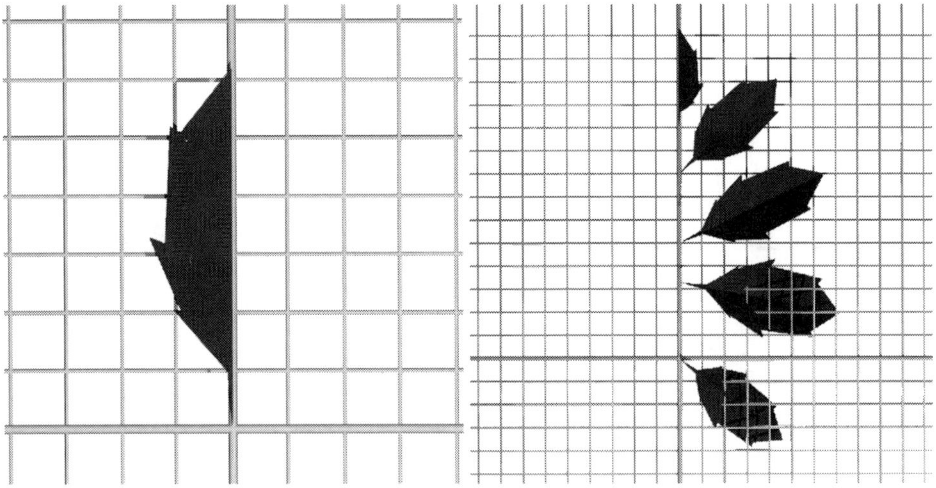

Figure 2.16 A leaf segment is multiplied into one half of a branch through a sequence of xform transformations. A grid has been rendered with the leaves to show their orientation in 3D space. The grid is located on the xy plane and is comprised of thin cylinders on .1-foot centers.

Now for the actual definition of the first leaf:

```
!xform -n 1a -ry -10     -rz -125 -ry 25  -s .12 -t 0 0 0 leaf_1.rad
!xform -n 1b -ry -10 -mx -rz -125 -ry 25  -s .12 -t 0 0 0 leaf_1.rad
```

The rest of the leaves progressively rotate toward the *y*-axis while the *z* value is increased, creating a curved leaf cluster.

```
!xform -n 2a -ry 20     -rz -100 -ry 20 -s .15 -t 0 .04 0 leaf_1.rad
!xform -n 2b -ry 20 -mx -rz -100 -ry 20 -s .15 -t 0 .04 0 leaf_1.rad

!xform -n 3a -ry 25     -rz -65 -ry 0 -s .14 -t 0 .06 0 leaf_1.rad
!xform -n 3b -ry 25 -mx -rz -65 -ry 0 -s .14 -t 0 .06 0 leaf_1.rad

!xform -n 4a -ry 10     -rz -45 -rx 20 -s .12 -t 0 .1 .025 leaf_1.rad
!xform -n 4b -ry 10 -mx -rz -45 -rx 20 -s .12 -t 0 .1 .025 leaf_1.rad
```

Note that the final xform command adds only half of a leaf to the tip of the branch. The complete *leaves_1.rad* file will be mirrored (see Figure 2.17) in the final flower file, creating both sides of the top leaf.

```
!xform -n 1 -ry 30 -mx -rz 0 -rx 35 -s .10 -t 0 .125 .05 leaf_1.rad
```

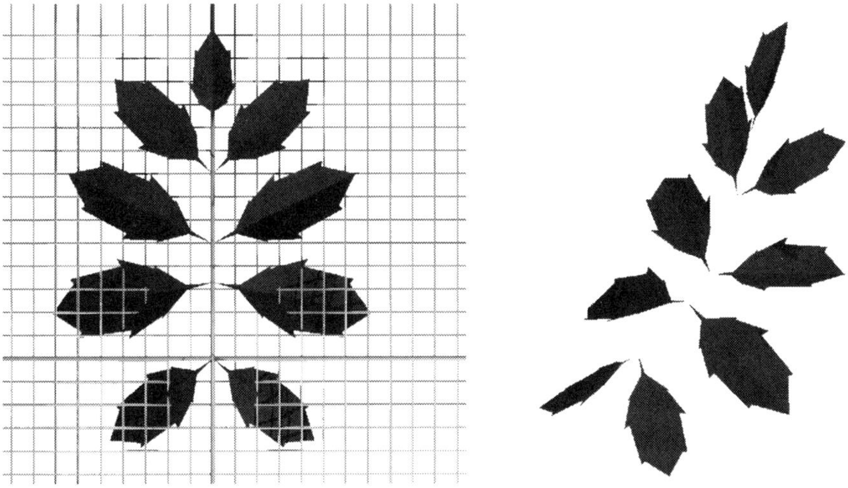

Figure 2.17 Mirror of the branch segment in *flower_1.rad* (left), and a perspective view of the branch without the grid (right).

2.4.12 Creating *flower_1.rad*

After the creation of a simple rosebud, the *leaves_1.rad* file will be mirrored and located on the flower stem. Add the following flower bud and stem material to the *material1.rad* file:

```
void plastic red1
0
0
5 1 0 0 0 0

void plastic green3
0
0
5 0 .8 .1 0 0
```

The bud is made from a cone and a sphere. Again, note the simplicity of the form. Great detail is not required because close-up images of the vase are unlikely. The insertion point will be the middle of the rosebud base. Add the following rosebud and stem to *flower_1.rad*.

```
red1 cone rose_c
0
0
8   0  0   0
    0  0  .075
    .02  0

red1 sphere rose_s
0
0
4    0   0 0 .02

green3 cone stem1
0
0
8     0 0 -.01
      0 0 -.03
      .02 .004

green3 cylinder stem2
0
0
7     0 0 -.03
      0 0 -.4
      .004
```

Now for the addition of the leaves. Two branches will be added to frame the rosebud in a pleasant manner. Figure 2.18 shows the result. Note the use of scale and rotations to disguise the fact that both branches are identical in shape. The xform array argument `-a ... -i` is also introduced here. Let's look closely at the first branch definition.

```
!xform -n lvs -s 1 -a 2 -mx -i 1 -rx 45 -t 0 0 -.075 leaves_1.rad
```

This command could be read

```
# Using xform, insert an object with the name (-n) lvs.
# Scale (-s) the surfaces by 1 then,
# Use array (-a) to make 2 copies of leaves_1.rad, mirroring each
# copy (-mx) about the yz plane. -i 1 declares that there will be one
# iteration of the array. It also serves to terminate the array
# manipulations.
```

Figure 2.18 A sprig of leaves frame the simple rosebud.

```
# Then rotate (-rx) both copies +45 degrees around the x-axis, following
# the right-hand rule.
# Finally move (-t) the copies to 0 0 -.075

# xform formal definition:
#
# xform [-a...-i] [-n] [-rx] [-ry] [-rz] [-s] [-t] file1 [file2...filen]
```

The second branch is scaled to be much smaller. It is rotated in a downward plane by adding `-rz 140`.

```
!xform -n lvs -s .7 -a 2 -mx -i 1 -rx -65 -rz 140 -t 0 0 -.125 leaves_1.rad
```

2.4.13 Creating *baseboard_1.rad*

To complete the scene, a baseboard is needed along the back wall. It will be painted the same color as the furniture, so no more definitions will be added to the *material1.rad* file. Again, sketching the shape of the baseboard provides the coordinates for the genprism polygon generator. The extruded molding is rotated and set in place by piping the genprism output through xform.

```
!genprism frame_brown baseboard1 \
7    0 0  0 -.1    .05 -.1    .1 -.08   .4 -.08  \
    .5 -.04    .5  0  -1 0 0 8  | xform -ry -90 -t 8 0 0
```

2.5 Assembling *scene1.all*

The whole scene can now be assembled and viewed for the first time. Though it would have been possible to lump all the individual geometry descriptions into one large file by constructing them in their final locations, it provides greater flexibility when you create a series of individual object descriptions and then collect them into a scene. The individual files begin to form a library, enabling files to be inserted in future scenes, and, as you discovered by building the rose, objects defined in separate files can be moved within a scene with great ease. The collector file is located in the *scene1* directory along with the *material1.rad* file, which means that all references to object files in the subdirectories should include appropriate paths.

The table and vase were made in their final locations, so they can be written directly into the *scene1.all* file by using the **!cat** (concatenate) command. These !cat statements are the equivalent of cutting and pasting the contents of *table_1.rad*, *vase1.rad*, and *wall_ceiling.rad* into *scene1.all*. A single !cat command could be followed by the three scene description files, but to make the listing easier to read, we will list them individually.

```
!cat    lib/table_1.rad
!cat    lib/vase1.rad
!cat    lib/wall_ceiling.rad
```

The stool and luminaires are located in the scene using the xform command.

```
!xform  -n stool1     -t   0 0 -4     stool_1.rad

!xform  -n light1     -t  -3 0  6.5   lamp_shade1.rad
!xform  -n light2     -t   3 0  6.5   lamp_shade1.rad

!xform  -n baseboard  -t  -4 4  0     lib/baseboard_1.rad
```

Finally, the floor will be constructed, using the xform array option.

This 2D array will multiply the contents of *tile_4.rad* into a 4-by-4 grid. This will result in an 8-foot-square floor made up of 64 tiles. Recall that `-a n` declares the beginning of the array, which will loop `n` times. `-i 1` states that only one iteration is required, and the position of `-i` in the command line marks the end of the array loop. Any transformation instructions located between the initial `-a` and `-i` options are progressively incremented by their initial values during each pass.

```
!xform -n floor -t -4 -4 0  -a 4 -t 2 0 0  -a 4 -t 0 2 0  -i 1 tile_4.rad

# The array function within xform is most powerful. This xform statement
# creates a 4 x 4 array of tile_4.rad. It could be read as follows:
#
# Move the insertion point of tile_4.rad to the xyz coordinate -4 -4 0
# Then make 4 copies of tile_4.rad, each copy located 2 feet further
# along the x-axis.
# For each of these copies, make three additional copies by increasing
# the y values by 2 ft.
#
# The result is an 8' by 8' tiled floor
```

2.6 Rendering Scene 1

Now that all the geometry has been assembled and appropriately located, the materials and geometry can be converted into the final octree. At the command prompt, enter the following:

```
% oconv material1.rad scene1.all  >  scene1.oct
```

Because the scene contains light sources, the ambient light value is set to a fraction of the previous levels (`-av 1 1 1`); otherwise, the effect of the direct lighting component would be masked by flat shading. We will discuss the art of determining reasonable ambient light values in the Scene 2 tutorial. Note that the vantage point (-vp) and ambient light values (-av) are the only arguments included in the rview command line. Rview has a set of default values for all its variables, which can be viewed on the command line by entering

```
% rview -defaults
```

Only alterations to these defaults need to be declared. View the following image:

```
% rview -vp 0 -15 4 -av .02 .01 .04 scene1.oct
```

Create a record of this vantage point by entering the following in the `rview` command window:

```
view scene1.vf
```

This instructs rview to write a file in the current directory, called *scene1.vf*, which contains a complete description of the view. Any file name can be used. The *.vf* filename extension has been added to identify the file's function, but is not required.

Now close rview by typing `q` or `quit` in the command window. You could check the view by entering rview again, but this time, override the `-vp -vd -vu` defaults by pointing to the new view file. The -vf argument is used to indicate that a view file follows.

```
% rview -vf scene1.vf -av .01 .01 .03 scene1.oct
```

With a view file and octree in hand, a final picture can be produced using the rpict program. Though rview enables a rapid viewing of the scene, its main function is to check geometry and to establish interesting viewing locations. Rpict works in the background, generating high-resolution pictures. In other words, use rpict for all final pictures and note that, unlike rview, it does not allow you to watch the picture rendering. To let you know that rpict is actually running, the following example uses a timer that reports the picture's progress by giving the percentage of the image that is completed. Rpict requires values for the pixel width and height of the final picture. Look at the default values of rpict by entering

```
% rpict -defaults
```

Do not be distressed by the dozens of arguments that are part of rpict. Only advanced users require knowledge of them all, and in Scene 2 the rad program will come to our rescue. For now, we will accept most of the default values and add to the command line only those we want to change. Enter the following command sequence to produce *scene1.pic:*

```
% rpict -vf scene1.vf -x 750 -y 750 -av .01 .01 .03 -t 30 scene1.oct > scene1.pic
```

This line could be read as follows:

```
# Call the program rpict and, using the view file (-vf) scene1.vf,
# create an image that is -x 750 by -y 750 pixels in size with an ambient
# value (-av) of .01 .01 .03. Every -t 30 seconds, report the progress
# of rpict as the octree scene1.oct is rendered into (>) the final image,
# called scene1.pic.
```

Once the rendering is completed, use the ximage program to view the picture, which is shown in Figure 2.19.

```
% ximage scene1.pic
```

Congratulations! You have constructed and rendered your first *Radiance* image.

But the rendering shows that the pendant luminaires are really inappropriate for this corner of our up-tempo espresso bar! The lighting must be reconsidered.

After evaluating several options, we decide to eliminate the pendants and try some recessed downlights and a few stylish wall sconces.

Figure 2.19 A complete rendering of the initial design.

2.7 Creating Basic Lighting

To explore this new lighting scheme, additional luminaires need to be created. To cover all bases, we will light the environment using the three basic approaches to interior lighting design: light to look at (decorative), light for objects to be seen (accent), and general lighting to see by (ambient).

2.7.1 Creating *downlight_a1.rad* and *light1.rad*

Recessed downlights will provide the ambient, or general, lighting. It is indeed possible to puncture the ceiling and insert all the geometry of the visible components of a downlight, including the reflector, lamp, and ceiling trim, but what is most critical to our scene is the effect of the light emitted from this luminaire, not its subtle structural details. In fact, this type of luminaire is designed to be reasonably well concealed. When was the last time you studied the interior of a recessed downlight while sipping cappuccino in an elegant coffee shop?

Keeping simplicity in mind, we will locate a disk of light with a diffuse distribution very close to the ceiling. The disk will appear to be the luminous opening of a downlight while requiring no detailed geometry and no puncturing of the ceiling surface.

This soft-light luminaire can take advantage of a low-wattage, warm-colored fluorescent light source. The model we will use incorporates two 18-watt lamps and should provide an illumination of about 100 lux at floor level. Each lamp initially emits 1200 lumens, but since we want to evaluate their typical effect, we will use their average, or design output, of 960 lumens (85%). The luminaire itself will absorb at least 25% of the lamps' light, so our disk will need to emit $960 \times 2 \times 75\% = 1450$ lumens. The opening of the downlight is 6 inches in diameter. This is now all the data we need to use lampcolor to calculate the radiance of the .25-foot-radius ring.

```
% lampcolor
Enter lamp type [halogen]: warm white
Enter length unit [meter]: feet
Enter lamp geometry [polygon]: ring
Ring radius [1]: .25
Enter total lamp lumens [0]: 1450
Lamp color (RGB) = 172.189867 107.858175 34.402984
```

Because we are including more than one light source, it is useful to create a file similar in function to *material1.rad* that contains only light data. Place the following light description in a new file, called *light1.rad*, located in the *scene1* directory.

```
void light lightring
0
0
3 172.189867 107.858175 34.402984
```

Now describe the recessed downlight in a file called *downlight_a1.rad* in the *lib* subdirectory. Modify the ring with `lightring` so it will inherit the radiance of our fluorescent downlight.

```
lightring ring downlight
0
0
8 0 0 0
  0 0 -1
  .25 0
```

2.7.2 Creating *downlight_b1.rad*

A halogen accent light will be applied to the table area, giving focus to the flower and vase and anything on the tabletop. *Radiance* has a built-in *spotlight,* which is useful for exploring the impact of various beam widths and intensities on the scene. The parameters discovered by using this prototype process can aid in the selection of actual spotlight photometry from the thousands of narrow-beam reflector lamps and luminaires. The "real" photometry of the selected luminaire can then be applied to the scene using the **ies2rad** function, which will be introduced in Scene 2.

The spotlight material uses a simple diffuse light source whose edges are clipped into a cone. The cone width is specified in the material description file along with a direction vector and its red, green, and blue radiance. This cone of light can then be applied as a material modifier to the emitting surface. In our case, the spotlight is recessed, so, again, we will use a ring. To help an object stand out in a scene, you can increase its illumination so that it appears several times brighter than its surroundings. Following this observation, we will make our accent downlight emit at least four times the intensity of the general downlight to help draw attention to the table and vase. Include the following in the *light1.rad* file, located in the *scene1* directory:

```
# The center of this cone of halogen light has several times the intensity
# of the center of the fluorescent downlights.
# Note that spotlight "clips" the diffuse output into a cone

void spotlight lightring2
0
0
7 1344 888 85   40 0 0 -.1

# spotlight definition:
#
# Using no modifier (void), create a spotlight material called lightring2(id).
# nothing on this line 0
```

```
# nothing on this line 0
# 7 variables follow, amount of red, green, blue, cone_width in degrees,
# and a direction vector, x y z. The amplitude of the vector affects the
# output intensity.

# spotlight formal definition:
#
# mod  spotlight  id
# 0
# 0
# 7    red  green  blue  width  xv yv zv
```

In a file named *downlight_b1.rad* located in the *lib* subdirectory, create the emitting geometry for the spotlight:

```
lightring2 ring downlight2
0
0
8 0 0 0
  0 0 -1
  .25 0
```

2.7.3 Creating *fixture1.rad*

The light to look at is a modern decorative wall sconce. It can be described as a luminous square that is held out from the wall by four red enamel posts. A lamp is located between the wall and the luminous square. The light from the lamp casts shadows of the porcelain posts onto the wall surface, creating an "x" shape pattern as shown in Figure 2.20. In reality, the rear lamp would radiate through the translucent square. To keep this example simple, the luminous square will be considered an independent light source that is attenuated to approximate a glowing translucent surface, based on the radiance of the lamp behind it.

The lamp behind the front surface is visible when viewed from the side, so a decorative globe lamp is installed. This is the same lamp we used in the ill-fated pendant luminaires. The lamp will be dimmed to create a more intimate environment, so use 300 lumens to calculate its radiance.

The luminous square will be created in the same manner as the downlights, but instead of a ring, the surface will be a 1-foot-square polygon. Approximately 30% of the lamp's light would be transmitted through this surface. Lampcolor can be used to calculate the radiance values for the panel based on this 100-lumen approximation.

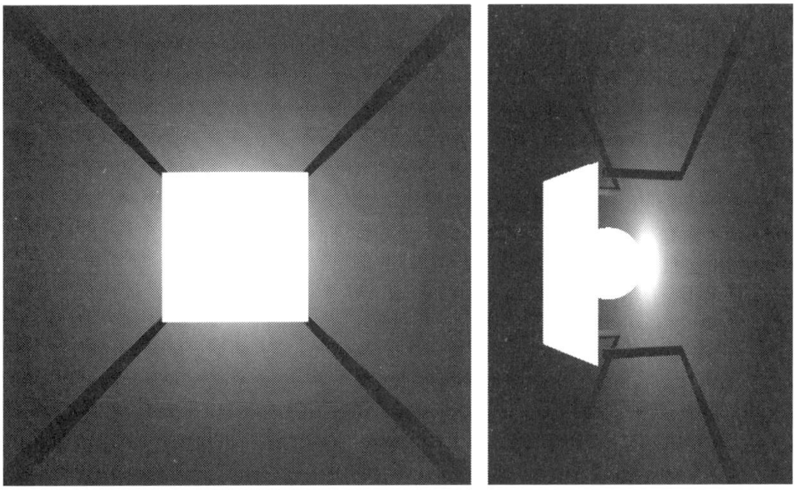

Figure 2.20 Two views of the decorative wall fixture. The image on the right exposes the globe lamp, which casts the shadow patterns on the wall surface. The front panel has been created as its own light source and assigned a radiance that represents the quantity of light that would pass through it if it were made of translucent glass. Because all visible light material in *Radiance* is opaque, the globe lamp does not add its radiance to the front panel. Therefore, our model is a reasonable representation of a translucent luminaire.

Add these two light sources to the *light1.rad* file:

```
# warm light for decorative 1-foot-sq. light panel
void light diffuse
0
0
3  2.6 1.7  .6

# warm globe lamp behind decorative panel, spherical r = .2
void light lumensf
0
0
3  15.794  10.413  3.993
```

Now build the description of the decorative wall sconce in a file called *fixture_1.rad*. The insertion point is at the center rear of the luminaire.

```
# luminous square
diffuse polygon lens
0
```

```
0
12  -.5     -.5    -.5
     .5     -.5    -.5
     .5     -.5     .5
    -.5     -.5     .5

# lamp behind the luminous square
lumensf sphere bulbf
0
0
4   0 -.25 0 .2

# posts that support the luminous square
red_porcelain cylinder post_sw
0
0
7      -.45     0      -.45
       -.45     -.45  -.45
        .025

red_porcelain cylinder post_se
0
0
7       .45     0      -.45
        .45     -.45  -.45
        .025

red_porcelain cylinder post_ne
0
0
7       .45      0       .45
        .45      -.45   .45
        .025

red_porcelain cylinder post_nw
0
0
7      -.45      0       .45
       -.45      -.45   .45
        .025
```

2.8 Reevaluating Scene 1

Incorporate the new lighting additions into the *scene1.all* file, then eliminate the pendants by inserting the # symbol at the beginning of each line. This will leave their deactivated description in place and on reserve for future explorations.

Now let's design the new lighting. First the spotlight will be located above the flower and vase, providing dramatic focus to the table area.

The diffuse downlights will flank the table and provide a nice, airy, general illumination during the daytime. It is likely that these will be turned off at night; this will heighten the visual drama created by the spotlight.

The wall sconces are located above the mirror height, which keeps them out of the patrons' reach and improves the visual composition of the scene. By rotating the sconces 45 degrees, a more interesting shadow pattern is created.

The adjusted *scene1.all* file looks like this:

```
#  scene1/scene1.all
#                        This file is used to place all objects

# directly insert descriptions that are constructed in location
!cat ./lib/table_1.rad
!cat ./lib/vase_1.rad
!cat ./lib/wall_ceiling.rad

# add two stools, one is turned out a little
!xform -n stool1          -t -2.0 0 0  lib/stool_1.rad

!xform -n stool2  -rz 30   -t  2.5 0 0  lib/stool_1.rad

# reserve for a different project
#!xform -n light1  -t -3 0 6.5  lib/lamp_shade_1.rad
#!xform -n light2  -t  3 0 6.5  lib/lamp_shade_1.rad

# add a four-by-four array of the tile units

!xform  -n floor  -t -4 -4 0  -a 4 -t 2 0 0  -a 4 -t 0 2 0  -i 1 \
       lib/tile_4.rad

# add the flower to the vase and scale accordingly
!xform  -n rose -s 2.5  -rz -30 -ry 2 -t 0 0 5.05 lib/flower_1.rad

# hang the mirror on the wall, leaning slightly outward
!xform  -n mirror -rx 5 -t 0 3.7 5 lib/mirror_1.rad
```

```
# locate the two decorative wall sconces
!xform  -n fix -ry 45  -t -2.75 4 6.5 lib/fixture_1.rad
!xform  -n fix -ry 45  -t  2.75 4 6.5 lib/fixture_1.rad

# add two diffuse downlights...note the use of the array command
!xform  -n dl_a1 -t -3 -1   7.99  -a 2 -t 6 0 0 lib/downlight_a1.rad

# add one spotlight on the ceiling above the vase
!xform  -n dl_b1 -t -0 -.5  7.99  lib/downlight_b1.rad

# insert the baseboard
!xform  -n baseboard -t -4 4 0   lib/baseboard_1.rad
```

Because we have separated the light descriptions from the other materials, *light1.rad* must be added to the oconv command line. Update the octree of Scene 1:

```
% oconv  material1.rad  light1.rad  scene1.rad  >  scene1.rad
```

2.9 Rendering and Filtering the Final Scene 1 Picture

Now render the final picture! This time, we will create a rendering that is twice the desired size. By filtering this larger picture into a smaller one, we eliminate many of the jagged edges and increase the image quality. We can make this filtered picture by using a longhand or shorthand approach. First, the longhand method. Two discrete steps are executed, resulting in the creation of one large and one smaller high-quality image.

```
%rpict -vf scene1.vf -x 1500 -y 1500 -av .01 .01 .03 -t 30 scene1.oct > scene1_b.pic
```

This is followed by the pfilt picture filter command:

```
%pfilt -1 -x /2 -y /2 -e +1 scene1_b.pic > scene1_bf.pic
```

This reduces the image size by one half (`-x/2 -y/2`). The pfilt -1 argument establishes that the picture will be passed through the filter once. The exposure is then opened one f-stop (`-e +1`), and the output redirected into a new image file called *scene1_bf.pic*. It should be noted that the *Radiance* image format also stores the original luminance values of the rendering. Altering the exposure of the image does not change these hidden values. Regardless of the exposure setting, a technical analysis of the lighting metrics derived from the image data remains constant.

A more efficient approach is to pipe the output of rpict directly into the pfilt command. The need for *scene1_b.pic* is eliminated.

```
%rpict -vf scene1.vf -x 1500 -y 1500 -av .01 .01 .03 -t 30 scene1.oct | \
            pfilt -1 -x /2 -y /2 -e +1 > scene1_bf.pic
```

When the rendering is complete, view the final 750-by-750-pixel Scene 1 picture as shown in Figure 2.21 (See also Plate 10 following page 328.):

```
%ximage scene1_bf.pic
```

After reviewing the image, we conclude that the resulting design is powerful and evocative and ready to be presented to the client! If the color of the walls or tiles changes, making simple changes in the *material1.rad* file and rerendering the scene will result in updated simulations of the final design of the cafe.

Figure 2.21 The final rendering of the Scene 1 exercise. (See also Plate 10 following page 328.)

2.10 Summary of the Scene 1 Exercise

This simple exercise has introduced the basic methods and conventions that are needed to create the beginnings of a photoaccurate picture, but we have only begun to uncover the capabilities of *Radiance*.

Our image is illuminated with light that comes directly from each light source, and we have not yet instructed *Radiance* to compute the contribution of interreflected light. This is the light that bounces from one surface to another, providing a more accurate representation of ambient light values throughout the space.

Though the materials in Scene 1 seem appropriate for the cafe, only color, specularity, and roughness have been used. Textures, such as the irregular surface found on handmade tiles or patterns such as woodgrain, could certainly enhance the floor or tabletop. And what about additional curved surfaces such as those that are needed to model a goblet or the handle of a coffee cup?

With increased complexity comes the need for greater organization. As you have observed, the greatest control over the placement of an object is achieved when it is created in a file of its own. A complex scene might be composed of dozens of files.

We could enhance the images we have produced using rpict, though they are already striking, by selecting alternative rendering and filtering parameters, such as increasing the number of rays sampling each pixel or improving antialiasing techniques.

So the Scene 1 exercise should be viewed as a stepping stone on the path toward learning how to release the full power of *Radiance*. The basic mechanism of modifying one description with another will be built on, so that more interesting materials and surfaces can be created. The process of building a shape with genbox and genprism exposes a format that is the basis of several geometry generators capable of producing exotic curved surfaces. Finally, the steps needed to organize and convert text files into octrees, and octrees into images, will be turned over to a powerful project manager program, which, once set up, will simplify the rendering of a complex scene.

Radiance generally provides several methods by which to accomplish a task. Though there are numerous approaches to building a complex 3D model and viewing it under light, some prove to be more efficient than others. The Scene 2 exercise follows a methodology that has evolved through applying *Radiance* to many large and detailed scenes. As you begin the project, keep in mind that some of the Scene 1 methods used to introduce *Radiance* basics will be replaced with more effective strategies.

CHAPTER 3

Scene 2 Tutorial

The interior of a small art gallery has been chosen for the Scene 2 exercise. The exercise concentrates on the visual impact of the interior. During the day, the entrance foyer is illuminated by daylight, which enters through two large windows and a pair of glass doors. The interior gallery is illuminated by indirect daylight from a central skylight. Direct daylight entering the skylight system is distributed throughout the gallery by a large overhead reflector. The nighttime illumination is provided by a series of aimable tracklights and recessed fluorescent luminaires. The gallery displays several artworks, including a large mounted photograph of the Scene 1 rendering, a few sculptures, and a collection of pottery artifacts, as well as appropriate furnishings.

The structure of this part of the tutorial will differ from the Scene 1 jump-start exercise. Now that you have some familiarity with the look and feel of *Radiance*, we will begin the exercise by focusing on several complex functions. These new tools will then be used in the construction of Scene 2.

3.1 Physically Based Lighting

To evaluate the visual impact of the art gallery, accurate descriptions of the light emitted from tracklights, linear fluorescents, and daylight need to be applied to the scene. Scene 1 was illuminated using luminaires based on some reasonable assumptions, but it would be a difficult task to find real luminaires that closely matched their distribution of light. The interior light sources for Scene 2 will use luminaire photometry that has been measured following controlled procedures. These data are then converted into a standardized text format that lighting analysis programs can read. Many luminaire manufacturers will provide photometric files of their product lines in this format. These files have an *.ies* extension, and examples can be found in the *Radiance* directory called *lib/source*. The daylight component will be based on resources that are built into *Radiance*. The data are derived from Commission Internationale de l'Eclairage (CIE) standards that closely model daylight observations that have been collected by scientists and engineers for decades. The resulting descriptions of sky light and sunlight will simulate the daylight illuminating our gallery.

3.1.1 Photometry Files

Radiance includes the **ies2rad** program to convert luminaire photometry written in the Illuminating Engineering Society of North America (IESNA) format into *Radiance* descriptions of light. In its simplest form, an IESNA photometric file includes an array of angles and intensities, along with a crude description of the luminaire's "luminous aperture," expressed in either feet or meters. Ies2rad can use this geometry to create a polygon, cylinder, or ring that distributes light in the described pattern. To create the emitting surface in the correct scale, ies2rad needs to know whether you are modeling the scene in feet or meters. If you are using feet, then use **-df** (default feet); otherwise, the program assumes that you are working in meters.

Two files are created by ies2rad and are given the extensions *.rad* and *.dat*. The *.dat* file contains a table of data specifying the distribution of light in a *Radiance* format. This is an auxiliary file and does not need to be directly handled by you. The statements in the *.rad* file use the information in the *.dat* file to attenuate the light description. The *.rad* file is then located, aimed, or copied in the scene by using **xform**. Unless the aiming, intensity, and color of the lighting is constantly changing, such as in a theater, it is useful to locate the ies2rad statements in one file and then manipulate the luminaire's location and aiming in another file. If you follow this convention, less processing time is required when you create a new octree after re-aiming or copying an existing luminaire type. It is not necessary to rerun the ies2rad program unless you have changed the luminaire's color or intensity. When you are creating the octree before rendering, the *.rad* file needs the data in the *.dat* file, so keep both in the same directory.

A typical ies2rad statement points to the *.ies* source file and includes parameters that establish the intensity, color, and distribution of the light. In the following example, the photometry of a PAR38 floodlight is converted into *Radiance* files named *type_S1*.

```
% ies2rad -df -t defaults -m .85 -c 1 1 1 -o type_S1  ies_lib/par38fl.ies
```

If we look at the contents of the *type_S1.rad* file, the relationship between *type_S1.dat* and *type_S1.rad* becomes apparent. *type_S1.dat* contains the PAR38 luminous intensity distribution data. These data modify the light material, which in turn modifies the **ring** geometry. The ring, called *type_S1.d*, is now a light source that has the photometric distribution of the PAR38 floodlight. All these details are automatically handled for you by the ies2rad program.

```
### type_S1.rad
#
# ies2rad -df -t default -m .85 -c 1 1 1 -o type_S1
# Dimensions in feet
# <PAR38FL   Beam spread: 47.6'
# 150-watt luminaire, lamp*ballast factor = 1

void brightdata type_S1_dist
4 flatcorr typeS1.dat source.cal src_theta
0
1 0.85

type_S1_dist light type_S1_light
0
0
3 85.6565 85.6565 85.6565

type_S1_light ring type_S1.d
0
0
8
     0 0 0
     0 0 -1
     0 0.2
```

Note that the floodlight enters the coordinate system as a luminous ring centered at 0 0 0 and pointing downward. To locate the floodlight in our scene, the aiming file would contain an xform command similar to this:

```
!xform -n track1_flood1 -rx 45 -rz 90 -t 10 10 7.5 type_S1.rad
```

Though there are many approaches to aiming the photometry of the `track1_flood1` luminaire, ours is tilted upwards (**-rx**) 45 degrees, then rotated to the right (**-rz**) 90 degrees, before being located beneath the track at 7 feet 6 inches above the floor. If you follow a consistent sequence of rotations for each luminaire, the task of predicting the aiming outcome is greatly simplified.

The ies2rad arguments include values that can alter the color and intensity of the luminaire's light. This example uses the color argument `-c 1 1 1` (RGB), to indicate that we are using white light and that the intensities of light described in the *par38fl.ies* file will not be modified. To simulate the color and intensity of light that would pass through a pink filter, these color values might be changed to `-c .8 .3 .4`. When the `-t default` option is used, ies2rad acquires color information from the -c values. If the -t value is the name of a common type of lamp, the program gets the appropriate color information from the *lamp.tab* database instead. Replacing `-c 1 1 1` with `-t halogen` would change the light color to match the spotlight that we constructed in Scene 1. The **lampcolor** program and the ies2rad -t option share the same database.

Most lamps' initial lumen output is significantly higher than their lumen output towards the end of their useful life. Design lumens represent the average output of a lamp. If *Radiance* is to accurately predict the average illumination levels of a scene, we need to reduce the initial lumens of the halogen PAR38 lamps to their design lumen output of 85%. This is accomplished by setting the value of the **-m** multiplier option to .85. This multiplier can also be used to test the effect of dimming the lamp (though the red shift of the filament is not automatically included) to explore the visual effect of lamps with the same photometric distribution but with different lumen values.

The **-o** <name> option is used to name the *.rad* and *.dat* output files. If the -o option is omitted, the default *.rad* and *.dat* filenames will have the same prefix as the input photometry filename.

Though this section covers most of the frequently used ies2rad options, you might look through the *Radiance* manual pages included on the CD-ROM for the details of additional features.

3.1.2 Creating Photometry Files from Printed Photometric Data

If you do not have access to a particular IESNA-format photometric file, but have only the published photometric data from luminaire or lamp catalogs, you can create your own ies2rad input files. When you are interpreting the data from charts and graphical descriptions, there may be inaccuracies. Keep this in mind when you begin to evaluate the visual appearance of a scene. The approach that follows is used to describe a distribution of light that is symmetrical about the *z*-axis. Though it is possible to handcraft IESNA-format photometric files that describe complex distributions of light, it can become a very tedious task. You might also discover that there are insufficient data to create a reliable 3D distribution.

Rather than delving into all the definitions, keywords, and format variations of the *IESNA Standard File Format for Electronic Transfer of Photometric Data LM-63-95*, we need only understand the basic anatomy of the format. This will enable us to create bare-bones text files that ies2rad will be able to convert into *Radiance* distributions of light. To acquire a current version of the IES photometric format standard, contact the Illuminating Engineering Society of North America.

Our simple file will have two parts. The first section will contain text descriptions of the luminaire, lamp, and catalog number.

```
This is a test file for a bare MR16 halogen lamp.
Catalog: MR16-50w floodlight
Note that this is a 12-volt lamp.
```

The comment section is terminated by a line that begins with `TILT=`. Unless the lamp is an HID source, the equal sign is followed by the word `NONE`.

```
TILT=NONE
```

Thirteen numbers follow; they describe several aspects of the photometry and related data. A new line is indicated by an asterisk (*):

```
*<number of lamps> <lumens per lamp> <candela multiplier>
 <number of vertical angles> <number of horizontal angles>
 <photometric type> <units type>
 <luminous opening width> <luminous opening length>
 <luminous opening height>
*<ballast factor> <reserved for future use. Set to 1>
 <input watts>
```

This is followed by the arrays of angles and related candela values:

```
*<vertical angles>
*<horizontal angles>
*<candela values for verticals at the 1st horizontal angle>
*<candela values for verticals at the 2nd horizontal angle>
*.
*.
*<candela values for verticals at the last horizontal angle>
```

Before we can create our ies2rad input file, we need to acquire the photometric data, consisting of a series of angles with associated intensities (candela values). These photometric data are generally presented in either a polar or a Cartesian graph. The graphs in Figure 3.1 represent identical distributions of light.

In the case of this MR16 photometry, the Cartesian graph provides the greatest detail. One method of acquiring the list of angle-candela values would be to sample the angles at equal distances. We might sample the data set every degree and record the associated candela value. Alternatively, we could create a smaller and equally accurate data set by recording the angle-candela values at the points where the slope of the line changes.

Eight pairs of angle-candela values reasonably depict the photometric data described by the Cartesian graph in Figure 3.2. The graph does not indicate the angle at which the candela value is 0, so we will have to extrapolate one. If the slope

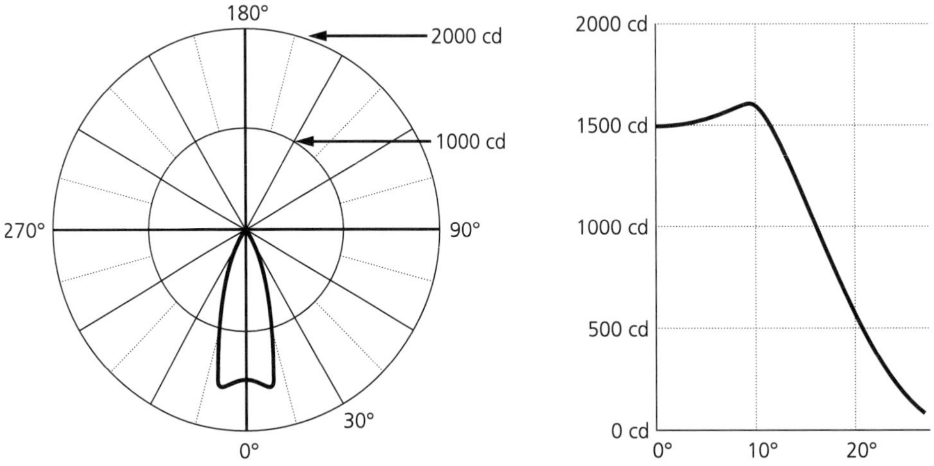

Figure 3.1 Polar (left) and Cartesian (right) graphs of a photometric file.

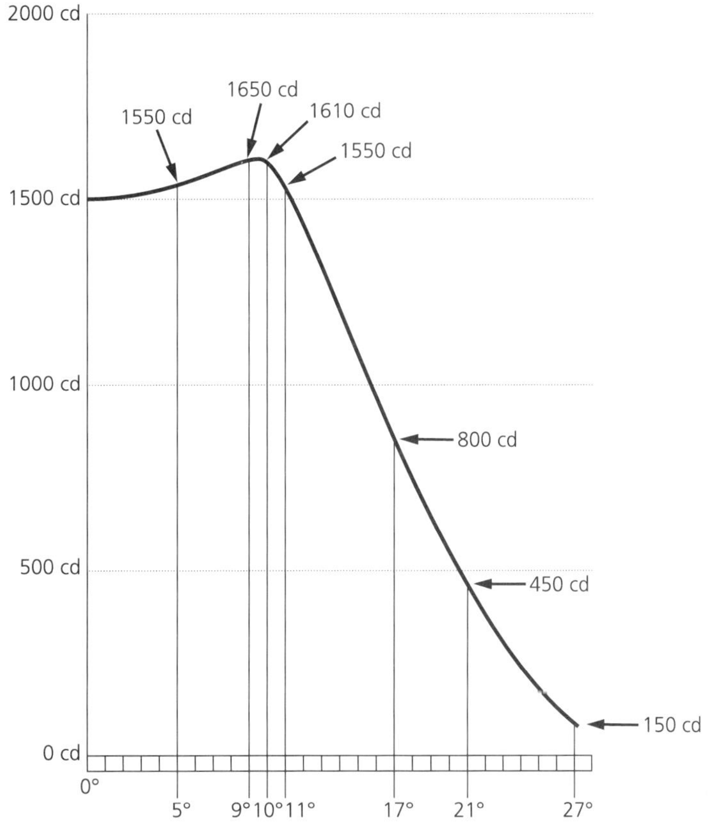

Figure 3.2 Determining the values for an IES photometric file.

of the line at 27 degrees remained constant, it would intersect the 0 candela value at about 30 degrees, so we will use this value to create the cutoff angle or the edge of the cone of light.

If we were to rotate this photometric distribution about the vertical axis, it would describe the symmetrical cone of light emitted by our MR16. The IESNA photometric format will instruct ies2rad to perform this rotation if the horizontal angle is 0 and the final value in the angle-candela array is either 90 or 180. Now we can construct our ies2rad input file.

```
This is a test file for an bare MR16 halogen lamp.
Catalog: MR16-50w-floodlight
Note that this is a 12-volt lamp.
TILT=NONE
```

```
1 650 1 10 1 1 1 -.16 0 0
1 1 50
0.00 5.00 9.00 10.00 11.00 17.00 21.00 27.00 30.00 90.00
0
1500 1550 1650 1610 1550 800 450 150 0 0
```

If you define the width of the luminous opening as a negative value (–.16), ies2rad will create a disc of material light with a diameter of .16 feet. To produce a 2-inch-square emitter, the width and length would be assigned values of .16. Remember that after ies2rad has processed our file, the center of the cone of light will point downward in the –*z* direction.

3.1.3 Generating the Sky and Sun

Gensky is a program that generates the sky dome and direct sunlight component for daylighted scenes. To illuminate the scene with the sky component, gensky produces the **skyfunc** modifier, which can be used to create a sky-component light source. This procedure will be described shortly. Should the scene be located somewhere other than San Francisco, gensky requires that the new geographic location be specified in degrees of longitude and latitude, along with the angle of the meridian, which establishes the appropriate time zone. The month, date, and time (24-hour clock) are added to generate specific daylight and sky conditions. Several optional sky descriptions are provided; they range from clear to cloudy. The direct-sunlight component can be switched on and off as required. Gensky assumes that +*y*-axis = north, +*x*-axis = east and +*z*-axis = up.

Gensky can contribute to our scene in three ways. First, it can create an impressive glowing sky dome, providing a background for exterior scenes. Interior environments can also look out onto this backdrop through windows and skylights.

To create a 180-degree sky dome for Bloomington, Indiana (latitude 39.1 degrees, longitude 86.3 degrees, meridian 75 degrees) at 1:00 PM on May 31, we would use the following descriptions:

```
!gensky 5 31 13 -a 39.1 -o 86.3 -m 75 -s

skyfunc glow sky_glow
0
0
4     .8 .8 1 0
```

```
sky_glow source sky
0
0
4      0 0 1 180
```

The gensky program creates skyfunc, which is used to modify the luminance of sky_glow. In turn, sky_glow modifies a source whose geometry appears to be a huge hemisphere centered about the +*z*-axis. Our scene is contained within this luminous dome, which depicts the sky for a specified time and place.

This is our first encounter with the surface called *source*. Actually, it is not really a surface, but a direction and an angular diameter. The sun, for example, would be represented as a source with a very narrow angular diameter. This replaces the need to locate a giant sphere of sunlight, 93 million miles away from our scene! In our glowing-sky example, a 180-degree source provides the effect of an infinitely distant dome.

A second application of gensky arises when the luminance of the sky needs to be accurately distributed through windows or doorways to illuminate an interior environment. The process begins by creating surfaces across these interior openings. An invisible light-emitting material called *illum* is used to modify this surface. Skyfunc is then converted into a modifier that conveys the daylighting distribution to the illum surface so that it invisibly radiates light into the room as though it were coming from the distant sky. The room is lighted accurately and the view of the exterior remains unimpeded.

For each window to distribute daylight from the appropriate sector of the sky, the invisible illum light sources must be created with the correct orientations. If the illum source is rotated at a later time, the lighting distribution of a west-facing window might suddenly be entering the room from the north!

The following description creates an invisible plane across a 4-foot-square window and broadcasts light from the western sky to an interior. Remember that the right-hand rule is very significant in this definition, because the order of the vertices that define this polygon determine which side of the illum surface will emit light. These descriptions could be appended to the previous gensky statement:

```
skyfunc brightfunc window_bright
2 winxmit winxmit.cal
0
0
```

```
window_bright  illum window1_light
0
0
3    .8    .8    .1

window1_light  polygon  window1_opening
0
0
12
        0    6    6.5
        0    2    6.5
        0    2    2.5
        0    6    2.5
```

The third common use of gensky is to illuminate the scene with the direct-sunlight component. Before we proceed, remember that while average illumination levels for an office interior might be 500 lux, an exterior surface at noon might register 50,000 lux. This 100:1 ratio is impossible for your computer's monitor to display accurately, so it is improbable that you will find an exposure level that serves both conditions effectively—just as in photography, if you open the exposure of the camera to see the details in a shadowed area, the surrounding sky becomes overexposed and appears white. Conversely, setting the exposure to the bright sky will obscure the details in the shadowed areas. The lesson here is to evaluate interiors and exteriors in separately exposed renderings. *Radiance* includes the **pcond** image-filtering program, which will compress a high-contrast picture so that more details become visible, but this is a postprocessing tool and is not always applicable. Thus, when using **rview** to initially explore an interior daylighted scene, do not panic when areas of the image appear too dark or are glaring white. Simply adjust the exposure with the interactive **exposure** command to optimize the visibility of different areas of the scene.

The sun is activated automatically when gensky is executed. To turn off its effect, include the **-s** argument in the gensky command line. When the sun is active, a ground ambiance value is calculated and inserted into a skyfunc comment line. If this value is 18 and you are evaluating an exterior scene, you might add an ambient value of `-av 18 18 18` to the rpict statement.

Because the direct component of the sun can have a very high intensity, the ambient value (**-av**) is much higher than Scene 1's atmospheric interior.

We need to digress briefly from the gensky discussion to establish a method for deriving an ambient value for scenes, such as our daylighted interior, that contain a broad range of luminance values. The following approach employs a technique that produces useful scene-specific ambient values.

1. Create an octree of the scene, then establish a useful vantage point using rview.
2. Type `e` or `exposure` in the rview command window and select a surface in the scene. Rview will normalize the exposure of the scene to the luminance at this point.
3. Select several surfaces using the `e` command until the exposure of the scene is optimized.
4. If you enter `exposure =` on the rview command line, the absolute exposure of the scene is revealed.
5. A reasonable ambient value can be determined by dividing the absolute exposure value by 2.

There is no absolute method for determining the -av value for all lighting conditions. Other approaches will be presented throughout this book, but the exposure/2 method meets our current needs. You will find that ambient values for a daylighted interior scene will generally range from about `-av 1 1 1` to `-av 4 4 4`. Where the luminance values within a scene vary tremendously, as in our daylighted scene that includes both outdoors and indoors, the rpict -aw parameter should be set to 0 so that the rendering process will not modify our ambient values. Otherwise, a setting of between `-aw 32` and `-aw 128` is reasonable for most scenes, ranging from indoor-only to outdoor-only.

The skyfunc description can be viewed by writing the output of the gensky command into a file.

```
% gensky 5 31 13 -a 39.1 -o 86.3 -m 75 > text.file
```

Now we can discover what is contained in the skyfunc description:

```
% more text.file

# gensky 5 31 13 -a 39.1 -o 86.3 -m 75
# Solar altitude and azimuth: 72.3 13.3
# Ground ambient level: 18.0

void light solar
0
0
3 7.16e+06 7.16e+06 7.16e+06

solar source sun
0
0
4 -0.070061 -0.295437 0.952790 0.5
```

```
void brightfunc skyfunc
2 skybr skybright.cal
0
7 1 3.24e+01 3.03e+01 1.45e+00 -0.070061 -0.295437 0.952790
```

In addition to the ground ambient level and the description of skyfunc, the source of the sun is revealed with its .5-degree angular diameter.

As we have mentioned, pictures rendered under full sunlight will appear to be very white and "burned out" when you use default rendering and filtering values. If you have not already determined an optimal exposure in rview, this "burnout" can be solved by reducing the exposure by a factor of -4 or -5, as shown in this pfilt command. Alternatively, change the -1 argument to -2 and pfilt will attempt to optimize the exposure for you.

```
% pfilt -1 -e -5 sunlight.pic > sunlight_filtered.pic
```

You now have access to all the descriptions of light most commonly used in *Radiance*. In Scene 1, we created distributions of light to approximate hypothetical recessed and decorative luminaires. Scene 2 will include photometry in the IESNA format that has been derived from real luminaires and geographically accurate daylight. However, if we use only the direct component of light and an ambient value derived from the exposure setting, the shaded areas will appear artificial and flat. The missing element is known to lighting designers as ambient light, while illumination engineers label it the indirect component. These terms describe the illumination that bounces off surfaces and reveals details in shaded areas.

3.2 Indirect Light

Indirect light cannot be put into a scene description format or read from an IESNA photometry file. Its effect is determined only after the direct components of the lighting design have been reflected by surfaces in the scene. If sunlight enters a room and strikes a blue carpet, the indirect component produced by light bouncing off the carpet will add a blue cast to the ceiling. Turn off the sun and the blue ceiling component disappears. This is not an artifact—indirect light is created as a consequence of the interaction between direct light and the objects in the scene.

When the indirect component is called for, *Radiance* adds many calculations to the rendering process. Images that take minutes to complete under direct light might render for hours when interreflection is added. A balance should be struck between rendering time and the resolution and quality of the resulting image. Rpict uses many arguments that can influence this rendering-time-versus-image-quality optimization. A listing of the -default settings for rpict reveals the argument names, the initial values, and a description of their function.

```
% rpict -defaults
-i-                                # irradiance calculation off
-vtv                               # view type perspective
-vp 0.000000 0.000000 0.000000     # view point
-vd 0.000000 1.000000 0.000000     # view direction
-vu 0.000000 0.000000 1.000000     # view up
-vh 45.000000                      # view horizontal size
-vv 45.000000                      # view vertical size
-vo 0.000000                       # view fore clipping plane
-va 0.000000                       # view aft clipping plane
-vs 0.000000                       # view shift
-vl 0.000000                       # view lift
-x 512                             # x resolution
-y 512                             # y resolution
-pa 1.000000                       # pixel aspect ratio
-pj 0.670000                       # pixel jitter
-ps 4                              # pixel sample
-pt 0.050000                       # pixel threshold
-bv+                               # back face visibility on
-dt 0.050000                       # direct threshold
-dc 0.500000                       # direct certainty
-dj 0.000000                       # direct jitter
-ds 0.250000                       # direct sampling
-dr 1                              # direct relays
-dp 512                            # direct pretest density
-dv+                               # direct visibility on
-sj 1.000000                       # specular jitter
-st 0.150000                       # specular threshold
-av 0.000000 0.000000 0.000000     # ambient value
-aw 0                              # ambient value weight
-ab 0                              # ambient bounces
-aa 0.200000                       # ambient accuracy
-ar 32                             # ambient resolution
-ad 128                            # ambient divisions
-as 0                              # ambient super-samples
-me 0.00e+00 0.00e+00 0.00e+00     # extinction coefficient
```

```
-ma 0.000000 0.000000 0.000000     # scattering albedo
-mg 0.000000                       # scattering eccentricity
-ms 0.000000                       # mist sampling distance
-lr 6                              # limit reflection
-lw 0.005000                       # limit weight
-t 0                               # time between reports
-w+                                # warning messages on
```

The family of rpict parameters with labels that begin with -a affect the way *Radiance* handles the indirect lighting calculation. Changing some of these values enables a very intricate scene to be rendered with great detail, while a different set of values will optimize the rendering of a simple planar scene. The -ab argument turns on the indirect calculation when its value is greater than 0. For most scenes, one ambient bounce is sufficient to reveal shaded areas with reasonable accuracy. The art gallery interior requires a minimum of two ambient bounces for the daylight to be distributed throughout the room. Direct sunlight enters the skylight and strikes the reflector, some of this light bounces toward the ceiling, and finally some of this ceiling light bounces toward the artwork and the surrounding surfaces. If several views of the same scene are required, including -af <filename> within each rpict statement will create an ambient file that accumulates and makes available indirect lighting data that all the rendering processes can share. This can really speed up the rendering time of a sequence of images in addition to improving their overall quality. If the geometry or light sources in the project change, the ambient file should be erased. The next time you execute rpict, a new ambient file will be created.

The following statement renders an image using one ambient bounce of light and creates a scene.amb so that other views in this sequence will be processed more quickly. There is a chance that this simple statement might produce a reasonable image, but it is more likely that you will want to adjust the rpict default rendering parameters to refine the quality of the image.

```
% rpict -vf view.vf -x 512 -y 512 -ab 1 -af scene.amb -t 60\
      scene.oct > scene.pic
```

Some printers have a draft setting, which produces fast output but grainy characters, and a high-resolution setting, which can create publication-quality text. Switching between these settings is analogous to altering rendering parameters to improve the quality of a picture. Though it might be very interesting to study the impacts of the dozens of rpict parameters, it can become a frustrating and time-consuming exercise to optimize the rendering of a picture using a random trial-and-error method. To address this issue, *Radiance* includes two programs that improve your chances of expediently rendering a high-quality picture. These rendering optimization programs generate a complete set of rpict and pfilt parameters based on information that you provide. These values can be further optimized as you become familiar with the details of the rendering process. In addition, these programs automate the process of checking for changes and updating octree files, setting up rendering statements, and even filtering the resulting pictures. The experience and wisdom that emerge through the settings produced by these optimization programs will quickly improve your understanding of the art and the nuances of creating a high-quality picture.

3.2.1 Using rad

Rad and **trad** are programs that set up a rendering procedure and optimize the rendering process based on a few general parameters that you provide. Actually, trad is just a graphical interface to rad. It calls rad, which then calls the other *Radiance* programs to do the actual work. Rad directly processes data to automate much of the rendering procedure. It interacts with text data in the form of a *Radiance* input file, normally identified by the *.rif* extension. We will explore the rad program in this tutorial, exposing the details that both programs handle.

A rad input file can replace the individual oconv, rpict, rview, and pfilt statements that we used to render the images of Scene 1. To do this, the *.rif* file requires a list of all scene description, lighting, material, and view files. These are organized under various headings, along with the names you want to use for the octree files and images. Several other parameters are set, which include entering a low, medium, or high value for the rendered image quality. The higher the quality, the longer the rendering time. What follows is a typical *.rif* file, set up for a daylighted interior.

```
### scene2_test.rif
#
# Example rad input file to render a portion of Scene 2
AMBFILE= scene2d.amb
DETAIL= Medium
EXPOSURE= -2
INDIRECT= 1
OCTREE= scene2d.oct
PENUMBRAS= False
PICTURE= pics/scene2_test
QUALITY= Medium
REPORT= 2
```

```
RESOLUTION= 480
UP= Z
VARIABILITY= Medium
ZONE= Interior 0 40.1 0 25.5 0 19.4
MATERIALS= lib/building.mat lib/sky_d.mat lib/luminaire.mat
RENDER= -aw 0
SCENE= sc2light.rad lib/walls.rad lib/ceiling.rad lib/floor.rad
view= s -vp -20 12 6 -vd 1 0 0 -vo 22
```

This *scene2_test.rif* file is put into action with the simple command line

```
% rad scene2_test.rif
```

Note that one indirect bounce is specified and that the resolution of the resulting image is 480 pixels square. This scene takes about one hour to render on a reasonably equipped 90-MHz Pentium-based computer running Linux.

The manual includes a comprehensive description of *Radiance* input file variables. A brief and practical description of the less obvious rad file variables is given below:

- *PENUMBRAS:* These are "soft shadows." The edges of a sharply defined circle of light, such as the Scene 1 spotlight, would be diffused if penumbras were activated by specifying a value of *True*. Generally, penumbras contribute significantly to rendering times. A value of *False* turns penumbras off.
- *REPORT:* The rendering progress is reported by including the *-t <seconds>* argument in an rpict command. REPORT serves this function in a *.rif* file, but its increments are in minutes.
- *RESOLUTION:* This line declares the final maximum dimensions of the image in pixels. If one dimension is provided, rad uses this as the limit for both horizontal and vertical dimensions. If two dimensions are listed, the first will specify the horizontal image size, and the second, the maximum vertical size.
- *VARIABILITY:* If light varies significantly over the surfaces in the scene, such as shafts of sunlight penetrating a gloomy warehouse, a value of *High* is appropriate. On the other hand, a uniformly lighted office would have a *Low* variability. *Medium* applies to environments with moderately diverse luminance patterns.
- *ZONE:* The values that follow *ZONE* inform rad whether the area of interest is *Interior* or *Exterior* and provide the dimensions of the volume that you want to visualize. Three pairs of numbers are required to describe the minimum and maximum x, minimum and maximum *y*, and minimum and maximum *z* coordinates of the scene. Care should be taken to provide reasonably accurate values because many rpict parameters are derived from this information.

- *view:* The view information can be specified in several formats. If three images are to be rendered, three separate view headings are included. To vary the names of the output images, an identifier (optional) can be inserted immediately following `view=`. In the previous example, s would be appended to the *PICTURE* identification, so the image would be called *scene2_test_s.pic.*
  An existing view file is specified by preceding the file name with the *-vf* argument. Alternatively, a string of view parameters such as *-vp* and *-vd* will also specify a view.

Additional headings, such as oconv, render (for rview or rpict), and pfilt, can be included, followed by a list of options and values. This is where you can adjust or override the settings that rad has generated. For example, you could force rad to include pfilt box filtering by adding the line

```
pfilt= -b
```

or turn off the rad-generated -aw option by including

```
rpict= -aw 0
```

To view the settings that rad would execute, the **-n** option (do not execute) and the **-e** option (list all actions and settings) can be added to the rad command line.

```
% rad -n -e scene2.test.rif
```

This results in a description of the previous *.rif* file settings followed by a comprehensive listing of the proposed rendering sequence.

```
rpict -t 120 -vu 0 0 1 -vp -20 12 6 -vd 1 0 0 -vo 22 -dp 512 -ar 22 -ms
0.7 -ds .3 -dt .1 -dc .5 -dr 1 -sj .7 -st .1 -ab 1 -af scene2d.amb -aw
1024 -aa .2 -ad 400 -as 64 -av 8 8 8 -lr 6 -lw .002 -aw 0 -x 64 -y 64
-ps 1 scene2d.oct > /dev/null

rpict -t 120 -vu 0 0 1 -vp -20 12 6 -vd 1 0 0 -vo 22 -x 960 -y 960 -ps 6
-pt .08 -dp 512 -ar 22 -ms 0.7 -ds .3 -dt .1 -dc .5 -dr 1 -sj .7 -st .1
-ab 1 -af scene2d.amb -aw 1024 -aa .2 -ad 400 -as 64 -av 8 8 8 -lr 6 -lw
.002 -aw 0 scene2d.oct > scene2_test_s.unf

pfilt -1 -e -4 -r 1 -x /2 -y /2 scene2_test_s.unf > scene2_test_s.pic
rm -f scene2_test_s.unf
```

All the choices that rad has made are now exposed. We are provided with an opportunity to review these details and fine-tune a few variables before activating the image-making process. The *.rif* files and the rad command will be explored further after we have built and assembled all Art Gallery scene descriptions.

As you work through the Scene 2 project, you will gain valuable insights about *.rif* files and the parameters that rad controls. Then you will be ready to explore the trad interface, which automates the editing and execution of *.rif* files. Figure 3.3 illustrates the trad graphical interface resulting from the following command:

```
% trad scene2_n.rif
```

3.2.2 Viewing through Walls

Now that we can render the effect of interreflected light, we need a way to peer into the room to see the results. This was not an issue in Scene 1 because the corner of the cafe was open on three sides. A movie set often leaves out a wall so that the director and camera have full view of the whole scenic environment, but if we leave a wall out of our model, we provide the ambient light with an escape route and invalidate the interreflection calculation!

Rpict and rview apply "clipping planes" to the scene, enabling you to see through walls without interfering with the interreflection of light. The application of clipping planes is illustrated in Figure 3.4. The forward clipping plane eliminates all visible surfaces in front of the vantage point to a distance specified by the **-vo** parameter. If a 1-foot-thick wall is 10 feet in front of the virtual camera location, setting -vo to 11.5 feet would make the wall disappear and you would be peering into the scene on its other side. An aft clipping plane can be activated, which limits

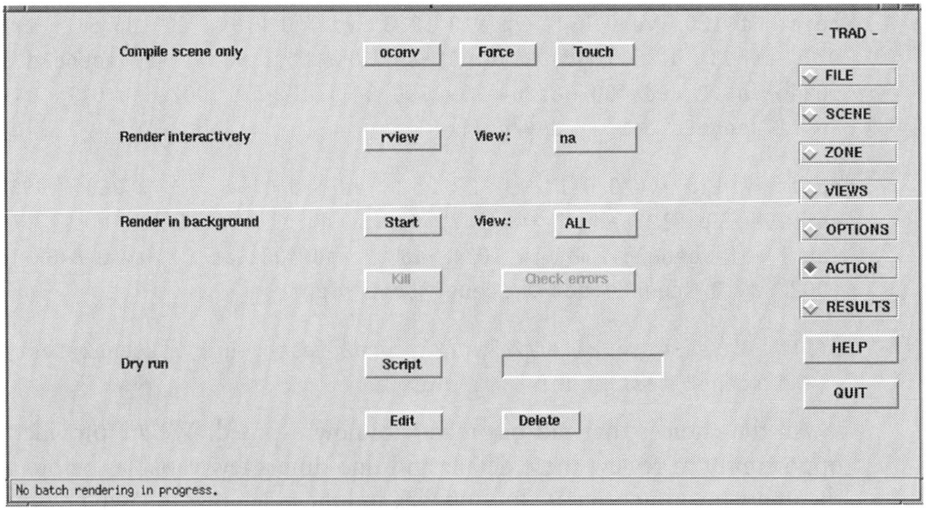

Figure 3.3 The trad graphical interface.

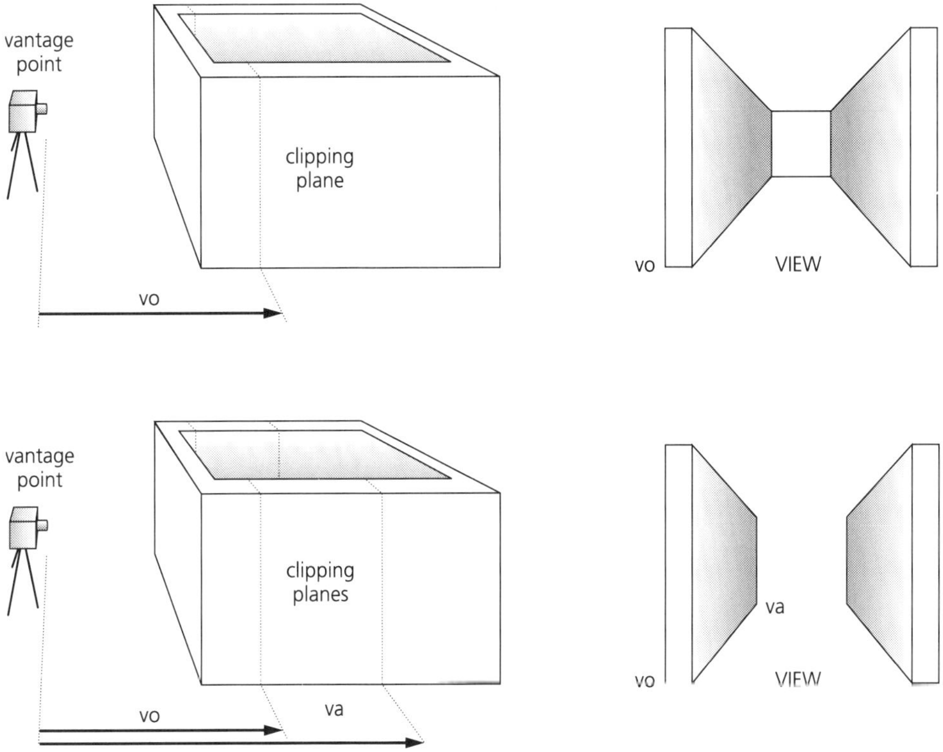

Figure 3.4 The fore (vo) and aft (va) clipping planes.

the distance you can see into the room. If we add `-va 20` to the rpict or rview command, everything past this distance becomes a black void. Peering through walls or creating a thin section through a complex building structure are just two of the possible applications. The default value for -vo and -va is 0, which deactivates the clipping plane effects.

3.3 Adding Textures and Patterns to Materials

The minimum requirements for a surface to become visible are the presence of light, a material modifier, and someone to view it! We have seen this principle in action throughout our work on Scene 1. You have no doubt noticed that the material definition also includes a modifier option. Textures and patterns can modify a material, creating new surface effects that are limited only by our imagination and our ability to manipulate or write functions.

To meet the needs of most users, *Radiance* provides a library of exciting texture- and pattern-generating functions. However, if you have reasonable math and programming skills, you can also use the set of tools provided by *Radiance* for inventing your own textures and patterns.

Modifying a material by giving it a texture creates the impression that you can touch and feel its surface variations. These "bumps" affect the general luminance and highlights of the object. Most textures are generated by **texfunc**, which calls texture-producing procedures. The procedure, in this case, is a mathematical description of the surface variations. Another method creates the texture by using surface normal data that have been stored in a file. It is aptly named **texdata.**

Patterns affect the color or reflectance of a material. In the case of transparent or translucent materials, they modify transmittance. There are many ways to acquire patterns. They can be drawn in a paintbox program, scanned from photographs, downloaded from the Internet, or generated through procedural functions. You then determine how the pattern is applied or mapped to polygons, cylinders, and spheres. You saw a pattern function at work when we explored the skyfunc output of gensky. The variations of luminance across the sky dome were applied using brightfunc.

The family of pattern types is given below:

- Functions: **Brightfunc** and **colorfunc** describe patterns using procedural functions. Brightfunc affects luminance variations of a material; colorfunc affects both luminance and color. In the language of the artist, these functions affect value and hue.
- Data: **Brightdata** and **colordata** use data from a file to vary the luminance and color of a material. A *Radiance* image is also a data file, and a special implementation of colordata, called **colorpict**, is used to map *Radiance* picture files to material surfaces.
- Text: **Brighttext** and **colortext** generate text fonts. Brighttext is used for black, white, or shades of gray; color text is generated by colortext.

So how do we incorporate textures and patterns into a scene? We define a pattern, apply it to a material, and use it to modify a surface. This identifier-to-modifier inheritance system can be extended to include several material characteristics. Let's look at a simple pattern function and apply it to one of the floor tiles that were constructed in Scene 1.

Now suppose that the interior designer changed the floor tile specification from a clear ceramic finish to faux granite. Since granite is extremely granular, the new finish can be approximated by applying a randomized pattern of flecks to the tile material.

The brightfunc procedure that can create these flecks calls on a random noise generator. Several types of random noise are available in *Radiance*. Regular noise is used to generate softer visual variations; fractal noise is used for sharper effects. We will use fractal noise to construct the granite pattern.

To demonstrate the inheritance process, create a description for granite by calling the *dirt.cal* function from the *Radiance* library. In a file named *test_pat.rad*, insert the granite function, the base material, and a surface generator to create the tile. Note the ID-to-modifier inheritance pattern as the `granite` modifies the `plastic tile_gray` that modifies the `granite_tile`. Figure 3.5 shows the resulting material.

```
# brightfunc pattern that looks like granite
void brightfunc granite
4  dirt  dirt.cal  -s .01
0
1     .6

# gray semi_gloss material that inherits the granite pattern
granite  plastic  tile_gray
0
0
5  .45  .4  .4  .04  .03

# tile surfaces with a flecked gray semi_gloss finish
!genbox  tile_gray  granite_tile  1 1 .1 -b .025
```

A closer look at the *dirt.cal* brightfunc format reveals that there are two variables that alter the granite effect.

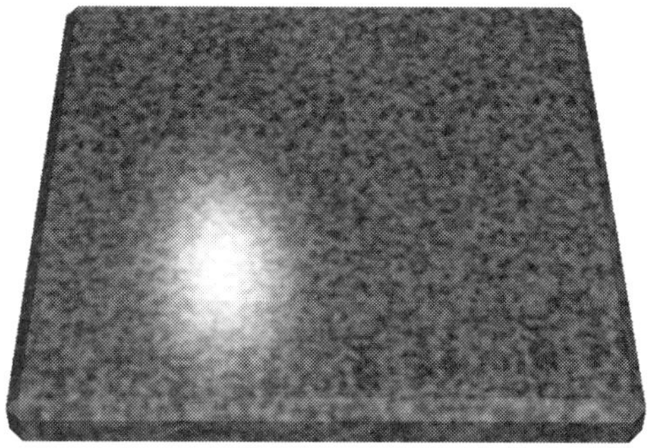

Figure 3.5 Granite pattern generated by the brightfunc *dirt.cal* function.

```
mod brightfunc  id
4 refl  function_file   scale n
0
1 amount_of_effect
```

The scale factor n increases or decreases the size of the flecks. In fact, any transformation can be included here, provided that you update the number of arguments at the beginning of the line. You could rotate this simple noise function by adding -rz 90, but that would create as much visual change as rotating a tray of sand—very little!

In this case, scale has significant influence, because it can vary the surface pattern from large splotches to the fine pattern of emery cloth. The amount_of_effect variable controls the intensity. An intensity of .1 renders the flecks barely visible; a value of .7 is quite noticeable.

Radiance enables any number of patterns and textures to be inserted into the inheritance stream of a material. This is a very powerful feature, which enables the construction of extraordinarily detailed effects. To illustrate this technique, we will add a second pattern to the tile. If the interior designer specified a seasoned maplewood tile, granite flecks would be reduced to a subtle mottling effect, the woodgrain pattern added, and the color changed. Again, the *Radiance* library is summoned.

```
# brightfunc pattern that adds character to wood
void  brightfunc  mottled
4  dirt  dirt.cal   -s .01
0
1 .30

# apply woodgrain pattern
mottled   brightfunc   maple
4  zgrain  woodpat.cal    -s .04
0
1 .55

# maple definition found in material.rad in Radiance library
maple  plastic  tile_maple
0
0
5  0.689  0.511  0.298  .025  .025

# old maple tile with a soft luster finish
!genbox  tile_maple  tile  1 1 .1 -b .025
```

The orientation of the woodgrain pattern produces a harsh crossgrain, which does not resemble the softer-looking maple parquet tile specified by the interior designer. Because the woodgrain function produces a 3D pattern, it can be rotated 90 degrees about the *y*-axis to generate a long-woodgrain effect. Edit the maple brightfunc description to change the direction of the woodgrain by adding another transformation:

```
# apply edge grain wood pattern
mottled brightfunc maple
6  zgrain  woodpat.cal  -s  .04  -ry 90
0
1 .50
```

Though the maple pattern is now quite satisfactory, the smooth ceramic luster of the tile is inappropriate. To add the appearance of porous wood, a texture function can be added to the inheritance stream. If you maintain the current specularity and roughness values, a waxed-wood effect is achieved, as illustrated in Figure 3.6. The final definition of the wooden tile combines the effects of two patterns, a texture and a plastic material to describe its surface appearance.

```
### maple wood tile with waxed finish
void  brightfunc  mottled
4  dirt  dirt.cal -s .01
0
1 .30

mottled brightfunc maple
6 zgrain woodpat.cal  -s .04 -ry 90
0
1 .55
```

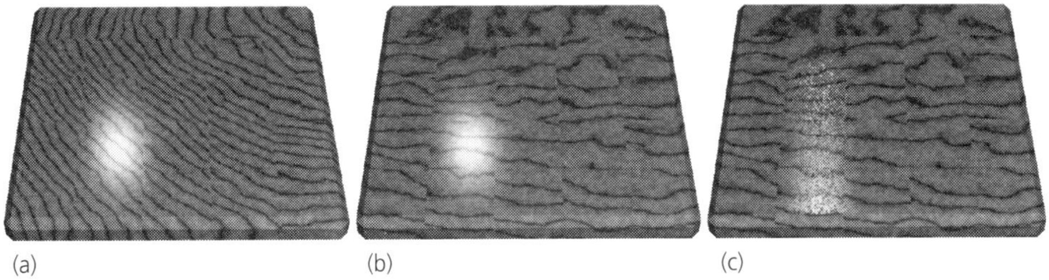

Figure 3.6 Examples of maplewood tiles: (a) crosscut tile, (b) long-grained tile, and (c) long-grained tile with waxed-wood texture.

```
maple  texfunc grainy
6  xgrain_dx ygrain_dx zgrain_dx woodtex.cal -s .005
0
1  .075

grainy  plastic  tile_grained_maple
0
0
5  .689  .511  .298  .025  .025

!genbox  tile_grained_maple  tile  1 1 .1 -b .025
```

The family of texture and pattern functions have similar-looking definitions. Before applying one of these library resources, list its contents and read the header so that you know what variables to include in the scene description.

```
% more ...ray/lib/dirt.cal
{
     Dirt pattern.
     This is probably the simplest application
     imaginable for the fractal noise function.

     A1 - degree of "dirtiness"; 1 is very dirty.
}
dirt = 1 - A1*.5*(1+fnoise3(Px,Py,Pz));
```

Review the granite and mottled definitions, observing how the variables in the *dirt.cal* listing are related to their scene descriptions. Our primary interest is the pattern effect and not the equation that produces it, so unless you are mathematically inclined, it's fine to skip over the parametric equations. Later in this tutorial, the gensurf exercise will give you ample opportunity to become familiar with including equations in a *Radiance* function.

```
# textfunc formal definition:
#
# mod textfunc id
# 4+ xpert ypert zpert function_file  transformation
# 0
# n A1 A2 .. An

# brightfunc formal definition:
#
# mod brightfunc id
```

```
# 2+ refl function_file transformation
# 0
# n A1 A2 .. An
```

Some texture and pattern functions require you to set several values. This example lists the information from the *brick.cal* header and gives a typical brightfunc scene description that could be used to modify an exterior wall material.

Header:

```
brick.cal  Brick patterns
  A1     = Grout width
  A2     = Nominal layer height
  A3     = Nominal brick spacing
  A4     = Offset
  A5     = Brick brightness
  A6     = Grout brightness
```

Scene description:

```
  # rows of offset bricks with white grout.
  void brightfunc  brick_pattern
  4 brick  brick.cal  -s 1
  0
  6  .05  .4  .95  .5  .3  .7
```

3.3.1 Mapping a Picture onto a Polygon

A special-purpose colordata function, called **colorpict**, can be used to map a picture onto a surface. This is a very useful function, which enables rendered or scanned pictures to be hung on walls or mapped to objects within the scene.

The image to be mapped must be in the *Radiance* picture file format (*.pic*). Because this format is not in general use, *Radiance* includes several filters to convert its pictures to and from common formats such as *.tif* and *.ppm*. The following example converts a *Radiance* picture into the *.tif* format, then, by including **-r** (reverse) in the command line, converts the picture back to its original *Radiance* format. The original floating point values will be compromised.

```
% ra_tiff    picture.pic picture.tif
% ra_tiff -r picture.tif picture.pic

# ra_tiff formal definition:
#
# ra_tiff [-r reverse] [-b grayscale] input_image output_image
```

Though pictures can be mapped to polygons, cylinders, and spheres, other surfaces are not yet supported. Our example will place the final picture from the Scene 1 exercise on a canvas so that we can hang it on the wall in the Scene 2 art gallery.

The colorpict function scales the shortest dimension of the picture to 1, then locates its lower left corner at 0 0 0 in the *xy* plane. Assuming that the *z*-axis is up, it's as though the picture were placed on the floor facing upward. However, the picture remains invisible until it is placed on a canvas! Once the canvas and the picture have been merged together, the artwork can be located in a file and placed anywhere in the gallery by using xform.

The first step in this process is to define the canvas material. We will use a bright white surface so as not to influence the original coloring of the image.

```
void  plastic  titanium_white_canvas
0
0
5  .9  .9  .9  0  0
```

Our Scene 1 picture is square, and regardless of its pixel size, it will be scaled to a one-unit square. We want to create visual impact with our art, so it will be enlarged to fit a 6-foot-square canvas.

```
void  colorpict  cafe_image_data
9 clip_r clip_g clip_bp scene1.pic picture.cal pic_u pic_v -s 6
0
0
```

This colorpict scene description first clips the picture's color values so they will not exceed an intensity of 1 and glow! The *picture.cal* function handles the coordinates of a flat picture, and the `pic_u` and `pic_v` locate the image in the *xy* plane. All we need to do is name the colorpict description (`cafe_image_data`), insert the name of the picture (*scene1.pic*), and establish the appropriate scale (`-s 6`). Because we want the canvas to be vertical, we can rotate the picture to a standing position by adding `-rx 90`.

```
void colorpict cafe_image_data
11 clip_r clip_g clip_b scene1.pic picture.cal pic_u pic_v -s 6 -rx 90
0
0
```

The image data and the canvas material are now ready to be merged. This is accomplished by using the **alias** command, which maps one name to another. This simply means that one entity can have two names.

```
# alias formal definition:
#
# mod  alias  additional_id  original_id

void  alias  The_Boss Bruce_Springstein
```

But if the alias command is modified, only the new identifier acquires these additional properties.

```
Alter_ego  alias  mr_hyde doctor_jekyll
```

Through this process, we can continue to use the same stock of canvas for many artworks with different names.

```
cafe_image_data  alias cafe_art  titanium_white_canvas
```

Finally, a surface is modified by the image material and the art is ready to hang!

```
cafe_art  polygon  cafe_painting
0
0
12  0 0 0
    6 0 0
    6 0 6
    0 0 6
```

The `titanium_white_canvas` definition could be added to a project's material file; the rest of the definitions could be listed in a unique library file named after the theme of the picture.

3.4 Complex Surfaces

All primary surface elements have been introduced in the Scene 1 exercise. You should be quite familiar with polygons, spheres, and the family of cones. A complex surface, such as the exterior of an automobile, might be modeled in a CAD program, written to a file in the *.dxf* or *.mgf* format, and filtered into a *Radiance* scene description. Though this import feature is tremendously useful, it is difficult to edit individual surfaces after they are converted into the *Radiance* format because these files are generally filled with thousands of lines of unintelligible polygon descriptions. **Dxfcvt** and **mgf2rad** are two of several *Radiance* programs that provide these file format conversion services.

Despite the convenience of importing a "CAD-sculpted" object, there are great benefits from modeling a complex surface using the tools that *Radiance* provides.

Intelligible and concise scene descriptions, control over every component of an object, smooth surfaces, and efficient rendering times top the list. To engage this next level of surface generators seriously, you need to have a comfortable relationship with math. On the other hand, if you can learn to change a few variables and are agreeable to some experimentation, you can approximate almost any shape.

To introduce the concept of describing a surface by directly applying mathematical relationships, let's look at the illum description that we created in Section 3.1.3. An invisible polygonal source broadcasts the light from the western sky into a room. If this polygon were broken into several surfaces, the distribution of light into the room may be more accurate under some circumstances.[3] Of course, you could divide the larger polygon into smaller ones by creating a series of longhand polygon definitions, but there is a more efficient approach.

Here is the original polygon definition with its normal pointing in the +*x*, or eastern, direction.

```
window1_light  polygon    window1_opening
0
0
12
        0     6     6.5
        0     2     6.5
        0     2     2.5
        0     6     2.5
```

The same polygon can be created using this gensurf command, the only difference being the addition of .1 to the polygon name:

```
# single windowpane that radiates western skylight
!gensurf  window1_light  window1_opening \
  '1' '6-t*(6-2)' '2.5+s*(6.5-2.5)' 1 1

window1_light  polygon  window1_opening.1
0
0
12
  1 6  6.5
  1 2  6.5
  1 2  2.5
  1 6  2.5
```

3. Large source subdivision is discussed in Chaper 11 and illum ouput distributions are discussed in Chapter 13. More detailed daylighting examples are given in Chapter 6.

3.4.1 Gensurf

Gensurf produces polygon descriptions. Unlike genbox and genprism, it has the capability of generating extraordinarily complex surfaces that can be defined using several techniques. First, let's look at one of the basic definitions of gensurf, then see how our polygon was produced.

```
#gensurf mat name 'x(s,t)' 'y(s,t)' 'z(s,t)' m n [ -s ]
```

Following the familiar material and name format, the three sets of single quotes contain, respectively, *x*, *y*, and *z* vertex information. The two single values at the end of the line control the number of vertices that will be generated. A value of `m` = 4 generates 5 passes, where `s` begins at 0 and is incremented by 1/`m` or .25 until `s` = 1. If four-sided polygons are being created, their total number will not exceed `m` × `n`. If equations in the command produce a surface resembling jagged mountains, including the -s argument softens their rough edges. If you are familiar with mathematical expressions, the following *Radiance* manual excerpt summarizes this relationship:

> S will vary from 0 to 1 in steps of 1/m, and t will vary from 0 to 1 in steps of 1/n. The surface will be composed of 2*m*n or fewer triangles and quadrilaterals.

In our single `window1_opening.1` polygon, all *x* values will be 1.

This gensurf command generates the following polygon descriptions. There are two *y* values:

```
when t = 0, 6 - 0*(6-2) = 6
when t = 1, 6 - 1*(6-2) = 2
```

and two *z* values:

```
when s = 0, 2.5 + 0*(6.5 - 2.5) = 2.5
when s = 0, 2.5 + 0*(6.5 - 2.5) = 6.5
```

Gensurf then assembles the vertices and creates the polygon. Of course, this is a convoluted way to describe a single polygon, but if you need to break a surface into many equal facets, this mechanism becomes a good choice.

Now suppose that we want to break this 4-foot-square window into an array of four individual panes. We also want to reverse the normals of the windows, so that they radiate the light of the eastern sky toward the west. Simply change the `m` and `n` values to 2 and reverse the order in which each polygon is created. Note the changes to the *y*-value portion of the definition:

```
# four window panes that radiate eastern skylight
!gensurf window1_light window1_opening \
 '0' '2 + t*(6 - 2)' '2.5 + s*(6.5 - 2.5)' 2 2

window1_light  polygon  window1_opening.1
0
0
12
     0    2    4.5
     0    4    4.5
     0    4    2.5
     0    2    2.5

window1_light  polygon  window1_opening.2
0
0
12
     0    4    2.5
     0    4    4.5
     0    6    4.5
     0    6    2.5

window1_light  polygon  window1_opening.3
0
0
12
     0    2    4.5
     0    2    6.5
     0    4    6.5
     0    4    4.5

window1_light  polygon  window1_opening.4
0
0
12
     0    4    6.5
     0    6    6.5
     0    6    4.5
     0    4    4.5
```

The real power of gensurf becomes evident when it is used to generate nonplanar surfaces. The following sequence begins with a flat surface, and when a simple sine function is applied, the surface takes on its curved shape, as shown in Figure 3.7. `Sin(2*π*t)` describes one complete sine wave cycle.

```
# creates a single square polygon on the xy plane with vertices
#     11 11 0   1 11 0   1 1 0  1 11 0
!gensurf white wave \
     '11 - s*(11 - 1)' \      # x dimension is 10 units
     '11 - t*(11 - 1)' \      # y dimension is 10 units
     '0' \                    # z value of all vertices = 0
     1 1                      # create a single polygon

# applies a sine function to the z values of the surface
# 7 individual polygons are created, with z values that vary
# in amplitude between -2 and +2.
!gensurf white wave \
     '11 - s*(11 - 1)' \
     '11 - t*(11 - 1)'\
     '2*(sin(2*PI*t))' \
     1 7
```

If you increase the number of samples, more polygons are generated and the surface becomes smoother. Finally, if you include the -s option, Phong shading is applied to the surfaces during rendering, creating a very smooth appearance (Figure 3.8). It is quite possible to create thousands of polygon descriptions with a

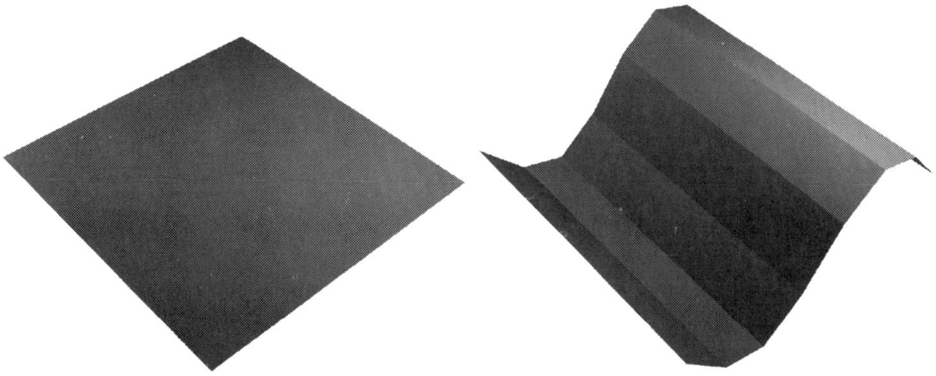

Figure 3.7 The surface on the left is flat because all vertices' z values are the same (0). The z values of the surface on the right have been modulated by applying a sine function to the gensurf command.

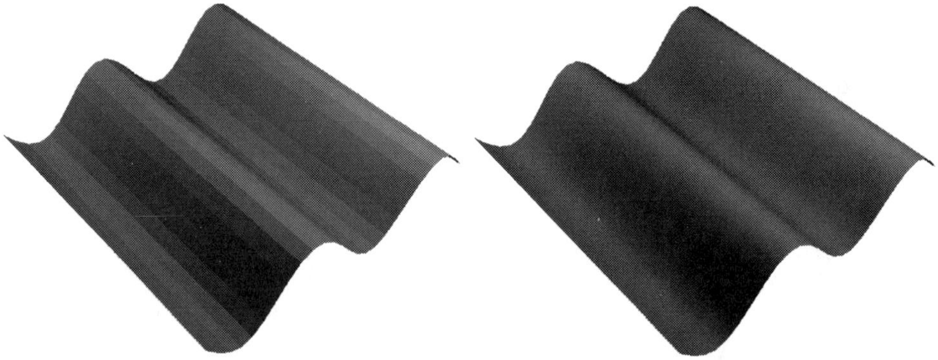

Figure 3.8 Adding more polygons helps to smooth the surface (left). Adding the -s Phong shading option increases this smoothness (right).

single gensurf command, so be careful not to get carried away with detail where it may not be needed. Be guided by the relationship between the final image's resolution and the size of the object in that image.

If we were to view these examples using the methods we have learned so far, we would create a scene description file, convert it into an octree, and then view it with rview or rpict. *Radiance* also provides the **objview** function, which automates this process. This function takes a scene description file as its argument, creates an octree, adds some light sources, and automatically generates a view of the object in rview. To view these gensurf examples using objview, simply create a material file and a scene description file, then pass them to objview. The following example uses a scene description file called *testwave.rad.*

```
% objview wave.mat testwave.rad

# objview formal definition:
#
# objview [material files] scene files
```

Note that the resulting view centers the object in an interactive rview window. Explore the following objects using objview:

```
# surface describes two sine wave cycles, with amplitude from +1 to -1
# 25 polygons are created.
!gensurf white wave \
     '11 - s*(11 - 1)' \
     '11 - t*(11 - 1)' \
     '1*(sin(4*PI*t))' \
     1 25
```

and

```
# add Phong shading
!gensurf white wave \
     '11 - s*(11 - 1)' \
     '11 - t*(11 - 1)' \
     '1*(sin(4*PI*t))' \
     1 25 -s
```

Parameters such as magnitude can be added to the gensurf description. Note how the **-e** option adds an expression that modulates the amplitude of the sine-wave effect (see Figure 3.9).

```
# surface describes 4 sine waves. amplitude
# of z is modulated by an additional magnitude function,
# varying in amplitude from 0 to 1
# 100 polygons are generated.
!gensurf white wave \
     '10 - s*(10 - 0)'  \
     '10 - t*(10 - 0)'  \
     'mag(s,t)*1*(sin(8*PI*t))'\
     1 100 \
     -e 'mag(s,t)=t'
```

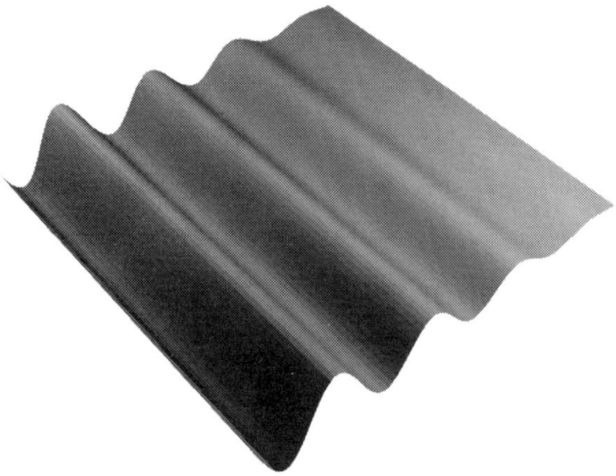

Figure 3.9 By applying simple functions to the *z* vertices, the gensurf command can generate complex "smooth" shapes.

The preceding example varies the *z* values of the gensurf along the *y*-axis only. Suppose that we also want to modulate the height in the *x* direction. Currently the polygon grid is defined with 100 divisions in the *y* direction and one long segment in the *x* direction. To modulate the height in the *x* direction, more than one segment is required! The magnitude currently modulates the height in the *y* direction, taking its values from the t variable. If you add an additional expression that modulates the s variable, the height can also be varied in the *x* direction. The following gensurf command increases the number of divisions from 100 (1 × 100) to 875 (25 × 35) and modulates the *z* values in the *x* and *y* directions, producing a series of "mounds" (Figure 3.10).

```
# surface has .25' deep depressions and .25' high mounds
# the modulation decreases over the panel
# the surface is 5' x 5'
!gensurf white waves \
 '5 - s*(5 - 0)' \
 '5 - t*(5 - 0)' \
 'mag(s,t)*.5*sin(5*PI*t)*sin(7*PI*s)' \
 25 35 -s \
 -e 'mag(s,t)=t'
# end waves.rad
```

The skills of constructing exotic surfaces by including equations in the gensurf description are acquired through practice. Three sets of equations follow; they have been included to provide a point of departure for your future explorations of the

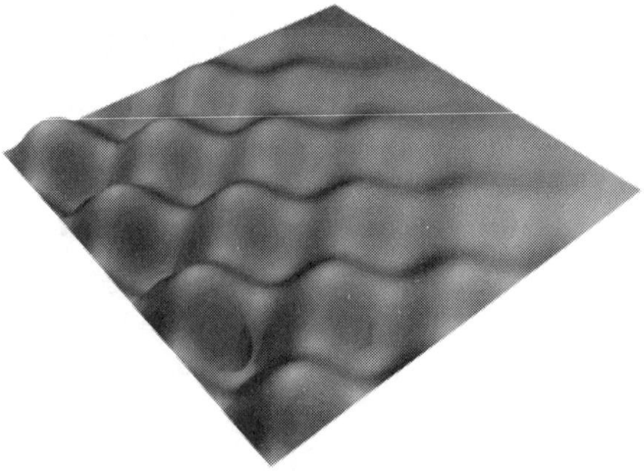

Figure 3.10 The magnitude of *z* (height) is varied in both the *x* and *y* directions.

parametric capabilities of the gensurf polygon generator. Insert them into a gensurf description, view the shapes they produce, and enjoy the variations created by modifying the equation values.

Equation set 1.

Crystal sphere.

```
'sin(PI*s)*cos(2*PI*t)' 'cos(PI*s)' 'sin(PI*s)*sin(2*PI*t)' 7 10
```

Equation set 2.

Round bowl (depth = 4, rim = 0, center at 5,5). Add a multiplier to x to generate an oval bowl.

```
sq(x) : x*x
z(x,y) = if (sq(4) - sq(x-5) -sq(y-5),
sqrt(sq4)-sq(x-5)-sq(y-5)),0);
```

Equation set 3.

Random landscape—*noise2.cal* generates the variations.

```
Z(x,y) = noise2(x,y)*std_deviation + avg_height
```

Another approach to creating a surface with gensurf is to incorporate a data set. The following "tent" shape is generated by describing a mesh of surface patches and using a list of real numbers for the z values of the vertices. You place these real numbers sequentially in a data file that can have no comment lines. Our *tent_height.dat* file contains the following values:

```
0 2 3 2 0
0 3 4 3 0
0 3.5 4.5 3.5 0
0 3.5 4.5 3.5 0
0 3 4 3 0
0 2 3 2 0
```

Now include the *tent_height.dat* file name in the gensurf command. Note that if four vertices create a nonplanar polygon, it is split into two triangular polygons. Figure 3.11 shows the resulting tent shape.

```
# 10 x 10 units in plan view.
# Surface raised into a tent using tent_height.dat values for z
# Tent divided into 4 x 5 = 20 primary elements.
# Some elements are split because they would otherwise be nonplanar.
!gensurf white ground 10*s 10*t tent_height.dat 4 5
```

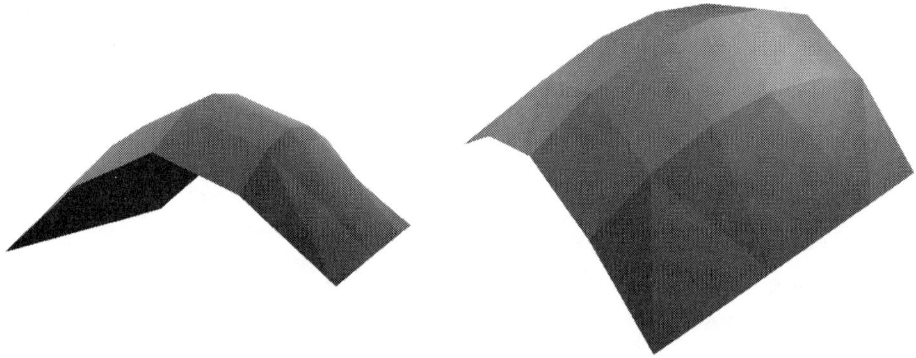

Figure 3.11 Tent shape described by creating a mesh of patches, then applying the vertices' heights from a data file. The use of data files can provide explicit control of dimensions.

Now that you have seen gensurf at work, its formal definitions should provide further insights into the ways it can be used to model a wide variety of shapes.

```
# gensurf formal definitions:
#
# gensurf mat name 'x(s,t)' 'y(s,t)' 'z(s,t)' m n [-e expr][-f file][-s]
# gensurf mat name 'x(s,t)' 'y(s,t)' dfile m n [-e expr][-f file][-s]
# gensurf mat name dfile dfile dfile m n [ -s ]
```

3.4.2 Genworm and Genrev

The **genworm** and **genrev** generators do not create polygon descriptions. Instead, genrev uses cones, and genworm uses cones and spheres, to create the description of an object. The size of the file, and eventually the amount of memory that these descriptions occupy, are generally tiny compared to the amount of memory occupied for similar polygonal shapes generated by gensurf. To create a smooth curved object with gensurf, the surface must be divided into many small facets. This can result in thousands of polygons in the scene description file. On the other hand, if the smooth shape can be constructed with a few dozen cones and spheres, the file will be smaller, more memory will be available during rendering, and rendering time will be significantly reduced.

There are several methods to define the curve that genrev and genworm use to construct an object. The following examples are constructed from a sine curve that is derived directly from the `sin` function. Depending on your mathematical prowess, you may wish to build upon these illustrations to produce even more exotic shapes. We will concentrate on the fundamentals of one function and encourage experimentation.

Radiance calculates angles based on radians. Those who are more familiar with using degrees to describe an angle might find this awkward at first, but converting between units is trivial. There are 2π radians, or 360 degrees, in a circle. Degrees and radians can be converted using the following formulas:

$$\text{radians} = \text{degrees} \times \pi / 180$$

$$\text{degrees} = \text{radians} \times 180 / \pi$$

One full cycle of a sine wave travels through 360 degrees, or 2π. One half of a sine wave can be described by plotting the sine function values for 0 through π. We will use the resulting shape and genworm to describe the tubular arch illustrated in Figure 3.12.

```
# genworm formal definition:
#
# genworm mat name 'x(t)' 'y(t)' 'z(t)' 'radius(t)' number_of_segments \
  [ -e expr ][ -f file ]
## t will vary from 0 to 1 in steps of 1/number_of_segments
## The number_of_segments = number of cones
## The number of spheres = number of cones + 1
```

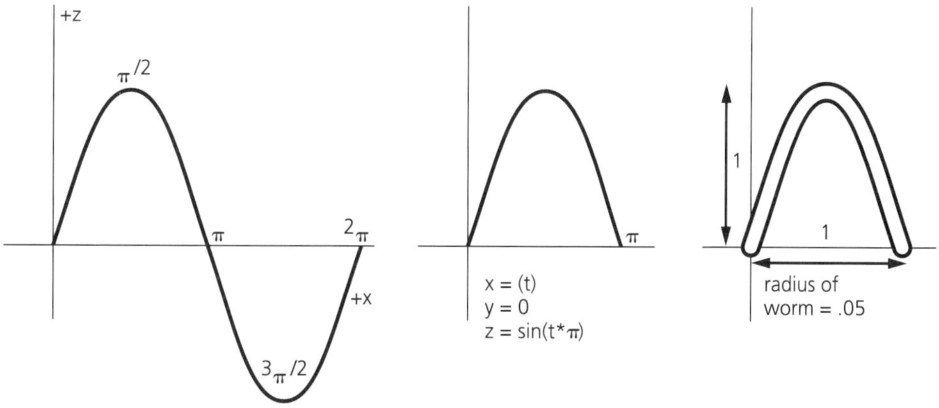

Figure 3.12 Using a trigonometric function to create a genworm.

Our arch shape will be composed of 20 segments, and the cones will have a diameter of .05. We are locating the arch in the *zx* plane, though we could locate it in any plane by reordering the appropriate genworm arguments or by piping the output through xform and then applying rotation commands. The genworm command that creates the tubular arch is as follows:

```
# creates an arch from 20 cones and 21 spheres in the zx plane
!genworm white arch '(t)' 0 'sin(t*π)' .05 20
```

The same segment of sine wave can be used by genrev to describe an upside-down bundt-cake pan (Figure 3.13). This time, the curve is rotated about the *z*-axis and cylinders are fitted to the shape. Unlike genworm, genrev always rotates the curve about the *z*-axis. Of course, the shape can be rotated or located elsewhere by piping the output of the genrev command through xform.

```
# genrev formal definition:
#
# genrev mat id 'z(t)' 'radius(t)' number_of_segments
#  [ -e expr ][ -f file ][-s ]
## t will vary from 0 to 1 in steps of 1/number_of_segments
## The number_of_segments = number of cones
## -s smooths the transitions between adjacent cylinders
```

The cake pan description that follows is constructed from 20 cones. The bottom and top radii and the height of each cone are determined by the sine function. Finally, Phong smoothing technique is applied to reduce the appearance of ridges on the surface.

```
!genrev white bundt_cake_pan 'sin(t*π)' '(t)' 20 -s
```

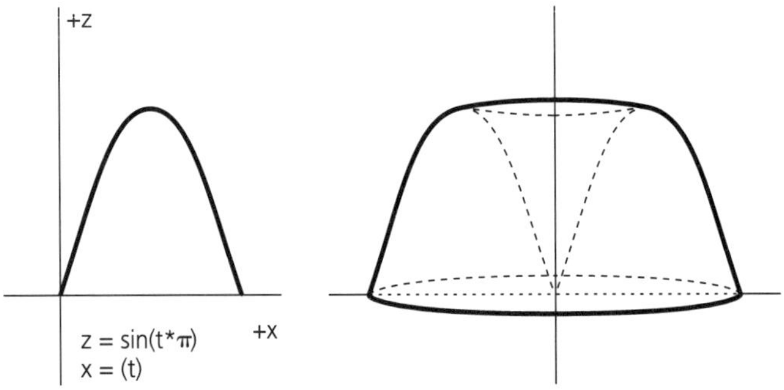

Figure 3.13 Creating a bundt pan from half of a sine wave and genrev.

3.4.3 Hermite Curves

Radiance provides an additional method to describe curves that can be used by generator functions. When a free-form or whimsical curve is required, we can use this alternative method to generate shapes without having to deal with convoluted strings of trigonometric functions and equations. The penalty, though, is our need to experiment with the new method until the shape is correct.

Hermite curves are defined by a beginning point and an ending point in the *zx* plane. Each of these points has a direction vector that influences the shape of the curve. The curve can be modulated between a straight line and an "S" shape by varying the location, orientation, and length of these vectors. To produce a complicated squiggle, several hermite curves would need to be joined together because each hermite curve can include only one inflection point.

Varying the length and orientation of the vectors can be likened to holding a piece of spring steel between your outstretched hands and then twisting your wrists. Turn both wrists upwards and an arch shape is described by the steel strip. Now twist one wrist downwards and an "S" shape is formed. Moving your hands farther apart flattens the "S" shape. With this concept in mind, imagine that the bottom hand is pushing and the top hand is pulling the spring steel against the fixed points that anchor the ends of the curve. This is how the vectors influence the shape. The mathematical relationship of the vector slopes, the magnitudes, and the positions of the anchor points is predetermined for us. Only through experimentation can you really begin to predict the outcome of a particular hermite declaration. Let's build a hermite curve in the *zx* plane between the points p_0 and p_1. The coordinates of these points would be

$$p_0(p_{0x}, p_{0z}) \text{ and } p_1(p_{1x}, p_{1z})$$

Now let's add the points that describe the displacement of the direction vectors:

$$r_0(r_{0x}, r_{0z}) \text{ and } r_1(r_{1x}, r_{1z})$$

The beginning direction vector is defined as p_0r_0 and the ending direction vector is p_1r_1, as shown in Figure 3.14.

The format for our *zx*-plane hermite curve places all the *z* values in one list and the *x* values in another. The order in which these values are listed is very significant. First the beginning and ending points are listed, followed by the tips of the beginning and ending vectors. *t* terminates the line and will vary from 0 to 1 in steps of 1/(number of segments).

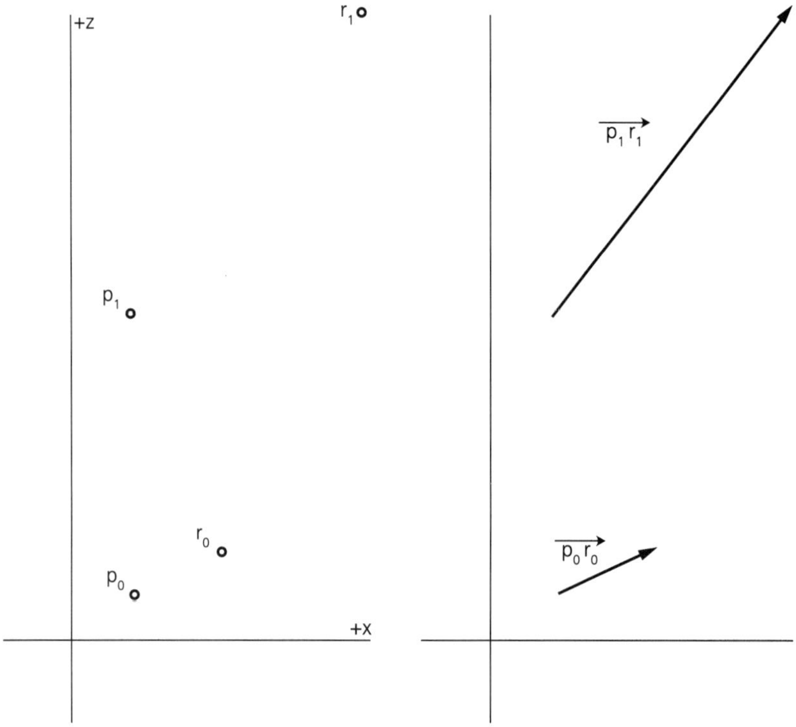

Figure 3.14 The points and vectors used in a hermite definition.

hermite $(p_{0z}, p_{1z}, r_{0z}, r_{1z}, t)$

hermite $(p_{0x}, p_{1x}, r_{0x}, r_{1x}, t)$

To create the stick illustrated in Figure 3.15, insert values for these hermite descriptions into a genworm function that produces a 15-segment tube with a radius of .025.

```
!genworm white stick\
     'hermite (.3,.3,.4,.9,t) '\
     '0'\
     'hermite(.1,1,.1,1,t)'\
     .025 15
```

The same hermite-curve description can be included in a genrev function, resulting in a vase-like shape (Figure 3.16). Note that the shape is open, with no lid or bottom.

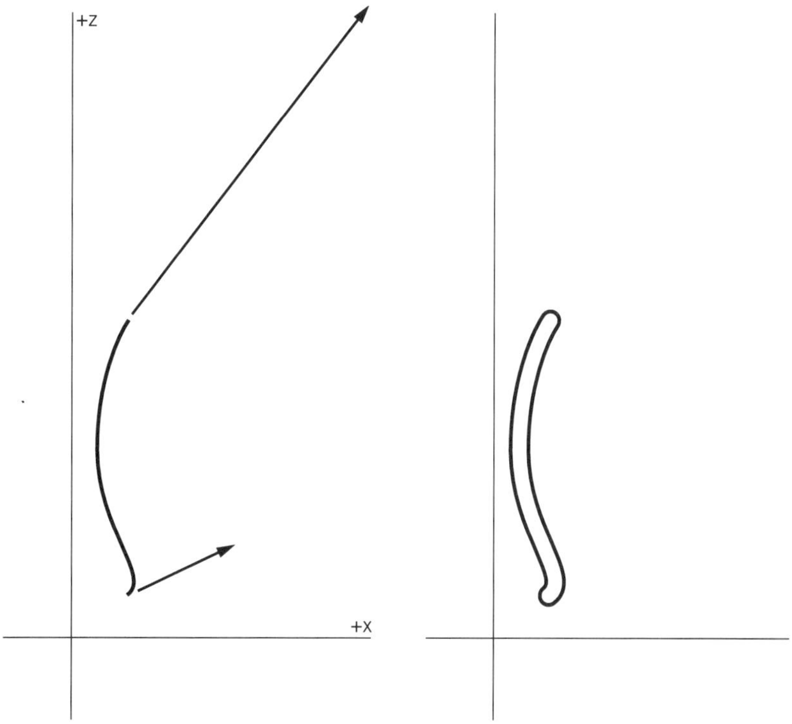

Figure 3.15 Using a hermite curve and genworm to create a curved stick.

```
!genrev white vase_shape\
     'hermite(.1,1,.1,1,t)'\
     'hermite (.3,.3,.4,.9,t)'\
     15 -s
```

More sophisticated objects can be constructed by assembling genrev shapes. The goblet that is described below and illustrated in Figure 3.17 combines a cup top with a stem base.

```
# combines two genrev shapes into a goblet
!genrev  pottery goblet_top \
     'hermite(.4,1,.4,1.1,t)' \
     'hermite(.025,.25,.3,.025,t)' \
     12 -s
```

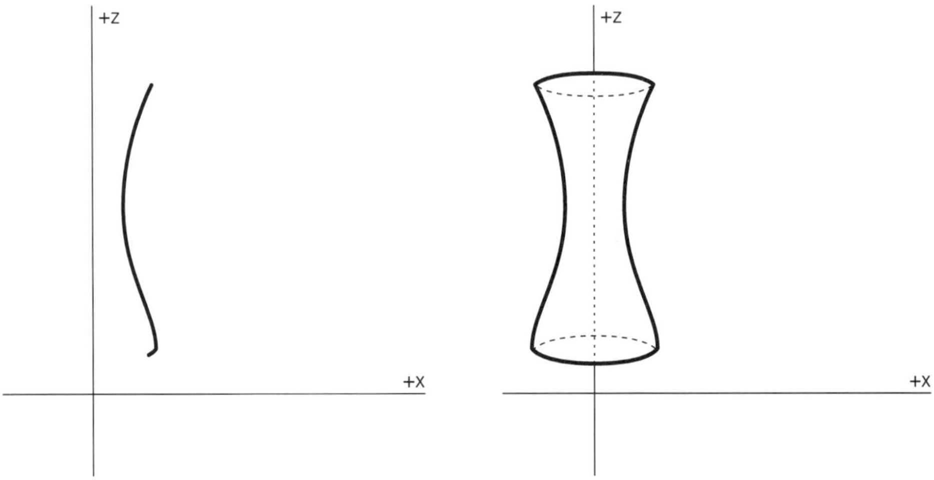

Figure 3.16 Using a hermite curve and genrev to describe a vase.

```
!genrev  pottery goblet_base \
     'hermite(0,.4,-.2,1.5,t)' \
     'hermite(.2,.025,.22,.2,t)' \
     12 -s
# end goblet
```

Some objects, such as the teacup shown in Figure 3.18, can be created by combining a genrev cup and a genworm handle. In this case, both shapes are derived from hermite curves.

```
# teacup created using a genrev cup and a genworm handle.
# the cup is one unit tall.

!genrev china tea_cup\
     'hermite(.18 ,1, -1.5, 1.5,t)'\
     'hermite(.2,.85, .6, .8,t)'\
     12 -s

!genworm china tea_cup_handle\
     'hermite(.5,.85,1.5,-1.5,t)'\
     '0'\
     'hermite(.15,.9,1,-1,t)'\
     .07 12

# end teacup.rad
```

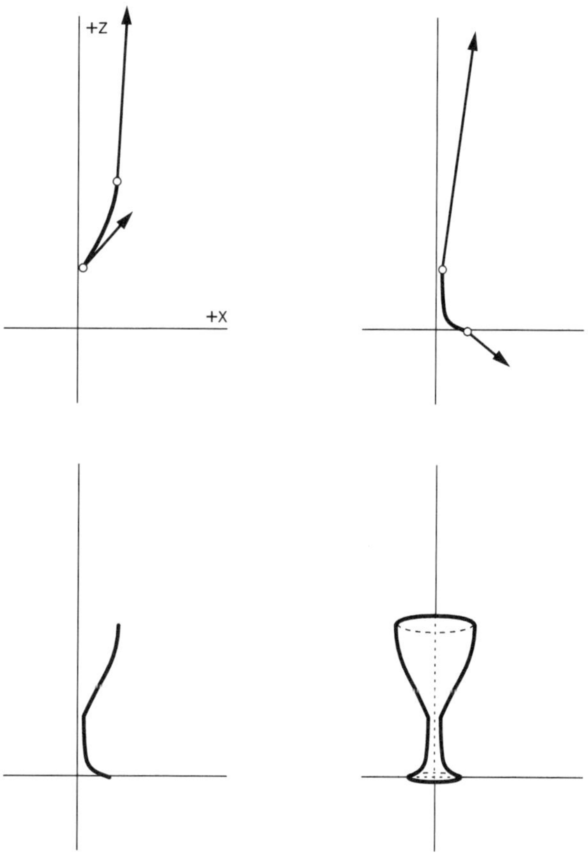

Figure 3.17 The hermite curves used to create a goblet with genrev.

Though a bone china cup is very thin, our teacup has no thickness at all. The complete description of a teacup and saucer follows. Note the use of a ring to join the inner and outer cup surfaces. The inner cup surface uses the same genrev description as the outer surface, then xform is applied to make it smaller and raise it slightly.

```
# China teacup and saucer. Teacup is 1 unit tall
# cup handle is on the right side of the cup

!genrev china tea_cup_outer\
     'hermite(.18 ,1, -1.5, 1.5,t)'\
     'hermite(.2,.85, .6, .8,t)'\
     12 -s
```

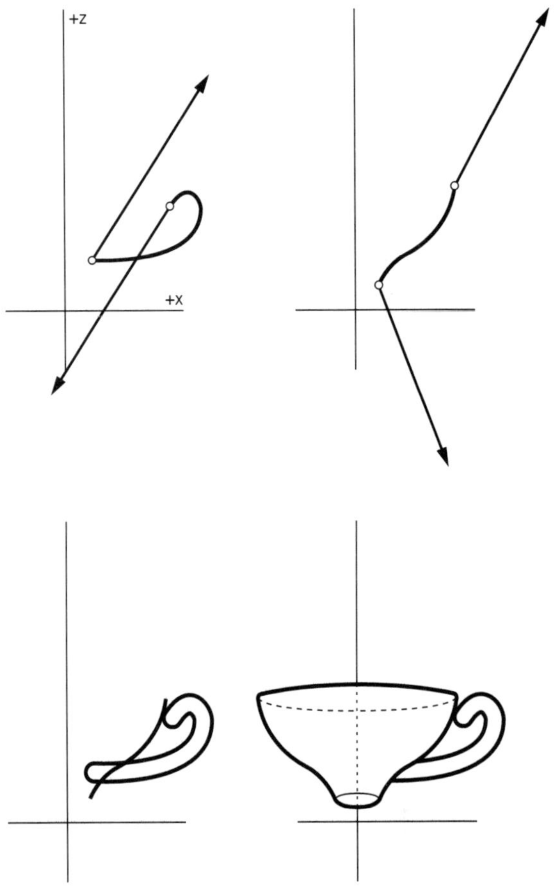

Figure 3.18 Creating a tea cup with genrev and genworm.

```
!genrev china tea_cup_inner\
     'hermite(.18 ,1, -1.5, 1.5,t)'\
     'hermite(.2,.85, .6, .8,t)'\
     12 -s | xform -s .95 -t 0 0 .05

china ring tea_cup_rim
0
0
8       0       0       1
        0       0       1
          .85    .8075
```

```
china ring tea_cup_base_inner
0
0
8      0      0     .25
       0      0     1
       .475   0

!genworm china tea_cup_handle\
     'hermite(.5,.85,1.5,-1.5,t)'\
     '0'\
     'hermite(.15,.9,1,-1,t)'\
     .07 12

!genrev china tea_saucer\
     'hermite(.05 ,.15, .45 , 1,t)'\
     'hermite( 0 ,1.4, 2.5 , 5,t)'\
     12 -s

# end teacup.rad
```

3.4.4 Anatomy of a Procedural Function

Though many rendering programs provide catalogs of surfaces, textures, and patterns, few enable you to invent your own. So far, this tutorial has been guilty of a similar omission by simply providing you with prepackaged functions, such as the granite pattern. The truth is that if you have the skill to describe a material or surface in a *Radiance* procedural function, you are free to create your own inventory of resources.

We will expose the anatomy of two functions that will provide the colored carpet pattern and the adobe wall texture for the Art Gallery. The primary purpose of annotating these examples is to tempt the mathematically inclined user to explore Chapter 4 of this book dedicated to function and script writing. The annotations describe the strategy behind the structure of the function, while also revealing the tool set that enables you to create your own. If you feel intimidated by the descriptive comment lines, do not worry; *Radiance* already provides a reasonable collection of surface, texture, and pattern functions that meet a broad set of needs.

The first function will be used to create the colored carpet pattern for the gallery floor. You add a colored pattern to a scene by including a colorfunc description. The format for a colorfunc pattern is as follows:

```
# colorfunc formal definition:
#
# mod  colorfunc   id
# 4+ red green  blue functionfile  transformations
# 0
# n A1 A2.. An
```

In this case, the function file will be called *carpet.cal.*

Before using a function, you need to know how many variables are available and what they control. This information is located in the header of the *.cal* file. The header is like the first few comment lines in a scene description file. Instead of using a line beginning with a #, the convention is that anything contained within curly brackets is considered a {comment}. The *carpet.cal* header explains the effect of each parameter. The remaining comment lines are for the brave of heart who want some insight into the way the function works.

```
{
 carpet.cal
     carpet pattern function called by colorfunc
     red green  blue =    carpr carpg carpb
     Scale pattern to tuft size with the -s option

     A1 - tuft red color
     A2 - tuft green color
     A3 - tuft blue color
     A4 - degree of variation
}

                                    { carpet tuft position }
{ Varies from [(1-A4),1] based on Perlin 3D noise function, a random
 wave function over 3D space, with scalar value everywhere between about
 -1 and 1. Sense of this is 0 means bottom of tuft and 1 means top
 (carpet surface). }
carpt = 1 - A4*(.5+.5*noise3(Px,Py,Pz));

                                    { exponent for carpet color }

{ Takes [(1-A4),1] range and maps it to [1,(1+4*A4)] for #
 interreflections }
carpe = 1 + 4*(1-carpt);
```

```
                                { coefficient (with fuzzies) }

{ Takes square of carpt as general shading coefficient (self-shadowing)
 and multiplies by some fractal noise hovering around 1 with a base
 frequency 10 times the tuft frequency (fuzzies). The noneg() function
 guarantees positive results for outlying values of the noise
 functions. }
coef = noneg( carpt*carpt * (1 + .25*A4*fnoise3(Px*10,Py*10,Pz*10)) );

                                { carpet color }
{ Final color is shading coefficient times carpet color raised to the
 power of the number of interreflections, which causes both darkening
 and deepening of color in between tufts. }
carpr = coef * A1^carpe;
carpg = coef * A2^carpe;
carpb = coef * A3^carpe;
{end carpet.cal}
```

The carpet function can be applied to a surface by first describing the carpet pattern, then using it to modify a material, which in turn modifies a surface.

```
void colorfunc carp
6 carpr carpg carpb carpet.cal -s .2
0
4 .7 .5 .08 .8
# A1 A2 A3 A4

carp plastic carpmat
0
0
5 .8 .8 .8 0 0

carpmat polygon carpet
0
0
12
     0  0  0
     0 20  0
    20 20  0
    20  0  0
```

The second function creates the texture of an adobe surface. With this pattern, unlike the previous one, the visual effect of a texture is dependent on the direction of light that strikes the surface. A light source that is perpendicular to the surface does not show this texture, but a grazing angle reveals the shadows and highlights of the surface variations, which look like trowel marks.

This function requires only one variable, and again, the scale factor will play a significant role in modifying the effect to meet our requirements.

```
{       abobe.cal
        adobe texture called by texfunc
        perturbations in x y z = cdx cdy cdz
        applies to any large, flat surface.
        scale texture with the -s option
        A1 - overall magnitude
}

{ Basic texture is scaled gradient of 3D Perlin noise function.
  Additional perturbation is added when in_crack is true. }
dx = A1  * noise3a(Px, Py, Pz) + if(in crack, cdx, 0);
dy = A1  * noise3b(Px, Py, Pz) + if(in_crack, cdy, 0);
dz = A1  * noise3c(Px, Py, Pz) + if(in_crack, cdz, 0);

{ First, compute crack coordinate system, which is at 3 times original
  bump scale and has additional fractal noise added for irregularity over
  an even larger scale. }
fn3 = fnoise3(Px, Py, Pz);
cu = Px/3 + fn3/30;
cv = Py/3 + fn3/30;
cw = Pz/3 + fn3/30;

{ Test in_crack returns true (positive) when Perlin noise in crack
  coordinate system is about -.4 times the fractal noise function at the
  same point. }
in_crack = inside(-.02, noise3(cu, cv, cw) + .4*fnoise3(cu, cv, cw), .02);

{ Final crack perturbation is 5 times as large as normal gradient at that
  point in Perlin function, meaning it will yank the surface normal one
  way or the other along that wiggly line where in_crack is true,
  yielding an apparent discontinuity in the surface. }
cdx = 5*A1*noise3a(cu, cv, cw);
cdy = 5*A1*noise3b(cu, cv, cw);
cdz = 5*A1*noise3c(cu, cv, cw);
{end adobe.cal}
```

The adobe texture is applied to a surface by defining the texture, modifying a material with the texture, then using the material to modify the final surface.

```
void texfunc adobe
6  cdx  cdy  cdz  adobe.cal  -s  .1
0
1  .015
#  A1

adobe plastic stucco_white
0
0
5  .8  .7  .5  0  0

stucco_white polygon wall
0
0
12
       0      0      0
      20      0      0
      20      0     20
       0      0     20
```

There is great latitude for invention when you are devising a useful function. The effort can result in a permanent solution for generating a family of surfaces, textures, or patterns. The parametric components of the adobe and carpet functions demonstrate the versatility of a well-written function by being able to produce many variations of wall texture and carpet styles. We will use these functions in the Art Gallery. The functions *carpet.cal* and *adobe.cal* are included on the CD-ROM.

3.5 Building the Art Gallery

The Scene 2 Art Gallery is now ready for construction. The gallery is a modest structure, composed of a small lobby entrance and a showroom. It has been designed for a part of the world known for its blue summer skies. Ceilings are vaulted, and during most days the interior is illuminated by the sun. To provide a maximum of display surface and to protect art from direct sunlight, the gallery incorporates an indirect skylight system. All wall and ceiling surfaces are neutral in color and have an adobe-like stucco finish. Floors are covered with a blue pile carpet. The building, as shown in the Figure 3.19 plan view, is 40 feet wide and 25 feet

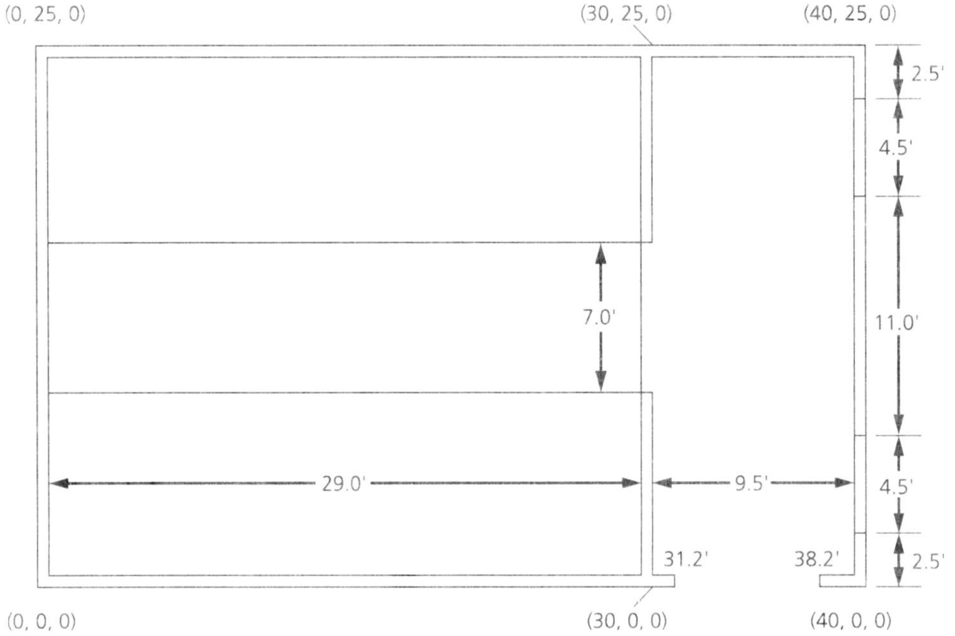

Figure 3.19 The Art Gallery ground plan.

deep, and the height of the structure does not exceed 19 feet 6 inches. The building is oriented in an east-west manner, with the main entrance on the south side. The southwest corner of the building is located at 0 0 0.

The project is set up by creating a *scene2* project directory with a series of subdirectories.

```
% mkdir scene2
```

The *lib* subdirectory contains all structural components.

```
% mkdir scene2/lib
```

To help us manage the many files needed for the Art Gallery project, several additional subdirectories will prove useful: *art_lib, ies_lib, lib, pics,* and *view_lib.*

The first order of business is to create the building material list, which is located in the *lib* subdirectory. The first entries include adobe plaster of two colors, a red roof material, and a blue carpet description.

```
### building.mat
#
# adobe texture function
void texfunc ad
6 cdx cdy cdz adobe.cal -s .1
0
1 .02

# wall adobe material
ad plastic stucco_white
0
0
5 .8 .7 .5 0 0

# high-reflectance adobe material for ceiling
ad plastic stucco_white2
0
0
5 .85 .85 .85 0 0

# carpet pattern function
void colorfunc carp
6 carpr carpg carpb carpet.cal -s .02
0
4 .7 .8 .9 .7

carp plastic carpet_blue
0
0
5 .7 .8 .9 0 0

void plastic red_roofing
0
0
5 .6 .05 .05 .03 .03
#end building.mat
```

The Art Gallery building surfaces will be described in three major files, called *floor.rad*, *walls.rad*, and *ceiling.rad*. We will begin construction from the ground up by creating a single carpeted-floor polygon. This is stored in the file called *floor.rad*.

```
carpet_blue polygon floor
0
0
12      .01     .01     0
     39.99      .01     0
     39.9     24.99     0
       .01    24.99     0
```

The walls are designed as simple shapes and will be constructed using the polygon-generator functions genprism and genbox. Dimensions are derived from the plan presented in Figure 3.19 and the elevation shown in Figure 3.20. The genprism walls are constructed flat on the ground before being "raised" into position. *Walls.rad* contains the following descriptions:

```
### walls.rad
#
# north wall has no openings and is made using a simple genbox
!genbox stucco_white wall_north   40  .5 10.5  | xform  -t 0 24.5 0

# south wall with door opening. wall_south1 is a door header.
!genbox stucco_white wall_south1  31.2 .5 10.5
!genbox stucco_white wall_south2   7   .5  2.5  | xform  -t 31.2 0 8
!genbox stucco_white wall_south3  1.8  .5 10.5  | xform  -t 38.2 0 0

# west wall is a complex shape requiring the genprism function.
# The wall is constructed on the ground before being raised.
!genprism stucco_white wall_west 8 \
     0 25 0 0 10.5 0 14 10.15 \
     19.4 10.15 19.4 14.85 14 14.85 10.5 25 \
     -1 0 0 5 | xform -ry -90 -t .5 0 0

# center wall partition requires an archway. Simply copy the west wall
# genprism description, insert 4 more vertices to define the doorway,
# then move it into position
!genprism stucco_white wall_center 12 \
     0 25 0 16 8 16 8 9 \
     0 9 0 0 10.5 0 14 10.15 \
     19.4 10.15 19.4 14.85 14 14.85 10.5 25 \
     -1 0 0 .5 | xform -ry -90 -t 30 0 0
```

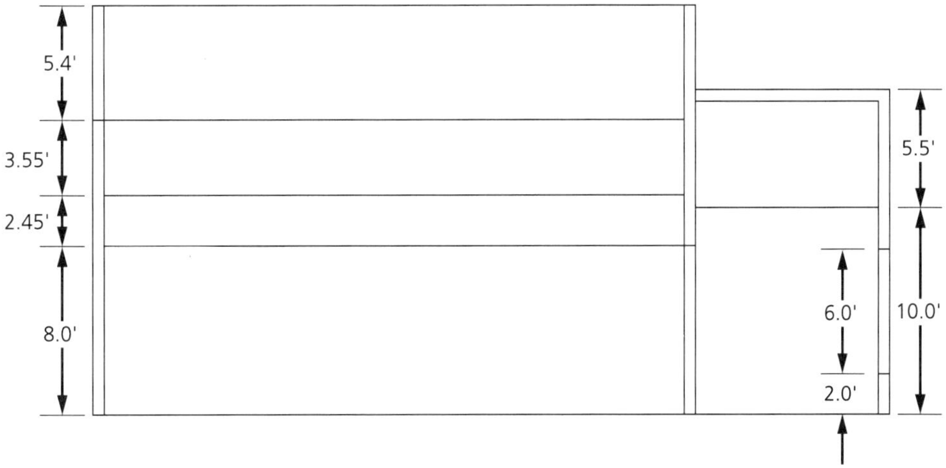

Figure 3.20 East-west section of the Art Gallery.

The east wall contains two windows. The wall is created in one description by carefully outlining the wall and windows in a genprism command. Figure 3.21 shows the required coordinates.

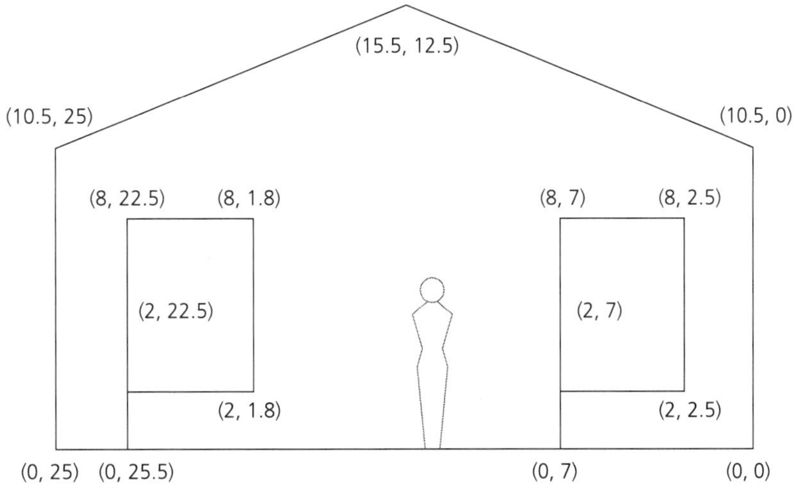

Figure 3.21 Coordinates of the Art Gallery east wall.

```
## east wall with 2 windows
!genprism stucco_white wall_east 17 \
     0 25 0 22.5 8 22.5 8 18 2 18 2 22.5 0 22.5 \
     0 7 8 7 8 2.5 2 2.5 2 7 0 7 \
     0 0 10.5 0 15.5 12.5 10.5 25 \
     -1 0 0 .5 | xform -ry -90 -t 40 0 0
```

The sides of the skylight aperture are enclosed by two long boxes.

```
## skylight walls
!genbox stucco_white wall_skylight_s 29.95 .5 5.4 | \
     xform -t .01 10.15 14
!genbox stucco_white wall_skylight_n 29.95 .5 5.4 | \
     xform -t .01 14.35 14
# end walls.rad
```

Now the ceiling/roof units can be constructed (see Figure 3.22) and raised onto the walls. The roofing material rests on top of the ceiling units and overhangs the walls by .2 foot. Because the ceiling and roof surfaces are nearly the same size and move through similar transformations, it is convenient to list their descriptions in related pairs.

```
### ceiling.rad
#
# ceilings, roofs, and daylight reflector

# ceiling and roof elements constructed together
!genbox stucco_white2 ceiling_south_w 29.98 11.2 .5 | \
     xform -t 0.01 0 -.5 -rx 21 -t 0 0 10.5
!genbox red_roofing roof_south_w 30.18 11.4 .1 | \
     xform -t -.19 -.2 0 -rx 21 -t 0 0 10.5

!genbox stucco_white2 ceiling_north_w 29.98 11.2 .5 | \
     xform -t 0.01 -11.2 -.5 -rx -21 -t 0 25 10.5
!genbox red_roofing roof_north_w 30.18 11.4 .1 | \
     xform -t -.19 -11.2 0   -rx -21 -t 0 25 10.5

!genbox stucco_white ceiling_south_e 9.99 13.45 .5 | \
     xform -t 0 0 -.5 -rx 21 -t 30 0 10.5
!genbox red_roofing roof_south_e 10.19 13.65 .1 | \
     xform -t 0 -.2 0 -rx 21 -t 30 0 10.5
```

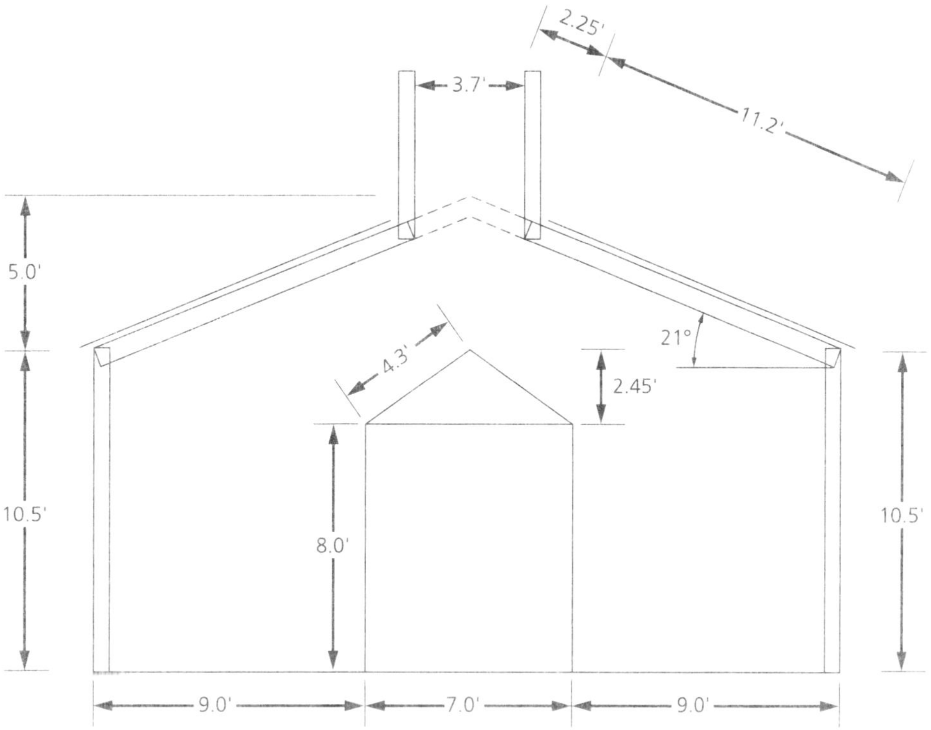

Figure 3.22 North-south section of the Art Gallery.

```
!genbox stucco_white ceiling_north_e 9.99 13.45 .5 | \
     xform -t 0 -13.45 -.5 -rx -21 -t 30 25 10.5
!genbox red_roofing roof_north_e 10.19 13.7 .1 | \
     xform -t 0 -13.5  0   -rx -21 -t 30 25 10.5

# art gallery indirect reflector located beneath the
# long skylight aperture, to reflect daylight toward the
# ceiling and interior walls.
!genprism stucco_white2 reflector 3 \
     0 -3.5 2.45 0 0 3.5 -1 0 0 29.98 | \
     xform -ry -90 -t 29.99 12.5 8
# end ceiling.rad
```

Finally, it's time to add the doors and windows so our structure will be habitable and ready for occupancy! The exterior double doors (Figure 3.23) are constructed using two files. One contains a description of a single door; the other inserts the door into a doorframe. This method enables the doors to be hinged open by simply altering two -rz variables.

The following door materials are included in the *building.mat* file. The *door-base.rad* and *door2x.rad* files describe a pair of closed doors.

```
# door and doorframe materials
void plastic frame_mat2
0
0
5 .1 .5 .7 .02 .02

void metal sill_mat
0
0
5 .6 .6 .6 .85 .05

void plastic handle_mat
0
0
5 .6 .1 .1 0 0

void glass door_glass
0
0
3 .9 .9 .9
# end building.mat
```

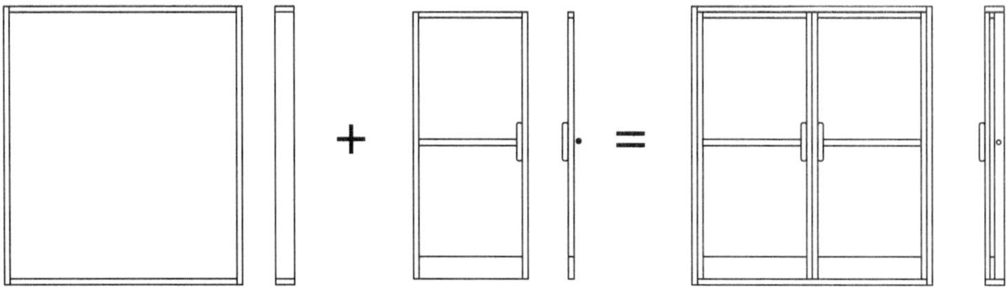

Figure 3.23 Constructing the entrance doors.

```
### doorbase.rad
#
# single glass door with handle and emergency latch
# this door is sized to fit into the doorx2.rad frame

# mullions that support the glass
!genbox frame_mat2 mull_l  .1   .1 7.85 | xform -t   0  0  .05
!genbox frame_mat2 mull_t 3.19 .1   .1  | xform -t  .1  0 7.8
!genbox frame_mat2 mull_r  .1   .1 7.85 | xform -t 3.29 0  .05
!genbox frame_mat2 mull_b 3.19 .1  .45  | xform -t   .1 0  .05

# glass panel
door_glass polygon door_window
0
0
12   .1  .05  .15
    3.29 .05  .15
    3.29 .05  .85
      .1  .05 7.85

# simplified exterior handle and interior emergency opener
frame_mat cylinder exterior_door_handle
0
0
7 3.25 -.1 3
  3.25 -.1 4
   .05

frame_mat cylinder interior_emergency_handle
0
0
7  .05 .1 3.5
  3.35 .1 3.5
   .05
# end doorbase.rad
```

```
### door2x.rad
#
# a double doorframe with two doors that can be opened
# requires:  doorbase.rad
# unit is 7' wide, 8' tall, and .5' deep
# insertion point is front lower left corner.

# construct the doorframe and sill
!genbox frame_mat jambl  .1 .5 8
!genbox frame_mat jambt 6.8 .5  .1   | xform -t  .1   0    7.9
!genbox frame_mat jambr  .1 .5  8    | xform -t 6.9   0    0
!genbox sill_mat sill   6.8 .55  .05 | xform -t  .1  -.05 0

# insert each door. Note that the doors can be opened by
# changing the -rz values. A negative value opens both doors outward
!xform -n door_w -rz -0     -t  .1 .1 0 doorbase.rad
!xform -n door_e -rz -0 -mx -t 6.9 .1 0 doorbase.rad
#end doorx2.rad
```

To insert the complete double door into the south wall of the art gallery, the following line is added to the *walls.rad* file:

```
!xform -n s_doors -t 31.2 0 0 doorx2.rad
# end walls.rad
```

The two windows in the east wall are identical in shape, so a single description can be located in a *windows.rad* file and then inserted twice into the *wall.rad* data set. The windows and doors are in the same style and from the same manufacturer, so there is no need to create any new material descriptions.

```
### window.rad
#
# single 4.5' x 6' window with frame
# insertion point is front lower left corner

!genbox frame_mat framel  .1 .5 6
!genbox frame_mat framet 4.3 .5  .1 | xform -t  .1 0 5.9
!genbox frame_mat framer  .1 .5 6   | xform -t 4.4 0 0
!genbox frame_mat frameb 4.3 .5  .1 | xform -t  .1 0 0
```

```
!genbox frame_mat sashl  .1 .1 5.8 | xform -t  .1 .3  .1
!genbox frame_mat sasht 4.1 .1  .1 | xform -t  .2 .3 5.8
!genbox frame_mat sashr  .1 .1 5.8 | xform -t 4.3 .3  .1
!genbox frame_mat sashb 4.1 .1  .1 | xform -t  .2 .3  .1

# glass panel
door_glass polygon door_window
0
0
12   .2  .35   .2
    4.3  .35   .2
    4.3  .35  5.8
     .2  .35  5.8
# end window.rad
```

To insert the windows into the east wall, the following description is added to the end of the *walls.rad* file:

```
# insert windows into the apertures located in the east wall
!xform -n se_window -rz 90 -t 30  2.5 2 window.rad
!xform -n ne_window -rz 90 -t 30 18   2 window.rad
# end walls.rad
```

This completes the structural components of the Art Gallery. In the next section, we add daylight, followed by the electrical lighting system and the furniture. Then, finally, the art can be moved in!

3.5.1 Creating the Art Gallery *illum* Daylight Sources

To accurately bring daylight into the art gallery, invisible illum light sources will be applied to each of the door, window, and skylight apertures. As described earlier in Section 3.1.3 of this tutorial, illum will be modified by the appropriate sky luminance for a particular location, time of day, and date. The gensurf discussion detailed the way to break up a large window illum surface into several smaller "panes," so all that remains is to create the specific gensky and illum descriptions for the Art Gallery.

To explore the ways the gallery will appear in both daylight and evening light, we will need two gensky descriptions. Though it is possible to edit a single description to switch between day and evening, separate files provide a less cumbersome approach. The daylight description is in a file called *sky_d.mat*, located in the *lib* subdirectory. The gensky command includes the +s option, which adds the direct-sunlight component. The description creates the sky light and sunlight for Bloomington, Indiana, at 1:00 PM on June 21.

```
### sky_d.mat
#
# creates a daytime sky and sky_illum

# 06/21 at 1:00 pm in Bloomington, Indiana.
# First day of summer!
!gensky 6 21 21.25 -a 39.1 -o 86.3 -m 75 +s

     skyfunc glow skyglow
     0
     0
     4 .8 .8 1 0

     skyglow source sky
     0
     0
     4 0 0 1 180

# procedure for mapping sky luminance to the
# invisible material illum. The data in
# skyfunc is created by gensky.
skyfunc brightfunc winbright
2 winxmit winxmit.cal
0
0

winbright illum sky_illum
0
0
3 .88 .88 .98
#end sky_d.mat
```

The *sky_n.mat* describes the evening sky at 9:15 PM on the preceding evening.

```
### sky_n.mat
#
# creates an evening sky and sky_illum

# 06/20 at 9:15 pm in Bloomington, Indiana.
# The evening of the summer solstice.
!gensky 6 20 21.25 -a 39.1 -o 86.3 -m 75 +s

 skyfunc glow skyglow
 0
 0
 4 .8 .8 1 0

 skyglow source sky
 0
 0
 4 0 0 1 180

# procedure for mapping sky luminance to the
# invisible material illum. The data in
# skyfunc is created by gensky.
skyfunc brightfunc winbright
2 winxmit winxmit.cal
0
0

winbright illum sky_illum
0
0
3 .88 .88 .98
#end sky_n.mat
```

The new illum material, labeled `sky_illum`, is applied to the gallery window apertures via invisible surfaces, which, in turn, convey light from the sky to the building interior. The orientation of each `sky_illum` surface is significant and must be carefully designed so that western-sky light does not enter through an east-facing window!

There are two basic strategies for including descriptions of daylight in a room. The first method involves deliberately subdividing each daylight illum source into smaller panels. This is absolutely necessary if we need to create individual panes in a mullion window, and useful if we want to optimize rendering times by maintaining control of the number of illum subdivisions. When you create your own subdivisions of an illum source, it is good practice for each illum surface to have approximately the same area so that the accuracy of the daylighting will be consistent throughout the room. Subdividing these panes into even smaller elements will increase the accuracy of the daylight effect while directly increasing rendering time! In our case, we will subdivide the exterior double doors into four illum panels to account for the two door windows, which are split in the middle by the emergency-exit push bar. Each window aperture is covered by two invisible "panes" to improve the interior distribution of daylight. To control the way *Radiance* handles our first method of subdividing illum sources, we must set the rpict -ds parameter to 0 when we render the picture. These gensurf descriptions are included in the *walls.rad* file.

```
# Art Gallery: lobby area daylighting
# (using explicit illum subdivisions and rpict -ds 0)
# illum in south wall, south glass_door
!gensurf sky_illum idoor_s \
     '31.2 + t*(38.2-31.2)' '0.51' '0 + s*(8-0)' 2 2

# illum in east wall, north window
!gensurf sky_illum iwindow_e_n \
     '39.49' '18 + t*(22.5-18)' '2 + s*(8-2)' 2 1

# illum in east wall, south window
!gensurf sky_illum iwindow_e_s \
     '39.49' '2.5 + t*(7-2.5)' '2 + s*(8-2)' 2 1
```

This first method can also be applied to the skylight illum source, as shown in Figure 3.24. The interior gallery area is illuminated indirectly via a skylight aperture and a reflector. Because the skylight is 4 feet wide and 28 feet long, we will divide its illum surface into eight "panes" to maintain size consistency with the win-

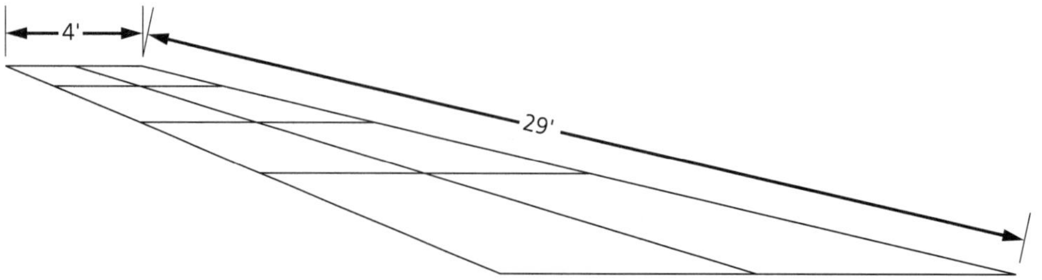

Figure 3.24 Using gensurf to divide the illum skylight source into eight panes.

dow and door illum surfaces. If we were to include the mullions that support the skylight glazing, we would subdivide the skylight illum into panes of those sizes. By adding this final description to the *walls.rad* file, we have completed the installation of our daylighting components using explicitly subdivided illum sources.

```
# Art Gallery: gallery daylighting
# (using explicit illum subdivisions and rpict -ds 0)
# illum at top of skylight aperture
!gensurf sky_illum skylight \
    '1 + t*(29-1)' '10.5 + s*(14.5-10.5)' '19.4' 2 4
# end walls.rad
```

Radiance does have an alternative method for subdividing large light sources, such as our windows. This alternative method automatically subdivides a source until the width of the source divided by the distance to the point being illuminated is less than a specified ratio. (See Chapter 11 for technical details.) Of course, this increases the rendering time, but the results are generally excellent. This feature is activated by providing the rpict -ds parameter with a value other than 0. In fact, *Radiance* sets the rpict default value of -ds to .25. In other words, when calculating the illumination of a point located 4 feet away from a 4-foot-wide illum source, *Radiance* will adaptively subdivide the illum into at least 1-foot widths. This approach is computationally expensive for points close to a large source where greater accuracy is required. On the other hand, *Radiance* will not subdivide an illum when calculating the illumination for distant points.

Because the exterior door in the building is physically divided into four quadrants by the door frame and the emergency exit bars, we need to keep these explicitly created illum subdivisions. Because we are not including mullions in any of the other windows, we could let *Radiance* automatically subdivide the illum sources for us. Using this second method, our illum daylight descriptions would look like this:

```
# Art Gallery: lobby area daylighting
# (using automatic illum subdivision set by the rpict -ds parameter)
# illum in south wall, south glass_door
!gensurf sky_illum idoor_s \
    '31.2 + t*(38.2-31.2)' '0.51' '0 + s*(8-0)' 2 2

# illum in east wall, north window
!gensurf sky_illum iwindow_e_n \
    '39.49' '18 + t*(22.5-18)' '2 + s*(8-2)' 1 1
```

```
# illum in east wall, south window
!gensurf sky_illum iwindow_e_s \
     '39.49' '2.5 + t*(7-2.5)' '2 + s*(8-2)' 1 1

# Art Gallery: gallery daylighting
# (using automatic illum subdivision set by the rpict -ds parameter)
# illum at top of skylight aperture
!gensurf sky_illum skylight \
     '1 + t*(29-1)' '10.5 + s*(14.5-10.5)' '19.4' 1 1
# end walls.rad
```

3.5.2 Creating and Aiming Tracklights in the Gallery

Though our gallery now enjoys the benefits of an indirect daylight system, a flexible tracklighting scheme is required to make the art adequately visible on cloudy days and during the evening hours. At first glance this might seem like a straightforward task, but actually several issues need to be addressed.

If we are simply locating the photometry of a single reflector lamp type somewhere in the gallery and have no concern for modeling the physical luminaire, our task remains trivial. We would use the ies2rad program to generate a *Radiance* description of a photometric file and then aim the lighting distribution at our art (see Section 3.1, Physically Based Lighting, at the beginning of this chapter). This would create several light-emitting rings or polygons hovering near the ceiling of the gallery. But we want to explore the detailed impact of the tracklighting system. This includes seeing which reflector lamps best illuminate a particular work of art as well as discovering how the placement, size, and color of the track heads affect the space. Will the track heads cast distracting shadows during the daytime? Will they visually interfere with the artwork?

Let's begin by organizing the lamp inventory. To simplify the appearance and maintenance of the tracklighting system, we decide to use PAR38 lamps and only one model of track luminaire. Five particular PAR38 lamps seem to provide the necessary variety of beam spreads and intensities, which range from a 90-watt narrow spot to a 150-watt quartz flood. When each of these IESNA-format photometric files is converted into a *Radiance* description, we will give it a generic name. The generic name, *typeS1* for example, can be used to locate the light with an xform command wherever a 90-watt flood is needed. If a lamp manufacturer suggests substituting a more energy-efficient 75-watt flood, you could insert its IESNA-format photometric file into the ies2rad program, but keep the same *typeS1* output name. The effect of the lamp could then be evaluated without the bother of globally renaming the individual occurrences of the lamp type.

To keep the active lamp inventory organized and readily accessible, the IESNA-format photometric files are located in the *ies_lib* subdirectory, and we use two local files to alter the installed lamps' intensities between their day and night settings. *lights_n.cvt* creates the *Radiance* spotlight descriptions used at night. Variations of this approach could be used to dim or color any grouping of luminaires. In our case, the -m multiplier applies a light loss factor to the luminaire's output. The -c color option has been set to white light (1 1 1), but by changing these RGB values, the effect of colored filters or exotic lamp colors can be added to the luminaires.

```
# !/bin/csh -f
### lights_n.cvt
#
# file for maintaining active Scene 2 photometry
# for nighttime settings.
# Turn off a circuit: -m  0
# Turn on a circuit:  -m >0 (.8 for reasonable LLF)
#spotlights for the art gallery
ies2rad -df -t default -m .8 -c 1 1 1 -o lib/typeS1 ies_lib/90pfl.ies
ies2rad -df -t default -m .8 -c 1 1 1 -o lib/typeS2 ies_lib/90psp.ies
ies2rad -df -t default -m .8 -c 1 1 1 -o lib/typeS3 ies_lib/90pns.ies
ies2rad -df -t default -m .8 -c 1 1 1 -o lib/typeS4 ies_lib/q150p38t.ies
ies2rad -df -t default -m .8 -c 1 1 1 -o lib/typeS5 ies_lib/q150p38s.ies
#end lights_n.cvt
```

Note the absence of the ! from the beginning of each ies2rad command. The "!" tells oconv and other scene parsers that an executable program follows. But we will maintain the inventory separately from the *Radiance* rendering procedure by making the *lights_n.cvt* file an executable shell script. This is accomplished by the following command:

```
% chmod 755 lights_n.cvt
```

Now, when *lights_n.cvt* is executed at the command line, the ies2rad output files are updated to the current nighttime settings:

```
% lights_n.cvt
```

In nontheatrical environments, once the lighting layout and lamps have been established for a particular time of day or event, it is unlikely that they will be altered. Similarly, with *Radiance*, once the lighting conditions for a particular environment have been designed, the focus of activity shifts to exploring the location and finish of each object in the space and visualizing the scene from various vantage points. Though we could rerun the ies2rad commands by including them in a material file, which would execute them every time we created a scene octree, we have elected to make this a separate process. The *Radiance* lighting files need only to be updated after an ies2rad command has been modified. This boils down to an issue of organization and modeling practice rather than an issue of *Radiance*'s capabilities.

The five files that follow are the root IESNA-format photometry sources for our *typeS* series; they are located in the *ies_lib* subdirectory.

```
IESNA91
90pfl.ies
90-watt PAR38 flood
TILT=NONE
1 1270 1 29 1 1 1 -.4 0 0
1 1 90
0 1.25 2.5 3.75 5 6.25 7.5 8.75 10 12.5 15 17.5 20 22.5 25 27.5 30 35 40
45 50 55 60 65 70 75 80 85 90
0
3411.7 3367.9 3235 3079.5 2938 2804.6 2685.1 2570.6 2422.5 2110.6
1739.9 1277.1 878.5 594.5 417.6 315.6 256.5 200 184.1 173.4 143.5 118.3
90.4 62.8 44.5 35.2 30.4 25.8 22.5

IESNA91
90pns.ies
90-watt PAR38 narrow spot
.
.
IESNA91
90psp.ies
90-watt PAR38 spot
.
.
IESNA91
Q150P38F.ies
150-watt quartz PAR38 flood  Beam spread: 47.6'
.
.
IESNA91
Q150P38S.ies
150-watt quartz PAR38 spot   Beam spread: 10.5'
.
.
```

Next, we need to create a complete tracklight, insert one of our lamp types, and prepare it for aiming. This is actually more complex than it appears.

Following the ies2rad conventions, the photometric description in the *typeS1.rad* file has been created at 0 0 0, pointing downward in the -*z* direction. A review of the contents of the *typeS1.rad* file shows the emitter to be a .2-foot-radius ring. A simple cylinder and endcap can be constructed around the ring light source, which can then be attached to the track by means of a yoke. But how do you aim the luminaire while also keeping the yoke anchored on the track? The first part of our solution involves describing the lampholder and photometry in one file and the yoke in another. These files are in the project *lib* subdirectory.

```
### luminaire.mat
#
# track system surface finish

void plastic enamel_white
0
0
5 .7 .6 .5 .03 0.02
# end luminaire.mat

### track_S1.rad
#
# track lampholder with typeS1 photometry
# lampholder in feet
# suspension yoke in track_y.rad

enamel_white cylinder  housing1
0
0
7     0     0     0
      0     0     .6
       .21

enamel_white ring  housing2
0
0
8     0     0     .6
      0     0    1
      .21   0
```

```
# insert photometry into the aperture of the cylinder
!xform -n lamp1 typeS1.rad
# end track_S1.rad

### track_y.rad
#
# tracklight yoke
# yoke in feet
# use with track_xx.rad lampholder

!genbox enamel_white yoke_stem .1  .1 .1 -r .02 | xform -t -.05 -.05 .35
!genbox enamel_white yoke_top  .5  .1 .05       | xform -t -.25 -.05 .3
!genbox enamel_white yoke_lft  .04 .1 .3        | xform -t -.25 -.05 0
!genbox enamel_white yoke_rgt  .04 .1 .3        | xform -t  .21 -.05 0
# end track_y.rad
```

Now we are able to rotate the luminaire and yoke about the *z*-axis while independently tilting the luminaire about the *x*-axis. The following description fragment illustrates the method:

```
!xform -n ls -t 0 0 -.5 -rx 45 -rz 20 -t 6 20.5 11.1 lib/track_S1.rad
!xform -n ly                   -rz 20 -t 6 20.5 11.1 lib/track_y.rad
```

Track_S1.rad is lowered 6 inches so that the rear of the cylinder is aligned with the yoke. The luminaire is then rotated around the *x*-axis (tilt angle). Finally, both the luminaire and the yoke are rotated around the *z*-axis before being translated to their track location. Though adjustments to the tilt are only applied to the *track_S1.rad* file, any change in the *z*-axis rotation or location of the track must be applied identically to both files. Examples of tilted and rotated tracklights are shown in Figure 3.25.

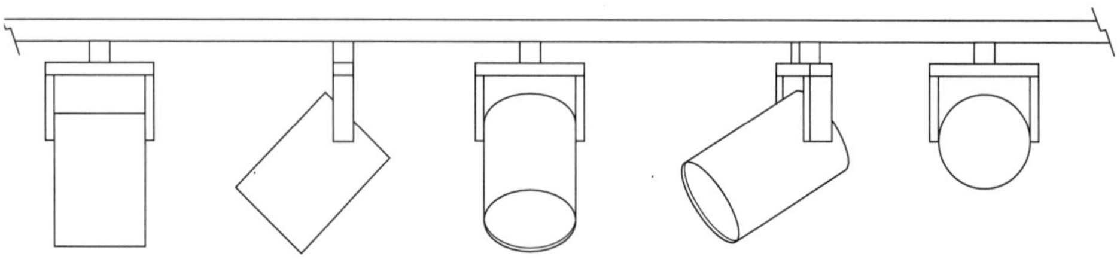

Figure 3.25 Tracklight luminaires aimed in many directions.

The other four tracklight lampholders can also be assembled. Each is identical to *track_S1.rad*, except for the photometry and the appropriate renaming of the file. The edited *track_S1.rad* and additional lampholder description files are in the *lib* subdirectory on the CD-ROM and are identified below:

```
track_S2.rad    #cylinder + typeS2.rad photometry
track_S3.rad    #cylinder + typeS3.rad photometry
track_S4.rad    #cylinder + typeS4.rad photometry
track_S5.rad    #cylinder + typeS5.rad photometry
```

The Scene 2 electric lighting system file includes descriptions of the track and of all aimed luminaires. Each luminaire is individually named with some reference to its location so that error messages or re-aiming requirements can be handled expediently. As the lighting scheme becomes more intricate, the benefits of careful preplanning and organization become evident. Hundreds of uniquely aimed luminaires can be realistically managed using this approach. The following file aims nine tracklights with five different lamp types from two lengths of ceiling-mounted track.

```
### sc2light.rad
#
#  electric lighting systems for Scene 2.
#  active photometry is listed in light.cvt.
#  If photometry is updated, then execute:
#    light_n.cvt

# south ceiling track followed by individual tracklights
!genbox enamel_white track1 24 .15 .15 | xform -t 3 4.35 11.55

!xform -n 11s -t 0 0 -.5 -rx 45 -rz 180 -t 6 4.35 11.1 lib/track_S4.rad
!xform -n 11y                   -rz 180 -t 6 4.35 11.1 lib/track_y.rad

!xform -n 12s -t 0 0 -.5 -rx 45 -rz 180 -t 12 4.35 11.1 lib/track_S4.rad
!xform -n 12y                   -rz 180 -t 12 4.35 11.1 lib/track_y.rad

!xform -n 13s -t 0 0 -.5 -rx 40 -rz 180 -t 18 4.35 11.1 lib/track_S4.rad
!xform -n 13y                   -rz 180 -t 18 4.35 11.1 lib/track_y.rad

!xform -n 14s -t 0 0 -.5 -rx 30 -rz 180 -t 24 4.35 11.1 lib/track_S4.rad
!xform -n 14y                   -rz 180 -t 24 4.35 11.1 lib/track_y.rad

!xform -n 15s -t 0 0 -.5 -rx 40 -rz -95 -t 26 4.35 11.1 lib/track_S5.rad
!xform -n 15y                   -rz -95 -t 26 4.35 11.1 lib/track_y.rad

# north ceiling track followed by individual tracklights
!genbox enamel_white track2 24 .15 .15 | xform -t 3 20.5 11.55
```

```
!xform -n 21s -t 0 0 -.5 -rx 45 -rz 5 -t 6 20.5 11.1 lib/track_S1.rad
!xform -n 21y                   -rz 5 -t 6 20.5 11.1 lib/track_y.rad

!xform -n 22s -t 0 0 -.5 -rx 45 -rz 5 -t 12 20.5 11.1 lib/track_S2.rad
!xform -n 22y                   -rz 5 -t 12 20.5 11.1 lib/track_y.rad

!xform -n 23s -t 0 0 -.5 -rx 45 -rz 5 -t 20 20.5 11.1 lib/track_S3.rad
!xform -n 23y                   -rz 5 -t 20 20.5 11.1 lib/track_y.rad

!xform -n 24s -t 0 0 -.5 -rx 45 -rz -30 -t 26 20.5 11.1 lib/track_S4.rad
!xform -n 24y                   -rz -30 -t 26 20.5 11.1 lib/track_y.rad
#end sc2light.rad
```

3.5.3 Adding Recessed Linear Lighting to the Art Gallery

The daylight reflector system in the gallery delivers reasonable light levels to the walls, but creates a shadowed effect in the middle of the space. To solve this problem, and to provide nighttime lighting, recessed linear fluorescent luminaires will be installed in the base of the reflector structure. As we discovered during the Scene 1 project, it is not necessary to pierce the ceiling when we position recessed luminaire photometry. We will use this technique to locate a light-emitting polygon just below the ceiling surface.

There are many varieties of recessed fluorescent downlights! The search for the most appropriate luminaire begins with querying your luminaire resources and acquiring the necessary IESNA photometric files. A semispecular parabolic baffle luminaire is ideal for our application, because it will light the center of the gallery while exhibiting very little distracting glare. In addition, the luminaire is reasonably energy-efficient.

```
IESNA91
[TEST] 1001.IES
[MANUFAC] DOWNLIGHT CORPORATION
[LUMCAT] dl-4
[LUMINAIRE] dl-4-24-T8-PBSS
[LAMP] F032/41K
[OTHER] parabolic baffles, semi specular
TILT=NONE
   2 2900. 1.0 19 5 1 1 .42 4.00 .00
1.0 1.0 64.
 .
 .
```

This file is located in the *ies_lib* directory—see the CD-ROM for a complete listing—so what remains is to update the *light_n.cvt* and *light_d.cvt* files. Following our generic labeling practice, we will call this luminaire *typeRLF* (recessed linear fluorescent). This ies2rad command is added to the *.cvt* files:

```
# 4' x .5' recessed linear fluorescent luminaires
ies2rad -df -t default -m .8 -c 1 1 1 -o lib/typeRLF2 ies_lib/1001.ies
```

Now a row of *typeRLF* can be included in the *sc2lights.rad* file. Each unit is 4 feet long and 6 inches wide. The units are designed to be joined into a continuous row, so the array option in xform will simplify the installation. The following lines are appended to the *sc2lights.rad* file:

```
# Direct louvered recessed fluorescents
!xform -n rlfd -rz 0 -t 11 12.5 7.99 -a 5 -t 4 0 0 -i 1 lib/typeRLF2.rad
```

To extend the daylighted ceiling effect into the night, recessed fluorescent luminaires will be located on the upper surface of the gallery daylight reflector. During the daytime, these will be turned off, but at night they will provide indirect light, which will contribute to the airy atmosphere of the gallery. Because these luminaires will not be viewed directly by the public, glare-reducing baffles are not required. For ease of cleaning, we will install prismatic lenses on these upward-facing luminaires. If we locate them close to the edge of the daylight reflector, they will distribute their light more effectively over the ceiling and be easier to maintain.

This alternative *1000.ies* file is included in the *ies_lib* photometry library:

```
IESNA91
[TEST] 1000.IES
[MANUFAC] DOWNLIGHT CORPORATION
[LUMCAT] dl-4
[LUMINAIRE] dl-4-24-T8-AP
[LAMP] F032/41K
[SEARCH]
[OTHER] acrylic prismatic
TILT=NONE
   2 2900. 1.0 19 5 1 1 .42 4.00 .00
1.0 1.0 78.
.
.
```

Another ies2rad command, located in the *light_n.cvt* file, creates and updates the *Radiance* indirect linear lighting data files.

```
# 1000.ies = prismatic indirect linear fluorescent.
# Significant Light Loss Factor (.6) from surface dust.
ies2rad -df -t default -m .6 -c 1 1 1 -o lib/typeRLF1 ies_lib/1000.ies
```

Though we plan to turn this luminaire off during daylight hours, we will include it in the *light_d.cvt* file in case we need to experiment with rainy-day lighting. Note that the luminaire is "turned off" with the `-m 0` option.

```
# 1000.ies = prismatic indirect linear fluorescent.
# Significant Light Loss Factor (.6) from surface dust.
ies2rad -df -t default -m 0 -c 1 1 1 -o lib/typeRLF1 ies_lib/1000.ies
```

Finally, the prismatic luminaires are located by this entry in the *sc2light.rad* file:

```
# Indirect recessed prismatic fluorescents
!xform -n rlfin -rx 145 -t 6 15.75 8.35 -a 5 -t 4 0 0 -i 0 lib/typeRLF1.rad
!xform -n rlfis -rx -145 -t 6 9.25 8.35 -a 5 -t 4 0 0 -i 0 lib/typeRLF1.rad
```

3.5.4 Lobby Lighting

The lobby is a transitional area between the outside world and the visual excitement of the gallery. In keeping with its function, its lighting will be simple and unobtrusive. The ambient light for the lobby will be provided by several wall sconces, which will bathe the ceiling with diffuse light. This lighting system will also serve as security lighting at night, and will likely be turned on during the day (no skylights in the lobby!). Energy-efficient compact fluorescent lamps will provide the illumination. A small number of ceiling-mounted tracklights will accent the lobby art and furniture during the evening hours.

To reduce the brightness of the wall above the sconces and to distribute light toward the center of the ceiling slopes, we select a small sconce with an asymmetrical light output. The following *2001.ies* file is located in the *ies_lib* photometry library:

```
IESNA93
File: 2001.ies
Report: test001
Manufacturer: Sconce Company
Lamp: 26-watt quad tube fluorescent, 1800 lumens
Cat Number: 2001-ws-26
Notes: Asymmetrical distribution, tilt 180 degrees for indirect
TILT=NONE
1 1800 1 37 9 1 1 0.8854 0.2813 0
1 1 28
.
.
```

Light_n.rad and *light_d.rad* are updated by adding the following command to each:

```
#2001.ies = indirect wall mounted sconce
ies2rad -df -t default -m .8 -c 1 1 1 -o lib/typeWM1 ies_lib/2001.ies
#end lights_n(d).cvt
```

In this situation, unlike that of the recessed fluorescents, we need to construct a physical wall sconce that will house the light source. A construction approach is illustrated in Figure 3.26. *Sconce.rad* is a description of a complete wall sconce; it is found in the *lib* subdirectory:

```
### sconce.rad
#
# Asymmetric indirect luminaire
# Photometry from 2001.ies (26-watt compact fluorescent)
# insertion point at top rear of bracket. Luminaire protrudes
# 1.05 feet and is 1 foot wide.

!genprism enamel_white housing 3 -.4 0 0 -.25 0 .25 -1 0 0 1 \
        | xform -ry -90 -t .5 -.5 0
!genprism enamel_white bracket 3 -.4 0 0 -.25 0 .25 -1 0 0 .5 \
        | xform -ry -90 -rz -90 -t 0 -.5 0

!xform -n sconce -rz -90 -ry 180 -t 0 -.5 .01 typeWM1.rad
# end sconce.rad
```

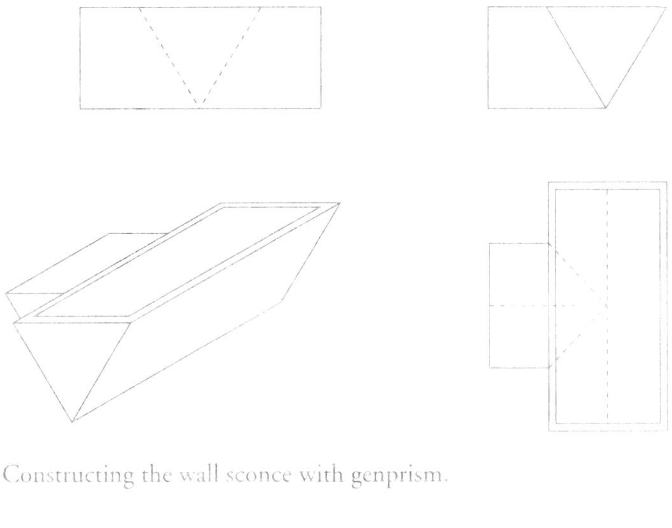

Figure 3.26 Constructing the wall sconce with genprism.

Now we can locate wall sconces to flank the front entrance and both sides of the gallery arch. The top of the sconce is set at 6 feet 3 inches, providing adequate distance from the ceilings and keeping the light source invisible to all but the tallest of patrons! The sconces are installed through the following lines in *sc2light.rad*:

```
# lobby indirect sconces
#gallery arch: lobby wall
!xform -n sc_sw -rz 90 -t 30 8.5 6.25 lib/sconce.rad
!xform -n sc_nw -rz 90 -t 30 16.5 6.25 lib/sconce.rad
# front door
!xform -n sc_e -rz 180 -t 30.7 .5 6.25 lib/sconce.rad
!xform -n sc_w -rz 180 -t 38.7 .5 6.25 lib/sconce.rad
# gallery arch: gallery wall
!xform -n sc_se -rz -90 -t 29.5 8.5 6.25 lib/sconce.rad
!xform -n sc_ne -rz -90 -t 29.5 16.5 6.25 lib/sconce.rad
```

If these wall sconces also included a downlight component, we would add them to the scene using an alternative method. The IES photometric format is based on a point-source description. If we were to locate the IES description of this new photometry on top of the geometry of the original sconce, the downlight component would be blocked by the luminaire housing. To overcome this obstacle, the `ies2rad` command includes the -i option, which discards the IES photometric format's "luminous opening" geometry and replaces it with an invisible illum sphere of a specified radius. This sphere should be just large enough to enclose the luminaire's geometry, as shown in Figure 3.27. The photometric distribution is then mapped to this illum sphere and the luminaire geometry no longer interferes with the outward radiating photometry. Luminous panels constructed from glow material could be placed on the luminaire to represent the luminous openings so that the visual impact of the luminaire could be evaluated. If this glow material were defined with a radius that did not exceed the radius of the illum sphere, the light emanating from the sconce would be accurately represented. This technique is particularly applicable when you evaluate the illumination and visual impact of chandeliers and other complex luminaires.

If we were to describe our sconce using an illum source, we would need to replace the existing luminous upper panel with glow material and change the ies2rad command to the following:

```
#2001.ies = indirect wall mounted sconce using an illum sphere
ies2rad -df -t default -m .8 -c 1 1 1 -i .6 -o lib/typeWM1 ies_lib/2001.ies
#end lights_n(d).cvt
```

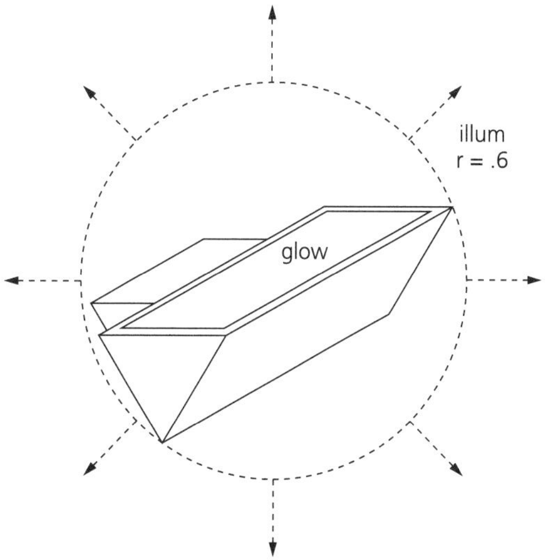

Figure 3.27 An illum sphere is used when the luminaire surfaces might interfere with a point-source photometric distribution of light.

Two short lengths of track and a few tracklights are added to *sc2light.rad*. This completes the lobby lighting:

```
# south lobby track
!genbox enamel_white track3 8 .15 .15 | xform -t 31 4.35 11.55

!xform -n 31s -t 0 0 -.5 -rx 0 -rz 0 -t 33 4.35 11.1 lib/track_S4.rad
!xform -n 31y                  -rz 0 -t 33 4.35 11.1 lib/track_y.rad

!xform -n 32s -t 0 0 -.5 -rx 0 -rz 0 -t 37 4.35 11.1 lib/track_S4.rad
!xform -n 32y                  -rz 0 -t 37 4.35 11.1 lib/track_y.rad

!xform -n 33s -t 0 0 -.5 -rx 37 -rz 90 -t 35 4.35 11.1 lib/track_S4.rad
!xform -n 33y                   -rz 90 -t 35 4.35 11.1 lib/track_y.rad

!xform -n 34s -t 0 0 -.5 -rx 35 -rz 0 -t 36 4.35 11.1 lib/track_S4.rad
!xform -n 34y                   -rz 0 -t 36 4.35 11.1 lib/track_y.rad

# north lobby track
!genbox enamel_white track4 8 .15 .15 | xform -t 31 20.5 11.55

!xform -n 41s -t 0 0 -.5 -rx 0 -rz 0 -t 33 20.5 11.1 lib/track_S4.rad
!xform -n 41y                  -rz 0 -t 33 20.5 11.1 lib/track_y.rad
```

```
!xform -n 42s -t 0 0 -.5 -rx 0 -rz 0 -t 37 20.5 11.1 lib/track_S4.rad
!xform -n 42y                   -rz 0 -t 37 20.5 11.1 lib/track_y.rad

!xform -n 43s -t 0 0 -.5 -rx 37 -rz 90 -t 35 20.5 11.1 lib/track_S4.rad
!xform -n 43y                    -rz 90 -t 35 20.5 11.1 lib/track_y.rad
```

Our basic lighting scheme has now been implemented. We will revisit the *sc2light.rad* file when we finally light the art after it is constructed and installed. For now, we have some work light to see by.

3.5.5 Creating the Furniture

The Art Gallery furniture is selected from a commercial product line. Its design elements include chrome metal tubing and materials such as black and yellow laminate and yellow vinyl. This modern furniture will suit the style of the gallery while providing patrons and employees with a comfortable and functional environment.

The curved chrome tubing supports for the furniture are based on segments of an arc. We will use genworm and the equation of a circle for the construction. Though it is possible to make the curves using gensurf, it would take thousands of polygons to give the surfaces a smooth appearance. This in turn would create much larger files and add to rendering time. Genworm is most efficient in its use of cones and spheres to build object descriptions, and in this case it will produce the best effect. If the furniture is viewed in extreme close-up, we might have to increase the number of segments per arc to avoid seeing individual cone segments, but in general our files will remain small and the chrome will appear smooth.

If a circle of a given radius is described about the axis of a 2D plane, the x and y values of any point on the circle can be determined by using the sine and cosine of the angle of rotation, as illustrated in Figure 3.28.

The equation of a circle can also be used to define an arc with genworm. In conjunction with the inner radius of the tube and the number of cone segments, a curved pipe results. Genworm locates a sphere at each end of the shape, so we do not have to seal the ends.

```
!genworm material pipe 'tx(t)' 'ty(t)' 0 r 10 \
            -e 'r:.1;R:1;Tmax:45*PI/180' \
            -e 'tx(t)=R*cos(t*Tmax)' -e 'ty(t)=R*sin(t*Tmax)'
```

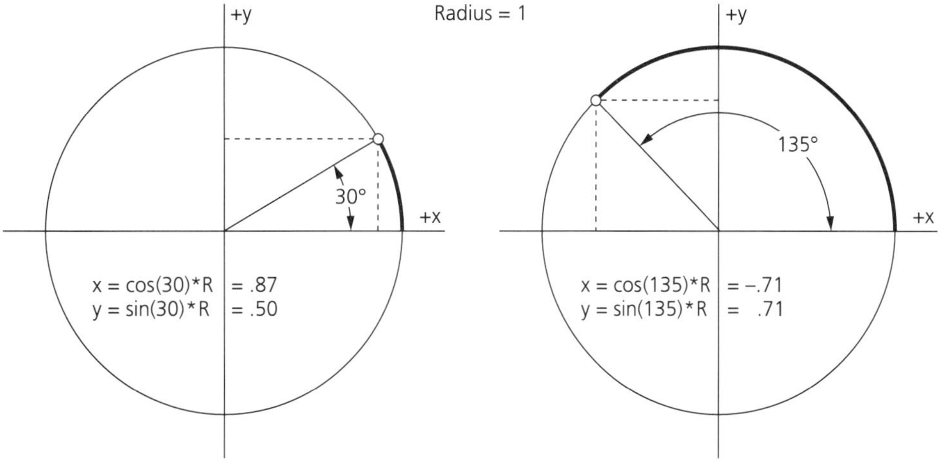

Figure 3.28 Using the equation of a circle to describe arcs.

This genworm command creates a .1-foot-radius pipe bent into a 45-degree arc with a radius of 1 foot. The pipe is composed of 10 cone/sphere segments of equal length. By modifying these variables, we will construct the chrome supports for our furniture. A directory called *scene2/art_lib* will store our furniture, works of art, and related material files:

```
% mkdir art_lib
```

The material for the furniture is defined in *furniture.mat*.

```
### furniture.mat
#
# file contains all furniture material

void plastic table_color
0
0
5 .1 .1 .1 .025 .025

void metal pipe_color
0
0
5 .7 .7 .7 .9 .02
```

```
void plastic seat_color
0
0
5 .8 .6 .05 0 0

void plastic desktop_color
0
0
5 .8 .6 .05 0 0

void plastic deskmid_color
0
0
5 .1 .1 .1 .025 .025
# end furniture.mat
```

Building a simple lobby chair (Figure 3.29) will demonstrate the construction methods used to create most of the furnishings. Note how xform manipulates the genworm constructions to form the chair frame in *chair_c1.rad*. Remember the right-hand rule when you are tracking the rotations!

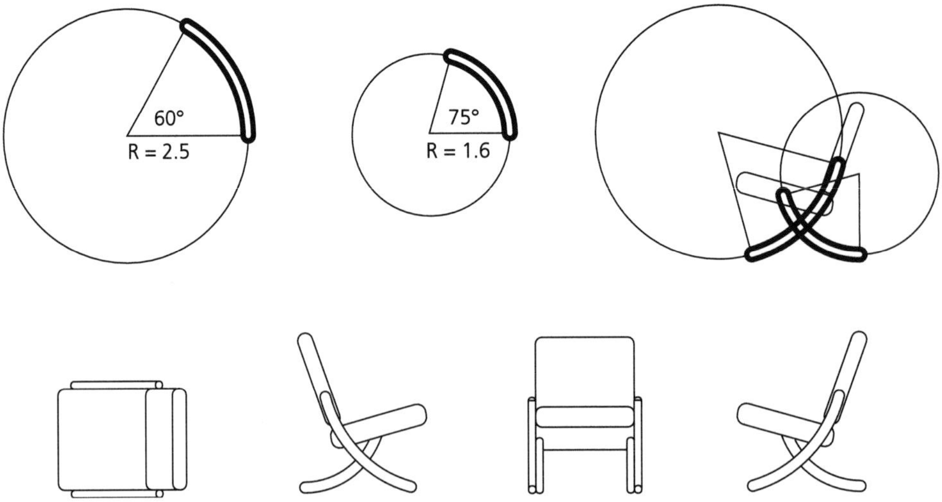

Figure 3.29 Constructing a chair with curved legs.

```
### chair_c1.rad
#
# reception area chair with no arms
# insertion point is at floor level, at center front of the seat

#left side support
!genworm pipe_color l_side 'tx(t)' 'ty(t)' 0 r 15 \
              -e 'r:.075;R:2.5;Tmax:60*PI/180' \
              -e 'tx(t)=R*cos(t*Tmax)' -e 'ty(t)=R*sin(t*Tmax)'\
              | xform -rz -75 -rx 90 -rz 90 -t -1.0375 -.3 2.5

!genworm pipe_color l_leg 'tx(t)' 'ty(t)' 0 r 15 \
              -e 'r:.075;R:1.6;Tmax:75*PI/180' \
              -e 'tx(t)=R*cos(t*Tmax)' -e 'ty(t)=R*sin(t*Tmax)'\
              | xform -ry 90 -rz 180 -t -.925 2.5 1.65

#right side support
!genworm pipe_color l_side 'tx(t)' 'ty(t)' 0 r 15 \
              -e 'r:.075;R:2.5;Tmax:60*PI/180' \
              -e 'tx(t)=R*cos(t*Tmax)' -e 'ty(t)=R*sin(t*Tmax)'\
              | xform -rz -75 -rx 90 -rz 90 -t 1.0375 -.3 2.5

!genworm pipe_color l_leg 'tx(t)' 'ty(t)' 0 r 15 \
              -e 'r:.075;R:1.6;Tmax:75*PI/180' \
              -e 'tx(t)=R*cos(t*Tmax)' -e 'ty(t)=R*sin(t*Tmax)'\
              | xform -ry 90 -rz 180 -t .925 2.5 1.65

# front seats
!genbox seat_color seat 2  2 .4  -r .15  | xform -rx -15 -t -1  0   1.3
!genbox seat_color back 2 .3 1.9 -r .125 | xform -rx -20 -t -1 1.75 1.3
# end chair_c1.rad
```

Once a detailed object has been created, variations can be built rapidly. A lobby sofa is constructed simply by copying the *chair_c1.rad* file into *sofa1_c1.rad* and applying the following changes to the seat cushion widths and to the xform commands that will relocate the supporting pipe structures and recenter the seat:

```
### sofa1_c1.rad
#
# sofa has a 5'-wide cushion
# insertion point is at floor level, at center front of the seat
```

```
#left side support
!genworm pipe_color l_side 'tx(t)' 'ty(t)' 0 r 15 \
        -e 'r:.075;R:2.5;Tmax:60*PI/180' \
        -e 'tx(t)=R*cos(t*Tmax)' -e 'ty(t)=R*sin(t*Tmax)'\
        | xform -rz -75 -rx 90 -rz 90 -t -2.5375 -.3 2.5

!genworm pipe_color l_leg 'tx(t)' 'ty(t)' 0 r 15 \
        -e 'r:.075;R:1.6;Tmax:75*PI/180' \
        -e 'tx(t)=R*cos(t*Tmax)' -e 'ty(t)=R*sin(t*Tmax)'\
        | xform -ry 90 -rz 180 -t -2.425 2.5 1.65

#right side support
!genworm pipe_color l_side 'tx(t)' 'ty(t)' 0 r 15 \
        -e 'r:.075;R:2.5;Tmax:60*PI/180' \
        -e 'tx(t)=R*cos(t*Tmax)' -e 'ty(t)=R*sin(t*Tmax)'\
        | xform -rz -75 -rx 90 -rz 90 -t 2.5375 -.3 2.5

!genworm pipe_color l_leg 'tx(t)' 'ty(t)' 0 r 15 \
        -e 'r:.075;R:1.6;Tmax:75*PI/180' \
        -e 'tx(t)=R*cos(t*Tmax)' -e 'ty(t)=R*sin(t*Tmax)'\
        | xform -ry 90 -rz 180 -t 2.425 2.5 1.65

# seat
!genbox seat_color seat 5  2 .4  -r .15  | xform -rx -15 -t -2.5  0   1.3
!genbox seat_color back 5 .3 1.9 -r .125 | xform -rx -20 -t -2.5 1.75 1.3
# end sofal_c1.rad
```

An executive desk chair is required for the manager of the gallery (Figure 3.30). It is based on the previous lobby chair and includes arms and a headrest. Note the use of the array -a and the -mx mirror option to duplicate and mirror the chair's

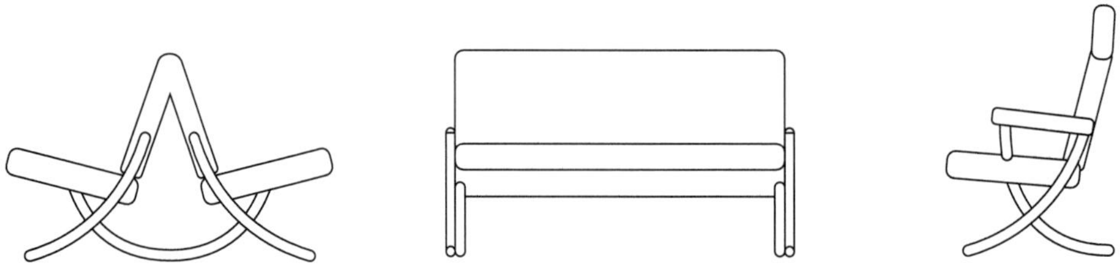

Figure 3.30 The back-to-back sofa and desk chair for the Art Gallery.

right arm to the left arm location. This procedure simplifies the construction and can be applied successfully because the chair is centered on the *yz* plane. *Deskc_c1.rad* is located in the *art_lib* directory.

```
### deskc_c1.rad
#
# Executive desk chair with arms and headrest
# insertion point is at floor level, at center front of the seat
.
.
# seat
!genbox seat_color seat 2 2 .4     -r .15  | xform -rx -5 -t -1  0   1.15
!genbox seat_color back_l 2 .3 1.9 -r .125 | xform -rx -15 -t -1 1.75 1.3
!genbox seat_color back_u 2 .3 .75 -r .125 | xform -rx -5 -t -1 2.2  3.0
!genbox seat_color arms .35 1.5 .2 -r .05  | xform -rx -5 -t .82 .7 2 -a 2 -mx
# end deskc_c1.rad
```

The final seating unit is a double-sided sofa, to be located in the center of the gallery (see Figure 3.30). The rear legs are reconstructed to support both the front and rear seating units. This time, the mirror option becomes an even greater asset, simplifying the positioning of the additional legs and seat cushions.

```
### sofa2_c1.rad
#
# back-to-back sofa has a 5'-wide cushion
# insertion point is at floor level, at center of unit

#left side support
!genworm pipe_color l_side 'tx(t)' 'ty(t)' 0 r 15 \
              -e 'r:.075;R:2.5;Tmax:60*PI/180' \
              -e 'tx(t)=R*cos(t*Tmax)' -e 'ty(t)=R*sin(t*Tmax)'\
              | xform -rz -75 -rx 90 -rz 90 -t -2.5375 -2.8 2.5 -a 2 -my

!genworm pipe_color l_leg 'tx(t)' 'ty(t)' 0 r 15 \
              -e 'r:.075;R:1.6;Tmax:150*PI/180' \
              -e 'tx(t)=R*cos(t*Tmax)' -e 'ty(t)=R*sin(t*Tmax)'\
              | xform -ry 90 -rx -75 -t -2.425 0 1.65
```

```
#right side support
!genworm pipe_color r_side 'tx(t)' 'ty(t)' 0 r 15 \
        -e 'r:.075;R:2.5;Tmax:60*PI/180' \
        -e 'tx(t)=R*cos(t*Tmax)' -e 'ty(t)=R*sin(t*Tmax)'\
        | xform -rz -75 -rx 90 -rz 90 -t 2.5375 -2.8 2.5 -a 2 -my

!genworm pipe_color r_leg 'tx(t)' 'ty(t)' 0 r 15 \
        -e 'r:.075;R:1.6;Tmax:150*PI/180' \
        -e 'tx(t)=R*cos(t*Tmax)' -e 'ty(t)=R*sin(t*Tmax)'\
        | xform -ry 90 -rx -75 -t 2.425 0 1.65

# front seats
!genbox seat_color seat 5 2 .4   -r .15  | xform -rx -15 -t -2.5 -2.5 1.3
!genbox seat_color back 5 .3 1.9 -r .125 | xform -rx -20 -t -2.5 -.75 1.3

#rear seats
!genbox seat_color seat 5  2 .4  -r .15  | xform -rx -15 -t -2.5 -2.5 1.3 -my
!genbox seat_color back 5 .3 1.9 -r .125 | xform -rx -20 -t -2.5 -.75 1.3 -my
# end sofa2_c1.rad
```

Creating the lobby desk poses some interesting problems (Figure 3.31). The desk unit is supported by two large arches, located at the front and the rear. The desk is shaped to rest on these arches.

But how do we expediently build this unusual concave shape into the desk unit? First we will describe and locate the front supporting arch, centered over 0 0 0, with its feet on the *xy* plane and the center plane of the arc in the *xz* plane. A second arch, which describes the end curves of the desk, is temporarily added to the data set. This will provide a template for the drawer unit shape, which we can then trace interactively while viewing the data in rview! If we do not have a drafting table or drafting program handy, the trace feature in rview provides us with the necessary coordinates so that we can construct a concave genprism to form the desk. This method is illustrated in Figure 3.32.

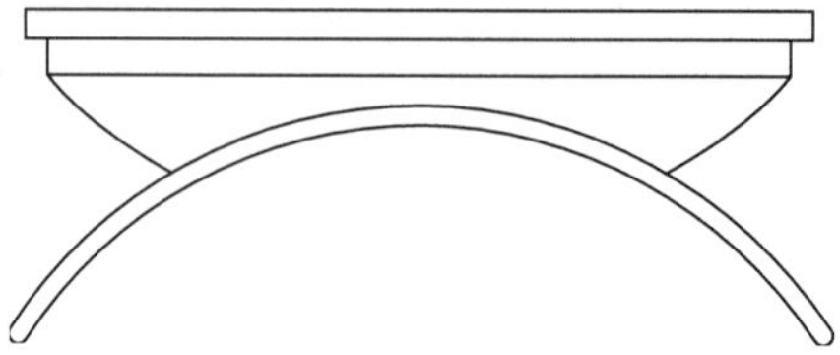

Figure 3.31 Front elevation of the lobby desk.

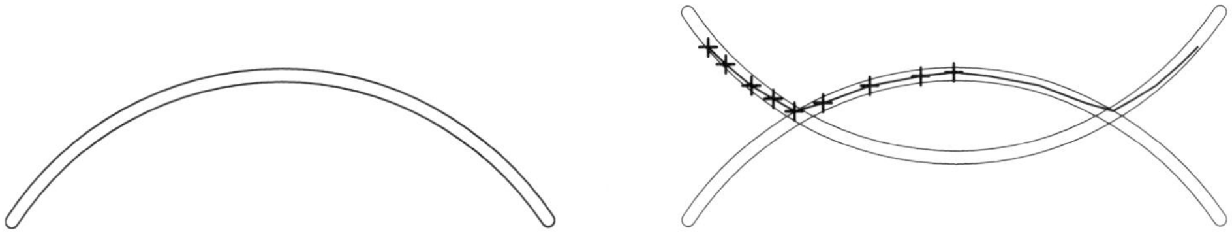

Figure 3.32 Using arches as templates for tracing the contour of the desk.

A preliminary *desk_c1a.rad* file contains the following descriptions:

```
# support structure at front of desk
!genworm pipe_color l_side 'tx(t)' 'ty(t)' 0 r 15 \
       -e 'r:.075;R:3.75;Tmax:120*PI/180' \
       -e 'tx(t)=R*cos(t*Tmax)' -e 'ty(t)=R*sin(t*Tmax)'\
       | xform -rz 30 -rx 90 -t 0 .1 -2

# This temporary arch is a template from which
# polygon and genprism coordinates can be determined
# using the trace command in rview.
!genworm pipe_color template 'tx(t)' 'ty(t)' 0 r 15 \
       -e 'r:.075;R:3.75;Tmax:120*PI/180' \
       -e 'tx(t)=R*cos(t*Tmax)' -e 'ty(t)=R*sin(t*Tmax)'\
       | xform -rz 210 -rx 90 -t 0 .1 4.5
```

Now convert the file into an octree and view the arches from the front using rview. If we include the -vtl option, a parallel view is configured instead of the default -vtv perspective view. An ambient value of `-av 1 1 1` will make the shape visible (Figure 3.33):

```
% oconv desk_c1a.rad > desk_c1.oct

% rview -vp 0 0 1.5 -vtl -av 1 1 1 desk_c1.oct
```

In rview, enter `trace` or `t` at the command line and select a series of points across the upper edge of the arch. The points should be sampled every 3 or 4 inches across the *x*-axis. Because the shape is symmetrical, the samples from half of the arc can be used to describe the whole concave shape. Write down these coordinates, then produce a polygon from the data and insert it into the *desk_c1.rad* file, using 0 for the *y* coordinate. Viewing this polygon will confirm whether the points you sampled produce the desired shape.

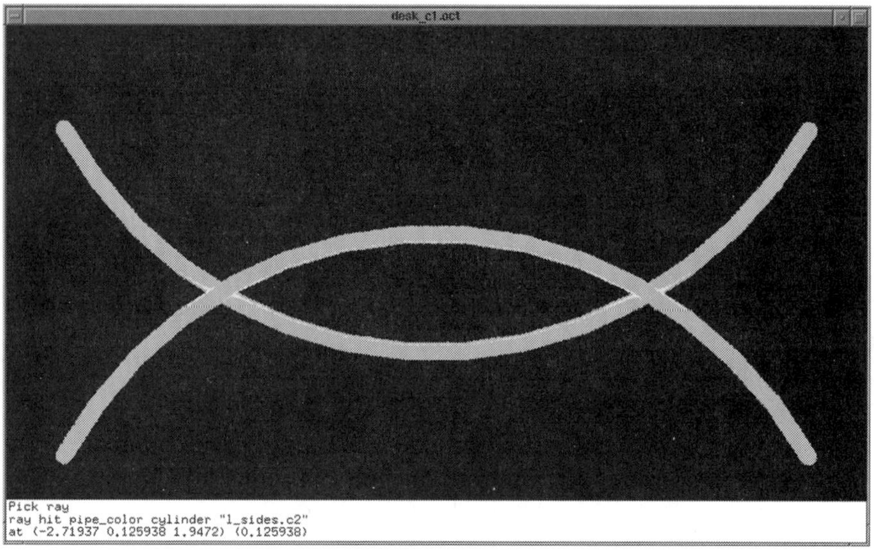

Figure 3.33 Rview can be used to acquire the coordinates of complex shapes.

The polygon, which is added to *desk_c1a.rad*, might look something like this:

```
deskmid_color polygon front
0
0
51 -2.9 .1  2.05
 -2.7 .1 1.85
 -2.4 .1 1.6
 -2.15 .1 1.45
 -1.9 .1 1.3
 -1.55 .1 1.4
 -1 .1 1.6
 -.4 .1 1.7
 0 .1 1.75
# Because the shape is symmetrical about x = 0, the description to
# the right of the center line can be derived by placing the left
# coordinates in reverse order.
 0.4 .1 1.7
 1 .1 1.6
 1.55 .1 1.4
 1.9 .1 1.3
```

```
 2.15 .1 1.45
 2.4 .1 1.6
 2.7 .1 1.85
 2.9 .1  2.05
# end front polygon
```

Return to rview and confirm that the polygon merges into the support arch with no gaps or protrusions (Figure 3.34). Now these points can be converted into the genprism that will describe the 3D base of the desk. The following command describes this shape and uses xform to move it into the correct position:

```
# Sculpted desk shape
!genprism deskmid_color front1 17 -2.9 2.05 \
 -2.7 1.85 \
 -2.4 1.6 \
 -2.15 1.45 \
.
.
 2.15 1.45 \
 2.4 1.6 \
 2.7 1.85 \
 2.9 2.05 \
 -1 0 0 -2.8  \
 | xform -rx 90 -t 0 .1 0
```

The final scene description of the desk is in the *art_lib* directory. Note that the descriptions used to derive the base shape have been commented out, leaving a record of the process.

```
### desk_c1.rad
#
# desk with concave drawer unit
# construction details remain in the file
```

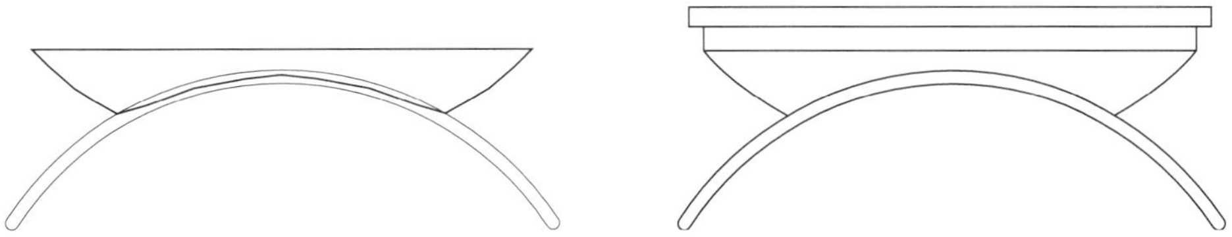

Figure 3.34 Testing and assembling the final desk description.

```
# as comment lines
# desk is 6.2' x 3' x 2.35' tall
# Insertion point is center front at floor level
# support structure at front of desk
!genworm pipe_color l_side 'tx(t)' 'ty(t)' 0 r 15 \
              -e 'r:.075;R:3.75;Tmax:120*PI/180' \
              -e 'tx(t)=R*cos(t*Tmax)' -e 'ty(t)=R*sin(t*Tmax)'\
              | xform -rz 30 -rx 90 -t 0 .1 -2

## This temporary arch is a template from which
## polygon and genprism coordinates can be determined
## using the trace command in rview.
#!genworm pipe_color template 'tx(t)' 'ty(t)' 0 r 15 \
#             -e 'r:.075;R:3.75;Tmax:120*PI/180' \
#             -e 'tx(t)=R*cos(t*Tmax)' -e 'ty(t)=R*sin(t*Tmax)'\
#             | xform -rz 210 -rx 90 -t 0 .1 4.5
.
.
# end desk_cl.rad
```

Four-foot-square coffee tables will be located in the gallery and used to display small pottery and precious-metal craft objects. These tables are approximately 15 inches tall and are constructed from chrome tubing and black laminate. The chrome tube frame that supports the black-laminate tabletop, shown in Figure 3.35, is constructed from four 90-degree chrome elbows and four cylinders.

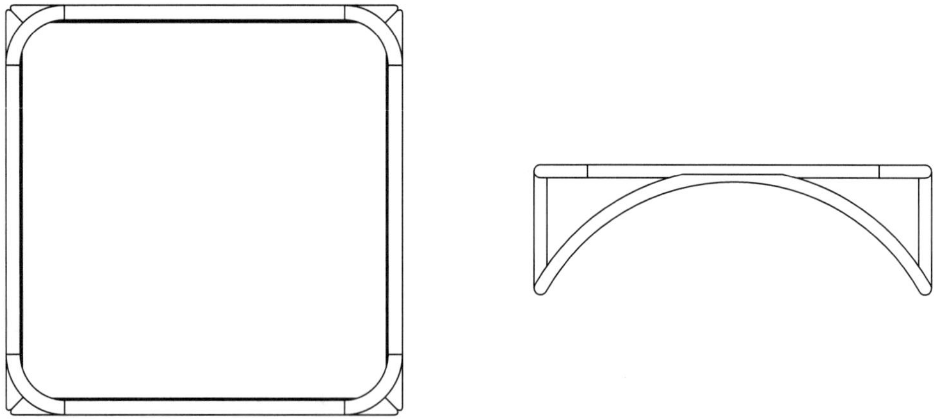

Figure 3.35 Plan view and side elevation of the coffee table.

The legs are formed from 120-degree segments of a 2.3-foot-radius arc, which are rotated and then translated into position. This *tble4_c1.rad* scene description is in the *art_lib* directory.

```
### tble4_c1.rad
#
# 4-foot-square coffee table. 1.3' tall
# insertion point at floor level in middle of table

!genworm pipe_color se_side 'tx(t)' 'ty(t)' 0 r 8 \
              -e 'r:.075;R:.5;Tmax:90*PI/180' \
              -e 'tx(t)=R*cos(t*Tmax)' -e 'ty(t)=R*sin(t*Tmax)'\
              | xform -rz -90 -t 1.5 -1.5 1.25

!genworm pipe_color ne_side 'tx(t)' 'ty(t)' 0 r 8 \
              -e 'r:.075;R:.5;Tmax:90*PI/180' \
              -e 'tx(t)=R*cos(t*Tmax)' -e 'ty(t)=R*sin(t*Tmax)'\
              | xform -rz 0 -t 1.5 1.5 1.25

.
.
pipe_color cylinder n_pipe
0
0
7 -1.5 2 1.25
  1.5 2 1.25 .075

!genworm pipe_color n_leg 'tx(t)' 'ty(t)' 0 r 15 \
              -e 'r:.075;R:2.3;Tmax:120*PI/180' \
              -e 'tx(t)=R*cos(t*Tmax)' -e 'ty(t)=R*sin(t*Tmax)'\
              | xform -rz 30 -rx 90 -t 0 2 -1.1

pipe_color cylinder s_pipe
0
0
7 -1.5 -2 1.25
  1.5 -2 1.25 .075

!genworm pipe_color s_leg 'tx(t)' 'ty(t)' 0 r 15 \
              -e 'r:.075;R:2.3;Tmax:120*PI/180' \
              -e 'tx(t)=R*cos(t*Tmax)' -e 'ty(t)=R*sin(t*Tmax)'\
              | xform -rz 30 -rx 90 -t 0 -2 -1.1
.
.
!genbox table_color table_top 3.8 3.8 .05 | xform -t -1.9 -1.9 1.25
# end tble4_c1.rad
```

Finally, a small 2-foot-square side table is constructed for the lobby. Though the tabletop is constructed similarly to the larger coffee table, its legs form a pedestal support structure.

```
### tble2_c1.rad
#
#side table 2' square, 1.3' tall
#insertion point at floor level at table center

!genworm pipe_color se_side 'tx(t)' 'ty(t)' 0 r 8 \
            -e 'r:.075;R:.5;Tmax:90*PI/180' \
            -e 'tx(t)=R*cos(t*Tmax)' -e 'ty(t)=R*sin(t*Tmax)'\
            | xform -rz -90 -t .5 -.5 1.25

.

!genworm pipe_color se_leg 'tx(t)' 'ty(t)' 0 r 9 \
            -e 'r:.075;R:1.25;Tmax:80*PI/180' \
            -e 'tx(t)=R*cos(t*Tmax)' -e 'ty(t)=R*sin(t*Tmax)'\
            | xform -ry 90 -t 0 -.75 1.325

!genworm pipe_color se_leg 'tx(t)' 'ty(t)' 0 r 9 \
            -e 'r:.075;R:1.25;Tmax:80*PI/180' \
            -e 'tx(t)=R*cos(t*Tmax)' -e 'ty(t)=R*sin(t*Tmax)'\
            | xform -ry 90 -t 0 -.75 1.325 -my

!genworm pipe_color se_leg 'tx(t)' 'ty(t)' 0 r 9 \
            -e 'r:.075;R:1.25;Tmax:80*PI/180' \
            -e 'tx(t)=R*cos(t*Tmax)' -e 'ty(t)=R*sin(t*Tmax)'\
            | xform -ry 90 -t 0 -.75 1.325 -rz 90

!genworm pipe_color se_leg 'tx(t)' 'ty(t)' 0 r 9 \
            -e 'r:.075;R:1.25;Tmax:80*PI/180' \
            -e 'tx(t)=R*cos(t*Tmax)' -e 'ty(t)=R*sin(t*Tmax)'\
            | xform -ry 90 -t 0 -.75 1.325 -my -rz 90

!genbox table_color table_top 1.8 1.8 .05 | xform -t -.9 -.9 1.25
# end tble2_c1.rad
```

We now have a collection of furniture ready to be moved into the Art Gallery. The following inventory lists the furniture files in the *art_lib* directory, including brief descriptions and insertion points.

3.5.6 Commercial Furniture Inventory

```
deskc_c1.rad    Executive Chair
                - 2 arms, headrest
                - ip at front center

desk_c1.rad     Executive Desk
                - 6.2 x 3 feet
                - ip at front center

chair_c1.rad    Lobby Chair
                - seat and arms only
                - ip at front center

sofa1_c1.rad    Lobby Sofa
                - 5' seat
                - ip at front center

sofa2_c1.rad    Gallery Back-to-Back sofa
                - 5' seats, back to back
                - ip at center of unit

tble2_c1.rad    Side table
                - 2' square
                - ip at center of unit

tble4_c1.rad    Coffee Table
                - 4' square
                - ip at center of unit
```

3.5.7 Creating the Art

Of course, the Art Gallery must include art! In addition to the picture of the Scene 1 tutorial, the gallery features several exciting sculptures, found in *art_lib*. The motive here is to demonstrate the power and efficiency of the *Radiance* scene description format. Some very complex objects can be created and manipulated with only a few lines of text and a little preplanning.

Feather (Figure 3.36) is a graceful mobile constructed from a simple `cone` and a genworm description. The quill shape is located in a file called *quill.rad*. Xform is then applied in the *feather.rad* file to create two arrays of *quill.rad*. The complete

Figure 3.36 Side view of the Feather sculpture.

shape is described in only seven lines of text! View this mobile from several angles and enjoy its soaring shape.

```
### feather.mat
#
void plastic  quill_material
0
0
5    .9 .8 .7 .03 .02

void plastic pearl
0
0
5    .8 .8 .7 .2 .03
# end feather.mat
```

```
### quill.rad
#
# The base "quill" component of the feather

quill_material cone vane
0
0
8 0 0 0  2 0 0  .1 .025
# end quill.rad

### feather.rad
#
# Builds the feather shapes and adds a "head" to the mobile

!xform -n f -a 50 -s .975 -ry -2.5 -rx .5 -rz 2 -t .2 0 .2 -i 1 quill.rad

!xform -n f -a 50 -s .95 -ry -2.5 -rx .5 -rz 2 -t .2 0 .2 \
  -my -i 1 quill.rad

!genworm pearl head '0' '2*sin(t)' '2*cos(t)'\
 '.3-(.5-t)*(.5-t)' 10 |xform -t 0 -1.3 -1.6 -rx 30 -rz 80 -ry 170 -s .6

## end feather.rad
```

Unfurled (Figure 3.37) is a whimsical sculpture that appears to have been constructed from a single length of rod. Note how the 180-degree genworm sections are assembled into a pseudo-spiral effect by matching their endpoints exactly. We can make the spiral begin to taper by applying a parametric function to the radius. Finally, the tip of the spiral breaks into a free-form wisp by applying a tapered hermite curve to the end segment.

```
### unfurled.mat
#

void plastic rod_color
0
0
5 .9 .8 .7 .04 .02
# end unfurled.mat
```

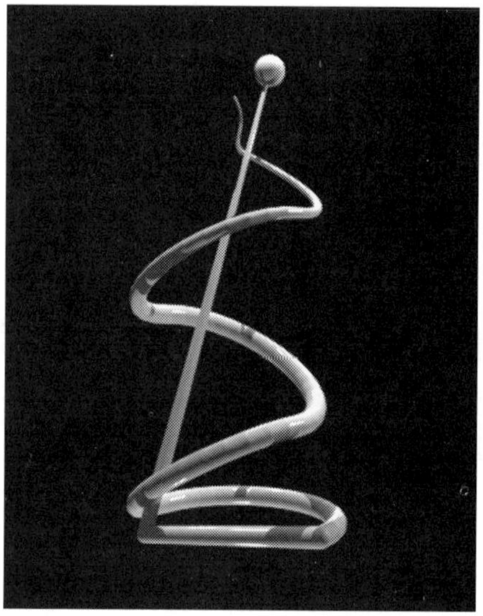

Figure 3.37 Unfurled is constructed with genworm, cones, and a sphere.

```
### unfurled.rad
#
# create a free-form sculpture from a continuous rod

# base constructed from 180 degrees of a torus
!genworm rod_color l_leg 'tx(t)' 'ty(t)' 0 r 15 \
              -e 'r:.1;R:1;Tmax:180*PI/180' \
              -e 'tx(t)=R*cos(t*Tmax)' -e 'ty(t)=R*sin(t*Tmax)'\
              | xform -rz 180 -t -.14 0 -.5

# connect tilted and rotated tori to create a pseudo-spiral
!genworm rod_color l_leg 'tx(t)' 'ty(t)' 0 r 15 \
  -e 'r:.1;R:1;Tmax:180*PI/180' \
  -e 'tx(t)=R*cos(t*Tmax)' -e 'ty(t)=R*sin(t*Tmax)'\
  | xform -ry 30

!genworm rod_color l_leg 'tx(t)' 'ty(t)' 0 r 15 \
 -e 'r:.1;R:1;Tmax:180*PI/180' \
 -e 'tx(t)=R*cos(t*Tmax)' -e 'ty(t)=R*sin(t*Tmax)'\
 | xform -ry 30 -rz 180 -t 0 0 1
```

```
# begin to taper the "spiral" by reducing the radius
!genworm rod_color l_leg 'tx(t)' 'ty(t)' 0 '0.1*((2-t)/2)' 15 \
 -e 'r:.1;R:1;Tmax:180*PI/180' \
 -e 'tx(t)=R*cos(t*Tmax)' -e 'ty(t)=R*sin(t*Tmax)'\
 | xform -ry 30 -t 0 0 2
.
.
# terminate "spiral" with a free-form tapering wisp
!genworm rod_color twist\
 'hermite (.3,.3,.30,.4,t) '\
 '0'\
 'hermite(0,.7,.5,1.1,t)'\
 '0.025*((2-t)/2)' 10 \
 | xform -t -.3 0 0 -rx -45 -rz 30 -t .496 -.82 3.29
.
.
# add a sphere at the top of the cone
rod_color sphere tip
0
0
4 .3 -1.1 4.2 .175
# end unfurled
```

The Tapestry installation is composed of a 6-foot by 4-foot panel of colored glass strips suspended 2 feet in front of a white wall. This art piece is designed to be viewed from the front and under specific lighting conditions. It is the sort of art that might be found in the lobby of a large corporation. We will use four files to create Tapestry. Of course, there are the material file *(tapestry.mat)* and the object description *(tapestry.rad),* located in *art_lib.* But in this case, we also need a specific lighting file and a new luminaire. Because the lighting comes with the art piece and will always be turned on when the gallery is open, we will separate these lights from the rest of the lighting files so that we can manage them more effectively. There is an additional file in the *scene2* directory called *tap_light.rad*, and *track_S4T.rad* is located in *scene2/lib.*

```
### tapestry.mat
#
void glass dk_green_g
0
0
3 .01 .2 .05
.
.
void glass yellow_g
0
0
3 .6 .6 .25

void plastic white_plaster
0
0
5    .8 .8 .8 0 0
#end tapestry.mat

### tapestry.rad
#
# A collage of colored glass.
# This file is a complete installation, and
# includes a screen and suspended glass
#
# Insertion point is at the center of the vertical screen,
# which measures 10' x 7.5'

dk_red_g polygon   11
0
0
12    -3    -2    -2
       3    -2    -2
       3     2    -.5
      -3    -2    -.5

yellow_g polygon   12
0
0
12     3    -2    -.5
       3    -2    -.5
```

```
     3    -2    .5
    -3    -2    .5
.
.
# horizon stripe
dk_blue_g polygon    h1
0
0
12    -3    -2.01    -.025
       3    -2.01    -.025
       3    -2.01     .025
      -3    -2.01     .025

# backing panel
!genbox white_plaster backing 10 .1 7.5 | xform -t -5 -.1 -4
# end tapestry.rad
```

The *tap_light.rad* file installs four critically located PAR38 floodlights that shine through the Tapestry glass panel and produce the overlapping shadows and color projections shown in Figure 3.38. When adding more luminaires, we must update the *.cvt* photometry handling file and, as we have mentioned, create a new luminaire file in the *lib* directory called *track_S4T.rad*. After completing the update, experiment with the location and aiming of the lamps and watch the color variations explode on the backing screen!

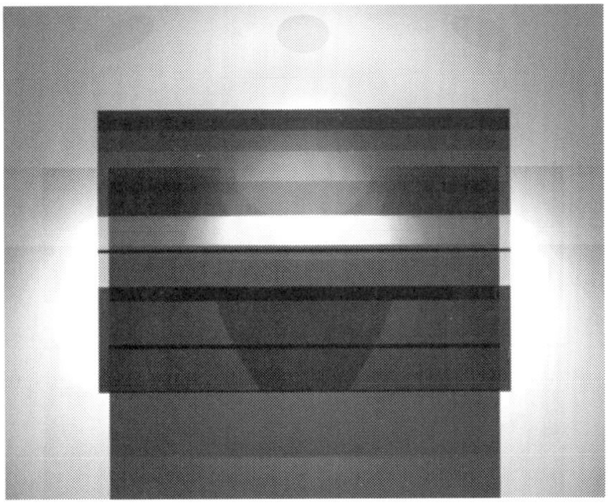

Figure 3.38 The Tapestry glass panel, illuminated with PAR38 floodlights.

```
### tap_light.rad      (located in scene2 directory)
#
#  Special set of luminaires that are part of the
# Tapestry installation

!xform -n par1 -rx 50 -rz 0 -t  2.5  -6.4 3.5 lib/track_S4T.rad
!xform -n par2 -rx 50 -rz 0 -t  0    -6.4 3.5 lib/track_S4T.rad
!xform -n par3 -rx 50 -rz 0 -t -2.5  -6.4 3.5 lib/track_S4T.rad
!xform -n par4 -rx 45 -rz 0 -t  0    -3.5 3.5 lib/track_S4T.rad
# end tap_light.rad

### track_S4T.rad      (located in scene2/lib)
#
#                      track lampholder with typeS4T photometry
#                      lampholder in feet
#                      suspension yoke in track_y.rad
#                      Part of the Tapestry installation

enamel_white cylinder    housing1
0
0
7      0 0 0
       0 0 .35
       .21

enamel_white ring        housing2
0
0
8      0 0 .35
       0 0 1
       .21 0

# insert photometry into the aperture of the cylinder
!xform -n lamp1 typeS4T.rad
# end track_S4T.rad
```

The Tapestry lighting is included in *lights_d.cvt* and *lights_n.cvt*, enabling different day and nighttime levels to be updated with changes to the rest of the lighting system.

```
# tapestry lighting
ies2rad -df -t default -m .8 -c 1 1 1 -o lib/typeS4T ies_lib/q150p38f.ies
```

Lotus is a small glass sculpture. Its shape is made by combining glass spheres, which are then hollowed out by using *antimatter* material as shown in Figure 3.39. (See also Plate 11 following page 328.) The antimatter declaration includes a list of existing material descriptions. It will interact only with surfaces modified by the materials on this list. Antimatter "subtracts" its shape from these surfaces. The surface of intersection acquires the properties of the first listed material. If the first-material position contains void, the surface of intersection remains transparent. Antimatter should be used selectively and with caution. A vantage point from within an antimatter shape creates unpredictable results and, if it intersects materials that are not listed in its definition, mottled artifacts can appear. Nevertheless, antimatter provides an ideal tool for constructing our glass sculpture.

```
# antimatter formal definition:
#

# modifier    antimatter    name
# n mat_1(or void) mat_2 .... mat_n
# 0
# 0
```

Each layer of lotus leaves is defined from its own material descriptions before it is combined into the completed sculpture. This strategy enables the layers to be

Figure 3.39 Lotus is constructed from spheres of dielectric and antimatter. (See also Plate 11 following page 328.)

individually sculpted with their own antimatter descriptions and avoids the surprise of unexpected shapes. The material definitions in *lotus.mat* should make this clear.

Windowpanes or other thin glass surfaces are generally made from the *glass* material type. This material has a fixed refractive index and, as demonstrated in the tapestry, can be colored. It is appropriate to use *Radiance* glass for most thin glass objects. But thick glass should be defined by a more elemental material type, called *dielectric*. In addition to color, this material requires a refractive index and a dispersion factor. If you vary its parameters, a large variety of transparent materials can be defined, such as water, ice, and, in this case of the lotus, lead-crystal glass.

```
# dielectric formal definition:
#
# modifier    dielectric    name
# 0
# 0
# 5     r    g    b          refractive_index   Hartmann's_constant
#       0:1  0:1  0:1               1:2>               <-12:30>
# black - transparent  vacuum - diamond   neg - pos dispersion

### lotus.mat

#
# lotus material file.

# outer lotus material
void dielectric glass_outer
0
0
5 .8 .8 .9 1.5 0

void antimatter      hollow_1

1 glass_outer
0
0
.
.
void antimatter      hollow_3
1 glass_inner
0
0
#end lotus.mat
```

```
### lotus123.rad

#
# This file creates the base of the lotus using
# 4 "glass" spheres. The bowl is scooped out
# by subtracting an antimatter sphere.
# Two additional sets of "lotus leaves" are
# then inserted into the hollowed bowl.
# Requires lotus_2.rad and lotus_3.rad
#
# Lotus is approximately 6" in diameter.
# Insertion point is at the center of the base.

glass_outer     sphere 11_sw
0
0
4 -1 -1 2.5 3

glass_outer     sphere 11_ne
0
0
4 1 1 2.5 3

glass_outer     sphere 11_nw
0
0
4 -1 1 2.5 3

glass_outer     sphere 11_se
0
0
4 1 -1 2.5 3

# Use an antimatter sphere to scoop out the bowl.
hollow_1     sphere bowl_1
0
0
4 0 0 5.5 4.0

# Apply an antimatter cylinder to flatten the bottom of the lotus.
# Note the surface normal directions of the rings that cap this
# cylinder.
```

```
hollow_1 ring clip_base_t
0
0
8 0 0 0.001
  0 0 1
  3 0

hollow_1 cylinder clip_base_m
0
0
7 0 0 0.001
  0 0 -1.6
  3

hollow_1 ring clip_base_b
0
0
8 0 0 -1.6
  0 0 -1
  3 0

# Insert two additional sets of lotus leaves:
!xform -n num2 -rz 45                lotus_2.rad
!xform -n num3 -s .6 -t 0 0 .75      lotus_3.rad
#end lotus123.rad

### lotus_2.rad
#
# middle lotus leaves inserted into lotus123.rad

glass_mid sphere 12_sw
0
0
4 -.75 -.75 2.75 2.5
.
.
hollow_2 sphere bowl_2
0
0
4 0 0 5.75 3
# end lotus_2.rad
```

```
### lotus_3.rad
#
# inner lotus leaves inserted into lotus123.rad

glass_inner sphere l3_sw
0
0
4  -.75  -.75  2.75  2.5
.
.
hollow_3 sphere bowl_3
0
0
4 0 0 5.75 3
# end lotus_3.rad
```

If Lotus is viewed in isolation, with no reflective objects around it, it will all but disappear. To view its shape clearly during the construction stages, try temporarily changing its material type to a reflective plastic. Alternatively, placing the lotus on a visible surface will reveal the refractive properties of its shape.

Six variations of the Wave wall hanging will be located throughout the lobby and gallery. The modulated surface of this art piece is based on the gensurf examples described previously in this chapter. Each variation is composed of 1750 polygons and differs only in color and texture. Let's build the Wave first; then we can explore a strategy for creating the variations efficiently. The following material and Wave description files are in the *art_lib* directory.

```
### waves.mat
#
#    material file for waves and wave instances

void    plastic sepia
0
0
5       .4 .25 .05 0 0

void    plastic blue
0
0
5       .15 .2 .8 0 0
```

```
void    metal pewter
0
0
5       .8 .8 .82 .85 .05

void    metal gold
0
0
5       .8 .6 .3 .85 .03

# end waves.mat

### waves.rad
#
#

# surface has .25'-deep depressions and .25'-high mounds
# the modulation decreases over the panel
# the art is 5' x 5' with its insertion point at center back
!gensurf sepia waves \
     '5 - s*(5 - 0)' \
     5 - t*(5 - 0)' \
     'mag(s,t)*.25*sin(5*PI*t)*sin(7*PI*s)' \
     25 35 -s \
     -e 'mag(s,t)=t' | xform -rx 90 -t -2.5 -.26 -2.5
# end waves.rad
```

When we assemble the scene, six variations of Wave can be installed by first creating five copies of *wave.rad*. Each of the additional Wave files would have a different name, use a different material type, and have a different xform placement.

Radiance provides an alternative method to locating copies of an object in a scene. To be eligible, the surfaces of each copy must not change, though the material of each copy could be different. This method creates an *instance*. The details of instance and its benefits will be discussed when we assemble the scene and use this method to locate each of the Wave variations. Meanwhile, we can prepare the wave description for this procedure by converting *wave.rad* into an octree. In the *art_lib* directory, execute the following command:

```
% oconv wave.mat wave.rad > wave.oct
```

The gallery displays small art pieces such as precious-metal and pottery goblets. It is also the custom to serve patrons a beverage, so cups and saucers are needed. The materials for these vessels are located in the *cups.mat* file in the *art_lib* directory.

```
### cups.mat
#
# materials for cups and goblets

void metal goldc
0
0
5 1 .7 .4 .9 .02

void metal silverc
0
0
5 .8 .8 .81 .9 .02

# champagne-like material
void dielectric clear_liquid
0
0
5 .8 .8 .6 1.1 0

# To apply a mottled pattern to the pottery
# so it has a more organic appearance, use the
# dirt.cal function.
# The alias command combines the function
# with the gray plastic material, which
# creates the final pottery effect.

void brightfunc dirty
4 dirt dirt.cal -s .02
0
1 .35

dirty plastic gray
0
0
5 .7 .7 .65 .02 .01
```

```
dirty alias pottery
 gray

# fine bone china material
void plastic china
0
0
5 .9 .9 .9 .03 .02
# end cups.mat
```

The goblet, champagne bowl, and teacup that follow are made with genrev and genworm generators. The furniture frames we created made heavy use of the equation of a circle to form the curves of the chrome tubing. These drinking vessels use the curved surfaces we demonstrated in Section 3.4.3, Hermite Curves. These files are in the *art_lib* directory.

```
### goblet.rad
#
# very simple goblet from 2 genrevs. 1 unit tall.
.
.

### champagne.rad
#
#champagne bowl with liquid. 1 unit tall.

!genrev goldc champagne_top \
      'hermite(.6,1,1,.8,t)' \
      'hermite(.025,.275,.05,0.005,t)' \
      16 -s

!genrev silverc champagne_top_in \
      'hermite(.76,1,.6,.8,t)' \
      'hermite(.0,.26,.-.1,0,t)' \
      8 -s

silverc ring champagne_rim
0

0
8     0      0      1
      0      0      1
      .275   .26
```

```
goldc cylinder champagne_stem
0
0
7     0       0      .2
      0       0      .6
      .025

!genrev goldc champagne_base \
      'hermite(0,.2,-.1,.35,t)' \
      'hermite(.2,.025,.5,.03,t)' \
      8 -s

clear_liquid ring champagne
0
0
8     0       0      .97
      0       0       1
      .245    0
#end champagne.rad

### tea_cup.rad
#
# China teacup and saucer. Teacup is 1 unit tall
# cup handle is on the right side of the cup
.
.
```

A wireless telephone will be located on the desk in the lobby. This device has an uncomplicated shape and is constructed using two genprisms and a genbox. Certainly the antenna could be constructed with a cylinder and a sphere, but unless we created an additional file, it would have to be explicitly positioned. Using genbox simplifies its placement because we can pipe the output directly through an xform command. Since it is unlikely that the antenna will ever be viewed closely enough to reveal its angular shape, the simpler genbox approach is most appropriate. Recall the advice in the Scene 1 project that warns against using too much complexity where the detail will not be seen.

```
### phone.rad
#
# desk phone set
# constructed in inch units: 3.5" x 9" x 4" tall
# insertion point: center front of base
```

```
!genprism accent_red p_base 6 \
        .5 0 8.5 0 9 1.5 8.5 2.65 0 1.5 0 .75 \
        -1 0 0 3.5 | xform -rx 90 -rz 90 -t -1.75 0 0

!genprism accent_red p_receiver 10 \
        .1 0 2 0 2 .2 6.5 .2 6.5 0 8.4 0 8.5 .1 \
        8 1.3 .5 1.3 0 .1 \
        -1 0 0 2.0 | xform -rx 90 -rz 90 -rx 8 -t -1.0 0 1.5

!genbox accent_red p_antenna 4 .25 .25 -b .075 \
        | xform -rx 90 -rz 90 -t 0 8 .75 -rx 8 -t -.125 0 1.5
# end phone.rad
```

Most retail environments proudly display their businesses' names. The owner of the Art Gallery has selected a large sign made of clear acrylic with gold-leaf lettering on its front surface. The first step in its construction is to acquire the materials. The following material file is in *scene2/art_lib*:

```
### sign.mat
#
# gold and acrylic sign materials

void dielectric acrylic
0
0
5 .98 .98 .98 1.4 0

void metal gold_leaf
0
0
5 .68 .27 .002 .875 .05

#end sign.mat
```

The sign is constructed in three steps. First we will make the acrylic plank. Then we will make a new surface by combining the ART GALLERY lettering and acrylic material. Finally, we will substitute this new surface for the original front polygon of the plank.

To construct the acrylic plank, we need to determine its coordinates and write individual polygon descriptions for each of the six faces. This could be accomplished longhand, or we could simply use genbox to write the polygon descriptions for us. The polygons for an 8.55-foot by 1.5-foot by .05-foot-thick acrylic sign are created by directing the output of the following genbox command into a file called *sign.rad.*

```
% genbox acrylic sign 8.55 .05 1.5 > sign.rad
```

The second task is to create the lettering and combine it with an acrylic surface. To accomplish this, we use the **mixtext** command and the Helvetica font provided by *Radiance* (*helvet.fnt*).

```
# mixtext    formal definition 1:
#
# mod        mixtext     id
# 4 foreground background fontfile textfile
# 0
# 9+   Ox Oy Oz
       Rx Ry Rz
       Dx Dy Dz
       [spacing]

# mixtext    formal definition 2:
#
# mod        mixtext     id
# 4+N foreground background fontfile
# A line with N words
# 0
# 9+   Ox Oy Oz
       Rx Ry Rz
       Dx Dy Dz
       [spacing]
```

Because we are placing only two words on the sign, the second definition is most appropriate because it includes the actual text in the command. In these definitions, the *O* (for origin) value `Ox Oy Oz` determines the top left corner of a character. The *R* values define a vector that begins at `Ox Oy Oz` and establishes the distance to the next character's origin. In our case, we want our characters to be located .75 foot to the *R* (for right) of each other, resulting in `Rx Ry Rz` values of .75 0 0. The *D* values define a vector that begins at the character origin and is aimed in a *D* (for downward) direction. If this vector is not perpendicular to the *R* vector, the characters will slant. We want our ART GALLERY text to lean slightly to the right, so the `Dx Dy Dz` will have values of -.1 0 -1.5. The -1.5 value establishes the downward distance to the next row of characters. Figure 3.40 illustrates this application of vectors to text. The description of the gold-leaf letters on an acrylic background follows.

```
void mixtext sign_mat
6 gold_leaf acrylic helvet.fnt . ART GALLERY
0
9
    .2    0    1.5
    .75   0    0
   -.1    0   -1.5
```

Now we edit the *sign.rad* file, replacing the modifier of the front polygon of the acrylic plank with our *sign_mat* material. This installs our lettering and completes the sign construction, pictured in Figure 3.41. *Sign.rad* is found in the *scene2/art_lib* directory.

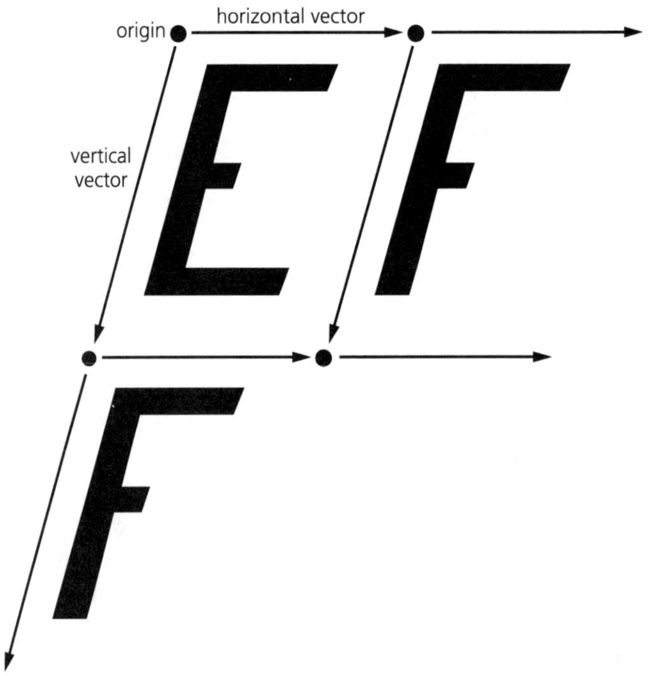

Figure 3.40 Vectors are used to describe the size, slope, and orientation of characters.

Figure 3.41 Art Gallery sign: gold letters on a clear acrylic panel.

```
### sign.rad
#
# creates an 8.55' x 1.5' x .05' thick sign
# clear acrylic background with gold lettering
# sign faces south (xz plane) with insertion point
# in the lower left rear corner

# gold text foreground with acrylic background
void mixtext sign_mat
6 gold_leaf acrylic helvet.fnt . ART GALLERY
0
9
    .2    0    1.5
    .75   0    0
   -.1    0    1.5

# Polygons generated by:
#    genbox acrylic sign 8.55 0.05 1.5
#
# replace the modifier of the front surface
# with the new sign_mat material:

sign_mat polygon sign.1540
0
0
12
    8.5    0    0
     .5    0    1.5
    0      0    1.5
    0      0    0
```

```
acrylic polygon sign.4620
0
0
12
    0    0    1.5
    0    0.05 1.5
    0    0.05 0
    0    0    0

acrylic polygon sign.2310
.
.
# end sign.rad
```

With all the art and furniture assembled, it's finally time to bring in the moving company and create our installation.

3.6 Assembling Scene 2

All the components of the Art Gallery, with the exception of tracklighting, are ready for assembly. Once the art and furnishings are in place, the lighting can be finalized and then the project will be ready to be rendered.

We need to create a few files that effectively collect and position the dozens of objects and materials that we have described so far. Though one collector file could serve in place of several, breaking the data into logically organized categories simplifies project management. These files are located in the *scene2* directory.

Let's start by assembling the building. Because the floor, walls, and ceiling were all built in place, our only task is to bond them together. *Sc2bldg.rad* is a small file that uses xform to find and include the building components. If we had used !cat instead of !xform, error messages would be issued for the *walls.rad* description when we were converting the scene descriptions into the final octree. The error messages would inform us that *windows.rad* and *door2x.rad* did not exist. This problem is corrected by using xform instead of cat. Why? Because for oconv to find a file, its location must be declared relative to the calling directory, or explicitly listed with the full path name. Xform, on the other hand, moves to the *lib* directory in this case, and is able to find the component files that are referenced in *walls.rad*. If the subdirectory files listed in a collector file do not have file dependencies, cat is a valid option.

```
### sc2bldg.rad
#
# collection of building scene descriptions

!xform lib/floor.rad lib/walls.rad lib/ceiling.rad
#end sc2bldg.rad
```

Each work of art has its own material file. In addition, we require a few more materials from which to build the pedestals that will support our sculptures. *Art.mat* serves as a collector file for all of these related materials; it is found in the *scene2* directory. Because each material is a self-contained description, cat is used to assemble them.

```
### art.mat
#
# file collects individual art materials
# for convenient handling
# and adds three additional materials.

!cat art_lib/tapestry.mat art_lib/unfurled.mat art_lib/feather.mat
!cat art_lib/furniture.mat art_lib/waves.mat art_lib/cups.mat
!cat art_lib/lotus.mat art_lib/sign.mat

void plastic accent_white
0
0
5 .8 .8 .8 0 0
.
.
# end art.mat
```

Finally, we can install our first exhibit! A floor plan of the space, shown in Figure 3.42, is useful for determining the coordinates of each artwork.

Scene_art.rad collects and locates all of the works of art and all the furnishings. The first installation is Tapestry. Note the inclusion of the Tapestry lighting file.

```
### scene_art.rad
#
#     this file contains art and furniture placement

# placement of the Tapestry installation and special lighting
!xform -n tap  -rz 90 -t .5 12.5 4.25 art_lib/tapestry.rad
!xform -n tapl -rz 90 -t .4 12.5 4.0  tap_light.rad
```

Lotus is only a few inches tall, so it is placed on a pedestal. The dimensions of Lotus are converted from inches to feet by using the scale option in xform.

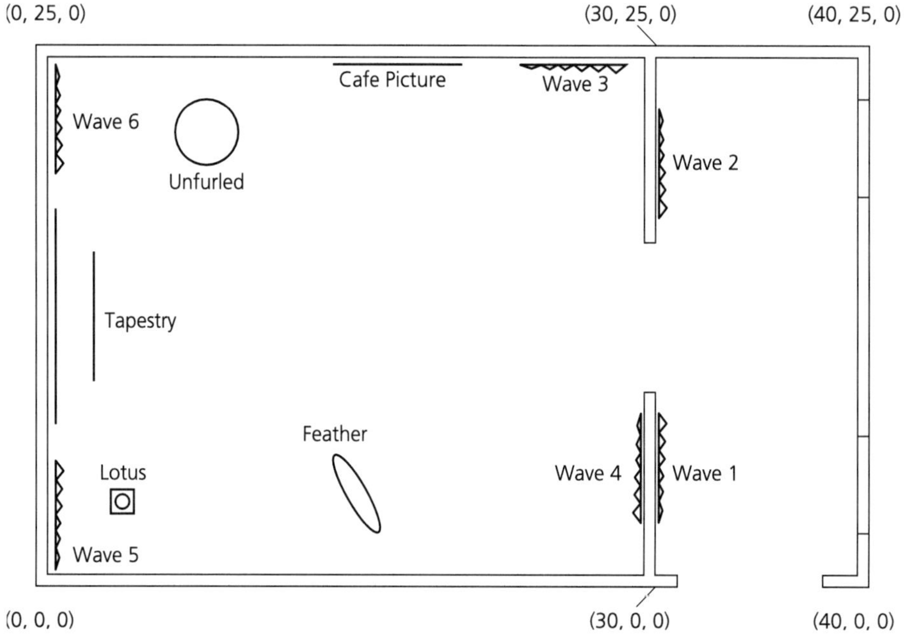

Figure 3.42 Ground plan of Art Gallery, showing the placement of art.

```
# make a pedestal and base to support Lotus
# Lotus was created in one unit = 1 inch scale
# to convert to feet, scale by .0833
!genbox accent_green pedestal 1 1 3 | xform -t 3.5 3.5 0

accent_white cone l_base
0
0
8    4 4 3
     4 4 3.25
    .4 .25

accent_green ring coaster
0
0
8    4 4 3.25
     0 0 1
    .25 0

!xform -n lotus -s .0833 -t 4 4 3.26 art_lib/lotus123.rad
```

Unfurled is also installed on a pedestal, and to contrast with the sculpture's pastel finish, the base is bright red.

```
# insert Unfurled on a low pedestal
accent_red cylinder u_base
0
0
7    8 21 0
     8 21 1.5
    1.5

accent_red ring u_baset
0
0
8    8 21 1.5
     0 0 1
     1.5 0

!xform -n unf -t 8 21 2.075 art_lib/unfurled.rad
```

The Cafe Picture and Feather are simple installations. Feather is suspended by monofilament line, which is so small in diameter that we will simply leave it out of the rendering. Because we have no interest in looking behind the picture, the Cafe scene also hovers, without a picture hook, in front of the wall.

```
# insert Feather. It is a mobile, so no base is required
!xform -n feath -s 1 -rz -60 -t 15 5 2.5 art_lib/feather.rad

# insert cafe_pic onto a wall (6' x 6' square)
!xform -n painting -t 14 24.4 2.5 art_lib/cafe_pic.rad
```

In Section 3.5.7, Creating the Art, we prepared the Waves wall hanging for installation by converting the description into an octree. Now instances of that octree are inserted into the gallery. For those familiar with CAD systems, inserting an instance is like inserting a block into a drawing. Only one description of the object really exists, and pointers to that description are located in the scene. In this way, hundreds of instances of a complex object can appear in a scene without proportionately increasing the size of the data set.

```
# instance    formal definition
#
# mod    instance    id
# 1+ octree_file transformation
# 0
# 0
```

We need to locate six instances of the original Waves wall hanging. By substituting different material names in the modifier position of the description, we are also able to vary the color and texture of each instance. This results in the placement of six 1760-polygon objects, but increases the data set as though fewer than two were installed.

```
# insert six instances of the Waves wall hangings

# first instance uses original waves.oct material
void instance wave1
9 art_lib/waves.oct -ry 90 -rz 90 -t 30 4 5
0
0

# additional instances are modified by new materials
blue instance wave2
9 art_lib/waves.oct -ry -90 -rz 90 -t 30 21 5
0
0

gold instance wave3
7 art_lib/waves.oct -ry 45 -t 25.75 24.5 5
0
0
.
.
pewter instance wave6
9 art_lib/waves.oct -ry 90 -rz 90 -t .5 21.5 5
0
0
```

To determine the coordinates of each piece, the placement of furniture is also explored on the floor plan (Figure 3.43) before being added to the *scene_art.rad* collector file.

```
## insert furniture
# gallery
!xform -n sofa2  -rz 180 -t 14    12.5 0 art_lib/sofa2_c1.rad
!xform -n 4_table1       -t 19    12.5 0 art_lib/tble4_c1.rad
!xform -n 4_table2       -t 26.5   3.5 0 art_lib/tble4_c1.rad
!xform -n chair1 -rz -90 -t 26.5 17.5 0 art_lib/chair_c1.rad
```

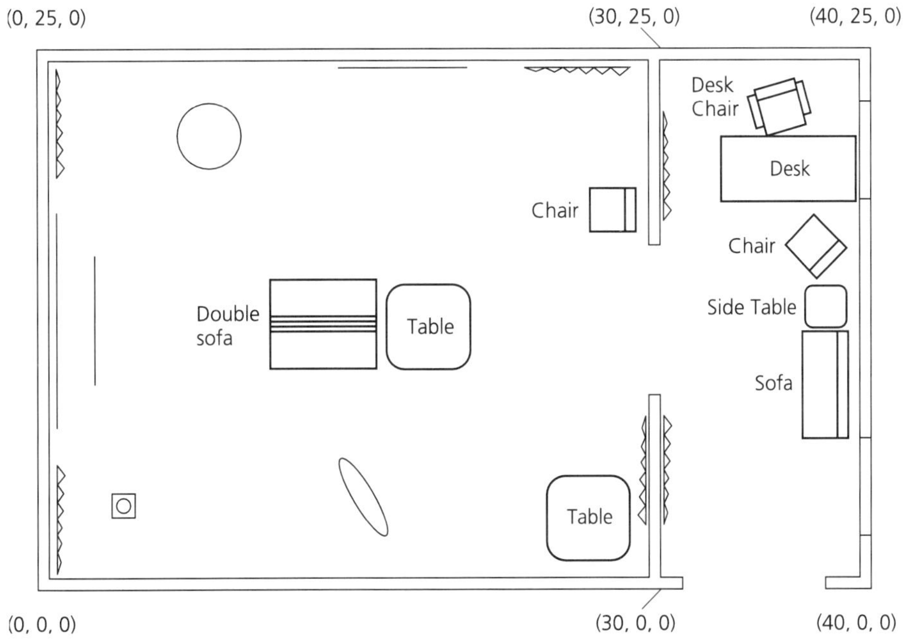

Figure 3.43 Ground plan of Art Gallery, showing furniture placement.

```
# lobby
!xform -n desk_chair -rz 15   -t 36.2 21.25 0 art_lib/deskc_cl.rad
!xform -n desk                -t 36.2 18    0 art_lib/desk_cl.rad
!xform -n chair2     -rz -135 -t 36.7 16.8  0 art_lib/chair_cl.rad
!xform -n 2_table             -t 38   13.1  0 art_lib/tble2_cl.rad
!xform -n sofa1      -rz -90  -t 36.5  9.25 0 art_lib/sofa1_cl.rad
```

The large tables are included in the gallery to display smaller craft items. A spiral arrangement of gold and silver champagne bowls fills the southeast table (Figure 3.44), and a water goblet is located on the table by the double sofa.

```
## insert items on tables
# create champagne bowls of eight different sizes in a spiral shape,
# about the insertion point. The arrangement is moved
# to the table in the corner of the gallery
!xform -n c1 -t 1.2 0 0 -s 1.5 -a 8 -s .9 -rz 50 -i 1 \
       -t -.4 0 0 -rz -30 -t 26.5 3.5 1.3 art_lib/champagne.rad

# locate a water goblet on the gallery coffee table
!xform -n c4 -t 18 11 1.3 art_lib/goblet.rad
```

Figure 3.44 A spiral arrangement of goblets on a large table.

A few signs of life suggest that people might actually visit and work in the gallery! Figure 3.45 shows two teacups and a telephone on the lobby desk and side table. (See also Plate 12 following page 328.)

```
# locate a teacup on the desk and one on the lobby table
!xform -n c2 -s .25 -rz -15 -t 35 20 2.45 art_lib/tea_cup.rad
!xform -n c3 -s .25 -rz  45 -t 38 13 1.3  art_lib/tea_cup.rad

# locate phone on desk
!xform -n p1 -s .0833 -rz 200 -t 38.2 20.2 2.45 art_lib/phone.rad
```

At last the gallery is completed by hanging our sign on the wall, and we can make the final preparations that will lead to our rendered pictures. These are the last entries in the *scene_art.rad* file...how welcome it is to encounter the final comment line!

Figure 3.45 View of the lobby from the front entrance. The cups, phone, and rotated chairs add a human element to the scene. (See also Plate 12 following page 328.)

```
# hang ART GALLERY sign on the lobby wall
!xform -n sign1 -t 30.75 24.44 6 art_lib/sign.rad
# end scene_art.rad
```

3.7 Lighting the Art

It's time to revisit the rough-in of the tracklighting system. With the art in place, we now have reason to hang additional luminaires, select appropriate lamps, and aim light at our masterpieces. The tracklighting component of the *sc2light.rad* file needs to be completely revised. Because lighting design is an interpretative art, feel free to visually evaluate what the following arrangement accomplishes, then change it and make it your own!

The new entries have been organized according to their functions. They are arranged according to the particular art piece that each is illuminating. This way, we are able to rapidly find and fine-tune the lighting of specific pieces. Our gallery area currently uses 20 tracklights. If 200 individually focused units were installed in a larger project, the benefits of this organizational strategy would be even more evident. A partial listing of *sc2light.rad* follows.

```
### sc2light.rad
#
# electric lighting systems for scene2.
# active photometry is listed in light_n.cvt and light_d.cvt
# If photometry is updated, then execute:
#  light_n.cvt or light_d.cvt

## south ceiling track followed by individual tracklights
!genbox enamel_white track1 24 .15 .15 | xform -t 3 4.35 11.55

# wave on sw wall
!xform -n l1s -t 0 0 -.5 -rx 45 -rz 95 -t 7 4.35 11.1 lib/track_S4.rad
!xform -n l1y -rz 95 -t 7 4.35 11.1 lib/track_y.rad

# lotus lighting
!xform -n l2s -t 0 0 -.5 -rx 2 -rz 180 -t 4 4.35 11.1 lib/track_S5.rad
!xform -n l2y -rz 180 -t 4 4.35 11.1 lib/track_y.rad

!xform -n l3s -t 0 0 -.5 -rx 5 -rz 92 -t 6 4.35 11.1 lib/track S4.rad
!xform -n l3y -rz 92 -t 6 4.35 11.1 lib/track_y.rad

# feather lighting
!xform -n l4s -t 0 0 -.5 -rx 40 -rz -90 -t 8 4.35 11.1 lib/track_S4.rad
!xform -n l4y -rz -90 -t 8 4.35 11.1 lib/track_y.rad

!xform -n l5s -t 0 0 -.5 -rx 10 -rz -90 -t 14 4.35 11.1 lib/track_S4.rad
!xform -n l5y -rz -90 -t 14 4.35 11.1 lib/track_y.rad

!xform -n l6s -t 0 0 -.5 -rx 15 -rz 90 -t 17 4.35 11.1 lib/track_S4.rad
!xform -n l6y -rz 90 -t 17 4.35 11.1 lib/track_y.rad

# wave on se gallery wall
!xform -n l7s -t 0 0 -.5 -rx 42.5 -rz -90 -t 23.5 4.35 11.1 lib/track_S4.rad
!xform -n l7y -rz -90 -t 23.5 4.35 11.1 lib/track_y.rad

# champagne bowl display
!xform -n l8s -t 0 0 -.5 -rx 5 -rz -95 -t 25 4.35 11.1 lib/track_S5.rad
!xform -n l8y -rz -95 -t 25 4.35 11.1 lib/track_y.rad

## north ceiling track followed by individual tracklights
!genbox enamel_white track2 24 .15 .15 | xform -t 3 20.5 11.55
```

```
# wave on nw gallery wall
!xform -n 21s -t 0 0 -.5 -rx 45 -rz 95 -t 7 20.5 11.1 lib/track_S4.rad
!xform -n 21y -rz 95 -t 7 20.5 11.1 lib/track_y.rad

# unfurled lighting
!xform -n 22s -t 0 0 -.5 -rx 35 -rz -90 -t 4 20.5 11.1 lib/track_S4.rad
!xform -n 22y -rz -90 -t 4 20.5 11.1 lib/track_y.rad

!xform -n 23s -t 0 0 -.5 -rx 0 -rz 5 -t 8 20.5 11.1 lib/track_S5.rad
!xform -n 23y -rz 5 -t 8 20.5 11.1 lib/track_y.rad

!xform -n 24s -t 0 0 -.5 -rx 45 -rz 90 -t 14.5 20.5 11.1 lib/track_S2.rad
!xform -n 24y -rz 90 -t 14.5 20.5 11.1 lib/track_y.rad

# cafe picture lighting
!xform -n 25s -t 0 0 -.5 -rx 40 -rz -10 -t 15.2 20.5 11.1 lib/track_S1.rad
!xform -n 25y -rz -10 -t 15.2 20.5 11.1 lib/track_y.rad

!xform -n 26s -t 0 0 -.5 -rx 30 -rz 0 -t 17   20.5 11.1 lib/track_S1.rad
!xform -n 26y -rz 0 -t 17   20.5 11.1 lib/track_y.rad

!xform -n 27s -t 0 0 -.5 -rx 40 -rz 10 -t 19   20.5 11.1 lib/track_S1.rad
!xform -n 27y -rz 10 -t 19   20.5 11.1 lib/track_y.rad

# wave on north gallery wall
!xform -n 28s -t 0 0 -.5 -rx 35 -rz 0 -t 25.5 20.5 11.1 lib/track_S4.rad
!xform -n 28y -rz 0 -t 25.5 20.5 11.1 lib/track_y.rad

# Direct louvered recessed fluorescents
!xform -n rlfd -rz 0 -t 11 12.5 7.99 -a 5 -t 4 0 0 -i 1 lib/typeRLF2.rad
.
.
#end sc2light.rad
```

3.7.1 Confirming the Lighting for Individual Art Pieces

To evaluate the effect of a group of luminaires on a particular work of art, rather than creating the complete scene octree, consider making a scratch file that contains only the elements under review. What would take minutes to prepare and view takes only seconds when the data set is tiny. For example, the direct lighting component on the Unfurled sculpture can be isolated and evaluated by creating a scratch file that looks like this:

```
### scratch_file.rad
#
# temporary file used to view elements of the design
# data are copied from existing files

#collect the necessary material files
!cat art.mat
!cat lib/luminaire.mat

## from sc2lights.rad
# unfurled lighting
!xform -n 22s -t 0 0 -.5 -rx 35 -rz -90 -t 4 20.5 11.1 lib/track_S4.rad
!xform -n 22y -rz -90 -t 4 20.5 11.1 lib/track_y.rad

!xform -n 23s -t 0 0 -.5 -rx 0 -rz 5 -t 8 20.5 11.1 lib/track_S5.rad
!xform -n 23y -rz 5 -t 8 20.5 11.1 lib/track_y.rad

# from scene_art.rad
# insert Unfurled on a low pedestal
accent_red cylinder u_base
0
0
7    8 21 0
     8 21 1.5
     1.5

accent_red ring u_baset
0
0
8    8 21 1.5
     0 0 1
     1.5 0
!xform -n unf -t 8 21 2.075 art_lib/unfurled.rad
# end scratch_file.rad
```

Now convert the file into an octree:

```
% oconv scratch_file.rad > scratch_file.oct
```

Then either render a small image with rpict or interactively explore the effect of the direct component of the lighting using rview. Try either of the following:

```
% rview -vp 8 4 5 -av .1 .1 .1 scratch_file.oct
```

or

```
% rpict -vp 8 4 5 -x 500 -y 500 -av .1 .1 .1 /
     scratch_file.oct > scratch_file.pic
```

Any adjustments you make in the *scratch_file.rad* can be pasted into the original data set. Make sure you remove the outdated settings!

3.7.2 An Alternative Method for Organizing the Tracklighting

The mark of a rich language is that an idea can be clearly expressed in several ways. Similarly, *Radiance* enables experienced users to individualize their approaches to building a complex scene description. The notion that two lighting designers can evolve different strategies to control the aiming of a complex light plot within *Radiance* testifies to the richness of the software.

What follows is an alternative method of creating lighting conditions identical to those produced by *sc2light.rad*. It employs some strategies that will be familiar to readers with programming and shell scripting experience; it yields a method of aiming a luminaire through a single command line. The file that follows is a modified version of *sc2light.rad* called *sc2light_alt.rad*.

```
#### sc2light_alt.rad
#
# An alternative approach to representing the tracklighting
# component of the electric lighting systems for scene2.
# active photometry is listed in light_n.cvt and light_d.cvt
# If photometry is updated, then execute:
#  light_n.cvt or light_d.cvt

# south ceiling track
!genbox enamel_white track1 24 .15 .15 | xform -t 3   4.35 11.55

# north ceiling track
!genbox enamel_white track2 24 .15 .15 | xform -t 3  20.5  11.55

# south lobby track
!genbox enamel_white track3  8 .15 .15 | xform -t 31  4.35 11.55

# north lobby track
!genbox enamel_white track4 8  .15 .15 | xform -t 31 20.5  11.55

# the individual track lights
!rcalc -i track_Lin.fmt -o track_Lout.fmt sc2track.pos
```

```
# Direct louvered recessed fluorescents
!xform -n rlfd -rz 0 -t 11 12.5 7.99 -a 5 -t 4 0 0 -i 1 lib/typeRLF2.rad
.
.
#end sc2light_alt.rad
```

The difference between *sc2light.rad* and *sc2light_alt.rad* is that all the individual tracklight commands have been replaced with a single call to `rcalc`, using an input record format called *track_Lin.fmt* that contains the single line

```
L $(typ) alt ${alt} azi ${azi} pos ${px} ${py} ${pz}
```

and an output record format called *track_Lout.fmt* containing the following:

```
### track_L.fmt
#
#                   track lampholder with $(typ) photometry
#                   altitude set to ${alt} degrees [-rx tilt angle]
#                   azimuth set to ${azi} degrees [-rz rotation]
#                   position sct to ${px} ${py} ${pz}
#                   lampholder in feet
#                   suspension yoke taken from track_y.rad

# the housing geometry
!( echo enamel_white cylinder housing1.${recno} 0 0 7 0 0 0 0 0 .6 .21 ; \
 echo enamel_white ring housing2.${recno} 0 0 8 0 0 .6 0 0 1 .21 0 ) \
     | xform -t 0 0 -.5 -rx ${alt} -rz ${azi} -t ${px} ${py} ${pz}

# insert photometry into the aperture of the cylinder
!xform -n lamp.${recno} -t 0 0 -.5 -rx ${alt} -rz ${azi} \
     -t ${px} ${py} ${pz} lib/type$(typ).rad

# insert suspension yoke
!xform -n y.${recno} -rz ${azi} -t ${px} ${py} ${pz} lib/track_y.rad
# end track_L.fmt
```

Notice that this looks very much like a *Radiance* scene description, except that a few variable fields have been added for the arguments we want passed through rcalc. Our new input file containing the actual positions of our luminaires, *sc2track.pos*, looks like this:

```
### sc2track.pos
#
# Tracklight positions, using the following format:
# L $(light_type) alt ${altitude} azi ${azimuth} pos ${tx} ${ty} ${tz}
#

# wave on sw wall
L S4 alt 45 azi  95 pos 7 4.35 11.1

# lotus lighting
L S5 alt 2 azi 180 pos 4 4.35 11.1
L S4 alt 5 azi  92 pos 6 4.35 11.1

# feather lighting
L S4 alt 40 azi -90 pos 8 4.35 11.1
L S4 alt 10 azi -90 pos 14 4.35 11.1
L S4 alt 15 azi  90 pos 17 4.35 11.1

# wave on se gallery wall
L S4 alt 42.5 azi -90 pos 23.5 4.35 11.1

# champagne bowl display
L S5 alt 5 azi -95 pos 25 4.35 11.1

# wave on nw gallery wall
L S4 alt 45 azi 95 pos 7 20.5 11.1

# unfurled lighting
L S4 alt 35 azi -90 pos 4    20.5 11.1
L S5 alt  0 azi   5 pos 8    20.5 11.1
L S2 alt 45 azi  90 pos 14.5 20.5 11.1

# cafe picture lighting
L S1 alt 40 azi -10 pos 15.2 20.5 11.1
L S1 alt 30 azi   0 pos 17   20.5 11.1
L S1 alt 40 azi  10 pos 19   20.5 11.1

# wave on north gallery wall
L S4 alt 35 azi 0 pos 25.5 20.5 11.1
```

```
# south lobby track
L S4 alt  0 azi  0 pos 33 4.35 11.1
L S4 alt  0 azi  0 pos 37 4.35 11.1
L S4 alt 40 azi 90 pos 35 4.35 11.1
L S4 alt 35 azi  0 pos 36 4.35 11.1

# north lobby track
L S4 alt  0 azi  0 pos 33 20.5 11.1
L S4 alt  0 azi  0 pos 37 20.5 11.1
L S4 alt 40 azi 90 pos 35 20.5 11.1
# end sc2track.pos
```

To change the location or orientation of a tracklight, we simply edit the appropriate line in the *sc2track.pos* file.

When we review this alternative method of representing the lighting system, two advantages surface. First, we need only a single line to specify each tracklight position, and this line is shorter and a little more self-explanatory. An *L* is followed by the lamp type, then the altitude and azimuth aiming angles, then its position in 3D coordinate space. Comments can be included in *sc2track.pos* because any extraneous text is ignored in the input file since it does not match rcalc's input record format.

The second advantage is that we have eliminated the need for separate *track_SN.rad* photometry files by combining the action of creating a tracklight with the action of naming a lamp type.

3.8 Light Color and Adaptation

As we approach the final process of setting up the renderings, we need to consider the influence of the color of light and visual adaptation.

Have you noticed how amber the incandescent lighting in a room can appear during the early evening when a window lets in bluish light? The contrast between the cool light from the sky and the relatively warm color of the electric light is very evident. When the light entering the room from the exterior diminishes as night falls, the interior light apparently becomes less amber. In fact, once it is dark outside, the interior light appears almost white. Now, there is no conspiracy between the electric light and the sky light. Your visual system has adapted to the interior light, and in the absence of a broader range of light color, the amber cast disappears and the sources appear white.

The same adaptation process influences the way you perceive the change of light color while watching a theatrical production. If a scene that is lighted with predominantly warm colors is crossfaded into a cool evening scene, it might appear *really* blue. As the scene progresses, the blueness evolves into a cold white light. This is not the work of the lighting designer; it results from the adaptation process occurring in your visual system. As another example, an incandescent-lighted room will appear much warmer in color if you have just been walking in the moonlight rather than working in the room all evening.

Since *Radiance* pictures provide snapshots, or frozen moments, the lamp color you use will depend on the point of view you wish to represent. To convey the effect produced as you enter the room from outdoors, `lampcolor HALOGEN` might be used to calculate the radiance of the incandescent light. On the other hand, to convey the apparent coloration of the room after the adaptation process is complete, white light would be most appropriate. Lampcolor has a `WHITE` category, specifically included to address this adaptation phenomenon.

Comparing the `HALOGEN` and `WHITE` lampcolor output for a tungsten-halogen 72-watt light bulb shows the unadapted and adapted radiance values that might be used to render two different perceptions of light color based on the preceding scenario. Taking the context of the scene into account, renderings that employ light sources with similar color temperatures are more accurately rendered using `WHITE` light.

```
% lampcolor
Enter lamp type [WHITE]: HALOGEN
Enter length unit [meter]: feet
Enter lamp geometry [polygon]: sphere
Sphere radius [1]: .1
Enter total lamp lumens [0]: 1035
Lamp color (RGB) = 217.968805 143.709329 55.109657

Enter lamp type [HALOGEN]: WHITE
Enter length unit [feet]:
Enter lamp geometry [sphere]:
Sphere radius [0.1]:
Enter total lamp lumens [1035]:
Lamp color (RGB) = 157.651327 157.651336 157.651336
```

We are interested in rendering our scene at 12:00 noon and at 9:15 in the evening. At noon, the main lighting source for the gallery is indirect daylight. This daylight is reflected from beige walls, blending the color of the direct sunlight with the cooler sky component. The illumination of the gallery is dominated by this unified light color, so it is appropriate to use `WHITE` light for the rendering.

The late evening scene is primarily lighted by the tracklighting and indirect fluorescent systems. The cooler effects of the early evening sky have slipped into the darkness of twilight and have little effect on the interior. The color of the indirect fluorescent light is modified by the beige wall color, reducing the color contrast between the fluorescent and halogen sources. Again, the occupant will likely be adapted to a unified color lighting scheme, making `WHITE` light the ideal choice for a representative rendering of the scene.

Currently, each of our ies2rad commands uses the `-t defaults` and `-c 1 1 1` options. As you recall from Section 3.1, Physically Based Lighting, `-t default` points the program to the -c value for color information. In this case, `-c 1 1 1` is equal to white light. If we want to change the PAR38s to halogen colored light, we replace the -t value with `HALOGEN`, and ies2rad will look up and use those color values found in *lamp.tab*.

If a situation arises in which a scene has been rendered under halogen light and needs to be evaluated under visually adapted conditions, there is an alternative to rerendering the scene with `WHITE` light sources. An option in the pfilt command changes the color balance of a picture and renders it as though it were illuminated by luminaires with a different lamp color. This option also provides a very rapid means of exploring the overall color effects of different light sources or color filters. The option is activated by -t followed by the name of a lamp located in the *lamp.tab* database.

To evaluate a scene under halogen light that was originally rendered under `WHITE` light, use the following command:

```
pfilt -1 -t halogen input_visually-adapted.pic > output_halogen.pic
```

Conversely, to see the visually adapted effect of an environment that was originally rendered under halogen light:

```
pfilt -1 -t WHITE input_halogen.pic > output_visually-adapted.pic
```

3.8.1 Rendering the Scene in Daylight

Let's set up the first batch of rendered pictures for the daytime lighting conditions by using a *Radiance* input file. Eventually we will pass this file to the rad program, which will generate settings for rpict and manage the rendering process. *Scene2_d.rif* is located in the *scene2* directory.

```
### scene2_d.rif
#
# scene2 daylight input file
AMBFILE= scene2d.amb
DETAIL= Medium
EXPOSURE= -2
INDIRECT= 2
OCTREE= scene2d.oct
PENUMBRAS= False
PICTURE= pics/scene2
QUALITY= Medium
REPORT= 2
RESOLUTION= 600 450
UP= Z
VARIABILITY= Medium
ZONE= Interior 0 40.1 0 25 0 19.4
materials= art.mat lib/sky_d.mat lib/building.mat lib/luminaire.mat
render= -aw 0 -av .2 .2 .2
scene= sc2light.rad tap_light.rad sc2bldg.rad scene_art.rad
objects= art_lib/wave.oct     art_lib/sign.rad     art_lib/goblet.rad
objects= art_lib/phone.rad    art_lib/tea.rad      art_lib/champagne.rad
objects= art_lib/sofa1_c1.rad art_lib/tble2_c1.rad art_lib/chair_c1.rad
objects= art_lib/desk_c1.rad  art_lib/deskc_c1.rad art_lib/tble4_c1.rad
objects= art_lib/sofa2_c1.rad art_lib/feather.rad  art_lib/cafe_pic.rad
objects= art_lib/fthrbase.rad art_lib/unfurled.rad art_lib/lotus_3.rad
objects= art_lib/lotus123.rad art_lib/lotus_2.rad  art_lib/tapestry.rad
objects= art_lib/lotus.mat    art_lib/cups.mat     art_lib/waves.mat
objects= art_lib/sign.mat     art_lib/unfurled.mat art_lib/furniture.mat
objects= art_lib/tapestry.mat art_lib/feather.mat
objects= lib/track_S1.rad lib/track_S2.rad lib/track_S3.rad
objects= lib/track_S4.rad lib/track_S4T.rad lib/track_S5.rad
pfilt= -r .6
view= da -vf view_lib/plan.vf
```

```
# view= db -vf view_lib/sectionx.vf
# view= dc -vf view_lib/section.vf
# end scene2_d.rif
```

Now let's review the key variable settings in this file.

A minimum of two bounces are necessary for light entering the skylight to be interreflected in the gallery. The first bounce illuminates the ceiling; the second bounce fills the room with light. To instruct rpict about this requirement, the `INDIRECT` parameter in *scene2_d.rif* is set to a value of 2. The efficient method of rendering several interreflection images from a particular octree is to create a shared ambient cache file. Our ambient cache file is created by `AMBFILE= scene2d.amb`.

It is convenient to store images separately from data files, so after creating the *scene2/pics* directory, we can use `PICTURE= pics/scene2` as the root name for each image.

The `VARIABILITY` of our image is set to Medium. This creates rendering variables that will accommodate the range of intensities from the bright ceiling to the darker areas under the reflector. If a shaft of direct sunlight entered the interior, we would set this value to High to account for the diverse range of luminance values.

The `materials=` listing includes files common to both the day and night renderings as well as the *lib/sky_d.mat* file, which specifically creates the daytime sky and illum values. Changing the contents of a material file does not generally require building a new octree unless the oconv command includes the -f option, resulting in a frozen octree. The advantage of a frozen octree is that it loads much faster because the inline commands do not need to be executed again. A frozen octree can also be moved to other directories or computers without moving its material files along with it. But beware: If you change a material definition and the related surface is in a frozen octree, the only way to update the octree with the material change is to rerun oconv.

The surfaces in our scene will be common to all renderings regardless of time of day. If we altered the location of a particular object described in the *scene_art.rad* file, rad would notice that the timestamp of the file had changed, resulting in the rebuilding of the octree. Similar to the UNIX make program, rad has the capability of tracking the timestamps of any files listed after `scene=` . These files become the arguments for the oconv command. The `objects=` variable provides the opportunity to list additional files that are not directly part of the oconv argument list. If the timestamp of these files is altered, the *scene2d.oct* file will be rebuilt automatically. In our case, we have listed the art pieces and their individual material files in `objects=` just in case they are modified.

To generate three different views of the Scene 2 project, three `view=` entries are required. The characters following the equal sign are appended to the root picture name and provide a convenient method for creating unique picture names. We also want our pictures to be rectangular. Note the values of the view horizontal (-vh) and view vertical (-vv) variables in the view files that follow. These represent the width and height of the image in degrees which are unequal and wil result in rectangular images. The following view files are in the *scene2/view_lib* directory on the CD-ROM.

```
### plan.vf
#
# plan view file that sets the clipping plane 34 feet in front of the
# vantage point. The view direction is down, resulting in an image
# that includes all objects with an elevation of 7 feet or less.
#
rview -vtv -vp 20 12.5 41 -vd 0 0 -1 -vu 0 1 0 -vh 60 -vv 45 -vo 34 -va 0

### sectionx.vf
#
# sectional view that clips the south wall, revealing the interior
# of the gallery and the complete indirect reflector system.
#
rview -vtv -vp 20 -25 6 -vd 0 1 0 -vu 0 0 1 -vh 60 -vv 45 -vo 34 -va 0

### section.vf
#
# sectional view that clips the west wall and peers into the gallery
# looking east. During daylight hours, this view reveals the design
# of the indirect daylighting system.
#
rview -vtv -vp -20 12 6 -vd 1 0 0 -vu 0 0 1 -vh 60 -vv 45 -vo 23 -va 0
```

An alternative to referencing a view file is to declare the view parameters at the `view=` variable. The following `view=` lines create the same vantage points as our view files.

```
view= da -vp  20  12.5 41 -vd 0 0 -1 -vh 60 -vv 45 -vo 34
view= db -vp  20 -25    6             -vh 60 -vv 45 -vo 34
view= dc -vp -20  12    6  -vd 1 0  0 -vh 60 -vv 45 -vo 23
```

Before we put rad into action, make sure that the appropriate lighting is installed.

```
% light_d.cvt
```

Now you are ready to produce your first sequence of images! Enter the following command at the prompt:

```
% rad scene2_d.rif
```

Several hours later, a wonderfully detailed plan view of Scene 2 will be placed in the *pics* directory, as shown in Figure 3.46. (See also Plate 13 following page 328.) Eventually, all three pictures will be located in the *pics* directory with these names:

```
% ls pics
% scene2_da.pic scene2_db.pic scene2_dc.pic
```

3.8.2 Rendering the Scene at Night

To render the nighttime pictures of the same views, we must first update the lighting levels to the evening values.

```
% light_n.cvt
```

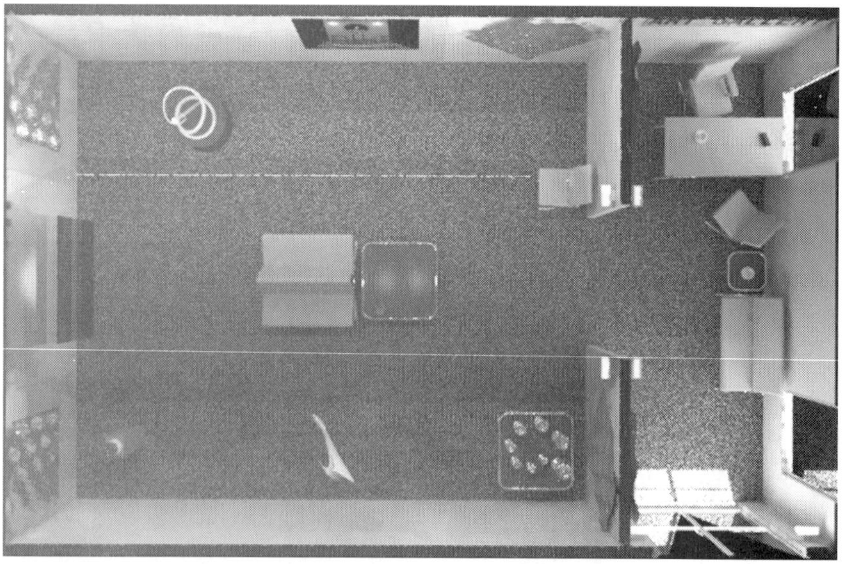

Figure 3.46 Picture *scene2_da.pic* presents a plan view of the daylighted scene. Note the patch of direct sunlight on the carpet by the front doors and the line of sunlight in the gallery, which has slipped past the edge of the skylight reflector. The lobby desk and chair are illuminated from the sky component; the art in the gallery is lighted by indirect daylight. (See also Plate 13 following page 328.)

We use a second *Radiance* input file, which switches to the nighttime sky and the evening lighting conditions. *Scene2_n.rif* (night) is produced by copying *scene2_d.rif* (day) and making the following changes:

```
### scene2_n.rif
#
# scene2 evening input file
AMBFILE= scene2n.amb
DETAIL= Medium
EXPOSURE= 1.1
INDIRECT= 1
OCTREE= scene2n.oct
.
.
materials= art.mat lib/sky_n.mat lib/building.mat lib/luminaire.mat
render= -aw 0 -av .07 .06 .04
.
.
view= na -vf view_lib/plan.vf
view= nb -vf view_lib/sectionx.vf
view= nc -vf view_lib/section.vf
# end scene2_n.rif
```

One of the significant alterations to this file is the reduction of the INDIRECT value. In daylight, the first bounce illuminates the ceiling. At night, the indirect fluorescents illuminate the ceiling directly, eliminating the need for the second daytime bounce (Figure 3.47). We could, of course, add several bounces, but the additional rendering time would not perceptibly increase the accuracy of the picture. Where computing resources are limited, most settings are optimized to create the most useful image rendered in the least amount of time.

To create the three images of Scene 2 at night, enter the following command at the prompt:

```
% rad scene2_n.rif
```

Two of the resulting images are pictured in Figures 3.47 and 3.48. (See also Plate 14 following page 328 for a color representation of Figure 3.48.)

Three more pictures will be added to the *pics* directory. Now create your own vantage points, edit the *Radiance* input files, render new views, and enjoy the visual consequences of your labor! Additional view files, which present what a patron might see when visiting the Art Gallery, are included in the *view_lib* subdirectory.

Figure 3.47 Picture *scene2_nc.pic* illustrates the effect of the indirect prismatic fluorescent luminaires that illuminate the ceiling. Only one ambient bounce is required for this light to reflect into the gallery below.

- *archview.vf*—Gallery from the entrance. Features the Tapestry hanging.
- *champ.vf*—Champagne bowl display
- *deskview.vf*—Front door from the lobby desk
- *doorview.vf*—Lobby from the front door
- *lotus.vf*—Close-up view of Lotus
- *picview.vf*—Cafe Picture and Unfurled

3.8.3 Reviewing the Daylighted Pictures

When we review *scene2_db.pic* and *scene2_dc.pic*, we notice that the upper third of each image is completely white, while the room interior is dingy (Figures 3.49 and 3.50). When a tremendous range of luminance values is present in a picture, only part of the scene can be optimized for viewing. Granted, these images are quite artificial in that the clipping plane is providing us with a view that only Superman's X-ray vision could produce, but the consequences of very high luminance ratios are clearly demonstrated.

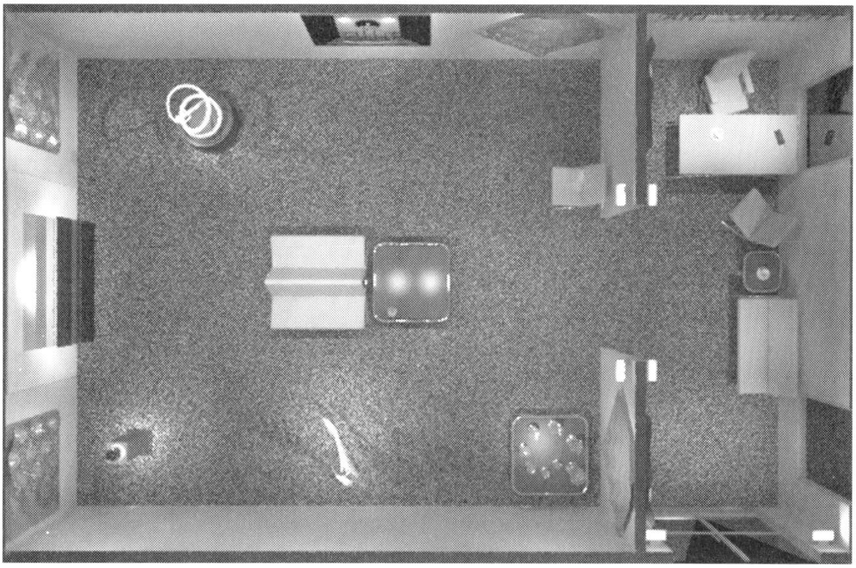

Figure 3.48 A plan view (*scene2_na.pic*) of the gallery reveals pools of light around each sculpture. The tracklights draw attention to the art and add to the visual interest of the room. (See also Plate 14 following page 328.)

Figure 3.49 *Scene2_dc.pic* reveals a large white area of glare that results from optimizing the picture's exposure for an area of the scene with lower luminance values.

Figure 3.50 Another view (*scene2_db.pic*) showing the overexposed upper regions.

The same effect can be observed if you take a picture of a person whose back is to the sun. If you set the exposure to the background, the face will be in complete shadow. Setting the exposure to the luminance of the face will turn the background into a blaze of glaring white. Is there a happy medium between these two extremes? Probably not, unless the subject's face lighting is increased or the sky clouds over. If we discover these conditions in an interior environment where visually critical tasks are to be performed, a lighting design expert must be brought in to remedy the situation!

Let's take a closer look at *scene2_db.pic*. The *scene2_d.rif* file established an exposure of -2. This setting creates a picture that shows both the ceiling and wall surfaces, but neither are optimized. Let's vary the exposure using the pfilt command and the -e option and compare the results.

```
% pfilt -1 -e -4   scene2_db.pic > scene2_db-4f.pic
% pfilt -1 -e -2.5 scene2_db.pic > scene2_db-25f.pic
% pfilt -1 -e -1   scene2_db.pic > scene2_db-1f.pic
```

View the three files using the ximage command (Figures 3.51, 3.52, and 3.53):

```
% ximage scene2_db-*f.pic
```

An exposure of `-e -4` clearly shows the sky and roof while turning the interior into a dark cave (Figure 3.51). *Scene2_db-25f.pic* has an exposure that shows the ceiling/reflector interreflection quite well, but the dingy-looking art below is disconcerting (Figure 3.52). Finally, *scene2_db-1f.pic* presents the art as though the viewer had been in the gallery for a while and had adapted to the interior lighting conditions. On the other hand, this exposure turns the upper third of the image into glare that obscures the roof and sky (Figure 3.53).

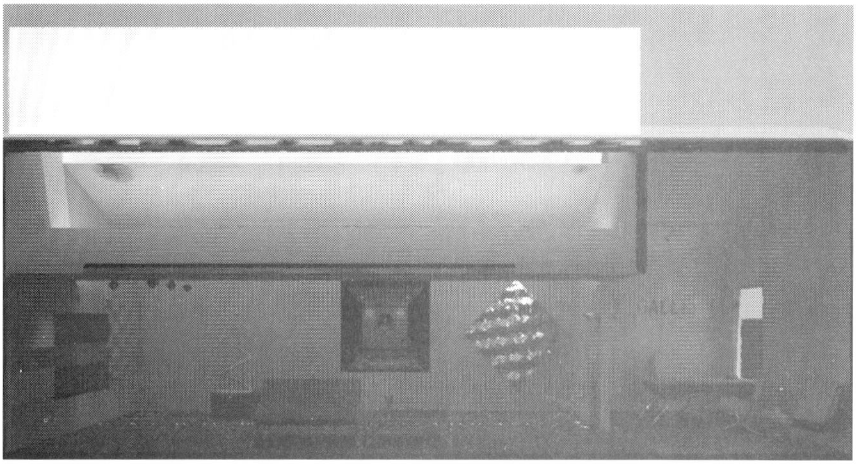

Figure 3.51 *Scene2_db-4f.pic* results from reducing the exposure by -4 using the pfilt command. Note that the roof and upper skylight are clearly visible, but the interior appears very dark.

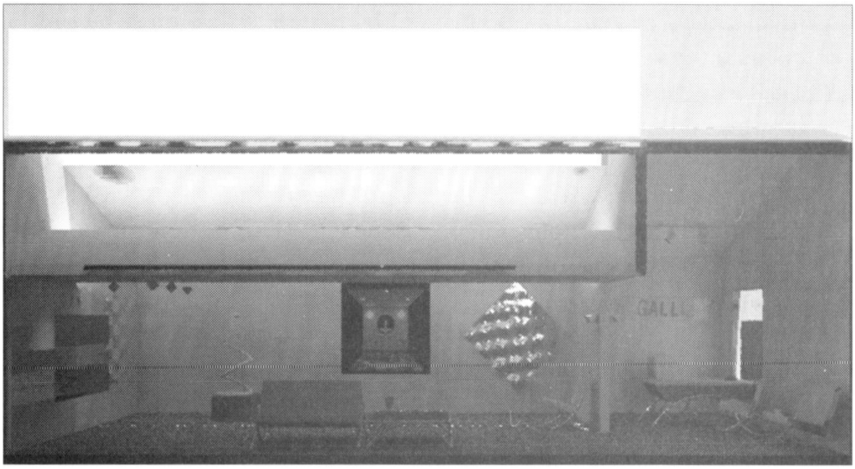

Figure 3.52 An exposure of `-e -2.5` optimizes the visibility of the ceiling and reflector system in *scene2_db-25f.pic*.

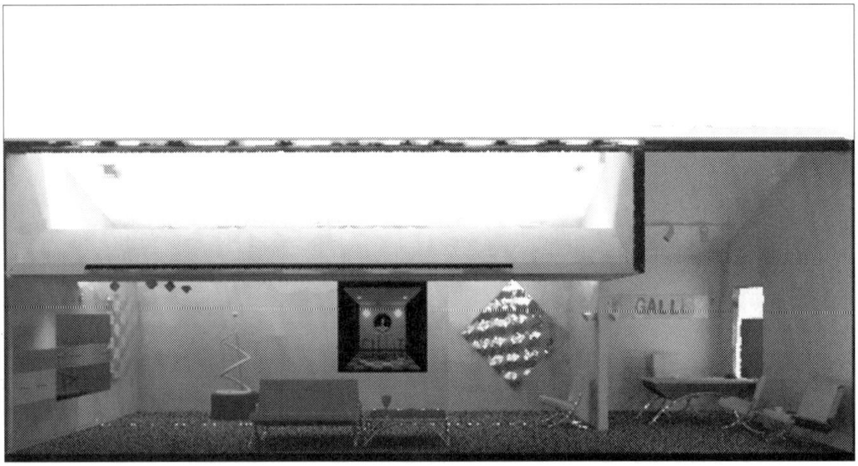

Figure 3.53 *Scene2_db-1f.pic* reveals the interior of the gallery quite clearly while the rest of the picture is obscured by glare.

The lesson here is to evaluate an environment from the vantage point of the occupant. Vantage points such as *archview.vf*, *doorview.vf*, and *lotus.vf* have views that are well within a range of acceptable luminance ratios.

An alternative approach uses the pcond program to condition the image through a variety of linear and nonlinear filters [LRP97]. Dim surfaces might remain unchanged while the exposure of a brighter zone is significantly reduced. This enables most of the details in a high-contrast image to be seen simultaneously. The harsh effects of glare can be masked by pcond, so we must be cautious when we evaluate the visual effect of a scene after a bold application of the filter. But generally, pcond provides a wonderful set of postrendering effects that increase the information that can be derived from a rendered image. The exposure of a picture can be based on human contrast sensitivity (-s). There is also the option of mimicking the human visual response to produce output that correlates strongly with a person's subjective impression of a scene (-h). This option can be modified (-h-) to represent what a person with perfect vision might see or to mimic certain human vision deficiencies (-h+), such as the inability to see color or contrast at low illumination levels. In addition, pcond can preprocess the color and contrast (-f) of a picture for an output device such as a film recorder or color printer. The general form of pcond is

```
# pcond [options] input [output]
```

To display our picture as perceived by a person with excellent sight (Figure 3.54):

```
% pcond -h- scene2_db.pic > scene2_db_p.pic
% ximage scene2_db_p.pic
```

After reviewing an image taken from *archview.vf* during the early afternoon, we notice that the Tapestry artwork appears dingy to a patron whose visual system is adapted to the brightly daylighted Art Gallery walls. The solution is to increase the artwork's illumination, but by how much? Should we increase the lamp wattage of the existing trackheads or hang additional units for daytime use only? The first step is to discover how much more light needs to be applied to the artwork.

This is accomplished by editing the *typeS4T* entry in the *lights_n.cvt* file. By doubling the multiplier from `-m .8` to `-m 1.6`, we have effectively increased the 150-watt PAR to a halogen 250-watt PAR38. A test rendering (Figure 3.55) now reveals the Tapestry artwork in its full glory. All that remains is to change the specification of these lamps to 250 watts and to note that a dimmer needs to be installed on this circuit so that the Tapestry lighting can be reduced at night for patrons whose vision is adapted to lower light levels.

Figure 3.54 *Scene2_db_p.pic* has been conditioned by pcond. The picture is adjusted for output to a typical 24-bit monitor and mimics the way a person might perceive the scene if that person could simultaneously view the interior and the exterior.

Figure 3.55 The Tapestry as viewed from the gallery entrance. Additional halogen lighting is needed for this artwork to maintain its visual impact during daylight hours. This illumination is reduced for compatibility with nighttime ambient lighting conditions.

3.8.4 Illumination Analysis

The desk in the entrance area often serves as the place where art catalogs are reviewed and contracts are negotiated. How do we know whether our lighting design for the lobby provides sufficient illumination to perform these tasks well? We have decided that the lobby lighting conveys the appropriate visual appeal during nighttime, but what of the lighting metrics?

One step of the analysis is to ascertain the illumination levels appropriate for these activities. The IESNA publishes a listing of visual tasks with their recommended ranges of illumination. The recommended illumination for reviewing photographs with moderate detail and for critical reading ranges from 500 to 1000 lux.

Radiance includes a program called **falsecolor**, which can be used to generate an illumination analysis. This is composed of a radiance picture of the scene with an overlay of isolux contour lines. Two input pictures of identical sizes are required. The first is an irradiance picture, which captures incident light levels and is created by adding the -i option to the rpict command line. This option affects only the final result, substituting a Lambertian surface and multiplying the irradiance by π. We will render our pictures using the nighttime sky and lighting levels.

```
% rpict -vf desk.vf... -i scene2n.oct > irr.pic
```

The second picture is a standard radiance image whose purpose is to provide a background reference for the isolux contour lines.

```
% rpict -vf desk.vf... scene2n.oct > rad.pic
```

Now we will use falsecolor to generate contour lines (-cl) from the irradiance picture and map them onto the radiance picture, as shown in Figure 3.56. (See also Plate 15 following page 328.) There are several options that control the scale, increment, and number of these contour lines. The following command produces five contour lines (`-n 5`) in equal increments between 0 and 1000 lux (`-s 1000`) and a legend with the label *Lux* (`-l Lux`).

```
% falsecolor -i irr.pic -p rad.pic -cl -n 5 -s 1000 -l Lux > Lux.pic
```

The contour lines on the resulting picture show that the surface of the desk immediately in front of the chair receives at least 700 lux and that most of the adjacent work area has an illumination greater than 500 lux. Not only does our scene look good, but the lighting system also delivers the illumination levels recommended to support the visual tasks performed at the desk.

The gallery is now ready to present its art in the best light!

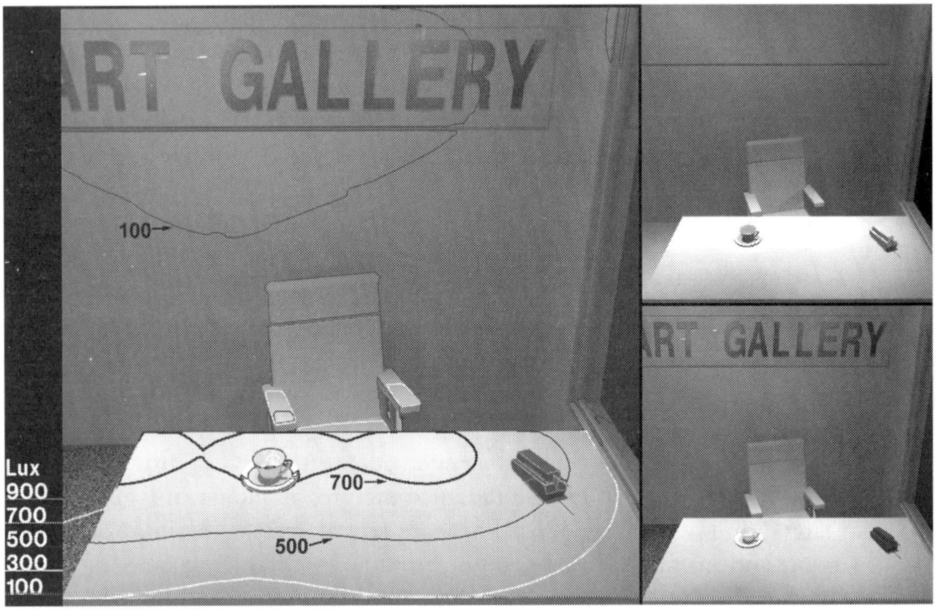

Figure 3.56 The large picture presents an isolux contour line illumination analysis of the desk area at night. The pictures on the right are small versions of the irradiance (top) and radiance (bottom) pictures used by falsecolor to generate the analysis. (See also Plate 15 following page 328.)

3.9 Scene 2 Summary

We have constructed, lighted, previewed, and analyzed an environment that does not yet exist. The images of the interior space not only look photorealistic, but are reasonably photoaccurate. The term *reasonably* refers to the important relationship between the accuracy of the scene descriptions in depicting the ways in which real materials interact with light and the accuracy of the final image in predicting how the scene might appear in the real world. "Reasonable" images are also dependent on the accuracy of the photometry and of the rad settings, which are derived from the values you have entered in the *Radiance* input file. If you ever have the opportunity to compare a *Radiance* picture with its real-world counterpart, "reasonableness" is also dependent on the accuracy and the orientation of the geometry used in the simulation.

There is an old adage that states, "Garbage in, garbage out." *Radiance* cannot control the credibility of its input data and rendering parameters—that's up to you. With a little effort, you can make *Radiance* produce images that have very little relationship with their real-world counterparts. On the other hand, if you provide *Radiance* with accurate data and carefully set the *Radiance* input file variables, tremendously valuable pictures will emerge.

These tutorials have only scraped the surface of the capabilities that *Radiance* offers. We hope you can use these scenes as your first stepping stones on a journey that is filled with visual rewards. Discovering the delicate nuances of a well-lighted scene and exposing the mistakes of a brave lighting design experiment are but two among the many benefits of mastering the power of rendering with *Radiance.*

CHAPTER 4

Radiance Scripting Techniques

It should be obvious by now that *Radiance* is based on the UNIX toolbox model, in which essential, orthogonal programs may be linked together in a command *pipeline* for a combined purpose. Our rendering pipeline has the combined purpose of taking us from a 3D model to a 2D image, and consists of the following steps:

model → compile → render → filter → display

A specific instance of this pipeline might be

```
% genbox red box 10 5 3 -r .5 \
        | xform -rz 20 -t 40 13 0 \
        | oconv basic.mat room.rad - \
        | rpict -vf good.vf \
        | pfilt -x /2 -y /2 -1 -e +2 \
        | ximage
```

Of course, this is not the way we usually render a scene, but *Radiance* is nevertheless designed to work with such a pipelined command model, and this facility is invaluable in customizing the system for specific problems.

In this chapter, we present some of the basic concepts and methods for *scripting*, which is simply command-level programming. We start with a discussion of the oft-used *Radiance* functional language (associated with files ending in *.cal*), giving examples of how and when it is applied. We then introduce several new utility programs that are useful in creating scripts. Next, we delve a bit deeper into C-shell programming, offering example script files that use built-in features of the UNIX C-shell. Finally, we show how scripting techniques can be used to solve two specific example problems that would otherwise require a lot of tedious file manipulation.

4.1 The *Radiance* Functional Language

At its most basic, the functional language used in *Radiance* is simply a means of defining real variables and functions in terms of other variables and functions, using standard algebraic expressions. Let's look at a simple example:

```
A(x) = sin(x)*cos(x);
```

This simply defines the new function `A(x)` as the sine of `x` times the cosine of `x`. (Sine and cosine are part of the standard function library, which is listed in the section called File Formats on the CD-ROM along with a more detailed description of language syntax and semantics.)

4.1.1 2D Plotting Utilities

We can plot this function using the *Metafile* graphics utilities provided as part of the *Radiance* distribution.[4] To create a basic plotting file, we add a few definitions to the function in a *.plt* file:

```
include = function.plt
title = "Test Function Plot"
xmin = 0
xmax = 2*PI
A(x) = sin(x)*cos(x)
```

4. The *Metafile* graphics format associated with *Radiance* should not be confused with Microsoft's Windows Metafile format, which was developed later.

We can then plot the above file using the **bgraph** program, sending the *Metafile* output to **x11meta** for display under X11:

```
% bgraph test.plt | x11meta
```

This results in a plot similar to the one shown in Figure 4.1. To produce a polar plot of the same function, the following bgraph options are applied:

```
% bgraph -polar +period '2*PI' test.plt | x11meta
```

This sets the plot type to polar and changes the period from the standard 360 degrees to 2π radians. The output is shown in Figure 4.2.

Because bgraph and its sister programs **igraph**, **dgraph**, and **gcomp** incorporate the functional language into their own input file syntax, the standard expression language is modified slightly. Specifically, definitions must be contained in a single line, unless the end-of-line is escaped with a backslash (\), and the semicolon at the end of the definition is optional, whereas it is required in most other circumstances.

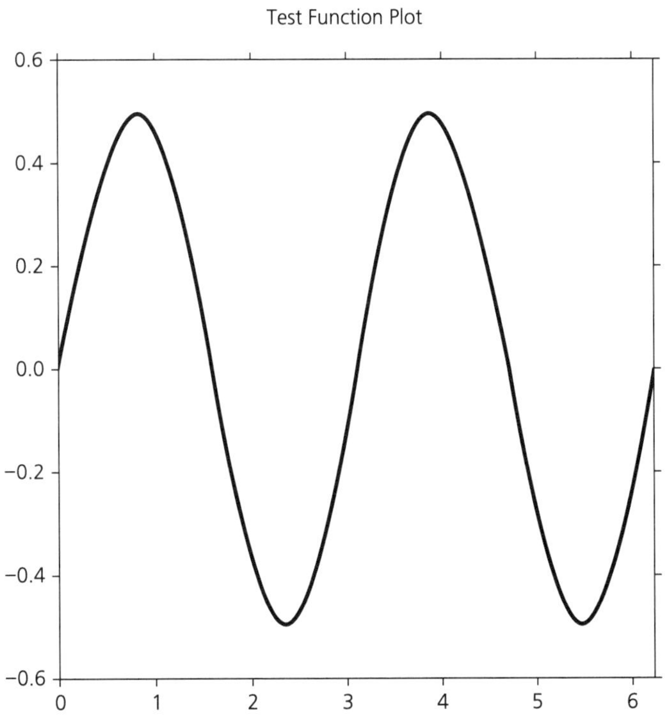

Figure 4.1 A Cartesian plot of sin(x)*cos(x) from bgraph.

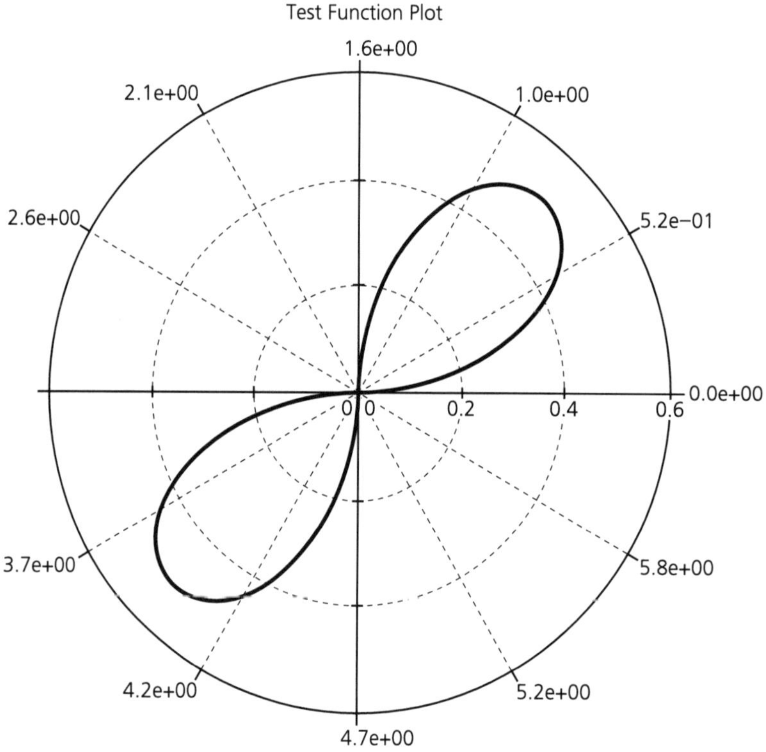

Figure 4.2 A polar plot of sin(x)*cos(x) from bgraph.

4.1.2 Calc and Rcalc

Let's look at another example showing how the functional language might be used, this time to perform some repetitive calculations. Included in the *src/cal/cal* directory of the standard distribution are a number of handy function files, including *trans.cal*, below:

```
{ --------------- trans.cal -------------- }
sq(x) : x*x;
n = 1.52;                   { index of refraction }
rn = sq((1-n)/(1+n));       { normal reflectivity }
                            { normal transmissivity }
tn(Tn) = (sqrt(sq(sq(1-rn))+4*sq(rn*Tn))-sq(1-rn))
                    / 2/rn/rn/Tn;
```

This function file computes the transmissivity for the *Radiance glass* primitive based on the normal transmittance, which is a much easier quantity to measure.[5] Note in the above file the addition of comments, which are enclosed in curly braces. Comments may appear anywhere except inside a number or name, and may be nested to any level. (This makes it easy to comment out definitions in a file without worrying about the comments that go with them.) Note also that definitions may continue over multiple lines in free format, and that each definition ends with a semicolon (;). In most files, new definitions will begin on new lines, but this is a convention to improve readability and is not required by the language syntax.

Since this file does not actually calculate anything, but only defines some variables and functions, we need some program to make use of it. For interactive use, the program **calc** is usually preferred. To use it, simply execute calc on the command line with the function files you wish to access as arguments. (It is possible also to read in files during a session using the "<" command.) Then type expressions on the standard input and calc prints results on the standard output. Below is an example.

```
% calc trans.cal
tn(.88)
$1=0.958415435
tn(.57)
$2=0.621392084
```

To exit the program, type the EOF character (`^D` on UNIX systems). Above, we have computed the normal transmissivity for an 88% transmittance glazing and a 57% transmittance glazing. The `$1=` and `$2=` outputs are shown, indicating that we may reuse these results in later expressions, such as

```
100*$1/$2
$3=154.236827
```

---

5. The "transmissivity" of a glass plate is the fraction of light that is not absorbed in the interior, and is always between 0 and 1. Since additional light is reflected at each interface, the total "transmittance" (i.e., the light that actually gets through the glass) is always less than this value, and also depends on the index of refraction.

If we wish to redefine the index of refraction, we can enter a new one as a replacement definition, like this:

```
n=1.33
tn(.88)
$4=0.916086355
tn(.57)
$5=0.593490428
```

Notice that our answers are now slightly different, since the definition of `tn(Tn)` depends on the index of refraction indirectly. This shows an important feature of this language—variables and functions are reevaluated every time. This means that changing a definition will affect all uses of that definition, wherever they may be. This provides us with much greater flexibility, though it can result in unnecessary calculations when variable and function definitions do not change. To improve efficiency in cases where we know our definitions will not change, we use the *constant attribute*. This attribute is indicated by substituting a colon (:) for the usual equal sign (=), as was done for the definition of the `sq(x)` function in *trans.cal*.

We know that we will never want to change the meaning of `sq(x)` (the square of x), so we feel safe giving this definition the constant attribute. However, in this particular file, we never make use of this attribute, since there are no cases where `sq(x)` is passed a constant expression such as `sq(5)`, which could be replaced immediately by the parser with 25. But if we *knew* that we would never want to compute the transmissivity of glass unless its index of refraction was 1.52, we could give the definition of `n` as a constant also, and of `rn` as well (since it depends only on `n`). This would then have the nice effect of percolating on down to the final definition of `tn(Tn)`, significantly reducing the compiled expression complexity. Specifically, the following file:

```
{ --------------- trans1.52.cal --------------- }
sq(x) : x*x;
n : 1.52;                    { index of refraction }
rn : sq((1-n)/(1+n));        { normal reflectivity }
                             { normal transmissivity }
tn(Tn) = (sqrt(sq(sq(1-rn))+4*sq(rn*Tn))-sq(1-rn))
                    / (2*rn*rn*Tn);
```

will be compiled and reduced to

```
tn(Tn) = (sqrt(0.840252843+4*sq(0.042579995*Tn))
                            -.916653066)
                    / (0.00362611194*Tn);
```

This saves quite a few operations during evaluation. In our particular case, it may not matter, since we are not going to spend much of our lives waiting for the calculation to be completed either way, but when these expressions are evaluated for procedural textures and patterns during rendering, the difference can be important. (Note how we collected variables in the denominator in the original file, to be sure that all constant subexpressions could be evaluated beforehand. The compiler is not smart enough to rearrange subexpressions to find all possible constant branches.)

What if we had a whole set of transmittances we wanted to convert to transmissivity values? We could sit there at the keyboard and enter them one by one and jot down the answers, but it might be easier to apply the **rcalc** program to perform the evaluations from a file.

To use rcalc, we simply create a file of transmittances, one per line, from which we wish to compute the transmissivity for standard glass with an index of refraction of 1.52. We then pass these data (which we have named *transin.dat*) to rcalc with the following arguments:

```
% rcalc -f trans1.52.cal -e '$1=tn($1)' transin.dat
```

The standard output will be the transmissivity corresponding to each transmittance in *transin.dat*, one per line. This may, of course, be redirected to a file if desired. The dollar sign followed by a number refers to a data column. If it appears as the left-hand side of a definition, it is interpreted as an output column assignment. If it appears in an expression, it is taken as an input column.

An even more powerful feature of rcalc is the ability to take formatted input and produce formatted output based on *templates*. A template is a (usually) short file showing what the input or output is expected to look like, with variable *fields* indicated with a special notation. Numeric (i.e., real) fields, such as those computed by expressions in our functional language, are enclosed in curly braces that begin with a dollar sign, like this:

```
${real_expr}
```

For input fields, the contents of the curly braces must be a variable name. For output fields, an expression may be used as well. String fields are used to pass unevaluated information from the input to the output, like this:

```
$(string_var)
```

String variables get their own name space, since they cannot be used in expressions. The rcalc **-s** option can be used to assign string variable values on the command line. (See the rcalc manual page on the CD-ROM for further information.)

Let's say we want to produce a set of material definitions for various transmittance glazings. We can use the following template (*glaz.fmt*) as our output format:

```
void glass glaz${pT}
0
0
4 ${t} ${t} ${t} ${n}
```

Then we execute `rcalc` using our *transin.dat* file from before:

```
% rcalc -f trans.cal -e 'pT=100*$1;t=tn($1)' \
            -o glaz.fmt transin.dat > glaz.mat
```

Note how we assigned the variable `pT` as the percent transmittance to use in the glazing name, and the variable `t` is the computed transmissivity value. The variable `n` also appears in the output format, and this is defined in the original *trans.cal* file as the standard index of refraction for glass. If we wanted to, we could return to a variable `n` and specify this in our input file as the second column on each line, then assign `'n=$2'` as an additional expression argument to rcalc. We could also give different transmittances for red, green, and blue and use these to assign different fields in the output format, or even expressions like these:

```
void glass glaz${pT}
0
0
4 ${Tn($1)} ${Tn($2)} ${Tn($3)} ${n}
```

The width of each numeric field in the output is determined by the width of each field in the template, so we can add spaces, if we like, to get more significant digits or to align columns in different output formats. (To get a dollar sign to appear as a literal in a format, you must use two dollar signs side by side.)

We will give other examples showing how rcalc can be used to construct *Radiance* scene descriptions toward the end of Section 4.2, Utility Programs. For now, it is better to focus on the *Radiance* generator programs that are tailored specifically to this task.

4.1.3 Function-Based Generator Programs

In the preceding two chapters, we saw some examples of using the functional language to define surface shapes as well as textures and patterns. In this chapter, we want to go into a little more detail on the mechanics and thought processes involved in designing and applying functions. We start with the simplest generator employing functional input, **genrev**.

The genrev program takes a 2D parametric curve that defines the radius and height as a function of an independent parameter (t), which varies from 0 to 1, as shown in Figure 4.3. Evaluation takes place at *N* evenly spaced points in t.

Let's generate a torus as a simple example. We use the parametric equation for a circle, then add an offset that is the major radius of the torus. The genrev command looks like this:

```
% genrev tmat torus 'r*sin(2*PI*t)' \
        'R+r*cos(2*PI*t)' 12 -e 'R:8;r:1.5'
```

The greater radius is defined with the constant R; the minor radius is defined with the constant r. The number of segments (cones) into which the torus will be divided is set to 12 in this example. If our material (tmat) is a *dielectric,* or some other type that cares about surface orientation, then we need to control the directions in which our surfaces face. According to the genrev manual page, the surface faces outward when z(t) is increasing, and inward when it is decreasing. (For consistency, this also means that the surface faces up if z(t) is constant and r(t) is decreasing.) In our example, this has the desired effect of orienting our surfaces outward, as seen in Figure 4.4.

Since this example was so simple, there was no need to create a separate function file, and we put it all on the command line. The way genrev actually works internally is by defining z(t) and r(t) functions equal to the expressions given in the

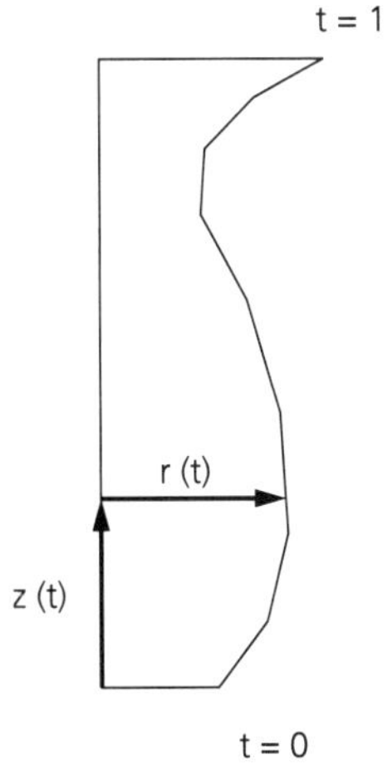

Figure 4.3 A simple vase defined parametrically with two functions, r(t) and z(t), where t varies from 0 to 1.

third and fourth command line arguments.[6] These functions are then evaluated at $N+1$ values of t to make N cone segments. For a more complicated object, we would likely define the actual z(t) and r(t) functions in a separate file, like this:

```
% genrev omat object 'z(t)' 'r(t)' 24 -f object.cal
```

The file *object.cal* would then contain definitions for the functions z(t) and r(t) as well as any supporting functions and variables we might need.

To take a more complicated example, let's look at a bicubic patch generated with **gensurf**. This program tessellates functional surfaces defined in terms of two independent parameters, s and t, each varying from 0 to 1. We'll use the one-dimensional hermite basis function [FDFH90] to build up a surface patch using the following file:

```
{
        hpatch.cal - Hermite bicubic form for gensurf.
}

x(s,t) = hermite(x0(s),x1(s), x0t(s),x1t(s), t);
y(s,t) = hermite(y0(s),y1(s), y0t(s),y1t(s), t);
z(s,t) = hermite(z0(s),z1(s), z0t(s),z1t(s), t);

x0(s)  = hermite(x00, x10, x00s, x10s, s);
x1(s)  = hermite(x01, x11, x01s, x11s, s);
x0t(s) = hermite(x00t, x10t, x00st, x10st, s);
x1t(s) = hermite(x01t, x11t, x01st, x11st, s);
```

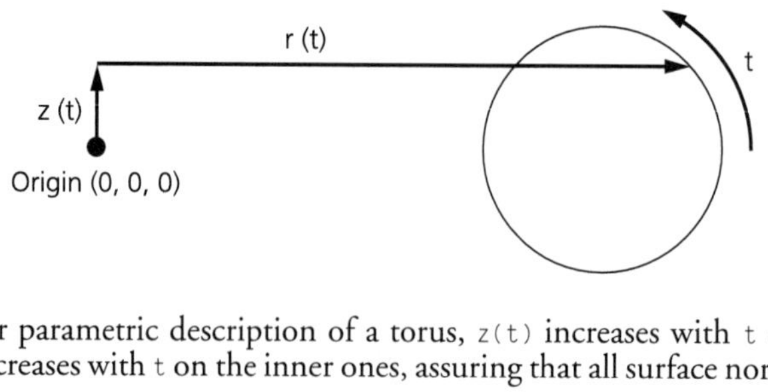

Figure 4.4 In our parametric description of a torus, z(t) increases with t on the outer cone segments, then decreases with t on the inner ones, assuring that all surface normals face the exterior of the torus.

6. The actual names used for these functions are selected so as not to interfere with user variable and function definitions, so that z and r may be used for other purposes.

```
y0(s)  = hermite(y00, y10, y00s, y10s, s);
y1(s)  = hermite(y01, y11, y01s, y11s, s);
y0t(s) = hermite(y00t, y10t, y00st, y10st, s);
y1t(s) = hermite(y01t, y11t, y01st, y11st, s);

z0(s)  = hermite(z00, z10, z00s, z10s, s);
z1(s)  = hermite(z01, z11, z01s, z11s, s);
z0t(s) = hermite(z00t, z10t, z00st, z10st, s);
z1t(s) = hermite(z01t, z11t, z01st, z11st, s);
```

The hermite basis function is defined internally by gensurf as

```
hermite(p0,p1,r0,r1,t) = p0 * ((2*t-3)*t*t+1) +
                         p1 * (-2*t+3)*t*t +
                         r0 * (((t-2)*t+1)*t) +
                         r1 * ((t-1)*t*t);
```

The object we will make is a leaf, which is an unusual patch because it is pinched at the base and the tip as shown in Figure 4.5. The stem is built with calls to **genworm**, a program that takes a parametric function for a 3D curve with varying radius and turns it into *N* cones (or cylinders) joined by spheres at the joints.

The specific parameters used to define the leaf lobes are given in the following file:

```
{
        leaf.cal - Bicubic patch for leaf.
}

                { Our corner points }
x00 = 0;           y00 = 0;          z00 = 0;
x01 = 0;           y01 = 0;          z01 = 0;
x10 = 0;           y10 = 0;          z10 = 2;
x11 = 0;           y11 = 0;          z11 = 2;

                { Our partials in s }
x00s = 0;          y00s = .5;        z00s = 0;
x01s = 4;          y01s = .5;        z01s = .5;
x10s = 0;          y10s = -.2;       z10s = 1;
x11s = 0;          y11s = -.2;       z11s = 1;
```

```
            { Our partials in t }
x00t = 0;       y00t = 0;       z00t = 0;
x01t = 0;       y01t = 0;       z01t = 0;
x10t = 0;       y10t = 0;       z10t = 0;
x11t = 0;       y11t = 0;       z11t = 0;

            { Our second derivatives }
x00st = 0;      y00st = 1;      z00st = 0;
x01st = 0;      y01st = -1;     z01st = 0;
x10st = 0;      y10st = -.5;    z10st = 0;
x11st = 0;      y11st = .5;     z11st = 0;
```

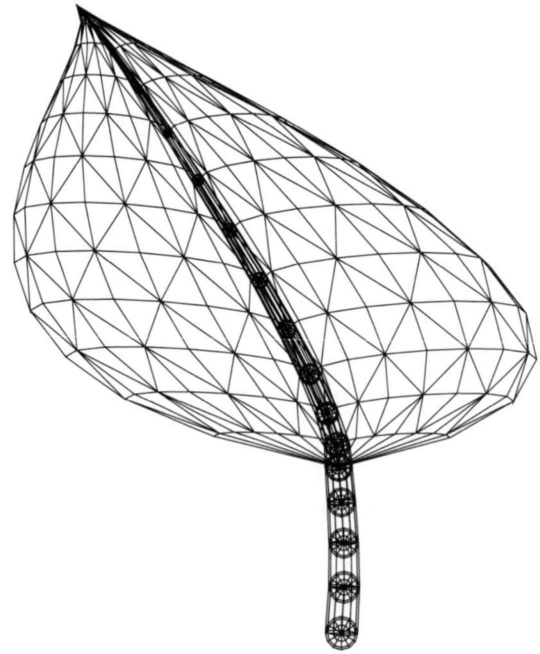

Figure 4.5 Line drawing of a leaf constructed from bicubic patches with a worm for the stem.

This file is then applied along with *hpatch.cal* in a straightforward manner, shown in this scene description file:

```
#
# Leaf
#

void trans leaf_mat
0
0
7 .404 .577 .158 .04 .05 .05 .1

void plastic stem_mat
0
0
5 .5 .65 .052 0 0

!gensurf leaf_mat leaf.right 'x(s,t)' 'y(s,t)' \
      'z(s,t)' 12 8 -f leaf.cal -f hpatch.cal \
      | xform -a 2 -mx

!genworm stem_mat stem 0 \
      'hermite(y00,y10,y00s,y10s,t)' \
      'hermite(z00,z10,z00s,z10s,t)' \
      '.03*(1.02-t)' 12 -f leaf.cal

!genworm stem_mat stem_end 0 \
      'hermite(y00,y00-.3,-.2,-.4,t)' \
      'hermite(z00,z00-.2,-.2,-.1,t)' \
      '.03*(1+.2*t)' 4 -f leaf.cal
```

Note how the patch is mirrored by **xform** to create a symmetric leaf shape, and the leaf parameters are used to create a stem that follows the inside contour. The final genworm call adds extrapolation to the origin in the reverse direction to create a stem. Since the stem lies in the *yz* plane, the genworm argument describing the function for *x* is simply 0.

Uniform rational spline surfaces may also be created with the aid of the standard file *src/cal/cal/patch3w.cal:*

```
{
      patch3w.cal

      Uniform Rational Patch
```

```
      Define Px(i,j), Py(i,j), Pz(i,j) and W(i,j),
           nrows, ncols
}
                          { default basis functions }
br(a,b,c,d,s) = b3(a,b,c,d,s);
bc(a,b,c,d,t) = b3(a,b,c,d,t);
b3(a,b,c,d,p) = bezier(a,b,c,d,p);
                          { default patch interpolation }
rint = interpolate;
cint = interpolate;
interpolate = 1;

x(s,t) = patch(s,t,Px);
y(s,t) = patch(s,t,Py);
z(s,t) = patch(s,t,Pz);

patch(s,t,p) = bc(P2(s,c0(t)+1,p), P2(s,c0(t)+2,p),
               P2(s,c0(t)+3,p), P2(s,c0(t)+4,p), cf(t))/
               bc(W2(s,c0(t)+1), W2(s,c0(t)+2),
               W2(s,c0(t)+3), W2(s,c0(t)+4), cf(t)) ;

P2(s,j,p) = br(W(1+r0(s),j)*p(1+r0(s),j),
             W(2+r0(s),j)*p(2+r0(s),j),
          W(3+r0(s),j)*p(3+r0(s),j), W(4+r0(s),j)*p(4+r0(s),j), rf(s)) ;

W2(s,j) = br(W(1+r0(s),j), W(2+r0(s),j),
          W(3+r0(s),j), W(4+r0(s),j), rf(s)) ;

r0(s) = rmult*floor(clamp(s)*npr);
rf(s) = s*npr - floor(clamp(s)*npr);
c0(t) = cmult*floor(clamp(t)*npc);
cf(t) = t*npc - floor(clamp(t)*npc);

rmult = if(rint, 4, 1);
cmult = if(cint, 4, 1);
npr = if(rint, nrows/4, nrows-3);
npc = if(cint, ncols/4, ncols-3);

clamp(p) = if(p, if(1-p, p, .9999999), .0000001);
```

The file below illustrates one example of a rational Bezier patch to describe the flukes of a whale. Note how the select library function is used to construct arrays of coefficients.

```
{
      fluke.cal

      Parameters for Bicubic Rational Patch
      of half of one whale fluke
      (mirror twice for flukes).
}
nrows = 4;
ncols = 4;

Px(i,j) = select( (i-1)*ncols+j,
          0.5, 0.32262, 0.193578, 0.104524,
          0.5, 0.286804, 0.00901883, -0.169621,
          0.5, 0.194508, 0.0453709, -0.108177,
          -0.18969, -0.29474, -0.37360, -0.457331
      );
Py(i,j) = select( (i-1)*ncols+j,
          -0.5, -0.486028, -0.512917, -0.491699,
          -0.166667, -0.08992, -0.1049, -0.142638,
          0.166667, 0.165846, 0.232517, 0.150724,
          0.528947, 0.544121, 0.555375, 0.555075
      );
Pz(i,j) = select( (i-1)*ncols+j,
          0, -0.0796445, -0.0990403,     0,
          0, -0.109165, -0.0800447,     0,
          0, -0.141696, -0.0659265,     0,
          0,      0,       0,      0
      );
W(i,j) = select( (i-1)*ncols+j,
         1,      1,      1, 0.519854,
         1,      1,      1,      1,
         1,      1,      1,      1,
         1,      1,      1,      1
      );
```

In the scene file, the following call mirrors the patch twice to make the flukes for the whale's tail:

```
!gensurf blue_glass s 'x(s,t)' 'y(s,t)' 'z(s,t)' \
        8 8 -f patch3w.cal -f fluke.cal \
        | xform -t 0 .478 0 -s .35 \
        -ry -90 -a 2 -mx -a 2 -my
```

4.1.4 Patterns and Textures

So far, there has been nothing very mysterious about how function files operate or how they are accessed. Definitions are taken from command line arguments and files named in the current directory, and all the variables that are used or needed are explicitly given. If a variable or function is redefined, the old definition is forgotten in favor of the new one. (Constants are, of course, a treacherous exception to this rule because their values may be compiled into other subexpressions.) Some of this self-evident nature is lost in the application of the functional language to procedural patterns and textures. Specifically:

- Function files are sought in the list of directories specified by the RAYPATH environment variable rather than always being taken from the current directory. The first directory with a matching file is the one used. (If a filename begins with a period (.), a slash (/), or a tilde (~), no search takes place.)
- Each function file gets its own name space so that reusing a function or variable name does not interfere with its use in other files. A single global context contains functions and variables defined by the system and the initialization file, *rayinit.cal.* Redefining a global name causes it to be hidden in the local context, but does not affect its use in other file contexts.
- Critical to patterns and textures are global variables and functions that transfer the parameters of the current scene primitive and ray intersection. These are described in the header comments of *src/rt/rayinit.cal* and in the File Formats section on the CD-ROM.

Let's revisit our simple dirt pattern from Chapter 3, showing how this process works. The following scene file segment defines a fractal noise pattern:

```
void brightfunc dirty
4 dirt dirt.cal -s 2.8
0
1 0.75
```

When the renderer first uses this pattern, it searches for the file *dirt.cal* in the list of directories indicated by the `RAYPATH` environment variable. This file can be found in the standard *Radiance* library directory (*/usr/local/lib/lib/ray/dirt.cal* by default). It looks like this:

```
{
	Dirt pattern.

	This is probably the simplest application
	imaginable for the fractal noise function.

	  A1	- degree of "dirtiness";
			  1 is very dirty.
}

dirt = 1 - A1*.5*(1+fnoise3(Px,Py,Pz));
```

The first thing to notice is that the variables `A1`, `Px`, `Py`, and `Pz`, as well as the function `fnoise3()`, are not defined in this file or by the primitive itself. Where are they defined? If we check the global initialization file, *src/rt/rayinit.cal*, we see in the header comments that `fnoise3()` is a library function defined by the system, and `Px`, `Py`, and `Pz` are the transformed ray intersection coordinates. We see also that `A1` is defined as `arg(1)`, which returns the first real argument from our scene primitive, 0.75 in this case. Since our primitive has an associated transformation (`-s 2.8`), the coordinates passed to `fnoise3(Px,Py,Pz)` will be scaled by 1/2.8 from their original values. This has the effect of enlarging the noise pattern so that the fundamental period is 2.8 instead of 1.

Let's look at another example, this time using the smooth noise function, `noise3()`. We wish to create the appearance of color flecks on a floor surface. The easiest way to get more or less evenly spaced flecks is to use a threshold on our noise function. We choose a level that the noise function will rise above about the right proportion of the time, giving the desired proportion of fleck to background. (We will leave this level as a parameter for maximum flexibility.) When our noise evaluation is above the threshold, we use the fleck color; when it is below, we use the background color. The average fleck spacing will be determined by the noise frequency, which is controlled by its position arguments. Our **colorfunc** primitive looks like this:

```
void colorfunc flecked
4 red grn blu fleck.cal
0
7 0.75 1 1 1 0.7 0.3 0.1
```

The real arguments will correspond to the fraction of background, followed by the foreground color (RGB) and the background color (RGB). Our *fleck.cal* file looks like this:

```
{
      A fleck pattern.  Arguments are:

      A1 -            approx. background fraction
      A2, A3, A4 -    foreground color
      A5, A6, A7 -    background color
}
infleck = (noise3(Px,Py,Pz)+1)/2 - A1;
red = if(infleck, A2, A5);
grn = if(infleck, A3, A6);
blu = if(infleck, A4, A7);
```

The first expression takes our noise function and maps it from its original range of −1 to +1 to a range of 0 to 1. This is then compared to the given threshold argument so that if it is greater, `infleck` is positive (true) and the subsequent `if()` statements return the foreground, rather than the background, primary values. You will notice that we have not explicitly given the fleck spacing, but left it as the default of 2 (minimum) associated with the unscaled `noise3()` function. Since it is easy to change this by adding a scaling transform to the primitive, we choose not to complicate our function more than we need to.

On the other hand, what if we wanted our flecks to look more like streaks? Since we cannot preferentially scale one axis over another, we need to have some way to individually control the scales of the three axis directions. So we can create a new file, called *streak.cal*:

```
{
      A streak pattern.  Arguments are:

      A1 -            approx. background fraction
      A2, A3, A4 -    foreground color
      A5, A6, A7 -    background color
      A8, A9, A10 -   scales for X, Y and Z
}
infleck = (noise3(Px/A8,Py/A9,Pz/A10)+1)/2 - A1;
red = if(infleck, A2, A5);
grn = if(infleck, A3, A6);
blu = if(infleck, A4, A7);
```

Noise Functions

There are two main noise functions in the current version of *Radiance,* `noise3(x,y,z)` and `fnoise3(x,y,z)`. Both have nominal ranges of −1 to 1, both have autocorrelation distances of 1, and both are defined over 3D space. Figure 4.6 shows the two functions along an arbitrary line through 3D space. We see that the Perlin noise function [Per85] [Arv91, p. 396], `noise3(x,y,z)`, is relatively smooth, whereas the fractal noise function, `fnoise3(x,y,z)`, varies wildly. In fact, fractal noise can be mimicked by summing Perlin noise functions evaluated at higher and higher rates, but it takes longer than the direct method implemented here. In general, Perlin noise is good for smoothly varying phenomena and fractal noise is good for natural phenomena, which have a rougher appearance. Three additional functions, `noise3x(x,y,z)`, `noise3y(x,y,z)`, and `noise3z(x,y,z)`, give the partial derivatives of the Perlin noise function at the specified point and are useful in texture generation and when a gradient field is needed. (The gradient of a fractal is undefined.)

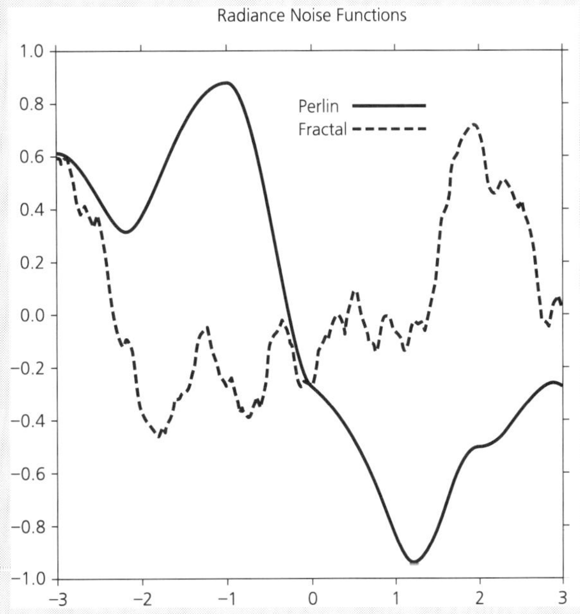

Figure 4.6 The Perlin noise function, `noise3(x,y,z)`, and the fractal noise function, `fnoise3(x,y,z)`, evaluated along arbitrary lines through 3D space.

One of the nicest features of the noise functions is that since they are defined over 3D space, they can be applied easily to the design of solid textures. A solid texture is defined everywhere in a volume, even if it is evaluated only at the surface boundary. As a simple example, take a block of wood. Only the surface of the wood block is visible, yet the woodgrain is present throughout the block, and can be most easily described as a solid texture rather than as an image mapped onto the block surface. This saves even more time if the solid object is complicated, such as a wood or marble sculpture.

Our primitive now must have three additional real arguments, scaling the *x*-, *y*- and *z*-axes independently. Note that we have not changed the names of our variables. If we had a scene using both *fleck.cal* and *streak.cal*, would this cause a problem? Recall that each function file gets its own unique name context, so these sorts of conflicts are avoided. (As an advanced exercise, see if you can combine these two files into one, using `arg(0)` to test whether or not `A8-A10` were specified.)

Next, let's look at a slightly more complicated example, a corrugated roof texture. For a texture (as opposed to a pattern), we want to compute a surface normal perturbation that will give the illusion of variation in the surface shape. This is not as accurate as varying the actual surface geometry, since self-shadowing and silhouette features will be absent, but it looks similar and is much less expensive computationally (and memorywise), so we accept it as a useful approximation.

We want our perturbation to move the surface normal from what it was (perpendicular to the original surface) to what it would be if we actually had a corrugated geometry as shown in Figure 4.7.

Let's start by assuming the corrugation is aligned with the *y*-axis, and that our surface lies in the *xy* plane. That way, we know we only have to perturb our normal in the *x* direction.[7] We can easily transform the texture later, as we will show in our

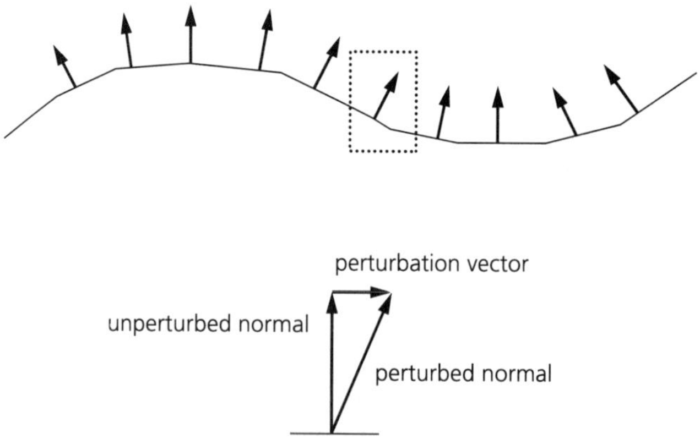

Figure 4.7 A corrugated surface we are simulating and a vector diagram showing unperturbed and perturbed surface normals.

7. Since our perturbed normal need not be normalized to a unit vector and we will not be taking it as far as 90 degrees from its orientation, our perturbation vector can be perpendicular to the original surface normal, which makes the math easier.

example. If we assume that our corrugated geometry follows the function of a scaled sine wave, our original and perturbed surface functions[8] are

```
              { Implicit function for xy plane }
F0 = Pz;                                { original plane }
              { Implicit function for corrugation }
F1 = Pz - A1*sin(2*PI*Px);              { target surface }
```

In general, the desired surface normal perturbation is equal to the difference between the gradient of our target surface function and the normalized gradient of the actual surface function (i.e., the true surface normal). Since the partial derivatives in *y* are zero and the partials in *z* cancel, we are left with only the *x* component of our perturbation vector:

```
              { Our computed perturbation vector }
dFx = -2*PI*A1*cos(2*PI*Px);
dFy = 0;
dFz = 0;
```

We could put these in a separate function file, but they are so simple that we might as well put them inline in our **texfunc** scene primitive:

```
# Add a transformation for 30-degree sloping
# roof with high end in positive x direction

void texfunc corrugated
10 -2*PI*A1*cos(2*PI*Px) 0 0 .
              -s 0.2 -rx 30 -rz -90
0
1 0.3

corrugated metal tin
0
0
5 .65 .65 .65 .8 .08

tin polygon roof
0
0
12
```

8. An implicit surface function defines a surface as $F(P_x, P_y, P_z)$==0; that is, the surface exists everywhere that $F(P_x, P_y, P_z)$ is zero.

```
    0    0    4
    9    0    9.2
    9    20   9.2
    0    20   4
```

The special entry "." for the function file name means that no file is needed (except the global initialization file). The `A1` variable accesses the first argument, which is 0.3 in this case, and could have been put into the formula directly. The transformation scales and rotates the corrugation function for our world units (meters) and roof position. Again, these things could have been worked into the formula, but it was left this way for clarity.

It is important to note that the way string arguments are parsed, any white space will separate one argument from the next, so it is imperative that expressions contain no white space. This rule does not apply in function files, of course, which have a free format that ignores white space.

Besides describing textures and patterns directly, the functional language can be used to define coordinate mappings for 2D scanned or precomputed patterns. A simple example of this was given in Chapter 3 for a picture on a wall and a tiled pattern on the floor. Let's look at tiling a scanned pattern onto a cylinder.

```
# A redwood bark pattern on a fallen log

void colorpict barkpat
11 noop noop noop redwbark.pic cyl.cal
       cyl_tile_u cyl_tile_v -s 1.75 -rx 90
0
2 1.64 1.5707

barkpat plastic bark
0
0
5 .2 .2 .2 0 0

bark cylinder log
0
0
7
    0    0    0
    0    21   0
    1.75
```

The standard library file, *cyl.cal*, contains the following definitions:

```
{
        cyl.cal - 2D coordinate mapping onto cylinder.

        Unit radius cylinder with axis along z.

        A1 = picture height/width
        A2 = unit scale for pattern
}

cyl_u = atan2(Py,Px)/A2;
cyl_v = Pz/A2;

cyl_tile_u = mod(cyl_u,max(1,1/A1));
cyl_tile_v = mod(cyl_v,max(1,A1));

cyl_match_u = tri(cyl_u,max(1,1/A1));
cyl_match_v = tri(cyl_v,max(1,A1));
```

Checking the real arguments, we see that `A1` is supposed to be the image height over width, which we determine with the **getinfo -d** option run on the library picture file, *redwbark.pic*. This returns `-Y 164 +X 100`, which corresponds to a picture aspect ratio of 1.64. The second real argument `(A2)` is the target length (scale) for the narrower picture dimension when it is mapped to the unit cylinder. Here, we chose a value of $\pi/2$ because we want there to be four image copies around the cylinder. (Note that we must give a numerical value for the real arguments to any primitive, though it would have been nice to enter this as `π/2` directly.)

The purpose of *cyl.cal* is to take our world coordinates (assuming a unit cylinder aligned with the *z*-axis for simplicity) to picture coordinates that must range between 0 and 1 in one dimension and between 0 and `A1` or `1/A1` in the other. (See sidebar on picture coordinates.) To accomplish this, we use the handy math function `atan2()`, which computes the azimuthal angle (in radians) based on the rectangular coordinates `Px` and `Py`. The second real argument from the scene primitive, `A2`, is needed to relate the scale of the pattern to the unit cylinder.

Since our log has a radius of 1.75 instead of 1 and is aligned with the *y*- rather than *z*-axis, we add a transformation to the end of the primitive to move the pattern into place. If we had also translated the log from the origin, we would also add in this translation so that `atan2()` would still work.

Note that the variable definitions for `cyl_match_u` and `cyl_match_v` in *cyl.cal* are not needed in our example. These definitions will still be loaded by the renderer along with the rest of the file, but will not result in any additional computation because they are never evaluated.

The first three string arguments to the **colorpict** primitive are the value-mapping functions, which may be used to adjust the picture pixel values for a particular application. In our tiling example, we use the `noop()` function, which leaves each value as it is. (See the sidebar on picture normalization.) If we had wished to use a color negative of our pattern, we could have defined the following functions:

```
                    { reverse color/greyscale }
invert_v(v) = noneg(1-v);
```

This would have required us to either edit *cyl.cal* or replace it with our own version to include this function, or add it to the others in *rayinit.cal.* The value-mapping function may take one or three arguments. If it takes only one, the argument passed is the original value for this color component. If it takes three, it is passed the red, green, and blue component values. A simple example of this is defined in *rayinit.cal*:

```
                    { compute grey (photopic) value }
grey(r,g,b) = noneg(.265074126*r + .670114631*g
                          + .064811243*b);
```

This computes the grey value for any color using the standard *Radiance* definitions of red, green, and blue. Another set of functions might be used to transform from one color system to another, like this:

```
                    { compute RGB from CIE XYZ }
red(x,y,z) = noneg( 2.565*x -1.167*y -0.398*z);
grn(x,y,z) = noneg(-1.022*x +1.978*y +0.044*z);
blu(x,y,z) = noneg( 0.075*x -0.252*y +1.177*z);
```

We have given just a few examples of the ways function files may be used in *Radiance* scene descriptions. There are many others. Besides patterns and textures, the functional language may be used to describe output distributions from lamps, sky luminance distributions, window transmission characteristics, surface reflectance functions, and combinations (mixtures). The possibilities are limited only by your imagination and your willingness to experiment.

Picture Coordinates

In *Radiance*, a picture may have any size. To simplify the coordinate-mapping process for the colorpict primitive, a standard image coordinate system is set up based only on the picture's aspect ratio (height/width). This way, changing the picture resolution will not necessarily affect the scene description. The smaller of the two picture dimensions will always be mapped between 0 and 1, and the larger picture dimension will be mapped from 0 to *M*, where *M* is the aspect ratio or the reciprocal of the aspect ratio, whichever is larger. Figure 4.8 shows the three possibilities.

If the picture has been flipped or rotated, the colorpict coordinates always refer to the original orientation. Therefore, if rotation or flipping is desired, it must be done in the coordinate-mapping function.

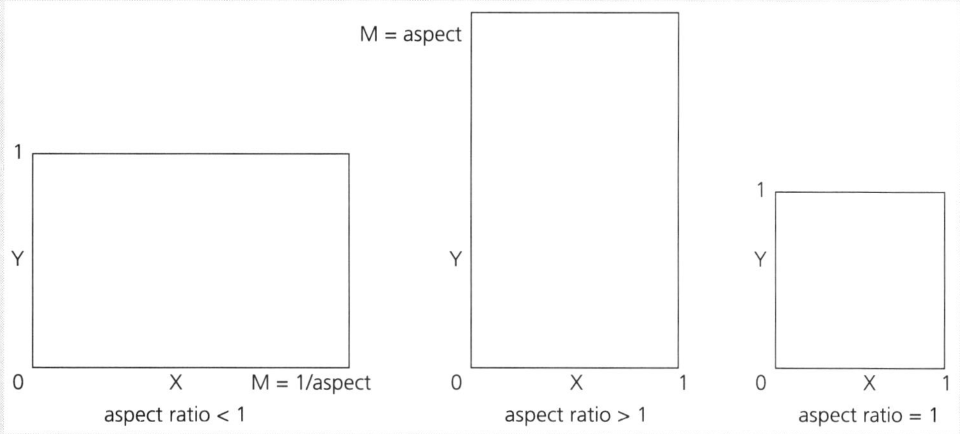

Figure 4.8 The mapping of picture coordinates in the colorpict primitive.

4.1.5 Image Processing

Image processing takes on a whole new dimension in *Radiance* because pictures contain floating-point color information at each pixel rather than the usual eight integer bits per primary of most image formats. (See the File Formats section on the CD-ROM and [Arv91, p. 80].) Because the original units of radiance (watts/steradian/m^2) are preserved, calculations may be performed based on these physical quantities. Visibility and glare may be predicted with tools such as **pcond** and **findglare**, and physical quantities may be visualized with **falsecolor**. More general operations may also be programmed via the functional language using the **pcomb** picture filter, which takes zero or more pictures of equal sizes and generates a combined output based on user-defined formulas.

In its programmable mode, pcomb has the following syntax:

```
% pcomb [-e expr] [-f func.cal] [[-o] pic1 ..]
```

Any number of function definition files may be given on the command line, followed by the picture file names. (The **-o** option tells pcomb to use the original radiance values, undoing any exposure adjustments that have been applied to the picture.) Computations on the picture(s) are defined using functions and variables native to pcomb, which are described in the manual page on the CD-ROM. A few of the more important ones are given here:

- **xmax, ymax:** The width and height of the input picture. (Picture rotations with **protate** will swap these values.)
- **x, y:** The current pixel position.
- **ri(n), gi(n), bi(n):** The red, green, and blue values for the current pixel in picture `n`.
- **li(n):** The photopic value for the current pixel in picture `n`.
- **ro, go, bo:** The user-assigned output variables for the current red, green, and blue pixel components.
- **lo:** Alternate greyscale output variable assignment.

To give you an idea how this works, we will give a simple example of multiplying the pixel values of two pictures together:

```
% pcomb -e 'ro=ri(1)*ri(2)' -e 'go=gi(1)*gi(2)' \
            -e 'bo=bi(1)*bi(2)' pic1 pic2 > pic1_2
```

The three expressions could have been put into a file instead, or combined as one -e option argument with semicolons between the definitions. The point is that the expressions for `ro`, `go`, and `bo` could return any positive value. A whole world of possibilities opens up.... Let's look next at an example in which a picture's physical values are really needed.

If we want to accurately simulate a negative's exposure for a particular black-and-white film, we need the film response function, which in this case is stored in the following table giving density ($-\log_{10}$(transmittance)) versus a normalized exposure, which is computed from the *Radiance* pixel value thus:

```
{ -------------- negative.cal -------------- }
{
       Set these constants for 35mm photograph:

              Fstop - aperture f-stop
              Speed - exposure time in seconds
              ASA   - film speed (ISO ASA)
              { WE is 179 lumens/watt for RGB }
              dens(e)- density function for
                           log10 of normalized exposure
              (density is -log10(transmittance))
}
{ From IES Lighting Handbook, 1987 Application
      Volume, section 11, page 24}

K : WE*PI/200;                        { conv. factor }
E : K * Speed * ASA / Fstop^2;        { multiplier }

lo = 10^-dens(log10(E*li(1)));        { output value }
```

To get the function `dens(e)` from our table:

```
# Density versus log exposure, log10(lux-seconds)
# for Kodak Tri-X Panchromatic film
# see Kodak Web site for more information
# http://www.kodak.com
-3.37       0.157
-2.80       0.197
-2.42       0.30
-2.08       0.45
-1.68       0.67
-1.18       1.00
-0.68       1.35
-0.37       1.61
-0.127      1.80
-0.0098     1.87
```

we use the **tabfunc** program:

```
% tabfunc -i dens < dens0.dat > dens0.cal
```

Picture Normalization

There are generally two cases in which pictures are applied as patterns. In the first case, the picture corresponds to a piece of artwork or some printed material, and only a single copy of it is mapped into the scene. The type of picture that is appropriate is usually one whose pixel values correspond to reflectances, so the average value will vary depending on average reflectance. The `clip()` function is often used for value mapping to ensure that reflectances do not exceed 1. In the second case, the picture corresponds to a repeating pattern on some larger surface, such as a tiled floor. The type of picture appropriate is usually normalized to an average value of 1, so that the material primitive will carry the average reflectance. The `noop()` function is usually specified for value mapping, since the reflectance multipliers may take on arbitrary values (corresponding to highlights, for instance). Be aware, when you are using these files, of which type of picture you have. This is most easily determined by displaying them with ximage or some similar display program. If about half their values are greater than 1 (washed out so −e −1 makes them look about right), they are normalized images for tiling. (See the **normpat** manual page on the CD-ROM for additional information.)

We will discuss tabfunc a little more later, but for now it is enough to know that the above command translates our table into a linearly interpolated function, `dens(x)`, based on the given *x* and *y* values. Putting this together with *negative.cal*, we can apply pcomb as follows to compute our negative:

```
% pcomb -e 'Speed:1/60;Fstop:2.8;ASA:100' \
        -f dens0.cal -f negative.cal -o input.pic > negative.pic
```

The output will be a black-and-white negative image based on the given 35mm camera settings and this specific film. The pcomb -o option is important to guarantee that we are working with the original radiance values, in case *input.pic* has already passed through **pfilt** with an exposure adjustment.

To give another example of how a general filter such as pcomb can be used, let's say we wanted to simulate a veil at a certain distance from the view point. We start with a rendering that has an associated z-buffer (generated with the rpict **-z** option).

We convert the z-buffer to a *Radiance* picture using the **pvalue** program, which needs the image size (not stored in the file) and options specifying that it is a short floating-point greyscale data file without a header. The command looks like this:

```
% pvalue -h `getinfo -d < input.pic` -r \
       -b -df input.zbf \
       | pcomb -e D:20 -f bveil.cal input.pic - \
       > bveil.pic
```

The `getinfo -d` command in back-quotes yields the correct resolution string for pvalue, and the other options are appropriate for converting a z-buffer file into a *Radiance* picture, which is then passed to pcomb as the second picture (using "-" to indicate reading from the standard input). The file *bveil.cal* is given here:

```
{ --------------- bveil.cal ---------------- }
{
       Compute a veil at distance D for picture.
}
T : 0.1;        { veil transmittance }
mult = if(gi(2)-D, T, 1);
ro = mult*ri(1);
go = mult*gi(1),
bo = mult*bi(1);
```

The `mult` variable gets an assignment of `T` (0.1) if the distance from the z-buffer is greater than `D`, and 1 otherwise. This multiplier is then applied to all three primaries equally. (We use `gi(2)` for the z-buffer value, rather than `li(2)`, for efficiency; the values are the same, since it is a greyscale picture.) The net result is a picture with the appearance of a veil at the distance `D` (20 world units in our example).

4.2 Utility Programs

We have seen scripting examples using the functional language, and in a few of these we needed help from other utilities such as cnt and tabfunc, which generate or manipulate tabular data and other ASCII text files not specific to *Radiance*. One of the most powerful utilities is in fact rcalc, which is not only programmable via the functional language, but works with almost any fixed-record text file format.

In this section, we will look quickly at a few of the essential utility programs, then give an rcalc scene-building exercise.

4.2.1 Cnt, Lam, and Total

The three simplest utilities, **cnt, lam,** and **total,** provide basic generation and manipulation of tab-separated columnar data. The first of these is cnt, which is a basic counter for data generation. It is often used as input to rcalc to create data records according to some enumerated script. The syntax is

```
% cnt N [M ..]
```

If only one integer argument is given, cnt produces that number of output records, one per line, starting with 0 and ending with $N - 1$. If two arguments are given, $N \times M$ records are produced, with two columns per line, the second column running from 0 to $M - 1$ for each change of the first column, which starts at 0 as before and ends at $N - 1$. The algorithm extends for any number of command-line arguments, corresponding to any number of nested counter variables printing out in columns. Here is a simple example with two counters:

```
% cnt 3 2 > index2.dat
% cat index2.dat
0	0
0	1
1	0
1	1
2	0
2	1
```

The second utility, lam, simply joins (laminates) lines from multiple input files, using a tab as the default separation character. This is usually the simplest way of combining data from two sources in one input stream, usually destined for rcalc. Let's look at combining the above file with another output from cnt:

```
% cnt 5 | lam index2.dat -
0	0	0
0	1	1
1	0	2
1	1	3
2	0	4
2	1
```

The second argument to lam is a hyphen, which reads from the standard input. Note that the last line is missing its third column because the input from `cnt 5` produces only five lines, and there were six in *index2.dat*.

The third utility is total, which sums together input columns, producing one total per data column. This is normally a simple sum, but can be an arithmetic or geometric mean instead, or one of several other options. (Real input values are assumed.) If we pass the output from the previous command into total, we get

```
% cnt 5 | lam index2.dat - | total
6       3       10
```

Even though the final column has fewer entries, total still gives the sum of whatever values are there.

4.2.2 Histo and Tabfunc

Similar to total, **histo** computes statistics on input data. The difference is that histo computes the frequencies of values in user-specified bins (i.e., a histogram). The syntax is as follows:

```
% histo min max n
```

where `min` is the lower limit, `max` is the upper limit, and `n` is the number of bins. (If `min` and `max` are integers and one bin is desired for each integer value, `n` should be left off.) The output from histo will be `n` records (lines), with the leftmost column giving the central value for each bin and as many more output columns as there were input columns. The first record will be the count(s) in the first bin, and so on to the last bin on the *n*th line. To continue with the previous example, let's pass the output of cnt and lam to histo:

```
% cnt 5 | lam index2.dat - | histo 0 4
0       2       3       1
1       2       3       1
2       2       0       1
3       0       0       1
4       0       0       1
```

The final program we discuss before getting on to rcalc is tabfunc, an extremely useful utility that bridges the gap between data files and function files. As input, tabfunc takes a set of data like the one above, with the independent value in the leftmost column and the dependent value(s) in the columns to the right. The output is a function definition for each column named on the command line. In the above example, we can name just the first two dependent data columns (the second and third columns on the input) and the output will be as follows:

```
% cnt 5 | lam index2.dat - | histo 0 4 \
     | tabfunc f1 f2
f1(x):select(x--1,2,2,2,0,0);
f2(x):select(x--1,3,3,0,0,0);
```

If the output is written to a file and handed as input to rcalc or to one of the other programs that accept function definitions, we have effectively imported this data to the functional language. The evaluation `f1(2)` will return the second dependent value at 3, which is 2 in this case. If the data represented discrete sampling on a continuous function, we could use the tabfunc **-i** option to get a linearly interpolated set of functions instead of the discrete ones shown above. This works for unevenly spaced data as well, so long as the independent variable is monotonically increasing or decreasing. (Completely unordered data can be passed first through `sort -nu` to satisfy this condition.)

4.2.3 Rcalc

We saw earlier, in the first section, a simple example using rcalc to generate glass primitives from transmittance data. Now let's look at an example in which rcalc is used to generate scene geometry that would be difficult or awkward to create with any of the standard generator programs. In this example, we are given the 3D coordinates of the knots of a net (or hammock) that is on a simple 20-by-60 grid. If we wanted to create a continuous surface, the data input options of gensurf would serve us well. In this case, though, we want instead to connect the points with cylinders rather than with polygons.

Our knot positions are given row by row, one 3D point per input line, and each row in the net with 20 knots (taking 20 lines in the file). To connect a knot with the next one in this row, we need to collect adjacent lines in the file for rcalc, using lam like this:

```
% tail +2 knot.dat | lam knot.dat - \
       | rcalc -e 'n:20' -s nm=row \
       -f inrow.cal -o cyl.fmt > net.rad
```

The **tail** command skips the first knot, then passes this to lam to laminate with the original file with an offset of 1. Thus, each knot is joined with the one next to it on lines handed to rcalc. The file *inrow.cal* looks like this:

```
{ --------------- inrow.cal --------------- }
{
      Connect knots in a row of length n.
}
CRAD: 0.05;          { cylinder radius }
cond = recno - n*floor(recno/n) - 0.5;
x0 = $1; y0 = $2; z0 = $3;
x1 = $4; y1 = $5; z1 = $6;
r : CRAD;
```

The key setting in this file is the `cond` variable, which is a special variable for rcalc that is positive when a record is to be produced and nonpositive otherwise. (If it is not defined, it is assumed to be always positive.) In this file, the variable is defined to exclude the joiner between the last knot in one row and the first knot in the next row. The last line will have only one knot in it, but it will not matter because `cond` will exclude it. The file *cyl.fmt* output format is simply

```
netmat cylinder $(nm).${recno}
0
0
7
      ${  x0   } ${  y0   } ${  z0   }
      ${  x1   } ${  y1   } ${  z1   }
      ${  r    }
```

Notice the extra space in each field that allows the values to have a reasonable number of significant digits. The name is given partially by the command-line assignment of the string variable `nm` and partly by the input record number, which rcalc starts counting at 1.

Once we have all the connectors within rows, we want to add the connectors between rows. To do this, we need to do a little file manipulation, since rows are not next to each other in the *knot.dat* input file. Again, we combine tail and lam:

```
% tail +21 knot.dat | lam knot.dat - \
      | rcalc -e 'm:60;n:20' -s nm=col \
      -f incol.cal -o cyl.fmt >> net.rad
```

The file *incol.cal* follows logic similar to that of *inrow.cal*:

```
{ --------------- incol.cal --------------- }
{
        Connect knots between m rows.
}
CRAD: 0.05;            { cylinder radius }
cond = (m-1)*n + 0.5 - recno;
x0 = $1; y0 = $2; z0 = $3;
x1 = $4; y1 = $5; z1 = $6;
r : CRAD;
```

The `cond` definition in this case prevents connection of the last row to the nonexistent one after it. In the next section we look at putting these commands into a more general shell script.

4.3 C-Shell Programming

The UNIX C-shell (*/bin/csh* on most systems) is most commonly used for interactive command-line processing. It provides basic quoting and "globbing" (file-matching) functionality, command path searching, pipelines, and a fairly powerful and confusing history mechanism for modifying and reissuing recent commands. It also provides basic looping functionality, built-in commands, and variable setting.[9] We have chosen the C-shell to illustrate scripting techniques not because it is the best shell or even the easiest to learn, but because it is common to most UNIX systems and probably more familiar than the other shells, such as the Bourne shell and the Korn shell. Also, most of the techniques we will demonstrate can be translated painlessly to these other shells, so it is not necessary to abandon your favorite shell to take advantage of this material.

One of the most common and straightforward uses of a shell script (file) is as a place to collect a set of commands for a combined function, such as generating an object. By gathering together useful command combinations, we add functionality to our system and customize it for our particular application. For example, we can

9. We cannot offer a complete introduction to the programming or features of C-shell in this book, so please consult the UNIX manual pages.

put the commands from the previous example into a C-shell script for generating simple nets from knot positions. The script file might look something like this:

```
#!/bin/csh -f
#
# Take knot data and generate a net grid.
#
if ($#argv != 6) then
       echo Usage: $0 mat name crad knot.dat N M
       exit 1
endif
set mat=$1
set name=$2
set crad=$3
set kdfile=$4
set N=$5
set M=$6
set tmpfiles=(/tmp/cyl$$.fmt)
onintr quit    # quit on interrupt
cat > /tmp/cyl$$.fmt << _EOF_
$netmat cylinder \$(nm).\${recno}
0
0
7
       \${  \$1  } \${  \$2  } \${  \$3  }
       \${  \$4  } \${  \$5  } \${  \$6  }
       $crad
_EOF_
tail +2 $kdfile | lam $kdfile - \
       | rcalc -s nm=$name.row -o /tmp/cyl$$.fmt \
       -e "cond=recno-$N*floor(recno/$N)-0.5"
@ nlskip = $N + 1
tail +$nlskip $kdfile | lam $kdfile - \
       | rcalc -s nm=$name.col -o /tmp/cyl$$.fmt \
       -e "cond=($M-1)*$N+0.5-recno"
quit:
rm -f $tmpfiles
```

The first line of the script file tells the system which shell interpreter to use and should be given as shown for the C-shell. You must also set the executable bit on the file by executing:

```
% chmod +x mknot
```

Note how some changes were made to the original commands to avoid having too many temporary files. (We get away with just one, which we could have eliminated also.) Temporary files are best avoided in shell scripts because interrupting the script often means leaving the temporary files on the system. Even when we are careful, adding a catch (`onintr`) for signals and removing our temporary file if the script is interrupted, there are still any number of errors that might cause the script to abort, leaving */tmp/cyl$$.fmt* on the system. (The *$$* notation substitutes the shell process ID for uniqueness.) Notice also the care we take in quoting and use of the dollar-sign character, since this is how we access C-shell variables as well as the format fields in rcalc. The output of each scene-generating command is left to go to the standard output of the shell script, which can then be redirected by you to a file (or the script can be used directly in an inline command in a scene description file).

Many of the programs in *Radiance* are in fact C-shell scripts that execute a set of more basic C programs. A good example of this is the falsecolor program, which uses pcomb and **pcompos** to process *Radiance* pictures for different types of value visualization. Looking at the file *src/px/falsecolor.csh*, we see that C-shell scripts can look quite complicated. One advantage of working with an interpreted language, however, is that changes can be made and tested quickly, and execution can be traced with appropriate options. (We recommend testing *csh* scripts with **-fex** to echo commands and quit if there is an error.)

4.3.1 Scene Animation

Another common application of shell scripting is for scene animation. One of the simplest animations is moving the sun position throughout the day using the **gensky** program. Such a daylight scripting example is given later in Chapter 6, and an animation script for **ranimate** is demonstrated in Chapter 9. Let's combine these here to create a script that ranimate can use to animate the sun position.

The ranimate command takes as one of its control variables the name of a script (or other command) whose last argument is the frame number. This script then produces the octree appropriate for that frame on its standard output. Assuming we have everything we need except the sky description in an octree named *scene.oct*, the following script will produce a sequence of sun positions over 25 frames on the summer solstice:

```
#!/bin/csh -f
#
# Add sun and sky according to frame index
#
set ti=(6 6.5 7 7.5 8 8.5 9 9.5 10 10.5 11 \
11.5 12 12.5 13 13.5 14 14.5 15 15.5 16 \
16.5 17 17.5 18)
gensky $ti[$1] 6 21 -a 43.2 -o 27.5 -m 30 \
      | oconv -f -i scene.oct - sky.rad
```

Another example of scene animation might be moving some object around the space:

```
#!/bin/csh -f
#
# Move a ball according to the frame index
#
set pi=("3 2.5 4" "4 2.7 4.1" "5.1 2.9 4.18" \
"6.25 2.8 4.15" "6.6 2.75 4.12" "7 2.5 4.1")
xform -t $pi[$1] ball.rad \
      | oconv -f -i scene.oct -
```

We can imagine animating any number of scene parameters, from lighting or geometry, as shown here, to materials and combinations of all three. Camera positions and exposure are usually controlled by ranimate, but this too can be written into shell scripts by the truly adventurous.

4.3.2 Data Generation and Plotting

At the very beginning of this chapter, we gave a brief introduction to some of the data-handling and plotting programs included with *Radiance*. Let's look now at how these programs can be combined with shell scripting to do specific kinds of lighting analysis.

Let's take a simple example of a rectangular room over which we want to compute illuminance levels at the workplane (height = 0.75 meter). The room dimensions are 3 by 5 meters, with the origin at one corner of the floor and the rest of the floor in the positive quadrant of the *xy* plane.[10] The compiled scene is stored in *room.oct*, and our script looks like this:

```
#!/bin/csh -f
#
# Plot a 4x6 grid of lux values.
#
cnt 4 6 \
        | rcalc -e '$1=3*($1+.5)/4;$2=5*($2+.5)/6' \
                -e '$3=1;$4=0;$5=0;$6=1' \
        | rtrace -h -I -ovp -ab 1 $* room.oct \
        | rcalc -e '$1=$4;$2=$5' \
                -e '$3=179*($1*.265+$2*.670+$3*.065)' \
        > values.dat
set xv=(`cnt 4 | rcalc -e '$1=3*($1+.5)/4'`)
set cv=(A B C D)
# Put out the plot file
cat << _EOF_
include=curve.plt
title="Lux vs. Position"
xlabel="Y Position (meters)"
ylabel="Workplane Illuminance (lux)"
legend="X Position"
_EOF_
# One curve per row (X value)
foreach i (1 2 3 4)
        echo "$cv[$i]label=$xv[$i]"
        echo $cv[$i]data=
        rcalc -e 'eq(a,b):if(a-b+1e-7,b-a+1e-7,-1)' \
                -e 'cond=eq($1,'"$xv[$i])" \
                -e '$1=$2;$2=$3' values.dat
        echo \;
end
```

The first long command in this file computes a 4-by-6 grid of illuminance values using **rtrace** and any rendering options passed to the script on the command line and converting from the radiance output units of watts/steradian/m^2 to lumens/m^2

10. We could use the **dayfact** script to compute this for us, be we want to plot the results with bgraph rather than look at the contour plots from falsecolor.

(lux) using the standard conversion factors. The addition of *xy* positions at the beginning of each record is used later to pick out the four rows to plot as separate curves. The output of the whole script is a bgraph plot file, which can be converted to PostScript or displayed under X11 like this:

```
% doplot -av .2 .2 .2 | bgraph > plot.mta
% x11meta plot.mta &      # X11 display
% psmeta  plot.mta | lpr # Print w/ lpr
```

Here we have named our script file `doplot` and made it executable beforehand with

```
% chmod +x doplot
```

Another thing to notice in this script is the assignment of the array variable `cv`, which gets the output of a command that computes the *x* coordinates of our sample points. The C-shell has some shortcomings in its ability to quote and separate arguments, and more complicated tasks quickly become difficult to follow. For this reason, we recommend using other shells such as the Bourne shell or Tcl [Ous94] when the going gets tough.

4.4 Advanced Examples

Let's look now at some scripting techniques for solving a couple of very different problems. In the first problem, we wish to place airplanes on the tarmac of an airport model. In the second problem, we want to animate changes in an electrochromic glazing system.

4.4.1 Plane Placement Problem

For our airport model, we have some aerial photography showing the layout of our runways, taken on a sunny day. We want to apply this in our scene description as a pattern, but, unfortunately, the photographs include images of the planes that happened to be there at the time. This would not be a problem, except that a low-altitude view of the tarmac with this pattern shows all the planes flattened on the runway. What we want to do is replace these flat planes with 3D models, then erase the original plane images using an image editor. Assuming we want the 3D plane models in the same positions, how do we go about determining what these positions are and place our models accordingly?

The method we arrived at was to generate a high-resolution *Radiance* rendering of the airport from above that shows all the planes we wish to replace in the original pattern. We then display this picture with ximage, and pass the output to rtrace to recompute ray intersections with the tarmac. The command looks like this:

```
% ximage airport_aerial.pic \
      | rtrace -h -op airport.oct \
      | lam - - > plane.pos
```

The output of the ximage command is the ray origin and direction for each pixel in the picture where the middle mouse button is pressed. For each plane, we press the middle mouse button first on the nose and second on the tail so we know the position, size, and orientation. These rays must then go to rtrace, which computes the actual intersection points with the tarmac, and these go into lam to join every two points into one line in the file, so we have one plane per record in *plane.pos*.

After this task is completed, we can go about positioning our actual plane models in the scene. We actually have three plane models to work with: a Boeing 737 for small planes, a Douglas DC-10 for medium planes, and a Boeing 747 for large planes. The 737 is approximately 30 meters in length, the DC-10 is about 56 meters, and the 747 is about 79 meters. Therefore, we use the following criteria in determining which model to use:

length < 43 meters:
  use Boeing 737 model.

43 meters ≤ length < 67 meters:
  use Douglas DC-10 model.

length ≥ 67 meters:
  use Boeing 747 model.

We know we will have to apply a scaling factor, a rotation, and a translation to each plane model. Since there will be many copies of each plane, we decide to use the *instance* primitive to minimize memory requirements in our scene. Our output format for rcalc looks like this:

```
############# plane.fmt ############
void instance $(name).${recno}
13 $(name).oct -t ${-nose} 0 0
               -s ${ sf } -rz ${ rz }
               -t ${ nx } ${ ny } ${ nz }
0
0
```

Our file to compute the transformation looks like this:

```
{ ----------- pxfm.cal ------------- }
{
      Compute plane transformation.
      Assumes that plane starts out with nose
      in positive x direction, z is up.

      Define for this plane model:
            nose - x coordinate of nose
            tail - x coordinate of tail
}
{ scene position coordinates }
nx = $1; ny = $2; nz = $3;
tx = $4; ty = $5; tz = $6;
{ plane length }
plen = sqrt((nx-tx)^2+(ny-ty)^2);
{ scale factor }
sf = plen / (nose-tail);
{ Z rotation }
rz = -180/PI * atan2(ny-ty, nx-tx);
```

Our plane position generator will then have three rcalc commands, one for each plane type:

```
#!/bin/csh -f
#
# putplanes
#
# Generate planes from position file,
# which should have 2 3D points per line;
# the first point is the nose and
# second point is the tail.
#
# Our 737 planes:
rcalc -s name=737 -e 'nose:12.3;tail:-18.1' \
      -e 'cond=43-plen' \
      -f pxfm.cal -o plane.fmt $1
```

```
# Our DC-10 planes:
rcalc -s name=dc10 -e 'nose:27.4;tail:-28.3' \
      -e 'cond=if(43-plen,-1,67-plen)' \
      -f pxfm.cal -o plane.fmt $1

# Our 747 planes:
rcalc -s name=747 -e 'nose:36.9;tail:-42.2' \
      -e 'cond=if(67-plen,-1,1)' \
      -f pxfm.cal -o plane.fmt $1
```

Note the assignments of the `cond` variable according to the criteria we established earlier. This command can then be executed on the command line directly, or put into our scene file like this:

```
!putplanes plane.pos
```

Remember to set the executable bit on `putplanes` first with **chmod**.

4.4.2 Electrochromic Glazing Animation

In this example, we wish to generate an animation of an office scene from a single viewpoint, where the transmittance of a pane of electrochromic glass is changed in controlled response to the sun's coming out from behind the clouds (see the Website *radsite.lbl.gov/electro/*). As input, we have the office model and the following table showing the transmittance as a function of voltage and time, and the fraction of sunshine making it through the clouds.

```
################## anim1.tab ##################
Vtime Rtime   Red     Green   Blue    Volts  Sun
0     0       0.743   0.786   0.458    0     0
0.1   0.1     0.586   0.687   0.435    0     0.15
# controls react to solar emergence
0.33  0.33    0.443   0.588   0.410    1.3   1
0.45  0.45    0.297   0.471   0.376    1.3   1
0.68  0.68    0.184   0.362   0.336    1.3   1
1.05  1.05    0.0998  0.259   0.289    1.3   1
1.74  1.74    0.0488  0.176   0.240    1.3   1
2.85  2.85    0.0224  0.117   0.195    1.3   1
4.6   4.6     0.0100  0.0769  0.155    1.3   1
4.7   7.62    0.0052  0.0543  0.127    1.3   1
5    17.6     0.0026  0.0366  0.100    1.3   1
5.1  17.7     0.0026  0.0361  0.100    1.3   1
```

```
5.2   17.8    0.0026  0.0362  0.100   1.3    0.15
# controls react to solar obscuration
5.3   17.9    0.0052  0.0543  0.127  -0.3   0
5.43  18.03   0.0100  0.0769  0.155  -0.3   0
5.58  18.18   0.0224  0.1172  0.195  -0.3   0
5.88  18.48   0.0488  0.1769  0.240  -0.3   0
6.29  18.89   0.0998  0.259   0.289  -0.3   0
6.72  19.32   0.184   0.362   0.336  -0.3   0
7.15  19.75   0.297   0.471   0.376  -0.3   0
7.62  20.22   0.443   0.588   0.410  -0.3   0
8.05  20.65   0.586   0.687   0.435  -0.3   0
# full bleaching, voltage returns to zero
9.7   22.3    0.743   0.786   0.458   0     0
9.8   22.3    0.743   0.786   0.458   0     0
```

Animl.tab shows the progression of our animation, with the video time (lapse) on the left, the actual time next, and then the transmittance coefficients, input voltage, and fraction of sun penetration.

We could simply rerender the entire scene at each time step as the glass transmittance gradually changes from clear to dark, but since the lighting can be broken into linear components, it is much faster to render the components separately beforehand and recombine them with appropriate coefficients.

Our scene is shown in Figure 4.9. There are three illumination components we need to separate: the direct solar component, the sky component, and the monitor screen. We assume that the sky distribution and intensity do not change with the appearance and disappearance of the sun behind a cloud, and that the monitor is unaffected by changes to the glazing transmittance.

To render the three component pictures, we modify our scene so that the first version has a sun and no sky description (and no window), the second has a sky with no sun (and no window), and the third has no sun or sky but a window (for reflection) and the glow of the monitor screen.

As we can see from *Animl.tab*, both our video time (lapse) values and our actual elapsed times are at irregular intervals. We want our video to track the time lapse values, but we need a method to interpolate these irregular points. Fortunately, the tabfunc program does exactly this with the -i option:

```
% tabfunc -i rt tr tg tb 0 sm < animl.tab \
      animl.cal
```

Figure 4.9 Our electrochromics demonstration scene. The rendering can be separated into three components: the sun (not shown), the sky, and the monitor screen.

The first input column is not named, because video time serves as our independent variable. We use the null identifier 0 for the voltage column, since we do not plan to use this data in our animation. If we look at the *anim1.cal* output of tabfunc, we see some obscure and difficult-to-read function definitions. Handing this file to calc or rcalc, though, we can get back our original values and interpolated values between. Try the following simple command to compute the elapsed time and average (photopic) transmittance as a function of video time:

```
% rcalc -f anim1.cal -e '$1=rt($1)' \
      -e '$2=27*tr($1)+67*tg($1)+6*tb($1)'
```

If we enter the video time value for the fifth record on the standard input, 0.68 minutes, we will get an elapsed time of 0.68 and an average transmittance of 31%. If we enter 5.58 minutes, we get 18.18 minutes and 9.6% transmittance, which corresponds to the sixteenth entry in our table. Next, we can enter a video time of 4.9 minutes and get an elapsed time of 14.27 minutes and a transmittance of 3.6%. This corresponds to values interpolated linearly between the tenth and eleventh table entries.

After we have rendered our three component pictures, we need to combine them in the appropriate way for each video time increment. Assuming we are computing only every tenth video frame, our time increment is 1/3 second at 30 frames/second, and our animation command looks like this:

```
% cnt 1764 | rcalc -e 't=$1/60' -f anim1.cal \
        -e 'T=27*tr(t)+67*tg(t)+6*tb(t)' \
        -o animcom.fmt | sh -x
```

The total video time, 9.8 minutes, seems extremely long for a sequence showing the sun coming out from behind a cloud and then going back again, and indeed we found the result to be boring in the extreme, so we readjusted the actual frame time to about 1/4 of the original. The number of frames (1764) was probably overkill in the end.

If we examine the above command, we notice that the final output of rcalc is passed to the Bourne shell, where the real work is done. In fact, we have hidden most of what is going on here in the output format file, *animcom.fmt:*

```
: Starting frame ${recno} ------------------
pcomb  -c ${tr(t)} ${tg(t)} ${tb(t)} sky_fin.pic \
       -c ${tr(t)} ${tg(t)} ${tb(t)} \
       -s ${sm(t)} sun fin.pic \
       mon_fin.pic > temp.pic
pcond -h temp.pic \
       | pcompos -l "${t}min. Tvis=${T}%" - 0 0 \
       | ra_avs \
       | compress > anim1/ec_${recno}.avs.Z
rm -f temp.pic
```

This shows an interesting and very powerful method of constructing scripts. By having rcalc produce the commands the shell executes, we gain much greater control over command arguments. Looking at the output of the rcalc command without the final pass to `sh -x`, we see records that look like this:

```
: Starting frame       13 ------------------
pcomb  -c 0.524684 0.644135 0.424785 sky_fin.pic \
       -c 0.524684 0.644135 0.424785 \
       -s 0.717391 sun_fin.pic \
        mon_fin.pic > temp.pic
pcond -h temp.pic \
       | pcompos -l "0.2min. Tvis=59.87%" - 0 0 \
```

```
        | ra_avs \
        | compress > animl/ec_13.avs.Z
rm -f temp.pic
```

Let's examine this sequence, which is similar to the sequence produced for each frame of the animation. The first call to pcomb applies our transmittance coefficient to the sky component picture, and both the transmittance and the independent solar coefficient are applied to the sun component picture. No coefficients are applied to the monitor picture because it is not affected by solar obscuration or window transmittance. This combined picture is then processed for human vision by pcond, and passed to pcompos to have an appropriate label attached. The final picture is then passed to `ra_avs` and `compress` to convert it to a compressed AVS file for subsequent transfer to video.

4.5 Conclusion

We have presented examples of *Radiance* scripting techniques to give a flavor and sense of the possibilities available with the UNIX toolbox model. Without ever writing a line of C code, one can do almost anything imaginable by combining the various rendering, filtering, and utility programs included in *Radiance*. Combining this knowledge with the C-shell and other command interpreters, we can create new command scripts that permanently extend the functionality of our system for ourselves and our fellow users.

PART II

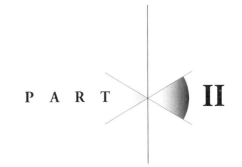

APPLICATIONS

CHAPTER 5

Lighting Analysis

by Charles Ehrlich

This chapter focuses on the accurate modeling and simulation of architectural environments for conducting real-world lighting analyses. We will present examples showing how to collect accurate data about material characteristics, how to model complex luminaires, how to set up advanced lighting analyses, and how to convincingly present the results to your client. Although the focus of this chapter is lighting analysis, the data collection techniques presented at the beginning are relevant to all applications of *Radiance*. In other chapters, you have gained a working knowledge of the use of various *Radiance* material types, including *plastic, metal, light,* and *glow.* You are comfortable with the UNIX command-line environment and the suite of tools available in *Radiance,* including **oconv**, **rview**, **rpict**, and **pfilt**. It is also helpful if you are generally familiar with the use of a high-end painting package such as Adobe Photoshop or CorelDraw.

This chapter, like each of the applications chapters that follows, is intended to be understandable with minimal reference to other parts of the book. However, you may find that Chapter 11, Direct Calculation, and Chapter 12, Indirect Calculation, help you to better understand how *Radiance* performs its calculations. The Reference Manual on the CD-ROM is by far the most important resource, because it lists all the details about *Radiance* primitives and their attributes. The topic of converting light source distribution data from IES-format files is also discussed in other chapters; here, we will discuss in some detail the creation of the candlepower distribution curves for light sources when you do not have luminaire photometry available on electronic media.

This chapter is structured somewhat differently from the previous chapters in that it is a discussion of *Radiance* modeling methods and not a step-by-step tutorial. The figures and example input files are used to illustrate the textual discussion. Therefore, there is a less cohesive flow between the disparate topics covered in the chapter. If you find yourself a bit overwhelmed by all the minutiae, we recommend stepping back and perhaps reviewing one of the tutorial chapters before getting too lost. And to help you decide whether *Radiance* is the right tool for your lighting analysis needs, this chapter begins with a discussion of how you might perform a needs analysis.

Does Radiance Fit Your Needs?

How do you decide whether *Radiance* is the appropriate tool for the analysis of your specific illuminated environment? To answer this question, you need to know what you get from *Radiance* as opposed to the other simulation tools at your disposal. You also need to know how much you need to learn about your specific illuminated environment and how much money you have to spend on computer software and hardware. And, most important, you need to know what input requirements are placed on you.

Most people are familiar with the process of reading software reviews to learn about the features available in the latest versions of their favorite programs, but few have spent time conducting a needs analysis. You need to conduct a needs analysis to minimize the effect of the "gee-whiz" factor on your decision to purchase or use any particular software. Deciding which tool to use involves the mapping of your information needs to the tool that most appropriately provides the features you need, with the fewest unnecessary bells, whistles, and costs.

If you are new to the field of lighting analysis, you also need to obtain a list of available software to choose from, because, as we all know, seeing the range of available features informs us of the kinds of features that might be useful in the future. Toward this end, you can look for the latest annual IESNA Software Survey issue of *Lighting Design and Application*.[11] The first thing that you will notice is that

11. *Lighting Design and Application*, vol. 26, no. 9, September 1996, p. 39, contains the latest Lighting Design Software Survey and Luminaire Design Software Survey. Website: *www.iesna.org*. IESNA, 120 Wall Street, 17th Floor, New York, NY 10005. Reprints: 212-248-5000, x111.

there are two sections: lighting design and luminaire design. *Radiance* is not a luminaire design tool. For that task, you must use one of the other tools listed in the second section of the survey.

Complex luminaire modeling is presented in this chapter insofar as it is necessary to create a physically accurate simulation of an illuminated environment. Special modeling techniques must be used so that the resulting analysis will look right when viewed in a full-color rendering and will also provide accurate numerical results. If only one of these two features is important to you, then perhaps *Radiance* is not the appropriate tool for your task. Another factor that must be considered is cost. *Radiance* for the UNIX platform is available at no cost from Lawrence Berkeley National Laboratory via anonymous ftp for the foreseeable future. This is not to say that there are no costs associated with the introduction of *Radiance* into your work flow. Training is vital, expensive, and often found in hard-to-reach places. If you have never worked in a UNIX environment, you will probably have to learn to install and administer UNIX and to compile the *Radiance* source code before you can even begin learning how to use the tool. (The DOS version of *Radiance* is discussed below.)

There are many commercial rendering programs that can create astonishingly real-looking images. It is important to keep in mind that most rendering programs use algorithms that are not based on the physical properties of light and surfaces; consequently, when you use them, artistic talent is needed to create visually realistic renderings. The fact that most other rendering programs produce an image that looks like an actual built environment is purely coincidental and, in our opinion, highly suspect. If purely artistic photorealism is your primary concern, *Radiance* may still be appropriate for you if the cost of these other rendering programs (or the cost of the artistic talent and computer hardware that they demand) is prohibitive, or if they present an a priori limitation on the size or complexity of the type of environment that you can render. Pay close attention to the other rendering programs' limits on number of light sources, number of surfaces, orientation and shape of surfaces, and types of surface and material primitives supported. Also inquire about the relationship between rendering time and increasing numbers of surfaces and light sources. Furthermore, if you intend to use a rendering tool to depict an actual built environment, with *Radiance* you can concentrate on accurately modeling the scene rather than wasting your time finding artistic workarounds for other rendering programs' limitations.

As we have mentioned earlier, the authoritative source of information about other lighting analysis software is the IESNA Software Survey published annually in *Lighting Design and Application*. Many of the programs listed there are luminaire manufacturer–supported products, provided to you at minimal cost in order to promote the sale of the manufacturer's products. A few tools have serious modeling limitations or require large amounts of RAM to be truly useful. Some tools use radiosity-based algorithms; some use ray tracing–based algorithms. Radiosity tools offer the advantage of a single calculation for all subsequent views of the same scene and include indirect light bounced off interior walls. This assumes, of course, that the lighting in the scene is view-independent (i.e., only diffuse, Lambertian surfaces are used). Also, the processing and memory requirements often increase dramatically with scene complexity. Ray tracing offers the advantage of accurately rendering specular and transparent surfaces in complex environments. However, most ray-tracing tools suffer from the inability to account for diffuse interreflections. Radiosity-based hybrid models such as Lightscape offer a postprocessing algorithm for specular highlights, but continue to have very expensive hardware requirements and strict 3D surface geometry modeling requirements. Ray tracing–based hybrid tools such as *Radiance* offer specular and transparent surfaces and accurate direct and indirect lighting calculations.

Since the summer of 1995, a DOS version of *Radiance* has been available as part of the ADELINE software package. ADELINE—Advanced Day and Electric Lighting New Environment—is a product of the International Energy Agency, Solar Heating and Cooling, Task XXI initiative and is actively being developed as a multinational collaboration. ADELINE is a strong first attempt to link together several related software packages with a comprehensible user interface for the purpose of designing daylighted spaces. The graphical user interface is a Microsoft Windows–like DOS program that connects the various programs together through pull-down menus. Included with the package are SCRIBE, a simple 3D modeling program; SUPERLITE, a radiosity-based daylighting tool by Lawrence Berkeley National Laboratory; and the DOS version of *Radiance*. It also includes supporting programs for importing DXF files and exporting various kinds of data from SUPERLITE to the DOE-2 thermal simulation program. The internationally agreed upon price is $450 US. Check the ADELINE Website for more information: *radsite.lbl.gov/adeline/HOME.html.*

In our opinion, the use of *Radiance* for accurate architectural simulations is meaningful and worthwhile only if two or more of the following conditions are present:

- Concern about the distribution of light from a specific luminaire within a specific illuminated environment
- Concern about the physical accuracy of the image
- Concern about human visual performance, including visual discomfort and glare
- For simulations: complexity beyond the capabilities of radiosity-based simulation tools

- For renderings: complexity beyond the capabilities of other powerful rendering tools
- A desire to learn something about light and architecture (and *Radiance*) and sufficient time to do so
- Unwillingness to spend thousands of dollars on software that does not perform all the necessary tasks involved in accurate lighting design and analysis

Major Hurdles

Everyone agrees that *Radiance* has a very gradual learning curve. This chapter is structured around the four major hurdles that we have overcome during our learning process. The four tasks involved in completing a successful lighting analysis with *Radiance* are collecting and measuring data, modeling complex luminaires, performing validated analyses, and presenting results to a possibly naive audience. The easiest of these tasks is collecting the necessary data about surface material properties from the responsible parties and getting them to commit to their material choices. The first section of this chapter contains a detailed discussion of various methods for collecting this real-world data so that you will not get stuck in the "garbage in, garbage out" syndrome.

The next easiest task is the modeling of complex luminaires, or the modeling of luminaires for which no IESNA candlepower distribution data are available in electronic format. The second section of this chapter goes into detail about the use of "impostor geometry" to accurately model both the geometric appearance of a luminaire and the luminous appearance of the luminaire as its light interacts with other surfaces in your scene.

The second most difficult task is setting up and performing analyses using the array of tools provided with *Radiance*. Paramount to the success of such analyses is meticulous and repeated validation of the model with the preliminary results. This process requires a user who is rigorously skeptical about all data that might present themselves. The analysis isn't done until all the garbage input has been corrected and validated. The third section presents several common analysis methods and offers some tips for validating your model and recognizing garbage input data.

By far, the most difficult task that we have faced in our lighting analysis projects has been the education of our clients about the value and meaning of an accurate lighting simulation, which all too often happens when we are presenting final results from the simulation. Your challenge, if you decide to use *Radiance* in your routine lighting analyses, is to become so thoroughly knowledgeable about physically based lighting analysis principles and the physics of light that you can convincingly explain in five minutes or less the basic difference between a *Radiance* image and an image from a generic architectural rendering package. If you are new to the field of physically based rendering, you may find the *Radiosity Bibliography* to be a useful resource.[12] The final section of this chapter discusses some of the issues you may face when performing and presenting *Radiance*-based lighting analyses.

5.1 Data Collection

Before you learn advanced luminaire modeling and analysis techniques, you need to learn real-world data collection techniques. These include finding and understanding architectural drawings for geometric data and using special devices or techniques to measure or approximate surface reflectance and chromaticity data. Some of these techniques involve the use of readily available tools such as the MacBeth Color Checker Chart and a camera, while other methods require the purchase of more expensive and esoteric equipment such as the Colortron by Light Source Images, Inc. Don't despair if you don't have the capital to invest in expensive hardware, because one of the techniques we present uses nothing more than a calibrated greyscale chart and your computer's properly adjusted RGB monitor.

5.1.1 Tools of the Trade

This chapter presents a number of tools, both hardware and software, that you may find worthwhile to have on hand. The examples provided will refer to these tools by their manufacturers' common names when the specific features of one device are being elucidated, and will refer to the generic device names when no specific features are important. The use of any particular named product by no means implies a recommendation of that product or a guarantee that it will work for your particular purpose. The names and addresses you'll need to find these devices are given in the Supplemental Information section at the end of this chapter.

5.1.2 Use Methods Appropriate to the Task

A relevant corollary to the rule "garbage in, garbage out" is "Expectations of simulation output accuracy should not exceed the accuracy of the input data." For example, if surface reflectance without color is being provided as input for *Radiance*

---

12. *Radiosity Bibliography*, maintained by Ian Ashdown, is available electronically from *http://www.ledulite.com/library-/rrt.htm* and *ftp://ftp.ledalite.com/pub/radbib97.bib.*

materials, the usefulness of modeling light sources with specific *xyY* chromaticities is questionable unless it is for academic purposes or for demonstration of optical principles. Likewise, if surface reflectance alone is important to you and you are not interested in the accurate representation of color, there is no need to invest in expensive equipment for the collection of surface chromaticity, although color does affect photometric results owing to the use of the RGB system.

This exercise will revolve around the development of a materials file for a typical open-plan office space. The plan of this office space is presented in Section 5.2, Luminaire Modeling. We will name this file *office.mat*. The *.mat* extension is a convention we use so that we can distinguish files containing only materials from those containing surfaces and materials. Your first task is to create the skeleton of your materials file with your favorite text editor and write down some simple descriptions of the various surfaces that you think are important for your analysis. The more prevalent a particular surface is in the room, the more heavily its characteristics will affect the accuracy of the simulation. Look through manufacturer catalogs for as much data as you can find. Gather samples of these materials and label them or identify them with a common name in your *office.mat* file. Below is an example text file that could be a skeleton of your project materials file.

```
## office.mat
# white ceiling tiles
# off-white paint for walls
# maroon cloth partitions
# dark blue carpet
# dark maroon baseboards
# light wooden door
# dark wood desk surface
# brass door knob
# metallic window frames
# grey tinted vision glass
# interior transom glass
```

Each of the common names of the surface materials in your project is a comment in your materials file. Each comment will be followed by the appropriate *Radiance* primitive.

5.1.3 Estimating Average Surface Reflectance and Transmittance

If surface color is not important for your simulations, there is certainly no reason to complicate your *Radiance* model with surface color information. Material surface characteristics based solely on the average hemispherical reflectance will allow you to accurately predict illuminance levels and generate handsome images. A simple, rule-based estimate of the average reflectance and transmittance will suffice for most architectural applications. The more you know about the physics of surface optical properties, the more accurate your estimates will be. Estimates of average surface properties are also useful for subjecting data provided by manufacturers, or collected by more advanced techniques, to a reasonability test.

The best way to approach the analysis of surface materials for *Radiance* is to start with the most general surface characteristics such as reflectance, and move on to more specific surface characteristics, such as specularity and roughness. The four most often used *Radiance* material types for architectural applications are plastic, metal, light, and *glass*. In the first exercises in this data collection methods section on surface reflectance, we assume you are measuring the properties of reflective media that can be modeled with plastic and metal. Light and glass are discussed later, in Sections 5.1.11 and 5.1.12.

Greyscale Chart Analysis Method

The precise name for the unit of reflectance that *Radiance* uses for input is *hemispherical reflectance,* which refers to the ratio of total flux leaving a surface to the total flux incident upon a surface as measured by a spectroradiometric device when illuminated by an equal-energy light source. We have had good success in estimating diffuse surface reflectance by comparing the surface with a greyscale chart. (See example in Figure 5.1.) You can purchase a greyscale chart from many photography and graphic arts stores, or you can assemble one yourself using neutral-density reflectance samples that you might find in a color palette from a graphic arts ink

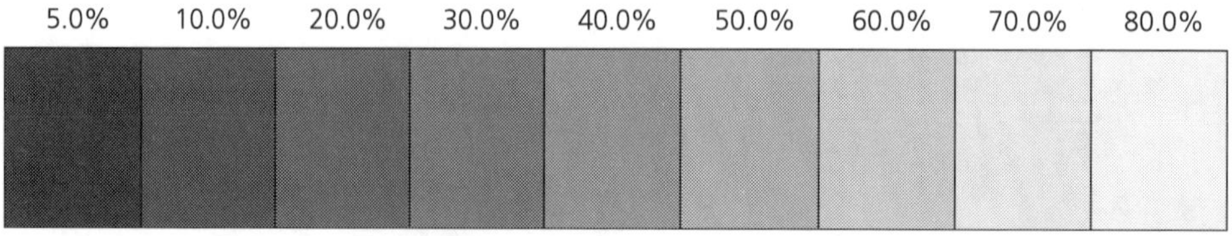

Figure 5.1 An example greyscale chart. (Caution: Do not use this chart to measure your samples, because the printing ink density is unknown.)

supplier. Lighting designers who may prefer to use the Munsell system are advised that the *luminous reflectance* scale of the Munsell system does not use the appropriate units for *Radiance*.[13]

While a greyscale chart assembled with samples that are 10% whole-number reflectances will work, it does not allow as much accuracy in the darker reflectance values. Consider that a change from 80% to 70% reflectance (one increment on a whole-number, percentage greyscale chart) is a decrease of 12.5%, whereas a change from 20% to 10% reflectance is a 50% decrease. For this reason, you may wish to provide additional samples below 30% reflectance. Also remember that very few diffuse materials have a hemispherical reflectance value greater than 80%.

To use the greyscale chart you have assembled or purchased, place the chart on top of the surface of interest. Be sure that you do not see any specular reflections. Squint so that your view of the sample and the greyscale chart is blurred. Find the grey patch that most closely matches the surface brightness. If the surface brightness lies between two grey patches, estimate whether the sample is closer to one patch or the other, or whether it lies equally between the two patches. By simple interpolation, you can estimate the actual surface reflectance within 5%. Keep track of these numbers in your *office.mat* file.

```
## office.mat
## surface reflectances estimated with grey chart
# white ceiling tiles
# reflectance = .72

# bright green carpet
# reflectance = .55

# off-white paint for walls
# reflectance = .65

# maroon cloth partitions
# reflectance = .35

# dark maroon baseboards, shiny
# reflectance = .01

# light wooden door
# reflectance = .55
```

13. *The Munsell Book of Color* by the Munsell Color Company and other products are distributed by the MacBeth Corporation, New Windsor, New York.

```
# dark wood desk surface
# reflectance = .35

# metallic window frames
# reflectance = .65

# grey tinted vision glass

# interior transom glass
```

Luminance Meter Reflectance Analysis Method

If you have access to an illuminance or luminance meter, there are simple experimental methods you may prefer to use. The assumption of these simple methods is that the surface is purely diffuse, meaning that it does not reflect more light in one direction than in another. For more complex types of surfaces, the use of a spectrophotometer device that employs an integrating sphere is advisable. Because of numerous other uncertainties, this method should not be the primary method used to estimate reflectance. By placing a sample of a known reflectance next to the surface of interest, you can measure the amount of light leaving each surface and compute the reflectance based on a simple ratio between the two samples. If you are using an illuminance meter, a black cylinder placed over the probe turns it into a makeshift luminance probe. For our purposes, the units are not important as long as they are consistent between measurements. When you are using a modified illuminance meter, be sure that the "cone of view" of the device is within the bounds of the sample. Also take precautions to ensure that you are not significantly changing the amount of available light as you measure the two samples.

```
Known reflectance standard is 30% reflectance
Reflectance standard and sample illuminated by sky
Radiance of standard measured at 100 cd/m^2
Radiance of sample is 35 cd/m^2
Reflectance ρ of sample is:
      100/0.30 = 35/ρ
      ρ= 35 * 0.30 / 100 = 0.105
```

5.1.4 Estimating Surface Color

To use this method, you will need access to a computer with an RGB monitor and a sophisticated graphics painting package that has a color picker that shows red, green, and blue values. You will need to estimate the average hemispherical reflectance (see definition above) in order to measure your estimated color. You must have a sample of the surface material that you wish to measure that is small enough to hold and easily manage next to your computer monitor. Furthermore, you need to calibrate your computer hardware and/or software to the gamma response curve of your monitor. (See the exercise in the next section called Determining Your Monitor's Gamma.) Before we begin this exercise, a word about some of the assumptions about color that *Radiance* uses is in order.

The units of color that *Radiance* uses are red, green, and blue hemispherical reflectance as measured by a radiometric device when illuminated by an equal-energy light source. These red, green, and blue values are very similar to the primary colors used in computer RGB monitors, although there is no widely accepted standard. The CIE chromaticity coordinates that *Radiance* uses to define its red, green, and blue are presented at the end of Chapter 10. Because the success of this estimation technique depends upon knowing your color monitor's output response function, you need to determine the proper gamma setting. For the PC and UNIX platforms, *Radiance* image display and conversion utilities and the public domain `xv` program have a **-g** command line option that allow you to specify the gamma correction value, and interpret the `DISPLAY_GAMMA` environment variable. A visit to the following Website is recommended before proceeding:

www-graphics.stanford.edu/gamma-corrected/gamma.html

This site discusses the way several computer platforms address the gamma issue and provides suggestions for accurately measuring and adjusting for the gamma of your monitor and computer. Keep in mind that gamma correction is cumulative when it is persistent across software applications, as in the Macintosh gamma control panel. *Radiance* also uses a gamma correction setting that is cumulative with other persistent gamma settings imposed by your computer hardware or operating system. Because the gamma setting of your monitor is so crucial to the success of this surface color estimation technique, a more in-depth discussion is provided in Section 5.1.5.

The process of estimating the color of a surface starts with launching your favorite graphics painting program and going to the color picker. (A sample screen is shown in Figure 5.2.) Hold the sample perpendicular to the monitor with one edge resting adjacent to a white area of the screen near the color picker's patch. Move in close to the monitor such that your field of view is largely influenced by the monitor and wait 10 to 15 seconds for your eyes to adapt to the color temperature of your monitor. Adjust the color picker such that the chosen color matches the sam-

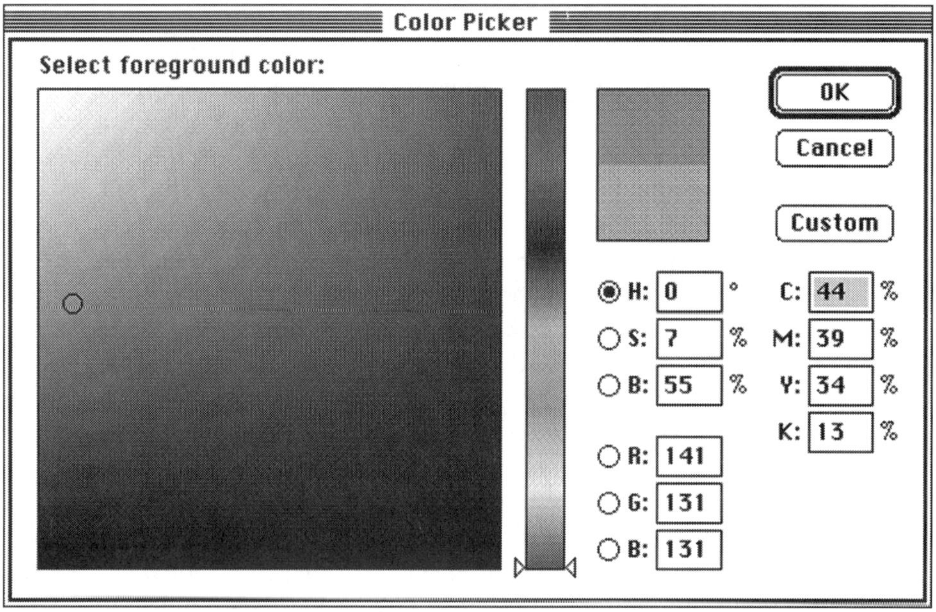

Figure 5.2 The Adobe Photoshop® Color Picker.

ple as closely as possible. This may require switching among different color-picking methods like hue, value chroma, and red, green, blue. We want to compute the corresponding red, green, and blue values for your *office.mat* file. Keep in mind that this method is susceptible to error because your sample is not being completely illuminated by the light of the monitor. The more you can eliminate ambient light, the more accurate your estimates with this method will be. This method is recommended only when no other method is available.

Determine the domain in which the red, green, and blue values are displayed. Some color pickers range from 0 to 255, while others range from 0 to 65,535. Divide the measured red, green, and blue values by the domain of your color picker and adjusted by your monitor's gamma to come up with decimal fractions of red, green, and blue. Then apply the `grey(red, green, blue)` procedure to determine the photopic reflectance of the surface material. If this computed value does not equal the average hemispherical reflectance that you estimated or measured (it will usually be different), divide the computed value by the measured value to determine a correction factor. Apply the correction factor to each of the red, green, and blue values to derive the input parameters for the *Radiance* materials plastic and metal. Recompute the photopic reflectance of the derived red, green, and blue colors to convince yourself that you did things correctly.

The example below shows how the **calc** program can be used with this method to determine the color of the off-white paint for walls. Calc is instructed to load the *Radiance* initialization file, called *rayinit.cal,* which will be located in the *Radiance lib* directory or somewhere else specified by your `RAYPATH` environment variable:

```
% calc /usr/local/lib/ray/rayinit.cal
gamma=1.8
f(x)=(x/256)^(1/gamma)
r=f(141)
g=f(131)
b=f(131)
grey(r,g,b)
$1=0.696829595
```

You have calculated that the average reflectance of the sample using only the RGB values you estimated would be 88.4%. Since you estimated that the total reflectance of the off-white paint for walls should be 72.0%, you need to determine the scaling factor for the RGB values (`$2` below) and apply this scaling to the original RGB values to come up with the final values to use in *Radiance* (`$3, $4, $5`):

```
<still within the calc session above>
.72/$1
$2=1.03325118
$2*r
$3=0.741831781
$2*g
$4=0.712125682
$2*b
$5=0.712125682
```

You are now ready to record these values into your materials file as *Radiance* primitives. This process involves choosing an appropriate name for each of your materials. One system to use is to append `_mat` to the material name to distinguish it from patterns or other potentially confusing primitive types. If this is the first time (or the hundredth time) you have created a *Radiance* material file, you will find it helpful to consult the *Radiance* Reference Manual on the CD-ROM:

```
## office.mat
## surface reflectances estimated with grey chart
## surface chromaticity estimated with RGB monitor
## and adjusted by surface reflectance with:
## grey(r,g,b) = noneg(.265*r + .670*g + .0645*b);
```

```
# white ceiling tiles, diffuse
# reflectance = .72
void plastic ceiling_tile_mat
0
0
5 0.742 0.712 0.712 0 0
# bright green carpet
# reflectance = .55
```

5.1.5 Determining Your Monitor's Gamma

Included in the *Radiance* distribution in the *ray/lib/lib* directory is the file *gamma.pic*. To determine your monitor's gamma value, first adjust your monitor's brightness and contrast settings so that the dark area surrounding the visible pixels of your screen is dark but close to becoming light with a small adjustment of brightness. Adjust the contrast setting such that white areas of the monitor are as bright as they can be while keeping the black border still truly black. Issue the command

```
% ximage -g 1 -b ray/lib/lib/gamma.pic
```

to display this image on your computer monitor. It is an image of two columns of grey values immediately adjacent to a region of black and white horizontal lines. Squint and blur your eyes as you look at the image and find the grey value on the right side that most closely matches the black and white horizontal lines on the left side. Your eyes are sufficiently blurred if you cannot distinguish individual horizontal lines. The number next to this grey value is the gamma for your monitor. To implement the gamma value for *Radiance*, set the environment variable `DISPLAY_GAMMA` equal to this value. In UNIX C-shell:

```
setenv DISPLAY_GAMMA 1.3
```

In UNIX Bourne shell:

```
DISPLAY_GAMMA=1.3
export DISPLAY_GAMMA
```

This environment variable setting can be made part of your login or boot-up sequence in the same place where the `RAYPATH` variable is set. For example, the C-shell uses a file called *.login*, the Bourne shell uses a file called *.profile* and DOS uses the *autoexec.bat* file.

What Is Gamma?

A cathode ray tube (CRT) displays graphic information by converting an analog voltage signal to pixel luminance on the phosphorescent screen. Because of the physics of the interaction between the beam of electrons and the phosphors, all CRTs exhibit a nonlinear brightness response to input voltage. The response curve usually fits a power relationship:

$$\text{display\_luminance} = \text{input\_voltage}^{\text{gamma}}$$

and is referred to as the gamma curve. A gamma of 2.5 corresponds to the response curve shown in Figure 5.3.

To correct for this nonlinear relationship, an inverse gamma function is applied to the input voltages going to the monitor. To determine whether the gamma is correctly adjusted is to verify that an input voltage of 50% corresponds to a pixel brightness that is at the midpoint of the monitor's output range. The *gamma.pic* file provided with *Radiance* in the *ray/lib/lib* directory contains carefully selected grey patches adjacent to a band of alternating 0% (black) and 100% (white) lines, shown in Figure 5.4.

When you blur your vision, the black and white stripes coalesce on your retina, allowing you to perceive an average of black and white lines. This is an accurate representation of how bright your monitor should be when a 50% grey patch is displayed. By matching one of the grey patches on the right with the perceived grey on the left, you have determined how the computer needs to adjust its analog out-

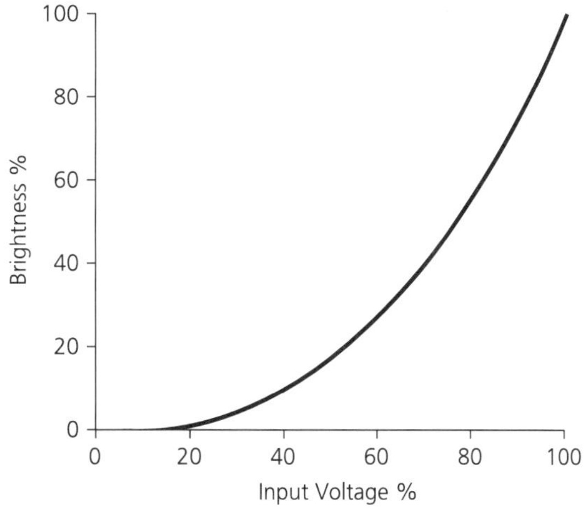

Figure 5.3 A plot of a gamma curve of 2.5.

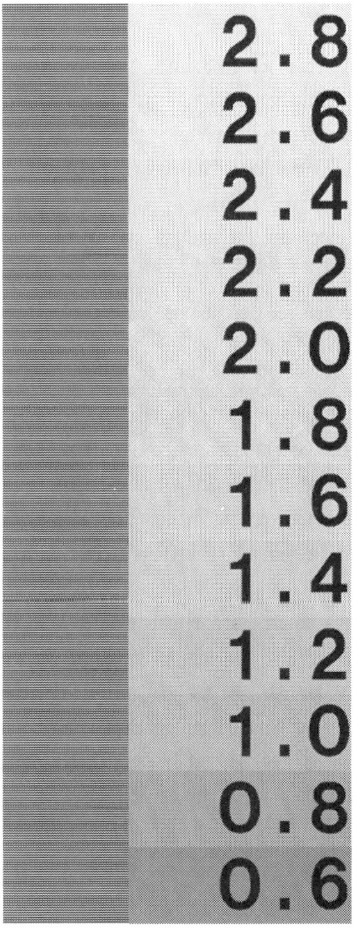

Figure 5.4 The *Radiance* gamma testing image.

put voltage signal. If you apply the corresponding gamma value to an inverse power function, a 50% grey (.5 .5 .5 RGB signal) will match your monitor's analog output of 50%.

Unlike most graphics software, *Radiance* does not adjust its stored pixel images with the gamma setting of your monitor. The **ximage** program maps these pixel values to monitor brightness by adjusting the output so that a monitor brightness is achieved. Furthermore, because a *Radiance* image contains a floating-point map of spectral radiance values, it is inappropriate to store gamma-corrected values in a

Radiance image file. Most software programs do not make this distinction, and consequently the accurate display of the resulting images becomes dependent on the particular computer monitor for which they were originally generated. If you set the `DISPLAY_GAMMA` value, *Radiance* display programs such as ximage and rview will adjust the displayed brightness of its digital images according to the inverse gamma response curve for your particular monitor while preserving the linear map of values in the image file. When you are converting *Radiance* images to other popular image formats such as TIFF or GIF, it is a good idea to know the gamma of the device to which the file is being sent and apply this correction factor to the converted TIFF or GIF image.

Some computers do not apply any gamma correction; others only partially correct monitor gamma. The details of how your particular hardware implements gamma correction are too complex for this applications chapter. The following list of URLs is provided for those who wish to explore this issue further:

www-cgi.cs.cmu.edu/afs/cs.cmu.edu/user/rwb/www/gamma.html

www-graphics.stanford.edu/gamma-corrected/gamma.html

www.seas.gwu.edu/student/gritz/gamma.html

radsite.lbl.gov/radiance/digests_html/v2n4.html#IMAGES

radsite.lbl.gov/radiance/digests_html/v2n5.2.html

radsite.lbl.gov/radiance/refer/index.html#cat5

5.1.6 Using a Luminance Meter to Measure Color

Some popular luminance meters have a *chromaticity* feature. Consult your meter's manual to learn the appropriate way to use this feature. The accuracy of data from such a meter is dependent on the lighting conditions. Applying the appropriate correction factor is left up to you. The chromaticity is usually provided in CIE *xyY* coordinates. To convert between CIE *xyY* coordinates and RGB, use the formulas in *ray/src/cal/cal/xyz_rgb.cal.* The useful function calls defined in this file are shown here:

```
{ xyz_rgb.cal (abbreviated)
compute RGB from CIE XYZ
}
R(X,Y,Z) : noneg(XYZ2RGB(0,0)*X + XYZ2RGB(0,1)*Y +
           XYZ2RGB(0,2)*Z);
G(X,Y,Z) : noneg(XYZ2RGB(1,0)*X + XYZ2RGB(1,1)*Y +
           XYZ2RGB(1,2)*Z);
B(X,Y,Z) : noneg(XYZ2RGB(2,0)*X + XYZ2RGB(2,1)*Y +
           XYZ2RGB(2,2)*Z);
```

To compute XYZ coordinates from *xyY*, we need the following formulas, executed using the calc command:

```
% calc xyz_rgb.cal
X=.34
Y=.53
myY=.523
myX=x/y*myY
myZ=(1-x-y)/y*myY
R(myX,myY,myZ)
$1=0.199308245
G(myX,myY,myZ)
$2=0.697338528
B(myX,myY,myZ)
$3=0.0443230583
```

A surface with measured *xyY* chromaticity coordinates of (.34 .53 .523) has a corresponding RGB value of (0.199 0.697 0.044). These values would be applied to a surfacc as follows:

```
## office.mat
<several lines omitted>

# bright green carpet
# reflectance = .523
void plastic bright_green_carpet_mat
0
0
5 0.199 0.697 0.044 0 0
```

5.1.7 What to Do When You Don't Have Material Samples

In the early phases of architectural design, it is very rare to know exactly which material will eventually be used in the space you are designing. Most often, you will have to rely on broad estimates and vague notions of color conveyed to you by the building owner. In these situations, we advise you not to request, or wait for, final material samples to be delivered. In the early design phase, it is safest to model your scene in grey to avoid any possibility that the designer or building owner will find your chosen color objectionable. A successful color scheme that we use for interior rooms in the early design phase includes only shades of neutral grey for the walls, floor, ceiling, and partitions, plus a brown wood-like color for desks and doors.

Using brass for all door hardware and dark black for baseboards adds just enough detail and color accent to convince the average rendering client that the images represent a simulation of an actual built environment. On several occasions, we have had to deal with stone-faced rejection of our renderings because the building owner or designer had a strong knee-jerk reaction to the designer's (or our) choice of color for a particular building material.

Yet another method for estimating material properties if you do not have material samples to work from is to use a library of predefined materials. Although the use of a list of materials is discouraged, in some cases having such a list to consult is valuable as a starting point. A list of common building materials is included with the *Radiance* and ADELINE packages in *ray/lib/lib/material.dat* and *adeline\plink\material.txt*, respectively. This list can also be found on the CD-ROM. The *IESNA Lighting Handbook* [IES93a] also includes a list of reflectances and transmittances of common building and lighting materials.

5.1.8 Using Calibrated Input Devices (Macbethcal)

A method of measuring the reflectance and chromaticity of material surfaces that is one step more sophisticated than the greyscale chart and RGB color monitor color picker method is the use of the **macbethcal** program. This program was developed to address the need to accurately capture color photographs of instrument panels in an air traffic control tower. The macbethcal program is the only public-domain, low-tech (not requiring special hardware) calibration method known to this author and can be used to calibrate all kinds of input and output devices and media, including photographic film, cameras, scanners, RGB monitors, film recorders, and lighting conditions. The use of macbethcal requires the purchase of a MacBeth Color Checker Chart, available at most professional photography supply stores for $30 to $50 US, or directly from the MacBeth Corporation in New Windsor, New York. Although reading the manual page is adequate preparation for you to begin using macbethcal, some discussion of the program here may help you get started using it more quickly and easily.

The idea employed in macbethcal is that if each link in the chain of image capture devices and media were calibrated to a known standard, fairly accurate and reliable real-world data could be measured from otherwise noncalibrated devices. The MacBeth Color Checker Chart was used as the reference standard because it is widely used, accepted, and readily available. A list of factors that influence the chromaticity of a surface to be measured with this method includes ambient and direct lighting conditions, camera flash, camera lens, camera exposure, film speed, film manufacturer, developing process, print paper media, scanner, scanner calibration parameters, and scanner exposure. The procedure for measuring surface chromaticity with a calibrated device is outlined here:

1. Note the lighting conditions and take steps to keep them constant during the photography session. Sky light or a good-quality camera flash is recommended instead of incandescent or fluorescent lighting.
2. Note the type of film being used and determine an exposure to be used for this batch of measurements. Keep the exposure and camera zoom constant.
3. Take a photograph of the MacBeth Color Checker Chart with the chart and camera in the same location and orientation that will be required for subsequent photographs of the surface materials.
4. Arrange as many of the surface material samples as possible in the same location as where the MacBeth Color Checker Chart was located. You may wish to apply labels to the samples for easy reference later.
5. Without changing any of the camera settings, photograph the arrangement of material samples.
6. Repeat steps 4 and 5 as necessary to capture all materials.
7. Develop the film at a reputable film developing establishment, using glossy print film (if you plan to scan the photograph rather than the negative). If you are using a slide scanner, slide film will also work, though negatives are preferred slightly for their greater dynamic range.
8. Investigate the software that controls your scanner hardware to determine the optimum settings to defeat any default calibration or automatic exposure compensation features. Write these settings down and save them to a default file, if possible, for reuse later.
9. Scan in photographs, negatives, or slides as required. If you are using a digital camera, steps 6–8 are meaningless. Save the scan of the MacBeth Color Checker Chart in a file called *mbscan.tif.* The *.tif* extension implies the use of the TIFF image file format.
10. Convert the scanner's TIFF (or similar) files into *Radiance* format with the corresponding image conversion program, such as `ra_tiff -r` for TIFF files, or `ra_t16 -r` for 16-bit Targa files, and so on. See the `ra_`*xxx* manual pages for more information. If you apply any nonstandard gamma correction during the image file conversion process, be sure to apply the same gamma correction the next time this calibrated device is used.
11. Create a calibration file for your image capture system using the scan of the photograph of the MacBeth Color Checker Chart. This involves the following commands:

```
ra_tiff -r mbscan.tif mbscan.pic
macbethcal -d debug.pic mbscan.pic my_scanner.cal
```

12. To find out how well the calibration process worked, view the *debug.pic* file to see an image with each of the scanned-in, uncalibrated MacBeth Color Checker Chart colors on the left, inset with the target color in the center and the corrected color on the right. Read the manual page for more information on how to evaluate the debug image.

```
ximage debug.pic
```

13. Apply the calibration to each of the remaining scanned images of material surfaces.

```
ra_tiff -r samples.tif | pcomb -f my_scanner.cal - \
> samples_calib.pic
```

14. View the calibrated samples image(s) with the ximage program and be prepared to write down the red, green, and blue values:

```
ximage samples_calib.pic
```

15. Move the cursor on top of each material and in turn, with the left mouse button, drag a rectangle across the color patch, then press the letter "C" on the keyboard. This computes the average RGB value of the area under the rectangle and displays it on the screen. Write down these values or type them into a file that associates the RGB triplet with the corresponding material name. Save these values in your material definitions file, *office.mat*.

```
## office.mat
## surface reflectances estimated with grey chart
## surface chromaticity estimated with RGB monitor
## and adjusted by surface reflectance with:
## grey(r,g,b) = noneg(.265*r + .670*g + .0645*b);
## chromaticity measured with calibrated photograph
## using macbethcal-generated file: my_scanner.cal

<some lines omitted>

## Material measured with scanned photographs
## calibrated with my_scanner.cal.
void plastic oak_wood_desk_mat
0
0
5 .3012 .4216 .2322 0 0
```

This method is recommended mostly for scanning patterns. Though it may be used as described to approximate colors, the absolute reflectance will not be accurate unless exactly the same lighting and exposure are used for the calibration shot and the angle of the samples and the Color Checker Chart are the same. For these and other reasons, the only method we can strongly recommend for measuring colors requires a calibrated spectrophotometer.

5.1.9 Using a Spectrophotometer

For the truly committed *Radiance* enthusiast, there is no better device to use for measuring surface material chromaticity than a spectrophotometer. There are many, many kinds of spectrophotometers, ranging in price from $1000 US to $100,000 US or more. Most of these devices require the use of a computer and special software, either to control the device itself or to download the data after measurements have been taken. Spectrometers that use an integrating sphere are more reliable for measuring the total hemispherical reflectance than those that do not. This discussion will be limited to two representative devices, in the low and middle price ranges.

On the low end, the Colortron, by Light Source Images Technologies, provides a 32-band sampling of your material using a tungsten light source in a 4-inch-long by 3-inch-tall, lightweight, hand-held enclosure. Its light source and sensor are focused on a small measurement patch, but it does not use an integrating sphere. It can measure diffuse reflectance (an estimate of total hemispherical reflectance) of matte and specular samples. It requires the use of a Macintosh or Windows computer with an RGB monitor to operate the device and collect data from the device. The user interface is flexible, well designed, easy to use, and actually fun. Unpublished tests performed on the device at Lawrence Berkeley National Laboratory (LBNL) found the device to be fairly linear; there were some concerns about the surrounding environment. While the manual does not provide any suggestions for controlling the environment surrounding the sample to be measured, LBNL tests showed that measurements could be adversely affected by the immediate surroundings. It is advisable to construct a simple black felt box in which to perform the calibration and measurements with the Colortron. When the material samples have been collected, the user interface provides a means to assemble a library of materials that can be saved for later reference or exported to a tab-delimited ASCII text file for use with *Radiance*. The output should be calibrated to an equal-energy light source and not to any of the other source choices, such as D75 or tungsten.

The other device we have experience with using is the Minolta CM-2002. This device costs between $10,000 and $20,000 US, depending on model options. It is a self-contained unit with a central processor; its LCD display is integrated into a hand-held, approximately 1-foot-tall by 6-inch-square molded enclosure. It contains two photosensors on an integrating sphere. It can measure total hemispherical reflectance with and without the specular component included. Therefore, a secondary derived characteristic that it measures is surface specularity, so long as the specular surface does not have a high degree of roughness. The CM-2002 is limited by the size of the aperture used to capture (exclude) the specular component. If there is too much surface roughness, the specularly reflected component will overlap the edges and be reflected in the integrating sphere. Measurements are at 40 bands of the visible spectrum between 400 and 700 nm. A serial interface application is used to download the data from the Minolta to your computer.

The output needed from one of these devices is a column-ordered ASCII file of reflectance values at specific wavelengths; it looks similar to the listing that follows. Don't worry if your file has values below 350 or above 780. They will be ignored during the conversion process.

```
#example output from a spectrometer
#visible range is approx. 350 to 780
#wavelength          reflectance
360                  .20238
420                  .28475
450                  .25376
485                  .33985
510                  .42013
540                  .52937
570                  .67935
600                  .74955
630                  .75021
660                  .76282
690                  .76744
720                  .74392
750                  .65327
780                  .48922
```

A combination of two function files is required to convert this kind of spectral data into *Radiance* RGB data. The first, called *cieresp.cal*, determines the CIE *XYZ* chromaticity coordinates for this spectral sample. The second function file, called *xyz_rgb.cal*, converts the *XYZ* coordinates into the RGB color space for *Radiance*. The *cieresp.cal* file shown below is greatly simplified, because the actual one, which can be found on the CD-ROM, is many pages in length.

```
{ cieresp.cal  (abbreviated)
  CIE standard response curves.
  Used by scripts illumcal, colorcal.
}
LEmax : 683;   { maximum luminous efficacy }
photopic(i) = LEmax * triy(i);
trix(x)=select(x-359,0.0001299,..., 1.25114e-06);
triy(x)=select(x-359,3.917e-06,..., 4.5181e-07);
triz(x)=select(x-359,0.0006061,...,0);
trix10(x)=select(x-359,1.222e-07,...,1.55314e-06);
triy10(x)=select(x-359,1.3398e-08,...,6.297e-07);
triz10(x)=select(x-359,5.35027e-07,...,0);
```

The application of *cieresp.cal* and *xyz_rgb.cal* is nontrivial, and since you may want to use these tools in the same way many times in the future, it is a good idea to put the required command sequence into a shell script. The file below is a C-shell script to convert from spectral reflectance values to CIE *XYZ* coordinates.

```
#!/bin/csh -f
# spct2xyz.csh: convert spectral data between
# 360nm to 830nm into CIE XYZ values.
# names of spectral data file(s) are given as arguments
# output is sent to stdout
foreach f ($*)
echo -n "inp=$f"
rcalc -f cieresp.cal -e 'cond=if($1-359,831-$1,-1)' \
-e 'ty=triy($1)' \
-e '$1=$2*trix($1);$2=$2*ty;$3=$2*triz($1);$4=ty' $f \
| total | rcalc -e '$1=$1/$4;$2=$2/$4;$3=$3/$4'
end
```

The following script converts the output of the script above to *Radiance* RGB coordinates:

```
#!/bin/csh -f
# xyz2rgb.csh: convert CIE XYZ coordinates
# from stdin to Radiance RGB values
# output is sent to stdout
rcalc -f xyz_rgb.cal \
-i 'inp=$(nm) ${iX} ${iY} ${iZ}' \
-e 'oR=R(iX,iY,iZ);oG=G(iX,iY,iZ);oB=B(iX,iY,iZ)' \
-o 'inp=$(nm) ${oR} ${oG} ${oB}'
```

A more sophisticated manipulation that produces material descriptions directly might also be possible, following examples from Chapter 4. The following runs convert two different spectral data sets into RGB values:

```
% spct2xyz.csh color1.dat color2.dat > mat_xyz.dat
% cat mat_xyz.dat
inp=color1.dat  0.25619   0.16016   0.15406
inp=color2.dat  0.27635   0.25153   0.35113

% xyz2rgb.csh < mat_xyz.dat > mat_rgb.dat
% cat mat_rgb.dat
inp=color1.dat 0.408938 0.0617396 0.160155
inp=color2.dat 0.275514 0.230526 0.370635
```

Of course, these commands could also have been given using a pipe with no intermediate file, like this:

```
% spct2xyz.csh color1.dat color2.dat \
| xyz2rgb.csh > mat_rgb.dat
```

5.1.10 Estimating Surface Specularity

The most effective tool that we have used to measure surface specularity is an integrating sphere–based spectrometer, such as the Minolta CM-2001. The specularity is the difference between the surface reflectance measurement made with the specular component included and the measurement made with the specular component excluded. A limitation of this device is that specular surfaces that are not close to being purely specular will be more prone to inaccuracy, because of the small aperture of the specular component exclusion port. Other heuristic, trial-and-error methods involve interactive viewing of a simulated surface as the specularity component is varied and comparison of the results to a physical sample. Here are some rules of thumb:

- The near-normal specularity of ordinary single-pane float glass is between 7% and 9% reflectance.
- The near-normal specularity of tinted single-pane float glass is between 4% and 7% reflectance.
- The specularities of most nonmetallic surfaces (i.e., the plastic primitive) rarely exceed 6%.
- Shiny, reflective metal surfaces usually have specularities above 50%.

For more examples of the specularity of common surfaces, see the *material.dat* file.

5.1.11 Estimating Surface Roughness

Surface roughness in *Radiance* is expressed as the root-mean-squared (RMS) facet slope of the surface. It is a measure of the average instantaneous slopes of a polished surface, which determines to what degree a semispecular highlight will be dispersed. Roughness cannot be used to model macro scale roughness—that is, surface imperfections visible to the naked eye. Roughness can be measured with expensive atomic-force microscopes and with some ellipsometers, but other than using one of these $100,000-US devices, the advisable method is to experiment with values within the acceptable range of 0.0 to 0.2 until the desired degree of scatter is achieved. The author of *Radiance* devised a clever bottomless black box with three LEDs around a viewing aperture, which he used to subject a semispecular surface to known lighting conditions. By using this box repeatedly and by remembering through experience which roughness values corresponded to which degrees of scattering of the specular highlight, he could reliably model semispecular finishes.

5.1.12 Measuring Surface Transmittance

When you are describing the properties of the *Radiance* glass primitive, it is important to remember to use the appropriate material property. *Radiance* uses transmissivity, a theoretical measure of the amount of light that penetrates a surface *excluding all interreflections* among opposite interface surfaces of the transmitting medium. Whereas the measurable quantity is called transmittance and includes interreflections, it is necessary to convert the measured transmittance to the theoretical transmission for the *Radiance* glass primitive.

There are many ways to measure surface transmittance. The simplest method involves the use of a constant light source, an illuminance meter, and a dark room. First, with the source turned off, take a dark reading on the illuminance meter when it is oriented the same way it will be when the source is pointed through the transmissive sample toward the illuminance meter. Next, turn on the source, allow the meter to settle, and record the value. Next, make sure that the relationship between the source and meter has not changed, place the transmissive sample between the source and the probe, and take another reading. Record the value. Subtract the dark reading from both of the measurements. Divide the "with-sample" measurement by the "no-sample" measurement, and the result is transmittance.

```
Dark reading is 1 lux
No sample reading is 540 lux - 1 = 539 lux
With sample reading is 450 lux - 1 = 449 lux
Visible Transmittance Tvis of sample is:

      Tvis=  449 / 539  = 0.83302
```

Convert this transmittance value to transmission using the procedure given in Chapter 4:

```
% calc trans1.52.cal
tn(0.83302)
$1=0.90740593
```

More advanced methods of measuring surface transmittance include the use of the Colortron and a stable light table source. Consult the Colortron manual for more information.

5.1.13 Measuring Luminous Flux

Sometimes it is unreasonable or impossible to determine the lamp specification and efficiencies for a particular luminaire, especially when you are rendering existing construction. In some cases, these luminaires have a diffuser that evenly transmits light in all directions. For these near-Lambertian types of light sources, there is a simple method to determine their light output (in radiance) for use with the *Radiance* light, glow, and illum material primitives.

1. Using a luminance meter, measure the luminance of the diffuser at several locations along the diffuser surface.
2. Calculate the average of these luminances in candelas/m^2.

3. Plug this average luminance into the following formula:

$$radiance(watts/steradian/m^2) = \\ average\ \ luminance\ (cd/m^2)/179(lumens/watt)$$

To verify your measurements and calculations, you may wish to take the process a few steps further by estimating the lumen output of the lamps inside the luminaire:

4. Measure the visible projected area of the diffusing lens in square meters.
5. Make an educated guess about the efficiency of the luminaire based on its age, discoloration, lamp age, and so on.
6. Plug these values into the following equation to obtain total lumen output:

$$lumens = \\ luminance(cd/m^2) \cdot projected\ \ area(m^2) \cdot luminaire\_efficiency \cdot \pi(steradians)$$

7. Divide the result by the number of lamps inside the luminaire.

If the result shows that your lamp lumens are a reasonable value for the known age and type of lamps you know are used (or expect to find there), you have modeled the luminaire accurately.

5.1.14 Measuring Lamp Color Temperature

The popular Minolta luminance meter model number CF-100 includes a chromaticity setting that allows the user to measure CIE *xyY* chromaticity coordinates. Consult the manual for this meter for more details. If our device measures an *xyY* value of (0.424 0.399 63), these coordinates can be converted to RGB using *xyz_rgb.cal:*

```
% rcalc -e 'ix=$1;iy=$2;iY=$3' -f xyz_rgb.cal \
-e 'iX=ix/iy*iY;iZ=(1-ix-iy)/iy*iY' \
-e '$1=R(iX,iY,iZ);$2=G(iX,iY,iZ);$3=B(iX,iY,iZ)'
.424 .399 63
^D
87.0934196      57.4293016      22.0304743
```

(This could, of course, be put into a script file, as in our previous example.) We can then use this RGB result to create the following *Radiance* material primitive:

```
void light halogen_light
0
0
3 87.0934196 57.4293016 22.0304743
```

5.1.15 Lamp Color Temperatures and Pfilt Options

As you may recall, it is suggested that you endeavor to use data only as accurate or complex as the accuracy of the simulation demands. This principle, when applied to the modeling of lamps, implies that in most situations, using lamp color temperature adds unnecessary accuracy and complexity. It is often unnecessary to model lamp color when only a single lamp type is being used, because the resulting image will appear unrealistically tinted by the color of the lamp. This discoloration will then be corrected by applying a color correction factor in the pfilt program. The net effect is to completely undo the work you did creating the colored light source in the first place. The exceptions to this rule are when multiple sources of different color temperatures are being used in the scene or when extreme lighting measurement accuracy is required. The latter is an exception because assuming a white source in a colored environment will introduce a slight error when you are calculating lighting (luminance and illuminance) values.

When the use of colored light sources is a requirement, some assumption about the performance of the human eye when it is adapted to an environment of colored sources of light must be established. Unfortunately, for complex environments with several source colors, no clear understanding of the eye's performance exists. There is, however, a simple and safe assumption, namely that the eye will tend to adapt toward the predominant source (which contributes the greatest amount of light in the scene). And although we know of no research to support the following hypothesis, it is also safe to assume that where no single light source dominates the lighting of the environment, the lumen-weighted average color can be used to adjust the displayed colors.

If a single lamp type predominates in the general area lighting, simply consult the *lamp.tab* file to find the corresponding name of the predefined lamp types. An example pfilt command that adjusts the displayed image for the color of a halogen source is

```
pfilt -1 -t halogen in.pic > out.pic
```

If *lamp.tab* does not contain your specific lamp type, you can add your measured chromaticity coordinates to the *lamp.tab* file or create your own lamp database and tell pfilt to use it with the following command:

```
pfilt -1 -f mylamp.dat -t my_lamp in.pic > out.pic
```

5.2 Luminaire Modeling

In this section, we delve into a few specific examples showing how the basic *Radiance* material primitives are interwoven with appropriate *Radiance* geometric primitives *(sphere, source, polygon, ring)* to produce complex, lighting-accurate luminaire models appropriate for real-world lighting analysis. You will be guided through the process of creating a complex luminaire in a somewhat complex-shaped room for the purpose of conducting a lighting analysis in the next section. You will draw on your experience in converting IESNA candlepower distribution files into *Radiance* data files.

5.2.1 Example Office Scene

You have been hired to help an architect design a layout of indirect luminaires in a computer-based office environment. The architect has supplied you with plan, section, and elevation drawings. Your task is to determine the optimum ceiling layout using this luminaire to provide uniform workplane illuminance of 500 lux. The client is also very concerned about the appearance of this luminaire, both on the bottom side of the luminaire and on the ceiling. The client understands that uniform ceiling luminance will provide the most glare-free environment for his employees' computer terminals.

You first survey the drawings and immediately notice that this office is not the average, flat-ceilinged office. The architect has designed a gradually, yet significantly, sloping ceiling from the core of the building to the perimeter. The shape of the floor plan is also odd; it is trapezoidal. After some thought, you realize that many of the radiosity-based algorithms are not appropriate for the task because this room has nonorthogonal surfaces. Furthermore, the standard spacing criteria provided by the manufacturer do not necessarily apply, because the distance from the ceiling to the luminaires will differ with each row. You therefore decide to embark on your first lighting analysis with *Radiance*. The architect has provided you with an AutoCAD 3D drawing (or *dxf* file) of the space as shown in Figure 5.5.

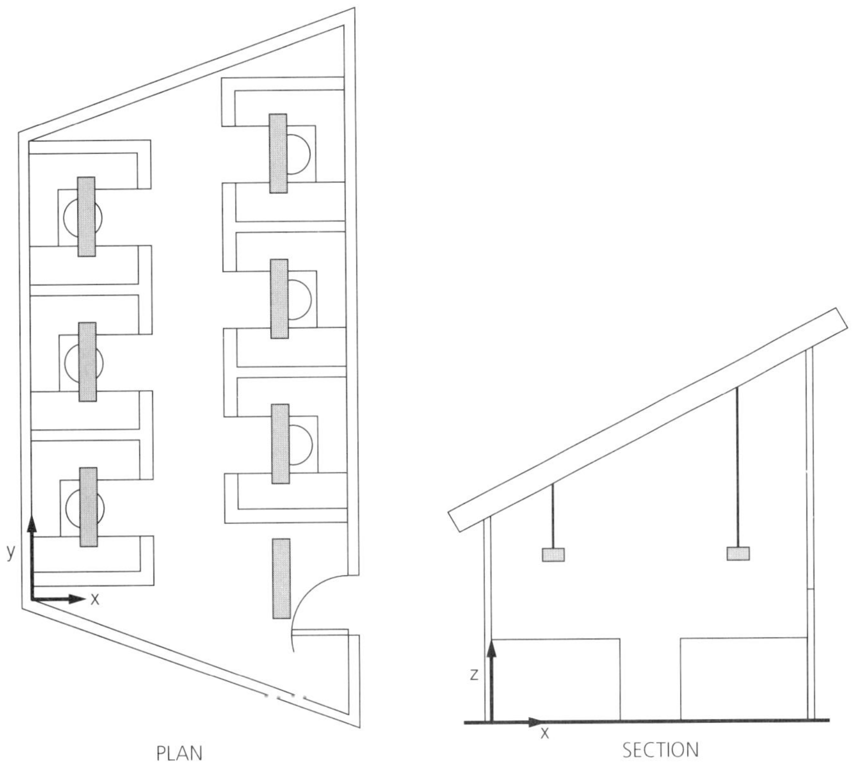

Figure 5.5 Office plan and section drawing showing luminaires in grey.

5.2.2 Using Geometry from CAD Programs

Several translators that are included with *Radiance* allow you to take advantage of external CAD programs and 3D data sets provided by the architect. Often there is more than one route from the original data set to the *Radiance* scene geometry, and different routes may improve the types of data and/or the quality of the data translated. (See Chapter 1 for a list of CAD translation utilities.)

Two of our favorite translators are **torad** and **radout**. They are both add-on utilities for Autodesk's AutoCAD R12 software and directly export *Radiance* geometry. The control screens for these utilities are very similar because the latter is an ADS-C version from the former AutoLisp utility. The torad control screen is shown in Figure 5.6.

```
 ______________________________________________________________________
|                   torad - radiance export facility                   |
| ____________________________________________________________________ |
|                                                                      |
| _ sampled entities _____________   _ write filetypes _______________ |
||  _                               | |  _                            ||
|| |X| Planarized faces of 3DFACEs | | |X| Geometry information      ||
||  _                               | |  _                            ||
|| |X| Extruded and flat TRACEs    | | |_| Master-Control            ||
||  _                               | |                               ||
|| |X| Extruded and flat SOLIDs    | |   WCS Rot. from E to X:  0.0  ||
||  _                               | |    _                          ||
|| |X| Extruded and flat CIRCLEs   | |   |X| Makefile                ||
||  _                               | |  _                            ||
|| |X| Extruded faces of ARCs      | | |_| Materials (all same)      ||
||  _                               | |  _           ___              ||
|| |X| Extruded faces of LINEs     | | |_| View:     |\/| Current    ||
||  _                               | |  _                            ||
|| |X| Extruded faces of 2D-PLINEs | | |_| Sun at position:          ||
||  _                               | |                               ||
|| |X| Constant width of 2D-PLINEs | | Long.:  -8.5    Month:  08    ||
||  _                               | | Lat.:   47.5    Day:    01    ||
|| |_| Closed 2s-polys as POLYGONs | | TZ.:    -1      Hour:   16.5  ||
||  _                               | |_______________________________||
|| |X| Faces of 3D-MESHes          |                                   |
||  _                               | _ sampling modes _______________ |
|| |X| Faces of POLYFACES          | | Sample entities by:           ||
||  _                               | |  _         _         _        ||
|| |_| Points as SPHEREs or BUBBLEs| | |X| Color |_| Layer |_| Toplayer||
||                                  | |                               ||
||                                  | | Seg./circle for arcs:   16    ||
||__________________________________| |_______________________________||
|                                          __________     __________   |
| Filename prefix:   ./myfile             |____OK____|   |__Cancel__|  |
|______________________________________________________________________|
```

Figure 5.6 The torad control screen.

To use torad and radout successfully, you must use only those AutoCAD primitives that each of them supports. Luckily, most commonly used entities are supported, except that torad does not support closed 3D PLINEs and the corresponding entities that rely on it, such as POLYMESH. Radout supports closed 3D PLINEs and is also up to seven times faster.

To use one of these AutoCAD add-on programs, de-archive the application's file into the *support* subdirectory. Launch AutoCAD, access the *File\Applications...* menu, and click on the *File...* button. For torad, find the *torad.lsp* file, or for radout, find the *rowin.exe* or *rodos.exe* file and click OK. This procedure need only be carried out once for each new drawing. The next time the drawing is loaded, again access the *File\Applications...* menu, select the program you want to use, and click the LOAD button. If the program is successfully loaded, you will then be able to access the torad or radout control screen by typing `torad` or `radout` into the AutoCAD text dialog screen.

Torad is currently available free of charge, and radout is available for a minimal shareware registration fee. Torad is available from the main *Radiance* ftp site:

ftp://radsite.lbl.gov/rad/pub/translator/torad.zip

Radout is available from Georg Mischler at

www.schorsch.com/autocad/radout/index.html

Those of you who may use AutoCAD on the DOS and Microsoft Windows platform may find this author's version of radout useful:

www.innernet.com/radiance/home.html

5.2.3 Collecting Luminaire Data

You contact the manufacturer of the specific luminaire that the architect would like to use, but, alas, they are unable to ship you one of their catalogs because they have run out. (Figure 5.7 shows what may be found in most luminaire catalogs.) They do, however, have IESNA candlepower distribution files that they will gladly provide for you. They assure you that in a few months all of their candlepower distribution files will be readily accessible for download via the Internet. You decide to accept the IESNA files, and you browse through the architect's library in search of a catalog of similar products. Luckily, you find one of similar size, rated wattage, type, and shape. Don't worry if you're not familiar with IESNA files, because we will go into some detail about the photometric database format so that you can create your own *Radiance* versions of other photometric database formats even if you don't have a conversion program.

CATALOG NO.:		2603T02EN
Lamp Type:	FO32T8 (EO)	Description:
No. of Lamps:	2	
Rated Lamp Lumens:	2900	
Ballast Input Watts:	61.4	Optical Efficiency: 85.1%
CIE-IES Classification:	Indirect	Lab Report No.: 2100342;

CANDELA DISTRIBUTION

	0	22.5	45	67.5	90	Flux Lumens
0	0	0	0	0	0	
5	0	0	0	0	0	0
15	0	0	0	0	0	0
25	0	0	0	0	0	0
35	0	0	0	0	0	0
45	0	0	0	0	0	0
55	0	0	0	0	0	0
65	0	0	0	0	0	0
75	0	0	0	0	0	0
85	0	0	0	0	0	0
90	0	0	0	0	0	
95	33	174	158	208	163	183
105	162	564	626	680	590	591
115	310	671	1076	1256	1165	912
125	476	719	1140	1415	1516	954
135	622	778	1098	1341	1453	823
145	747	841	1032	1207	1307	646
155	847	893	997	1082	1142	459
165	917	932	972	1000	1032	275
175	955	957	959	960	968	92
180	961	961	961	961	961	

POLAR CANDELA PLOT

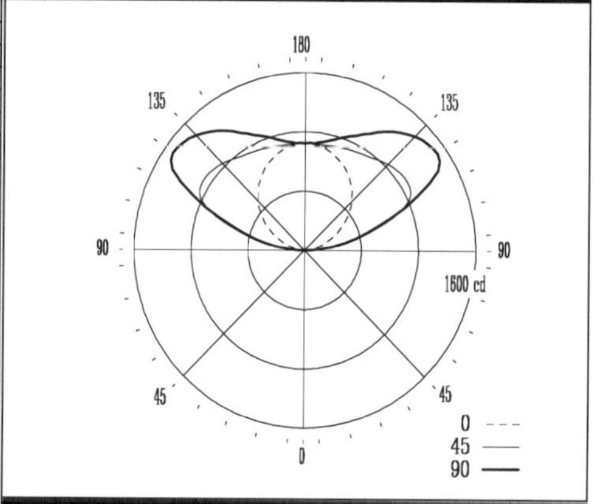

COEFFICIENTS OF UTILIZATION (%)

Ceiling	80				70			50			0
Wall	70	50	30	10	70	50	30	50	30	10	0
RCR											
0	81	81	81	81	69	69	69	47	47	47	0
1	73	70	67	64	62	60	57	41	39	38	0
2	67	61	56	52	57	52	48	36	33	31	0
3	61	53	48	43	52	46	41	31	28	26	0
4	55	47	41	36	47	40	35	27	24	22	0
5	51	41	35	31	43	36	30	24	21	19	0
6	46	37	31	26	39	32	26	22	18	16	0
7	43	33	27	22	36	28	23	19	16	14	0
8	39	30	24	19	33	25	20	17	14	12	0
9	36	27	21	17	31	23	18	16	13	10	0
10	34	24	19	15	29	21	16	14	11	9	0

*Based on a floor reflectance of 0.2

ZONAL LUMEN SUMMARY

Zone	Lumens	%Fixture	%Lamp
0-30	0	0.0%	0.0%
0-40	0	0.0%	0.0%
0-60	0	0.0%	0.0%
0-90	0	0.0%	0.0%
90-130	2639	53.5%	45.5%
90-150	4107	83.3%	70.8%
90-180	4933	100.0%	85.1%
0-180	4933	100.0%	85.1%

AVG LUMINANCE (cd/m^2)

	0	45	90
0	0	0	0
5	0	0	0
15	0	0	0
25	0	0	0
35	0	0	0
45	0	0	0
55	0	0	0
65	0	0	0
75	0	0	0

LUMINAIRE SECTION

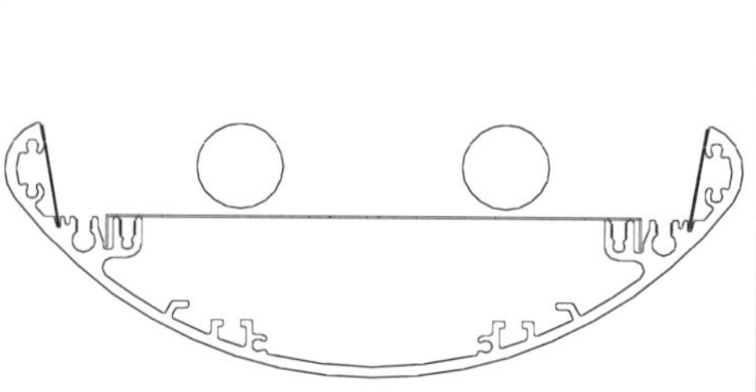

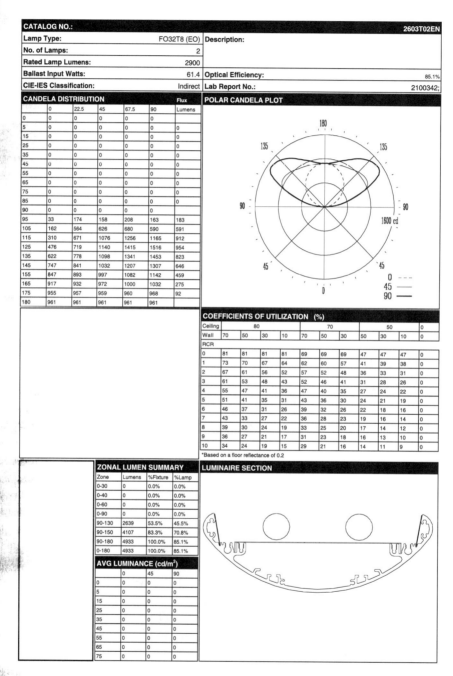

Figure 5.7 Manufacturer's luminaire specification sheet. (Copyright © Lightolier, Inc., Fall River, Mass. A division of Genlyte, Union City, NJ.)

The first fact you need to learn in order to design lighting-accurate luminaires is that for complex luminaires, the surface in *Radiance* responsible for emitting light can be a different one from that for describing the visible appearance of the location where the light is emitted. These invisible surfaces are called *impostors.* Complex luminaires may contain parabolic or louvered elements, chandeliers, translucent surfaces, or other macro-scale diffusing geometry. Because *Radiance* samples a light source with a single point on the emitting surface, it is necessary to create impostor surfaces to circumvent the complexities of the actual luminaire. It is not always possible for a backwards ray-tracing algorithm to follow all of the bounces of light far enough and reliably enough to reach a light source that is hidden behind louvers, diffracting lenses, convex or concave mirrors, and so on. This calculation is sometimes possible, but always expensive and the results will be unreliable. Besides, the candlepower distribution curves available for most luminaires already account for the complexity of the luminaires. What we need are some simple, invisible impostor surfaces to provide a place to "anchor" the candlepower distribution curves. A suspended direct/indirect luminaire is one type that requires impostor geometry for correct appearance.

The designer has supplied you with an IESNA candlepower distribution file for a direct/indirect luminaire. The first step in creating the appropriate model for this luminaire is to learn as much as possible about the IESNA file that the designer provides, and to verify that the designer intends to use the same number of lamps in this luminaire as is indicated in the IESNA file. To do this, you must inspect the provided file. Much of the difficulty of interpreting IESNA files is alleviated with Ian Ashdown's IES file parser; the latest version can also be downloaded from *ftp://ftp.ledalite.com/pub/ies_100c.zip.*

The header of an example IESNA file, *111621pn.ies*, is shown here:

```
REPORT NUMBER: ITL36346                    DATE:  11-28-1989
CATALOG NUMBER: 111621-PN-12HP-NN
LUMINAIRE: EXTRUDED SQUARE ALUMINUM HOUSING, WHITE PAINTED
      REFLECTORS, SEMI-SPECULAR PARABOLIC LOUVER, OPEN TOP.
LAMPS: THREE F40T12/CW, EACH RATED 3150 LUMENS.
BALLASTS: ONE EACH PHILIPS HM-140-TPS AND VALMONT 8G1022W
MOUNTING: SUSPENDED-DIRECT/INDIRECT
TILT=NONE
```

When this file is passed through the **ies_read** program, the following categories of summary information are produced. The entire file is included in the Supplemental Information section at the end of this chapter:

Photometric Data File Information
Luminaire Description
Lamp Data
Luminaire Dimensions
Electrical Data
Photometric Data
Calculated Information
Candela Distribution
Zonal Lumen Summary
CIE Classification
Coefficients of Utilization
Notes

Converting IESNA Candlepower Distribution Data

In other chapters of this book, some basic and more advanced uses of the **ies2rad** program are presented. In this chapter, we will discuss a nonstandard use of ies2rad to create a *Radiance* model for the direct/indirect suspended luminaire whose IESNA data file is shown above. For this luminaire, renderings from applying ies2rad in the usual way will be inaccurate and undesirable. (The version of *Radiance* included on the CD-ROM circumvents the problem described here, but the discussion is still a useful demonstration of imposter geometry.) A dark band, or "shadow," will encircle the room between the heights of the upper and lower edges of the light-emitting surfaces of the luminaire. This is because, relative to points within this band, the surface normals of these light-emitting surfaces are oriented away; therefore, no direct light source rays are traced to either of these light-emitting surfaces. However, the direct/indirect nature of this luminaire belies this computational limitation. There is some small component of the output distribu-tion that travels at near-horizontal angles to the luminaire. The fact that this small component is not included in the calculation causes the dark band to appear.

To circumvent the computational limitation, an "impostor geometry" is created that completely encloses the luminaire and provides the anchor for the IESNA candlepower distribution. The first step in this process is to convert the IESNA file in such a way that the area of emitting surfaces is equal to 1. This is accomplished by using the -i option of ies2rad, set equal to the radius of a sphere whose area is equal to 1:

```
projected_area (meter squared) = 1 = PI * (radius)^2
radius = sqrt( 1 / PI )
radius = .56419
```

This value is a constant and works regardless of the units of your scene.

```
% ies2rad -t white -i .56419 111621PN.IES
```

The `-t white` option tells ies2rad to create a pure white light source that does not have any coloration because of lamp color temperature, and the `-i .56419` is the special value for the enclosing sphere that creates a sphere with area equal to 1. The *Radiance* input file resulting from the above command, shown below, is called *111621pn.rad.*

```
# ies2rad -t white -i .56419
# Dimensions in feet
#<REPORT NUMBER: ITL36346       DATE:  11-28-1989
#<CATALOG NUMBER: 111621-PN-12HP-NN
#<LUMINAIRE: EXTRUDED SQUARE ALUMINUM HOUSING,
#<WHITE PAINTED REFLECTORS, SEMISPECULAR PARABOLIC
#<LOUVER, OPEN TOP.
#<LAMPS: THREE F40T12/CW, EACH RATED 3150 LUMENS.
#<BALLASTS: ONE EACH PHILIPS HM-140-TPS AND VALMONT #<8G1022W
#<MOUNTING: SUSPENDED-DIRECT/INDIRECT
# 147.5 watt luminaire, lamp*ballast factor = 1

void brightdata 111621pn_dist
5 corr 111621pn.dat source.cal src_phi4 src_theta
0
1 1

111621pn_dist illum 111621pn_light
0
0
3 0.999999 0.999999 0.999999

111621pn_light sphere 111621pn.s
0
0
4 0 0 0 .56419
```

The simplicity of knowing what the output of the luminaire is, excluding the effect of the area of the emitting surface, allows you to easily adjust the output to match the known area of the luminaire for which you are creating the impostor geometry. Usually, when creating a luminaire from scratch, you must divide the radiant output of the luminaire by the projected area of the emitting surfaces. However, in this case we are using a special function file that takes care of this for us. In this case, we are concerned about the appearance of the luminaire when it gets very close to surrounding surfaces, so a sphere cannot create a tight enough bound on the enclosed geometry. The **lboxcorr** function found in *source.cal* is appropriate for computing the projected area of a box. Lboxcorr requires as input the dimensions, in meters, of the impostor parallelepiped. You must first convert the dimensions of the luminaire (as reported from the ies_read program) from feet into meters:

```
< from  111621PN.TXT >

Luminaire Dimensions
--------------------
Width  =        0.41
Length =        4.00
Height =        0.51

% calc
.41*.3048
$1=0.124968
4.00*.3048
$2=1.2192
.51*.3048
$3=0.155448
```

The dimensions of our impostor geometry will be just slightly larger than those of the luminaire geometry. Rounding up the third decimal place results in the following dimensions: width = .125, length = 1.22, height = .156.

The next step is to create a rectangular box just larger than the visible geometry of the luminaire to be enclosed, which will provide the impostor geometry needed to accurately simulate the output distribution of this direct/indirect light luminaire. The inline command we will add to our file in place of the original impostor sphere geometry is

```
!genbox 111621pn_light 111621pn.s .125 1.22 .156 \
       | xform -t -.0625 -.61 -.078
```

The box is transformed such that the center of its volume is at the origin. This command replaces the sphere geometry in our original ies2rad output.

To ensure that you are using lboxcorr correctly, check the *source.cal* file:

```
{ source.cal (abbreviated)

boxcorr function corrects for distribution modeled
with a rectangular box. lboxcorr provides a more
accurate calculation for nearby surfaces, but requires
that the source box be centered at the origin.
The dimensions of the box, which must be aligned with
the x,y,z axes, are given in meters regardless of the
units being used in the scene file.

A1          - optional multiplier
A2,A3,A4    - X,Y,Z dimensions of axis-aligned box
                    (in meters!)
}
                    { local definitions }
lboxprojection = ( noneg(abs(Px-Dx*Ts)-A2/2)*A3*A4 +
                   noneg(abs(Py-Dy*Ts)-A3/2)*A2*A4 +
                 noneg(abs(Pz-Dz*Ts)-A4/2)*A2*A3 ) / Ts;

{ local box correction }
lboxcorr(v) = A1 * v / lboxprojection;
```

Back in our luminaire file, you can delete the lines referring to the sphere entity and allow the **genbox**-created surface to fall into place. Then change the illum description by changing `corr` to `lboxcorr` and entering the dimensions of the impostor geometry. As shown below, an efficiency factor of 75% was also applied as the first floating-point argument.[14]

```
void brightdata 111621pn_dist
5 lboxcorr 111621pn.dat source.cal src_phi4 src_theta
0
4 .75  .125  1.22  .156
```

14. For tables of lamp data, lamp aging, and typical luminaire efficiencies, you are encouraged to consult the *IES Lighting Handbook* and manufacturers' lamp catalog/technical manuals.

```
111621pn_dist illum 111621pn_light
0
0
3 0.999999 0.999999 0.999999

!genbox 111621pn_light 111621pn.s .125 1.22 .156 \
       | xform -t -.0625 -.61 -.078
```

We should discuss a few minor details about our luminaire before proceeding. In some cases, the impostor geometry will be significantly larger than the visible geometry. In the case of a pendant luminaire, there may even be some geometry that is both inside and outside the impostor-geometry emitting surface. In those cases, when these intermediate pieces of the geometry inside the impostor geometry are visible, it is important to think about how you will illuminate the parts of the geometry that are inside the impostor; otherwise, these parts will appear unnaturally dark or possibly even black. This lighting of the inside of the luminaire is achieved with the use of the glow primitive, with a radius of effect large enough to reach the farthest element of the luminaire. You need not worry about light from these glow surfaces affecting the surrounding scene, because *Radiance* assumes that any glow surfaces found on the back side of an illum are not intended to go beyond the illum (impostor geometry) boundary.

5.2.4 Modeling Sources of Different Color Temperature

As we mentioned earlier in Section 5.1.15, Lamp Color Temperatures and Pfilt Options, it usually makes sense to use uncolored light sources for optimal white balance in the results. However, there are certain cases, such as when more than one source color is present in a scene and the color differences are important to the evaluation, when lamp color is a desired input parameter.

The *ray/lib/lamp.tab* file contains a database of lamp chromaticities that are used with the **lampcolor** and ies2rad programs. Lampcolor is the program to use if you do not have IESNA candlepower distribution data, or if you are modeling a simple diffusely emitting luminaire. Here is an example session with the lampcolor program:

```
% lampcolor
Program to compute lamp radiance. Enter '?' for help.
Enter lamp type [D65WHITE]: daylight fluorescent
Enter length unit [meter]:feet
Enter lamp geometry [polygon]: <cr>
Polygon area [1]:43.0556
```

```
Enter total lamp lumens [0]: 2900
Lamp color (RGB) = 0.867251 1.189160 1.066163
Enter lamp type [D65WHITE]: ^D
```

This calculation determines that a luminaire modeled in feet, with a projected area of 43.0556 square feet and a total output of 2900 lumens from daylight fluorescent lamps, is equivalent to a *Radiance* light polygon with RGB values of (0.867251 1.189160 1.066163). The units of these RGB values is watts/steradian/m^2. Keep in mind that the *radiant* energy watts of *Radiance* units are not the same as the electrical wattage of a lamp.

5.2.5 Manual Entry of Candlepower Distribution Data

Sometimes you are unable to obtain luminaire data on electronic media, or the only data available are not in the IESNA standard format. In these cases, you will need to have a better understanding of the *Radiance* data file format as it relates to the description of candlepower distribution curves. Here is an example of the scene file and data file needed to describe an under-counter task light:

```
# light.rad
void brightdata light_dist
5 flatcorr taskD.dat source.cal src_theta src_phi2
0
0

light_dist light light_output
0
0
3 .0418 .0418 .0418

light_output polygon aperture
0
0
12
       -18      11.75   -1.875
        18      11.75   -1.875
        18      6       -1.875
       -18      6       -1.875
```

Keep in mind that in the above example, the first dimension listed after `source.cal` (`src_theta`) corresponds to the dimension listed first in the data file, while the second listed dimension (`src_phi`) corresponds to the dimension listed second in the data file. If the data for `src_theta` are interchanged with the data for `src_phi`, simply changing the listed order of these variables in the **brightfunc** entity effectively resolves this discrepancy.

You can insert comments anywhere in a data file by beginning the line with a # character (refer to Figure 5.8). The rest of the line then becomes a comment. No comments were allowed in data files before *Radiance* version 3.0. The first value in the data file is the number of dimensions of the data set. Next comes a definition of the way the theta values change. There are two methods of defining theta and phi values: explicitly and implicitly. The example above shows the explicit method, which begins with two zeroes, followed by the number of theta values, followed by a listing of the theta values. After the first-dimension (theta) values are defined, the phi-dimension values are defined implicitly, and must be uniform. Phi is defined implicitly by specifying the beginning and ending phi values (0, 180), followed by the total number of steps between the minimum and maximum. Following the definition of the second dimension, the actual value corresponding to the first values

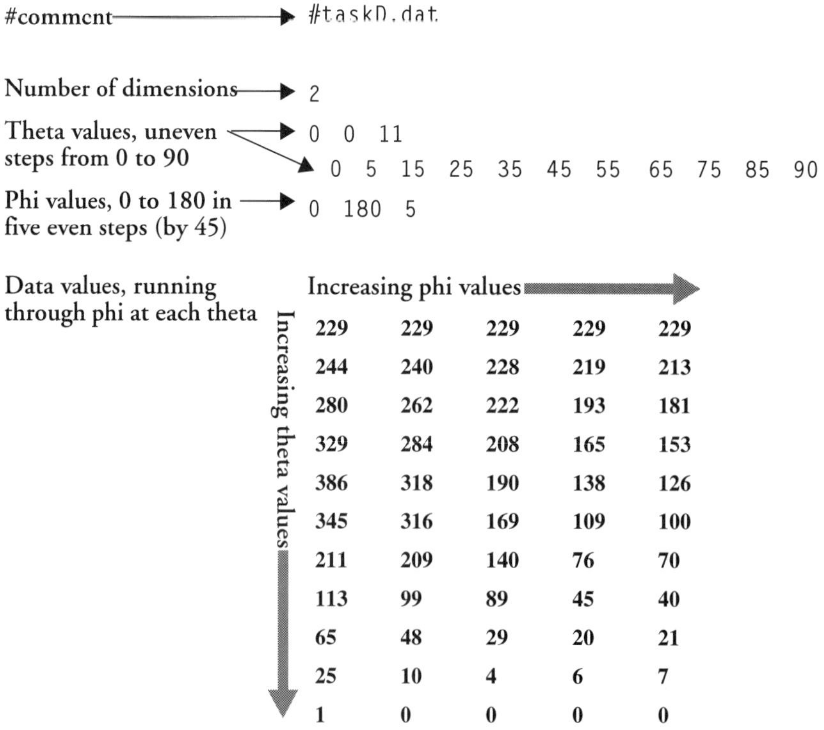

Figure 5.8 An example *Radiance* data input file containing luminaire candlepower.

of theta and phi is listed, followed by the value corresponding to the first value of theta and the second value of phi, on through the end of the phis. When all phis are exhausted, the next number is the value corresponding to the second value of theta and the first value of phi. This continues until all thetas and phis are exhausted.

5.2.6 Modeling Transmitting Media

Some luminaires use semitransparent surfaces to cover the bright light sources hidden inside. This can include downlights and other lensed luminaires. In addition, some daylight control products, such as curtains and fritted glass, are most appropriately modeled as a semispecularly transmitting medium. In these cases, it is important to know how to properly specify the *trans* material type to accurately model the appearance of the luminaire or other light-transmitting architectural element.

Specifying a trans material can be intimidating. It is one of the most confusing material entities in the *Radiance* repertoire. However, it is the simplest material that will trace direct source rays through a semispecular surface in order to determine the diffuse and specular transmitted components.

You will have to measure the following surface properties in preparation for the creation of a trans material type:

- Diffuse reflectance (RGB): The color will affect both diffusely reflected light (if there is any surface roughness) and transmitted light. Call the red, green, and blue components **Cr**, **Cg**, and **Cb**. Calculate the photopic average of the RGB and call this **Rd.**
- Reflected specularity: As with glass, this is the fraction of light that is reflected off the first surface in a mirror-like way. This we'll call **Rs**; it is equal to floating-point argument 4, A4.
- Surface roughness (RMS): Facet slope as in plastic. Call this **Sr.**
- Diffuse transmissivity: Fraction of light that passes all the way through the surface diffusely. Call this **Td.**
- Transmitted specularity: Fraction of light transmitted as a beam—that is, the fraction of light *not* diffusely scattered. Call this **Ts.**

The following formulas can be used to calculate the A7 through A1 parameters for the trans material:

A7=Ts / (Td+Ts)

A6=(Td+Ts) / (Rd+Td+Ts)

A5=Sr

A4=Rs

A3=Cb / ((1-Rs)*(1-A6))

A2=Cg / ((1-Rs)*(1-A6))

A1=Cr / ((1-Rs)*(1-A6))

The behavior of trans is regulated by the -st specular threshold rendering parameter. The following formula can be used to determine the appropriate -st setting for rview, rpict, or rtrace to ensure that the transmitted (and reflected) semispecular component will be rendered. The variables `A1` through `A7` are the first through seventh floating-point arguments to the trans primitive as calculated above.

St = A6 * A7 * (1 - grey(A1, A2, A3) * A4)

Unlike most other *Radiance* material primitives, the trans material is neither intuitive nor straightforward to apply. It is a good idea to keep ample notes for later reference when you are creating a trans material. Backing out your assumptions from an unannotated trans primitive is difficult.

5.3 Analysis Techniques

Now that you have these advanced luminaire modeling and data collection skills at your disposal, we will present additional techniques and examples that will help you ground your analysis in real-world terms. The preceding sections about data collection in this chapter are required reading.

5.3.1 Visualizing Light Distribution Using Falsecolor

One of the most common and important tasks for a lighting designer is to determine the luminance levels of the space being designed. There are a number of ways to achieve this. Probably the easiest way is to generate a *false-color* version of a precalculated image. False color means that instead of displaying colors in the image based on the wavelength of light reflecting off the surfaces, we assign a color value that corresponds either to the luminance or to the illuminance at those pixel locations. If the view is an irradiance calculation (`render= -i`, or `rtrace -I`), the resulting false-color image will represent illuminance values.

The *Radiance* tool for generating false-color images is, not surprisingly, called **falsecolor**. It requires as input one precalculated image file. It can also accept two precalculated image files when the result you wish to display is a contour map of illuminance values on top of an image of radiance values. This retains the visible colors of the scene while superimposing false-color bands or lines of different colors corresponding to the illuminance of the scene.

The most useful and informative view type for use with falsecolor is a plan view. To set up a plan view of your scene, you can use the built-in features of **rad** that allow you to specify the view type and direction by specifying the axis and direction along which the view is projected. (See the rad manual page.) Alternatively, the view parameters can be adjusted by hand. The following is a typical plan view file:

```
VIEW= -vtl -vp 5 5 5 -vd 0 0 -1 -vu 0 1 0 -vh 10 -vv 10
```

This creates a parallel projection view (`-vtl`) centered at 5, 5 at 5 units above the floor (`-vp 5 5 5`), looking along the negative *z*-axis (`–vd 0 0 –1`) with the top of the image pointed along the positive *y*-axis (`–vu 0 1 0`) with a width and height of 10 units (`–vh 10 –vv 10`). When you are using two images as input to falsecolor, it is important that the view parameters for both images be identical. Assume that you have calculated an irradiance image called *plan_irr.pic* and a normal radiance image called *plan_rad.pic*. To calculate a false-color image showing the illuminance levels in lux, use

```
% falsecolor -i plan_irr.pic -p plan_rad.pic -l Lux -cl > plan_fls.pic
```

The `-l Lux` parameter defines a label for this image that must correspond to the units of the `-i plan_irr.pic` image. It is your responsibility to make sure this is correct, because falsecolor does not check it for you. The **-cl** parameter specifies the use of contour lines that allow the greatest view of the underlying image.

Using the appropriate factor, the `-m multiplier` parameter of falsecolor can be used to convert between lux and footcandles or between nits and footlamberts. This exercise is left for you. The scale factor `-s scale` parameter is used to specify the maximum range over which the contour lines are spread starting from zero and, by default, are subdivided linearly. A logarithmic division is also available with the `-log decades` parameter. For log scales, the minimum value equals the maximum value (`-scale` option) divided by 10 to the number of decades.

5.3.2 Mimicking the Human Eye

The performance of the human eye is all too often equated with the performance of a camera. This oversimplification misses facts beyond the obvious one that humans have binocular vision and most cameras do not. It is popularly believed that if it is not possible to photographically reproduce an image of something, then that something is therefore not visible to the human eye. This belief, while grossly inaccurate, is still a limiting factor in the simulation expert's ability to represent images generated with *Radiance*. It is important to know in what ways the functioning of the human eye differs from photographic imaging, and it is equally important to know how to create *Radiance* views that are compatible with popular photographic reproduction techniques.

Matching Images and Views with Camera Prints and Lenses

One question beginning users of *Radiance* frequently ask is "How do I create an image that matches the 50mm-focal-length lens of my 35mm camera?" The seemingly obvious answer is to set the **-vh** and **-vv** parameters to the known horizontal and vertical view angles of the camera system that you wish to mimic, and set the resolution `-x` and `-y` values proportional to the -vh and -vv settings. However, the image dimensions do not end up as expected because the relationship between the *image* dimensions and the *view* parameters is nonlinear. The thing to remember is that final image resolution is automatically reduced along the smaller image axis, so that the aspect ratio follows the following formula:

```
view aspect = y/x = tan(vv/2)/tan(vh/2)
```

To specify exactly what the final resolution will be, the first step is to determine the aspect ratio of your final image dimensions.

```
aspect_ratio = image_height/image_width
```

The aspect ratio of 35mm photography (the negative) is approximately 23mm/34mm, or .6765, but it could be anything you want. After all, when a 35mm negative is printed onto 3.5-inch by 5-inch, or 4-inch by 6-inch, or 8-inch by 10-inch paper sizes, some of the image is cropped. The purpose of this exercise is to eliminate wasting computer time tracing unnecessary rays. The maximum output dimensions of your printer are another good aspect ratio to use. The following equation can be placed in a *.cal* file and used with the calc program to determine your viewing parameters.

```
{ view_param.cal
       Arbitrary aspect ratio:
       p = pixel aspect ratio (height/width=input)
       h = horizontal view angle (input)
       v = vertical view angle (output)
}
v = 114.6*atan(p*tan(h/114.6))

{      View parameters specific to 35mm photography
       f = focal length of lens (input)
       v35 = vertical view angle -vv (output)
```

COLOR PLATES

Plate 1 A *Radiance* rendering of a conference room. (Model courtesy of Anat Grynberg and Greg Ward Larson.)

Plate 2 A photograph of the conference room simulated in Plate 1.

Plate 3 A simulation of the same conference room with superimposed isolux contours (i.e., lines of equal illuminance). This emphasizes the numerical nature of the results, showing information that is critical for lighting analysis.

Plate 4 A *Radiance* rendering of a daylighted office space. (Model courtesy of Raphaël Compagnon and Jean-Louis Scartezzini, EPFL, Switzerland.)

Plate 5 A photograph of the office simulated in Plate 4. (Photograph courtesy of Raphaël Compagnon and Jean-Louis Scartezzini, EPFL, Switzerland.)

Plate 6 A model showing anisotropic reflection functions and patterns that can be defined in *Radiance.*

Plate 7 The model shown in Plate 6 with diffuse reflection functions as they might be modeled in a radiosity system.

Plate 8 The interior of the Indiana University Mellancamp Pavilion as rendered by *Radiance.* Input was translated from AutoCAD input. (Model courtesy of Scott Routen and Rueben McFarland.)

Plate 9 An exterior rendering of the model shown in Plate 8. (Model courtesy of Scott Routen and Rueben McFarland.)

Plate 10 The final rendering of the Scene 1 exercise. (See also Figure 2.21 on page 91.)

Plate 11 Lotus is constructed from spheres of dielectric and antimatter. (See also Figure 3.39 on page 189.)

Plate 12 View of the lobby from the front entrance. The cups, phone, and rotated chairs add a human element to the scene. (See also Figure 3.45 on page 209.)

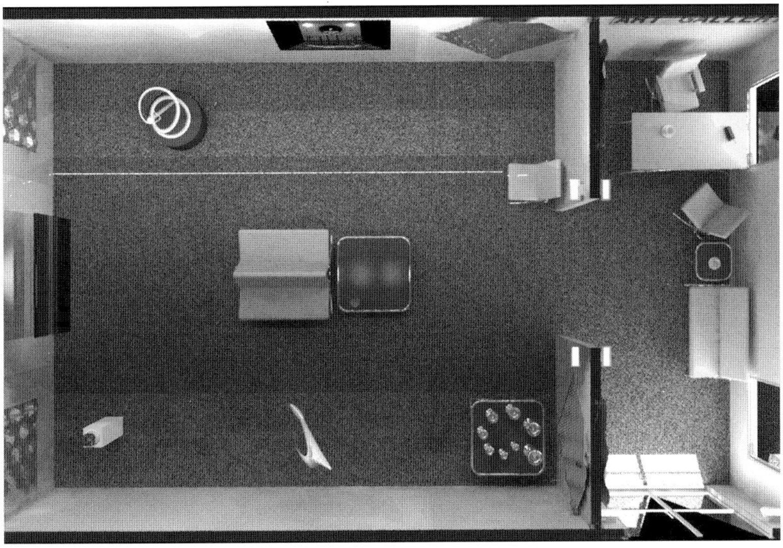

Plate 13 Picture *scene2_da.pic* presents a plan view of the daylighted scene. Note the patch of direct sunlight on the carpet by the front doors and the line of sunlight in the gallery, which has slipped past the edge of the skylight reflector. The lobby desk and chair are illuminated from the sky components; the art in the gallery is lighted by indirect daylight. (See also Figure 3.46 on page 222.)

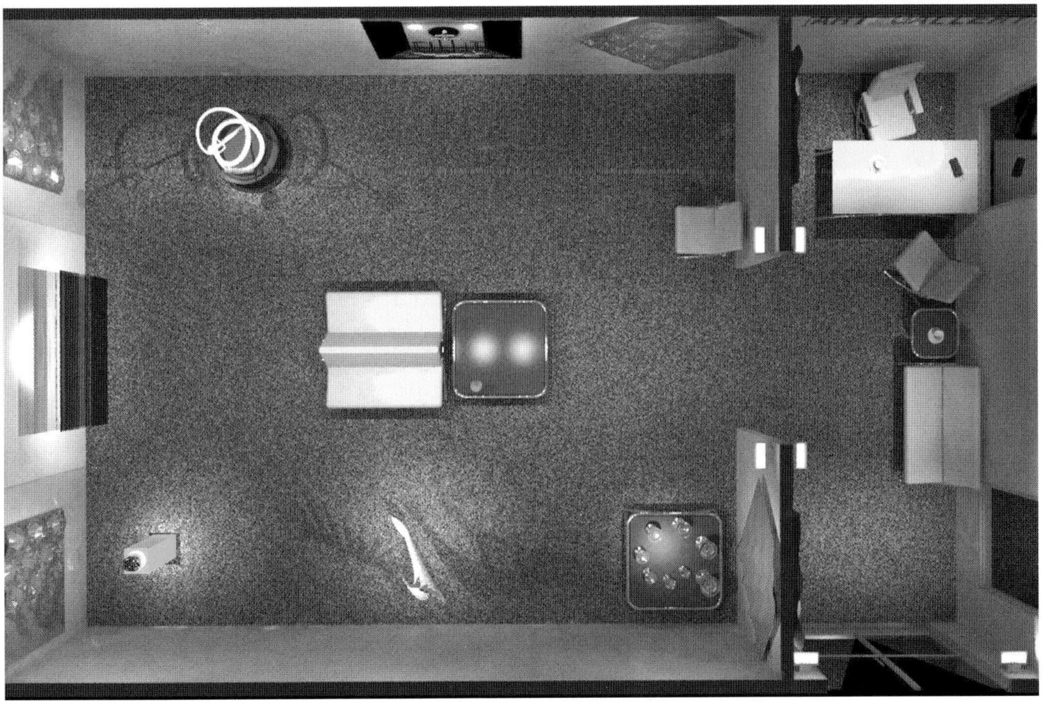

Plate 14 A plan view *(scene2_na.pic)* of the gallery reveals pools of light around each sculpture. The tracklights draw attention to the art and add to the visual interest of the room. (See also Figure 3.48 on page 225.)

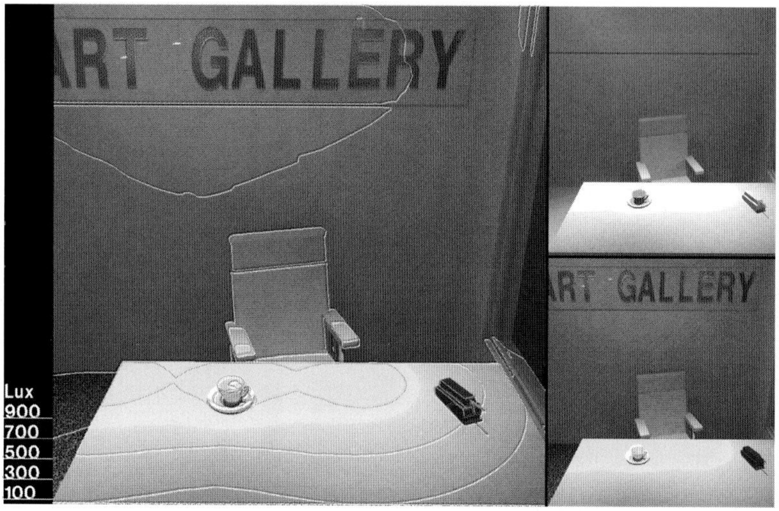

Plate 15 The large picture presents an isolux contour line illumination analysis of the desk area at night. The pictures on the right are small versions of the irradiance (top) and radiance (bottom) pictures used by `falsecolor` to generate the analysis. (See also Figure 3.56 on page 232.)

Plate 16 A daylight simulation of an atrium designed by Foggo Architects, U.K. (Model courtesy of John Mardaljevic.)

Plate 17 A *Radiance* concept image for the opening of *All's Well that Ends Well.* The underside of the umbrella (left) is illuminated by light reflected off the simulated slate floor. The dappled light patterns, in soft focus, are achieved by inserting a template into the ellipsoidal reflector spotlight beam. (See also Figure 8.1 on page 421.)

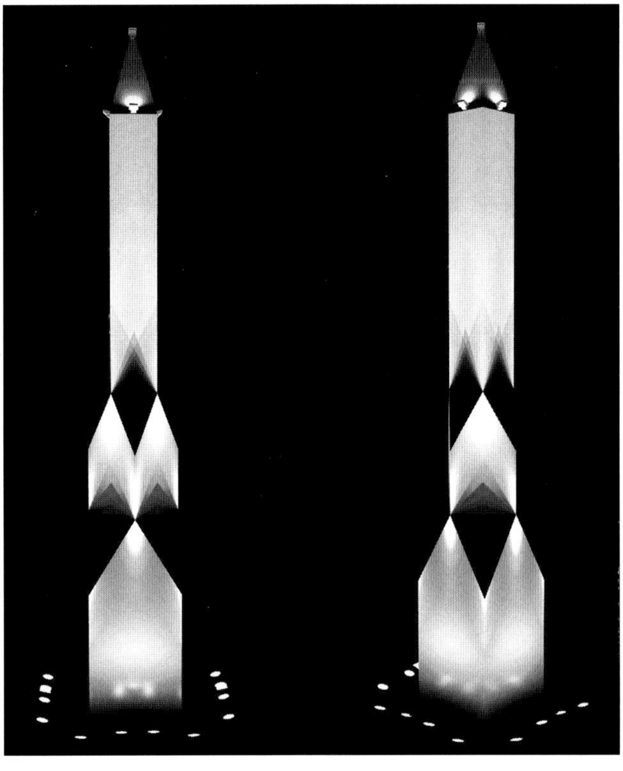

Plate 18 The complete effect of the final lighting design for the obelisk. (See also Figure 8.13 on page 450; model courtesy of Shakespeare Lighting Design.)

Plate 19 The illumination from thousands of luminaires is accurately depicted in this view of the Tsing-Ma suspension bridge in Hong Kong. (See also Figure 8.15 on page 452; lighting design courtesy of R. Shakespeare for Linbeck and Rausch, Lighting Consultants.)

Plate 20 *Mist* is used to simulate shafts of light passing through participating media. This *Radiance* picture is a keyframe from a simulation of a rock 'n' roll concert lighting sequence. (See also Figure 8.20 on page 459; model courtesy of Theater Computer Visualization Center, Indiana University.)

Plate 21 A deterministically ray-traced image of a simple model.

Plate 22 A pure Monte Carlo stochastic ray-traced image of the model shown in Plate 21.

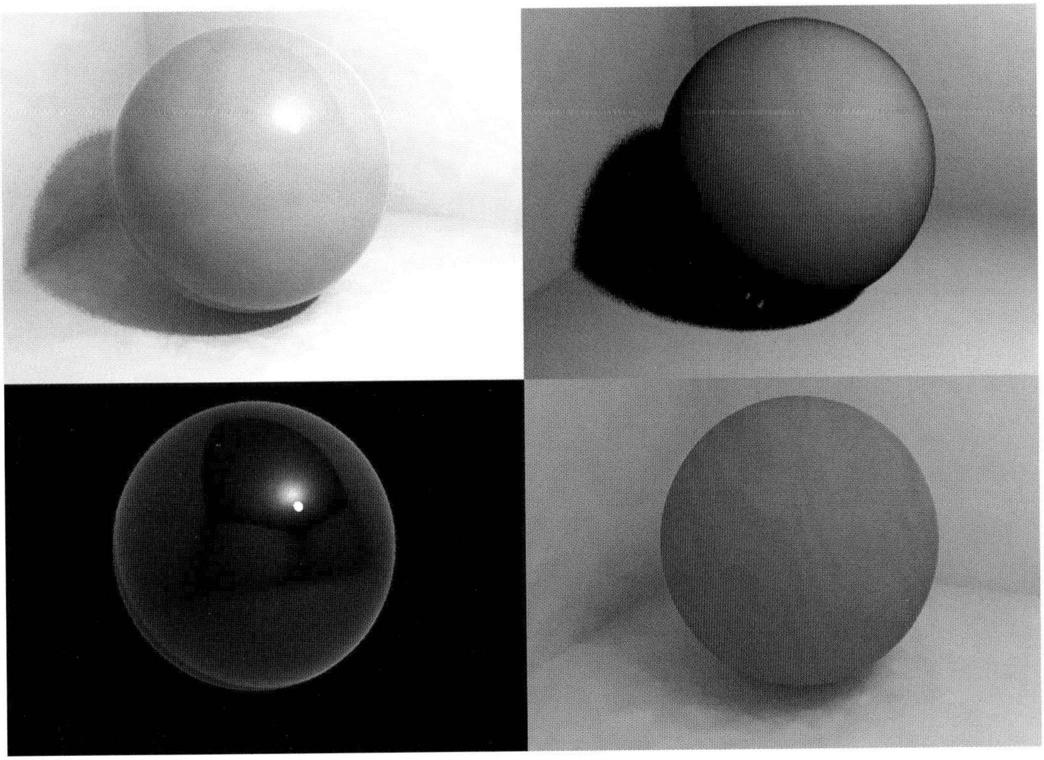

Plate 23 An artificial separation of the direct (upper right), indirect specular (lower left), and indirect diffuse (lower right) components, with the combined result (upper left).

Plate 24 The model shown in Plates 21 and 22 computed using a hybrid technique in a fraction of the time required by pure Monte Carlo ray tracing, yet producing more accurate, smoother results. (See Chapter 10 for details.)

Plate 25 A scene with three blocks, showing the placement of indirect irradiance calculation points. (See Chapter 12 for details.)

```
        h35 = horizontal view angle Ovh (output)
}
v35 = 114.6*atan(17/f)
h35 = 114.6*atan(11.5/f)
```

To use the first function to determine the view parameters for printing to a device that has a 1600-pixel by 2000-pixel maximum size (in landscape mode) when you want the horizontal view angle to be 80 degrees:

```
% calc view_param.cal
p=1600/2000
h=80
v
$1=67.7447729
```

The vertical (smaller) view angle would be 67.75 degrees. Alternatively, an alias can be defined in your *.login* file that would allow you to use a single command to determine your required viewing parameters. Be sure to include the comments so that when you come back to it some time in the future, you know how to use it:

```
# first input parameter is aspect ratio (h/w)
# second input parameter is horizontal view angle

alias vang \
'ev "114.6*atan((\!:1)*tan((\!:2)/114.6))"'

# The input parameter is focal length of lens
# aspect ratio of 35mm film is assumed

alias f135 \
'ev "114.6*atan(17/(\!:1))" "114.6*atan(11.5/(\!:1))"'
```

To use this alias to determine the horizontal and vertical view angles for a 50mm lens on a 35mm camera:

```
% f135 50
37.5588329 25.9074373
```

The horizontal view angle parameter is `-vh 37.5588329` and the vertical view angle parameter is `-vv 25.9074373`.

The next question you may have is "How do I use these parameters to come up with an image with the exact dimensions I want?" The answer is to put these -vh and -vv parameters into your *.rif* file, or into your other view files. Then set the `RESOLUTION` parameter in your *.rif* file, or set the `-x <xres> -y <yres>` parameters on the command line, to the maximum dimension of your larger view parameter. The other side of the view will be automatically reduced to the appropriate number of pixels. This method is used to eliminate the possibility that you will calculate images with nonsquare pixels—that is, that one of the view axes will be in a different scale from the other.

Film Speed and Radiance *EXPOSURE*

Sometimes a naive client may ask you, "At what exposure is this image taken?" It may be a naive question, but not having a ready answer could discredit you in the mind of your client, who is struggling to understand the images you are presenting. Therefore, having the following formula close at hand will allow you to answer your client's question:

```
{ exposure.cal
  Relationship between Radiance EXPOSURE and
  film photography exposure
       t = exposure time (in seconds)
       s = film speed (ISO ASA)
       K = 2.81 (conversion factor 179*PI/200)
       Output variables:
       f = f-stop
       E = Radiance EXPOSURE
}
K = 179*PI/200
E = K * T * S / f^2
f = sqrt( K * T * S / E )
```

To use this formula, first determine the exposure setting of your precalculated image by using

```
% getinfo < office1.pic
oconv office.mat office.rad
EXPOSURE=5.700000e-01
```

The exposure of the image *office1.pic* is .57. Then assume that the film speed is 100 and the shutter speed is 1/60 of a second, and calculate the f-stop with

```
% calc exposure.cal
t=1/60
s=200
```

```
e=.57
f
$1=4.05497703
```

The aperture size of this image at 1/60 second, with ASA 200 film (assuming 35mm photography), is approximately f/4. This comes from the *IES Lighting Handbook*, 1987 Application Volume, section 11, page 24. The formula is less accurate for extremes of exposure settings, so use it with caution.

Another use for this formula is to determine what a particular image would look like if it is exposed at 1/60 second on ISO ASA 100 (DIN 21) film at f/4. The following pfilt options would give you the answer:

```
% pfilt -1 -e `ev "2.81*1/60*100/4^2"` raw.pic > fin.pic
```

We recommend that you use this technique sparingly. The reason for this is that the eye does not behave like a camera (thank goodness). What is important to the eye is the overall brightness adaptation level, which is the subject of the next section.

Determining an Appropriate Ambient Value and Exposure for Images

The title of this section was chosen carefully, because the way the eye responds to light is not entirely well understood. A complete presentation of issues surrounding adaptation levels is beyond the scope of this book, but we can address the need to obtain a good estimate of the eye's adaptation with the techniques briefly presented here. The pcond program brings an enhanced understanding of the eye's behavior and a corresponding ability to automatically adjust the display of image luminances on a computer monitor or other output device. The new algorithm maps luminances to display brightness in a way that attempts to elicit the same response in the observer of the displayed image that an observer in the built space might experience. The details are discussed in the following section. However, it is still important to determine an appropriate average exposure for an image so that the rad program can set the background ambient value (`-av`).

This empirical method involves creating an interactive view of the image for which you wish to set the exposure. Since our goal is determining an appropriate ambient value, we must keep in mind the environment we are rendering. Is there daylight in the space? Are the lights very dim? Are there small areas of intense brightness in the peripheral vision? Set up a *.rif* file with the following parameters before beginning this exercise:

```
#background.RIF file for determining appropriate
# exposure and background ambient value
```

```
INDIRECT=2
QUALITY=MEDIUM
VARRIABILITY=HIGH
render= -i -av 0 0 0
```

Start an interactive session with

```
rad -o x11 background.rif
```

Once a substantial part of the image has been "filled in," use the rview `frame` command to concentrate further rays on a part of the scene that receives no direct light, such as a patch on the floor under a table. When this framed region has resolved, `trace` a ray into a representative direction and record the average irradiance of this ray:

```
128 refining...
: t
Pick ray           <click>
ray hit material polygon "surface_name"  <cr>
at (xpos, ypos, zpos)  <cr>
value (red_ir grn_ir blu_ir) (average_irradiance)
```

The relationship between average hemispherical radiance and irradiance is

```
radiance = average_irradiance/PI.
```

Your first estimate of the `EXPOSURE` variable will be the value computed with the above procedure. Let us assume that the computed value is 2. This would mean an -av setting of .63. Change the *.rif* file to reflect this -av setting and remove the irradiance calculation flag from the `render=` parameter line.

```
#background.RIF file for determining appropriate
# exposure and background ambient value
INDIRECT=2
QUALITY=MEDIUM
VARRIABILITY=HIGH
render= -av .63 .63 .63
```

Start another interactive view with our new *.rif* file and allow it to refine the image to a resolution of 32 or better. To verify that this ambient value setting is accurate, use the rview `set` command to turn off the ambient calculation with `set ab 0` and observe what happens to the dark, shadowed regions of the image. If the shadowed regions become significantly brighter, the ambient value parameter needs to be reduced. If the brightness does not change significantly, the ambient value parameter is an appropriate one. Once the image is sufficiently resolved, use the rview `exposure` command to adjust the display brightness to the average for the scene, then have rview report to you what this exposure value is and write it down:

```
128 refining...
: e 1    <cr, image is re-displayed>
128 refining...
: e =    <cr>
exposure (1.5123135)
```

To verify that this exposure will set the ambient parameter appropriately, use the following relationship:

```
-av {red green blue} = 0.5/EXPOSURE
```

If this relationship is true, then the `render= -av r g b` setting can be removed from the *.rif* file. The `EXPOSURE=` setting alone will accurately set the ambient value. However, if the average for the view seems too bright or too dark, you will likely have to adjust the exposure of the calculated image and keep the explicit setting of the ambient value.

Use the rview `exposure` to adjust the brightness of the image up or down. When you have a view that appears closest to your intuitive understanding of how bright the space should be, display the exposure setting with the `exposure =` command. The value returned is the *Radiance* `EXPOSURE` value.

You may wonder how such a subjective approach could achieve reliable results. Keep in mind that the eye is insensitive to large changes in brightness in the visual field, and can in fact quickly adapt to very bright small areas within the field of view. Thus, it would be accurate to say that the proper exposure depends on who is viewing the image, and under what circumstances the viewer is experiencing that view. For the purpose of determining a background ambient value, knowing one person's opinion of the appropriate exposure verifies that the ambient value parameter is set within the right order of magnitude.

Setting the ambient value parameter accurately is most important for scenes that use only the deterministic ray-tracing methods; in other words, `INDIRECT` is set to zero or -ab is set to zero. However, the ambient-value parameter is also used in multiple-bounce calculations. After the final ambient bounce is reached, that ray receives an intensity derived from the -av setting. The cumulative effect of the ambient values is reduced by the surface reflectance of the final surface it struck, and again by each intervening surface until it reaches the eye.

Visualizing Loss of Contrast, Color, and Acuity Using Pcond

You already know that a key to the power of *Radiance* is the fact that an image file is a pixel map of spectral radiance (or irradiance) values in a high-dynamic-range, floating-point data format. If you have used *Radiance* before, you have probably discovered that one of the most difficult features of *Radiance* has been finding the correct exposure for the scene. An assumption underlying this difficulty is that it is the user's responsibility to determine the appropriate display parameters that most accurately reproduce the psychophysical experience a viewer of that scene might have. In effect, the *Radiance* user has been burdened not only with the responsibility of creating an accurate mathematical representation of the environment, but also with the responsibility of accurately "photographing" the simulated environment. These two tremendous responsibilities are more than most casual users of *Radiance* can successfully master and, in effect, introduce the "art" of rendering back into what might otherwise be a purely synthetic procedure. Now, at last, there is a utility to help with this final task.

One of the most powerful features of *Radiance* that was not developed until release version 3.1 is the ability to simulate some of the eye's perceptual limitations [LRP97]. The new program called pcond provides powerful tools for easily manipulating *Radiance*'s "map of spectral radiance" into a displayed image that causes a response in the viewer that closely matches the response a viewer of the real-world equivalent environment might experience. Pcond uses a variety of mathematical techniques to determine an appropriate exposure and simulate loss of acuity and veiling glare, loss of focus, and loss of color sensitivity. Pcond is also a more efficient (faster and easier-to-use) tool for adjusting images for the color and brightness gamut of the output device. Using pcond is almost foolproof. If you want to adjust a final *Radiance* image for all of the "human" effects for display on an average CRT, the command to use is simply

```
pcond -h final.pic > final_eye.pic
```

If you have more information about the color space of your output device, the additional command line arguments to use for displaying on an RGB device such as a CRT are

```
pcond -h -p $DISPLAY_PRIMARIES final.pic > final_crt.pic
```

The above example assumes that you have set up an environment variable called `DISPLAY_PRIMARIES` containing the CIE *(x,y)* chromaticities of your CRT's red, green, and blue phosphors plus the *(x,y)* chromaticity of your CRT's pure white. The format of this environment variable is

```
setenv DISPLAY_PRIMARIES "xr yr xg yg xb yb xw yw"
```

The chromaticities of the white (xw,yw) are usually set to (.333, .333) in order to avoid introducing color-balance problems. The assumption is that your eyes are color-balanced to the CRT's white, and not color-balanced to some arbitrary "pure white" as measured by your chrominance meter. In these cases, it is best to rely on your eye's ability to adjust for pure white rather than to attempt to display a "color" of white that you are not used to viewing on your monitor (thereby forcing your eyes to readjust to this new white color balance).

If your display device is a film recorder for which you have a macbethcal calibration file and know the minimum and maximum luminance of the projected slide pixels, use

```
pcond -h -u 80 -d 100 -f film.cal final.pic > film.pic
```

The above example assumes that your maximum projected image luminance (a white recorded image) is 80 candelas/m^2 and the black level is 1/100 this value, or 0.8 candelas/m^2. If your display device is a printer with reflective media for which you also have a calibration file and you plan to view the print under 500 lux of available light, use

```
pcond -h -u 127 -d 40 -f print.cal final.pic > print.pic
```

The above example assumes that the reflective medium has a minimum reflectance of 2% and a maximum reflectance of 80% and is calculated as follows:

```
Max. luminance = 500 lux * .8 / PI = 127 cd/m^2
Dynamic range = 80 / 2 = 40:1
```

5.4 Conclusion

In this chapter, we have explored some useful techniques and pointed out some important caveats for lighting designers who wish to apply *Radiance* in their work. One of the principal lessons of this chapter is that the results you get with *Radiance* (or with any other simulation program) depend largely on the effort and care you put into the input side of the equation. In the case of *Radiance*, it is critical to have good light sources and material models to go with the geometric model in order to produce reliable results. It is also important to have some understanding of the underlying algorithms employed in the simulation, at least to the extent that the parameter settings affect the accuracy of the results. In particular, we recommend that you study the manual page on the CD-ROM for rad and understand the import of its numerous control variables. More advanced users will also wish to study the chapters in Part III, Calculation Methods, to gain further insight into what goes on inside the *Radiance* simulation engine.

Author's Biography

Charles Ehrlich has spent over eight years working with *Radiance* in various capacities. In 1990, he established a private consulting practice focused on the use of *Radiance* for lighting analysis, called Space & Light, currently located in Berkeley, California. His clients have included architects Mark Mack, Polsheck and Partners, Skidmore Oewings and Merril, and Cesar Pelli and Associates; lighting designers, including Horton Lees Lighting Design of New York; energy consultants, including Energy Simulation Specialists of Tempe, Arizona, Cunningham and Associates of San Francisco, and Stephen Winter and Associates of Norwalk, Connecticut; and lawyers, including Alan Moss of San Francisco. Space & Light has completed projects including the daylighting of the Inventure Museum in Akron, Ohio; exterior lighting of a skyscraper bank headquarters in Winston-Salem, North Carolina; a theater in San Francisco; the new International Lobby building at San Francisco International Airport; a terminal building interior at the Ben-Gurion International Airport; a library; a utility headquarters building; daylighting analysis for Wal-Mart stores; and several legal cases, including one train-pedestrian accident. Charles Ehrlich received his Bachelor of Architecture degree from the University of California at Berkeley, College of Environmental Design, in 1989.

Supplemental Information

Material Data Collection Device Manufacturers

Colortron
Light Source, Inc.
4040 Civic Center Drive, 4th Floor
San Rafael, CA 94903
Phone: 415-446-4200
Website: *www.ls.com/colortron.html*

Minolta CM-2001 Spectrometer
Minolta CM-2002 Spectrophotometer
Minolta CF-100 Luminance Meter
Minolta USA, Inc.
Instrument Systems Division
101 Williams Drive
Ramsey, NJ 07446
Phone: 201-818-3517

Fax: 201-825-4374
Website: *www.minoltausa.com/low/static/products.html*
(Click on the link to "Color Measurement and Appearance Instruments.")

Lambda 9 Spectrometer
Lambda 19 Spectrometer
Perkin-Elmer, Inc.
761 Main Avenue
Norwalk, CT 06859-0001
Phone: 203-762-1000
Website: *www.perkin-elmer.com:80/uv/index.html*

IESNA File Parser Output

```
              Ledalite IES Photometric Data File Utility
              ------------------------------------------

                           Version 1.00C

Photometric Data File Information
---------------------------------

File name: 111621pn.3s
File format: LM-63-1986
TILT file name = NONE

Luminaire Description
---------------------

REPORT NUMBER: ITL36346                   DATE:  11-28-1989
PREPARED FOR: LEDALITE ARCHITECTURAL PRODUCTS, INC.
CATALOG NUMBER: 111621-PN-12HP-NN

LUMINAIRE: EXTRUDED SQUARE ALUMINUM HOUSING, WHITE PAINTED
REFLECTORS, SEMI-SPECULAR PARABOLIC LOUVER, OPEN TOP.
LAMPS: THREE F40T12/CW, EACH RATED 3150 LUMENS.
BALLASTS: ONE EACH PHILIPS HM-140-TPS AND VALMONT 8G1022W
MOUNTING: SUSPENDED-DIRECT/INDIRECT
```

```
Lamp Data
---------

Number of lamps = 3
Lumens per lamp = 3150.00

Luminaire Dimensions
--------------------

Measurement units = Feet
Width = 0.41
Length = 4.00
Height = 0.51

Electrical Data
---------------

Ballast factor = 1.00
Ballast-lamp factor = 1.00
Ballast watts = 147.50

Photometric Data
----------------

Multiplier = 1.00
Goniometer type = Type C

Calculated Information
----------------------

Total Lamp Lumens: 9450.00
Luminaire Efficiency: 61.2 %
```

CANDELA DISTRIBUTION

	0.0	22.5	45.0	67.5	90.0	112.5	135.0	157.5	180.0	FLUX
0	1734	1734	1734	1734	1734	0	0	0	0	
5	1738	1733	1731	1724	1728	0	0	0	0	165
15	1651	1654	1677	1685	1687	0	0	0	0	473
25	1480	1489	1468	1471	1481	0	0	0	0	683
35	1254	1250	1226	1222	1252	0	0	0	0	778
45	936	892	903	927	978	0	0	0	0	717
55	337	376	500	557	603	0	0	0	0	425
65	26	31	78	156	181	0	0	0	0	93
75	7	9	12	17	23	0	0	0	0	13
85	3	4	4	4	5	0	0	0	0	4
90	0	0	0	0	0	0	0	0	0	
95	23	31	18	12	10	0	0	0	0	19
105	177	141	135	133	127	0	0	0	0	150
115	354	292	261	247	242	0	0	0	0	276
125	511	474	402	379	371	0	0	0	0	383
135	646	593	546	522	511	0	0	0	0	436
145	764	759	736	665	648	0	0	0	0	448
155	847	838	809	805	832	0	0	0	0	382
165	907	896	895	896	898	0	0	0	0	254
175	939	933	928	923	926	0	0	0	0	88
180	936	936	936	936	936	0	0	0	0	

ZONAL LUMEN SUMMARY

ZONE	LUMENS	%% LAMP	%% FIXT
0 - 90	3351	35	57
0 - 30	1321	13	22
0 - 40	2099	22	36
0 - 60	3241	34	56
90 - 120	445	4	7
90 - 130	828	8	14
90 - 150	1712	18	29
90 - 180	2436	25	42
0 - 180	5787	61	100

CIE Classification: Type III - General Diffuse

COEFFICIENTS OF UTILIZATION

RC	80	70	50	30	10	0
RW	70 50 30 10	70 50 30 10	50 30 10	50 30 10	50 30 10	0
0	66 66 66 66	62 62 62 62	53 53 53	45 45 45	38 38 38	35
1	61 59 57 55	57 55 54 52	48 47 46	41 41 40	35 35 34	31
2	57 53 49 47	53 49 47 44	43 41 39	37 36 35	32 31 30	28
3	52 47 43 40	49 44 41 38	39 36 34	34 32 30	29 28 27	24
4	48 42 38 34	45 40 36 33	35 32 30	31 28 27	27 25 24	22
5	44 38 33 30	41 36 32 29	32 28 26	28 25 23	24 22 21	19
6	41 34 30 26	38 32 28 25	29 25 23	25 23 21	22 20 19	17
7	38 31 26 23	36 29 25 22	26 23 20	23 21 19	20 18 17	15
8	35 28 24 21	33 27 23 20	24 21 18	21 19 17	19 17 15	14
9	33 26 21 19	31 25 21 18	22 19 16	20 17 15	17 15 14	12
10	31 24 20 17	29 23 19 16	20 17 15	18 16 14	16 14 12	11

Notes:

1. Coefficients of Utilization calculations are based on an effective floor cavity reflectance of 20 percent.

IES_READ Program

The ies_read program is copyright 1995–96
by Heart Consultants Limited
620 Ballantree Road
West Vancouver, BC
Canada V7S 1W3

Questions about this program should be directed to
Ian Ashdown
Research and Development Manager
Ledalite Architectural Products Inc.
9087A 198th Street
Langley, BC
Canada V1M 3B1
Phone: 604-888-6811
Fax: 604-888-0566
email: iashdown@ledalite.com
Website: *www.ledalite.com*

CHAPTER 6

Daylight Simulation

by John Mardaljevic

The primary goal of daylighting analysis is the reliable evaluation of the potential of a design to provide useful levels of natural illumination. This chapter will explain how *Radiance* can be used to predict the daylighting performance of an architectural design.

It is expected that you will already be familiar with the fundamentals of the *Radiance* system, and that you have some knowledge of the way the command-line interface operates. The diffuse indirect calculation is particularly important for daylighting analysis, so a good understanding of the key features of this method is desirable. If you are specifically interested in daylighting but are new to *Radiance*, this chapter, together with the general introduction, could serve as a starting point for investigating the system.

Daylighting analysis can take many forms. A comprehensive survey of all the ways in which *Radiance* can be used to address these issues would require a book in itself. To limit the discussion to a single chapter, some compromises have to made. Rather than give cursory mention to a multiplicity of techniques, we will describe a set of key procedures in detail. These are presented in the form of case study examples. Some of the examples are straightforward descriptions of how to get from A to B. Others are expanded to demonstrate, for instance, the correspondence between analytical solutions and *Radiance* predictions, or accuracy criteria and efficiency. If you already know some daylighting, you may wish to skip the first few case studies.

The chapter begins with an overview of daylight monitoring, with little or no mention of *Radiance*. Next, there is a general discussion about evaluation techniques and how, in broad terms, these influence the *Radiance* modeling and simulation. The bulk of the chapter is taken up with case study examples.

The important *Radiance* programs for this chapter, that is, those for which you will learn how to make informed choices for critical parameter values, are **rtrace, rpict, mkillum, gensky,** and the script **dayfact**. It is expected that you have already formed, from the general introduction, some appreciation of the function and use of the rtrace, rpict, and mkillum programs. We will use a handful of other *Radiance* programs, such as **oconv** and **rcalc**, as a matter of course.

6.1 Daylight: Monitoring, Sky Models, and Daylight Indoors

The source of all daylight is the sun. Scattering of sunlight in the atmosphere by air, water vapor, dust, and so on gives the sky the appearance of a self-luminous source of light. Here we are concerned only with daylight modeling for architectural purposes, so both the sky and the sun will be treated as light sources distant from the local scene. The brightness of the sun, or a point on the sky, will not be modified by scattering or absorption. In other words, the effects of participating media phenomena such as smog or haze on daylight will not be considered.[15]

The illumination produced by the sky depends on its luminance. Sky luminance varies according to a series of meteorological, seasonal, and geometric parameters that are difficult to specify. Characterizing the sun and sky for lighting simulation is equivalent to light source photometry for electric luminaires. Geometrically, the sky is simple to describe: the sky always has the same "shape" and "position." The brightness pattern of the sky, however, can be quite difficult to characterize for all but heavily overcast conditions. When clouds are present, the sky brightness distribution can change dramatically over very short time scales. For these reasons, it has been necessary to devise ideal sky brightness patterns known as *sky models*. These are used for the majority of daylight simulation applications. Sky models are used to generate sky brightness patterns from basic daylight quantities.

---

15. You are encouraged to investigate these effects at your leisure once you have grasped the requisite techniques.

6.1.1 Measuring Daylight

Continuous monitoring of the sky brightness began in earnest in the 1950s. There are now many locations in the industrialized world where 10 or more years of daylight data have been recorded and archived. The degree of monitoring varies from the most basic stations, which record integrated quantities averaged over time, to those that measure a comprehensive range of daylight metrics including the actual sky brightness distribution. They can be divided into classes as follows.

Basic

The longest time-series data from which daylight availability can be elucidated are the climatic or weather tapes [PO83]. These usually contain hourly integrated values of global and diffuse irradiance (Figure 6.1). Irradiance is a measure of the total energy flux (watts/meter^2) incident on a surface. The visible part of the radiant energy, the illuminance (lumens/meter^2), is calculated using a luminous efficacy

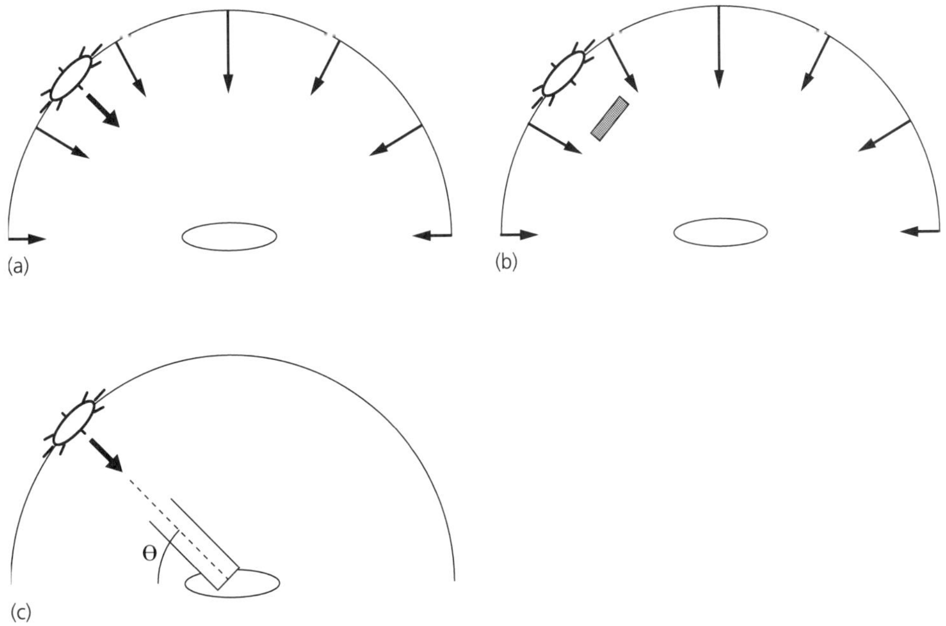

Figure 6.1 Basic daylight components: (a) global horizontal (sky and sun), (b) diffuse horizontal (sky only), and (c) direct normal (sun only).

model [Lit88]. Luminous efficacy, K, can be thought of simply as the ratio of illuminance to irradiance with units of lumens per watt:

$$K = \frac{683 \int S_\lambda v_\lambda d\lambda}{\int S_\lambda d\lambda} \tag{6.1}$$

where S_λ is the spectral radiant flux in watts per unit wavelength interval at wavelength λ and V_λ is the relative spectral response of the eye at that wavelength. See Supplemental Information in Chapter 10 for a plot of this function. Equivalently, the ratio of luminance to radiance, which gives the same value, may be used.

This ratio is not constant and will vary with solar altitude, cloud cover, and sky turbidity. Furthermore, under the same sky conditions, the luminous efficacy for direct-beam radiation will be different from that for the diffuse component.

Intermediate

Monitoring of the visible component of irradiation, the illuminance, is nowadays more common. An intermediate-level monitoring station will measure global and diffuse illuminance together with the corresponding irradiance values. More comprehensive monitoring would include measurements of the direct components of solar illuminance and solar irradiance. These direct solar components are measured normal to the direction of the sun (Figure 6.1), so the instruments that record these quantities are mounted on sun-tracking motorized drives.

In addition, some stations record the illuminance incident on vertical surfaces facing north, south, east, and west. Here, the four vertical photocells are screened from ground-reflected radiation and the illuminance recorded is that due to the sky only. Although the four vertical values can provide some indication of the azimuthal asymmetry in the brightness distribution, these are still integrated quantities.

Advanced

The finest level of detail is provided by stations that also measure the actual sky luminance distribution using a sky-scanning device. The number of measurements taken during each scan varies according to the instrument used. These data provide the measurements necessary to validate sky models. Measured sky brightness distributions may also be used directly in the lighting simulation [Mar95].

In addition to lighting quantities, many stations also record dry bulb temperature and relative humidity.

Basic daylight quantities provide the input to sky model generator programs. Global horizontal, diffuse horizontal, and direct normal are related as follows:

$$I_{gh} = I_{dh} + I_{dn}\sin\theta \tag{6.2}$$

where I_{gh} is the global horizontal irradiance, I_{dh} is the diffuse horizontal irradiance, I_{dn} is the direct normal irradiance, and θ is the sun altitude. The same relation holds for illuminance quantities.

6.1.2 Sky Models

The simplest sky model of them all is the Uniform Luminance Model, which describes a sky of constant brightness. It was intended to represent a heavily overcast sky. It has long been appreciated, however, that a densely overcast sky exhibits a relative gradation from darker horizon to brighter zenith; this was recorded as long ago as 1901. The Uniform Luminance Sky is therefore a poor representation of any actually occurring meteorological conditions and is generally not used for illuminance modeling.

The CIE Standard Overcast Sky, originally known as the Moon and Spencer Sky, was devised to better approximate the luminance distribution observed for overcast skies. Adopted as a standard by the CIE in 1955, this description is the one most frequently used for illuminance modeling. Normalized to the zenith luminance, it has the form

$$L_{\zeta} = \frac{L_{\zeta}(1 + 2\cos\zeta)}{3} \tag{6.3}$$

where L_{ζ} is the luminance at an angle ζ from the zenith and L_{ζ} is the zenith luminance. Comparisons with measured data have demonstrated the validity of the CIE Standard Overcast Sky model as a representation of dull sky conditions [KV93].

To describe the brightness distribution for clear sky conditions requires a considerably more complex mathematical representation. The complexity arises from a number of observed effects that are accounted for in the model. Among these are a bright circumsolar region, a sky luminance minimum that is at some point above the horizon, and a brightening of the sky near the horizon. The scales of these effects are related to the solar position and the relative magnitudes of the illumination produced by the sun and sky. Like the CIE overcast standard, the CIE clear sky model is normalized to zenith luminance and the sky luminance distribution is given by [CIE73]

$$L = L_\zeta \frac{(0.91 + 10e^{-3\theta} + 0.45\cos^2\theta)(1 - e^{(-0.32/\sin\gamma)})}{(0.91 + 10e^{-3(\pi/2 - \gamma_s)} + 0.45\sin^2\gamma_s)(1 - e^{-0.32})} \qquad (6.4)$$

where γ is the sky point altitude, γ_s is the solar altitude, and θ is the angle between the sun and the sky point. Note that the spectral distribution of skylight—its color—is not predicted by any of these models.

The overcast and clear CIE models are representations of extreme sky types—densely overcast or completely clear. Intermediate skies—that is, thin/moderate cloud cover and/or hazy atmospheric conditions—are more likely occurrences than totally clear or overcast skies for many geographical locations. Sky models generate continuous sky luminance distribution patterns. The discontinuous aspects of skylight—instantaneous cloud patterns—are not addressed.

6.1.3 Daylight Indoors—The Components of Illuminance

It helps to characterize the daylight entering a space by its origin—sun or sky—and the path by which it has arrived—directly from the source or by reflection (Figure 6.2). These categories will be particularly useful later on, when we relate light exchanges by reflection to ambient parameter settings.

6.2 Evaluation Techniques and Accuracy

Daylight simulation for interior spaces can be divided into two modes of evaluation:

- Quantitative, or numerical
- Qualitative, or visual

Quantitative data are usually presented in the form of line graphs, surface plots, or false-color maps, for example, of the distribution of illuminance across a plane. We use images to give an impression of what the finished building will look like, usually from several different viewpoints and under different lighting conditions. These modes are complementary rather than exclusive, and indeed often overlap. You may find that, even for purely numerical work, a few well-chosen images will facilitate the process of obtaining accurate predictions.

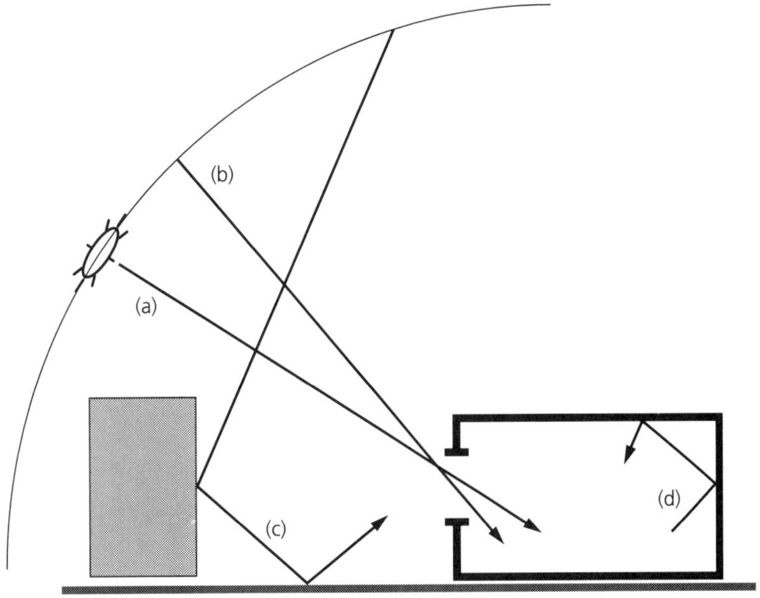

Figure 6.2 Components of daylight: (a) direct sun, (b) direct sky, (c) externally reflected, and (d) internally reflected.

For want of better criteria, we will distinguish between scenes that use the standard CIE overcast sky for illumination and the rest, which use any type of sky with sun. Overcast skies tend to be used for numerical work, which is aimed toward obtaining unambiguous quantities such as the daylight factor. Sunny sky conditions are particular to each sky, and the analysis under these circumstances will be more complex and less general than, say, a daylight factor evaluation. A few of the more common forms of analysis are described below for each of the two categories of illumination.

1. Standard CIE overcast sky conditions (daylight factor prediction)
  - Analysis of an architectural design to ensure compliance with, say, a statutory minimum daylight provision
  - Comparative evaluation of design options
  - Prediction of the daylight factor reduction caused by introducing new external obstructions to the local environment, such as a proposed nearby building
  - Visual impression of the scene accompanied by a false-color image of daylight factor (or illuminance values)

2. Skies with sun
   - Visual impression at certain times of day/year
   - Solar penetration/shading studies, such as a "movie" sequence of images
   - Effect of advanced glazing materials, such as a "movie" sequence and/or illuminance plots
   - Glare evaluation, such as locating sources of glare in an image and predicting indices for visual comfort probability

These are just some of the possibilities. The daylight factor approach is a standard technique and warrants detailed description.

6.2.1 The Daylight Factor Approach

The daylight factor at any point is the ratio of the interior illuminance at that point to the global horizontal illuminance under CIE standard overcast sky conditions. The daylight factor (DF) is normally expressed as a percentage:

$$DF = \frac{E_{in}}{E_{out}} \cdot 100 \qquad (6.5)$$

The interior illuminance is usually evaluated at workplane height (.Figure 6.3). Direct sunlight is, of course, excluded from the calculation. Because the overcast skies will generally be the dullest, the daylight factor method should be considered a "worst case" evaluation, primarily suited to calculating minimum values. Because the sky luminance does not vary with azimuth, the orientation of the scene about the *z*-axis has no effect on DF.

The conventional method to evaluate daylight factors, still very much in use, is from illuminance measurements taken inside scale models under artificial sky conditions. Unlike thermal, acoustic, or structural models, physical models for lighting do not require any scaling corrections. While a detailed physical model may indeed provide reliable results, such models can be very expensive to construct, especially if several design variants are to be evaluated. Increasingly, architects and design consultants are looking to computer simulation to offer an alternative solution approach.

Daylight factors are usually evaluated for uncluttered spaces. Since we are not interested in visual impression, the scene description usually accounts for only the important structural features of the space, and furniture and so on is not included.

Illuminance (and DF) are quantities that we derive from the irradiance predicted by the rtrace program. Often you will see that the irradiance values from the standard output of rtrace are converted directly to illuminance (or DF). Wherever in

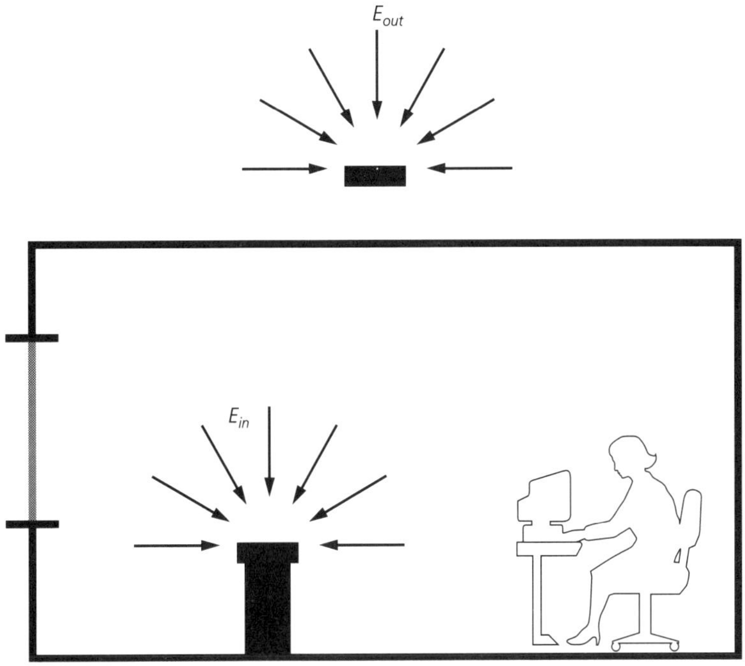

Figure 6.3 Internal and external horizontal illuminance.

the text we refer to illuminance (or DF) prediction, we shall use the term to mean irradiance prediction followed by conversion to the appropriate units. The following section describes, in general terms, how the mode of analysis influences the setting of key *Radiance* parameters.

6.2.2 Pictures, Numbers, and Accuracy

For a conventional office scene constructed with typical materials, an accurate (±10%) illuminance prediction usually requires four or more ambient bounces [Mar95]. We will see later that some of the other ambient parameters can be set to fairly low-resolution values without compromising too much the accuracy of the illuminance calculation. As most users will already have discovered, however, coarse ambient parameter settings can give fast renderings but usually produce blotchy images.

So why is it that parameters that might result in blotchy images can nevertheless give accurate illuminance predictions? The answer becomes apparent when we consider the relative complexity of DF (illuminance) prediction and image generation.

A screen-size image will comprise approximately one million pixels. Empty scenes look fairly boring, so we usually include tables, chairs, and so on, to make it look more like a real room. Depending on the view point, the image is likely to include several items of furniture. The more cluttered the scene from the view point, the harder the interreflection calculation has to work. This means more frequent sampling if we wish to avoid blotches, with the resulting computational overhead. Contrast this with an uncluttered space for DF evaluation. For an accurate prediction, it is essential that the first level of hemispherical sampling produce a good estimate of the irradiance gradient. DFs are usually evaluated at a relatively small number of points, say 50 to 500, across a plane. Furthermore, it is much easier to estimate irradiance gradients across one plane than across the hundreds of surfaces we are likely to see in the image (Figure 6.4). Because the first estimate is so important for DF calculations, we usually set a high value for -**ad**, but relax the parameters that determine the density of the ambient calculation. This allows us to use a high value for -**ab** without the simulations becoming unmanageable.

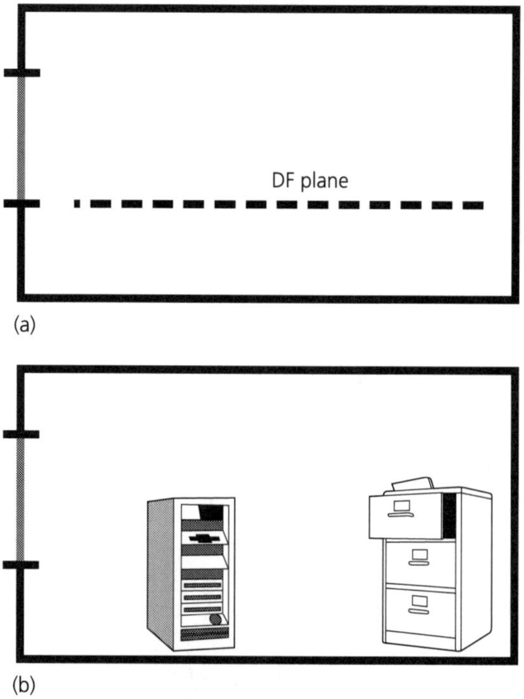

Figure 6.4 Illuminance calculation (a) can be used to calculate daylight factors. Image generation (b) can be used to render images with detail corresponding to need.

As we turn our attention now to image generation, the experienced user will already be aware that the cost of computing images rises with each successive bounce. Do images need more than one or two ambient bounces? First, we should decide what information we want our image to contain. Do we really want highly accurate (±10%) luminance values for every pixel in the image? One or two ambient bounces may give us pretty accurate luminance values, say, within 25%, for the majority of pixels in the scene, for example most of the wall, floor, and ceiling. But do we really want to crank up the number of ambient bounces to five or more just to add a little bit of luminance to each pixel, or possibly shade in what may be a tiny part of the scene? Given that sooner or later we will want to solve real-world problems, within real-world time constraints, the answer for the majority of us will be no.[16] The ambient calculation is one of the keystone features of *Radiance* and, used carefully, it can impart a tremendous impression of realism to a synthetic image. Note that it is the *directionality* of the ambient shading that lends this realism, for example the brightening of surfaces near a sun patch. This can be largely achieved with just one or two ambient bounces (possibly applied in conjunction with a mkillum-generated window). With increasing ambient bounces, the higher-level reflections tend toward a homogeneous and isotropic field of diffuse radiation. These higher-level reflections add little that can be noticed on a monitor to the pixel luminance already achieved with, say, -ab = 2. For image generation, the higher-order reflections are therefore best approximated by the careful setting of a constant ambient value (**-av**). How to choose a value for the -av parameter will be demonstrated in the case study examples. Absolute accuracy is required for illuminance prediction, and the constant ambient value is usually set to zero for these calculations.

For image generation, the conversion of a window to a light source using the mkillum utility can significantly speed up the production of smooth renderings. The technique works well as long as the total number of secondary light sources is kept reasonably small. For illuminance calculations, however, where -ab > 2 is usually essential, the preprocessing of windows to secondary light sources is generally not recommended. Similarly, for those rare occasions when images need to be rendered using a high value for -ab, it may be best to avoid using secondary sources and rely on the ambient calculation.

16. There will be exceptions; remember that these are recommendations, not rules.

6.2.3 Color Specification

How we specify the colors of the objects in our scene is another consideration. Color will influence the photometric results owing to interactions between surfaces. Visually, we perceive this in renderings as "color bleed," whereby a surface takes on some of the hue of other, usually more strongly colored, surfaces. This can be a significant effect, not just for the surface materials, but also for the sky and the sun if they are given a nongray radiance. If the RGB color values of materials are known from spectrophotometer measurements, these should be used in the simulations. If this information is not available, then for purely quantitative work, you are urged to specify gray reflection, transmission, and emission properties for *all* the materials and sources. For visual impression, however, if color data are not available, you will have to make a few good guesses. The setting of spectral radiance values for colored skies will be addressed in Section 6.7.4, Sky Spectral Radiance Values.

Having covered some of the basics, we will now demonstrate, using a series of case study examples, how to apply *Radiance* to the solution of realistic daylighting problems.

6.3 Case Study I: Creating the Luminous Environment

The sky and sun are, on an architectural scale, considered to be very distant from the local scene. In other words, the unobstructed view of the sky will be identical for all observers placed anywhere in the scene. The sky is therefore specified as a source solid angle rather than a dome of actual extent. From our local "flat Earth," the sky appears to be a luminous hemisphere. Thus, we model it as a source whose angle is 180 degrees, and we aim the center of the source directly upward, that is, toward the zenith.

Here we introduce a basic calculation technique fundamental to daylight prediction. The following example demonstrates the use of the rtrace program to determine the horizontal irradiance resulting from an unobstructed uniform sky.

6.3.1 Example: Uniform Sky

The scene file, which we will call *sky_uni.rad*, describes our entire scene, which is simply a hemispherical sky of unit radiance:

```
# uniform brightness sky (B=1)
void glow sky_glow
0
```

```
0
4 1 1 1 0
sky_glow source sky
0
0
4 0 0 1 180
```

By giving each of the spectral channels the same radiance (i.e., 1), we are defining a colorless, or "gray," sky. From this scene file, generate an octree, say

```
% oconv sky_uni.rad > sky_uni.oct
```

Now execute the rtrace program to determine the horizontal irradiance due to the uniform sky. A typical command might look like this:

```
% echo "0 0 0 0 0 1" | rtrace -h -I+ -w -ab 1 sky_uni.oct
```

which writes to the standard output the simulated spectral (RGB) irradiance values:

```
3.141593e+00  3.141593e+00  3.141593e+00
```

Because the Boolean irradiance switch is set to "on" (i.e., -I+), rtrace interprets the standard input as the measurement position (0 0 0) and orientation (0 0 1). In other words, rtrace will evaluate the irradiance at point 0 0 0 for a surface (an imaginary one) whose surface normal points upward (0 0 1). The output, therefore, is a triad of predicted values for spectral (RGB) horizontal irradiance. To convert the spectral irradiance triad to irradiance, use the following formula:[17]

$$I = 0.265 I_R + 0.670 I_G + 0.065 I_B \qquad (6.6)$$

Because the sum of the multiplying factors is 1, the achromatic irradiance equals 3.141593, which is of course the value for π. We will now compare this with an analytically derived result. For any hemisphere of radiance $B(\theta, \phi)$ the horizontal irradiance is given by

$$I = \int_0^{2\pi} \int_0^{\pi/2} B(\theta, \phi) \sin\theta \cos\theta \, d\theta \, d\phi \qquad (6.7)$$

where for a uniform sky, $B(\theta, \phi) = B$, and Equation 6.7 simplifies to

17. The coefficients should match those specified in *src/common/color.h*.

$$I = B\int_0^{2\pi}\int_0^{\pi/2} \sin\theta\cos\theta\, d\theta\, d\phi \tag{6.8}$$

$$= \pi B$$

which, for a sky of unit radiance, gives $I = \pi$. This value for irradiance is what the rtrace simulation predicted. Because the sky was of uniform brightness, all the samples return the same radiance, and we therefore get an exact answer. For any nonuniform sky, however, the prediction will never exactly match an analytically derived result. We see this in the next example. We shouldn't worry, though, because Monte Carlo–based algorithms were never intended to give exact solutions, but they can give very accurate ones.

6.3.2 Example: CIE Overcast Sky

A more realistic example applies the same rtrace technique to a CIE standard overcast sky. Inserting the CIE overcast sky brightness distribution function (Equation 6.3) into Equation 6.7, and evaluating, gives

$$I = \int_0^{2\pi}\int_0^{\pi/2} B_z\left(\frac{1 + 2\sin\theta}{3}\right)\sin\theta\cos\theta\, d\theta\, d\phi \tag{6.9}$$

$$= \frac{7}{9}\pi B_z$$

where B_z is the zenith radiance. As with the uniform sky, the analytical result is exact. However, before we can repeat the above test with rtrace, we need to be able to create skies that have nonuniform brightness distributions. To do this, we select a predefined brightness function that corresponds to the CIE overcast description, then use this to vary the brightness of the glow material. This is achieved by using the gensky program, which can generate descriptions for several sky types. We will first look at how gensky can produce CIE overcast skies. To do this, we use the **-c** option to designate the type of sky we want, but we will also use the **-b** option so we can specify a zenith radiance for the sky. (The sun angles need to be declared also, but these will not be used by gensky for the CIE overcast, so any values can be supplied). The command

```
% gensky -ang 45 0 -c -b 1
```

writes the following to the standard output:

```
# gensky -ang 45 0 -c -b 1
# Ground ambient level: 0.8

void brightfunc skyfunc
2 skybr skybright.cal
0
3 2 1.00e+00 1.56e-01
```

The comment lines echo the gensky command and recommend a *ground ambient level.* We will discuss the significance of this value later; for the moment, we will restrict ourselves to the meaning of the rest of the output. The last line of the gensky output has three (real) arguments. These are the number `2`, indicating the type of sky, the zenith radiance (`1.00e+00`), and the ground radiance (`1.56e-01`). The zenith radiance is what we expect, since we specified this as an input argument to gensky. The significance of the ground radiance we leave for later, because our simple scene, for now, will comprise only the sky.

The output from the gensky program provides a brightness function (`skyfunc`) that we can apply as a modifier to the glow material. The easiest way to include the modifier is to execute the gensky command in the description file. The contents of the file *sky_ovc.rad* would then be as follows:

```
# CIE overcast sky (Bz = 1)

!gensky -ang 45 0 -c -b 1

skyfunc glow sky_glow
0
0
4 1 1 1 0
sky_glow source sky
0
0
4 0 0 1 180
```

The RGB radiance that the sky now assumes is `skyfunc` *multiplied* by the RGB radiance specified for glow, which here is unity for each of the channels because we want a gray (overcast) sky.

Now we create the octree for this scene, just as before:

```
% oconv sky_ovc.rad > sky_ovc.oct
```

and then calculate the horizontal irradiance using rtrace (pipe the output through rcalc to obtain the achromatic irradiance directly):

```
% rtrace -w -h -I+ -ab 1 sky_ovc.oct < samp.inp | rcalc -e \
 '$1=$1*0.265+$2*0.670+$3*0.065'
```

which produces the value

```
2.434001
```

The exact theoretical value for irradiance from the CIE overcast sky is $7_{\pi}B_z/9 = 2.443451$, since $B_z = 1$. Our predicted value is in good agreement with this. Note also that rather than being supplied through the pipe by the echo command, the coordinates are now read from the file *samp.inp*.

6.3.3 Example: CIE Overcast Sky Defined by Its Horizontal Illuminance

The preceding example showed how to generate a brightness distribution based on the standard CIE overcast sky model. The absolute brightness of the sky, however, was normalized for the purposes of illustration. Furthermore, the input and output were in units of radiance or irradiance. Before we can tackle real-world problems, we need to be able to relate the more usual daylighting quantities of luminance and illuminance to the radiance and irradiance inputs required by gensky. Recall that although the *Radiance* system calculates in units of radiance/irradiance, we will use a constant value for the factor to convert these to luminance/illuminance, or vice versa.

Daylighting practitioners commonly describe a sky in terms of the diffuse horizontal illuminance that is produced by that sky. Recall that the CIE overcast model does not include the sun, so here the global horizontal illuminance will be the same as the diffuse horizontal illuminance. The CIE overcast sky can therefore be fully characterized by the horizontal illuminance, usually given in lux. A realistic horizontal illuminance for a (brightish) overcast sky is 10,000 lux. This is a convenient figure to work with; for example, a daylight factor of 5% corresponds to an illuminance of 500 lux. The gensky program gives us two ways in which we can generate a 10,000-lux CIE overcast sky. We can specify either the zenith radiance (-**b** option) or the horizontal (diffuse) irradiance (-**B** option). The second option is perhaps the more direct, and we shall use that for the next rtrace example.

Luminous Efficacy

This conversion factor is the *Radiance* system's own value for luminous efficacy and is fixed at K_R = 179 lumens/watt (lm/w). This should not be confused with the more usual daylighting value, which can be anywhere between 50 and 150 lm/w depending on the type of sky or light considered.

First, we need to modify the gensky command to produce a 10,000-lux sky. The irradiance that corresponds to this illuminance is 10,000/179 = 55.866 w/m^2. The line giving the gensky command should now look like this:

```
!gensky -ang 45 0 -c -B 55.866
```

The rest of the file remains as before. Let's now double-check that this sky is indeed what we specified. Run oconv as before, then execute a slightly modified rtrace command:

```
% rtrace -w -h -I+ -ab 1 sky_uni.oct < samp.inp | rcalc -e   \
 '$1=($1*0.265+$2*0.670+$3*0.065)*179'
```

The calculation returns the value

```
9977.17002
```

which is pretty close to our starting value of 10,000 lux, in fact within 0.3%. Notice that the irradiance output is now multiplied by 179 to convert it to illuminance (lux). So far, the only ambient parameter that we've set for the simulation has been -ab; all the other parameters will use the default settings. Since this scene comprises only a glow source, the parameters that relate directly to the density of the irradiance gradient calculation (i.e., **-aa** and **-ar**) will have no effect. Before we go on to more complex (i.e., realistic scenes), we will first have a look at the sky we have generated. To view the sky, start the **rview** program:

```
% rview -vta -vp 0 0 0 -vd 0 0 1 -vu 0 1 0 -vh 180 -vv 180 sky_ovc.oct
```

to give an angular fish-eye view of the entire sky. The view point will be useful later on, so save it in a file called *ang180.vf* using the rview command. A false-color image of the sky will show more clearly the CIE overcast sky luminance distribution:

```
% rpict -vf ang180.vf sky_ovc.oct   \
   | falsecolor -s 4000 -l cd/m^2 > ovc_lum.pic
```

The luminance scale in the **falsecolor -s** option was set too close to the approximate zenith luminance of the sky, found either from Equation 6.9 or by using the `trace` command in rview. The default label `nits` has been changed to the more familiar cd/m^2, which means the same thing. The false-color image shows what we expect to see from Equation 6.3: a brightness distribution depending only on altitude where the zenith luminance is three times that of the horizon.

6.3.4 The Ground "Glow": An "Upside-Down" Sky

Although it might seem too self-evident to point out, we should remind ourselves that at the horizon the sky "meets" the ground. An actual ground plane of finite extent, say, a disc of radius *r*, will always fall short of an "infinite" horizon. For any given view toward the horizon, we can make the gap (a black void) between the edge of the ground and the sky appear smaller by using a larger *r*. However, we can never make them meet. Furthermore, there are good reasons not to introduce an actual ground plane of inordinately large size: the resolution of an ambient calculation will be dependent on the maximum dimension of the scene.

To get around this problem, we use an upside-down sky to represent a luminous ground. To do this, we apply the `skyfunc` modifier to a 180-degree glow source, where the direction vector is pointing downward. To include a glowing ground in our scene, add the following lines to the file *sky_ovc.rad*:

```
skyfunc glow ground_glow
0
0
4 1 1 1 0

ground_glow source ground
0
0
4 0 0 -1 180
```

The glowing ground behaves differently from a glowing sky. Although the same modifier is used for both, *Radiance* can distinguish between the two by testing the *z* component of any ray's direction vector. Above the horizon, the sky-model brightness distribution is applied, but below the horizon, a constant brightness value is used.[18] Note that as with the sky, the ground brightness is achromatic. The

18. In fact, a sharp-cutoff mixing function ensures a continuous transition from ground to sky. This operates only about the horizon, leaving most of the sky independent of the ground's brightness and vice versa.

radiance value that will be used for the ground brightness was determined by the gensky program. It is based on two factors: the sky's (diffuse) horizontal irradiance and the "average ground reflectivity." The horizontal irradiance is either supplied as an argument to gensky or evaluated from the zenith radiance. The "average ground reflectivity" may also be supplied as a gensky argument (`-g refl`); otherwise, a default value of 0.2 is used (as will be the case for us). The value 0.2 (or 20%) is a typical value for ground plane reflectance. We can check the gensky-supplied value for ground radiance very easily using Equation 6.8, since the ground is in effect a luminous "hemisphere" of constant brightness. Execute the gensky command as it appears in the *scene* file:

```
% gensky -ang 45 0 -c -B 55.866
```

Recall that the last number of the gensky output for the CIE overcast sky is the ground radiance, which here is shown to be 3.56e+00 w/m^2. The illuminance from a hemisphere source of this brightness is $\pi(3.56 \times 179) = 2001.9$ lux, which is 20% (or 0.2) of the horizontal illuminance due to the sky. We shouldn't worry too much about using an "upside-down" sky for the ground, but we should be aware of the practicalities. Although the ground radiance is based on the sky's horizontal irradiance, putting something between the sky and the ground will not affect the brightness of either (Figure 6.5). In other words, no matter how built-up the model becomes, with nearby tall structures and so on, the ground radiance (where it is visible) will be the same as for an empty scene. By the same token, a single building is an obstruction. Therefore, all scenes should include a local ground plane that participates in the interreflection calculation. This will ensure that the ground plane brightness is a function of both the sky brightness and the local environment.

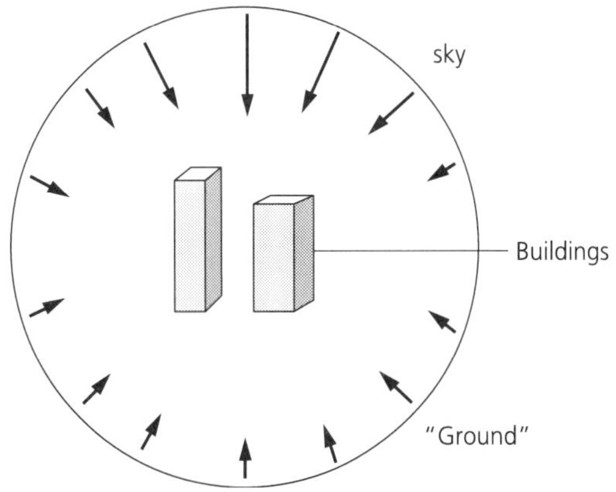

Figure 6.5 The luminous "envelope" describes luminance as a function of incident direction.

6.3.5 Summary

The scene we have constructed thus far is a seamless luminous envelope. The brightness of this envelope is based on a combination of a mathematical sky model and a ground plane reflectance model. We can specify the absolute brightness of this environment using physically meaningful quantities. Environments of this type will contain the rooms, office spaces, and so on, for which we wish to predict daylight quantities.

6.4 Case Study II: Predicting Internal Illuminances

In this example, we demonstrate how to predict DF levels for a simple scene. We show how to automate the execution of the rtrace program and how this can be used to test for convergence in the ambient calculation. The section concludes with an introduction to the dayfact script.

6.4.1 A Simple Space

The room we will use is 3 meters wide, 9 meters deep, and 2.7 meters high. These dimensions are typical of a deep-plan office module. The long dimension is aligned north-south; the room has a single south-facing window of width 2.6 meters and height 1.5 meters. The south wall is 0.2 meter thick and the window is set in the middle of this wall, so there are internal and external windowsills of depth 0.1 meter. The plan view of the room is shown in Figure 6.6. The room description is maintained in three scene files:

- *room.rad*—walls, floor, ceiling geometry
- *mat_gray.rad*—material description for walls, floor, ceiling geometry
- *window.rad*—window geometry and material description

6.4.2 Computing Daylight Factor Values

A typical analysis might begin by determining the daylight factor along the mid-point of the room. The file *samp1d.inp* contains the coordinates of the positions at which the DFs will be evaluated. Executing the rtrace command from a shell script is a convenient way to automate systematic explorations of parameter settings. The following script shows how to automate the DF calculation and test the sensitivity of the prediction to the number of ambient bounces. For this test, we cover the range `-ab 1` to `-ab 5`.

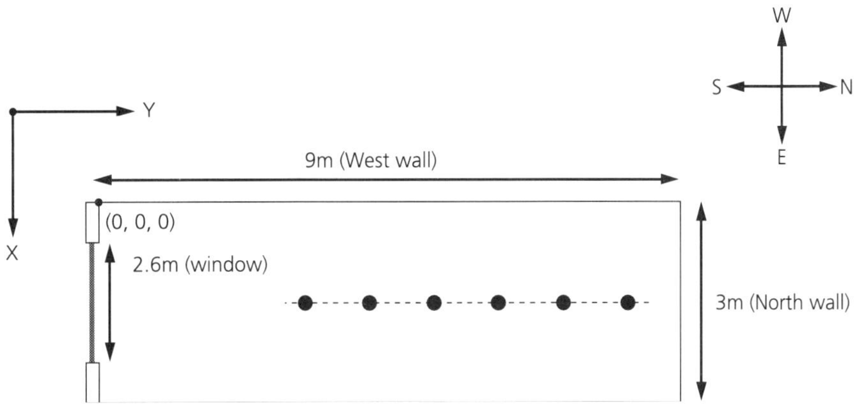

Figure 6.6 Plan view of room.

```
#!/bin/csh -f

# loop through ab
foreach ab (1 2 3 4 5)

echo "Ambient bounces" $ab

# Calculate DF

   rtrace -w -h -I+ -ab $ab -aa 0.2 -ad 512 \
     -as 0 -ar 128 scene.oct \
     < sampl.inp | rcalc -e\
     '$1=($1*0.265+$2*0.670+$3*0.065)*179/10000*100'

end
```

For all other parameter settings, the current rtrace defaults will, of course, be applied.[19] The predictions follow a characteristic pattern as shown in Figure 6.7: close to the window, the predictions for the range of -ab are relatively similar (17% to 20% at 0.5 meter). Farther away from the window, where interreflection becomes more important, they agree less (0.24% to 1.26% at 5 meters). We expect the predictions for -ab 5 to be greater than those for -ab 1, but sampling variance may mask that. We also expect the illuminance, and therefore the DF, to gradually

19. Some of these are declared in the script to allow comparison later on. Default values occasionally change when a new version of *Radiance* is released.

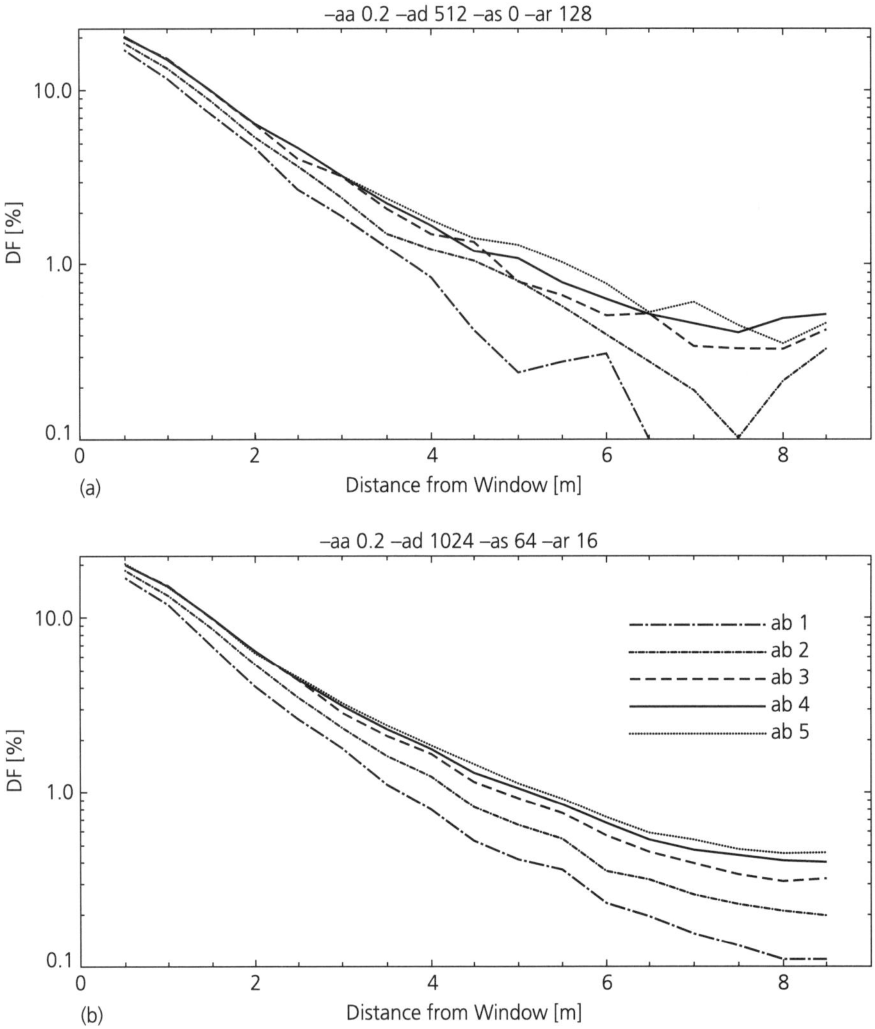

Figure 6.7 Daylight factor plots showing the effects of the -ab parameter. The top graph (a) uses fewer samples over the hemisphere, -ad 512 -as 0, than the bottom graph (b) which uses -ad 1024 -as 64.

decrease away from the window. The DF curves in Figure 6.7(a) nevertheless confound our expectations: the predictions are simply not good enough to show a consistent pattern in the data. This is especially noticeable at the rear of the room, where the curves are very jagged.

You may be relieved to learn that we don't *always* have to work through a series of -ab simulations before we can discover that one or more of the other ambient parameter settings was too coarse. We can, for many situations, use the `-ab 1` as a diagnostic to help us make better choices for some of the other settings. Recall that for `-ab 1`, the illuminance predicted will be that due to the portion of sky that is directly visible from the point of calculation, that is, the direct sky component. This component is usually the major contributor to the total illuminance at that point. If we get the direct sky component (`-ab 1`) wrong, our predictions for the total illuminance (-ab > 1) will be also poor. For this space, we know that some sky should be visible from all the points for which we want to predict the DF. Examination of the data for `-ab 1` reveals that for several points at the back of the room, the DF was predicted to be zero. This tells us that too few rays were spawned to guarantee adequate sampling of the window from all points in the DF plane. To remedy this, we should set -ad to a higher value, say 1024. We can further improve our estimates at `-ab 1` by enabling the ambient supersampling option (**-as**) in the rtrace calculation. The value we set for -as is the number of extra rays that will be used to sample areas in the divided hemisphere that appear to have high variance. In other words, for this scene, additional rays will be used to sample around the window—assuming, of course, that the ambient division sampling picked up the window in the first instance.

We now repeat the DF predictions with `-ad 1024` and `-as 64`. The ambient accuracy is the same as before, but the ambient resolution has been relaxed to `-ar 16`. These DF predictions look much better as shown in Figure 6.7(b). The curves are fairly smooth and the rank order is the same at all points along the DF plane. Which of these predictions, if any, are correct? Before we can answer this, we need to distinguish between *absolute* accuracy and *useful* accuracy. For daylighting purposes, it is important to obtain reliable predictions of the DF distribution in the critical range 10% to 0.5%. The recommended minimum DF for full daylighting is 5%, and the 1% value is generally considered to be a minimum below which the provision of daylight can be considered negligible. Thus, we need to be fairly certain of the DF down to the 1% level. There is little practical use in resolving the 0.1% DF boundary, or in distinguishing between the 0.02% and 0.05% levels. With this in mind, there is little to choose between the `-ab 4` and `-ab 5` curves. Would it be worthwhile predicting the DFs for -ab greater than 5? For this case, no. We can see from the curves that the difference between successive DF predictions for higher -ab gets smaller each time. Remember, the predictions will never be exact, so the DF curves for scenes like this will never be perfectly smooth. The basic tenets for setting the ambient parameters are

1. Set -ad high enough to capture the visible luminous features at the first bounce.
2. Give sufficient ambient bounces to redistribute the light.
3. Set the remaining ambient parameters to sufficiently high resolution to deliver *acceptably* smooth results.

6.4.3 The Dayfact Script

The dayfact script is a user-friendly interface to the illuminance prediction capabilities of rtrace. The script essentially performs the same rtrace illuminance calculation shown above, but in addition it can create contour plots of

- Workplane illuminance
- Workplane daylight factors
- Potential savings resulting from daylight illumination based on a given lighting design level

The script works out the points in the DF plane based on user-supplied values for the plane origin and dimensions. It also determines the global horizontal illuminance directly from the gensky arguments. Try the script out using one of the ambient parameter combinations from the preceding example.

Dayfact is a handy utility to have, but because it hides some of the workings of rtrace, we do not recommend that you use it to investigate convergence and so on. Application-specific shell scripts are far better suited to exploring these aspects of the ambient calculation. The contour-level defaults built into dayfact may not be ideal for everyone and cannot be overridden. Users who do want *Radiance* contour images are urged to use the falsecolor script. Taking a dayfact-produced illuminance picture as input, falsecolor offers a great deal of user control over contour levels, color mapping, and so on. See the falsecolor manual page for details. Alternatively, you can import the illuminance prediction data into a proprietary software package that can produce contour, surface plots, and so on. The next example shows how additional objects, ground plane, and so on affect the ambient calculation, and shows how to account for them correctly.

6.5 Case Study III: Introducing Complexity

In this section, we add a ground plane and a nearby building to our simple scene. We model the ground plane as a disc of, say, radius 20 meters, centered on the origin. The diffuse reflectance for the disc material is the same as the ground plane reflectance used in the gensky command (0.2, or 20%). We can guess that the effect of the ground plane will be to slightly lower the DFs calculated in the preceding example, because, as we mentioned earlier in the chapter, we are replacing (locally) a ground glow of constant radiance with a material whose brightness now depends on the geometry and reflectance of nearby objects as well as the sky (Figure 6.8). In the vicinity of the room, the calculated ground plane radiance will be less than the ground glow radiance because the room obscures some of the ground plane's view of the sky. Rtrace now has to evaluate the ground plane brightness during the simulation; we should therefore consider the additional cost to the ambient calculation. This is best explained using a simplified ray diagram to represent the ambient bounces (Figure 6.9). The ground component of internal illuminance is, in effect, "one bounce further away" with a ground plane than it is with a ground glow. The same will be true for nearby buildings that obscure the sky (glow)—the building facade brightness will have to be evaluated as part of the ambient calculation. To complete the modifications to the scene, we now add an external obstruction: a nearby building. We represent this using a box 9 meters square and 12 meters tall, which has a diffuse reflectance of 30%. The box is positioned so that

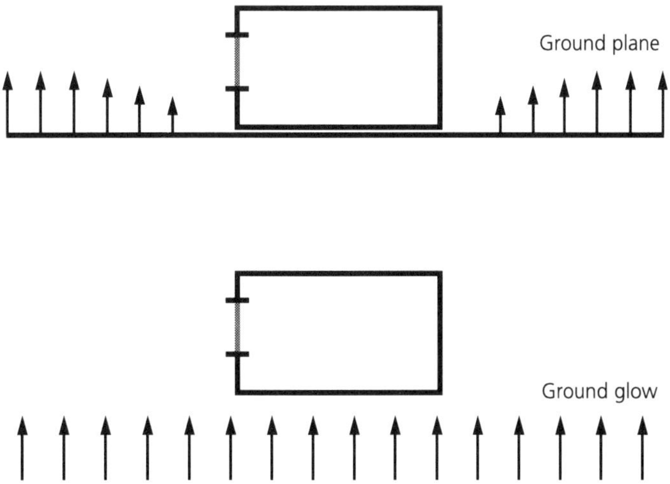

Figure 6.8 Ground plane versus ground glow.

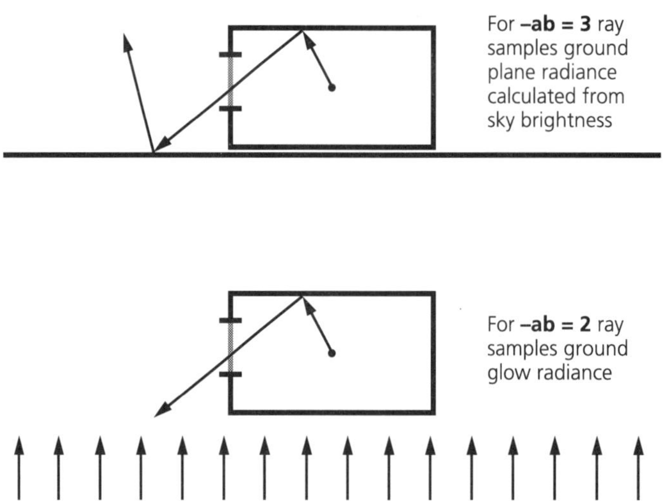
For **–ab = 3** ray samples ground plane radiance calculated from sky brightness
For **–ab = 2** ray samples ground glow radiance

Figure 6.9 Ambient bounces and the ground plane.

it faces the room window and obscures much of the view of the sky from inside the room. The DF predictions are repeated as before, only now we increase the maximum -ab to 7.

The results for two ambient accuracy settings are shown in Figure 6.10. The DF curves in Figure 6.10(a) are surely unsound: the `-ab 1` curve shows an *increase* in DF from 0.5 to 1 meter, and for higher -ab the DF at the rear of the room is *greater* than for the unobstructed case. Before we despair, let us examine the predictions obtained using the higher ambient accuracy in Figure 6.10(b). The DF curves now begin to make sense. Why the dramatic difference? This example was contrived to create the circumstances under which the irradiance interpolation algorithm would, for certain parameter combinations, perform relatively poorly. To appreciate why this has happened, we need to recognize that irradiance interpolation can occur across the points supplied to rtrace in the same way that it can across the surfaces (i.e., pixels) computed by rpict. In other words, hemispherical sampling (at the first level) will not necessarily be initiated from every point in the DF plane supplied to rtrace.

To understand the possible outcomes, we need to examine in more detail the way the simulation progresses. Hemispherical sampling at the first level will always be initiated from the first point supplied to rtrace provided that -ab ≥ 1. From the rays spawned at the first point, the ambient calculation will predict the way the indirect irradiance is changing about that point—this is the indirect irradiance gradient. The calculation also evaluates an estimation of error associated with the prediction

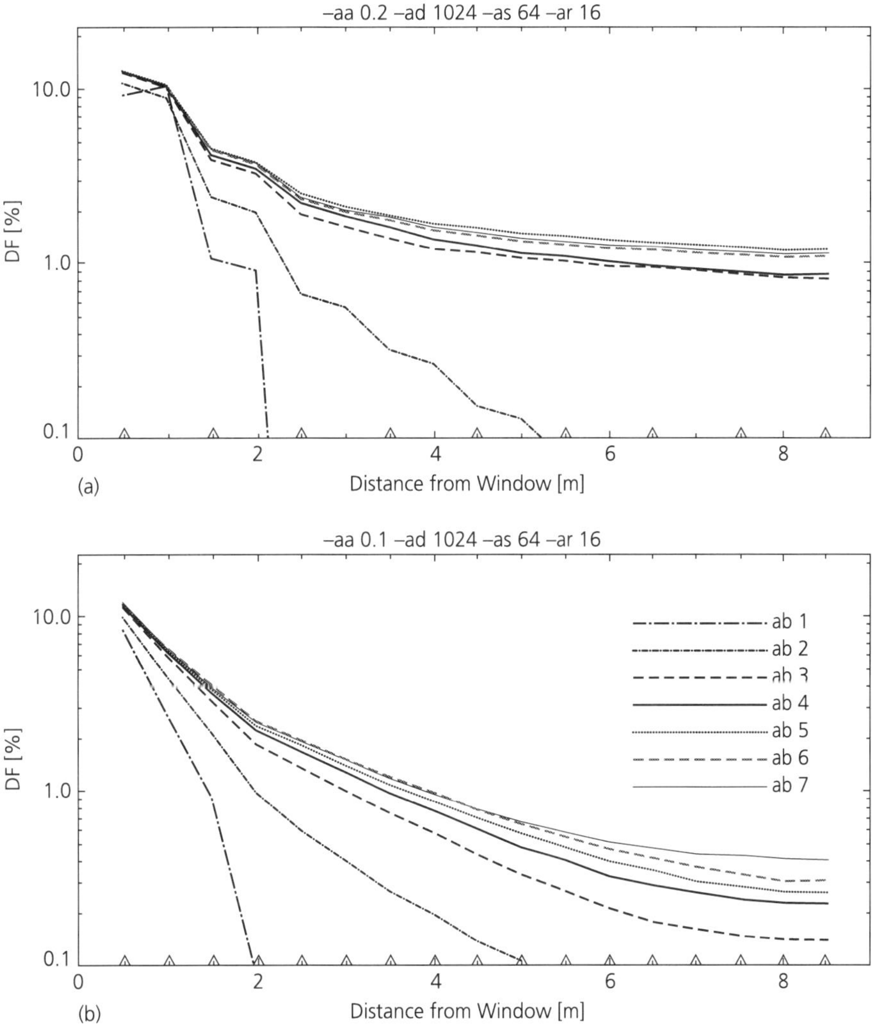

Figure 6.10 Daylight factor curves with ground plane and obstruction. The top graph (a) shows the -aa 0.2 setting, which results in an inappropriate interpolation. The bottom graph (b) shows better results with the -aa 0.1 setting.

for the irradiance gradient. These quantities, together with the ambient accuracy parameter, are used to determine a "radius of validity" for the gradient estimate. If the next point supplied to rtrace is within this radius, the indirect irradiance is evaluated from the gradient estimate and not from further hemispherical sampling. In other words, the value is obtained by a form of interpolation rather than by actual sampling. This is a somewhat abridged description of the way the ambient calculation operates; see Chapter 12 for a detailed explanation.

Factors that influence the scale over which interpolation may occur are

- Ambient accuracy (-aa)
- Ambient resolution (-ar)
- Maximum scene dimension

The minimum possible spacing between hemispherical sampling points is the maximum scene dimension multiplied by the ambient accuracy divided by the ambient resolution. We can confirm that the bad results for `-aa 0.2` arose from interpolation by plotting on the abscissa of both graphs the points in the DF plane from which hemispherical sampling was initiated (Δ markers). For `-aa 0.1`, sampling was initiated from all the points supplied to rtrace; for `-aa 0.2`, it was from every other point. Note that a doubling of the value for ambient resolution (i.e., from 16 to 32) would *not* necessarily have effected the same cure. This is because the -ar parameter acts as a limiting device. If you are already running up against the -ar limit, increasing the setting will result in a higher density of sampling. If the limit has not been reached, then increasing -ar should have no effect.

It should now be apparent why the ground plane size should be chosen with care. This is usually the largest surface in any scene, and its size will directly affect the sampling density for any given -aa and -ar. As a rule of thumb, the ground plane should be at least twice the maximum extent (horizontal or vertical) of the scene contents.[20]

We urge you to develop this exploration of the ambient calculation one or two stages further. Add or change, one at a time, features of the scene and investigate the effect that this has on the convergence characteristics of the ambient calculation. Try to anticipate the effect of changes in scene composition and/or parameter combination. The *Radiance* ambient calculation may appear difficult to control the first few times. However, by carrying out a handful of exploratory tests, you will begin to develop an almost intuitive sense of how to manage the simulation to good effect.

20. The dimensions of a scene can be obtained using the getbbox program.

6.6 DF Prediction: Tricks of the Trade

Here are a few hints on how to accelerate the modeling and evaluation process.

6.6.1 Appropriate Complexity

For illuminance (DF) prediction, it is not normally necessary to model nearby external obstructions in fine detail. Most building facades can be modeled using a single material whose reflectance is an area-weighted average of the reflectances of the major facade elements. It may be necessary to pay attention to surface finish, especially when the adjacent building is clad in mirrored glazing.

Where visual realism is not intended, the scale of modeling complexity should generally be commensurate with the scale of the effect of the modeled structures on internal light levels. A good example of putting this principle into practice might be a DF analysis for an office module in an atrium building (Figure 6.11). Nesting of a moderately detailed scene description in a simpler structure should not compromise the accuracy of the DF predictions, but it can produce significant savings in modeling time.

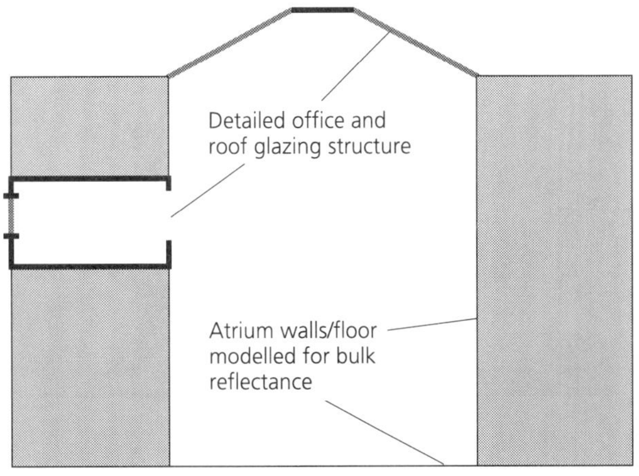

Figure 6.11 Nesting of a detailed office module in a coarsely modeled atrium building.

6.6.2 Views from the DF Plane

It often helps to visualize the scene from one or more view points along the DF plane. Choose a point in the DF plane, say, near the window, and generate a view looking directly upward—use the interactive previewer rview. Set the view type to hemispherical (**h**) and the view angles to 180 degrees. As the image resolution gradually improves, you will see a hemispherical projection view of the sky through the window. Set -av to some value to reveal the other surfaces. This makes it easier to understand the image, but what we are really interested in is the view of the sky. Compare the views with and without the external obstruction (Figure 6.12). The impact of the nearby building on internal light levels can be roughly estimated just from these images. Since the building obscures about half the view of the sky, the DF values will be approximately halved. This is a worst-case guess—it will, of course, depend on the facade reflectance. Examining a scene in this way will help you to appreciate the luminous environment "from a light meter's point of view."

6.6.3 The Ambient Exclude/Include Options

It is possible to limit the number of surfaces that participate directly in the indirect irradiance calculation. By limiting the scope of the ambient calculation, we can make significant savings in simulation time. This is achieved by telling rtrace not to include certain named material modifiers in the indirect calculation. Instead, the named materials will receive the constant ambient-value approximation. There is a complementary option called ambient include. With this option, only the named materials participate in the indirect calculation; the rest receive constant ambient-

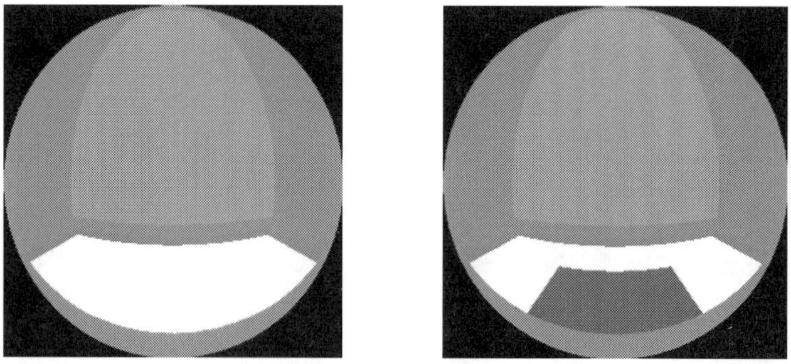

(a) (b)

Figure 6.12 Two views from the daylight factor plane: unobstructed view (a), and view with nearby building (b).

value approximation. We should take care to exclude only those materials that play no major part in the illumination of the space. The rtrace manual page explains how the options are enabled.

6.7 Case Study IV: Creating Skies with Sun

There are two *Radiance* sky generator programs. The "official" program, which is part of the standard *Radiance* release, is called gensky; it offers a selection of sky model types based on CIE standards. The other program is called **gendaylit**; it is one of the many *Radiance* extension programs, that is, it is not part of the standard release but is freely available to all users. We will discuss this program briefly near the end of this section.

6.7.1 Gensky

In addition to the standard CIE overcast model, the *Radiance* sky generator program can produce sun descriptions and sky brightness distributions that correspond to either the CIE clear or intermediate skies. The gensky program has several modes of operation, and unless you are careful, you can end up using a sky generated from default geographical parameters that are not appropriate to the intended location. Try the command

```
% gensky -defaults
```

to check what the current defaults are. Furthermore, if you do not explicitly specify parameters in the gensky command that are related to absolute sky and sun brightness, these quantities will be evaluated using standard functions. These quantities also may not be entirely suitable for your location.

The only way to be certain of the sky and sun brightness is to supply them as gensky arguments. The sky brightness can be specified in terms of either the zenith radiance (-**b** option) or the horizontal diffuse irradiance (-**B** option). The sun brightness is either given directly (-**r** option) or evaluated from the horizontal direct irradiance (-**R** option). Most users will want to generate sun and skies based on either measured or yardstick values for global horizontal and diffuse horizontal illuminance. For example, say we want to generate a sun and intermediate sky description from these measured quantities: a global horizontal illuminance of 66,110 lux and a diffuse horizontal illuminance of 41,881 lux. The sun position was recorded as altitude 49.6 degrees and azimuth 222.5 degrees. The altitude is the angle in degrees above the horizon and the azimuth is measured as degrees east of north. Note that this azimuth convention is different from the one used in *Radiance,* which is degrees west of south, so we need to subtract 180 degrees from the measured azimuth value. From the illuminance quantities, we need to deduce the correct gensky arguments for the -B and -R options—they are the easiest to figure out from what we have.

$$\text{horizontal diffuse irradiance} = \frac{\text{horizontal diffuse illuminance}}{\text{luminous efficacy}} \qquad (6.10)$$

$$233.97 = \frac{41881}{179}$$

and

$$\text{horizontal direct irradiance} = \frac{\text{hor. global ill.} - \text{hor. diffuse ill.}}{\text{luminous efficacy}}$$

$$135.35 = \frac{(66110 + 41881)}{179}$$

Thus, our gensky command, executed in a scene file, would look like this:

```
# Intermediate sky with sun
# Igh=66,110 lux, Idh=41,881 lux.

!gensky -ang 49.6 42.5 +i -B 233.97 -R 135.35

skyfunc glow sky_glow
0
0
4 0.986 0.986 1.205 0

sky_glow source sky
0
0
4 0 0 1 180
```

Remember that the material and surface specifications for the sky should follow the gensky command. This sky has a small blue excess specified for the glow material (see below). You may wish to generate a sun position based on an actual time of day, in which case the site latitude, longitude, and standard meridian need to be known. The following example demonstrates how to set these values. See also the gensky manual pages for the full list of options.

6.7.2 Time of Day Image Sequence

The progression of the solar beam in a space can be shown by images generated for different times of day. The creation of these can be automated by treating the gensky (or gendaylit) time parameters as shell variables. Here we show how to generate a dawn-to-dusk sequence of images. The location is Athens; the date is July 1. The geographical coordinates of Athens are 37.97 degrees N and 23.5 degrees E, but the site meridian on which local time is based is at longitude 30.0 degrees E, that is, two hours ahead of the time at the Greenwich meridian. The gensky command for an intermediate sky at noon on this day is

```
% gensky 7 1 12 +i -a 37.97 -o -23.50 -m -30
```

Note that negative angles are used for degrees east of Greenwich (or south of the equator). Experienced shell programmers all have their own styles and are likely to do things slightly differently. The example below illustrates just one of the many ways to automate scene and picture file creation.

```
#!/bin/csh -f
#
# Set month, day and geographical coordinates
#
set mon   = 07
set month = July
set day   = 01
set coord = (-a 37.97 -o -23.50 -m -30)

set ab =   2
set ad = 512
set as = 128
set ar = 64
set aa = 0.3

foreach hr (05 06 07 08 09 10 11 12 13 14 15 16 17 18 19 20)

set skypar = ($mon $day $hr +i $coord)
set gambv = `gensky $skypar | rcalc -i '# Ground ambient\ level: ${ga}' -e '$1=ga'`
if ($gambv == 0) goto SKYDARK
set inamb = `rcalc -n -e '$1='"$gambv"'/2'`
set inamb = ($inamb $inamb $inamb)

set ambpar = (-ab $ab -ad $ad -as $as -ar $ar -aa $aa -av $inamb)
```

```
oconv -i scene.oct '\!gensky '"$skypar" sky.rad > hr.oct

rpict -vf view.vf $ambpar \
     -x 1024 -y 1024 hr.oct \
    | pfilt -1 -e 0.06 -x /3 -y /3 \
    | pcompos - 0 0 '\!psign '"$month"' '"$day"' '"$hr"'h00' 0 0 > $month$day$hr.pic

rm hr.oct

SKYDARK:

end
```

We do not intend this book to be a treatise on shell programming, so we will describe this script purely in functional terms—what it does, rather than why we do it in this way. First, we define shell variables for the month (number and name), the day, and the geographical coordinates. We then define most of the ambient parameter shell variables. The `foreach` line starts the loop; here we cycle through all the hours listed in the parentheses. Next, we group all the gensky parameters into one shell variable: `skypar`. The four lines that follow are used to set a shell variable for the constant ambient value. The value itself is based on the ground ambient value, which is extracted from the gensky output; that is why we execute gensky here. This scene was very open, so the constant ambient value was set to half the ground ambient value: a rough estimate, but adequate for this task. Included here is a test for night (that is, zero-brightness) skies. Next, just to be neat, we group all the ambient parameters to one shell variable. Then we make the scene octree. There is no need to recreate the entire octree when we are changing only the sun and sky. So to maximize efficiency, we use the include option of oconv to specify a previously created scene octree. This octree contains everything but the sun and sky. You will notice that the gensky command is executed inline with oconv. The file *sky.rad* contains the material and source descriptions for the sky and ground glow materials. Remember that this always follows the gensky command or output. The rendering command looks a little daunting, but it is really quite straightforward. For each pass of this command,

1. A picture is generated; maximum dimension is 1024 pixels.
2. The picture is filtered down to one third the original size and the exposure is set.
3. A picture label based on the settings of the shell variables for month, day, and hour is created.
4. The label is added to the filtered image.

This could be achieved in four separate steps, each producing its own output, three of which would be discarded. By using the UNIX pipe, however, we avoid the intermediary output, creating only what we want to keep.

On completion, we are left with a sequence of images showing the illumination of the scene at various times of day. These could be combined into a single picture, or even used as the basis for an animation. The script could easily be changed to cycle through other parameters, say, month, day, building orientation, and so on.

On the CD-ROM, we have included an example animation sequence showing a daylit interior throughout the hours of a day. The exposure of the images was computed to correspond to human visual response using the new pcond program.

6.7.3 Gendaylit

Another *Radiance* sky generator program, gendaylit, (written by Jean-Jacques Delavnay) produces a description based on the Perez All-Weather model [PSM93]. With this model, the generator program determines the sky conditions (overcast, intermediate, clear, and so on) based on the input parameters. You are therefore spared having to choose a particular sky type. For this reason, it is perhaps the best sky model to use with a time series of measured illuminance data, for instance, for an automated set of simulations. The gendaylit program source code is included on the CD-ROM; its use is described in the accompanying manual page.

6.7.4 Sky Spectral Radiance Values

Spectral radiance values for nongray skies should be calculated so that they do not affect the overall sky luminosity. To ensure that this is the case, the following condition should hold:

$$1 = 0.275L_R + 0.670L_G + 0.065L_B \tag{6.11}$$

where L_R, L_G, and L_B are the RGB radiance values for the sky glow material. The same should be true for the ground as well.

6.8 Rendering Scenes Illuminated by Sunny Skies

So far, the emphasis has been on illuminance prediction and how to obtain highly accurate values. A lighting designer will have no problem interpreting these data, but this is only part of the story. The majority of people can only really appreciate an architectural design once they have seen the finished building. If you want to know in advance what it will look like, you need to visualize it somehow. The capabilities of the *Radiance* system make it particularly well suited to the rendering of architectural scenes under daylight illumination.

Recall that when we render a scene, we are not striving for absolute accuracy in the prediction of luminance for every pixel in the image. In fact, the accuracy criteria we employ for judging images include many subjective elements. With this in mind, we demonstrate in this section a few different approaches to image synthesis. You will by now be aware that it is impossible to recommend a single set of rendering parameters that can guarantee an efficient solution for every conceivable design type. It should, however, be possible to anticipate from the actual design and lighting conditions the best approach to solving the problem.

6.8.1 A Note about the Rad Program

This chapter is really intended for those users who will eventually want to carry out exacting quantitative work and/or produce high-quality renderings of daylight-illuminated scenes. For either of these tasks, it helps to gain a detailed understanding of how key features of the *Radiance* system work. A more direct route to producing renderings, however, is to use the **rad** program. This "executive control" program will automatically determine many of the parameter values based on a few intuitive variable settings. Rad will also construct a "rendering pipeline" for you. This could include fairly complex operations, such as a mkillum preprocess of windows. The rad program, therefore, screens you from many of the intricacies of the rendering process; it has greatly improved the overall usability of the *Radiance* system. Try out the rad program and see if suits your needs—its use is described in Part I, Tutorials (Chapters 1 through 3). Sooner or later, though, and particularly for research applications, you will want to exercise complete control over all aspects of the simulation. The sections that follow will show how this can be achieved.

6.8.2 The Simple Space Lit by a Sunny Sky

Recreate the simple room scene octree using the intermediate sky description. Include the ground plane but leave out the external obstruction. Use the rview interactive renderer to view the scene from somewhere at the back of the room, looking toward the window at about eye-level height. All that you will see at first is the sky through the window and the sun patch on the floor/wall. Initiate the interreflection calculation by setting the number of ambient bounces to 1. Restart the image with the command `new`.[21]

---

21. Note that further increases in the -ab value from within rview will not show up in the onscreen rendering (even after issuing a `new` command) because the cached values will be reused and they were computed with only a single bounce.

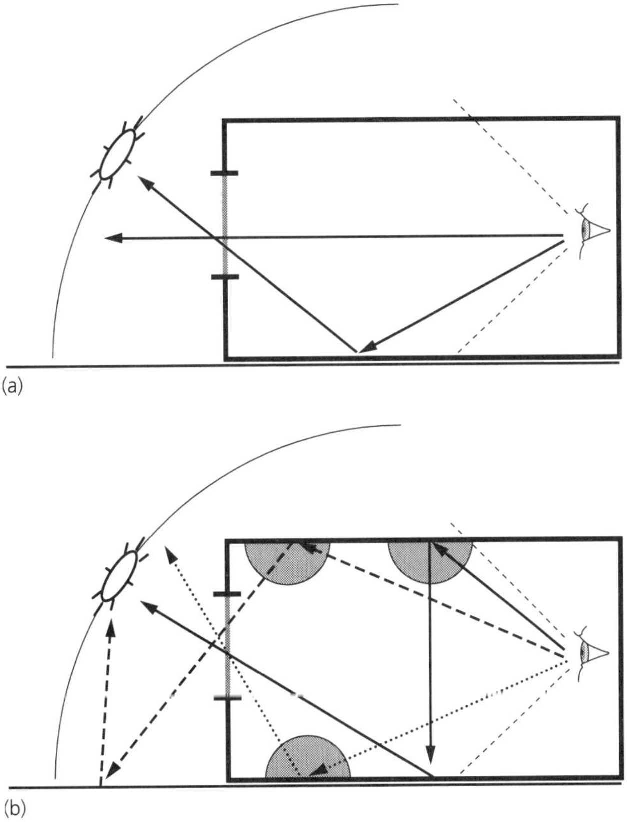

Figure 6.13 Possible light transfers for ambient bounces equal to 0 (a), and 1 (b).

You now begin to see more of the room, but it will appear blotchy because the default ambient parameter settings for rview are fairly coarse. At this stage in the chapter, we should be able to anticipate the pattern of light transfer in this scene for ambient bounce settings of 0 and 1. A pair of simplified ray diagrams illustrate some of the light transfers we can expect (Figure 6.13). With the ambient calculation switched off, we see the sky (glow) through the window and whatever sun patches are directly visible from the view point. With the interreflection calculation switched on, several other routes to the eye (that is, the camera) become possible via hemispherical sampling. Three of these are illustrated in the second diagram of the figure. Each one shows how a distinct component of internal illumination might be evaluated during the simulation. The point in the ray path where hemispherical sampling was initiated is marked by a shaded semicircle. The illumination components and the source origin are

1. The ceiling illuminated by the sun patch inside the room (solid rays)
2. The ceiling illuminated by the sun patch outside on the ground plane (dotted rays)
3. The floor inside the room illuminated by the sky glow (dashed rays)

It is important to appreciate the element of chance at work whenever hemispherical sampling is used. If the number of initial sampling rays (-ad) were set too small, the calculation might, for example, "miss" the sun patch even though it was "visible" from the point at which the rays were spawned. By the same token, an unrepresentative chance "hit" of a small sun patch by one of the sampling rays can produce a gross overestimate for indirect irradiance. In a rendering, the artifacts associated with ambient undersampling are all too apparent—bright and dark blotches. To avoid this, we need to set a sufficiently high value for the number of initial sampling rays.

Hemispherical sampling is generally too expensive to initiate at every surface visible from the eyepoint (that is, from every pixel). The calculation needs good indirect irradiance estimates from sampling at a limited number of locations. We then rely on the irradiance interpolation algorithm to estimate the in-between, or missing, values. To generate a fairly smooth rendering for the sunlit space, accounting for the first level of interreflection, we would need to set moderately high resolution values for the ambient parameters. To approximate the effect of the higher-level reflections, we should set a value for the -av parameter. In a later section (Visualizing a Highly Detailed Atrium Scene), we show how to obtain a good estimate for this parameter using rview. A rough guess, however, would be something in the range of 1/50 to 1/200 of the ground ambient value (obtained by executing the gensky command).[22] You may decide that `-ab 1` is insufficient to model the major light transfers, and that `-ab 2` is needed. In fact, this is almost certainly the case, because by using only one ambient bounce, we fail to account for the externally reflected component of *sky light*. This is likely to result in significant underestimation of the ceiling luminance near the window, since this part of the room has a good "view" of the (external) ground plane.

---

22. This range in percentage terms, 2% to 0.5%, corresponds approximately to the daylight factor about the middle of the room.

6.8.3 The Mkillum Approach

We can somewhat reduce the element of chance in our calculations for important light transfers by treating the window opening in a special way. The *Radiance* system allows you to select known sources of light (windows, skylights, and so on) and precompute light output distributions for them. They are then moved from the indirect (stochastic) calculation to the direct (deterministic) calculation. The program we use for this task is called mkillum. To illustrate the effectiveness of this approach, consider hemispherical sampling spawned at the rear wall of the room and also at the window plane. At the rear wall, the window subtends a solid angle that accounts for about 5% of the hemispherical "view" normal to the wall surface. Therefore, only about 5 in every 100 rays spawned from this point will directly sample the luminous environment through the window—even though we know the window to be the only "source" of illumination. The same sampling strategy at the window plane, however, will cause about half the rays to sample the sky and the remainder to sample the ground. This is how mkillum works; you direct the program to determine a light output distribution for the window based on the sampling of incident radiation and the glazing transmission properties. In any subsequent calculation or rendering, the glazing elements are treated as "secondary light sources." Note that mkillum can account only for the diffuse component of light that passes through the glazing; the direct and specular components are unaffected.

Mkillum parameters can be specified in the scene description file, but on first encountering the technique, you may prefer to control all aspects of the calculation from the command line. In this case, you must keep the window description, materials, and surfaces in a separate file. To create a scene octree with the modified window description usually requires three stages:

1. Prepare scene octree in the normal way.
2. Use mkillum to compute the light output distribution of named glazing elements, usually one or more polygons. On completion, the program will have created new window description(s) using a special light source material called *illum*. In addition, there will be data files, one for each illum surface, that contain the material's light output distribution.
3. Recreate the scene octree, replacing the original window description with the modified light source window.

The commands might be as follows:

```
% oconv room.rad window.rad sky.rad out.rad > scene.oct
% mkillum [rtrace options] scene.oct < window.rad > mkiwin.rad
% oconv room.rad mkiwin.rad sky.rad out.rad > mkiscene.oct
```

What rtrace settings you use will depend on which light transfers you think need to be modeled, and on the complexity of the external scene. A series of simplified ray diagrams[23] (Figure 6.14) shows what ab settings will account for these components of diffuse radiation incident at the window:

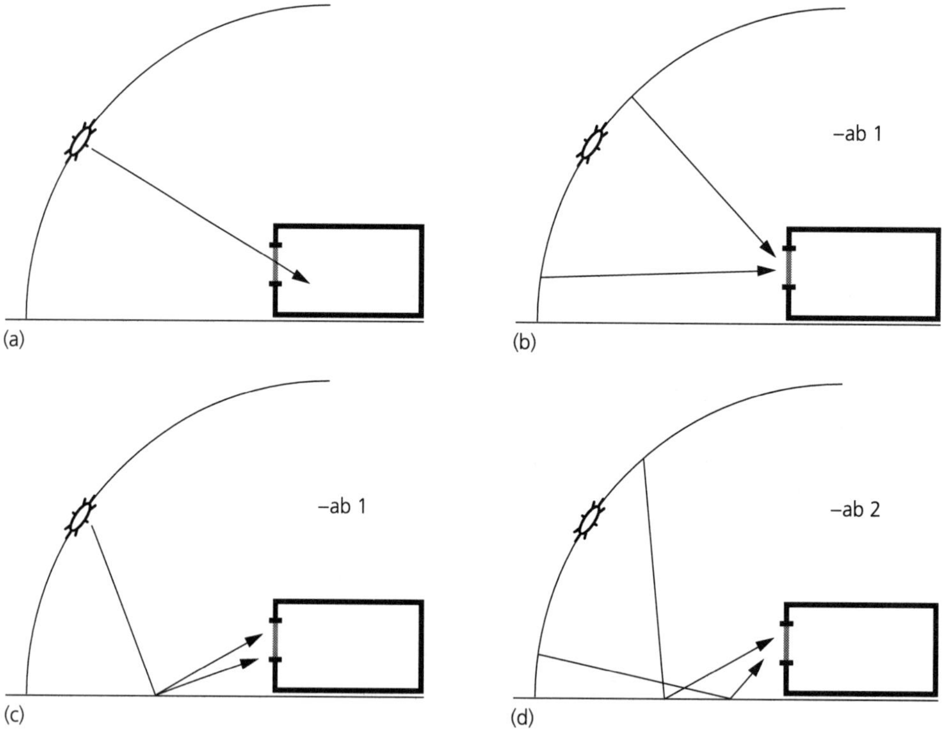

Figure 6.14 The direct solar component (a) is not accounted for by mkillum because it is part of the *Radiance* direct calculation. The direct sky component (b) is accounted for by mkillum, as is the indirect solar component (c), and the indirect sky component (d).

23. Here we ignore the fact that *Radiance* actually traces rays backward from the eye, and instead adopt the more intuitive convention that rays emanate from luminous sources.

- The diffuse component of light from the glow sky (b)
- The diffuse component of the first-order reflection of solar radiation from outside surfaces, for example the ground plane (c)
- The diffuse component of the first-order reflection of sky radiation from outside surfaces, for example the ground plane (d)

For the majority of scenes, setting –ab 2 is usually sufficient to account for most of the diffuse light transfer paths to a window

Ordinary *Radiance* light sources are opaque; if this were the case with the illum window, we would not be able to see through it. To avoid this, the illum sources have a dual nature. When treated in the direct component calculation, they behave like ordinary light sources, but when viewed directly, they revert to the original material description.

The mkillum approach requires a certain amount of user expertise to be implemented effectively for all but the simplest of cases. We therefore hope that if you are interested, you will take some time to familiarize yourself with the technique. The "Drafting Office" example in the *obj/virtual* subdirectory is a good place to start. The scene, devised by Greg Ward Larson, demonstrates fairly advanced use of the mkillum approach.

6.9 Visualizing a Highly Detailed Atrium Scene

Every design will present its own set of problems. With an ambitious project, even the experienced *Radiance* user is likely to chance upon one or more unforeseen difficulties. While these are undeniably frustrating at times, the possibility of discovering new techniques with *Radiance* usually serves to inspire the user—discovery is, after all, part of the fun. The visualization and analysis of a design known as the Foggo Atrium was one such project.

The IESD Center at De Montfort University, UK, was invited to participate in a case-studies design project for low-energy urban offices. The proposed design, by the architectural firm Peter Foggo Associates, was for a building that avoided air conditioning and made maximum use of daylight. The floor plan of the five-story building was fairly deep: 16.5 meters and 15 meters (upper two stories). The design would incorporate a linear atrium to provide core illumination. The lighting analysis brief called for both daylight factor prediction and visualization of the scene. The daylight factors were required to assess the effectiveness of external facade shading devices, and of the atrium as a provider of illumination. The images, on the other hand, were conceived to create a strong visual impression of what the design might look like.

A synthetic image of the atrium, Plate 16, shows the degree of complexity that was achieved for this model. The entire *Radiance* scene description was created from the command line. This task was not as horrendous as it might first appear. Once a basic office module had been worked up, it was easy to generate much of the structure using the repeated-transformation option in **xform**. In fact, the scene description consists of hierarchies of repeated transforms at various scales—for example, ceiling lights, a single office module, a row of office modules, and so on. For the daylight factors, however, a fully detailed office module was nested in a simple atrium model using the technique described in the section called DF Prediction: Tricks of the Trade.

6.9.1 Ambient Calculation Parameter Values

Having created the scene description, how do we go about selecting values for the ambient parameters? First, we need to decide what light transfers are needed to produce the major illumination components for the rendering we have in mind. This will depend to some degree on how we choose to illuminate the model, and on the view parameters. For open scenes, it is invariably the case that some direct solar illumination greatly enhances the impact of the rendering. Overcast-sky illumination looks dull and dreary in renderings and in real life. So we opt for a sunny sky description, in this case a CIE clear sky with sun. From what we know of the model geometry and orientation, we can decide on a viewpoint and make a good guess at the solar altitude and azimuth positions. A visual check with rview will tell us whether or not we have chosen well.

This atrium has numerous facade windows and many roof glazing elements. With so many potential sources of light, it would be very inefficient to calculate their contribution in the deterministic domain. Preprocessing of glazing elements to secondary light sources is therefore not advised for this type of building. Consequently, we will rely exclusively on the ambient calculation to model the interreflection.

The following sections show, step by step, how to make informed choices for ambient parameter values *before you begin any batch rendering.* Trial and error can be an instructive process. However, when, as here, the number of possibilities is nearly infinite, we need to drastically reduce the options before we do any exploring.

Setting -ab

Having settled on a view point and a sun position, we then set the ambient calculation parameters. The most important of these is, of course, the number of ambient bounces. We could go for a low-cost rendering and set `-ab 0`, but the final result, we know, would not be very convincing. At one ambient bounce, the sky and sun patch become potential sources of indirect illumination. At two ambient bounces, we have the potential to calculate indirect illumination for surfaces that have no direct line of sight to either sky or sun patch. This should be sufficient to give most of the surfaces that we can see a *calculated* diffuse irradiance. We approximate the effect of subsequent ambient bounces with a constant ambient value.

Setting -av and -aw

The constant ambient value option serves two functions. The first is to participate in the interreflection calculation, where it approximates the contribution of the higher-order reflections (see Chapter 12 for a description of the way this approximation is calculated). The other function is as sole provider of indirect illumination to surfaces excluded from the ambient calculation (see the Ambient Exclude/Include Options section, below). It usually pays to spend a moment or two to determine a "good" value for this parameter. With simple models, a value can sometimes be arrived at by analytical means. For the majority of scenes, however, it is more likely that you will need to base the estimate on calculated values. Here, we demonstrate how rview can be used to make a reasonable estimate for a constant ambient value. Where in the scene should we determine this value? The average radiance in the middle of the office floor at level 2 will be very different from the average radiance at the top of the elevator shaft. We decide by anticipating where in the scene the ambient calculation will expend the greatest effort. This is most likely to be for the office ceilings, many of which are visible from our viewpoint. Consequently, a "good" ambient value for the office spaces is what we should determine. This can be achieved in the following way:

1. Start the previewer rview with the irradiance option (**-i**) enabled, `-ab 1`, and maybe -ad set to higher than the default.
2. Wait a while for some detail to appear, then select a region in shade to refine (`frame` option). In this case, a bit of the ceiling at level 2 would be suitable.
3. After some further refinement, pick out and display the irradiance evaluated at a surface on the ceiling (use the `trace` option). We call this value *I*.
4. Recall that a uniform radiance that produces an irradiance, *I*, is simply I/π. (See Equation 6.8.)

Try this value (I/π) with the ambient bounces set to zero. Does it give similar indirect illumination for the same surface? If yes, this is the value to use.

The ambient weight parameter -aw, if enabled (i.e., -aw > 0), will modify the default ambient value in a moving average as new indirect irradiances are computed. This may produce more accurate renderings for scenes where the luminance extremes, and therefore the indirect contributions, are not too great. However, this is rarely the case for renderings with daylight, and it is usually safest to disable this option, setting `-aw 0`.

Setting -ad and -as

Having decided on values for -ab and -av, how do we go about setting the remaining ambient parameters? The sun patches on the floor and structure of the atrium will be significant sources of indirect illumination. To capture these potential sources, we should use a relatively large number of ambient divisions, in this case `-ad 1024`. Ambient supersampling should therefore be set to about one half or one quarter of this value.

Setting -aa and -ar

Our view of the atrium will reveal an enormous amount of fine-scale detail, for example the numerous ceiling lights and acoustic baffles. None of these objects is seen really close up, but we still want to calculate values for them rather than use a constant ambient approximation. Otherwise, we would not see, in the shading, the local illumination effect of the sun patch. Exact shading for each and every surface, however, is not really necessary; moderate irradiance interpolation errors over the scale size of a ceiling fixture should not be too conspicuous in the final image. Thus, a moderately accurate value should suffice. For this rendering, `-aa 0.3` was used.

Having settled on a value for -aa, we can base the ambient resolution on a minimum separation for indirect irradiance values in the cache. In other words, for distances less than this minimum, the calculation will always resort to interpolation, rather than initiate more sampling, regardless of the error estimate associated with that interpolation. This prevents the calculation from expending massive effort resolving irradiance gradients over negligible scales. Strictly speaking, this distance gives the scale at which the interpolation accuracy *begins* to deteriorate from the -aa setting. How do we decide on a magnitude for this scale? It often helps to evaluate this scale for a range of -ar and then to choose the value that gives the best compromise between speed and accuracy. The scene dimension, D_{max}, is found from the scene octree using the -d option of **getinfo**. For this atrium, it was 99.2 meters. The minimum separation for cached irradiances, S_{min}, is given by

$$S_{min} = \frac{D_{max} \times \text{-aa}}{\text{-ar}} \quad (6.12)$$

For `-aa 0.3`, the S_{min} for a range of -ar are given in Table 6.1. The third column gives the approximate relative cost of the calculation based on a minimum ambient resolution of 32. From these values, we can make a reasonably informed choice for -ar and anticipate the trade-off between accuracy and speed. For the minimum -ar listed, the potential exists for poor irradiance interpolation over scales of about 1 meter. These could be quite conspicuous from our view point, whereas (potentially) inaccurate shading over scales smaller than about 0.25 meter is far less likely to impair image quality. Higher resolution is of course possible, but at some cost. With this in mind, an ambient resolution of 128 seems a reasonable compromise.

S_{min} [m]	-ar	Relative cost
0.93	32	1
0.47	64	4
0.23	128	16
0.12	256	64

Table 6.1 Minimum separation and relative computational cost for a range of -ar settings.

Ambient Exclude/Include Options

Having set the parameters that control the computation of indirect irradiance, we should decide whether we want to exclude any materials from this calculation. Excluded materials will use the ambient value approximation directly, rather than a calculated indirect irradiance. Depending on the scene, we can make significant savings in rendering time by applying this option. How do we decide what to leave out? Exclusion criteria could be any of the following:

- Surfaces not visible from our view point (and unimportant in terms of light transfer)
- High-detail areas (the -ar parameter may already impose a partial restriction here)
- Surfaces that have a small diffuse reflectance (say, less than 5%)
- Surfaces that will appear very small in the final image
- "Sticks"—surfaces that will appear as thin lines in the final image

Some of the surfaces of the Foggo Atrium model that did not participate in the rendering ambient calculation (and the reasons for their exclusion) were

1. External facade detail including light shelf surfaces (not visible)
2. Window frames (sticks)
3. Windowsills (small)
4. Atrium roof vent slats (detail and small)
5. Atrium roof glazing bars (sticks)
6. Black handrail supports (low diffuse reflectance)

As we can see from the final image, Plate 16, these exclusions hardly detract from the quality of the rendering.

Note: It is easier to apply this technique if you segregate the materials into include and exclude types when you first construct the scene. In CAD terms, it helps to build up the model, layer by layer, with these requirements in mind.

Ambient File Use and the "Overture" Calculation

For a daylight rendering, the lion's share of the computation is invariably taken up by the ambient calculation. It makes sense, therefore, to save the cached indirect irradiance values to a file so they can be reused for later renderings. With a well-populated ambient file, it can be surprising how little time additional renderings take to complete, especially when there is significant overlap between views. There are rules that have to be observed when reusing ambient files. The most important of these rules is that you must always set the same combination of ambient parameters for every rendering that uses the ambient file. There is a special exception to this (see below). Also, the ambient exclude (or include) list should not change after the ambient file has been created.

Interpolation accuracy can be improved if the "presentation" (i.e., large) image is rendered using an already partially populated ambient file. The creation of the initial ambient file is known as an "overture" calculation. The ambient parameters values for the "overture" calculation should be those we have made the case for above. We use the same view parameters that are intended for the "presentation" image, but we generate the ambient file for a small picture size, no larger than, say, 64 by 64 pixels. We then reuse the ambient file to render a larger "presentation" image. The overall cost of the rendering will not be much greater than that of a one-pass approach, but the results can be significantly better.

Having created the ambient file with the "overture" calculation, you can, with caution, relax *some* of the ambient parameters for the larger renderings. The parameter revisions could be one or both of the following:

- Reduce -ad and -as by about 50%
- Slightly increase -aa (i.e., by 0.05 or 0.10)

The other ambient parameter settings should not be changed. If you do decide to change any of the -ad, -as, or -aa settings after the "overture" calculation, you should be aware that the modifications will not be reflected in the header of the ambient file. Thus, you need to track both the picture and the ambient file headers to obtain a complete record of the parameter settings for an image.

6.9.2 Batch Rendering

The ambient parameter values are set and we are ready to make the first rendering. Starting with the "overture" calculation, we generate a small image and save the ambient file. The "presentation" image we have in mind is a rendering at approximately the resolution of the monitor display: about 1000 pixels square. We rarely show images at the resolution at which they were rendered; alias artifacts always look unpleasant and greatly detract from the impression of realism. The highest quality is achieved by creating the rendering at two or three times the eventual size, then scaling it down using the **pfilt** program. We could go directly from the "overture" calculation to an (unfiltered) presentation image about 3000 pixels square. This is quite a leap and may take some time to render. In this case, we might prefer to reassure ourselves with an intermediate-sized image, say, 500 pixels square. This should provide sufficient detail for us to appraise the effectiveness of the ambient calculation. For certain scenes with multiple ambient bounces, you may find that it is the "overture" calculation that takes the longest, and that subsequent renderings, regardless of size, are completed relatively quickly. In this case, don't be too concerned if the "overture" calculation seems to be taking a long time to generate a small image.

Rendering time can be like kitchen cupboard space—it doesn't matter what you *need*, you always fill up what's *available*. It makes sense, therefore, to batch-render a series of images, say, overnight or over the weekend. Automate the rendering from shell scripts and keep track of the progress by setting the -e and -t options of rpict.

A Critical Appraisal of the Atrium Rendering

The viewpoint and lighting were chosen to create a striking impression rather than to show a typical view. The low view point was deliberately chosen to reveal specular reflections from the "terrazzo" floor and the nearby water feature. This effect is perhaps too exaggerated, and the floor itself has something of the appearance of calm water in a murky pool. It is in fact the uniformity of the floor that is the problem, rather than the specular component. If the floor had been divided up into slabs or tiles, and these given slightly different material properties, the final result would be much more convincing. If each tile had a small random component applied to its surface normal, giving us a slightly uneven floor, the rendering would be better still. These issues are related to material properties and to the way the model was constructed; what about the contribution of the indirect calculation?

In terms of overall impression, the diffuse shading looks pretty good. The indirect illumination effect of the sun patch is readily apparent, and the shading on the underside of the walkways between the elevator shafts is particularly realistic. At a finer level of detail, even individual ceiling fixtures don't look too bad, though there does appear to be some erroneously bright shading at the very smallest scales. Errors of this proportion were anticipated when we set the -aa and -ar parameters. On larger scales, we can see no evidence of light blotches, so our -ad and -as parameters were adequate for this scene.

6.9.3 Summary

From the limitless number of conceivable ambient parameter combinations, we have arrived at a set of values that we hope will either give acceptable results immediately or require only minor amendment. For each parameter, we have shown how the choice is influenced by the building design, the illumination, and the view point. The same approach could be applied to many architectural rendering problems.

However thoughtful our selection of ambient parameter values, we are unlikely to hit on the ideal combination that delivers the best compromise between speed and accuracy. Even if we stumbled across this magic combination, how would we know? Unless we tried out zillions of other combinations, we never would. Thus, we shouldn't worry about this too much. It is important, though, to have good ballpark values to begin with. Thereafter, we should be able to anticipate the effect, to a greater or lesser degree, of any subsequent parameter modifications. After all, our goal is to provide workable solutions to real-world problems.

6.10 Conclusion

Accurate simulation of the quantity and distribution of daylight in an architectural space is now a realistic prospect. The *Radiance* system can be used to predict illumination levels and visual appearance under daylight conditions for virtually any building design. In this chapter, we have looked at just some of the ways in which *Radiance* can be applied to solving daylight problems. We hope that daylight designers will find the techniques of value and use them to solve their own lighting problems. More important, we hope that the majority will be inspired to take a closer look at the system and the possibilities it offers.

Author's Biography

John Mardaljevic is a Research Fellow at the Institute of Energy and Sustainable Development (IESD), De Montfort University, Leicester, UK. He received his B.Sc. (1982) in physics and his M.Phil. (1988) in astrophysics, both from the University of Leicester. In 1990, he took up a research assistant post with De Montfort University. His first work there was on a project to assess dynamic thermal simulation programs for passive solar design. In 1991, he began to look into daylighting design tools for complex spaces, in particular atrium buildings. The *Radiance* system seemed particularly well suited to coping with modern atria: complex designs with a large number of specular or semispecular reflecting surfaces. As data from the International Daylight Measurement Program became available, the emphasis of Mardaljevic's work shifted toward validation and novel approaches to illuminance prediction—specifically, a comparison of sky model performance based on internal illuminance predictions and the formulation, implementation, and validation of the daylight coefficient approach for the *Radiance* system. This technique offers the potential for an efficient evaluation of the internal illuminance due to any sky condition by reusing precomputed illuminance values from a discretized sky. These studies form the basis of a recently completed Ph.D.

In addition to pure research, Mardaljevic has used *Radiance* to create renderings and to provide design advice for various architectural projects. To date, these have included atria (daylight factor and visualization), artificially lit offices, shading analysis (a preprocess for thermal simulation programs), and the evaluation of the visibility of a large-scale video display screen against daylight-produced glare.

From 1993 until his return to De Montfort in 1996, Mardaljevic worked as a research assistant at the University of Aberdeen, Scotland. Based at the Marine Laboratory, Aberdeen, he worked on oceanographic and ecosystem modeling projects. He has published papers on astrophysics, marine science, and illumination modeling. He is married and has a daughter.

CHAPTER 7

Roadway Lighting

by Erich Phillips

Although it was not originally conceived to do so, *Radiance* can be used to model lighting on roadways. In fact, *Radiance* is one of the most useful tools available to model lighting, illuminance, luminance, contrast, visibility, glare, and the brightness of retroreflective materials in and around the roadway. After a brief section on the basics of roadway lighting, we will encourage you to jump right in by constructing a roadway in *Radiance*. Using this *Radiance* model, the following items will be discussed and examined: the uses of illuminance and luminance as roadway lighting metrics, small target visibility (STV), and disability glare, or veiling luminance.

7.1 Roadways and Lighting

The lighting of roadways has long been of concern to those interested in roadway safety as well as to those interested in commerce along the roadway. Space does not permit a very detailed description of the basics of roadway lighting. For a more detailed description of roadway lighting, the interested reader is referred to the handbook published by IESNA [IES93a, Chapter 24]. An entire chapter of that handbook is devoted to roadway lighting. Alternatively, one could consult the American National Standards Institute (ANSI) standard practice for roadway lighting published by the IESNA [IES83] [IES93b].

Historically, roadway lighting has been specified by the illuminance on the pavement from fixed light sources near the roadway, which we commonly call streetlights. The illuminance on the pavement is usually reported as an average and a uniformity ratio. The uniformity ratio is simply a measure of the variability of the illuminance, and is commonly reported as the ratio of the average to the minimum illuminance.

The lighting can also be specified by the luminance of the pavement from a particular viewpoint on the roadway. The advantage of this approach is that luminance is more directly related to what we see than illuminance and therefore, in theory, more directly related to the visibility of objects on the roadway. The disadvantage is that measurements or calculations of pavement luminance are more difficult to make than measurements or calculations of pavement illuminance. In the case of calculations, which are of more relevance to readers of this book, even the simplest of luminance calculations require some knowledge of the material properties of the environment. In the case of roadway lighting, pavement is the material of primary interest. At most angles, pavement reflectance can be assumed to be fairly diffuse. However, it is well known that at certain combinations of viewing and source angles, pavement reflectance becomes highly specular.

Neither pavement illuminance nor pavement luminance is directly related to the visibility of objects on the roadway. The visibility of these objects is, however, of paramount importance to the roadway user. Often, it is the lighting of the roadway environment that determines the visibility of some important object on the roadway, be it another vehicle, a piece of debris or pothole, an animal, or a pedestrian. The visibility of such an object may be very important in determining the events that lead up to an accident. If we know enough about the lighting environment on a roadway, and about the object of interest, we can estimate the distance at which the object will be detected by a reasonably alert observer. From such an estimate, we can determine whether such a driver would have sufficient time to perceive and react to the object [Phi90].

Radiance is a highly useful tool for evaluating both the illuminance and the luminance of a roadway environment. It can be used as a design tool, and also as a way to visualize a design before it is built. In addition, *Radiance* can be used as a tool to assess the visibility of objects on the roadway.

Before we can discuss any of these topics further, we need to build a simple test roadway.

7.2 Building a Road

The files that follow make up a *Radiance* description of a roadway, complete with a staggered arrangement of streetlights. Let's examine them one at a time.

```
######road.rad######
pavement polygon pave_surf
0
0
12
   0   -1200    0
  48   -1200    0
  48    1200    0
   0    1200    0

!genbox concrete curb1 6 2400 .5 | xform -e -t -6 -1200 0

!genbox concrete curb2 6 2400 .5 | xform -e -t 48 -1200 0

!xform -e -t 23.6667 -1200 .001 -a 2 -t .6667 0 0 solid_yellow.rad

!xform -e -t 12 -1200 .001 -a 120 -t 0 20 0 -a 2 -t 24 0 0 dashed_white.rad

grass polygon lawn1
0
0
12
  -6   -1200    .5
  -6    1200    .5
-506    1200    .5
-506   -1200    .5


grass polygon lawn2
0
0
12
  54   -1200    .5
  54    1200    .5
 554    1200    .5
 554   -1200    .5
```

This file creates a 2400-foot by 48-foot pavement polygon, bordered by 6-foot-wide concrete sidewalks. The sidewalks are bordered by 500-foot-wide swatches of grass. The pavement area is subdivided into four lanes, two traveling in each direction. The lanes are delineated by pavement markings, the basic building-block files for which are described below.

```
######dashed_white.rad######
white_paint polygon lane_dash
0
0
12
  -.1667  0  0
   .1667  0  0
   .1667  8  0
  -.1667  8  0

######solid_yellow.rad######
yellow_paint polygon center_stripe
0
0
12
  -.1667     0  0
   .1667     0  0
   .1667  2400  0
  -.1667  2400  0
```

Next, the description of the scene contains a staggered arrangement of streetlights, repeating every 240 feet, staggered on opposite sides. The offset of the stagger is 120 feet. This arrangement is described in the following file.

```
######lights_s.rad######
!xform -e -t -1 -1200 0 -a 11 -t 0 240 0 light_pole.rad
!xform -e -rz 180 -t 49 -1080 0 -a 10 -t 0 240 0 light_pole.rad
```

The above file refers to the *light_pole.rad* file, which consists of a combination of the luminaire itself, a vertical support pole, and a horizontal mounting pole.

```
######light_pole.rad######
!xform -e -rz -180 -t 6 0 30 luminaire.rad

chrome cylinder pole
0
0
```

```
7
  0    0    0
  0    0   32
 .3333

chrome cylinder mount
0
0
7
  0    0    30.1667
  6    0    30.1667
 .1667
```

The *light_pole.rad* file refers to the *luminaire.rad* file, a description of the light fixture itself. This file is based on the photometric measurements of an example roadway lighting fixture published in the 1983 ANSI standard for roadway lighting [IES83, p. 31]. The data were originally in IES photometric data file format, processed by the *Radiance* program **ies2rad**.

```
######luminaire.rad######
# ies2rad
# Dimensions in feet
#<EX2
#<TEST REPORT UNKNOWN
#<CATALOG # UNKNOWN
#<COBRAHEAD WITH REFRACTOR
#<HPS
#<200 WATT
#<DATA TAKEN FROM EXAMPLE IN
#<FHWA `ROADWAY LIGHTING HANDBOOK'
#<DATED 1983
#<END
# 220-watt luminaire, lamp*ballast factor = 1

void brightdata ex2_dist
6 corr ex2.dat source.cal src_phi2 src_theta -my
0
1 1
```

```
ex2_dist light ex2_light
0
0
3 2.492 2.492 2.492

ex2_light sphere ex2.s
0
0
4 0 0 0 0.5
```

The ies2rad program also generates a data file, called *ex2.dat*, that contains the photometric data in *Radiance* format. This file and the original IES-format file, called *ex2.ies*, can be found on the CD-ROM provided with this book.

To complete the scene description, the **gensky** program was used to generate the following sky distribution:

```
######night_sky.rad######
# gensky 6 15 12 -s
# Ground ambient level: 5.054647
#
# Want ground ambient level for night sky to be 5e-4, so glow materials
# scaled accordingly
#

void brightfunc skyfunc
2 skybright skybright.cal
0
7 -1 11.620399 8.936111 1.637813 0.033302 -0.250539 0.967533

skyfunc glow ground_glow
0
0
4 1e-5 8e-6 5e-6 0

ground_glow source ground
0
0
4  0  0  -1  180
```

```
skyfunc glow sky_glow
0
0
4  2e-6  2e-6 1e-5 0

sky_glow source sky
0
0
4  0 0 1 180
```

Normally, gensky is used to generate a sky that would account for the illumination from the sun and the sky. The **-s** parameter directs the removal of the sun. In order to simulate a night sky, the sun was removed and the red, green, and blue values that gensky computed for the sky distribution (the *glow* types in the above file) have been multiplied by 10^{-4}. This results in a ground ambient level of about 5×10^{-4}, which was found to be appropriate for nighttime. In this case, gensky is simply used as a convenient way to generate a glowing dome (the sky) that approximates the ground ambient radiance values one would get from a typical nighttime sky.

Lastly, the following file contains the material descriptions that are referred to in the preceding *Radiance* scene description files.

```
######materials.rad######
void plastic pavement
0
0
5   .07   .07   .07   0  0

void plastic concrete
0
0
5   .14  .14  .14  0  0

void plastic yellow_paint
0
0
5  .7   .7   .01  0 0

void plastic white_paint
0
0
5  .7   .7   .7   0   0
```

```
void plastic grass

0
0
5  0  .1   .02  0  0

void plastic 20%_gray
0
0
5  .2  .2  .2  0 0

void metal chrome
0
0
5  .2  .2  .2  .05  .05
```

Note that the pavement reflectance is described as if pavement were a completely diffuse material. As we have mentioned previously, we know that at certain source and viewing angles, the pavement reflectance has a strong specular component. Unfortunately, not enough data have been collected to allow us to create a material description in *Radiance* to describe this reflectance satisfactorily. The measurement of such reflectance data for pavement is a current research topic, and we expect that in the not-too-distant future there will be enough information to create a satisfactory material description. In many situations, modeling pavement as a diffuse reflector will suffice. We must simply be aware of the limitations. We have included an alternative material description in a file called *r3.rad*, which is of the *metdata* type. The data for this material description come from the 1983 ANSI standard for roadway lighting [IES83]. The limitation of these data is that the reflectance values were measured at one viewing angle only. For this reason, a very small fraction of the pixels in a typical image will be affected by the data. For the interested reader, the *r3.rad* file; the associated data file, *r3.dat;* and a calculation file, *roadsurf.cal*; are included on the CD-ROM.

At this point, we have finished creating a roadway, complete with streetlights. The next step is to generate the octree file using the **oconv** command.

```
% oconv materials.rad road.rad lights_s.rad \
 nignt_sky.rad > scene.oct
```

The following command generates a plan view of the roadway:

```
% rpict -x 500 -y 2000 -vtl -vp 28 150 4 -vd 0 0 \
 -1 -vu 0 1 0 -vh 100 -vv 400 -vs 0 \
 -vl 0 scene.oct | pfilt -x 200 -y 800 -e -r .6 \
 -1 -e 200 > scene.pic
```

In the above command, the output of **rpict** is piped directly into the **pfilt** command, which is used to antialias and generate a picture of the proper exposure (Figure 7.1(a)). The curbs, lanes, and staggered arrangement of the streetlights are clearly visible in this image.

In the next few sections, we will look at the roadway in a few different ways.

7.3 Roadway Lighting Metrics

To evaluate the illuminance of the roadway, the **-i** option of rpict or **rview** can be used. This option computes the irradiance and the corresponding photometric

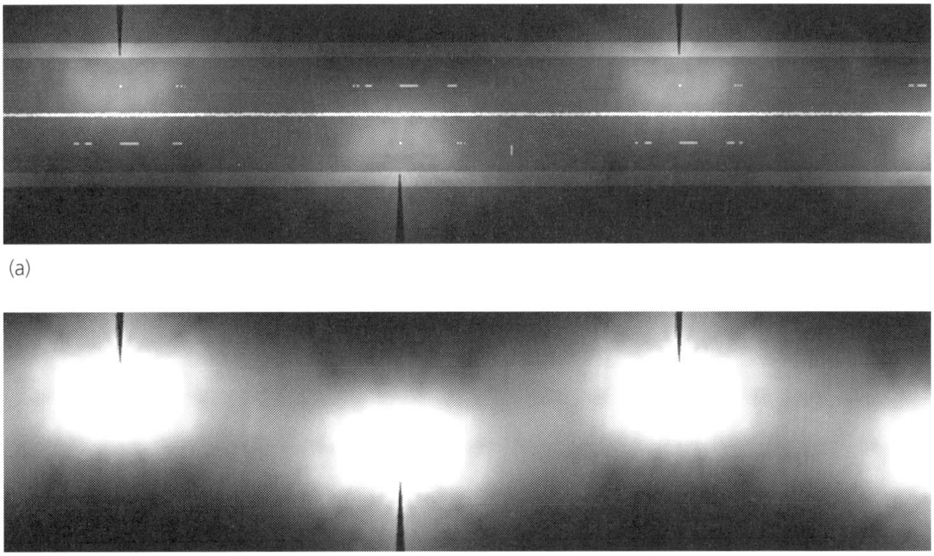

(a)

(b)

Figure 7.1 A parallel aerial view of the test roadway scene (a). The roadway scene computed as irradiance values (b).

quantity illuminance rather than the radiance and corresponding luminance. The resulting image is shown in Figure 7.1(b).

```
% rpict -i  -x 500 -y 2000 -vtl -vp 28 150 4 \
 -vd 0 0 -1 -vu 0 1 0 -vh 100 -vv 400 \
 -vs 0 -vl 0 scene.oct | pfilt -x 200 -y 800 -e \
 -r .6 -1 -e 200 >  scene_illum.pic
```

Next, the **falsecolor** command is used to generate the contours and composite the contours and the picture; the resulting image is shown in Figure 7.2.

```
% falsecolor -i scene_illum.pic -p scene.pic \
 -cl -s 12 -n 12 -l Lux > lux.pic
```

The roadway lighting metrics of average illuminance and uniformity can be calculated from Figure 7.1(a), by using the **I** option of the **ximage** command. One would simply draw a box to cover the roadway over a sufficient length to capture one repeat of the staggered streetlight arrangement, then type the letter "I." If we do this with the image in Figure 7.1(b), we find that the average illuminance in the enclosed region is approximately 4.1 lux. The minimum illuminance can be identified by eye and read directly from the image in Figure 7.2 as approximately 0.9 lux. Thus, for this roadway design, we would report that the average illuminance is 4.1 lux with a uniformity ratio of 4.5.

The luminance of the pavement on a roadway depends on the point of view of the observer. For this reason, the pavement luminance, when used as a roadway lighting metric, is always measured or calculated from the point of view of a standard observer. This position is expressed in the following view point file:

```
######eye.vp######
rview -vtv -vp 28 -273 4.75 -vd 0 0.999856 -0.0169975 -vh 25 -vv 12.5
```

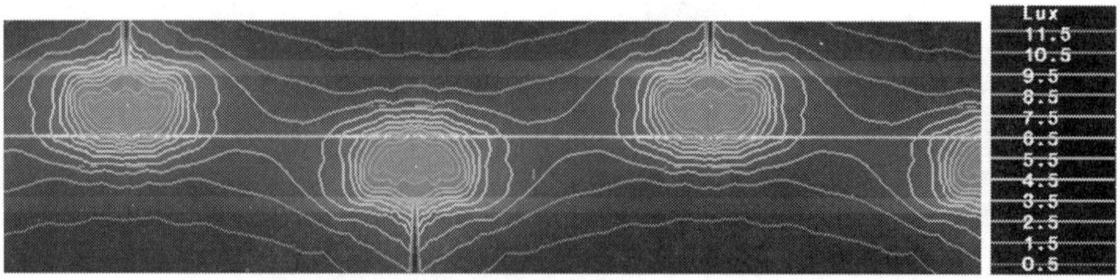

Figure 7.2 Isolux contours superimposed on Figure 7.1(a) using the irradiance values computed and shown in Figure 7.1(b).

The standard observer is 273 feet away from, and 4.75 feet above, the section of pavement of interest. This seemingly unusual choice arises from the fact that the IESNA has adopted 4.75 feet as the typical eye height of a driver. Thus, for a viewing angle of 1 degree down, the eye is looking at the pavement 273 feet away. All this is reflected in the above view point file. Figure 7.3 is a view of the roadway we created above from this point of view. The pavement area of interest is directly in the center of the image.

In Figure 7.4, we have the same view as in Figure 7.3, but the pavement material description has been changed to account for the specular nature of the reflection at some angles. As discussed above, we do not have enough information to account for such reflection at all angles, but for the sake of comparison, the following approximation has been used. The following descriptions were substituted into the *materials.rad* file:

Figure 7.3 The roadway scene as viewed from a typical driver's height above the road.

Figure 7.4 The same scene shown in Figure 7.3, but with a semispecular road surface.

```
void plastic pavement
0
0
5   .07   .07   .07   0.002  0.001

void plastic concrete
0
0
5   .14  .14  .14
```

The specularity and roughness parameters were determined by trial and error from actual pavement measurements. You should be cautious when using these values, because they may not apply in all situations.

The final category of roadway lighting metric that we will mention is small target visibility (STV). The easiest way to understand STV is to imagine the following: We are standing on a roadway that has some combination of streetlights. In front of us on the roadway are a series of 7-inch-square targets, perpendicular to the pavement surface, arranged in a regular array of rows and columns. The reflectance of each of these targets is a 20% gray. As you look up and down the roadway, some of these targets will appear lightly colored against a dark background and others will appear darkly colored against a light background. These appearances are determined by the geometric arrangement of streetlights and by where each target happens to be within this arrangement. One other thing we notice is that some of the targets virtually disappear because the brightness of the target is nearly equal to the brightness of the background. What we are discussing is the variance in the luminance contrast of the targets and their backgrounds. The visibility of each of these targets is directly related to this contrast.

STV is a weighted average of the visibility of each of the targets in this array [Phi93]. The idea is that by varying the photometric output of the streetlights, as well as their geometric placement, one tries to maximize STV, or to achieve some stipulated level of STV. Such a roadway design would, in theory, provide better visibility of objects on the roadway, and therefore better safety.

In the following figures, such an array of targets has been put on our example roadway by incorporating the following file into the scene description.

```
######target_array_s.rad######
!xform -e -t 2.71 6 0 -a 8 -t 6 0 0 -a 10 \
 -t 0 12 0 target.rad
```

The *target_array_s.rad* file refers to the following file, which describes the STV target itself:

```
######target.rad######
!genbox 20%_gray stv_target .58 .1667 .58
```

The above target array, incorporated into the scene description and viewed from the camera position described in the *eye.vp* file above, is shown in Figure 7.5.

To demonstrate the effect of light pole placement, an alternate light pole placement is used. Instead of using the *lights_s.rad* file, the following file, *lights_o.rad*, is used.

```
######lights_o.rad######
!xform -e -t -1 -1200 0 -a 11 -t 0 240 0 light_pole.rad
!xform -e -rz 180 -t 49 -1200 0 -a 11 \
 -t 0 240 0 light_pole.rad
```

Figure 7.5 The staggered streetlight arrangement with targets incorporated to test visibility.

This produces an array of streetlights with a spacing of 240 feet, in which the streetlights are opposite one another rather than staggered. To compare these two alternatives directly, a different array of STV targets is used.

```
######target_array_o.rad#######
!xform -e -t 2.71 8 0 -a 8 -t 6 0 0 -a 15 |
 -t 0 16 0 target.rad
```

This array has eight columns of targets, spaced 6 feet apart, and each column has sixteen members spaced 15 feet apart. The following commands are then used to generate two different scenes:

```
% oconv materials.rad road.rad lights_s.rad \
 target_array_o.rad nignt_sky.rad > scene_s.oct
```

```
% oconv materials.rad road.rad lights_o.rad \
 target_array_o.rad  nignt_sky.rad > scene_o.oct
```

Now we have two slightly different roadway scenes, one with a staggered arrangement of streetlights, and the other with the streetlights arranged opposite one another. The average illuminance and luminance of these two alternatives are the same. For this reason, the more traditional means of assessing roadway lighting would not distinguish them, except in uniformity, for which the staggered arrangement would be judged better because it is more uniform. Figures 7.5 and 7.6 illustrate these two different scenes, the staggered and opposite arrangements, respectively.

Figure 7.6 Visibility targets shown in a scene with streetlights in an opposing arrangement.

Note that the contrast of the targets is lower, on the average, with the staggered arrangement than with the opposite arrangement. This is true despite the fact that the staggered arrangement would be judged better using the average illuminance or the average luminance method, because of its lower uniformity ratio. To facilitate the two comparisons, we have generated a view of each target in the first six columns of targets on the roadway as viewed from the standard observer eye point (273 feet away, 4.75 feet above the pavement). Each of these images of an individual target is then composited using the **pcompos** command to generate a single image for each arrangement of streetlights. The resulting images are shown in Figures 7.7 and 7.8 for the staggered and opposite arrangements, respectively. In these images, a direct comparison of the contrast and the resulting visibility of each corresponding target can be made. Recall that the STV is a weighted average of the visibility of each individual target in the array. Thus, STV accounts for the visibility or contrast of all of the targets in one lumped parameter. This feat can also be accomplished quite easily by looking at Figures 7.7 and 7.8 and letting your visual system do the "averaging" for you. What you see is a verification of what we saw in Figures 7.5 and 7.6, that the average contrast and visibility is higher for the opposite arrangement of lights than for the staggered arrangement.

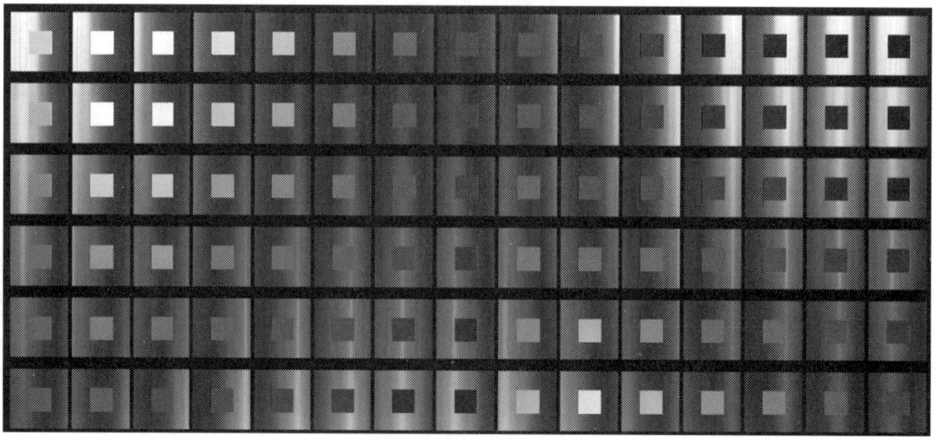

Figure 7.7 Close-ups of the small targets from the staggered arrangement (Figure 7.5).

7.4 Veiling Luminance

In the last section of this chapter, we will address a problem that everyone has experienced when driving at night. This is the phenomenon called veiling luminance. Whenever there is an area in our visual field that is significantly brighter than the average for the rest of the scene, the potential for glare exists—for example, when we see an oncoming vehicle with its high-beam headlights on, or when a vehicle with bright headlights approaches us from behind and we pick up the reflected image of the beams in our rearview mirror. There are two common terms for glare in the parlance of roadway lighting. One is *discomfort glare;* it is measured by the degree to which a glare source causes discomfort. The other is called *disability glare;* it is related to the fact that glare can actually reduce the contrast of objects in the scene, disabling or decreasing one's ability to see them. One way to describe disability glare is through the concept of veiling luminance. Veiling luminance can be thought of as a veil of luminance, or brightness, that emanates from a glare source. This "veil" is caused by scattering of light within the eye. The optical media of the eye are not perfectly transparent, and some light energy is lost from the imaging rays due to scattering. This scattering causes a portion of the light energy to be diverted from the image of the light source to other regions of the retina. The fraction of light energy scattered away from an imaging ray in a particular direction is inversely dependent on the angle between the imaging ray and the direction of the scattered ray. More specifically, the magnitude of this veil of luminance depends on the illuminance of the glare source at your eye and the difference between the

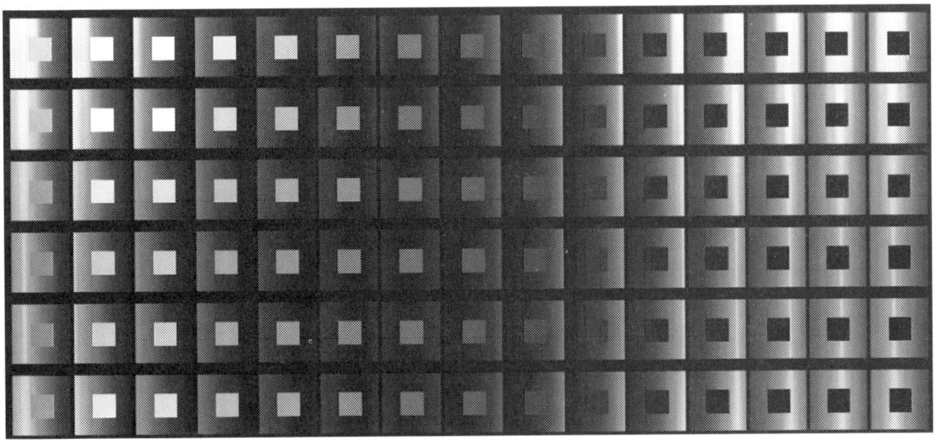

Figure 7.8 Close-ups of the small targets from the opposing arrangement (Figure 7.6).

direction vector between your eye and the glare source and the direction vector of your gaze. In other words, the closer an object is to the glare source, in terms of angle, the greater the veiling luminance. The greater the illuminance of a glare source at your eye, the greater the veiling luminance. The veiling luminance as a function of angle has been measured empirically, and can be described by the following equation [Fry54]:

$$L_v = (9.2E)/(\theta^2) \tag{7.1}$$

This equation allows us to predict for each angle of view (or direction, in *Radiance* parlance), the veiling luminance for each glare source in a scene. If we add up the contribution of veiling luminance from each glare source, we can compute the total veiling luminance at each angle of view in a scene. How is it that veiling luminance affects the contrast of an object? The following equation is a description of the contrast of an object.

$$C = (L_{object} - L_{background})/L_{background} \tag{7.2}$$

where C is the contrast, L_{object} is the luminance of the object, and $L_{background}$ is the luminance of the background. One can see from this equation that the contrast is positive when the object is brighter than the background, negative when the object is less bright than the background (like the letters on this page), and zero when the object is equal in brightness to the background.

In the presence of glare, the veiling luminance adds to the luminance of both the object and the background.

$$C = ((L_{object} + L_{veil}) - (L_{background} + L_{veil}))/(L_{background} + L_{veil}) \tag{7.3}$$

where L_{veil} is the veiling luminance. L_{veil} is canceled from the numerator, leaving us with the following equation:

$$C = (L_{object} - L_{background})/(L_{background} + L_{veil}) \tag{7.4}$$

If the magnitude of the veiling luminance, L_{veil}, is large compared to the magnitude of the numerator in the above equation, the contrast is significantly reduced in the presence of the glare source. In fact, as L_{veil} gets larger and larger, the contrast can approach zero. This is why in the presence of oncoming headlamps, otherwise visible objects on the roadway can sometimes disappear.

Imagine a *Radiance* image that includes a small, bright light source. Each pixel in the image represents an angular section of the visual field—a rectangular cone, if you will. The size of this cone depends on the resolution of the image. For any image with enough resolution to actually be called an image, we can approximate each pixel as one angle, or direction, within the visual field. If we knew the illuminance reaching the eye from the bright light source in the image, we could compute the veiling luminance from that light source for each pixel in the image. Recall that veiling luminance is a fairly simple computation that requires the illuminance at the eye and the angle from the light source to the direction of gaze. The direction vector for any particular pixel in the image defines the angle of gaze, and the illuminance at the eye from the bright light source can be computed from its luminance and angular size. If this computation were done for every pixel in the scene, it would, in effect, result in a second image that depicted the veiling luminance profile. This second image would be the same size as the original image, and every pixel in it would contain the veiling luminance for the corresponding pixel in the original image.

To implement such a calculation in *Radiance*, we can use the **findglare** command. This command takes an existing image and finds within it the potential sources of glare. We also need the following calculation file, *veil.cal*, which implements the above equation for veiling luminance.

```
######veil.cal######
{
  Add veiling glare caused by bright sources to an image.
  Input is direction and illuminances of sources as can
  be determined by findglare.

  N :    Number of glaring sources
  SDx(i) :  x component of normalized direction to source i
  SDy(i) :  y component of normalized direction to source i
  SDz(i) :  z component of normalized direction to source i
  I(i) :  illuminance due to source i in normal direction
    (multiply the luminance by the solid angle)
}

PI : 3.14159265358979323846;
bound(a,x,b) : if(a-x, a, if(x-b, b, x));
Acos(x) : acos(bound(-1,x,1));

mul(t) : if(.5*PI/180-t, 9.2/.5^2, 9.2/(180/PI)^2/(t*t));

Dx1 = Dx(1); Dy1 = Dy(1); Dz1 = Dz(1);  { minor optimization }

angle(i) = Acos(SDx(i)*Dx1+SDy(i)*Dy1+SDz(i)*Dz1);
```

```
sum(i) = if(i-.5, mul(angle(i))*I(i)+sum(i-1), 0);

veil = le(1)/179 * sum(N);

ro = ri(1) + veil;
go = gi(1) + veil;
bo = bi(1) + veil;
```

This calculation file needs as input the number of glare sources, the direction vector to each glare source, and the illuminance of each source at the eye. All these quantities can be determined from the findglare command. At this point, an example is in order. We will start with the roadway scene with the staggered arrangement of light poles, and the arrangement of STV targets found in the *target_array_s.rad* file. To this we will add two oncoming headlamps, first on low-beam and later on high-beam. We need the files *lowbeam.rad* and *highbeam.rad*. These files were generated by the ies2rad command and come from photometric tests performed on a headlamp. These two headlamp files and the associated data files *lowbeam.dat* and *highbeam.dat* can be found on the CD-ROM. These files were transformed using the xform command, first to orient the headlamps and then to place them in the proper positions in the roadway scene.

```
% xform -rz -90 -rx -90 -t 14 300 2 \
 -a 2  -t  4 0 0 lowbeam.rad > lowbeams.rad
% xform -rz -90 -rx -90 -t 14 300 2 \
 -a 2  -t  4 0 0 highbeam.rad > highbeams.rad
```

These commands place pairs of oncoming headlamps on the road—low-beams and high-beams, respectively. The following commands were executed to generate the views seen in Figures 7.9 and 7.10:

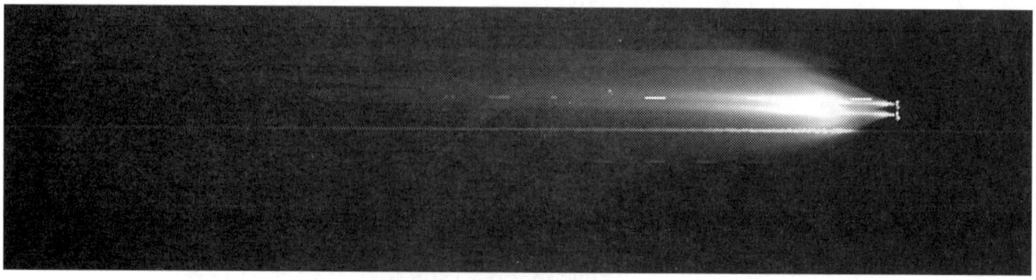

Figure 7.9 A car heading toward the targets with its low-beams on.

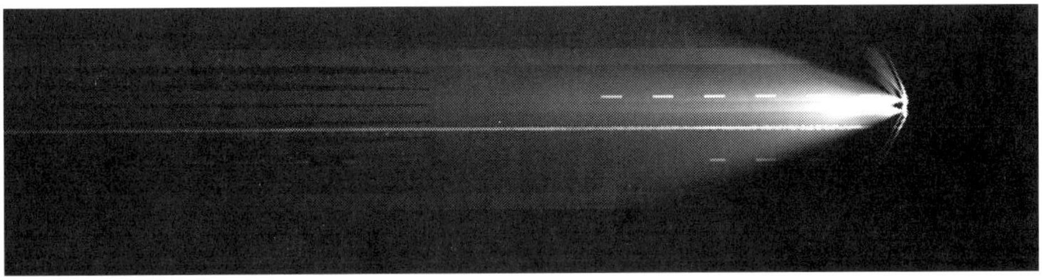

Figure 7.10 A car heading toward the targets with its high-beams on.

```
######Figure 7.9######
% oconv materials.rad night_sky.rad road.rad \
 target_array_s.rad lowbeams.rad | rpict -vtl \
 -vp 28 150 4 -vd 0 0 -1 -vu 0 1 0 -vh 100 -vv 400 \
 -vs 0 -vl 0 -av .00001 .00001 .00001 -t 60 -x 500 \
 -y 2000 | pfilt -r .6 -1 -e 2000 \
 -x 200 -y 800 > target_nl_low.pic

######Figure 7.10######
% oconv materials.rad night_sky.rad road.rad \
 target_array_s.rad highbeams.rad | rpict -vtl \
 -vp 28 150 4 -vd 0 0 -1 -vu 0 1 0 -vh 100 -vv 400 \
 -vs 0 -vl 0 -av .00001 .00001 .00001 -t 60 -x 500 \
 -y 2000 | pfilt -r .6 -1 -e 2000 -x 200 \
 -y 800 > target_nl_high.pic
```

Figures 7.9 and 7.10 illustrate top views of the headlight beams, low-beams and high-beams, respectively. The target array reveals itself as the long shadows seen in the bottom portion of the picture. Note that in these images, the streetlights are off.

Next, let's create the same two scenes with the streetlights on, using the following commands to generate the images seen in Figures 7.11 and 7.12:

```
######Figure 7.11######
% oconv materials.rad night_sky.rad road.rad \
 lights_s.rad target_array_s.rad lowbeams.rad \
 | rpict -vtv -vp 28 -273 4.75 \
 -vd 0 0.999856 -0.0169975 -vu 0 0 1 -vh 6 -vv 3 \
 -vs 0 -vl 0 -x 3000 -y 1500 > target_low.pic

 % pfilt -r .6 -x 800 -y 400 -1 -e 5 \
 target_low.pic >  target_low.pic
```

Figure 7.11 Looking into low-beams and the staggered-streetlight arrangement.

Figure 7.12 Looking into high-beams and the staggered-streetlight arrangement.

```
######Figure 7.12######
% oconv materials.rad night_sky.rad road.rad \
 lights_s.rad target_array_s.rad highbeams.rad \
 | rpict -vtv -vp 28 -273 4.75 \
 -vd 0 0.999856 -0.0169975 -vu 0 0 1 -vh 6 -vv 3 \
 -vs 0 -vl 0 -x 3000 -y 1500 > target_high.pic

 % pfilt -r .6 -x 800 -y 400 -1 -e 5 > target_high.pic
```

These figures look almost identical, although the luminance of the high-beams is considerably greater than that of the low-beams. This is because in both cases the RGB values of the headlamps in the image files far exceed the average luminance of the scene, and therefore appear as white. Now let's use the findglare command to locate the glare sources, and ultimately create some images that include the veiling luminance.

```
% findglare -t 1000 -c -r 4000 \
 -p target_low.pic > target_low.glr

% findglare -t 1000 -c -r 4000 \
 -p target_high.pic > target_high.glr
```

The resulting files, *target_low.glr* and *target_high.glr*, are shown below.

```
######target_low.glr######
findglare -t 1000 -c -r 4000 -p target_low.pic
VIEW= -vth -vp 28 -273 4.75 -vd 0 1 0 -vu 0 0 1 -vh 180 -vv 180 -vs 0 -vl 0
FORMAT=ascii

BEGIN glare source
    -0.024000  0.999702  -0.004500  0.000001  346186.000000
    -0.017000  0.999845  -0.004500  0.000001  257760.000000
END glare source
BEGIN indirect illuminance
    0  0.367515
END indirect illuminance

######target_high.glr######
findglare -t 1000 -c -r 4000 -p target_high.pic
VIEW= -vth -vp 28 -273 4.75 -vd 0 1 0 -vu 0 0 1 -vh 180 -vv 180 -vs 0 -vl 0
FORMAT=ascii
```

```
BEGIN glare source
    -0.024000  0.999702  -0.004500  0.000001  1348944.000000
    -0.017000  0.999845  -0.004500  0.000001  1506464.000000
END glare source
BEGIN indirect illuminance
    0  0.372724
END indirect illuminance
```

The output of the findglare command between the `BEGIN glare source` and `END glare source` lines is what we need for the next step. The first three columns are the *x*, *y*, and *z* components of the direction vector between the eye point and the glare source. The fourth column is the solid angle of the glare source as seen from the eye point. The fifth column is the luminance of the glare source. The product of the fourth and fifth columns (the solid angle and the luminance) is the illuminance of the glare source at the eye point. Note that the output is the same for the low-beams and the high-beams except for the luminance column; the high-beams have four to five times the luminance when seen from this angle.

Recall that the calculations directed by the *veil.cal* file require as input the number of glare sources, the direction vector to the glare sources, and the illuminance at the eye for each glare source. These parameters are lumped together in the following calculation files, *target_low_glr.cal* and *target_high_glr.cal:*

```
######target_low_glr.cal######
SDx(i): select(i, -0.024000, -0.01700);
SDy(i): select(i, 0.999702, 0.999845 );
SDz(i): select(i,  -0.004500, -0.004500);
I(i) : select(i, 0.000001*346186.0, 0.000001*257760.0  );
N : I(0);

######target_high_glr.cal######
SDx(i): select(i,  -0.024000, -0.017000 );
SDy(i): select(i,  0.999702, 0.999845);
SDz(i): select(i,  -0.004500, -0.004500);
I(i) : select(i,  0.000001*1348944.0, 0.000001*1506464.0);
N : I(0);
```

These files present, in combined form, the components of the direction vector from the eye point to the *i*th source, the illuminance at the eye due to the *i*th source, and the number of glare sources. The **pcomb** command can be used to combine images or to perform pixel-by-pixel calculations and combine the results with images. Here is how the pcomb command is used to compute the veiling luminance due to all glare sources and combine the result with the image in our headlamp examples:

```
% pcomb -f target_low_glr.cal -f veil.cal \
 target_low.pic | pfilt -r .6 -x 800 -y 400 -1 \
 -e 5 > target_low.veil.pic

% pcomb -f target_high_glr.cal -f veil.cal \
 target_high.pic | pfilt -r .6 -x 800 -y 400 \
 -1 -e 5 > target_high.veil.pic
```

The resulting images are shown in Figures 7.13 and 7.14 for the low-beams and the high-beams, respectively.

Compare these with Figures 7.11 and 7.12, which show the same scene and the same exposure, but without the veiling luminance. The contrast and visibility of the targets is reduced in the presence of oncoming low-beams, and virtually eliminated in the presence of oncoming high-beams.

This procedure illustrates quite well the versatility of *Radiance*. The calculation of veiling luminance is fairly straightforward, and *Radiance* is flexible enough to allow you to include whatever calculations you wish. The *uses* of *Radiance* are defined and limited only by the *users* of *Radiance*.

Figure 7.13 Veiling luminance calculation applied to Figure 7.11, simulating the glare effects resulting from oncoming low-beam headlights.

Figure 7.14 Veiling luminance calculation applied to Figure 7.12, simulating the glare effects resulting from oncoming high-beam headlights.

(Since the writing of this chapter, version 3.1 of *Radiance* was released, including the program **pcond**, which performs veiling glare simulation as part of its visibility reproduction repertoire.)

Author's Biography

Dr. Phillips received his B.S. in biophysics from the University of Michigan in 1980, and his Ph.D. in biophysics from the Johns Hopkins University in 1985. Dr. Phillips's research background is in the field of vision physiology.

In 1987, Dr. Phillips left academia to join Failure Analysis Associates as a consultant in the areas of vision and lighting. In 1994, Dr. Phillips left Failure Analysis Associates and joined Forensic Technologies International Corporation (FTI), where he is currently the director of FTI/Anamet. Dr. Phillips is a member of several professional organizations, including the Illuminating Engineering Society of North America (IESNA). Dr. Phillips is an advisory member of the Roadway Lighting Committee of the IESNA.

FTI Corporation is the nation's only litigation consulting firm offering engineering and scientific analysis, high-tech visual communication services, and jury research and market analysis. Much of Dr. Phillips's consulting work has been in the area of roadway lighting, often in relation to vehicular accidents where vision and visibility is an issue. He is often consulted by attorneys, insurance companies, and municipalities in courtroom matters, and has qualified to testify as an expert witness both in federal court and in many state courts.

CHAPTER 8

Dramatic Lighting

The appreciation and use of theatrical lighting design techniques are increasing throughout the lighting profession. In many cases, designs are driven by artistic and emotional effect while the metrics of illumination are relegated to the back seat. Only after the visual direction of the design evolves and the implementation is being considered do the engineering metrics become more prominent.

Photoaccurate images can play an invaluable role in both of these design phases. In fact, when you explore a visual effect in *Radiance*, both the quality and the quantity of light are always present. While you might be focusing on how a form is being revealed, the lighting metrics are continually updated and readily available beneath the surface of the *Radiance* picture. The methods by which you have built the simulation and the accuracy of your scene descriptions seriously influence the usefulness of the image; if care is taken, extraordinarily detailed insights can result. Seeing the emerging design benefits the designer, the design team, and ultimately the audience who will perceive the lighted result.

Dramatic lighting involves taking artistic risks. The risks increase when designers are unsure whether their ideas can be implemented in the real world. *Radiance* has its place here. If the idea has been accurately described, *Radiance* will show the visual consequences to you and to all who are involved. This enables brave ideas to be developed and then presented to others for evaluation. Refinements are rapidly incorporated, and much of the ambiguity surrounding a lighting design idea is dispelled.

8.1 Stage Lighting Design

Dramatic lighting is born in the theater, where the designer uses light to create a panoply of effects, from brooding emotional atmospheres to dazzling moments of spectacle.

The lighting orchestration of a theater spectacle represents the most complex example of lighting design. Hundreds upon hundreds of instruments (the theater term for luminaires), in different colors, with different photometric distributions, at ever-changing intensities, make up the stage lighting designer's palette.

Radiance is a wonderful tool for stage lighting designers to use during all phases of the design process. In early design development, designers can use *Radiance* to explore and confirm their own lighting ideas. Later, the most promising *Radiance* images can be used to convey these lighting ideas to the rest of the design team. An example is shown in Figure 8.1. (See also Plate 17 following page 328.) Finally, in the short period of time allocated for physically lighting the production, more time can be apportioned to fine-tuning the visual elements that were born in the pictures, whereas if the lighting were built from scratch, less time would be available to explore the subtle nuances that separate mediocre stage lighting from artistry.

Whereas the objects in the Chapter 3 art gallery were static, elements within a stage picture are continually moving. Let's begin by exploring an approach to managing scenic elements before engaging the peculiarities of stage lighting.

First, within any given scene, identify those objects that do not move. These might include walls, most furniture, a corpse, and so on. Convert these scene descriptions into a single octree file. Remember to locate the material description file before the scene descriptions it modifies. The **-f** option will produce a frozen octree that will speed up the viewing process. Don't use the -f option until you are reasonably satisfied with your scene description, because once a file is frozen, changes to the material file are not automatically incorporated when the file is viewed or rendered.

```
%oconv -f scene.mat static_set.rad > static_set.oct
```

Figure 8.1 A *Radiance* concept image for the opening moments of *All's Well that Ends Well.* The underside of the umbrella (left) is illuminated by light reflected off the simulated slate floor. The dappled light patterns, in soft focus, are achieved by inserting a template into the ellipsoidal reflector spotlight beam. (See also Plate 17 following page 328; model courtesy of R. Shakespeare, lighting designer)

Now convert each object that moves within the scene into an individual octree file.

```
% oconv -f actor.mat actor.rad  > actor.oct

% oconv -f scene.mat teatrolly.rad > teatrolly.oct
```

Actors...? Until recently, the expense of obtaining the model of an actor was prohibitive, and the hours involved in modifying its appearance into a character were excessive. Luckily, more affordable actors are now available, from less detailed models, best suited to distant views, to more complexly constructed actors with a variety of clothing and hairstyle options. Three examples are shown in Figure 8.2. But beware! Off-the-shelf models are rarely posed for dramatic action! You will need a modeler to manipulate your prepackaged actors into the poses appropriate for your scene. Alternatively, programs such as POSER (by Fractal Design) will provide you with reasonably detailed models of both sexes in a variety of body types, and will allow you to position their body parts into appropriate gestures. Again, a modeler is required, but this time its function is to separate the actor into components that have the same material attributes, such as pants, shirt, hair, skin, and so on. These layers can be assigned distinct material attributes when they are converted into parts of *Radiance* scene descriptions.

Figure 8.2 Three actor models. The 3500-polygon dancer (left) was created in POSER, and her clothing was assigned in a modeler. The 6000-polygon man was built in a modeler from a MANNEQUIN (by Biomechanics Corp. of America) primitive. The 20,000-polygon woman (right) is a purchased data set and requires a modeler to alter the pose.

The most common method of converting these data sets into *Radiance* description files is through the `dxfcvt` filter. If you are using a program such as POSER, save the actor in `dxf` format. Then enter the following on the command line:

```
% dxf2rad -i actor.dxf -orad actor
```

The conversion process creates two files. In this case, they are *actor.rad* and *actor.mod*. The following listings show the typical contents of `dxfcvt` output files. Note that the *.mod* (material) file lists only the identifier label. This label is also located in the modifier position in the *.rad* file:

```
# actor.mod       created by dxfcvt
# geometry data are defined in actor.rad

FACE
HAIR
NECK
JACKET
.
.
.
TRIM
DRESS
# EndofFile
```

```
# actor.rad  created by dxfcvt
# a list of all modifiers is in actor.mod

FACE polygon FACE_0
0
0
9
0.11069  0.527603 5.05504
0.113735 0.479578 5.04787
0.169419 0.421523 5.05683

FACE polygon FACE_1
0
0
9
0.113735 0.479578 5.04787
0.075637 0.427378 5.02995
0.148344 0.375963 5.0407
.
.
.
DRESS polygon DRESS_2425
0
0
12
-0.354645 0.388856 4.02655
-0.376306 0.425202 4.03244
-0.646867 0.463816 0.112031
-0.635022 0.383869 0.112031
# EndofFile
```

Edit the material file *actor.mod* and assign the appropriate *Radiance* materials to each of the labels that have been named after the layers you created in your modeler program.

```
# actor.mod       created by dxfcvt
# geometry data are defined in actor.rad

void  plastic  FACE
0
0
5  0.76  0.62  0.58  0.00  0.00
```

```
void  plastic  HAIR
0
0
5  0.4  0.3  0.15  0.00  0.00

void  plastic  NECK
0
0
5  0.75  0.62  0.56  0.00  0.00

void  plastic  JACKET
0
0
5  0.10  0.10  0.15  0.00  0.00
.
.
.
void  plastic  TRIM
0
0
5  0.04  0.05  0.04  0.00  0.00

void  plastic  DRESS
0
0
5  0.1  0.1  0.15  0.00  0.17
# EndofFile
```

The imported model of the actor is ready to be inserted into the scene after it has been converted into an octree file.

The `dxf` filter creates scene descriptions using polygons. The more polygons, the smoother the clothing and skin. An actor constructed with about 5000 polygons can appear reasonably natural if not viewed in close-up. If close-ups are required in a scene, be cautious of using actors with more than 15,000 polygons, because data sets approaching this size will have a significant effect on the speed of the rendering process.

Finally, we need to create the scene's collector file, in which we will assemble the mobile and static set, props, and actors. Each of these octree files is located in the scene as an *instance.* In the following example, note how *static_set.oct* is simply inserted and not transformed from its original location. The fewer the transformations, the less delay time between repositioning an object and viewing the result.

```
# stage.all
#
# collector file example

#insert static components of set
void      instance     static
1         static_set.oct
0
0

# locate actor named Miss Prism, scaled down to 95% and turned
# 30 degrees counterclockwise, 2 feet stage left and 2 feet
# upstage from the center of the proscenium arch.
void      instance     miss_prism
9         actor.oct     -s .95 -rz 30  -t  2   2   0
0
0

#locate the teatrolley in front of miss_prism
void      instance     teatrolley
9         teatrolly.oct     -s 1 -rz 120 -t  3  1   0
0
0
# end of stage.all
```

This moment of our scene is now ready to be combined with its lighting and converted into the final octree so that it can be viewed.

In the Art Gallery simulation, we created spotlights and aimed them at art pieces. We can draw from the approaches used in that tutorial, but stage lighting is a much more complex event. Let's look at the issues and solutions connected with photometry, color, aiming, and dimming that lead to the accurate simulation of stage lighting orchestration.

8.2 Measuring and Modeling "Stage Lighting"

Stage lighting is evaluated using the designer's subjective response to a scene, and thus is far removed from the objective metrics of foot-candles, candelas, lumens, and nits. Consequently, stage lighting designers have not paid much attention to photometric data. This is not to say that stage lighting designers are indifferent to the photometric details of the equipment they select for a project. However, their evaluations generally have been based on the visual effect that the instrument delivers, not on its photometric description.

A cone of light can be described in two ways. One is based on its visual effect; the other, on its photometric distribution. Both are inextricably intertwined, but whereas the illumination engineer relies on technical specifications to select a luminaire, stage lighting designers have relied primarily on their visual memory of the effect the instrument produces and on a few crude metrics.

However, stage lighting designers are becoming more aware of the value of photometric data. For one thing, many stage lighting designers are being drawn into the world of architectural lighting, where knowledge of photometrics is indispensable. Increasingly stringent energy codes in the lighting industry have drawn manufacturers to make their stage lighting equipment more energy-efficient. In turn, instrument manufacturers are beginning to advertise the efficiency of their product lines by comparing their photometry (generally consisting only of beam angle, field angle, and center beam candlepower) with that of their competitors. At the same time, engineering visualization tools, led by *Radiance*, now have sufficient resolution and accuracy to be useful to the stage lighting artist. During this period of transition, when stage lighting manufacturers' published data are not yet as comprehensive as most architectural photometric files, where do we obtain the physically based photometry files that will enable us to model stage lighting in *Radiance?*

8.2.1 Stage Lighting Photometry

The workhorse of stage lighting is the ellipsoidal reflector spotlight (ERS). Its cone of light can be shaped with shutters, sharpened, softened, or used to project the pattern of a template. We could create a general photometric description of this instrument by using the center beam candlepower, field angle, and beam angle provided by the manufacturer. The distribution of most ERSs is such that the beam angle is two thirds of the field angle, as shown in Figure 8.3. This beam/field relationship is commonly referred to as a cosine distribution.

Typically, if we fit the cosine curve to the beam and field angles provided by the manufacturer, we can derive sufficient data to build an IES-format photometric file (see Chapter 3). A limitation of this approach is that we are constructing a photometric distribution from only three sample points, and we have no idea whether the edges of the cone of light (cut-off angle) are in sharp or soft focus. Accordingly, renderings produced with this photometry are of questionable accuracy. Until comprehensive testing procedures are used by the stage lighting industry and the

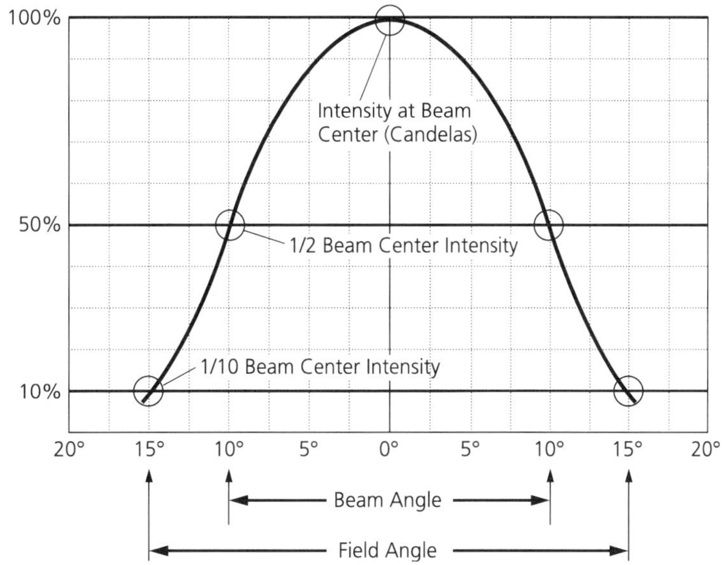

Figure 8.3 The photometry of an ellipsoidal reflector spotlight is commonly aligned so that its beam angle is two thirds of its field angle. This relationship is referred to as a cosine distribution. In turn, if you know the intensity of the beam center, the field angle, and the beam angle, a representative distribution of light can be approximated. In this example, the beam angle (at 50% peak candela) is 20 degrees, while the field angle (at 10% peak candela) is 30 degrees. This graph describes the changes in intensity across the beam of light as a percentage of center beam intensity (peak candela).

resulting data files are made available to the designer, we need to measure our own photometry. This is no mean task, given that the photometric description for a standard stage lighting instrument, with its versatile optics, is much more complex than that of a typical architectural luminaire.

A reasonable strategy creates three photometric files for a single ERS with cosine distribution. One file describes the effect of the beam with the lens in sharp focus. The other two files describe soft focus, with the lens tube slid in and slid out. These three distributions are graphically illustrated in Figure 8.4. An ERS can also be aligned, by adjusting the lamp/reflector relationship, into what is termed "peak focus." This distribution maximizes the center beam candlepower. Similarly, three additional photometric files can be constructed to describe these arrangements in sharp and soft focus. These six files represent the most common variations of a single ERS spotlight.

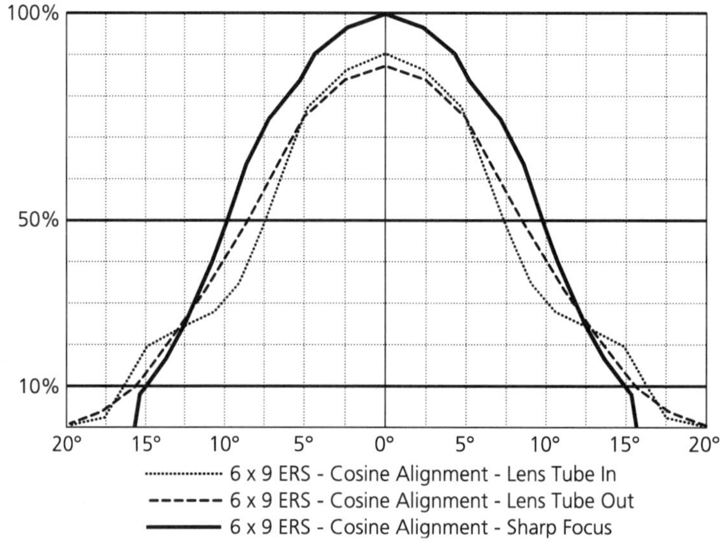

Figure 8.4 This 6″ × 9″ ellipsoidal reflector spotlight is cosine-aligned and its photometry measured for sharp focus, lens tube in and lens tube out. Note the variations in the photometric distributions, particularly near the edges of the cone of light. Similar photometric data can be collected with the instrument aligned in peak focus.

Because *Radiance* is physically based, and because we do not have IES-format photometric files that have been measured by independent test labs following IES-recommended testing procedures, we will have to measure our own instruments. What follows here and in Figure 8.5 is a description of a practical measuring procedure, but you are encouraged to review the *IES LM-11 IES Guide for Photometric Testing of Searchlights* and *LM-35 IES Approved Method for Photometric Testing of Floodlights* for complete procedures.

To create a reasonably accurate photometric description of an ERS with a field angle of more than 10 degrees, we need an illuminance meter, a tripod on which to mount the instrument, and a darkened space. The lens of a 6-inch- or 8-inch-diameter ERS should be at least 30 feet from the illuminance meter. At this distance, the diameter of the lens begins to approach that of a point source, and the measured data can be stored in the IES photometric format's point source description. It is also wise to measure an instrument within its application distance, and again a 30-foot throw is quite typical. If the field angle is less than 10 degrees, as in a narrow followspot, the meter should be located about 100 feet from the lens. At this distance, the illuminance is more likely to obey the inverse-square law, so a point source description remains valid. Adjust the alignment of the ERS to a cosine dis-

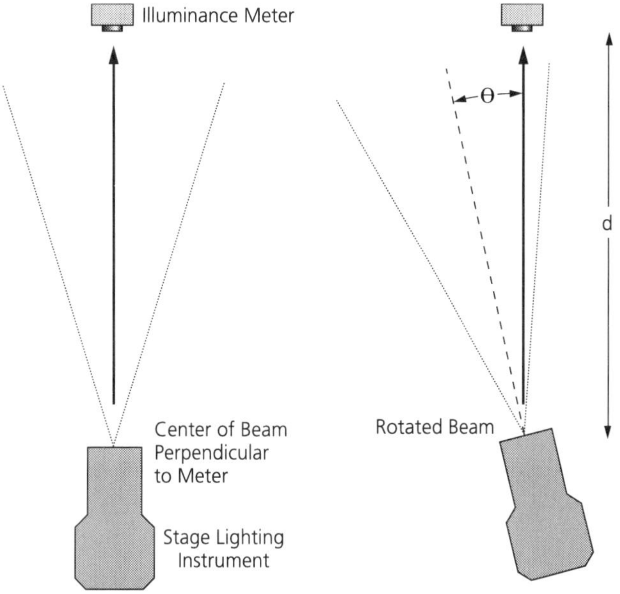

Figure 8.5 To measure the photometric distribution of an ERS or Fresnel stage lighting instrument, locate the luminaire on a tripod at least 30 feet from an illuminance meter. Rotate the luminaire so that its beam of light scans over the meter, while recording the related FC levels and angles (θ). Divide the FC level by d^2 to calculate the intensity (candelas) at a particular angle.

tribution and position the lens of the instrument as close to the pivot point of the tripod as possible. Now aim the center of the cone of light at the illuminance meter. The meter must be parallel to the plane of the lens. Record the ambient illumination while the instrument is turned off. Now turn the instrument on to full intensity and record the illumination. Rotate the instrument horizontally through 1 degree increments, while recording the associated foot-candle levels. Because an ERS has a fairly symmetrical lighting distribution, one sweep of the instrument will reasonably describe its photometry. Subtract the ambient illumination from these foot-candle levels and divide each by the distance from the meter to the lens plane, squared, to calculate the intensity in candelas at each angle.

$$\text{intensity (candelas)} = \text{Illumination (FC)} \times d^2 \text{(feet)} \qquad (8.1)$$

Because we are sweeping the beam of light over the meter, the meter-to-lens distance remains constant and no cosine adjustment is required.

The same approach can be used to measure the photometric distribution of a Fresnel. In this case, three files describe the light output with the lens/lamp relationship in spot, mid, and flood positions.

Ies2rad produces output files that enable complex photometric distributions to be accurately inserted into a scene. An ies2rad input file for a sharp focused 6″ × 9″ ERS in cosine alignment follows. The instrument uses a 1000-watt lamp, and the intensity of the beam center is 38,000 candelas. This file is in a very basic IES photometric format; it is described in the Scene 2 tutorial in Chapter 3, Section 3.1.2.

```
6x9ERS 1KW  (BRAND X)
ERS COS B/A=20 F/A=30 CUTOFF=16
FEL 1KW T/H LAMP 27500 LUMENS 300 HRS
BCCP=38000CD

TILT=NONE
1 27500 1 11 1 1 1 -0.5 0 0
1 1 1000
0.0   2.5   4.0   6.0   7.5   10.0  12.0  15.0  15.5  16.0  90.0
0.0
38000 36670 34200 31540 28120 19000 11400 3800  3040  0     0
```

Instead of having only a single photometric file derived from the scanty information provided by the manufacturer, we now have an array of physically based photometric files that more accurately describe the typical lighting effects produced by each instrument. When lighting a scene, you can now choose a file that most closely represents the way the instrument would be focused to achieve the desired stage lighting effect.

8.2.2 Color Changes Resulting from Dimming

Another lighting attribute of particular concern to theater lighting designers is the color shift resulting from dimming tungsten halogen lamps. In industrial and architectural lighting, most light sources are selected according to their color temperatures and average lumen outputs. The only reduction of lumen output results from light loss factors, and the only color shifts result from the aging of the lamp.

In theater, most lighting instruments use tungsten halogen lamps. The effect of a shaft of sunlight might be achieved with an instrument turned up to full intensity (3200 degrees K). That same instrument might also be required to provide the effect of the dim golden glow of a candle in a night scene (2400 degrees K). Rather than adding a color filter to the instrument, you can achieve this color shift by reducing the voltage to the lamp, or, in other words, dimming the instrument. The intensity of a lamp is most often controlled by using a fader or keypad on a scale from 0% (off) to 100% (full). The level of a control channel typically affects the voltage output of a dimmer, following the square law relationship. The resulting lamp lumen output is not equal to the control value, with the exception of full on or off. If the control channel is set to 100%, the lamp should produce its rated output and specified color temperature. If the control channel is set to 30%, the lumen output is dropped to 10% and the color temperature reduced to 2400 degrees K. Other dimming curves can be programmed into a modern stage lighting control system, but the square law profile is often set as the default. Table 8.1 lists control channel levels, each with its associated lumen output multiplier and an RGB representation of the lamp's color temperature. Values are shown for tungsten halogen lamps with color temperatures of 3200 degrees K and 3000 degrees K.

Ies2rad can be used to create a *Radiance* description of a dimmed tungsten halogen light source. The following example converts the photometry of an ERS with a 3200 degree K lamp into a *Radiance* light source that could produce the bright

		3200 degree K lamp			3000 degree K lamp		
Control level	Lumen output multiplier	R	G	B	R	G	B
100%	1.00	1.377	0.913	0.351	1.450	0.890	0.292
90%	.81	1.407	0.904	0.326	1.481	0.880	0.268
80%	.64	1.440	0.893	0.299	1.517	0.868	0.243
70%	.50	1.479	0.881	0.270	1.559	0.854	0.216
60%	.35	1.527	0.865	0.237	1.610	0.837	0.186
50%	.25	1.584	0.845	0.201	1.672	0.816	0.152
40%	.16	1.660	0.820	0.158	1.751	0.788	0.115
30%	.09	1.760	0.785	0.112	1.864	0.748	0.070
20%	.04	1.876	0.743	0.065	1.876	0.743	0.065
10%	.01	1.876	0.743	0.065	1.876	0.743	0.065
0%	.00						

Table 8.1 Lamp output and color are functions of dimming level for 2 lamp types.

sunlight effect we have described. The **-c** option provides the color description, and the **-m** value is used as a lumen multiplier. The test lumen output of the *6x9ers.ies* file is unaffected when the multiplier is set to 1.

```
% ies2rad -l default -df -m 1.00 -c 1.377 0.913 0.351 -o channel1 6x9ers.ies
```

To change the sunlight effect to the dim golden glow of a candle, we would reduce the control channel to a setting of 30%. This effect can be emulated by changing the -m and -c values to the chart's percentages of lumen output and RGB data that are correlated with a control channel level of 30%.

```
% ies2rad -l default -df -m 0.09 -c 1.760 0.785 0.112 -o channel1 6x9ers.ies
```

This procedure can be used to approximate the color temperature change and decrease in intensity resulting from dimming for any instrument with a 3200 degrees K or 3000 degrees K tungsten halogen lamp.

8.2.3 Color Filters

Hundreds of color filters (often referred to as *gels*) are available to the theater lighting designer. A salmon tint might be selected to represent the light of a romantic sunset, or a deep blue to evoke an eerie night. Desktop photospectrometers (such as Colortron, by Light Source) enable you to acquire your own color data from a variety of materials, including gels, but luckily there are several sources of published color filter data. *Color Science for Lighting the Stage,* by William Warfel and Walter Klappert (Yale University Press, 1981), provides a comprehensive listing of color filter data in the CIE *Yxy* format. A color filter database is also included in the GELFILE software (by Systems Design Associates). In addition, several manufacturers provide spectral transmission curves with their gel samples.

To convert a list of CIE *Yxy* color data to *Radiance* RGB color values, we can use the *xyz_rgb.cal* script, located in the *Radiance* library, and an input format description file (*input.fmt*) containing

```
$(name)    ${transmission}    ${myx}    ${myy}
```

An input color file (*cie.in*) of any length can be produced by following this input format:

```
ltstraw    85.28          .465    .418
straw      82.32          .509    .445
amber      70.32          .533    .425
red         7.21          .695    .281
pink       70.63          .482    .388
```

```
dkpink     30.58              .549    .313
ltblue     63.51              .422    .404
blue       24.09              .291    .343
dkblue      5.71              .204    .187
```

The output format is defined in a file (*output.fmt*) containing

```
$(name)   ${myR}   ${myG}   ${myB}
```

and an additional script called *mycvt.cal* converts this input and output data.

```
myX = myY*myx/myy;
myY = transmission/100;
myZ = myY*(1-myx-myy)/myy;
myR = R(myX,myY,myZ);
myG = G(myX,myY,myZ);
myB = B(myX,myY,myZ);
```

Now execute the following **rcalc** command to create a file called *gel.lst.*

```
%rcalc -o output.fmt -i in.fmt -f mycvt.cal -f xyz_rgb.cal cie.in > gel.lst
```

The result is an output file called *gel.lst,* containing RGB filter colors listed by name:

```
ltstraw  1.343    0.727     0.137
straw    1.421    0.669     0
amber    1.414    0.492     0
red      0.370    0         0.002
pink     1.330    0.510     0.166
dkpink   0.965    0.062     0.121
ltblue   0.851    0.590     0.211
blue     0.140    0.279     0.257
dkblue   0.019    0.057     0.209
```

If you store these data in a library, the process needs to be performed only once for a particular set of color filters. These RGB values can be inserted with the -c option into ies2rad, which creates the effect of putting the color filter into the instrument. The example that follows produces the effect of inserting a blue gel into the beam of an ERS.

```
% ies2rad -l default -df -m 1 -c 0.140 0.279 0.257 -o channel1 6x9ers.ies
```

8.2.4 Spectral Transmission Data

If spectral data for a color filter are available, we can use features of the Material and Geometry Format (MGF), included with the *Radiance* distribution, to convert this data into CIE *Yxy* values. Then the procedure described in the preceding section can be applied to convert the results into *Radiance* RGB values.

Spectral transmission data for color filters are generally included with the sample books distributed by filter manufacturers. It is useful to know what these spectral data represent. The manufacturer of the blue filter described in Figure 8.6 used a 2856 degree K illuminant in measuring the transmission data. The resulting spectral curve captures the transmission characteristics of the filter. This is not the spectrum of 2856 degree K light passing through the filter. Instead, the data represent the amount of light transmitted through the filter at each wavelength, as a percentage of the unfiltered test illuminant. The result is transmission data that are reasonably independent of the color temperature of the test light source.

By itself, this transmission data is not very useful until we combine it with the spectral data of a lamp. These elements are combined by simply multiplying together the filter transmission and light source spectral values for each wavelength. Figure 8.6 also describes the spectra resulting from placing our blue filter in the path of a 2856 degree K incandescent light source (the light source spectra have been scaled to fit within the range of the graph).

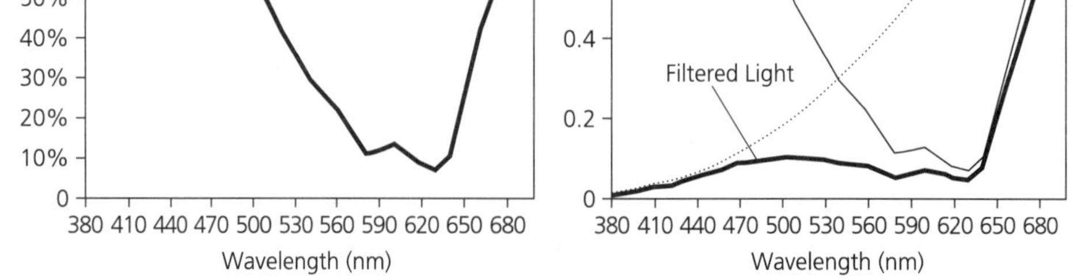

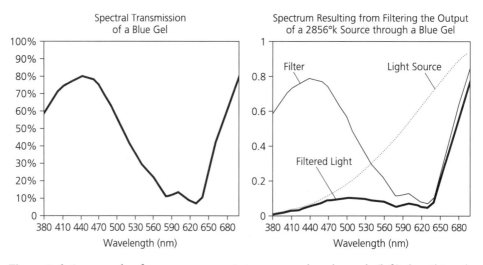

Figure 8.6 An example of a percent transmission vs. wavelength graph (left) describing the spectrum of a blue color filter. Data can be collected from the graph and combined with the spectrum of a light source to produce a description of filtered light (right).

8.2.5 Converting Spectral Data into *Light*

We can convert light source and filter spectral data into RGB values and use them in ies2rad to produce a *Radiance* light description. This is the process:

1. Acquire spectral data from the color filter manufacturer's charts (Figure 8.6) and organize the values in 10-nanometer (nm) increments. These 10-nm steps are convenient to use with other MGF-generated tables. If the transmission data are extremely varied, a higher sample rate is needed to capture the details.
2. Generate the spectra of an incandescent light source at the appropriate color temperature, using the `mgfilt` program. The following command sequence produces a list of spectral data for a 2856 degree K tungsten lamp ranging between 380 nm and 780 nm in 10-nm increments:

```
%mgfilt c,cspec
%cct  2856
cspec 380 780 0.0830 0.1025 0.1245   ... 2.0451
```

3. Multiply the filter's transmission values by the illuminant's spectra at each visible wavelength.

```
Wavelength (NM)                380      390      400      ...700
Color Filter (% Transmission     0.580    0.640    0.700    ...0.800
2856 degree K Light source       0.0830   0.1025   0.1245   ...1.6780
Combined spectral data           0.048    0.066    0.087    ...1.342
```

4. Place the combined spectral data in a file and convert it into a CIE *xy* value.

   First create a file (*spectrum.in*) which lists the spectra of the blue gel as an MGF color description:

```
# Spectrum of a blue filter
m new_blue =
       c
       cspec  380  700  0.048  0.066  0.087  ...1.342
```

   `m new_blue =` declares that a material named `new_blue` will be defined and `c` indicates that color information follows. In reality, only the `cspec` values will be processed, but MGF requires a complete material definition. The first two values of `cspec` define the range of the spectral data. In our case, the data begin at 380 nm and end with 700 nm. The number of values that follow determines the spacing of the spectral transmission samples. Our 33 values will be spaced 10 nm apart.

```
( 700 NM - 380 NM )/(33 - 1) =  10 NM between values
```

Now execute the following `mgfilt` command to generate the CIE *xy* values of the spectral data and then view the output:

```
% mgfilt c,cxy  spectrum.in > cie_xy.out

% more cie_xy.out
c
cxy 0.2954 0.3281
```

5. Use the % transmission provided by the filter manufacturer as the CIE *Y* value for the gel and complete the CIE *Yxy* color description.

```
35.000.29540.3281
```

6. Finally, we can convert our color-filtered CIE *Yxy* data into RGB values, ready for use in an ies2rad function call. Place the following in a file (*blue.in*):

```
new_blue  35.00  0.2954  0.3281
```

Then execute the rcalc command,

```
% rcalc -o output.fmt -i in.fmt -f mycvt.cal -f xyz_rgb.cal blue.in >> gel.lst
```

which appends our new RGB filter (`new_blue 0.2399 0.3879 0.4081`) data to the end of the *gel.lst* file. If the color temperature of the light sources used to derive the data in our library are different, combining these filters in a scene without additional conversions will produce dubious results. Appropriately, the color filter data obtained from GELFILE and the color description we just calculated from spectral data are both based on a lamp with a color temperature of 2856 degrees K.

8.2.6 Combining the Effects of Dimming and Color Filters

The same spectral conversion techniques can be used to describe the red-shift effect on a tungsten halogen lamp and color filter combination at any dimmer setting. Simply change the argument in the `mgfilt` command line to the desired color temperature and recalculate the combined result. The following command generates the spectra for a tungsten halogen light source that is dimmed until its color temperature is 2400 degrees K.

```
%mgfilt c,cspec
%cct  2400
```

Figure 8.7 describes the spectra resulting from combining `new_blue` gel with a tungsten halogen lamp at its rated color temperature of 3200 degrees K and with the lamp dimmed to 2400 degrees K. Note how the blue component is diminished between the 440 nm–530 nm range at the lower color temperature.

8.2.7 A Practical Approach to Managing Dimming, Color Filters, and Photometry

As we have just demonstrated, the effect of a color filter changes significantly when an instrument is dimmed. If a pale blue filter is added to an instrument, its light appears blue at 100%, but at 10% it emits only a murky green light. Since virtually every instrument in a stage lighting design will have a color filter and will be dimmed, we need to incorporate these effects into our pictures for them to be accurate simulations of the way the stage will appear. Again, rcalc will come to the rescue, along with *xyz_rgb.cal* and a script called *instr.cal.* They will generate an ies2rad command line that combines the effect of dimming the lamp and including a color filter with the photometric distribution of each instrument.

Here is an example of the contents of an input data file called *lights.in:*

```
i: 6x9ers.ies ch1 .240 .291 .343 3200 .5
i: 612ERS.ies ch2 .057 .204 .187 3000 .3
```

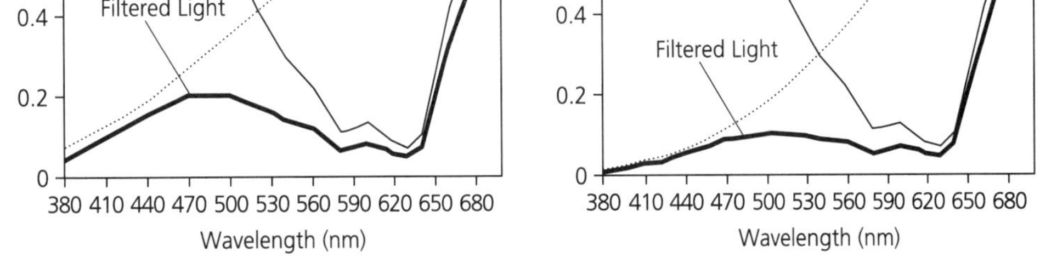

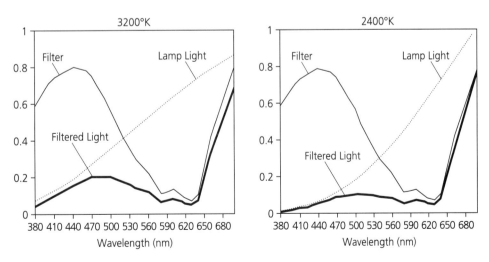

Figure 8.7 The spectrum of filtered light produced by combining a tungsten halogen source and a color filter is significantly altered by dimming. Note how the blue component is reduced at the lower color temperature (right).

and the file (*instr.fmt*) which defines the input format:

```
i: $(iesf) $(radf) ${Ygel} ${xgel} ${ygel} ${Tlmp} ${Clmp}
```

This input file uses a specific format beginning with the name of the ies2rad input photometry file. This is followed by the output file name `$(radf)`, the CIE *Yxy* gel color values `${Ygel} ${xgel} ${ygel}`, the color temperature rating of the lamp `${Tlmp}`, and the control channel level `${Clmp}` (0–1 scale). This example results in four ies2rad output files (*.dat* and *.rad* for each entry). We could use xform to locate and aim the light sources *ch1.rad* and *ch2.rad* in a scene.

An abbreviated listing of the script that manages the conversion process, called *instr.cal*, follows. Note the `Tilla : 2856` entry. This variable should be set to the color temperature of the illuminant used in deriving the color filter data.

```
{instr.cal
The following table of color temperature indexed by lamp output was
generated using Klappert's formula . . .
}

{
Constants and functions for instrument control
}
Tmax : 3300;          { color temperature corresponding to max. table value }
cto(s) : s*s;         { standard control function (square law) }
mta(t) : (t/Tmax)^8;  { adjusted maximum value for color temp t }
Tilla : 2856;         { color temperature of test Illuminant }
Milla : mta(Tilla);   { adjusted maximum for Illuminant A }
                      { normalized RGB color for Illuminant A: }
Rilla : ltr(Milla)/Milla;
Gilla : ltg(Milla)/Milla;
Billa : ltb(Milla)/Milla;

{
       Compute gel RGB color based on Yxy with Illuminant A
}
Xgel  = Ygel*xgel/ygel;
Zgel  = Ygel*(1-xgel-ygel)/ygel;
Rgel  = R(Xgel,Ygel,Zgel)/Rilla;
Ggel  = G(Xgel,Ygel,Zgel)/Gilla;
Bgel  = B(Xgel,Ygel,Zgel)/Billa;
```

```
{
        Compute RGB multiplier from gel and color temperature
}
Mlmp = mta(Tlmp);          { adjusted maximum output }
Mset = Mlmp*cto(Clmp);     { adjusted output at control setting }
Rout = Rgel*ltr(Mset)/Mlmp;
Gout = Ggel*ltg(Mset)/Mlmp;
Bout = Bgel*ltb(Mset)/Mlmp;
```

Finally, put the following line in a file called *iesi.fmt* to format the output into a sequence of ies2rad commands:

```
ies2rad -t default -df -c ${Rout} ${Gout} ${Bout} -o $(radf) $(iesf)
```

To run the script and automatically execute the ies2rad commands, enter the following command:

```
%rcalc -f xyz_rgb.cal -f instr.cal -i instr2.fmt -o iesi.fmt lights.in | sh -x
```

To stop the command from echoing the output, you can remove the -x. If you want to save the output and execute the ies2rad commands at a future time, write the output into a file:

```
%rcalc f xyz_rgb.cal f instr.cal i instr2.fmt o iesi.fmt lights.in > save.lights
```

The contents of *save.lights* follow. Note that the -m multiplier option is not used. Instead, the reduced lumen output due to dimming is wrapped within the -c color specification.

```
ies2rad -t default -df -c 3.63603  6.83586  5.54444  -o ch1 6x9ers.ies
ies2rad -t default -df -c 0.196607 0.469553 0.900838 -o ch2 612ers.ies
```

To execute the ies2rad commands contained in *save.lights*, change the file permissions to executable and enter *save.lights* on the command line.

```
% chmod 755 save.lights
% save.lights
```

The benefits of this process are immense. The effect of any stage lighting instrument, tungsten lamp, or gel can be accurately dimmed and viewed. You can engage in this process interactively when you need to manipulate the lighting levels of a scene. Simply change the control channel settings in *lights.in* and execute the rcalc command to update the scene's lighting descriptions.

8.2.8 Adaptation and the Color of Light

Our discussion of colored light for the stage has avoided the issues involved in color adaptation and normalization. If the stage is illuminated with no color filters and no instruments are dimmed, it is reasonable to use white light (`-c 1 1 1`) in every ies2rad command to depict the way the actors will appear to an audience member who has been watching the stage for a while. More typically, though, the audience is presented with frequent changes in the illumination. Each of these changes might incorporate different combinations of colored light at a variety of different intensities. Trying to predict the full effect of color adaptation on an audience member whose color environment is in flux is far beyond the scope of this book.

However, you will note that a white screen illuminated by a 3200 degree K *Radiance light* source, generated by *instr.cal*, appears yellowish. This is because our functions that convert from CIE color space to RGB color values use white light to depict a 6000 degree K illuminant. If you are adapted to daylight (a color temperature somewhere in the range of 5000 degrees K to 7000 degrees K), the light emitted by a tungsten halogen lamp will indeed appear yellow! Modern theaters generally attempt to exclude daylight, so to better portray the color experience of an audience member, we could represent a 3200 degree K illuminant as white instead of yellow. This is accomplished by editing the *instr.cal* file so that final RGB values are divided by the RGB value of a 3200 degree K source (1.377 0.913 0.358).

```
Rout = Rgel*ltr(Mset)/Mlmp/1.377;
Gout = Ggel*ltg(Mset)/Mlmp/0.913;
Bout = Bgel*ltb(Mset)/Mlmp/0.358;
```

In general, these changes result in a more acceptable color representation of the effects of stage lighting.

8.2.9 Organizing the Light Plot

Two methods of organizing a modest number of individually aimed light sources were presented in Chapter 3, but we did not require separate control over each of these luminaires, nor did we need to explore many focus options. A third approach, tailored to the demands of stage lighting design, is needed to organize the instruments and the multitude of color and intensity variations that convey changes in such things as time, location, and mood. The simplest strategy places the ies2rad program and the xform command positioning the light source in the same file, conveniently locating the color, intensity, photometry, and all aiming variables for a given instrument close to one another. Since we have no need to look at the lighting instruments themselves (which are generally masked from audience view), but only the effect of the light they emit, the geometry of the instrument housings will not be included in our theater lighting files.

The following is a typical entry in a lighting file for a theatrical scene. It locates a stage lighting instrument with a straw-colored gel, so that it will light the left side of an actor's face at a 45 degree vertical angle (downlight = 90 degrees, horizontal light = 0 degrees, uplight = –90 degrees).

```
!ies2rad -l default -df -m 1.0 -c 1.343 0.727 0.137.7 -o ch1 6x9ers.ies
!xform -n ch1,lightpipe1_1 -rz 0 -rx 45  -rz 45 -t 15 -15 26 ch1.rad
```

When you are manipulating hundreds of instruments, you should list command options in a consistent order to make it easier to review the data. The **-n** option is listed first; it can be used to assign a unique name to each instrument, composed of its control channel and its location in the theater.

Without adding any transformations, the center axis of a beam of light enters the scene at 0 0 0, pointing downward in the $-z$ direction. The first rotation in our options list spins this cone of light 0 degree around the z-axis. In this case, no action is performed, but if we were aiming a 1000-watt PAR64, we could use the first **-rz** option to rotate its elliptical photometric distribution around the center of its beam into the desired orientation. The **-rx** option tilts the photometry 45 degrees from vertical, followed by the second -rz option, which provides the horizontal rotation. The cone of light is then moved to its location on the first lighting pipe with the `-t 15 -15 26` translation.

It might be convenient to control a second, identically configured instrument with this same channel, in which case there would be no need for an additional ies2rad command. Simply add a second xform command to locate the new instrument.

```
ies2rad -l default -df -m 0.10 -c 1.343 0.727 0.137 -o ch1 6x9ers.ies
!xform -n ch1,lightpipe1_1  -rz  0  -rx  45 -rz 45 -t 15 -15 26  ch1.rad
!xform -n ch1,lightpipe1_2  -rz  0  -rx  45 -rz 45 -t 8  -15 26  ch1.rad
```

If we want to change the photometry of the second instrument to a soft focus 6″ × 9″ ERS, a new ies2rad command is required:

```
!ies2rad -l default -df -m 1.0 -c 1.343 0.727 0.137.7 -o ch1 6x9ers.ies
!xform -n ch1,lightpipe1_1 -rz 0 -rx 45 -rz 45 -t 15 -15 26 ch1.rad

!ies2rad -l default -df -m 1.0 -c 1.343 0.727 0.137 -o ch1a 6x9ers_soft.ies
!xform -n ch1,lightpipe1_2 -rz 0 -rx 45 -rz 45 -t 8 -15 26 ch1a.rad
```

Although you could assign different -m values for two instruments in the same channel, this practice would conflict with the way channels are applied in theater lighting. If you keep the levels, expressed by the -m value, consistent within each channel, at a later time you can translate the levels to the actual lighting control console in the theater. Once you have refined your concept image, why disregard your lighting levels? If your physical instruments are hung and focused in the same way as your simulation and you retain the channel settings, your concept image has not only conveyed your idea to the rest of the design team, but in addition, your channel levels can provide a "jump start" for lighting the actual scene on the stage.

A variation of this strategy keeps all xform data (aiming and location) in one file:

```
!xform -n ch1,lightpipe1_1 -rz 0 -rx 45 -rz 45 -t 15 -15 26 ch1.rad
!xform -n ch2,lightpipe1_2 -rz 0 -rx 45 -rz 45 -t  8 -15 26 ch2.rad
```

and all other lighting attributes (color, photometry, channel level) in another file:

```
i: 6x9ers.ies    ch1    .240    .291    .343    3200    .5
i: 612ERS.ies    ch2    .057    .204    .187    3000    .3
```

The disadvantage of this final approach occurs when it is necessary to traverse two files while making changes to both the aiming and the quality of light. This becomes particularly awkward when you are creating key frames for moving light sequences (robotic controlled instruments).

The big advantage of this approach surfaces when your instrument selection, placement, and aiming are finalized. If the -f option is not used when you are making the octree for the lighting and the scene geometry, changes to color and intensity can be viewed without an octree rebuild, reducing the time delay between changing a series of levels and viewing the consequences with rview. Though it is not as immediate as the real-time response experienced during a level set in the theater, the speed of the visual feedback provided via the monitor becomes very useful. As processing speed increases and becomes more affordable, so will the usefulness of this offline editing technique.

This final approach also has the advantage of using simulated control settings that are directly correlated with the real stage lighting control system. Because we are mimicking the square law dimming curve in our simulation, channel levels may not require additional conversions when being ported to the lighting control console.

Here is a summary of the significant steps that lead to a concept picture:

1. Create a database of the photometry and filter data that reflects the inventory required for your lighting design.

2. Acquire/build the set and actor data sets; convert them to an octree format using oconv, and organize them for rapid rendering.
3. Arrange the lighting data into an appropriate file format with all instruments at full intensity.
4. Build a complete octree from the scenic and lighting data.

```
% oconv stage.all  lighting.all >  scene.oct
```

5. Change lighting levels by updating *Radiance* light descriptions using ies2rad commands, then view the scene.

```
% rview -vf scene.vf -av .01 .01 .01 scene.oct
```

6. Make adjustments to the lighting levels, close the old rview window, and open an updated simulation.
7. After fine-tuning the lighting of a scene, set up a *Radiance* input file and render a concept picture at the desired resolution using **rad**, as described in Chapter 3. Because stage lighting is mostly dependent on the direct lighting component, one ambient bounce is sufficient to add the effect of interreflected light.

Remember that if you re-aim a luminaire or move an element of the scene, the octree must be updated using the oconv command.

8.2.10 Shaping the Beam of Light

When ellipsoidal reflector spotlights are focused to the stage, shutters are often used to shape the cone of light. Figure 8.1 depicts the dappled effect produced by placing a template in an instrument. Though you could collect very detailed photometric reports that describe the effect of inserting shutters or templates in each instrument, such an approach is impractical. Shutters and templates can be placed in an infinite number of arrangements and their effect sharpened or softened by sliding the lens tube of the instrument. Hundreds of photometric files would not capture the range of effects produced by one instrument!

A solution to this problem takes advantage of the IES point source description of a light source and the ray-tracing techniques used by *Radiance*. A sharp-focused shadow is produced when an opaque object is inserted into a cone of light emitted by a point source. Similarly, a polygon will cast a sharp shadow when inserted into a beam of light that has been created by the ies2rad function. However, this harsh-edged boundary between light and shadow looks very artificial and would rarely be used on the stage.

The effect of a real shutter or template can be captured in a photograph, as shown in Figure 8.8. If a transparency of this photograph is located in the light beam, the shadow patterns of the physically based shutter or template are accurately mimicked. The transparency can be moved within the light beam to produce the desired effect. In addition, the photometric distribution of the instrument is unaffected in the nonshadowed areas.

Three different images of a shutter will meet most needs. Aim an ellipsoidal reflector spotlight at a white screen and insert a shutter. Adjust the focus from sharp to lens-in and lens-out, recording each arrangement on a photograph. Scan the photo and isolate the shutter segment using photo-editing software. Convert the shutter image into the *Radiance* picture format by using the filters provided with the distribution. If the picture is in TIFF format, it can be converted using the `ra_tiff` program.

```
% ra_tiff  shtr_sft.tif     shtr_sft.pic
```

Because hundreds of template patterns are commercially available, the general effect of a template can be tested on a scene by scanning its silhouette from a catalog image and softening its edges using photo-editing software. An example appears in Figure 8.9. After you determine the most effective patterns, the same photographic method can be used to capture the effect of the real templates. Again, three images of a template pattern are required so that the whole range of focus options is available to the scene.

Templates range from simple silhouettes cut out of thin metal to color and monochrome images applied to heat-resistant tempered glass. We will use the latter to illustrate the process of inserting a captured shape into the beam of a 6″ × 9″ ERS.

First scan and edit the template image and convert it into a *Radiance* picture. To map the picture onto a glass square, create a file containing the following scene description:

Figure 8.8 The bottom edge of this image was derived from a photograph of the effect of a shutter inserted into an ellipsoidal reflector spotlight with the lens tube slid out.

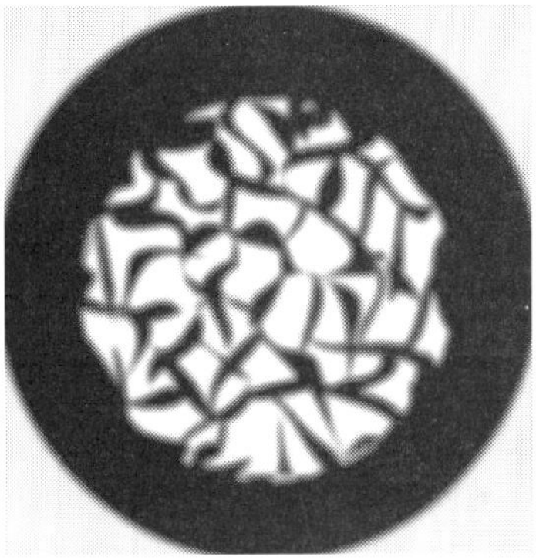

Figure 8.9 A picture of a soft-edged template pattern.

```
# softgobo.rad
#
# map a picture onto a glass surface

void colorpict gobo
9 red green blue softgobo.pic picture.cal pic_u pic_v
                -s .5
0
0

gobo glass pattern
0
0
3  .9  .9  .9

pattern polygon template
0
0
12
   0    0    0
   .5   0    0
   .5   .5   0
   0    .5   0
# end softgobo.rad
```

Because many copies of this template might be required in the scene, convert the file into an octree so we can use the instance function to locate it in the beam of light.

```
% oconv  -f  gobosoft.rad   >  gobosoft.oct
```

A template is designed to fit into the gate of an ERS so that its effect fills the whole beam of light. Shutters are also inserted in this plane. To simulate this effect, locate an instance of the template just in front of the light source. This distance needs to be adjusted for each beam width, so that the edge of the template image lines up with the edge of the beam of light, as shown in Figure 8.10.

Because ies2rad positions the point source of our photometry at 0 0 0 facing in the $-z$ direction, we can locate the center of the template just below this point and it will intercept the center of the cone of light. In the case of a 6″ × 9″ ERS, this is approximately 6 inches in front of the light source (`-t -.25 -.25 -.5`). To place the template in the scene, simply add the transformations that locate the instrument. The following file inserts *gobosoft.oct* into our channel 1 instrument on the light pipe.

```
#  tmplts.rad
#
# this file is used to locate templates and shutters into instruments
```

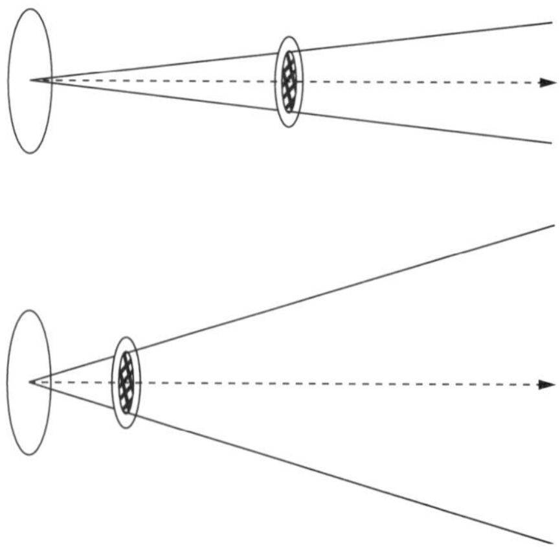

Figure 8.10 The width of the beam of light determines the placement of the template in front of the emitting geometry.

```
void instance template_ch1
15  gobosoft.oct  -t -.25 -.25 -.5 -rz 0 -rx 45 -rz 45 -t 15 -15 26
0
0
#end tmplts.rad
```

If *tmplts.rad* is included in the octree used to view the scene, and channel 1 is turned on, the effect of the template can be evaluated. With this same technique, shutters can be used to model the shape of a beam of light. This technique can even be applied when you are evaluating images projected on the scenery, provided that you have the photometry of the projector.

Once you are satisfied that your lighting idea is useful, your *Radiance* images are ready to be shared with the rest of the production team. The inventory of instruments, lamps, gels, and templates necessary to achieve your design has been tested in simulation and is ready to be installed in the theater. Though unexpected situations always arise, you have already confronted and overcome many problems by focusing each instrument in simulation, thus saving valuable stage time. Finally, the channel levels used to paint your *Radiance* pictures can be loaded into the lighting control console, ready to be evaluated and adjusted as you bring the real actors into the appropriate light.

Of course, the use of color filters, dimmers, and shaped beams of light is not limited to the stage! The picture on the front cover of this book illustrates the evocative effect produced by combinations of framing projectors, templates, spotlights, and color filters in the lobby of a large hotel.

8.3 Dramatic Architectural Lighting on the Skyline

Unlike most theater productions, the lighting of a building facade is likely to remain unchanged for decades. Add to this fact the considerable expense of installing and maintaining a large architectural lighting design, and the result is an air of caution that often subdues the lighting design process. This caution can lead to a situation in which expensive mockups of the proposed effects are produced, and some of the bravest and best ideas are rejected as being too extravagant to be explored.

If we consider the most prominent architectural and engineering triumphs in our cityscapes, such as skyscrapers and bridges, to be giant urban sculptures, they deserve special treatment. These landmarks can become beacons at night, conveying the nighttime character of a city. There is an increasing awareness of the power of light and shadow to sculpt the nighttime image of a building rather than to merely floodlight its facade in a blaze of uniform whiteness. *Radiance* can benefit the users of both approaches, but it really shines when the esthetic effect of the structure's lighting takes priority. Even the most adventurous of ideas can be explored in a *Radiance* simulation in a fraction of the time, and at a fraction of the expense, of a physical mockup. There is less need to be cautious when an accurate and relatively inexpensive simulation is central to the discussion. A photoaccurate image dispels ambiguity and often directs the client toward the more subtle consequences of a possible lighting design.

To illustrate how *Radiance* can show a client very subtle differences in a lighting design, let's look at the simple obelisk (Figure 8.11) that tops the NationsBank building in Atlanta, Georgia. This spire overlooks the city and is one of its more prominent features during the day. Until the opening night of the 1996 Olympics, it was unlighted and disappeared after sunset. The *Radiance* pictures in Figure 8.12 played a critical role in determining which lighting approach would best suit the project, and in allowing the client to play a more active role in determining the final appearance of its building.

The pictures (Figure 8.12) present four ways the sides of the obelisk could appear. Each picture results from a different arrangement of spotlights and floodlights. The sculptured effect in the upper-right picture, achieved by balancing

Figure 8.11 Previously unlighted obelisk atop the 1000-foot NationsBank building in Atlanta, Georgia.

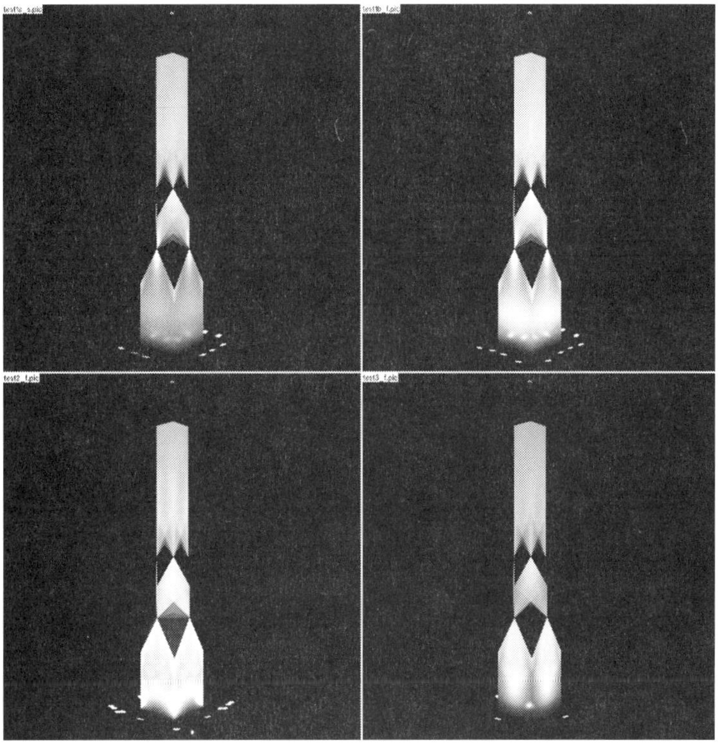

Figure 8.12 Four variations of a lighting design for the obelisk. (Model courtesy of Shakespeare Lighting Design)

highlights with the floodlighting, won the approval of the client. The simple floodlighted approach depicted in the lower-right image was considered the least desirable.

Four images can be assembled into a single *Radiance* picture by using the **pcompos** command. Figure 8.12 illustrates some additional features, including automatic labeling (**-la**) and control of the white space (`-s 10 -b 1 1 1`) between pictures. The command that produced the composite picture is

```
% pcompos -la -a 2 -s 10 -b 1 1 1 test3.pic test2.pic test1b.pic test1a.pic > spire_4.pic
```

The `-a 2` option instructs pcompos to create a column of pictures two images wide.

The lighting for the spire top was added, and a second set of pictures was used to evaluate the completed lighting scheme, as shown in Figure 8.13. (See also Plate 18 following page 328.) Compared with traditional lighting design presentation and analysis methods involving arrays of illumination values, inaccurate sketches, and only a vague idea of the way the project will actually look, integrating photoaccurate images into the design process wins hands down.

The usefulness of a *Radiance* picture is not limited to the concept and design development phases of the project. Although a numeric record of the precise aiming of each luminaire is stored in the xform commands, it is useful to see where the center of each beam of light is actually aimed. A practical method to show aiming is to create a narrow cylinder of luminous material and use xform to locate it on the axis of the beam of light. If you start the cylinder several feet from the light source, the illumination is not masked significantly and the spire remains visible (Figure 8.14).

Figure 8.13 The complete effect of the final lighting design for the obelisk. (See also Plate 18 following page 328; model courtesy of Shakespeare Lighting Design)

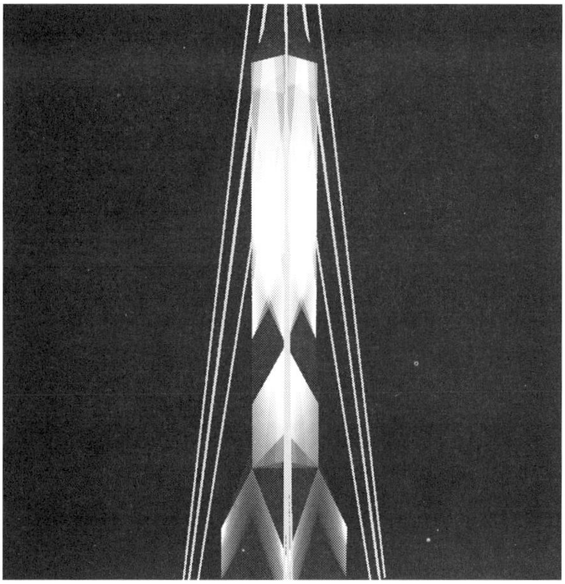

Figure 8.14 The aiming of a floodlight can be viewed by locating a cylinder along the beam's axis. (Model courtesy of Shakespeare Lighting Design)

The cylinder is defined in its own file:

```
#  glow_rod.rad
#
#  cylinder, starting 5 feet along the axis of an ies2rad-generated floodlight.
#  vary the length according to the maximum throw distance.
#  made of a cyan glowing material

void glow luminous
0
0
4   0 10 10 0

luminous  cylinder   shaft
0
0
7    0  0  -5
     0  0 -150
     .125
#end glow_rod
```

Then this file name is inserted at the end of the xform command, which also locates the luminaire:

```
# sw corner luminaires, aimed at upper spire
ies2rad -df -t default -m .7  -c  1  1  1   -o  zone1  ./lights/parcsi.ies
!xform -n sw -rx 173.5 -rz -45 -t -11   -11   934  zone1.rad  glow_rod.rad
!xform -n sw -rx 171.5 -rz -45 -t -10.3 -10.3 933  zone1.rad  glow_rod.rad
!xform -n sw -rx 170.8 -rz -45 -t -9.4  -9.4  933  zone1.rad  glow_rod.rad
!xform -n sw -rx 172.5 -rz -45 -t -11.5 -11.5 935 zone1.rad glow_rod.rad...
```

Immense projects, such as the illumination of the architecture of a sequence of bridges, can be rendered with *Radiance*, but when thousands of light sources are included, considerable computing resources are required. Figure 8.15 is a *Radiance* simulation that includes all roadway, tower, and cable lighting proposed for the illumination of the Tsing-Ma suspension bridge, part of the Lantau Fixed Crossing in Hong Kong. (See also Plate 19 following page 328.)

Figure 8.15 The illumination from thousands of luminaires is accurately depicted in this view of the Tsing-Ma suspension bridge in Hong Kong. (See also Plate 19 following page 328; lighting design courtesy of R. Shakespeare for Linbeck and Rausch, Lighting Consultants)

Pictures such as this enable the visual impact of the architectural features to be compared with signage visibility and roadway lighting. Distant views enable the nighttime impact to be aesthetically evaluated, and provide a resource for exploring potential conflicts with navigational visibility. After it is determined that the appearance of the structure is appropriate, the metrics of the illumination can be reviewed and fine-tuned so that they meet the technical requirements of the contract.

Figure 8.16 shows the illumination of an isolated section of one of the 700-foot towers. Visual studies, complete with an illumination analysis (Figure 8.17), assist in luminaire selection, location, and aiming. Each component can be scrutinized and judged on its technical and esthetic contributions years before implementation.

It seems that almost every design project presents some new challenge to a lighting designer. Similarly, when you are rendering with *Radiance*, each project is likely to require different resources and strategies to achieve the most meaningful results. The bridge and the obelisk were organized in the same way as were the theater lighting design examples. This enabled a variety of photometry to be swapped in and

Figure 8.16 Checking the illumination results after aiming 12 high-intensity spotlights at the northeastern face of the tower. (Model courtesy of Shakespeare Lighting Design)

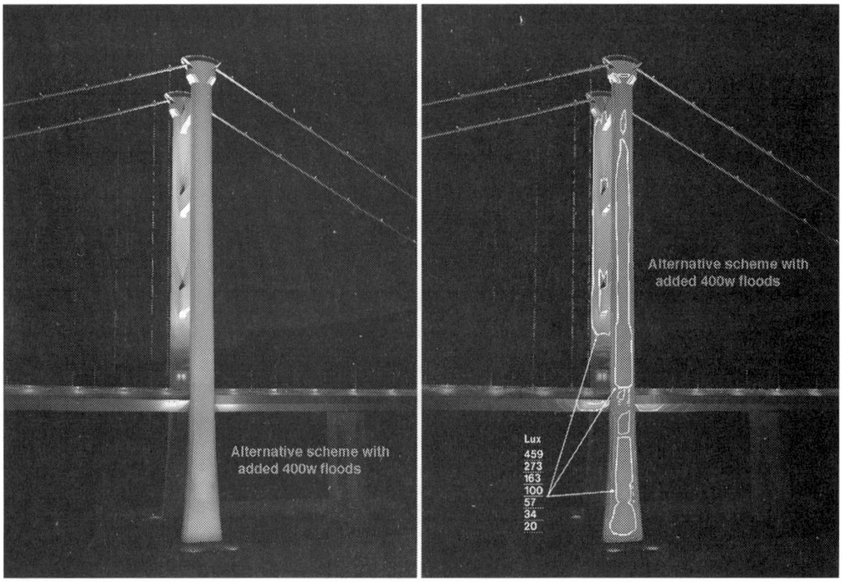

Figure 8.17 These images were submitted to the client, illustrating the effect of adding additional floodlighting to the base of a tower. An isolux analysis of the same rendering confirms the effectiveness of the solution. (Model courtesy of Shakespeare Lighting Design)

out and aimed easily. Though they are not presented here, this file strategy also facilitated studies adding color filters to the bridge's floodlights. The fixed roadway lighting and cable beacons, on the other hand, were set up with the ies2rad commands in files separated from the luminaire xform commands. This approach is fully illustrated in Chapter 3. Finally, it is up to you to determine which of the scene-building strategies presented in this book best suits the challenges of your own projects.

Whether it be for theater or for an element of the skyline, accurately depicting the visual impact of a lighting idea is a critical step in enhancing the appearance of the world around us. Light can be extraordinarily evocative, and with *Radiance* pictures as part of the process, collaboration among artists, engineers, consultants, producers, and architects is made much easier.

8.4 Special Tool Kit

The remaining portion of this chapter explains how *Radiance* can be used to model some of the more challenging components of dramatic lighting.

8.4.1 Lines of Light

"Lines of light," whether from cold cathode, neon, or optical fiber sources, have been particularly challenging to render accurately. From 1000 feet, you might clearly see the edge of a building that has been outlined using a T5-15-millimeter cold cathode tube. If a vantage point in a simulation is 1000 feet from a 15-millimeter cold cathode tube, the width of the tube is but a fraction of the width of a pixel, unless your picture is gigantic. Until the recent releases of *Radiance*, the only way to "find" these lines of light was to increase the number of samples per pixel during rendering with rpict. This added significant time to the process and produced an unsatisfactory image. The very distant lines appeared as though they were being viewed through a broken comb.

Radiance now does an admirable job of finding even the tiniest light sources in a scene, as shown in Figure 8.18. The example that follows constructs three variations of cold cathode tube and locates them 10, 120, 220, 520, and 1020 feet from the vantage point. Approximate radiance values for the cathode color called Brilliant Blue (which actually appears more like bright cyan!) have been provided. If you need to model a specific linear light source accurately, consult the manufacturer for color and lumen output values.

```
#  cc_x3.rad
#
# describe three "Brilliant Blue" cold cathode tubes:
#                                               T6-20 mm  120ma
#                                               T6-20 mm   90ma
#                                               T5-15 mm   30ma
# each is 10 foot tall and located on 5' centers

# T6-20 mm 120ma  BB Cold Cathode  -  213  lumens/ft
# rgb values calculated using lampcolor:  0   28.234950  31.207050
void glow illum1
0
0
4  0  28.234950  31.207050  0
```

Figure 8.18 The impact of "lines of light" on the Times Square building in Hong Kong was explored in an animation rendered with *Radiance*. This picture is a frame from the video. (Lighting design courtesy of R. Shakespeare for Linbeck and Rausch, Lighting Consultants)

```
illum1 cylinder  20mm-120ma
0
0
7    0   0   0
     0   0   10
       .0328

# T6-20 mm 90ma  BB Cold Cathode  - 161  lumens/ft
# rgb values calculated using lampcolor:   0   21.440915  23.697854
void glow illum2
0
0
4  0  21.440915  23.697854   0

illum2 cylinder 20mm-90ma
0
0
```

```
7    5   0   0
     5   0   10
     .0328

#  T5-15 mm 30ma BB Cold Cathode  - 121  lumens/ft
# rgb values calculated  using lampcolor :  0   21.406282   23.659575
void glow illum3
0
0
4  0 21.406282   23.659575  0

illum3 cylinder 15mm-30ma
0
0
7    10   0   0
     10   0   10
     .0246
#end  cc_x3.rad

#  many_cc.rad
#
# locate cc_x3 at 0', 100', 200' 500' 1000'. Clusters are offset
# enabling all to be viewed from   -vp 5 -20 5

!xform -n closest   -t   0  0   0    cc_x3.rad
!xform -n left-20   -t -20  0  100   cc_x3.rad
!xform -n right20   -t  20  0  200   cc_x3.rad
!xform -n left-20a  -t -20  0  500   cc_x3.rad
!xform -n right20a  -t  20  0 1000   cc_x3.rad
#end many_cc.rad
```

The resulting image demonstrates the ability of *Radiance* to find and reasonably represent each of these cold cathode tubes, even those 1020 feet from the vantage point. The picture (Figure 8.19) was rendered in less than a minute on a 90-MHz Pentium processor.

8.4.2 Adding the Effects of Mist to a Scene

Mist is a *Radiance* material that provides such effects as fog, steam, suspended dust, and water vapor. As light is traced through a participating medium (the computer visualization term for small particles in the air), it is scattered, absorbed, and

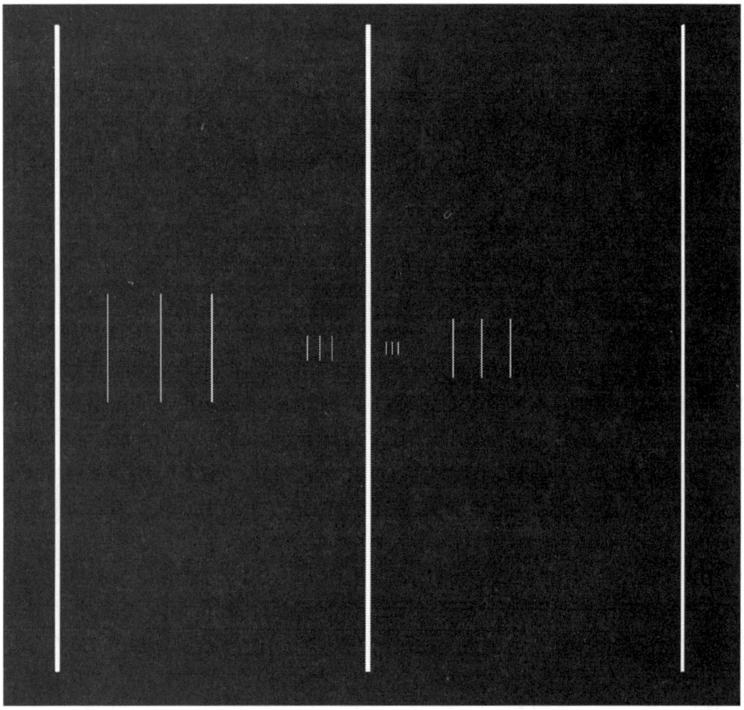

Figure 8.19 Each group of three lines is a simulation of cold cathode tubes. Distance from the observer to each group is 20, 120, 220, 520, and 1020 feet.

reflected. Most commercial software makes no attempt to include an accurate depiction of these effects because the computational burden can be enormous. Instead, such programs provide planes and triangles of fake-looking luminous white, which are called "fog."

Radiance includes a very efficient method for inserting discrete volumes of participating media. If you follow the guidelines, only a small increase in rendering time results from a startlingly powerful effect. This technique is particularly well suited, but not limited, to simulating the shaft of light from a lighthouse on a misty night or the beams of light slashing through the haze of a rock 'n' roll concert, as shown in Figure 8.20. (See also Plate 20 following page 328.) Though it could fill the whole volume of the scene, a participating medium is included most effectively when its effect is localized around the distribution of each light source. This strategy is illustrated by observing car headlights when there is a light haze in the air. With the headlights off, the scene appears to be reasonably clear. Turn on the headlights and two shafts of light illuminate the air in front of the car. To model this

Figure 8.20 *Mist* is used to simulate shafts of light passing through participating media. This *Radiance* picture is a keyframe from a simulation of a rock 'n' roll concert lighting sequence. (See also Plate 20 following page 328; model courtesy of Theater Computer Visualization Center, Indiana University)

localized effect, we would wrap the distribution of light from the car headlights in a cone of mist material. As a viewing ray intersects the mist surface surrounding the distribution of light from a headlamp, the mist calculation is turned on. Samples are taken at defined distances until a particular limit is reached or the ray leaves the medium by passing through the other side of the mist volume. The additional mist calculations are localized to the area where the effect is likely to be observed, so the rendering time for the rest of the scene remains unaffected.

The following example builds a scene depicting the effect of an ellipsoidal reflector spotlight shining through stage fog. Though the scattering, reflection, and absorption metrics of stage fog are not available, the values used in this example have been estimated by comparing the simulated effects with actual observations. A sphere has been inserted into the beam of light to illustrate the difference between the flat "fog" provided with many renderers and the accurate shadow that *Radiance* produces in the participating medium. This approach is illustrated in Figure 8.21.

Let's look at the scene description, then work through the resulting details, shown in Figure 8.22.

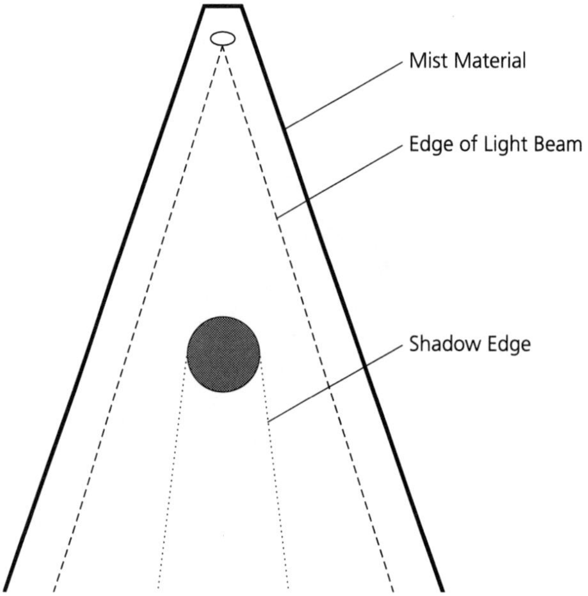

Figure 8.21 The cone of mist material encompasses the complete light beam. The top of the cone is capped with a ring of mist material, but as the length of the cone generally extends beyond the view of the scene, the bottom is not capped.

```
# misty.rad
#
# simulates the effect of a spotlight shining through stage fog.
# a ball is located in the beam, leaving a shadow effect in the mist.

# create chl.rad, a light description of the 6" x 9" ERS photometry
!ies2rad -df -t default -m 1  -c  1  1  1   -o chl 6x9ers.ies

# insert chl.rad into the scene, naming it down_light
!xform -n down_light -t 0 0 0  chl.rad

# define the mist material properties and its associated light source
void mist boundary
1    down_light.chl.d
0
7    0    0    0      .4    .4    .4     .45
```

Figure 8.22 Rendered picture of our mist description.

```
# describe a cone of light that encloses the ERS's beam of light
boundary cone edge1
0
0
8  0 0 1
   0 0 -20
   1  10

# cap the top with a ring of mist
boundary ring cap1
0
0
8  0 0 1
   0 0 1
   0 1
```

```
# define a material for the floor and ball
void plastic white
0
0
5 .9 .9 .9 0 0

# insert a sphere into the beam of light
white sphere ball
0
0
4 0 0 -11 1

# add a stage floor
!genbox white screen 20 20 .1 | xform -t -10 -10  -20
#end misty.rad
```

A detailed description of mist and its control parameters can be found in Chapter 14, Single-Scatter Participating Media (Mist), so only the information necessary to render a picture is included here. The default global participating media arguments in rview and rpict are set to 0. If we do not provide alternative mist values, the picture will render using values found in our local mist scene descriptions, and if these are incomplete, the mist effect will not be rendered. Please see Chapter 14 for definition of the mist variables **-me**, **-ma**, and **-ms**.

When we run rpict or rview, we will set the global extinction coefficient to `-me .02 .02 .02` and the scattering to `-ma .3 .3 .3`. Light scattering through stage fog does not appear to have a significant forward direction, so a value of `-mg .35` will be tried. Finally, we will sample the medium every 6 inches by setting `-ms .5`. If a complex template pattern were inserted into the beam, a closer sample distance, such as `-ms .2` would be used to capture the details of the shadow shapes, resulting in a higher-resolution picture and increased rendering times.

Note that the mist description included in *misty.rad* has several values in addition to the list of associated light sources:

```
# define the mist material properties and its associated light source
void mist boundary
1    down_light.chl.d
0
7    0    0    0      .4    .4    .4     .45
#  rext  gext  bext    ralb  galb   balb   gecc
```

These mist values can individualize participating media volumes within the same scene.

A total of 0, 3, 6, or 7 values must be listed. If no entries are present (0), all of mist's global values will be applied. The first three values are extinction coefficients that will be added to the global values set with the rview/rpict command. If values of 0 0 0 are used, the global values will be used without modification. These can be followed by scattering albedo and scattering eccentricity values that override the global settings. To demonstrate this relationship between global and local mist values, we have substituted new values for scattering albedo and eccentricity in *misty.rad*, so the global mist values defined in the following rview command will not affect our image:

```
rview -vp  0 -28 -11  -me .05 .05 .05 -ma .3 .3 .3 -mg .5 -ms .5 misty.oct
```

Troubleshooting Mist

If your scene description files seem to be in order but everything shows up in a picture except the mist effect, the culprit might be the light name you associated with each mist description.

When an object is manipulated by xform, *Radiance* appends a prefix to the object name. Additionally, *Radiance* appends a *.d* to the name of the emitting surface when it is described in the ies2rad output file (*.rad*). When *Radiance* looks for the name of a light source listed in a mist description, *Radiance*'s internal name for that light may be different from the name you first gave it. The examples that follow expose this internal naming system. In a complex lighting simulation, your files might be organized in one of the following ways, with files A and C open so that you can make changes to color, intensity, and aiming.

VARIATION 1:

File A	ies2rad commands (e.g., `ies2rad ..-o ch1 6x9ers.ies`)
Files B1... n	ies2rad command output file, mist definition, and mist surface descriptions (e.g., *mist_ch1.rad* includes `!xform -n ml1 -t 0 0 0  ch1.rad`)
File C	collector file used to aim each luminaire-mist file (e.g., `!xform -n lum1 -t -15 10 20  mist_ch1.rad`)

Each File B would have contents similar to those of *misty.rad*, omitting the ies2rad command and the *sphere*, **genbox**, and *plastic* definitions. The name of the light source in the `mist` definition is a combination of

```
[B: xform -n ml1] .  [A: ies2rad -o ch1]  .d  = ml1.ch1.d
```

VARIATION 2:

File A	ies2rad commands (e.g., `ies2rad ..-o ch1 6x9ers.ies`)
File M	mist definitions, perhaps listed with other material files
Files B1... n	individual mist surface descriptions and ies2rad output files (e.g., *mist_ch1.rad* includes `!xform -n ml1 -t 0 0 0  ch1.rad`)
File C	collector file used to aim each luminaire-mist file (e.g., `!xform -n lum1 -t -15 10 20  mist_ch1.rad`)

You might think that the only difference between Variations 1 and 2 is the separation of the mist definitions into a material file. But in Variation 2, unless you add the File C `xform -n name` to the light source in the `mist` definition, no mist effect will appear. In this case, the light source is named:

```
[C: xform -n lum1 ] . [B: xform -n ml1] . [A: ies2rad -o ch1] .d  = lum1.ml1.ch1.d
```

VARIATION 3:

File A	ies2rad commands (e.g., `ies2rad ..-o ch1 6x9ers.ies`)
File M	mist definitions, perhaps listed with other material files
File B1... n	individual mist surface descriptions (e.g., *mist1.rad*, . . .)
File C	collector file used to aim each luminaire and mist file (e.g., `!xform -n lum1 -t -15 10 20  ch1.rad  mist1.rad`)

This file structure is the simplest to maintain because each component file serves only one function. In this case, the name of the light source in the mist definition is

```
[C: xform -n lum1 ] . [A: ies2rad -o ch1] .d  = lum1.ch1.d
```

Finally, if the mist effect appears in your picture, but is not where you expect it, move your vantage point so that it is not located inside a cone of mist material!

8.4.3 The Star Filter

A postrendering star filter is included in the pfilt toolbox. If appropriate values are applied to the image, the brightest areas appear as though viewed through a diffraction grating. When added to a still picture, this "sparkle" can help to convey the twinkling effect of tiny Christmas tree lights or the flicker of a candle flame. As with many *Radiance* options, experimenting with the star filter will provide insights into how it might prove useful in your own pictures. Figure 8.23 illustrates the effect as applied to a simulation of an illuminated carillon. This is a single frame from an

Figure 8.23 A star filter has been applied to this frame of a *Radiance* animation of a carillon for Times Square, Hong Kong. (Lighting design courtesy of R. Shakespeare for Linbeck and Rausch, Lighting Consultants)

animation of *Radiance* pictures that shows the effect of the small lights "dancing" with bell music. The sparkle, added by the star filter, helps to convey the charm of the experience.

Let's look at the command that produced the star filter patterns on the carillon picture.

```
% pfilt   -2 -h 5 -n 6 -s .00001  clck.pic  clckstar.pic
```

`-h lvl` Sets intensity considered "hot" to `lvl`. Areas of the image that are above this level will begin to exhibit star diffraction patterns (see below). The default is 100 watts/steradian/m^2.

`-n N` Sets the number of points on star patterns to `N`. A value of 0 turns star patterns off. The default is 0.

`-s val` Sets the spread for star patterns to `val`. This is the value a star pattern will have at the edge of the image. The default is .0001.

The -2 option is actually the pfilt default setting, which selects two passes of the filter. This is necessary to create the star effect. The `-h 5` sets the threshold level. If we want to include the small lights in the effect, this value can be reduced until the desired effect is achieved. The six points in the star effect are set with the -n option and the extent of the star effect is controlled by the value following -s.

8.5 Large Data Sets

Radiance does have physical limits. A large project, such as the suspension bridge or a production involving dozens of actors, may produce warnings and even fatal errors when you try to create the octree for the scene. Unfortunately, there is no sure way to predict whether a data set will bring oconv screeching to a halt. Perhaps the problem is brought about by the size and spacing of objects, the kinds of primitives used, the scales involved, oconv options, or the number of surfaces. Of course, the configuration and memory resources of your computer play a major role in all this.

The Diagnostics section of the oconv manual pages presents a listing of various error messages, what they mean, and what may have caused them. You should turn to this resource first to identify the probable cause.

If the data sets for the project appear error-free and you suspect that there just may be too many surfaces, you might try to divide the scene descriptions into smaller components. If an octree of each component can be produced, there is a chance that you will be able to assemble the whole project successfully. To solve the problems with the large suspension bridge mentioned earlier in this chapter, 15 component files were produced. Each file described an isolated section of the structure or the surrounding landscape, such as the northeast tower or the southwestern land mass. A few objects were extraordinarily long and thin, so these descriptions were rewritten and split into several parts. Though this increased the number of surfaces slightly, it reduced the ratio of the smallest to the largest object, which seemed to help significantly. Finally, alternative approaches were used to model the cables, drastically reducing the number of polygons while only slightly reducing the apparent detail of the surfaces.

With the exception of the lighting descriptions, an octree was made for each component file:

```
% oconv -f  bridge.mat  e_tower.rad   >    e_twr.oct
% oconv -f  bridge.mat  w_shore.rad   >    w_shr.oct ...
```

All were assembled successfully by using the oconv -i option to include the files that were already in octree format:

```
% oconv -f fl.lgt st.lgt cl.lgt  -i e_twr.oct  -i w_shr.oct ..> bridge.oct
```

A variation of this method follows the approach used to incorporate actors in a scene, and is described in Section 8.1, Stage Lighting Design, earlier in this chapter. Octree files are inserted into the collector file as instances and accomplish the same thing as the previous oconv command line. Unless the locations of components change, the only advantage of the collector file arises when parts of the lighting or structure need to be studied. Individual descriptions can be turned off by commenting them out.

```
# bridge.all
# collector file for complete bridge project

!xform -n tower -t 0 0 0 fl.lgt
!xform -n road  -t 0 0 0 st.lgt

# The cable lighting is turned off
#!xform -n cable -t 0 0 0 cl.lgt

void instance e_tower
1 e_twr.oct
0
0

void instance w_shore
1 w_shr.oct
0
0
.
.
#end bridge.all
```

An octree of the bridge is produced with the following command:

```
% oconv  -f bridge.all  >  bridge.oct
```

8.6 Summary

The art of rendering with *Radiance* is built on experimentation, on wisdom shared by its users and its developer, and on insights you gather while building projects and exploring the ways scenes or structures might someday appear. We hope this chapter has provided a few tools and a splash of inspiration, contributing to your own journey in rendering dramatic applications of light.

CHAPTER 9

Animation

by Peter Apian-Bennewitz

Computer-generated animated films are useful for architectural simulations mainly in two ways: for *walk-throughs* and for *scene animation*. During a walk-through, the viewer is shown different perspectives of the building interior or exterior, which enhance the visualization of complex 3D architectural spaces. The viewer might be guided to move around a detail of the scene (e.g., demonstrating glare at a computer screen), to move along a certain route (e.g., to simulate a tour through a planned museum), or to "look around" from a fixed point (e.g., for a complete panoramic view). These movements are specified by a "camera path." Some examples of *scene animation* are the motion of the sun during the day, the changing light sources in stage lighting, and the varying shading elements for daylighting.

We will start with a simple sketch defining the basics of animation, then describe key parameters of the camera. The specification of the camera path is treated in detail, since it is worth knowing the power of a simulated camera that, freed of all physical constraints, is ready to follow your desired path in space and time. The same applies to scene animation, in which objects can follow complex paths. Next, hints are given on how to organize the data needed for an animation and how to use parallel rendering to finish the animation before your boss's retirement. The last section explains how to record your animation on film or video.

9.1 Basics

The basic idea with animation is to make changes from one frame to the next that are small enough to be integrated smoothly by the eye and large enough to be interesting. A real-time animation of a hummingbird beating its wings would be a blur, and a real-time animation of a flower opening its petals would be a bore. Likewise, a moving camera should be neither too fast nor too slow for human vision. Panning (rotating the camera) too fast is particularly bothersome, since continuity of the entire image is lost, instead of just the foreground, as with camera translation.

9.1.1 Real Cameras

Since the Lumière brothers showed an astounded audience the first moving images projected by their cinématograph in 1895, the basic principle of film and animation has remained the same: Presenting nearly identical still pictures to the eye at 40 to 70 frames per second (fps) creates the illusion of continuous motion, because of the finite time resolution of the eye and the image-processing parts of the brain. The minimal frequency needed depends on the contrast and brightness of the images.

Different techniques use 18 fps (old amateur 8mm film, where every frame is chopped three times during projection to generate 46 fps), 24 fps (standard cinema, in which every frame is chopped twice), 25 fps (Europe's PAL TV signal, interlaced to simulate 50 fps), 30fps (the U.S. NTSC TV signal, interlaced to simulate 60 fps), 60 fps (standard computer screens), and the 72 fps of modern computer screens (no noticeable flicker, even for bright spots).

For lighting simulations, the best brightness and contrast can be achieved with classical 70mm film (for example, *2001: A Space Odyssey*); bright TV projection techniques rank next (contrast approximately 1:100). The contrast ratios of normal phosphor screens are lower (approximately 1:30). However, the cost for classical film material and projection is high, and the electronic projections are steadily improving in resolution and contrast.

Traditionally, films are recorded by a movie camera, whose characteristics are now mimicked by a camera model in computer animation. The three rotational degrees of freedom are called *pan* (rotation around the vertical axis), *tilt* (looking up or down), and *spin* (rotation around the optical axis). The camera is mounted on a standard "head" on top of a tripod, which can be translated in the horizontal plane and moved vertically. Reproducing this mechanical setup in a computer camera model makes it easy to operate for people acquainted with real cameras. The necessary transformation to the notation used by **rpict** (position and view vector) is simple and is done, for example, in the program **rshow**.

Real cameras expose the film or the electronic chip (CCD) for a certain amount of time (e.g., 1/60 sec shutter for 16mm Arriflex cameras), during which a moving object is recorded not as sharply frozen, but as slightly blurred ("motion blur"). During projection, this blur adds to the impression of a continuous movement and is therefore worth reproducing in computer animation, even if it increases computation time. Another parameter is the focus and depth of field of most real lens system: Since people are used to depth of field, both from their eyes and from "real" movies, simulating these parameters in computer animation creates a better representation of the "real world," although it too requires more rendering time.

9.1.2 Specifying the Camera Path

For a walk-through animation, the camera movement should be smooth and to the point, showing the viewer the interesting parts of the scene. A jerky motion would probably cause queasiness and distraction. Specifying a smooth motion quickly and easily requires a little mathematical background.

The motion of a rigid object through space is specified by the 3D trajectory of its center of mass plus three variables specifying the object's orientation (pan, tilt, spin). All six variables are functions of time; the first three constitute a three-component vector. The orientation variables and further camera parameters (e.g., depth of focus or zoom) are one-dimensional, time-dependent variables. Each can be given as a mathematical function; however, specifying *one* function for the *full* path may result in a very complicated function. It's much easier to break it down into small, piecewise functions that are suitably connected. This leads to the concept of "control points" through which an interpolated curve should pass. This algorithm is combined with a graphical user interface in rshow, a program written by this author for scene preview and camera animation. In the following section, the mathematics are given for those who like to understand the background.

9.2 Interpolation Methods

Once the general path of the camera has been specified with a sequence of control points, we must choose a method for interpolating these points to get all the in-between camera positions for each frame. There are many reasonable ways to do this, and our choice will affect the speed (rate) and smoothness (acceleration) of different parts of the animation.

9.2.1 Geometric Path

Control points in 3D space, mathematically termed P_i, are given. Figure 9.1 shows an example in which the control points and curve are lying in the *xy* plane. To interconnect these points, cubic functions $f(s) = a_3s^3 + a_2s_2^2 + a_1s + a_0$ are used for each coordinate, in which the parameter *s* varies from 0 to 1 between two control points. The coefficients a_i for each function f_i between points P_i and P_{i+1} are calculated by the algorithm to achieve a smooth transition to the neighboring functions. For linear functions, this smooth transition would only mean that two neighboring functions f_i and f_{i+1} meet at P_i (mathematically termed $C^{(0)}$ continuity). Cubic functions can do better, and the tangents of f_i and f_{i+1} are the

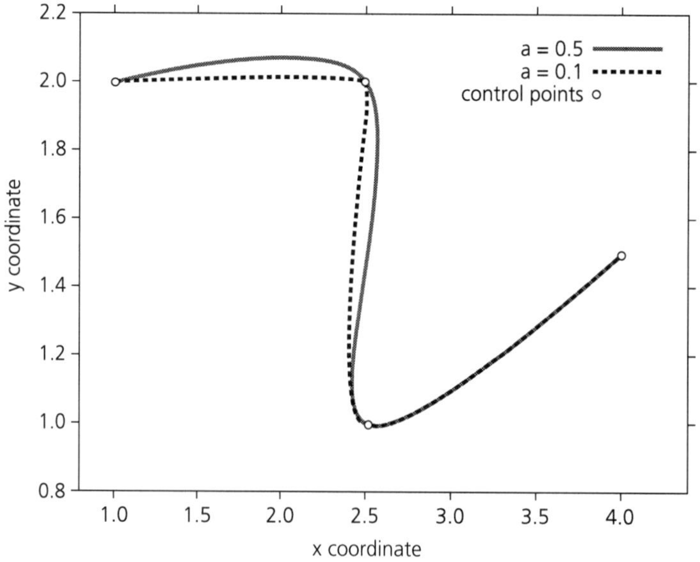

Figure 9.1 2D plot of splines with varying coefficient *a* and control points.

same at P_i ($C^{(1)}$ continuity). These curves are called splines. User-supplied parameters may relax the mathematical continuity to allow kinks even in paths made of cubic splines.

There are a number of spline-based interpolation methods, such as Catmull-Rom [CR74], Cardinal, hermite, and the newer X-splines. [MT87] gives an overview. For newer spline interpolations, see [BS95]. We chose the hermite splines proposed by Kochanek and Bartels (1984). For the parameter s, a point $V(s)$ between P_i and P_{i+1} is given with vectors T and P and matrix **H** as

$$V(s) = T\mathbf{H}P^T$$

$$T = [s^3 s^2 s]$$

$$P = [P_i P_{i+1} D_i D_{i+1}]$$

$$D_i = a(P_{i \div 1} - P_{i-1})$$

$$\mathbf{H} = \begin{bmatrix} 2 & -2 & 1 & 1 \\ -3 & 3 & -2 & -1 \\ 0 & 0 & 1 & 0 \\ 1 & 0 & 0 & 0 \end{bmatrix}$$

Note that s is in general *not* equal to the curve length along the spline. The interpolation is termed *local* because the function f_i depends only on P_i and four neighboring points: P_{i-2}, P_{i-1}, P_{i+1}, P_{i+2}. Hence, moving control points interactively requires only the recalculation of the splines next to the point moved. For the parameter a, Figure 9.2 shows that changing a for P_2 affects only the splines around P_2, whereas the spline between P_3 and P_4 remains the same.

These splines would allow additional control using the further parameters *bias* and *continuity,* which are used for a more refined calculation of the tangent vector D_i. These parameters are currently not used in rshow, mostly because sharp bends are not needed in a camera path.

The user-supplied parameter a specifies the "stiffness" of the curve at P_i, as is demonstrated in Figure 9.2. The two splines differ by the a value at P_2; a smaller value generates a tighter bend at P_2. Note that setting $a = 0.5$ gives the Catmull-Rom spline formulation.

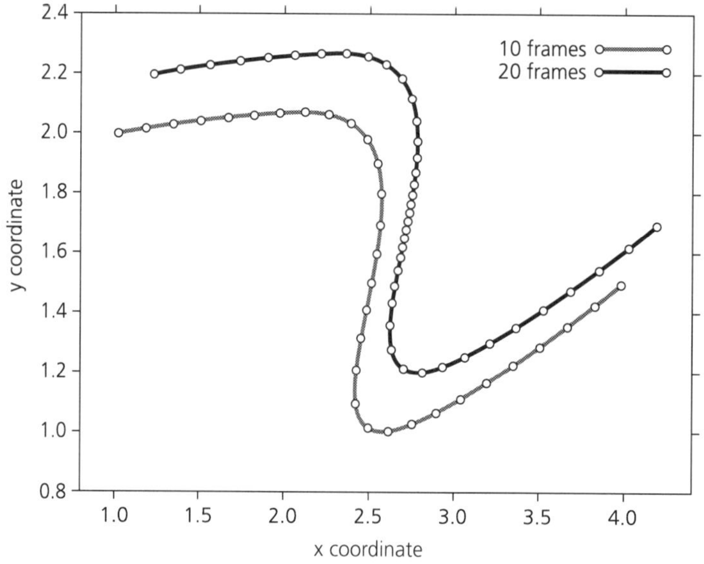

Figure 9.2 2D plot of splines with different velocities.

9.2.2 Camera Velocity and Time-Dependence

To be useful in describing the camera path, the geometric, spatial curve must be further processed: the camera should move along the path with user-specified, usually smoothly changing speed. In rshow, the user specifies camera speed in terms of the time between two control points in units of frames. The position along the spatial spline is then itself a hermite spline of the frame number n (termed temporal spline). The spatial position of the camera for a given frame n is calculated by first getting the length along the spline for n, looking up the corresponding spline function f_i between the two control points, calculating the spline parameter s for the position, and feeding s to the spatial spline functions. This results in a user-selectable, smooth movement along the spatial spline.

To indicate speed, the trajectory is plotted with a tick mark for each frame. Higher densities of marks along the trajectory indicate slower movement. This plot is sometimes called a *P-curve.*

The speed interpolation is shown in Figure 9.2: each tick mark along the curve indicates a frame. In the first example, there are 10 frames between all control points; in the second example, which is shifted in the plot to differentiate the two examples, the number of frames between P_2 and P_3 is set to 20. This results in a lower camera speed, as indicated by the denser ticks. All other camera parameters (e.g., pan angle) are interpolated using one-dimensional spline functions.

Hermite splines have a tendency to "over-swing," as shown in Figure 9.1 at P_2, a tribute to the $C^{(1)}$ continuity. For one-dimensional variables, such as pan, this is not desired (e.g., first swinging the camera a bit to the left before taking a long swing to the right). To avoid this, the *a* parameter should be chosen small, or additional control points should be inserted. For the temporal splines, this "over-swing" might occur when a high frame number is used between two spatial close control points: if your camera moves backward along the curve for some frames, lower the frame number between the control points or lower the temporal *a* parameter.

9.3 Getting the Rendering Organized

When generating a long, animated sequence, it is a good idea to make some rough guesses as to the disk space and CPU time requirements and to check that the camera and scene motion you have are what you want. One program that can help with this process is **ranimate**, which we will describe in this section along with some important checks and techniques.

9.3.1 Disk Space

The animation procedure poses one crucial question: Do you have enough disk space to hold all data during animation, including input files, temporary files, and final output picture files?

If you do, you may opt for a parallel approach: first generate all the input files needed, check for errors, start rendering (probably in parallel on multiple machines), check for completeness, convert to a format suitable for output (also parallel on multiple machines), and then record sequentially to videotape. Luckily, parameters needed for subsequent operations need not to be set on earlier phases: for example, during rendering with rpict, you don't have to worry about the best exposure setting for the complete animation. This is set in the final stage when converting the completely rendered *Radiance* picture files to an appropriate output format (e.g., PPM). Also, you can use rshow to check the octrees before starting the ray tracing. Depending on the graphics workstation and scene complexity, rshow runs faster than rpict in most cases.

If your animation does not fit on disk as a whole, the above steps are applied to a group of frames at a time. This requires that all parameters be set from the beginning and that a special program keep track of what has been done so far, in case a machine or disk crashes. The *Radiance* program ranimate is intended to organize the different steps; an example will be given later. Ranimate can also automatically transfer finished picture files from disk to tape, thereby saving the work and freeing disk space.

To estimate the required disk space, we take a look at file sizes. Picture sizes depend on the final resolution, which varies from TV (PAL 768-by-576 pixel, NTSC 646-by-486 pixel) to 70mm film (2400-by-1100 pixel, for a film with 50 lines/mm average resolution and 48.6mm-by-22mm film area). Because your images will probably contain a high degree of detail, the compression used by rpict, **pfilt**, and **ximage** to store *Radiance* images in a file will not reduce the file size very much. For example, expect about 1 MB per frame for TV resolution. For rendering in sequences, the output frames may be stored in a more compact format before final complete transfer to tape. For example, the JPEG image format can be used:

```
ra_ppm -e -2 abc.pic | cjpeg > abc.jpg
```

JPEG compression is high, but is subject to loss because it weeds out data that the typical eye cannot resolve anyway.

Input files (e.g., octrees for *instance* primitive, pictures for *colorpict* primitive, function files, **mkillum** data files) can be anything from a few kilobytes to dozens of megabytes. Changes during a scene animation may affect a fraction (e.g., a shade element is tilted) or the whole scene (e.g., simulated erosion of ancient walls). You have to test and find out how many megabytes will change before deciding to generate all scene data at once or to use ranimate to generate scene data on the fly for each frame when needed.

9.3.2 CPU Time Needed

At 25 fps, a rather short 10-second animation requires 250 frames. Supposing each frame takes two hours on your workstation (of course, this depends on CPU power and on the scene), the job will take 10 days. To speed this up, *Radiance* offers two methods: parallelization, and reusing information from one frame to the next. On a network of workstations, parallelization will be framewise: each machine renders one complete frame at a time using rpict, as described later in Section 9.3.5, Ranimate Tricks.

Images of an animation will look nearly the same from frame to frame; this suggests reusing information from one frame to the next. Thus, *Radiance* offers two ways to speed up rendering: sharing ambient files, as described in Chapter 12, and interpolating between two frames using the program **pinterp**. For pinterp, rpict is used to render every *n*th frame, with *n* varying between 3 and 5 for typical scenes. The in-between frames are approximated by interpolation. To achieve a better result than just blending the images, pinterp needs the depth information for each rendered frame. To record this, the **-z** option is used for rpict. Beware that the *z* files are uncompressed and may become rather large. Pinterp does the astounding job of merging the two frames and optionally rerenders missing pixels (e.g., hidden parts of the scene that are not included in either picture). Combined with **pmblur**, pinterp can also produce motion-blurred frames.

If your site offers a queue system for the workstations in your network (e.g., PSUB, NQS, or DQS), you should take advantage of it: your jobs will be more evenly distributed while maintaining balance with other people's needs for CPU time. Ranimate would be overloaded with the functions offered by NQS or PSUB, so you can either merge the queue commands into ranimate or disregard ranimate altogether.

Normally, all workstations render to one file server, causing potential bottlenecks in network bandwidth and I/O performance at the server. Since rpict writes a picture line by line, and rendering takes at least dozens of seconds per line, this is hardly a problem unless the number of workstations is extremely high. Bottlenecks may occur at start-up time, when multiple rpicts read the input files from a central server, but these short delays can be neglected.

We will now look at things to do before starting the animation and then explain how to use ranimate for parallelization.

9.3.3 "Preflight Checks"

Input data should be checked before you start rendering, especially because the animation is mostly started on an "fire-and-forget" basis, so mistakes will show up too late. Checks should include the following:

- Is your scene geometry consistent for all viewpoints, for example closed geometry and mapping of outside pictures? If you are using geometry input from CAD, are the *Radiance* files up to the latest version?
- Are material specifications finalized?
- When generating octrees with ranimate, does your generating script or program use temporary file names? If so, have you checked that a parallel run of the script does not clobber the same file?

- Does your camera path keep clear of obstacles (easily checked with rshow)?
- If you are using ranimate and interpolation by pinterp, do you see reflected images in highly specular, flat surfaces? If you do, the interpolation may give erroneous results and interpolation may not be advisable. The same applies to refracted images, such as those seen through a thick glass object (modeled by the *dielectric* material).
- You may want to prerender every tenth frame or so to double-check.
- All required input files should be copied into one dedicated directory to ensure data integrity while rendering is proceeding. Renderings take a long time, so you do not want to risk changing input data accidentally (e.g., fine-tuning a color) and thereby sabotaging the animation. One easy way to copy data is UNIX's cpio command (see the `cpio` manual pages—on some systems the parameters are `cpio -pdmvh`):

```
%echo "*.oct *.pic *.cal *.vf" \
| cpio -pdmvL /usr/local/renderdir/myrendering
```

9.3.4 Examples Using Ranimate

Suppose you have a workstation called tos00 and two other machines called sim02 and sim04 on the same network, and you want to use all three to render one animation. We first have to discuss some technical basics about your access to the remote workstations.

For simplicity, we assume that your user ID is the same on all three and that you can do an **rlogin** from tos00 to sim02 and sim04 without being prompted for a password. If not, contact your system administrator. If you can, you can also use the "remote shell" that is used internally in ranimate to distribute jobs to sim02 and sim04. We also assume that the *Radiance* programs rpict and pfilt are in a standard place on your workstation (on most systems it should be the */usr/contrib/bin,* or */usr/local/bin* directory). If this is not the case, either your system administrator should link them there, or you will have to write a little shell script to simulate an extended "remote shell." The latter course offers additional flexibility for special situations, but we will defer this discussion until the end of the next section.

Having made sure you are allowed to start rpict and pfilt remotely on sim02 and sim04, and locally on tos00, we now dig into the settings of the ranimate configuration file. Only a few are needed, while others provide extensions. To get you started easily and smoothly with a walk-through animation, we create a file called *ranfile* with the following lines:

```
START=1
END=30
VIEWFILE= /nfs/tos02/users/apian/rodik/ranimate_beacon.vf
RIF=      /nfs/tos02/users/apian/rodik/animate.rif
BASENAME= /nfs/tos00/usr/render/apian/ranimate/film.%03d
DIRECTORY=/nfs/tos00/usr/render/tmp
host=sim04
host=sim02
host=tos00
```

On the input side, your input file for **rad** is given by `RIF`, and the views are in the file specified by `VIEWFILE`. You want to render 30 frames (`START` to `END`), and in this case the view file should contain 30 lines of view specifications, as written by rshow or rview. Now we look at the output side of your animation. The rendered frames will be written to the `BASENAME` directory, and the frames will be named *film.001.pic, film.002.pic*, and so on, as specified by a directory for temporary files and a status file used by ranimate internally.

Starting ranimate is straightforward:

```
% ranimate ranfile &
```

The program will finish when all frames are done, and will write out lines telling you what it does on which machine. This verbosity may be switched off by using the **-s** option. If you want to know what ranimate would do but without actually starting any render jobs, you specify **-n** as a command-line option.

In this example, we assume you have network file access, via the Network File System (NFS), from the remote machine to the file server (tos00), so that all output files are gathered in one directory (*/nfs/tos00/usr/render/apian/ranimate* in this case). This is a necessary prerequisite for parallel rendering, because rpict bases its choice of which frames to render on which frames have already been created.

The default final image size is 640 pixels wide and has double `OVERSAMPLE`, meaning rpict calculates a width of 1280 pixels and pfilt samples this down to reduce noise in the image. As usual, the image height depends on the view aspect. You can set other image sizes and oversample rates like this:

```
RESOLUTION= 800 600
OVERSAMPLE=3
```

You can set the exposure for each frame with

```
EXPOSURE=-2
```

The `MBLUR` variable sets frame averaging for motion blurring:

```
MBLUR=5 0.5
```

This command calls `mblur`, which assumes that the shutter is open half the time between two frames (1/50 second for 25 fps) and five samples are used to simulate motion blur.

If you need to, you can get options for pfilt, pinterp, and rpict directly. For example, you may set rpict options like this:

```
% render= -av 2 2 2 -ab 1 -ad 5000 -as 200
```

For scene animation, the octrees are time-dependent and are generated by a program (or shell script) specified by `ANIMATE`:

```
ANIMATE= /nfs/tos02/users/koll/apian/r/models/rodik/gen_octree
```

The final argument in this program is the frame number; it is left to the external program to generate an octree depending on this frame number.

We'll give an example of scene animation using a UNIX shell script. For our uses, these are not too difficult to write, and they are portable across UNIX machines from different vendors. This one is written for the Bourne shell, but should be fairly easy to port to other shell types. The only two things you have to know about shells for these two examples are that a variable is assigned by = and used with a $, and that the `'abc'` notation means that the program `abc` is called and its output returned.

The *Radiance* input text file, or (to be more exact) some floating-point numbers in it, depend on the variable *f*, the frame number. The task is first to calculate other floating-point variables, such as time of day, from the frame number *f*, by using the *Radiance* program `ev`. Alternatives to `ev` include the standard UNIX program `bc`, which also features programming constructs like `for` loops. The second step is to use the floating-point number thus calculated in scene generation.

Now we'd like to simulate the sunlight in a museum during a day. For varying the sun position, the shell script is straightforward, since the sun is generated by a separate program (**gensky**) anyway. We would like an animation running from 8:00 AM until 6:00 PM in 30 frames. The file *static.rad* contains all static parts of our scene and is initially converted by `oconv -f` to *static.oct*. Recalling that ranimate calls this script with the first parameter equal to the frame number and expects an octree at `stdout`, we write

```
frame=$1
tmp=/tmp/sun.rad.$$
time_of_day=`ev "8 + 10 * $frame / 30.0"`
gensky 4 5 $time_of_day > $tmp
oconv -i static.oct -f $tmp
rm $tmp
```

Note that the name of the temporary file avoids clobbering of the same file by shell scripts running simultaneously: The variable `$$` contains the process ID, a number that is unique for each shell script running on one machine. Using the -i option of oconv avoids rebuilding the full octree for every frame, which saves time, since the static part may have complex geometry. We might add that this example is provided on the CD-ROM, but is not necessarily an ideal case of daylighting. It merely uses the direct sunlight in the room to show time during the day.

As another example, we simulate the rotating beacon of a lighthouse in the marine department of the museum. Let's see what the shell script looks like. We want to rotate the searchlight a full 360 degrees in 48 frames. First we write the rotating parts (spotlight definition and the lamp housing) to *beacon1.rad*. The final position of the lamp in the scene should be at coordinates 0 50 50.

```
frame=$1
tmp=/tmp/sun.rad.$$
rot_angle=`ev "360.0 * $frame/ 48.0"`
xform -rz $rot_angle -t 50 50 0 beacon1.rad > $tmp
oconv -i static.oct -f $tmp
rm $tmp
```

But we don't have to separate every moving part into its own file. We might as well change the input file directly by smuggling the number into the *Radiance* text file. For this, the UNIX program `m4` can be used, since it is intended to process text files and substitute variables, which is exactly what we want. The processing of text files offers more possibilities than the xform calls, but requires the extra program.

Now, for the same example but using the m4 program, we can use just *one* scene file, in which we substitute floating-point numbers to be animated by variable names. The beacon spotlight would then become

```
myspotlight_mat spotlight spotty1
0
0
7 1000 1000 1000 20 DIR_X DIR_Y 0
```

and we process this file using m4 in the shell script:

```
frame=$1
tmp=/tmp/sun.rad.$$
rot_angle=`ev "360.0 * $frame/ 48.0"`
dirx=`ev "sin( asin(1) * $rot_angle / 90.0 )"`
diry=`ev "cos( asin(1) * $rot_angle / 90.0 ) "`
m4 -DDIR_X=$dirx -DDIR_Y=$diry scene.rad > $tmp
oconv -f $tmp
rm $tmp
```

All input is passed unchanged, except for the substitution of DIR_X and DIR_Y by the floating-point numbers calculated in the shell script. The advantage is that all geometry remains in one file. The more moving objects your scene animation has, the more you want to separate geometry (in *scene.rad*) and time-dependent animation variables (in the shell script). To this we may add that the ugly sine/cosine calculations in this example could be moved into the m4 file for reasons of esthetics and principle.

If we name the above shell script gen_octree, the *ranfile* for ranimate is as follows:

```
DIRECTORY=    /nfs/tos00/usr/local/render/apian/ranimate
BASENAME=     /nfs/tos00/usr/local/render/apian/ranimate/anim.%d
ANIMATE=      gen_octree
VIEWFILE=     rshow.vf
START=        1
END=          48
EXPOSURE=     +1
host=         tos00
host=         sim02
host=         sim04
render=       -ab 1 -ad 1000 -as 200
```

9.3.5 Ranimate Tricks

Under rare circumstances, ranimate becomes confused about what it has done, or the user confuses ranimate by accidentally removing a picture file. To fix this, terminate the running ranimate, find out what picture files have what status, and hand-tweak the settings in ranimate's `STATUS` file to rerender or refilter the files. If ranimate caused incorrect rendering at frame 120 and left frames 110 to 119 rendered (`UNF` extension) but not filtered (`PIC` extension), you would set

```
Next render: 120
Next filter: 110
Next transfer: 110
```

When your animation is rendered and filtered up to the last frame, but you realize a frame is mysteriously missing in the middle, you set the `START` and `END` variables in the ranimate control file to this number and restart ranimate. Also see the next section about checking for consistency using `ra_bad`.

Sometimes you may want to replace the system remote-shell command (`rsh`) with your own shell script, for example to set up the `PATH` or `RAYPATH` variables before executing rpict. This script can be named `ranimate_rsh` and the `RSH` variable in the ranimate input file is set to `RSH=ranimate_rsh`:

```
#!/bin/ksh
HOST=$1
OPT=$2
shift; shift;
ADD_ONS="RAYPATH=/usr/local/radiance/models:/usr/local/radiance/lib:. ;
export RAYPATH"
ADD_ONS="$ADD_ONS;PATH=$PATH:/usr/local/radiance/bin"
#on HPUX and others substitue 'rsh' by 'remsh'
rsh $HOST $OPT "$ADD_ONS ; $* "
```

Note that the `shift` commands are used to access an arbitrary number of command-line options following the first two options given to this script. We assumed your host lines in the ranimate config file look like `host = sim02` without giving an extra user name. The reason for this is that ranimate calls the script with a varying number of arguments, depending on the `host` variable. Writing a smart script to detect this is left as an exercise for you.

If you're interested in learning more about the inner workings of ranimate, some of the details are described in Chapter 15.

9.3.6 Example Using an External Queue System

As an example of using a third-party queue system to distribute animation rendering across multiple workstations connected to a network, we use the PSUB software. We first start with a walk-through animation. Assuming that the file *cams.vf* contains view points (one per line), the main shell script looks like this:

```
VIEWS="cams.vf"
OPTS="-ab 1 -ad 1000 -t 600"
DIR=/nfs/tos00/usr/local/render/film
RAYPATH="$RAYPATH:`pwd`"
export RADIANCEOPTS RAYPATH

i=1; while [ $i -le `wc -l $VIEWS | awk 'print $1 ' ` ]
do
INFILE=input.oct
RADVIEW=`awk 'if ( NR == '$i' )  print $0 '  $VIEWS | sed 's/^rpict//' `
RADIANCEOPTS="$RADVIEW $OPTS -e $DIR/$i.e -o $DIR/$i.pic $INFILE"
        psub -l rpict -c conf -e /tmp/tb.$i.err rpict $RADIANCEOPTS

        done
```

We use the `awk` program to extract views from the view file, since this works for arbitrarily large view files. For additional scene animation, the `INFILE` variable would depend on `i` and point to the corresponding octree.

The `psub` command queues an rpict job for execution on the next available remote machine. If no machine is available, for example because they are already loaded with background jobs, or they are temporarily disabled for service, the jobs remain queued.

The rpict command is called by PSUB with the command `rpict $RADIANCEOPTS`, with the same environment as the shell script, which allows the `RAYPATH` environment variable to be passed to the executing rpict program. Note that the input and output files in this example are distributed by NFS, assuming that the file server exports its file system to the rendering workstations. With machines that are not accessible via NFS, all necessary input files have to be copied using PSUB itself, rcp, ftp, or whatever transfer protocol is available.

Only rarely will all jobs finish without at least one failing. Since no status file is used by this method during rendering, and *Radiance* currently does not append end-of-file markers at an image, the only possible check is to read every written frame on the file server and test for completeness. Note that this is 100% "bulletproof": no matter what strange illness of the network interfered with transfer between the rpict process and the file server, or what mistakes the user made during rendering, it *guarantees* that every pixel in every frame is valid. To do this as fast as possible, ra_bad was written. Reading file names from stdin, it returns filenames of incomplete or nonexistent pictures on stdout. This filter can easily be added to the above shell script, replacing the psub call with

```
if [ -n "`echo $DIR/$i.pic | rsh tos00 ra_bad`" ] then
      psub -l rpict -c conf -e /tmp/tb.$i.err rpict $RADIANCEOPTS
fi
```

Ra_bad runs faster on the file server, since even fast networks such as FDDI or ATM are slower than access to local disks. The above script allows for the possibility that the queuing for PSUB is not necessarily done on the file server.

After rendering, the frames are converted to output size by a standard shell script like this:

```
for in *.pic
do
      pfilt -1 -p 1 -m 0.3 -x 768 -y 576 $i > $i.tv
done
```

Depending on the ratio between the floating-point CPU power of the file server and the network bandwidth, this might be distributed by PSUB as well. As a final step, all picture files are transferred to video laserdisc (see below), using a program that reads *Radiance* picture files directly to save time that would otherwise be needed for file format conversion.

As a final example, we take a look at a program generating a sequence of *Radiance* input files. Using a very simple finite-element program to simulate the erosion of ancient walls, this example shows that output files are written for each time step. All files are than converted to octrees and rendered in parallel.

On the CD-ROM, two animations are included as MPEG files. The first one shows a walk through the library at Fraunhofer Institute for Solar Energy Systems in Freiburg, Germany, where the camera path was designed using rshow. The second one is an animation of scene, time of day, and camera, showing the erosion of the walls in an ancient city.

9.4 Output

Traditional animations are recorded on film. Computer animations are often written directly to video or even to a compressed file format for real-time playback on a personal computer. Since video is the most easily distributed format, we will pay particular attention to it in this section.

9.4.1 Available Media

The viewer wants to see your animation at the fps rate for which the animation was designed. Currently, there are three ways: classical film, standard TV, and replays on computer screens. Classical film provides high quality, but the costs of rendering this quality and recording on film (using fast film recorders) are high. Standard TV videotape will be the medium of choice for nearly all projects, since the equipment is an order of magnitude cheaper and the video can be played nearly everywhere and for a wide audience. Therefore, the next section is devoted to TV output. For replays on computer screens, the PC hardware coming to the market has built-in decoding hardware to play screen-sized animation in "real-time" (i.e., 24 fps). For you, as the animator, this has tremendous advantages. You don't need any special equipment at all to record your animation, since you can compress the frames to standard animation format (e.g., MPEG) using software. Most likely, there will be a world standard, so you don't need copies of your videotape in PAL, NTSC, or SECAM, and the animation can be merged with sound into presentations, info kiosks, or Web pages.

9.4.2 Recording to Videotape

Animations for architects and clients are mostly distributed on VHS tape, since this system is fairly common. The higher-quality MII or Betacam systems are used for broadcasting and to blend the animation into commercial films, which are further edited. For a high-quality signal, it is advisable to use the latter component recording techniques, which record each of the three TV color signals separately rather than merging them into one analog data stream (as in classical VHS).

For both systems, the two recording methods are the same: either you record onto tape at 25 fps or you record each frame individually. The latter stresses the tape and the recording mechanism of the recorder, because the fast-rotating recording head is moved back and forth on nearly the same tape position for every frame. Since only a few workstations provide uncompressed, broadcast-quality playback of your rendered frames at full speed (25 fps), special equipment is used on which the single frames for the film are recorded, buffered, and then played to the tape recorder at full speed in one go. Either an array of fast hard disks or a video laserdisc, allowing single-frame recording, is used as intermediate storage.

A few tips to avoid frustration: Each TV set clips about 30 pixels along the border of the full image (*overscan*), so be sure not to use your full TV resolution for titles and other text. Color is another limit. Neither PAL nor NTSC nor SECAM encoding was designed to cope with bright, fully saturated colors, simply because normal cameras hardly ever deliver such signals. A full-blown red or blue (i.e., RGB values of 255 0 0), easy to achieve with computer graphics, will not show sharp and crisp edges on TV ("chroma crawl"). Component recording devices cope better; VHS and SVHS are worse. Also, avoid "one-liners": two neighboring horizontal lines with different intensities (e.g., in line graphics or text) will flicker because of the interleaving of lines used for TV.

The programs rshow and `ra_bad` are not part of the standard *Radiance* distribution, but are available from *ftp.ise.fhg.de* and are included on the CD-ROM.

Author's Biography

Peter Apian-Bennewitz is a researcher at the Fraunhofer Institute for Solar Energy Systems ISE, Freiburg, Germany. He received his M.Sc. in 1989 from the University of Freiburg for designing and building a large-scale goniophotometer, and his Ph.D. in 1995 from the University of Freiburg for mathematical modeling of light-scattering material.

As optical scattering data of arbitrary samples became routinely available with the goniophotometer, Apian-Bennewitz used the data for input into *Radiance* by specially designed function files. This allowed much more detailed and validated studies on daylighting, using different materials for windows, roofs, light shelves, or baffles.

During the physical modeling, Apian-Bennewitz advised ISE on hardware to set up the daylight simulation group, including graphic workstations, video production, hard copy, and high-contrast projection systems. His preview program rshow plays a key role in designing and running animations with *Radiance*.

He is also actively involved in a variety of international consulting and simulation projects on daylighting, ranging from office spaces to large stadium roofs. Apart from rendered images, he is fond of the cinema of Welles, Truffaut, and Renoir and is affectionate to members of the *Panthera* and *Felis* species.

PART III

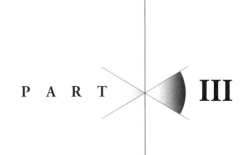

CALCULATION METHODS

CHAPTER 10

Deterministic and Stochastic Ray Tracing

Now that we've seen how to create scenes for *Radiance* and a bit of what it can do, let's take a look inside the software to understand how it works. This will help us to interpret the output as well as to generate better results by tuning the various parameters that control the calculation.

Radiance simulates light propagation in model environments using a *ray-tracing* approximation. This approximation assumes that light follows geometric (i.e., linear) ray paths between surfaces. Extensions are made to the original rendering method to include most significant light contributions, such as diffuse interreflection and secondary sources. These extensions will be explained in detail in the chapters that follow. In this chapter, we just give an overview of the basic rendering technique and explain its formulation. We will refer to this formulation repeatedly in the chapters that follow, so it is important to understand this material and know the basic difference between deterministic and stochastic ray-tracing methods.

10.1 Ray Tracing

The ray-tracing approach to rendering follows "view rays" from the virtual focus of an eye or camera through pixels in an imaginary image plane into the environment. These geometric rays intersect mathematically with the model geometry, as shown in Figure 10.1. Additional rays are "spawned" toward light sources and other surfaces to determine direct and indirect contributions to illumination at that intersection in a *recursive* process.[24]

Although ray tracing is appealing in its basic resemblance to the behavior of light, there are a few important differences. First and most obvious, real light travels in the opposite direction! Why do we follow it backward, then? The reason is economics. Following light from the sources onto the image plane, we would waste enormous resources on rays that never reach the view point. To take a typical example, a 512-by-512 rendering of a bare light bulb in a lightly colored room would take about a month on the world's fastest supercomputer using forward ray tracing.[25] The same rendering takes about three seconds using *Radiance*.

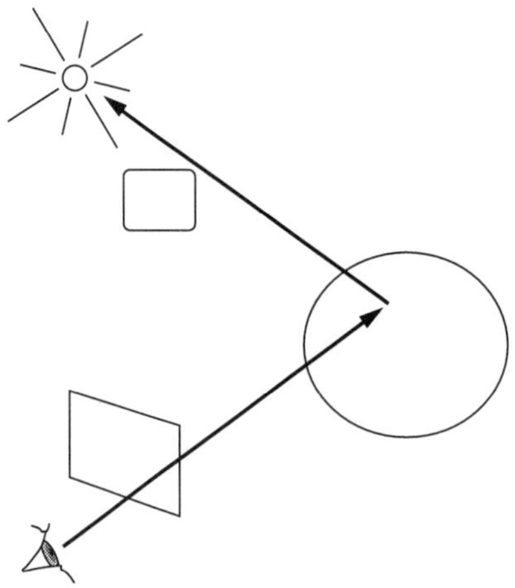

Figure 10.1 The path of a ray traced backward from the eye point into a scene.

---

24. A recursive method reformulates a problem in terms of a simpler version of the original problem. In this case, we are solving for the final value of a ray by tracing other rays and finding their values.

25. For this reason, most implementations of forward ray tracing collect rays on the surfaces rather than on the image plane, and generate an image as a separate step. Unfortunately, this requires either enormous data structures to maintain the directionality of incident rays or a diffuse assumption on the final reflection, which largely defeats the purpose of a Monte Carlo rendering technique.

The second thing you may notice is that we've put the image plane in front of the view point, whereas it really belongs behind. Actually, it makes little difference, since the image plane is imaginary—it only determines where to send a ray for a given pixel. A camera places the real image plane behind the virtual focus (which, in turn, is just behind the lens) and the image forms upside-down and backwards. The result is otherwise similar.[26]

The third caveat we will mention is that light does not always travel along geometric rays. In fact, light may be diffracted around corners when object details are very small (on the order of the wavelength of the light). However, since most objects we are interested in rendering are much larger than a micron, we can safely ignore diffraction in most of our simulations.

10.2 Deterministic versus Stochastic

The original ray-tracing rendering technique, as introduced by Whitted in 1980 [Whi80], used a strictly *deterministic* algorithm, which is to say that the same result would be achieved for a given rendering when it was repeated. By contrast, a *stochastic* algorithm employs random processes, which when repeated will generally give slightly different results. Although this is disconcerting, it is in fact the way light works in nature: photons are bouncing about randomly, and it is only their enormous number that gives light the appearance of stability at any given point.

We can illustrate the difference between deterministic and stochastic ray tracing with a simple example. Let us consider the ray sent from the intersected object to the light source in Figure 10.1. In a deterministic algorithm, the ray would be sent toward the exact center of the source every time. The resulting illumination would always come out the same. A stochastic algorithm, on the other hand, would choose a random direction in which to send the ray.[27] In some cases, the ray would reach the light source, but in other cases it might first intersect the intervening object or go off in a different direction entirely. This nondeterministic behavior shows up in the rendered image as noise, and a different rendering would give a different result. The average of all results thus obtained will be closest to the true answer.

---

26. Some ray tracers take into account lens effects such as depth of field by distributing rays over an imaginary lens. Although this technique is not employed by default in *Radiance*, it can be simulated using the **pinterp** program with **pdfblur**.

27. In fact, most computers are incapable of generating truly random numbers. More frequently, a "pseudorandom" number generation algorithm is employed. In *Radiance*, the generation of random values is modified even farther to reduce variance by employing a stratified sampling sequence due to Schlick [Sch91]. This can sometimes be seen in the "brushed" appearance of rough specular reflections.

If stochastic techniques cause noise, why would anyone use them? The simple answer is that they are more accurate on the average than purely deterministic approaches. Using the method described above, we can change an image with an artificially sharp shadow into one where a more accurate (though somewhat noisy) penumbra is evident. Taking this comparison to the extreme, Plate 21 shows a deterministically ray-traced image with three objects illuminated by two rectangular fluorescent fixtures in an otherwise empty room. The image looks nice and smooth, but the shadows are unnaturally sharp and there is no interreflection between surfaces. Plate 22 shows the same scene as rendered by a pure Monte Carlo (stochastic) algorithm. The image took many times longer to compute and the result is quite noisy, but many real effects missing from Plate 21 have been captured here. The shadow penumbras are visible, as are the effects of interreflection between the objects and room surfaces.

Clearly, neither algorithm is entirely satisfactory. The deterministic approach will never render all of the interactions and details we wish to see, and the stochastic approach takes forever to reach a reasonably noise-free solution. What we want is a technique that captures the best of both worlds, rendering all important phenomena, yet finishing in a reasonable time with a manageable amount of noise. This is the tightrope we walk in *Radiance*, a line first drawn by Cook in 1984 [CPC84][Coo86].

10.3 The Radiance Equation

In the simple example shown in Figure 10.1, we looked at the way we can follow light backward from the measurement point to an object and then to a light source. We have not illustrated the more general problem of accounting for all light contributions, from other surfaces as well as from sources. We do this by following each ray until it intersects a surface, where it may spawn more rays until we determine that enough rays have been computed, and the answer bubbles up from these many contributions.

This process is captured by the following integral equation, which is the whole basis of our calculation:[28]

$$L_r(\theta_r,\phi_r) = L_e + \iint L_i(\theta_i,\phi_i) f_r(\theta_i,\phi_i;\theta_r,\phi_r) \left|\cos\theta_i\right| \sin\theta_i d\theta_i d\phi_i \qquad \mathit{(10.1)}$$

Though it may look a bit scary to readers not used to staring at lots of Greek symbols, its essence is actually quite simple. The function being described is the value of a ray in a given direction, expressed in terms of luminance or radiance. (See the appendix at the end of this chapter.) Evaluating this function means evaluating the expression on the right-hand side, which sums together the emitted radiation and the convolution of all incoming radiation with the reflectance-transmittance function for the surface, f_r.

Notice that the $L_r(\theta_r,\phi_r)$ function is defined in terms of itself, because the incident luminance or radiance at a point on a surface must be the emitted or reflected luminance or radiance at a point on another surface. Thus, this equation captures the essential recursive nature of the ray-tracing process. Evaluating one ray implies evaluation of the other rays, and the process continues until the error is small enough to quit. In *Radiance*, the recursive process halts when one of the following is true:

- The intersected surface is a light source (for which the reflectance is approximated as zero).
- The ray has reflected more than a specified number of times. (Six is the default limit.)
- The ray "weight," which is the product of all previous reflectances, is below a specified value. (The default limit is 0.005.)

Let us consider just the integral portion of Equation 10.1, which is the most difficult bit. Multiplied together are the incoming luminance distribution, $L_i(\theta_i,\phi_i)$, and the bidirectional reflectance-transmittance distribution function (BRTDF), $f_r(\theta_i,\phi_i;\theta_r,\phi_r)$.[29] The combined integrand will therefore have peaks where one or the other of these functions is large. The incoming luminance function will peak around light source directions, and the reflectance-transmittance function will peak in specular directions. If we can remove these portions of the integral, the remainder will be more manageable.

---

28. This equation assumes no participating medium. This will be later amended in Chapter 14, when we discuss the implementation of participating media in *Radiance*, but we felt it would introduce unnecessary complexity at this point.

29. See [Gla95] and [NRHGL77] for a more complete discussion of this equation.

A purely deterministic solution to the integral would trace the same ray directions every time. In most ray tracers, one ray is directed toward the center of each light source in the scene, one ray is directed in the mirror direction (if the specularity is nonzero), and one ray is directed in the transmitted direction (for transparent materials). The unaccounted-for remainder is approximated by a constant ambient value set somehow by the user. The result is clean and quick, but not terribly accurate for most scenes.

A purely stochastic solution to the integral would trace rays in random directions, weighted by the BRTDF and the other terms in the integrand. (A better technique is to send uniformly weighted rays whose directions are chosen by the process of Monte Carlo inversion [Rub81] [SW92][Shi92].) This approach is slow and prone to noise, but is more accurate and general than any other, including radiosity methods. In fact, for the small class of scenes to which classic radiosity is suited, diffuse environments with large area sources, this method is just as fast for the same level of accuracy—even faster if the scene geometry is complicated.

In the hybrid deterministic/stochastic technique of *Radiance*, these approaches are mixed to obtain a balance between speed and accuracy. The direct component is computed with rays traced to random locations on the light sources. The specular indirect component is computed with rays distributed about the mirror and transmitted directions using uniformly weighted Monte Carlo sampling. Once these two prominent components are removed from the integral, the diffusely interreflected component is computed by occasional evaluation of the simplified integral at dynamically selected locations. These components are shown graphically in Plate 23, together with the combined result.

Plate 24 shows the same scene as in Plates 21 and 22, this time computed using the standard techniques employed in *Radiance*. The computation time was somewhere between those for the two previous images, yet the result looks smoother and is more accurate than the long-running Monte Carlo rendering.

The next three chapters in this section will detail these component calculations. Chapter 11 discusses optimizations in the direct calculation and what happens when there are many light sources, large area sources, and "virtual" light sources caused by mirror reflections and the like. Chapter 12 discusses the intricacies of the indirect calculation, how diffuse indirect values are computed, stored, and interpolated, and how specular indirect rays are sampled. Chapter 13 discusses the special treatment of "secondary" light sources, which are intense areas of redirected illumination such as skylights and windows. Chapter 14 explains the new single-scatter computation for participating media, then Chapter 15 goes on to address the issues of parallel rendering on a multiprocessor computer or across a local area network.

10.4 Supplemental Information

The photometric unit of luminance is the quantity of light passing through a point in a given direction, expressed in terms of lumens over area over solid angle. The lumen is the basic photometric unit, which corresponds to a canonical human observer's visual response to a quantity and spectrum of radiation. For light energy at a wavelength of 555 nanometers, a lumen is defined as 1/683 watt. This is the peak of the human $v(\lambda)$ visual response curve defined by the CIE (Commission International de l'Eclairage), shown in Figure 10.2. The radiometric unit of radiance is more basic, expressed in terms of power over area over solid angle, independent of wavelength. Because we wish to represent our results on computer displays and in color images, we break radiance down further into spectral contributions for the three primary phosphor colors, red, green, and blue. These primary colors are in turn defined in terms of the three CIE primaries. (The CIE $v(\lambda)$ defines CIE photopic (Y), and the long (X) and short (Z) channels are shown in Figure 10.2 as well.) For a thorough discussion of color metrics, see [WS67].

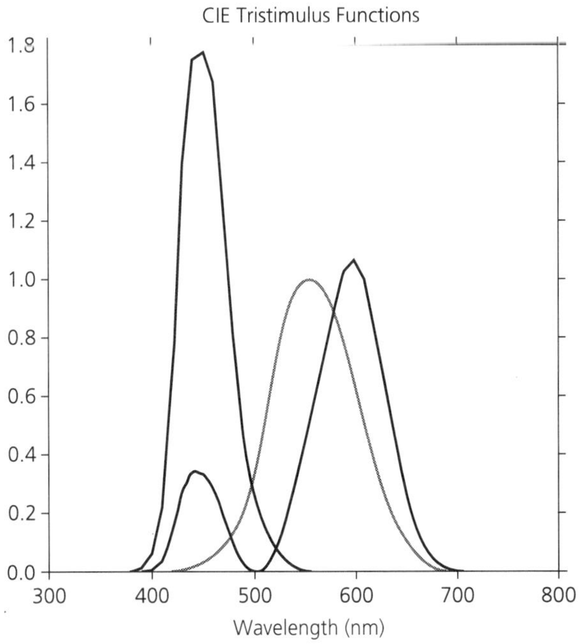

Figure 10.2 The standard CIE tristimulus curves.

The final conversion between CIE *XYZ* and *Radiance* values is determined by the chromaticity coordinates chosen to represent a canonical set of computer display phosphors. In version 3.1, the phosphor chromaticities are

Red	$(x,y) = (0.640, 0.330)$
Green	$(x,y) = (0.290, 0.600)$
Blue	$(x,y) = (0.150, 0.060)$

Equal-energy white is chosen as the balance point for conversions, since this is the assumed adaptation of the eventual observer. (See [Rog85] for details on converting between color systems.)

These three separate channels are processed simultaneously in the calculation. It would be possible to process more channels at a modest additional cost, but the current input format for *Radiance* uses only three.

CHAPTER 11

Direct Calculation

Because certain objects or surfaces contribute more significantly than others and are known in advance of any computation, we can treat them specially as light sources in a "direct calculation" and save ourselves a lot of hunting around. Recall the central radiance equation from Chapter 10:

$$L_r(\theta_r,\phi_r) = L_e + \iint L_i(\theta_i,\phi_i) f_r(\theta_i,\phi_i;\theta_r,\phi_r) \left|\cos\theta_i\right| \sin\theta_i d\theta_i d\phi_i \qquad (11.1)$$

Remember that we said the key to the efficient evaluation of this equation is removing any places we know where incoming radiance, L_i, or the surface reflectance function, f_r, is large. We see that light sources usually represent large values in L_i. There is nothing magical that decides what is part of the direct calculation and what is not—it's simply a matter of which sources we can identify. In most cases, this includes light sources, but may also include other objects that are reflecting or redirecting light in some way that we can compute a priori.

Light source testing (also called "shadow testing") has been a common feature of ray-tracing algorithms since the very beginning [Whi80] and is still one of the best ways to reduce noise and improve calculation efficiency. It is not without drawbacks, however. Here are a few:

- Calculation time tends to increase linearly with the number of light sources; that is, twice as many light sources means twice as long for a picture. This becomes unreasonable in large open spaces where hundreds of light sources tend to be the rule rather than the exception.
- Large area sources (large, that is, relative to the distance to the illuminated surface) must be subdivided to avoid inaccuracies and excessive noise. Doing this unconditionally means oversampling such sources at points far enough away that a single shadow ray would suffice.
- Light source reflections in mirrors are not included in most direct calculations, and finding such significant sources of illumination with undirected ray samples is usually impractical. The result is missing illumination or noise specks.

Radiance combats each of these problems with specially developed algorithms. Specifically:

- Selective Shadow Testing
  To avoid linear calculation growth with the number of light sources, *Radiance* sorts all potential direct contributions at each evaluation point and sends shadow rays as necessary to meet a given accuracy requirement. The result is that the speed is increased by a factor from 2 to 10 in environments with many light sources.
- Adaptive Source Subdivision
  Large area sources are adaptively subdivided into smaller ones based on the distance to the test point. This avoids solid angle and penumbra errors without introducing excessive sampling at more distant points.
- Virtual Light Source Calculation
  Source reflections from mirrors and other redirecting surfaces are managed in a "virtual light source calculation" that tracks virtual positions of light sources and follows rays through the appropriate reflections and refractions to find the original sources. Careful management of these virtual positions prevents the calculation from getting out of hand.

We will discuss each of these optimizations in this chapter in turn. In each case, we will present the basic problem and our solution to it, followed by a discussion of the limitations of the technique. We will then describe the associated rendering parameters and recommended settings. Finally, we will give some details of the algorithm with pointers to the actual C source code where it is implemented in

Radiance. To understand these explanations, it is important to be somewhat familiar with the source code in the *src/rt/* subdirectory. As a starting point, the reader may want to refer to the Source Tree Roadmap on the CD-ROM.

11.1 Selective Shadow Testing

At any given point in the scene, some sources will be more significant than others, and it is more important to determine shadow boundaries for these sources. Some sources may be behind the test point or pointing in another direction, and can be summarily ignored. (See Figure 11.1.) Others may be so distant or dim that their contribution is almost negligible, and sending sample rays in their direction is a waste of time. We cannot ignore all such sources, however, because this would result in a systematic underestimation of illumination. What we would like to do is test just enough sources so that the shadows look right, then approximate the missing illumination using statistics.

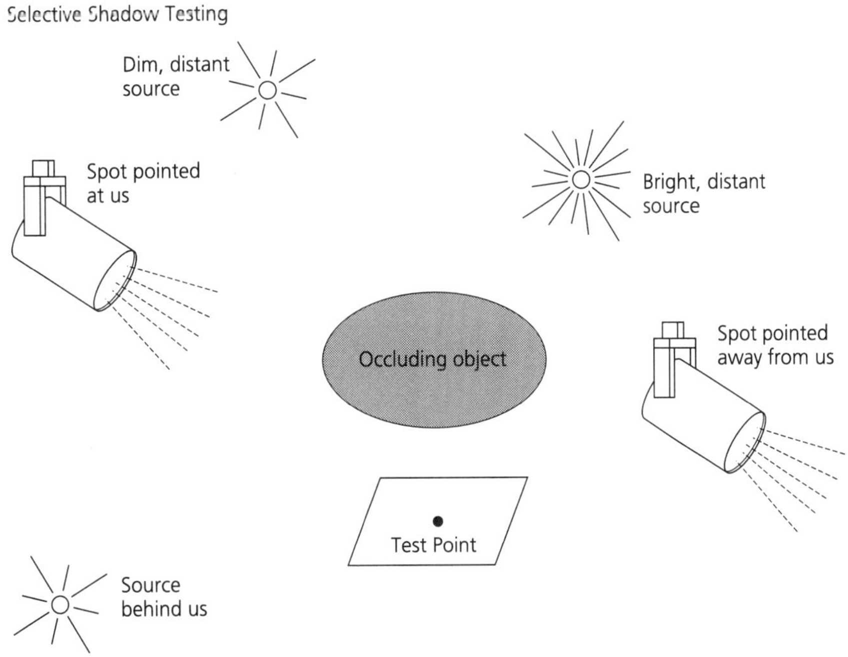

Figure 11.1 Which sources do we test for shadow?

As with many other algorithms in *Radiance*, we start with a simple observation such as this, then attempt to quantify or adapt it to gain some improvement in calculation efficiency. In this case, the translation from idea to algorithm is fairly simple [War91]:

1. A list of potential light source contributions at this point is sorted in order of decreasing magnitude. The potential contribution of a source considers size, brightness, and distance—everything except visibility, which is the most expensive part to compute and thus the part we wish most to avoid.
2. Light sources are tested for visibility, one by one from the top of the list, until the remainder of the list (or a portion thereof) is below some fraction of the accumulated total.
3. The contributions of the remaining (untested) sources are estimated based on visibility statistics gathered during previous shadow tests.

Figure 11.2 gives an example of this algorithm in action. The left column represents our sorted list of potential light source contributions for a specific sample point. We proceed down our list, checking the visibility of each source by tracing shadow rays, and summing together the unobstructed contributions. After each test, we check to see if the maximum remainder of our potential contributions has fallen below some specified fraction of our accumulated total. If we set our accuracy goal at 10%, we can stop testing after four light sources, because the remainder of the list is less than 10% of our known direct value. We could either add all of the remainder in or throw it away, and our value would still be within 10% of the correct answer.

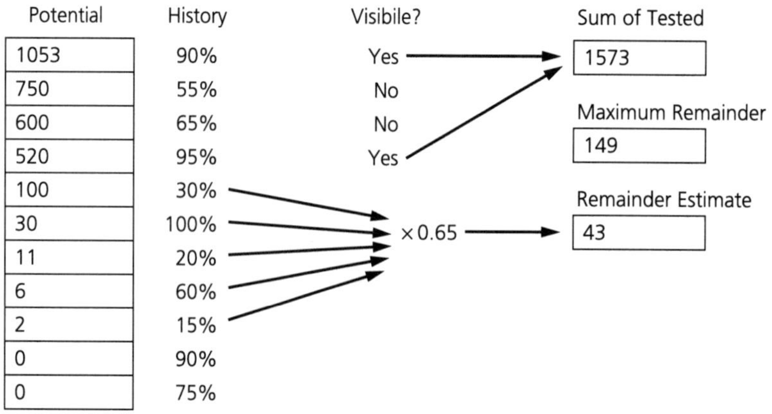

Figure 11.2 Selecting sources to test.

But we can do better than this; we can make an educated guess at the visibility of the remaining sources, using statistics. Taking the history of obstructed versus unobstructed shadow rays from previous tests of each light source, we multiply this probability of hitting an untested source by the ratio of successful shadow tests at this point over all successful shadow tests (2 / (.9 + .55 + .65 + .95) = 0.65 in this example), and arrive at a reasonable estimate of the remainder. (If any computed multiplier is greater than 1, 1 is used instead.) Our total estimate of the direct contribution at this point is then the sum of the tested light sources and our statistical estimate of the remainder, or (1573 + 43) = 1616 in this example.

The effect of the described algorithm is to assure that the desired accuracy value is met, while eliminating unnecessary source visibility tests. Note that if none of the large potential contributors are visible, the entire list may end up being tested, though this is generally a rare occurrence. This is because a point that is "visible" to the viewer is usually visible to nearby light sources as well.

A variation on the algorithm permits even greater savings in source tests by relaxing the accuracy goal. The user gives a "certainty" value that varies between 0 and 1, and this affects the stopping criterion. Whereas before we would compare to the maximum remainder, now we look at, at most, `n_shadcheck` sources, defined by

$$\texttt{n\_shadcheck} = \texttt{n\_contributions}^{\texttt{shad\_certainty}}$$

If the certainty value is 1, we base our tolerance criterion on the full remainder as before. If the certainty value is 0, we look at only one source beyond the current sum. Since there is usually only one source per shadow boundary, even with a certainty of 0, we will not miss any shadow boundaries that would make a difference above the tolerance level. Because shadow boundaries are what the eye notices, this is the most important factor. Certainty settings between 0 and 1 will provide relatively greater certainty that the tolerance criterion is met in absolute terms, with a consummate cost in the number of shadow rays followed. Even if the certainty is low, our statistical estimates of the remainder will tend to minimize any errors.

Figures 11.3 through 11.5 show a conference room in free fall. The scene contains 192 light sources, created by manually subdividing 24 fluorescent fixtures into 8 sections each. Figure 11.3 shows a rendering in which every source was tested at every point. Figure 11.4 shows the same scene rendered with a target accuracy of 0.2 and a certainty value of 0.5. Although only 20% as many shadow tests were used to make this picture, it still achieved an average pixel accuracy of 5% and is barely distinguishable from its fully calculated counterpart. Figure 11.5 shows the squared pixel difference between the two images times 100, indicating that the areas with the largest error are not in fact at the shadow boundaries, but tend to be in areas that are fully illuminated. This is where a statistical method will tend to

Figure 11.3 A test scene with complicated shadows.

Figure 11.4 The Figure 11.3 scene computed using only 20% of the original shadow rays.

Figure 11.5 Dark regions show where errors may be significant even though they are not apparent in Figure 11.4.

underestimate illumination by predicting shadows when there are none. However, since the eye is a rather poor judge of absolute levels, these areas do not stand out as artifacts in the image.

Figure 11.6(a) shows the fraction of sources tested for visibility in this scene as a function of the accuracy and certainty settings. Figure 11.6(b) shows the average error associated with each setting. Figure 11.6(c) shows the maximum pixel error for each setting. As we can see, the average error is generally well below the target value even when the certainty is fairly low. This attests to the ability of our statistical visibility estimates to avoid local error or global bias. Some individual pixels do have larger errors, but even with a 50% certainty value, we rarely exceed the target error even at a single pixel.

11.1.1 Limitations

Although this algorithm performs well with scenes containing a dozen to a few hundred light sources, the expense of computing potential contributions in scenes with thousands of light sources becomes quite significant. Since the technique gathers no absolute information about global visibility, it is not able to cull unimportant light sources completely from the calculation. When you are modeling a large

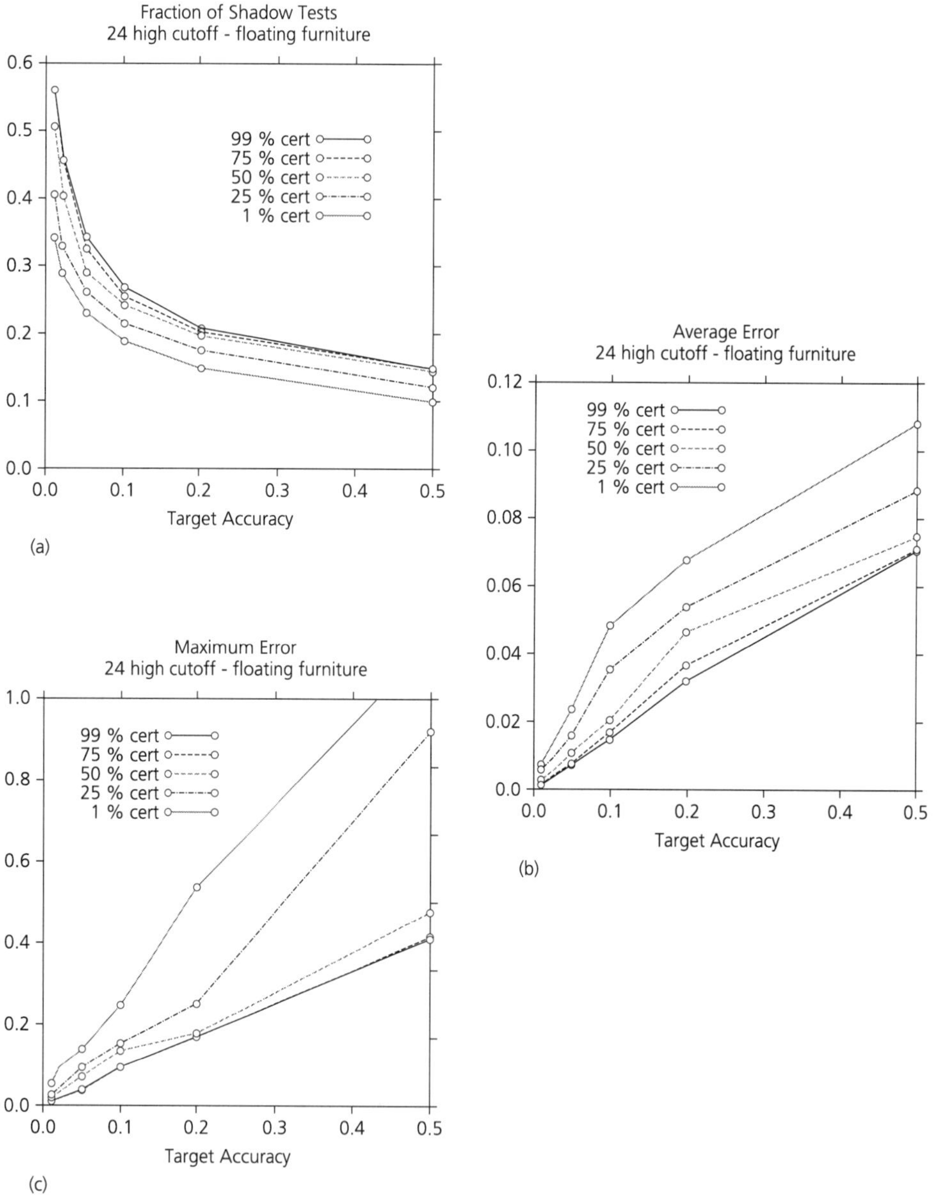

Figure 11.6 Plots of the fraction of source rays traced as a function of the -dt and -dc accuracy and certainty parameters (a); the average error associated with different target accuracies and certainties for our test scene (b); and the maximum pixel error as a function of accuracy and certainty settings for our test scene (c).

building complex, it is therefore important to include in the description only those light sources needed for the current view. In large open retail spaces or stadiums where many sources are visible, judicious application of the *glow* and *spotlight* material types can reduce the time spent in unnecessary calculations.

11.1.2 Relation to Rendering Parameters

There are essentially two parameters that control the selective source testing algorithm used in *Radiance*:

-dt Sets the *direct threshold*, which is equivalent to the target accuracy for the selective testing algorithm. If set to 0, every nonzero source contribution will be tested for visibility, disabling selective shadow testing.

-dc Sets the *direct certainty*. A maximum value of 1 means that the direct threshold will be the maximum allowed error under all conditions. A minimum value of 0 means that the threshold restricts only the maximum shadow error for any given light source. In-between values offer a greater or lesser degree of certainty that the given accuracy target will be met. (This setting is irrelevant if -dt is set to 0.)

Recommended Settings

The settings used by **rad** are determined solely by the `QUALITY` variable, as follows:

`QUALITY =`	**Low**	**Med**	**High**
-dt	0.2	0.1	0.05
-dc	0.25	0.5	0.17

Obviously, these settings may not always be ideal. If accuracy is particularly important, or if it is important to have a guarantee of accuracy, a higher certainty value may be indicated. If rendering speed is crucial and there are a large number of light sources, it may be possible to increase the threshold and set certainty to a small value and still get a usable result. If shadow appearance matters but absolute numerical accuracy is not critical, then a zero setting of certainty paired with a lower threshold value will yield a fast result without visible artifacts.

11.1.3 Algorithm Details and Source Code

The C code implementing the selective light source testing is in *src/rt/source.c* in the standard distribution. The main function is `direct(r,f,p)`, which is called by material functions with any diffuse component that necessitates light source testing. The three parameters passed are the intersecting ray `r`, a call-back function `f` that computes the direct coefficient for a particular source, and a pointer `p` to client-specific data that is passed to `f` along with the direction and solid angle of the source being tested. Many calls may be made to `f` for each call made to `direct`.

Glossing over the details, `direct` looks something like this:

```
direct(r,f,p) begin
        foreach source sample do
                compute coefficient by calling f()
                compute potential_contribution
                store potential_contribution in an array
        end foreach
        sort potential_contributions array
        compute partial_remainder of \
                potential_contributions by adding \
                fraction of list equal to dc_setting
        set total = 0
        set our_hit_rate = 0
        while partial_remainder > dt_setting*total do
                trace ray sample to next largest \
                        potential_contribution
                increment test_count for source
                if ray hit target then
                        add potential_contribution to total
                        increment hit_count for source
                end if
                add source hit_count/test_count to \
                        our_hit_rate
        end while
        divide our_hit_rate by number tested above
        foreach untested potential_contribution do
                set P = source hit_count/test_count * \
                        our_hit_rate
                if P > 1 then set P = 1
                add P * potential_contribution to total
        end foreach
        set r->return_value = total
end direct
```

Note that computing the `potential_contributions` array above requires that one be able to compute a source value without actually tracing a ray. (It would work also if one did trace the ray, but the whole point of selective sampling would be defeated.) We therefore implement a special function that follows rays to light sources without testing for intervening surfaces. This function, `srcvalue`, is also contained in the *src/rt/source.c* module. The standard C library function `qsort` is used to sort the `potential_contributions` array, and it is fast enough that it never contributes significantly to execution time for any scene we have tested.

11.2 Adaptive Source Subdivision

Large light sources can be a significant source of error in a standard ray-tracing calculation. If only a single sample ray is sent to each source, even if it is distributed randomly over the surface, the resulting value may be a poor estimate of visibility, because a large source is more likely to be partially occluded than a small one. Even if partial occlusion is not an issue, a standard estimate of the source solid angle (i.e., the portion of the projected hemisphere covered by the source) will likely be inaccurate. Although it is possible to come up with better approximations to the solid angle for large sources, they tend to be expensive to compute [Arv95].

A more robust approach, therefore, is to subdivide large area sources into smaller regions and sample the regions separately. This process is diagrammed in the example in Figure 11.7. This action is taken conditionally based on the size of the source relative to the distance to the test point in question. Even a large source may appear small if it is far away, and it would be wasteful to subdivide such a source for all samples. Likewise, a small source may appear large if a point is near enough to it, so we cannot decide a priori when subdivision is necessary.

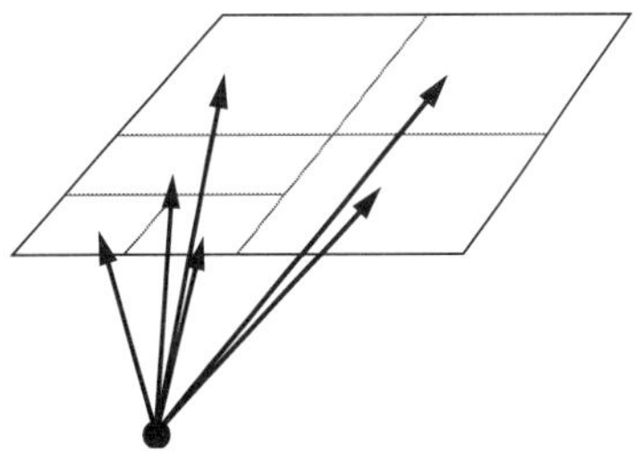

Figure 11.7 Adaptively subdividing a large area light source.

The algorithm for adaptive sampling is simple to describe, though the implementation is complicated by the different light source shapes supported in *Radiance*. The basic method is as follows:

1. If the maximum side length of a source is greater than a certain fraction of the distance to the source from this point (controlled by the **-ds** option), subdivide the source into two subsources along the longest axis.
2. Repeat process on each subsource until all pieces satisfy the relative size criterion.

There are two reasons for comparing the distance to the length of the longest side instead of the solid angle. The first is the difficulty of computing the solid angle for large sources—remember that this was one of the reasons for subdividing in the first place. The second is that the source may be oriented at a steep angle relative to the test point, in which case the closer part of the source may contribute much more than the rest, and it is important to subdivide until the nearby pieces are relatively small.

A second algorithm is used to distribute samples randomly over each subsource. This is an essential part of "distributed ray tracing" as introduced by Cook in 1984 [CPC84], which describes the application of stochastic techniques to reduce certain artifacts of deterministic rendering methods. As in Cook's work, *Radiance* employs a very basic jittering algorithm to sample over sources, which are approximated as rectangular volumes. More sophisticated algorithms that distribute samples over the visible surface are possible and have been implemented by others [SWZ96], but they use up valuable time in a part of the calculation that can scarcely afford it, and the net improvement in accuracy is slight.

11.2.1 Limitations

The jittered sampling approach limits the shape of light sources in *Radiance* to ones that are roughly rectangular (see Figure 11.8). Fortunately, a lot of leeway is allowed here, so even spheres, disks, and long cylinders may make effective light sources. However, a source that is shaped like a skinny *L* or something irregular must be subdivided into roughly rectangular subsources in the scene description file. Otherwise, the infamous "aiming failure for light source" warning will be issued when *Radiance* fails to sample it properly. Depending on the severity of the error, it may or may not be significant to the final result. This may also occur for a cylindrical light source if the radius is not small relative to side length, since a sample ray may miss the end and hit the inside or even pass straight through. (Cylinders whose radius is greater than one fifth of their length will automatically generate a warning for this reason.)

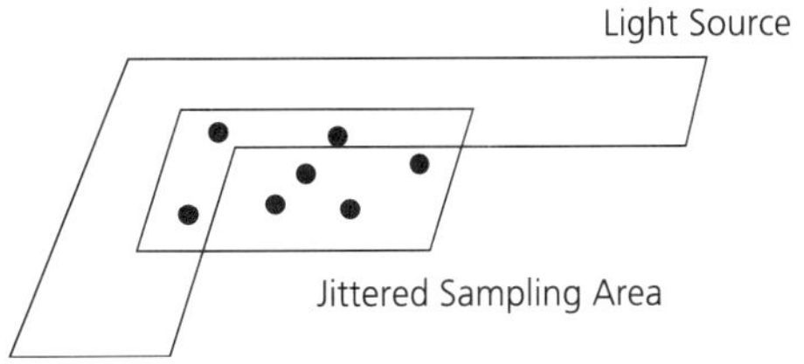

Figure 11.8 Jittered sampling of a nonrectangular light source. Since *Radiance* approximates the area as a parallelogram, which is not a good fit in this case, many ray samples miss the target, generating a warning message and degrading the calculation's accuracy and efficiency. This source should be divided into two roughly rectangular subsources.

A source will not be broken into more than `MAXSPART` subdivisions (a macro defined in *src/rt/source.h*). This avoids breaking a source up to ridiculous levels for points right next to it, which would be very expensive. An artifact of this limit may appear as unnatural scalloping on a windowsill when the window is treated as a light source.

Certain light source shapes are not subdivided adaptively because it would either result in sampling errors or would be otherwise ineffective. Specifically, neither the *source* nor the *sphere* shape is subdivided. Since a source is infinitely distant, the distance criterion is either never or always met; hence, it makes more sense to subdivide large sources initially or else relegate them to the indirect calculation by using them with a glow material type. As for spheres, if they are large relative to a point, they are also close, and a simple volumetric subdivision does not result in effective or accurate sampling. Fortunately, large spherical sources are relatively rare in practice.

11.2.2 Relation to Rendering Parameters

Two parameters control the adaptive source subdivision and jittered sampling in *Radiance*:

-ds Sets the *direct subsampling* threshold. If a source has a side that is longer than this fraction of the distance between the source and the test sample, the source is subdivided. A setting of 0 means that sources should never be subdivided, effectively switching this algorithm off for maximum speed at the expense of accuracy.

-dj Sets the degree of *direct jittering*. A value of 1 would force sampling over the full rectangular source volume, but is not recommended because some sources are far enough from rectangular that the corners will be missed. Generally, a setting of 0.65 or less is safe. A setting of 0 turns direct jittering off.

Recommended Settings

The settings used by rad are determined by the `QUALITY` and `PENUMBRAS` variables. For `PENUMBRAS` off (False), we get

`QUALITY =`	**Low**	**Med**	**High**
-ds	0	0.3	0.02
-dj	0	0	0

For `PENUMBRAS` on (True), we get

`QUALITY =`	**Low**	**Med**	**High**
-ds	0.4	0.2	0.01
-dj	0	0.5	0.6

Besides the aforementioned problem with errant samples, there is another reason why the direct jitter parameter is frequently set to 0; nonzero values increase the pixel variance in the image, and require greater sampling frequencies to reduce visible noise. This means setting the **-ps** option to 1 and possibly increasing the maximum number of samples per pixel by rendering a larger source picture for pfilt. This is expensive, but is the only way to completely eliminate unnaturally sharp shadows from the image. If false shadows are not a problem, then setting the rad `PENUMBRAS` variable to False can save quite a bit of rendering time.

11.2.3 Algorithm Details and Source Code

Two modules in *Radiance* implement the source sampling algorithms. Initialization code for computing the sampling volumes for different source types is contained in *src/rt/srcsupp.c*. Code for partitioning and sampling sources is contained in the file *src/rt/srcsamp.c*. Both modules reference data types and macros defined in *src/rt/source.h*. Rather than explaining in detail the sampling process, which is interwoven with too many other functions to be neatly described, we will point out some of the more important routines and data structures so that the adventurous reader can explore the code with some hope of sorting it all out.

- `SRCFUNC sfun[];`
  This array of structures is initialized in `initstypes` (in *src/rt/srcsupp.c*). It contains pointers to functions that initialize and partition sources. One structure is loaded for each valid source geometric type, and the type number (defined in *src/common/otypes.h*) is used as the index. Additional functions are provided for virtual source objects and materials, which are described in the next section.
- `SRCREC *source;`
  The dynamically allocated source list. This array is built in the function `marksources` (in *src/rt/source.c*, called once from `main` during initialization) based on the materials used by each scene surface. The material types light, spotlight, glow, and illum generally modify light source objects, and this is how they are identified. Surface-specific object initialization functions assigned to the `sfun` array are used to fill most of the `SRCREC` data structure. An additional call to `makespot` (defined in *src/rt/srcsupp.c*) is made for spotlight sources, and other fields are assigned for glow sources.
- `void initsrcindex(SRCINDEX *si);`
  This macro, defined in *src/rt/source.h*, initializes a source sample index. This index is later passed to `nextssamp`, described below.
- `double nextssamp(RAY *r, SRCINDEX *si);`
  This routine (in *src/rt/srcsupp.c*) is used to compute the next source sample direction based on the given ray origin and sample index. Object functions from the `sfun` array are called to partition sources as necessary. The value returned is the distance (in world space) to the light source, or 0 if no more source samples are required.
- `int srcray(RAY *sr, RAY *r, SRCINDEX *si);`
  This routine (in *src/rt/source.c*) assigns the next source ray `sr` based on an originating ray `r` and a sample index `si`. It is called from `direct` (also in *src/rt/source.c*) once for each potential source contribution. It calls `rayorigin` to initialize `sr` and `nextssamp` to get the direction. The function returns 1 on success, or 0 if no more samples are needed.

11.3 Virtual Light Source Calculation

What happens when light is reflected from a mirror? If we were modeling actual photons, we would have no trouble simulating this effect. Unfortunately, we are not following light forward from the sources, but backward from the camera, for the economic reasons mentioned in Chapter 10. We have just explained how we locate and sample light sources we have marked in the scene by directing rays at them, but how can we direct rays at sources that are reflected in mirrors or redirected by some other material? The solution applied in *Radiance* is to create a "virtual light source" for important specular source paths in our environment. If we follow rays directed at such virtual sources, the actual sources are found.

Figure 11.9 shows two examples of specular source paths and their associated virtual sources. Figure 11.9(a) shows a mirror reflecting a light source onto a surface. If we create a virtual light source on the opposite side of the mirror plane, we can trace sample rays to this virtual source that will be reflected back to the original source. The basic idea of "virtual worlds" was put forth by Rushmeier in 1986 [Rus86] and has been exploited with varying degrees of success by Wallace [WCG87] and others. The advantage of applying this method here instead of to a radiosity calculation is that only the light sources need be reproduced on the other side of the looking glass, not the entire environment. We have also extended the method to include other types of light redirection, such as the refraction in a prismatic panel shown in Figure 11.9(b). In this case, light rays are bent rather than reflected. So long as we can approximate the redirection as a general transformation

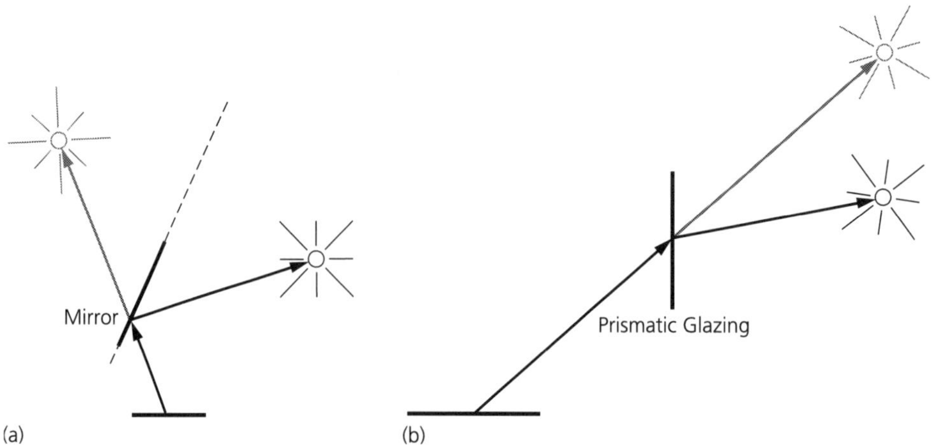

(a) (b)

Figure 11.9 Virtual light source created by a mirror (a), and virtual light source created by a prism (b).

of the source (i.e., there is little spreading or concentration of rays), virtual sources will work effectively.

What happens if light from a source is redirected by multiple surfaces? If we were creating virtual worlds, we would end up having to create virtual-virtual and virtual-virtual-virtual worlds and so on. Since we are only working with light sources, we can eliminate a lot of unnecessary duplication because most of the possible redirections implied by multiple objects are precluded by visibility constraints. Figure 11.10(a) shows a light source between two mirrors. Normally, we would have to create virtual sources plus virtual-virtual sources, but in this case, there is no possible path from the source to one mirror and then to the other, so creating virtual-virtual sources would be a waste of time. *Radiance* therefore tests the intersections of visibility cones against redirecting objects before creating virtual-virtual sources.

Likewise, we can pretest the visibility of sources to avoid creating virtual sources where no redirection can occur owing to intervening obstructions, as shown in Figure 11.10(b). Pretesting can also eliminate unnecessary intersection testing when the path between a source and relay object is completely *unobstructed.* If no pretest rays are occluded, a flag is set that avoids further testing once the relay object has been reached during shadow testing.

The density of these pretest samples is controlled by the **-dp** parameter. If this parameter is set to 0, pretesting is not used. This guarantees absolute shadow accuracy at the expense of testing some unnecessary source paths.

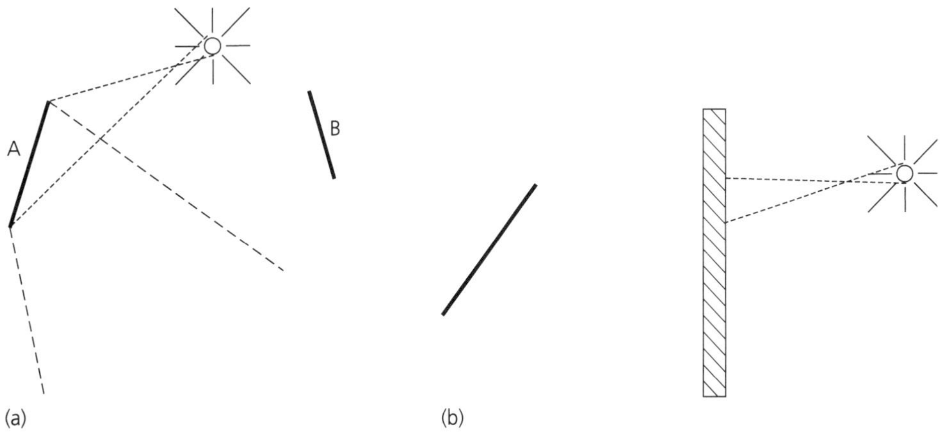

Figure 11.10 Rays reflected by the light source in mirror A not reaching mirror B because of the angles involved (a), and rays leaving the light source not reaching the mirror behind the wall (b). We don't have to create a corresponding virtual-virtual source for either situation.

11.3.1 Limitations

Only certain materials will result in virtual light sources. It is the user's responsibility to assign these materials to the important reflecting/redirecting surfaces. This avoids inadvertent growth of the calculation for surfaces that might have some small specular component but that are not particularly important to global illumination. There are currently three virtual source materials in *Radiance: mirror* for reflecting surfaces, and *prism1* and *prism2* for surfaces with one and two important redirections, respectively. Surfaces with more than two significant redirections are not currently supported. The common approach with prismatic glazings (which may have any number of redirections) is to use the `fprism_val` library function developed by the LESO group in Switzerland to find the most important transmission modes for a given incident angle [Com93]. (See the *lib/fprism.cal* file in the standard distribution for further information.)

The main limitation of the virtual light source calculation in *Radiance* is that it works only for planar relay surfaces. Currently, this includes *polygons* and *rings*. Any other surface type generates a warning when modified by a virtual source material, and no virtual sources will be created by it. Curved surfaces may, of course, be broken into smaller planar surfaces, but this is a fairly inefficient approach, since it will result in at least as many virtual sources as there are surfaces multiplied by the number of visible sources from those surfaces. This limitation hinders the application of *Radiance* to heliostats and specular luminaires, but these systems are best treated by a separate forward Monte Carlo method. (Writing such a program is left as an exercise for you.)

11.3.2 Relation to Rendering Parameters

There are essentially two parameters that control virtual light source calculation in *Radiance*:

-dr Sets the maximum number of *direct relays* from redirecting objects. When this parameter is set to 1, only virtual sources will be created. If it is set to 2, virtual-virtual sources will be created. Setting this parameter to 0 turns off the virtual light source calculation.

-dp Sets the virtual *direct pretest* density to the given number of samples per steradian; thus, larger objects closer to virtual source positions will receive relatively more samples. A setting of 0 turns presampling off.

Recommended Settings

The settings used by rad are determined by the QUALITY and DETAIL variables. Here are the settings for low DETAIL:

QUALITY =	Low	Med	High
-dr	0	1	3
-dp	64	256	1024

Here are the settings for medium DETAIL:

QUALITY =	Low	Med	High
-dr	0	1	3
-dp	128	512	2048

Here are the settings for high DETAIL:

QUALITY =	Low	Med	High
-dr	0	1	3
-dp	256	1024	4096

Since presampling occurs only once during initialization, the overall calculation time does not strongly depend on it. Doubling the presampling density may double this initialization time, but this is typically only a matter of seconds before moving on to the actual rendering. The number of direct relays is much more important, since it partially determines how many virtual sources will be created. In the worst case of a hall of mirrors, there may be exponential growth in the number of virtual sources, where -dr sets the exponent. This will affect both initialization time and, more significantly, time spent in the direct calculation running through all the potential source contributions, so think carefully about this setting if you have a lot of virtual source objects.

As noted in the section on limitations, a scene without virtual source materials will result in no virtual light sources, whatever the parameter settings.

11.3.3 Algorithm Details and Source Code

The virtual light source calculation is one of the most algorithmically complex components of *Radiance*. Although the basic idea is simple, the special tests involved to avoid runaway source creation are many. We will give a crude outline of the methods and routines involved, so that the adventurous reader can better explore the C code.

As for ordinary light sources, the handling of virtual light sources comes in at two places, once during the initialization and later during shadow testing. Initialization consists of finding and marking virtual light sources after all the ordinary sources have been found. Testing virtual light sources is essentially the same as testing ordinary sources, except that rays are intercepted by the virtual source objects (mirrors or prisms) and relayed to the originating sources. (Redirection may happen several times.)

The source files important to the virtual source calculation are *src/rt/source.h* for data structures and external declarations, *src/rt/virtuals.c* and *src/rt/srcsupp.c* for initialization, and *src/rt/source.c* for shadow testing. In addition, the initialization code works with special routines in the two other modules implementing each virtual source object type. For the mirror type, these routines are in the file *src/rt/m_mirror.c*. The routines for the prism1 and prism2 types are in the file *src/rt/m_direct.c*.

The principal data structures used for virtual sources are the same as those used for ordinary sources. The important aspects are described below:

- `SRCFUNC sfun[];`
  As described in the last section, this array of structures contains pointers to functions for each valid source geometric type. In addition, there are functions for flat geometric types needed to determine reflections, and so on, for virtual sources. For virtual source object materials (mirror, prism1, and prism2), there is a pointer to a function that computes the virtual source projection, which is needed for the creation of these sources. (See the `vproject` function, described below.)
- `SRCREC *source;`
  For each source, the size and position is calculated and stored in a standard configuration in this dynamically allocated array. The chief difference with virtual light sources is that their position is virtual—the target source is not really at the specified location; what is in that direction instead is the virtual source object, that is, the planar surface that relays to the actual source lying in another direction. The object the ray should relay to is indicated by the virtual source member

of this structure. Many virtual sources also have an associated "spot"—solid angle and direction—outside of which they are known not to be important. This is a fast way of culling unnecessary source tests.

The initialization of virtual light sources is the most complicated part of the process; it begins with a call to the function `markvirtuals` after all the ordinary sources have been added to the `source` array. We will briefly describe the purpose of the principal initialization routines below.

- `void markvirtuals();`
  Makes a pass through the loaded scene description, identifying surfaces modified by one of the virtual source material types (mirror, prism1, or prism2). A nonplanar surface modified by one of these materials generates a warning message and the process continues. Once all the redirecting objects have been identified, we loop through the ordinary light sources, adding virtual sources for each with a call to `addvirtuals`.
- `void addvirtuals(int sn, int nr);`
  Adds virtual light sources associated with the ordinary source `sn`, including up to `nr` redirections (initially set by the -dr parameter in this recursive call). This is a very short routine that checks a couple of conditions, then calls the `vproject` routine once for each virtual light source object (i.e., each redirecting surface identified in `marksources`).
- `void vproject(OBJREC *o, int sn, int n);`
  This routine calls the material-dependent functions to create virtual source projections for source `sn` in object `o`. For each valid projection, the routine `makevsrc` is called to do the real work of checking visibility and creating the virtual source entry in the `source` array. For each virtual source created, a recursive call is made to `addvirtuals` to make any associated virtual-virtual sources. (The `n` parameter is simply the decremented counter for the number of reflections as passed from the parent `addvirtuals` call.)
- `int makevsrc(OBJREC *op, int sn, MAT4 pm);`
  Attempt to create a virtual light for source `sn` redirected by object `op` according to transformation matrix `pm`. This routine is really at the heart of virtual light source creation, and it manages source visibility cones (`SPOT` structures) and checks whether or not a virtual source path is traversable. First we call `getdisk` to compute the visible disk from the source, and check against impossible visibility conditions for virtual-virtual sources. Next, we locate the virtual source position, using the given matrix, and compute a visibility cone from the size and location of the redirecting object. If the original source has an associated spot, we compute the intersection between our spot and theirs. If there is none, the virtual source is not visible and we return failure (−1). If the original source is

flat, we next check to see if we are behind it; if we are, we also return failure. Finally, we perform an empirical source visibility test by calling `vstestvis`. If this final test is passed, we allocate and assign the new `source` structure and return its index to `vproject`.

- `double getdisk(FVECT oc, OBJREC *op, int sn);`
  This function calls the object-specific function for `op` to compute the maximum disk (returned center `oc` and radius as value). If the source being considered for redirection `sn` is also a virtual source, we perform additional tests to see if the new object is on the affected side of the virtual source object. If the new disk is entirely on the same side of the redirection plane as the new virtual source position, there is no way for any ray directed at the virtual source to go from the new object to the old object for redirection, so we can return 0 to `makevsrc` so it will not create any virtual-virtual source.
- `int vstestvis(int f, OBJREC *o, FVECT oc, double or2, int sn);`
  Here lies the real power of the virtual source calculation, and also a possible pitfall. The idea is simple—we want to test for the visibility of the source `sn` in the object `o` (with precomputed center `oc` and maximum radius squared `or2`). Unfortunately, the only way we know to do this is to trace some rays from one to the other through our scene and check for obstructions. If our ray tests are completely obstructed, we assume that the light source is not visible, so no virtual source should be created. We indicate this by or-ing the `SSKIP` flag to the passed flags `f` and returning this value. If some of our rays make it and others do not, we return the original flags. If none of our rays are obstructed, we subtract the `SFOLLOW` flag so as to minimize future source testing. The pitfall of this calculation is that we might be wrong in assuming either that the source is fully visible or that it is fully obstructed, since we cannot exhaustively test all possible paths between the two. The density of our "presamples" is determined by the -dp parameter, which turns off this algorithm when set to 0. This is the only way to guarantee correct results, but at a commensurate cost.

When all the virtual sources have been found and entered into the `source` array, the actual ray-tracing process begins. During shadow testing, rays are directed toward the virtual source positions by the corresponding relay object functions. If a ray to a virtual source fails to intersect its relay object, its potential contribution as computed in `direct` is 0. Here are the important routines for virtual light source testing:

- `void direct(RAY *r, int (*f)(), char *p);`
  Detailed in pseudocode in the previous section on selective shadow testing, this routine calls `srcvalue` and checks the source flags assigned by `vstestvis` to decide whether or not to follow the full virtual source path.

- `void srcvalue(RAY *r);`
  Used to compute potential light source contributions for the `direct` function, this routine calls the appropriate object evaluation functions in order to relay the ray back to its original source, checking surface boundaries simultaneously. It does not actually check the ray for obstructions, which is done conditionally by `direct` later.

The real work of redirecting rays toward the actual light sources is carried out in the material-dependent functions for virtual source objects:

- `int m_mirror(OBJREC *m, RAY *r);`
  This function is associated with the mirror material type. It is nearly identical to one that would simply relay a ray in the mirror direction of a surface and modify the color according to its real arguments. The only difference is that it checks to see if the ray is being directed toward a virtual light source, and if so it indicates this in the new ray. (The other minor difference is that it applies surface normal perturbations in computing the new direction only if the ray is not headed toward a virtual source. This is to prevent unwanted noise and errors in the direct component.)
- `int m_direct(OBJREC *m, RAY *r);`
  This function is called for both prism1 and prism2 material types, and `redirect` to do the actual work of making the first or second ray redirection. For prism1 objects, only a single ray is redirected. For prism2 objects, two rays are generated unless we are looking for a virtual source, in which case only the designated direction is followed. The direction for each component is actually determined by a user-specified function file, which is called by `redirect` during its execution.

11.4 Conclusion

In this chapter, we have looked at those parts of *Radiance* that constitute the "direct" calculation, which includes light sources and any other significant component that can be identified a priori. In the next chapter, we will look at the "indirect" components, which include just about everything else. This will be followed by a chapter on promoting sources of illumination from the indirect to the direct calculation for reasons of efficiency. These we call *secondary sources.*

CHAPTER 12

Indirect Calculation

In *Radiance*, the indirect calculation includes all sources of illumination not found during the direct calculation. This includes light reflected and transmitted in specular directions (mirrored and refracted rays) as well as light bouncing diffusely between surfaces in all directions. Mathematically, direct contributions represent peaks identified a priori in the L_i function of the radiance equation (reprinted below), which we have seen how to account for in the preceding chapter. In this chapter, we examine the methods *Radiance* uses to integrate places where the BRTDF, f_r, is large. Moreover, we will explain the diffuse indirect calculation, the all-important treatment of the remainder of our integral, where neither L_i nor f_r is known to be large.

$$L_r(\theta_r,\phi_r) = L_e + \iint L_i(\theta_i,\phi_i) f_r(\theta_i,\phi_i;\theta_r,\phi_r) \left|\cos\theta_i\right| \sin\theta_i \, d\theta_i \, d\phi_i \qquad (12.1)$$

The basic approach to the treatment of specular and diffuse reflection is to send a small number of rays to sample the specular component, followed by a large number of rays to sample the diffuse component. To avoid geometric growth in the diffuse calculation, values are *cached* in a specialized data structure for reuse at nearby points. Briefly, the two strategies work as follows:

- Specular Sampling
  One ray is sent in each designated specular direction. If the component is pure (i.e., ideal reflection or refraction), the direction is completely determined. If the component is rough-specular, Monte Carlo importance sampling is used to determine the actual sample direction, and the contribution of light sources is computed separately as part of the direct component.
- Indirect Irradiance Caching
  Since light comes from undetermined reflections in the environment and contributes to diffuse reflection, we have little choice but to sample over the entire hemisphere at some point. We save ourselves from the dire implications of a pixel-independent calculation by caching our calculated values and reusing them efficiently.

In this chapter, we will look first at the specular component calculation, followed by the intricacies of the diffuse indirect computation. As in the preceding chapter, we will start with a basic explanation, followed by a discussion of the limitations of each technique. Then we will describe the associated rendering parameters, followed by details of the algorithms and pointers to the relevant C source code.

12.1 Specular Sampling

In *Radiance*, we take "specular" to mean any non-Lambertian component of surface reflection or transmission. This includes refraction through a dielectric medium (e.g., solid glass) as well as mirror-like reflection from a polished opaque surface or directional scattering from a translucent material. Virtually every material type in *Radiance* at least potentially has some specular component. A few materials, such as *dielectric* and *glass*, are purely specular, and require neither direct nor diffuse indirect calculations. Once the appropriate ray or rays have been directed and computed for these materials, the evaluation of our radiance equation is finished.

In the more common case of surfaces with some Lambertian and some specular component, the evaluation is a little more complicated. Part of the integral is computed in the direct calculation, since the BRTDF is evaluated in the direction of each light source (or subsource, if direct subsampling is on). We must therefore take care not to double-count light sources. Any ray that hits a light source during the indirect calculation must be ignored. Most of this tracking is managed with special ray flags, which are tested during the evaluation of light source materials.

In *Radiance*, reflectance is divided into as many as six components, depending on the specific material primitive being used. (See the document on *Radiance* materials on the CD-ROM for details on each material type.) Breaking reflectance into components permits us to tailor our sampling strategies efficiently.

For example, let us consider the two-component model used by the *plastic* material type. One reflection component is Lambertian (i.e., uniform over the hemisphere) and the other is specular or rough specular reflection centered about the mirror direction. The specular component represents a peak in the BRTDF, perhaps even a delta singularity.[30] By sampling this component separately, we can remove a large source of variance in our integral. We accomplish this in *Radiance* by sending a single ray in a direction distributed about the mirror angle according to the specified roughness value. If the roughness is zero, the specular ray is exactly in the mirror direction, and a clear reflected image results in the sampled surface. If the roughness is nonzero, we compute a random direction using Monte Carlo importance sampling to get an accurate glossy reflection. The Lambertian diffuse component is then computed either with a constant ambient value as in the original Whitted formulation [Whi80], or using Monte Carlo hemisphere sampling and value caching, discussed in the next section.

Other materials follow a similar strategy, sending rays in specular directions and then using a diffuse interreflection calculation to account for any diffuse components.

A few pictures will help to illustrate the relative importance of these components. Figure 12.1 shows the light source positions and sizes as seen from a sample point on the floor of a cabin model. Figure 12.2 shows the BRTDF evaluated at this point for a specific view direction. Figure 12.3 shows the combination of the BRTDF with the direct illumination pattern. Note that the largest contribution comes from the relatively small source near the specular highlight, illustrating the importance of using the reflectance function in the direct calculation. Figure 12.4 shows the indirect sources of illumination in this scene. Note that the source positions are dark, since they have already been taken into account. Figure 12.5 shows the BRTDF combined with the indirect illumination. Again, the specular highlight contains a significant (though not dominant) contribution. Sending a separate sample ray in the specular direction would probably pay off in this case.

30. A delta singularity, or "Dirac delta function," is a function that may evaluate to infinity at a point, but the integral in a region around this point is still finite. This construct is often used as a mathematical approximation to a physical quantity whose integral is more important than its value, such as BRTDF.

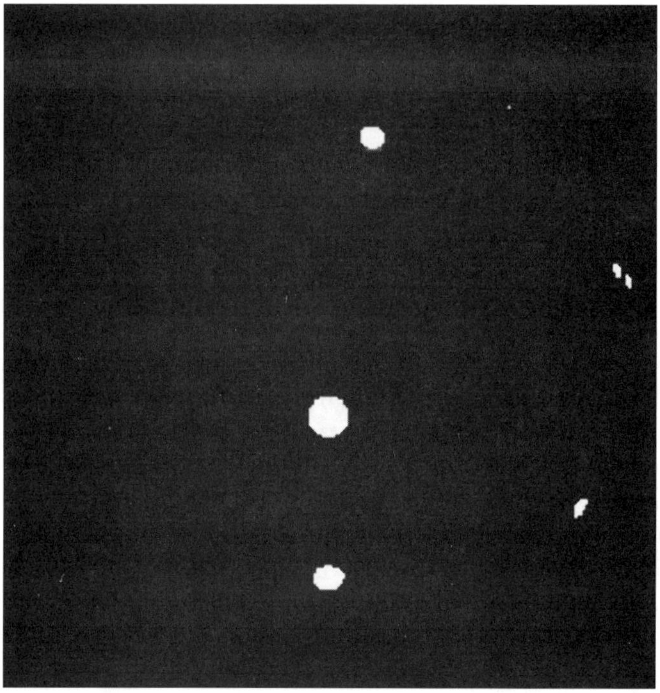

Figure 12.1 The light sources as seen from a point on the cabin model floor.

Figure 12.6 shows a diagram of incident and reflected ray directions, which we need to explain the reflection model and generation of sample directions for rough specular reflection. For an isotropic material, such as plastic or *metal*, our Gaussian reflection model is defined as follows:

$$f_{r,\,iso}(\theta_i, \phi_i; \theta_r, \phi_r) = \frac{\rho_d}{\pi} + \rho_s \cdot \frac{1}{\sqrt{\cos\theta_i \cos\theta_r}} \cdot \frac{\exp[-\tan^2\delta/\alpha^2]}{4\pi\alpha^2} \qquad (12.2)$$

where

ρ_d is the diffuse reflectance

ρ_s is the specular reflectance

δ is the angle between surface normal, $\hat{n}$, and the half vector between the incident and reflected directions, $\hat{h}$

α is the standard deviation (RMS) of the surface slope

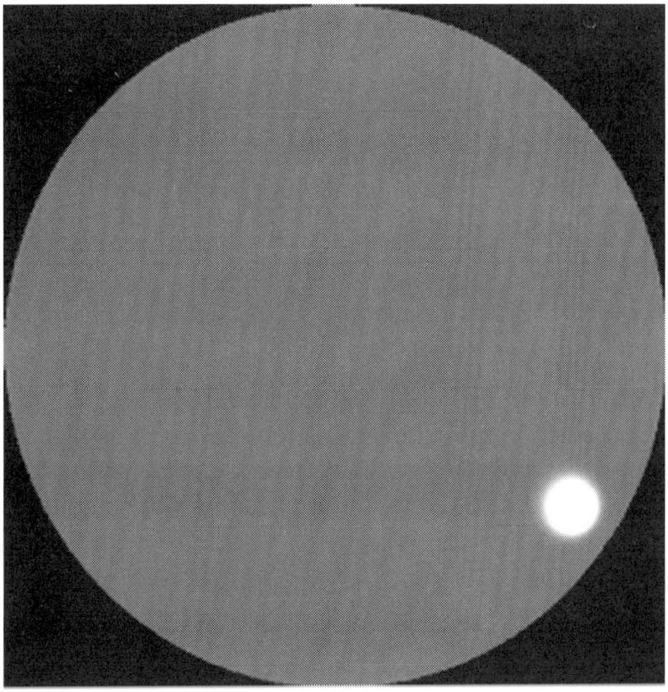

Figure 12.2 The cabin floor reflectance function magnitude for a specific viewing direction.

We generate two uniformly distributed random numbers, u_1 and u_2, in the range (0,1]. We then generate the angles δ and ϕ using the following equations, which are derived using standard Monte Carlo inversion techniques [Rub81]:

$$\delta = \alpha[-\log(u_1)]^{1/2} \qquad \textit{12.3a}$$

$$\phi = 2\pi u_2 \qquad \textit{12.3b}$$

where

ϕ is the azimuthal angle

u_1, u_2 are uniform random variables in the range (0,1]

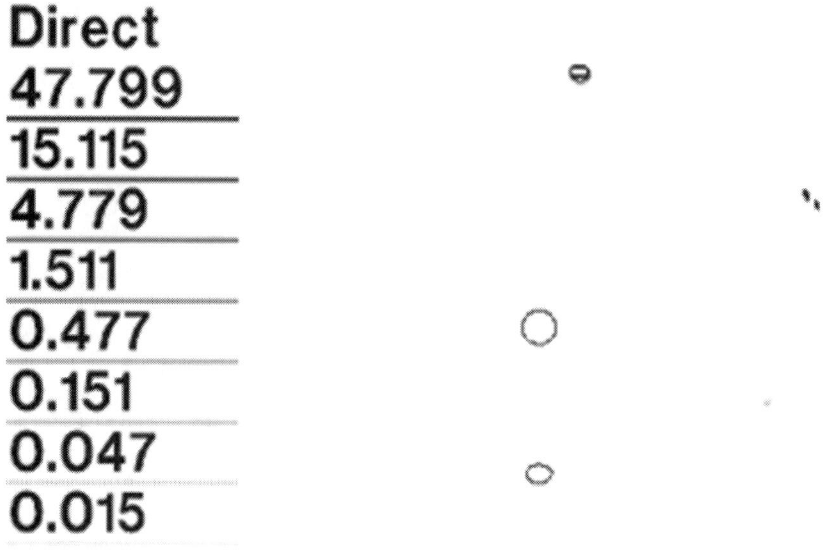

Figure 12.3 The direct component multiplied by the floor reflectance function.

At most, *Radiance* sends out one ray per specular direction in order to minimize the number of spawned samples. Antialiasing takes place for these samples, along with everything else on the image plane, via image reduction using the **pfilt** program. For anisotropic materials, such as *plastic2* and *metal2*, the above equations are modified to become

$$f_{r,\,aniso}(\theta_i, \phi_i; \theta_r, \phi_r) = \frac{\rho_d}{\pi} + \rho_s \cdot \frac{1}{\sqrt{\cos\theta_i \cos\theta_r}} \cdot \frac{\exp[-\tan^2\delta(\cos^2\phi/\alpha_x^2 + \sin^2\phi/\alpha_y^2)]}{4\pi\alpha_x\alpha_y} \qquad (12.4)$$

where

ρ_d is the diffuse reflectance

ρ_s is the specular reflectance

α_x is the standard deviation of the surface slope in the $\hat{x}$ direction

α_y is the standard deviation of the surface slope in the $\hat{y}$ direction

δ is the angle between the half vector, $\hat{h}$, and the surface normal, $\hat{n}$

ϕ is the azimuth angle of the half vector projected into the surface plane

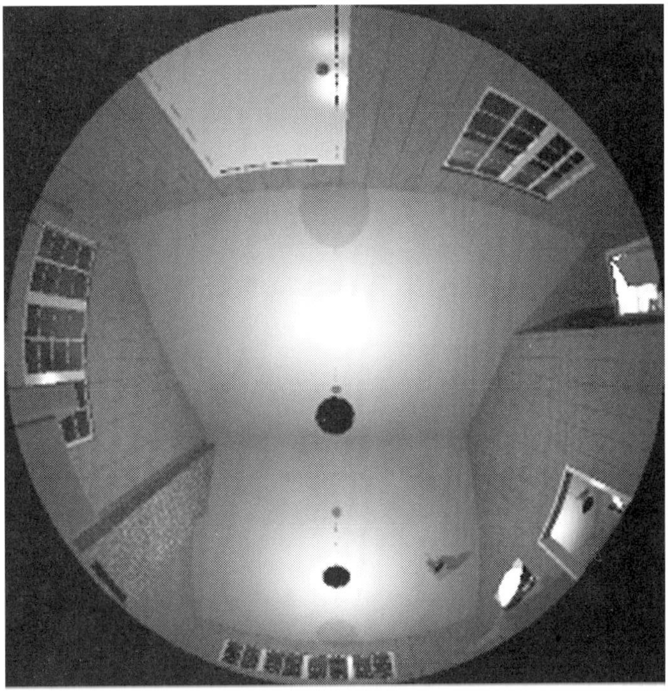

Figure 12.4 The indirect component as seen from the cabin floor.

$$\delta = \left[\frac{-\log(u_1)}{\cos^2\phi/\alpha_x^2 + \sin^2\phi/\alpha_y^2}\right]^{1/2} \qquad \textit{12.5a}$$

$$\phi = \tan^{-1}\left[\left(\frac{\alpha_y}{\alpha_x}\right)\tan(2\pi u_2)\right] \qquad \textit{12.5b}$$

where

ϕ is the azimuthal angle relative to material anisotropy

u_1, u_2 are uniform random variables in the range (0,1].

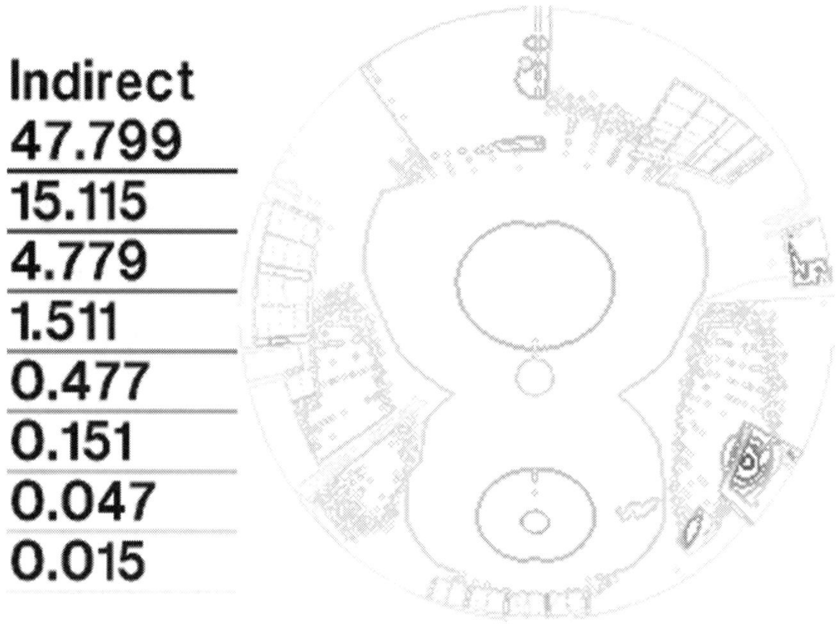

Figure 12.5 The indirect component multiplied by the reflectance function at the same scale as Figure 12.3.

The simplicity of the above formulas and the fact that they can be derived at all is a key benefit of the Gaussian reflectance models used in *Radiance*. These models were developed as approximations to measured surface reflectance data, and are guaranteed to be physically valid so long as the parameters are kept within the prescribed ranges [War92].

12.1.1 Limitations

Some materials cannot use Monte Carlo importance sampling because we have no general method for computing sample positions from arbitrary BRTDFs. The specular lobe will be sampled if the material is one of the standard *Radiance* types plastic, metal, *trans*, plastic2, metal2, or *trans2*, and the specular component is above the threshold set by the **-st** option. Specular components that belong to an arbitrary BRTDF type or are below the user-set specular threshold will be considered only during the direct and diffuse indirect calculations. That is, the assigned BRTDF will be evaluated in light source directions, then the total will be added into the diffuse indirect portion.

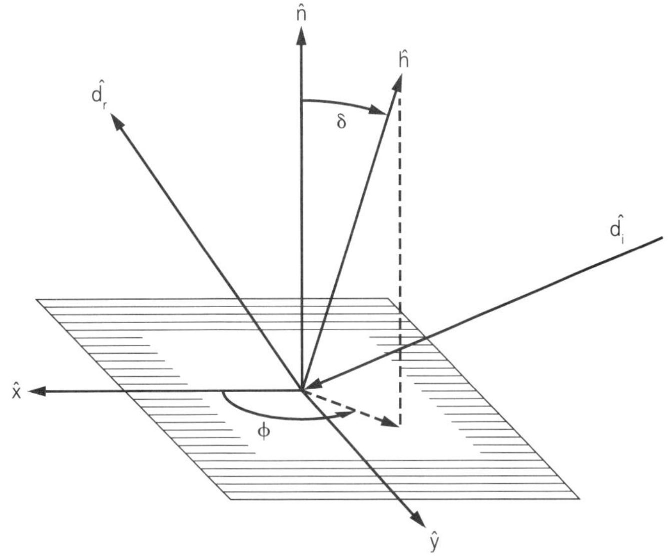

Figure 12.6 Ray reflection diagram, showing important vector directions.

The separation of reflection into diffuse and specular components, each with a constant multiplier, is a limiting approximation. Some materials do not fit this model very well because they become relatively more specular at high angles of incidence. It is impossible to model this effect in *Radiance* without compromising the energy balance of the diffuse indirect calculation, since a surface without a constant diffuse multiplier actually has no Lambertian component. As with any approximation, it is important to weigh the benefits against the costs, and the benefits of having a separable diffuse component are substantial.

12.1.2 Relation to Rendering Parameters

Two parameters control the specular indirect sampling in *Radiance:*

-st Sets the *specular threshold.* Any material whose specular component is above this threshold will have its highlight sampled by tracing a ray distributed about the transmitted or reflected direction. Materials whose specular components are less than or equal to this threshold will have this component added into the diffuse indirect calculation to maintain energy balance, but with a loss of directionality. A value of 0 means that any nonzero specular component will be sampled. A value of 1 means that no specular component will be sampled.

Reflection Models

A *reflection model* is a mathematical formula designed to mimic the light-scattering behavior of a class of materials. It may be derived from physical properties (e.g, [HTSG91]), or from fits to measured BRTDF values (e.g, [War92]). An *isotropic* model is one that has no dependency on the azimuthal orientation of the material; that is, it is rotationally invariant. Materials that fit this model include most plastics with uniform finishes and many painted surfaces. An *anisotropic* model is one that varies with the azimuthal orientation of a surface, such as brushed metal or varnished wood.

-sj Sets the *specular jitter* amount. A value of 1 means that the entire highlight will be sampled. A value of 0 means that only the highlight center will be sampled, creating artificially sharp reflections in rough specular surfaces. This may be desirable as a means to eliminate this source of variance in the image (at the cost of simulation accuracy). A value between 1 and 0 means that relatively more or less of the highlight will be sampled.

Recommended Settings

The settings used by **rad** are determined solely by the `QUALITY` variable, as follows:

`QUALITY =`	**Low**	**Med**	**High**
-st	0.5	0.1	0.01
-sj	0	0.7	1

In most cases, a specular jitter value of 1 does not cost significantly more than a lesser value and does not have any hidden drawbacks. The only problem with setting -sj to 1 is that it may increase pixel variance on some surfaces. If this is a problem, and having an artificially distinct reflection is not objectionable, this value may be reduced. As for the specular threshold, a setting around 0.1 generally ensures that metallic surfaces will have their highlights sampled and nonmetallic surfaces will not. This may be a problem for particularly dark plastics, whose highlight is relatively important even though the specular component may only be a few percent.

12.1.3 Algorithm Details and Source Code

In *Radiance*, similar material types are handled together by a designated module. Among material types with a sampled specular component, the routines to handle the types plastic, metal, and trans are in the module *src/rt/normal.c*. Routines to handle plastic2, metal2, and trans2 are in *src/rt/aniso.c*. Each of these modules has a similar structure, with a single function assigned to handle each of the three related material types. We will focus here on the workings of the *src/rt/normal.c* module, with the understanding that *src/rt/aniso.c* is mostly similar.

In *src/rt/normal.c*, there are three principal functions and one defined data structure, called `NORMDAT`. The function assigned to handle the three material types plastic, metal, and trans is `m_normal`. The material structure and the intersecting ray are passed to this function. After checking its arguments to make sure the material is at least grossly valid, `m_normal` loads a `NORMDAT` structure, which will be used in later calls to `direct` and `gaussamp`. Here are the `m_normal` and `gaussamp` routines in pseudocode:

```
m_normal(m, r) begin
        if shadow ray and not trans type then return
        check material arguments
        check for ray hitting back of material
        load NORMDAT structure nd
        if trans type then
                compute transmitted direction
                if roughness is zero then \
                        trace ray straight through
        end if
        if shadow ray then return
        if specular reflection is nonzero then
                compute reflected ray direction
                if roughness is zero then \
                        trace mirror ray
        end if
        if roughness zero and no diffuse then return
        if roughness not zero then \
                call gaussamp(r,nd)
        if diffuse reflection not zero then
                call ambient for front side
                add in ambient multiplied by diffuse refl
        end if
```

```
        if diffuse transmission not zero then
                call ambient for back side
                add in ambient multiplied by diffuse tran
        end if
        call direct(r,dirnorm,nd)
end m_normal

gaussamp(r, nd) begin
        if specular reflection and \
                        specular transmission are below \
                        -st sampling threshold then return
        compute surface coordinate axes
        if specular reflection above threshold then
                compute Monte Carlo reflected \
                        direction using -sj multiplier
                trace ray reflection
        end if
        if specular transmission above threshold then
                compute Monte Carlo transmitted \
                        direction using -sj multiplier
                trace ray transmission
        end if
end gaussamp
```

The `dirnorm` routine, also defined in *src/rt/normal.c*, is called by `direct` for each light source to compute the appropriate coefficient for each source direction and solid angle. It simply evaluates the BRTDF for the given direction, possibly using the solid angle to approximate an integral average. (The `direct` routine was given in pseudocode in Chapter 11.)

Some details have been glossed over or simplified in the above pseudocode to avoid confusion. Note the places in `m_normal` where a shadow ray is treated differently. A shadow ray is a ray traced by `direct` toward a light source for shadow testing. It is not necessary or useful to follow reflections from such a ray, so only direct transmission is considered. For materials with no transmitted component, a shadow ray always evaluates to zero.

The `m_aniso`, `diraniso`, and `agaussamp` routines in *src/rt/aniso.c* are roughly equivalent to the `m_normal`, `dirnorm`, and `gaussamp` routines we have just explained, except that they use the anisotropic reflection model and Monte Carlo sampling equations given earlier in this chapter (Equations 12.4 and 12.5).

Much of the work in computing reflection from surfaces with diffuse reflection or transmission is hidden in the call to the `ambient` routine, which we will discuss in the next section.

12.2 Indirect Irradiance Caching

After we have accounted for light source contributions and specular interreflections, we have captured the fastest-changing and therefore most visually significant components of the radiance equation. Unfortunately, we are not yet finished, because light also reflects diffusely between surfaces. Although the effects of diffuse interreflection are subtle (color bleeding, gradations in shadow regions), they are critical to the accuracy of the calculation and have an important influence on appearance in scenes with little or no direct lighting.

By *diffuse interreflection*, we specifically mean Lambertian contributions from surfaces not designated as light sources. In a standard Monte Carlo or path-tracing evaluation of the radiance equation, we would need to sample random ray directions over the hemisphere (or sphere, for diffuse transmission) at each pixel. This quickly becomes prohibitive, since it takes somewhere between 100 and 1000 rays to adequately sample the hemisphere at a given point—more if multiple interreflections are considered.

The approach taken in *Radiance* is the following: we sample the hemisphere at selected points, and interpolate values between these points. This works because the diffuse indirect component tends to change slowly over surfaces, so it is not necessary to recompute it at every pixel.

Point selection and interpolation are closely related. The interpolation algorithm searches the cached indirect irradiance values, and if none of the previously computed values are close enough to this point, a new calculation is invoked. (That is, the current point is "selected" for evaluation.) A value is "close enough" if it has a computed weight that meets the user-specified tolerance **-aa**. Before we go into detail about how values are stored and interpolated, we will first explain the basic calculation of indirect irradiance at a point.

12.2.1 Computing Indirect Irradiance

Indirect irradiance is the integral of radiance not emanating directly from light sources over the projected hemisphere. (Here, *projected* means *cosine-weighted.*) It is defined as follows:

$$E_{ind} = \iint L_{ind}(\theta_i, \phi_i) \cos\theta_i \sin\theta_i d\theta_i d\phi_i \qquad (12.6)$$

As with almost everything else in lighting, computing this quantity exactly is impossible, except in a few degenerate cases.[31] We therefore apply an approximation technique, which is Monte Carlo evaluation. We send a few hundred rays (the actual number is set by the **-ad** option) out over the hemisphere and collect the results into an average. The ray directions sampled are determined by standard Monte Carlo inversion techniques [Rub81]:

$$E = \left(\frac{\pi}{M \cdot N}\right) \sum_{j=0}^{M-1} \sum_{k=0}^{N-1} L_{j,k} \qquad (12.7)$$

where

$L_{j,k}$ is the indirect radiance in the direction $(\theta_j, \phi_k) = \left(\operatorname{asin}\sqrt{\frac{j+X_j}{M}}, 2\pi\frac{k+Y_k}{N}\right)$

X_j, Y_k are uniformly distributed random variables in the range [0,1)

$M \cdot N$ is the total number of samples and $N \approx \pi M$

Figure 12.7 shows the point locations on a hemisphere using the above sampling pattern. The lines indicate stratification boundaries; the points show where the actual rays passed through.[32] The area of each stratified region as projected onto the plane below is identical to that of every other region. This is why the rays may be given equal weight in the summation, which represents the optimal sampling condition when nothing is known about the integrand.

---

31. One such case is that in which all surfaces emit light identically and have the same diffuse reflectance value. Such a scene would be uniformly one color, and hence nothing would be visible.

32. Stratification reduces variance in a stochastic technique when applied to an integrand with some coherence, by spreading samples more evenly over the domain. Note that many other uniform sampling patterns are possible, and may even provide better coverage. This pattern was chosen for its simplicity and the simplicity of building other algorithms on top of it, such as the gradient calculation explained in the next section.

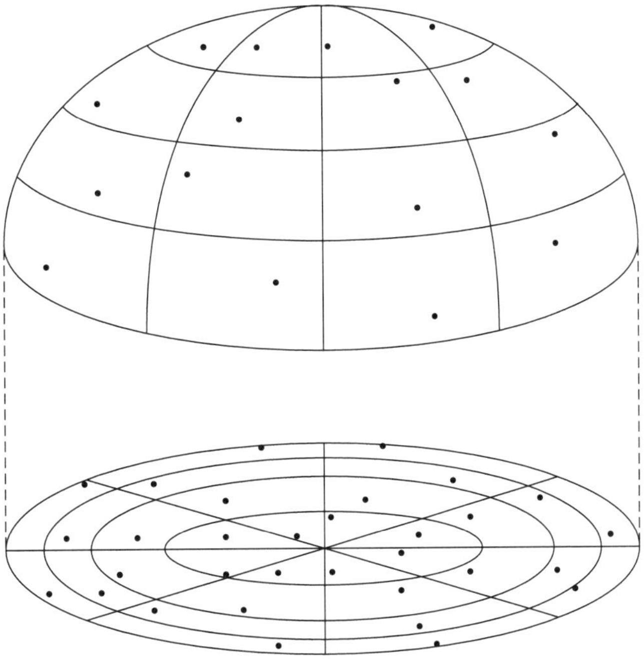

Figure 12.7 Sampling pattern used to compute indirect irradiance over the projected hemisphere.

In scenes where some light-scattering surfaces are much brighter than others, it may be more efficient to sample those regions more heavily. The **-as** option specifies a number of additional samples to send into the regions of the hemisphere with the highest variance, estimated by the difference in sample radiances taken in each neighborhood. Note that this technique is effective only if the number of initial samples (set by **-ad**) is large enough to discover all of the problem areas [KA91].

Figure 12.8 shows a hemispherical fisheye view from the floor of a conference room model. Figure 12.9 shows the values returned by about 2000 sample rays distributed according to our stratified sampling technique. Note that this number of samples is not adequate to identify objects in the scene visually, though it is more than enough to compute a good average value for indirect irradiance. Note also that the light sources in the scene appear dark. This is because we are computing *indirect* contributions, so any source that is intercepted returns zero in this part of the calculation.

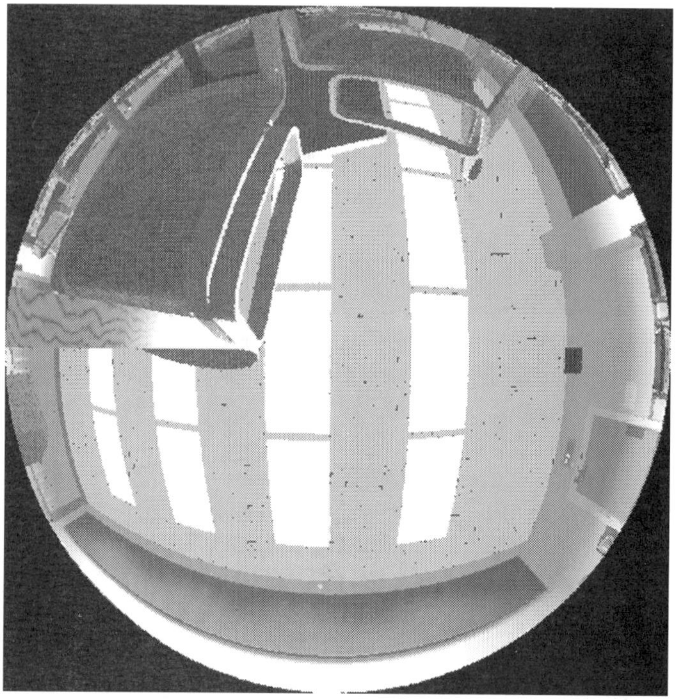

Figure 12.8 A hemispherical fisheye view from the floor of the conference room model.

In addition to computing the radiance in each direction, ray tracing also gives us the distance to each sample point, as shown in Figure 12.10. We can use this information to judge how quickly irradiance is changing over the surface, meaning we can use it to compute the gradient. The gradient is useful for improving the accuracy of our interpolation method as well as for telling us when we may need closer value spacing.

Irradiance Gradient Calculation

(The following explanation of irradiance gradients is excerpted from [WH92], which is included in its entirety on this book's CD-ROM.)

The hemispherical sampling tells us how much light is reflected from other surfaces visible from a point. The sum of these samples is simply the indirect irradiance at that point. How does this value change as we move our point from side to side or rotate our surface's orientation? If we had this information, we might be able to

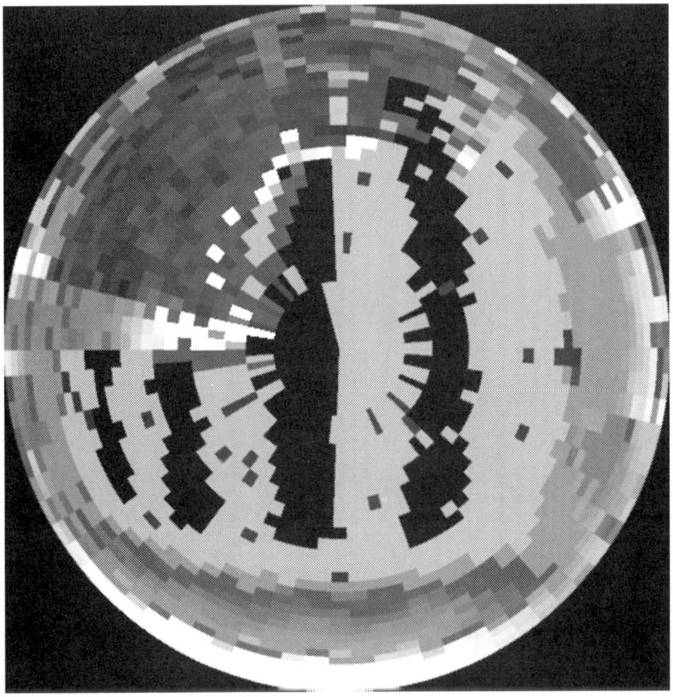

Figure 12.9 The sampling pattern used to compute the indirect irradiance value at this point.

use it to get a better approximation to nearby values, which of course we need for value interpolation. As we will see in this section, this *irradiance gradient* information is contained implicitly in our hemispherical sampling.

The irradiance gradient indicates how the irradiance field is changing as a function of position and orientation. It is the first derivative of a scalar field defined in a multidimensional space, and is usually represented as a vector. Since the irradiance in a scene is a function of five variables, three for the position and two for the direction, the irradiance gradient should be a five-dimensional vector. For computational convenience, we will compute instead two separate 3D vectors. One will correspond to the expected direction and magnitude of the *rotation gradient* and the other to the direction and magnitude of the *translation gradient*. Both gradient vectors will lie in the base plane of the sample hemisphere, which is the tangent plane of the sample. Thus, each vector will in fact represent only two degrees of freedom. This representation of the gradient is used because we

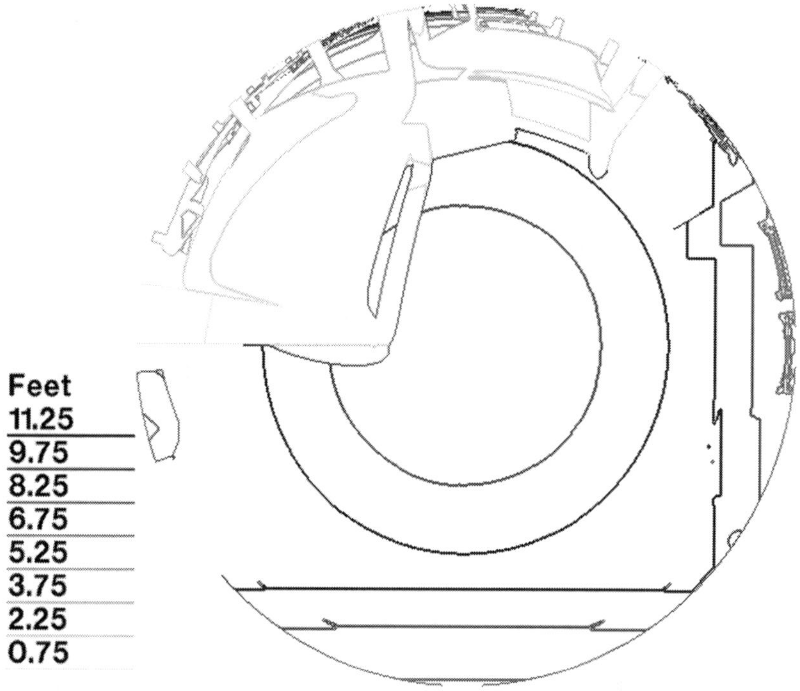

Figure 12.10 The distances to surfaces available during the sampling process.

interpolate only across a surface. Furthermore, the irradiance above and below most surfaces is discontinuous, and the gradient with respect to displacement in the polar direction is therefore undefined.

Our calculations of the rotation and translation irradiance gradients are based on very simple observations about the sampled environment. The sampling of rays over a hemisphere tells us much more than the total light falling on the surface. It tells us the distance, direction, and brightness of each contribution.

The directions and brightnesses tell us how irradiance changes as the sample hemisphere is rotated because they indicate how the cosine projection of those contributions affects the overall sum. To take a simple example, Figure 12.11(a) shows a single contributing surface. The background is assumed to be darker than the surface. If we rotate our sample hemisphere to face this surface, its contribution becomes proportionally larger than other contributions. If we rotate it away from the surface, its overall contribution is diminished. By summing over all such potential changes, we can compute the total rotation gradient for the hemisphere.

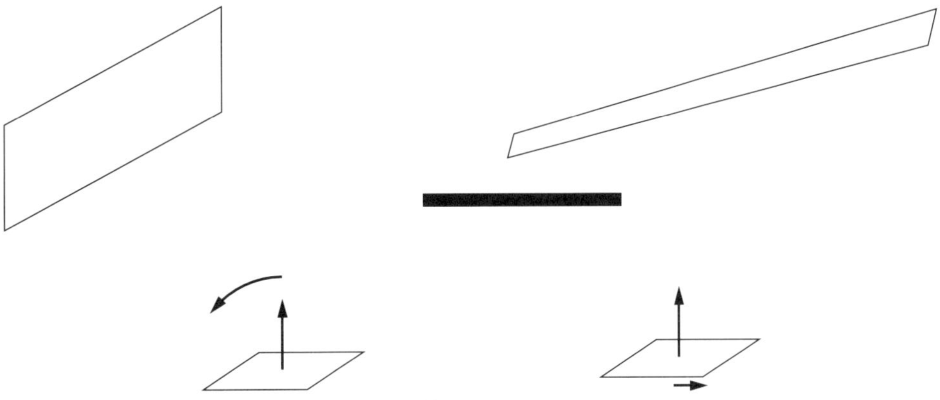

Figure 12.11 As the point in the rotation gradient example (a) rotates toward the bright surface, irradiance increases. Likewise, as the point in the translation gradient example (b) moves to the right, irradiance increases.

For the translation gradient, the distances to the contributing surfaces must be considered because occlusion plays an important role. In Figure 12.11(b), a darker surface occludes a brighter surface in the background. As the sample hemisphere is moved to the right in the diagram, the influence of the brighter background surface becomes stronger, and therefore the translation gradient is positive in this direction. By summing over all such changes, we can compute the overall gradient with respect to translation.

Figure 12.12 shows a top-down view of our hemisphere sampling pattern. The unit vectors $\boldsymbol{u}$ and $\boldsymbol{v}$ will be used to indicate the incremental gradients due to the radiance sample at point *(j,k)*.

The Rotation Gradient The rotation gradient is the partial differential of irradiance with respect to orientation. To compute this, we simply sum the differential of the cosine for each contributing sample. The formula is

$$\vec{\nabla}_r E = \frac{\pi}{M \cdot N} \sum_{k=0}^{N-1} \left\{ \hat{v}_k \sum_{j=0}^{M-1} -\tan\theta_j \cdot L_{j,k} \right\} \qquad (12.8)$$

where

$\hat{v}_k$ is the base plane unit vector in the $\phi_k + \frac{\pi}{2}$ direction

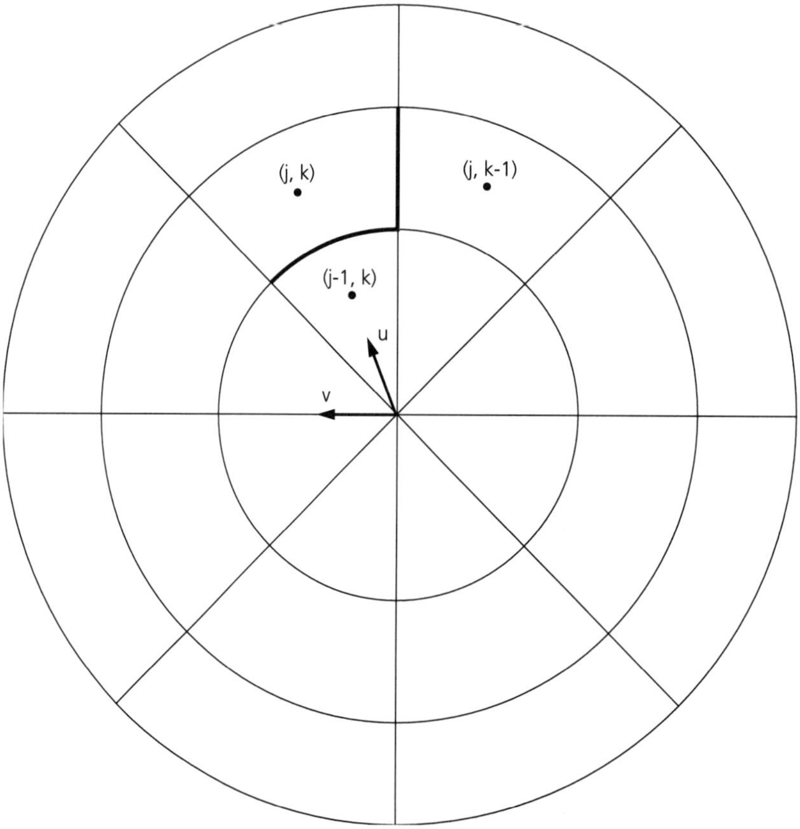

Figure 12.12 Samples and vector directions used to compute irradiance gradient.

The tangent appears in the summation because the differential of the cosine is the negative sine, and our sampling contains the cosine weighting implicitly, so it is necessary to multiply the sample values by the tangent (sine over cosine) to get back a sine weighting.

The Translation Gradient If we consider each hemisphere sample to be a little patch of known radiance at a known distance that covers an associated area, we can imagine what happens as we slide around in this environment. The patches move around according to their positions, occluding or exposing neighboring patches that are farther away, and being occluded or exposed by neighboring patches that are closer. Spend a few moments imagining this as it might take place in the hemisphere sampling shown in Figure 12.9. Of course, our samples are not the best representation of the environment, but as an approximation of irradiance they are perfectly adequate. And as an approximation to the gradient, we can suppose that each sample defines an independent patch at a certain distance.

We can approximate the gradient associated with a given hemisphere sample using the difference between it and neighboring samples, and the minimum distance along the boundary (for it is the closer boundary that appears to move faster). Looking at Figure 12.12, we can compute the gradient for the two boundaries shown in bold for sample *(j,k)*, then repeat this for each sample to get the overall sum. (Obviously, we will skip the inner border at the pole, since its length there is zero.) Here is the formula:

$$\vec{\nabla}_t E = \sum_{k=0}^{N-1} \left\{ \hat{u}_k \left(\frac{2\pi}{N}\right) \sum_{j=1}^{M-1} \frac{\sin\theta_{j_-} \cdot \cos^2\theta_{j_-}}{Min(r_{j,k}, r_{j-1,k})} \cdot (L_{j,k} - L_{j-1,k}) + \hat{v}_{k_-} \sum_{j=0}^{M-1} \frac{\sin\theta_{j_+} - \sin\theta_{j_-}}{Min(r_{j,k}, r_{j,k-1})} \cdot (L_{j,k} - L_{j,k-1}) \right\} \qquad (12.9)$$

where

$\hat{u}_k$ is the unit vector in the ϕ_k direction

$\hat{v}_{k-}$ is the unit vector in the $\phi_{k-} + \frac{\pi}{2}$ direction

θ_{j-} is the polar angle at the previous boundary, $\sin^{-1}\sqrt{\frac{j}{M}}$

θ_{j+} is the polar angle at the next boundary, $\sin^{-1}\sqrt{\frac{j+1}{M}}$

θ_{k-} is the azimuthal angle at the previous boundary, $2\pi\frac{k}{N}$

$r_{j,k}$ is the intersection distance for cell (j,k)

Though this may look nasty, computationally it is quite simple. In fact, the time required to compute the gradient is minuscule compared to the time spent tracing the actual ray samples, and the benefit is substantial. Our gradient approximation increases the value of our hemisphere samples by extracting implicit information about the environment, which we can use to improve interpolation accuracy and ensure that we are spacing our indirect calculations appropriately.

Irradiance Interpolation

(The reader is referred to [WRC88] for more detailed explanations of the following two subsections. This paper is included in printable form on the CD-ROM.)

The irradiance interpolation algorithm serves two essential purposes. The first is to interpolate between cached indirect irradiance values. The second is to determine when there are not enough values in the cache to permit interpolation, thus triggering a new hemisphere sampling at this point. In *Radiance*, we require only that a single usable value be in the cache for interpolation to take place. (It would be extrapolation in that case.)

The example in Figure 12.13 shows two previously computed indirect irradiances, *E1* and *E2*, and three sample points, A, B, and C. Point A is within the valid range of both *E1* and *E2*, and will use an interpolation of these two values. Point B is within range of *E2* only, and hence will be extrapolated from this single value. Point C is not within range of either value, so a new value will be calculated at this point, using the hemispherical sampling method. The result will then be stored in the cache for later reuse.

The dual purposes of interpolation and proximity evaluation are served very well by a weighted averaging strategy. The weights in this case are inversely proportional to the error predicted for using a particular cache value at a new position. In our example in Figure 12.13, interpolation at point A will use a weight for *E1* that is inversely proportional to the expected error of value *E1* at point A. Likewise, the weight for *E2* will be inversely proportional to its expected error at A. If a weight corresponds to an error greater than some user-specified tolerance (the -aa parameter), that cache value is not used. This defines the valid domain of a cached irradiance, which is shown as a circle around each value in our diagram.

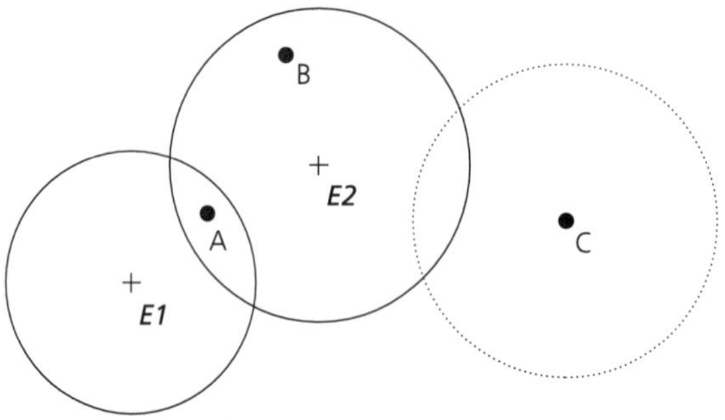

Figure 12.13 Indirect irradiances *E1* and *E2* were calculated previously and stored in the cache. Test points A and B are close enough for interpolation, but point C needs a new value.

But how can we compute the error to an unknown quantity? The best we can do is come up with a reasonable bound to the error, using some defensible assumptions. In *Radiance*, we assume the indirect environment contains no bright, concentrated sources, since these should have been treated in the direct component calculation. (Also, naive Monte Carlo sampling is a very poor way to locate such sources, so we would be in trouble even without interpolation if we did not remove them.) Here we introduce the *split sphere model*, which represents an environment with large rotation and translation irradiance gradients but with no concentrated sources. By evaluating the error in this environment, we arrive at a maximum estimate of error in arbitrary environments without concentrated sources.

The split sphere model is shown in Figure 12.14. Imagine two hollow hemispheres, one whose inside is perfectly black and one whose inside emits light at a constant level. A small surface element is placed at the center of the two hemispheres, facing their shared equator as they are brought together. We wish to evaluate the change in illumination on our surface element as it is shifted from one side to the other (the x direction), or rotated so that it sees more black or more white (the ξ angle).

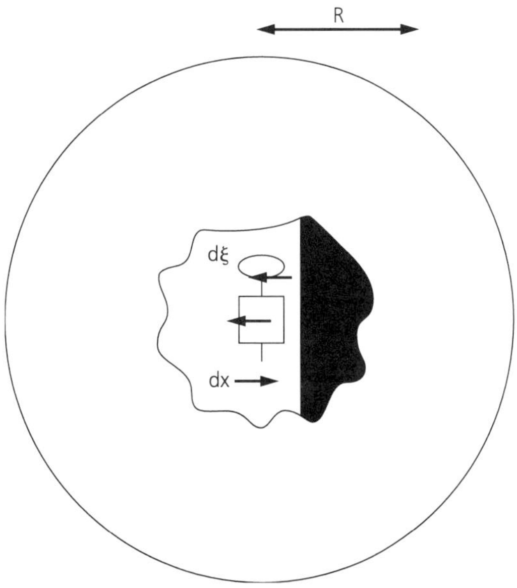

Figure 12.14 The split sphere model. A differential surface element is suspended at the center of a sphere split into light and dark hemispheres (as seen from the inside). The surface element faces the dividing line between dark and light, shown by a cutaway in this drawing.

The relative change in irradiance at our surface element due to motion in x or rotation in ξ is given by a first-order Taylor expansion based on the differential changes to the projected area of the light hemisphere:

$$\varepsilon \le \left|\frac{\partial E}{\partial x}(x - x_0) + \frac{\partial E}{\partial \xi}(\xi - \xi_0)\right| \tag{12.10}$$

$$\varepsilon \le \frac{4E}{\pi R}|x - x_0| + E|\xi - \xi_0|$$

Since our premise was that our environment behaves no worse than the split sphere model, we wish to generalize the above formula to translation or rotation in any direction. We accomplish this by replacing our independent variables with vector-derived quantities where motion in any direction or rotation about any angle produces an error similar to x and ξ above:

$$\varepsilon(\vec{P}) \le \frac{4}{\pi}E\frac{\|\vec{P} - \vec{P}_0\|}{R_0} + E\sqrt{2 - 2\vec{N}(\vec{P}) \cdot \vec{N}(\vec{P}_0)} \tag{12.11}$$

where

$\vec{N}(\vec{P})$ = surface normal at position $\vec{P}$

$\vec{P}_0$ = surface element location

E = illuminance at $\vec{P}_0$

R_0 = average distance to surfaces at $\vec{P}_0$

The average distance R_0 in the above equation is computed as the harmonic mean (reciprocal mean reciprocal) of distances determined during Monte Carlo sampling of the hemisphere. The reason for using a harmonic mean instead of a straight mean is that the value appears in the denominator, and averaging this way distributes the mean over the sum correctly.

As we have mentioned before, we apply the inverse of error in a weighted average of indirect irradiance:

$$E(\vec{P}) = \frac{\sum_{i \in s} w_i(\vec{P}) E_i(\vec{P})}{\sum_{i \in s} w_i(\vec{P})} \tag{12.12}$$

where

$$w_i(\vec{P}) = \frac{1}{\frac{\|\vec{P} - \vec{P}_i\|}{R_i} + \sqrt{1 - \vec{N}(\vec{P}) \cdot \vec{N}(\vec{P}_i)}}$$

$E_i(\vec{P})$ = computed illuminance at $\vec{P}_i$ extrapolated to $\vec{P}$

R_i = harmonic mean distance to objects visible from $\vec{P}_i$

$S = \{i : w_i \vec{P} > 1/a\}$

a = user selected constant

Note that we have dropped the constants in our error estimate, since they were valid only for the split sphere and are reasonably close to each other and to unity. Using the above weighted average, we are guaranteed not to introduce error greater than 1.4 times a in the split sphere environment. Other environments may be worse if they have concentrated sources not accounted for in the direct calculation, but the error will still be proportional to a. Thus, we have given the user a means to control the calculation error via a method for spacing and interpolating values that targets accuracy, rather than being purely heuristic. Furthermore, point locations can be arbitrary, so no meshing is required and no restrictions are placed on the scene geometry.

The value of $E_i(\boldsymbol{P})$ in Equation 12.12 is extrapolated from the cached irradiance at $\boldsymbol{P_i}$ and its associated gradient, and is computed as follows:

$$E_i(\vec{P}) = E_i + (\hat{n}_i \times \hat{n}) \,.\, \vec{\nabla}_r E_i + (\vec{P} - \vec{P}_i) \,.\, \vec{\nabla}_t E_i \tag{12.13}$$

where

$\vec{P}$ is the test point position

$\hat{n}$ is the surface normal at the test point

E_i is the irradiance value at sample i

$\vec{P}_i$ is the position of sample i

$\hat{n}_i$ is the surface normal at sample i

Why, if we have an expression for the gradient at each cached irradiance point, do we use the split sphere model for our weights? Why not just use the computed gradient as the error estimate and use that to compute the weights? We certainly could, but remember that the split sphere was estimating worst-case error, not actual error, and there are good reasons to prefer it. There will be places where the gradient is small even though there are nearby surfaces, simply because the surfaces have close to the same brightness. If we use this small gradient as our error estimate, we may end up using the cached irradiance value far from its original calculation point, where the gradient estimate may be way off because of a large second derivative. The split sphere model avoids this by overestimating the gradient where the second derivative may be large, thus spacing values more closely.

We may still want to use the gradient as a criterion in places where the computed gradient is larger than that predicted by the split sphere. This is a rare condition in practice, but when it arises, it is good to respond with denser value spacing. This highlights a basic principle of good sampling, which can be stated as follows:

Start with as many samples as you think you need to handle the worst case.
When you fail to converge, sample some more.

Sending ample initial samples is very important, because if you miss something at the beginning, there is no way later even to discover that it is missing [KA91].

The Irradiance Cache

So far, we have discussed the calculation of indirect irradiance and its gradient from hemisphere samples, and have noted that these values may be interpolated without regard to meshing or surface representation. However, we have not mentioned how the values are stored, or how the set S in Equation 12.12 is determined. Presumably, we are caching a great many of these values, so if we have to search through the entire list every time we interpolate, our algorithm is going to lose.

We could follow the course applied in radiosity algorithms and associate the values with surface positions, perhaps using a grid structure for indexing. This would provide us with quick lookup, but it would also introduce some new difficulties. We would need to restrict our geometry to primitives that could be sensibly divided into a *(u,v)* coordinate space. Spheres, a favorite for ray tracing, are problematic in this regard, as are many other shapes. Another drawback of surface association is that a given indirect irradiance value might be useful on more than one surface.

Take the case of a landscape that has been tessellated into many small polygons on a mesh. Adjacent polygons, if the landscape is fairly smooth, will have very similar indirect irradiances, and requiring a separate calculation for each would be overkill. If we tie our value lookup to surfaces, it is very difficult to share values with nearby surfaces. Finally, we have the general problem of partitioning a surface with irregularly spaced values that have very different valid domains. Plate 25 shows the indirect irradiance point locations for a simple scene with three blocks. It would be challenging to construct a partition of the floor surface that would provide convenient lookup of nearby irradiance values. A Delaunay triangulation might work, but making incremental changes to such a mesh as new calculation points are added is tricky [Hec94, p. 24], and looking up values without actually breaking the surface into smaller polygons (which would be wasteful of memory) is time-consuming.

For these and other reasons, we chose a more general approach for 3D range searching using an octree to determine the set *S*. This is not the same octree that is used to sort surfaces for ray intersection, but another data structure that is completely independent of the scene geometry. This way, we minimize constraints on the geometric representation while optimizing the search for nearby indirect irradiance values.

The idea for each octree node is to have a list of indirect irradiances whose centers are in the corresponding cube and whose valid domains are proportional to the cube size. Searching through the octree involves looking at all cubes that might contain values whose domains contain the point *P* in question. Figure 12.15 shows an example association between values and octree nodes where the cube size is greater than twice but not more than four times the valid domain radii of contained values. (The valid domain is equal to the harmonic mean distance to hemisphere samples, R_i, times the user-specified accuracy value, *a*.)

The recursive search algorithm can be described in pseudocode as follows (this is the `sumambient` routine mentioned in the source code section at the end of the chapter):

```
foreach value at this node
       if wi(P) > 1/a and di(P) >= 0 then
              include value
       end if
end foreach
foreach child node
       if P is within half the child's size \
                     of its cube boundary then
              search child node
       end if
end foreach
```

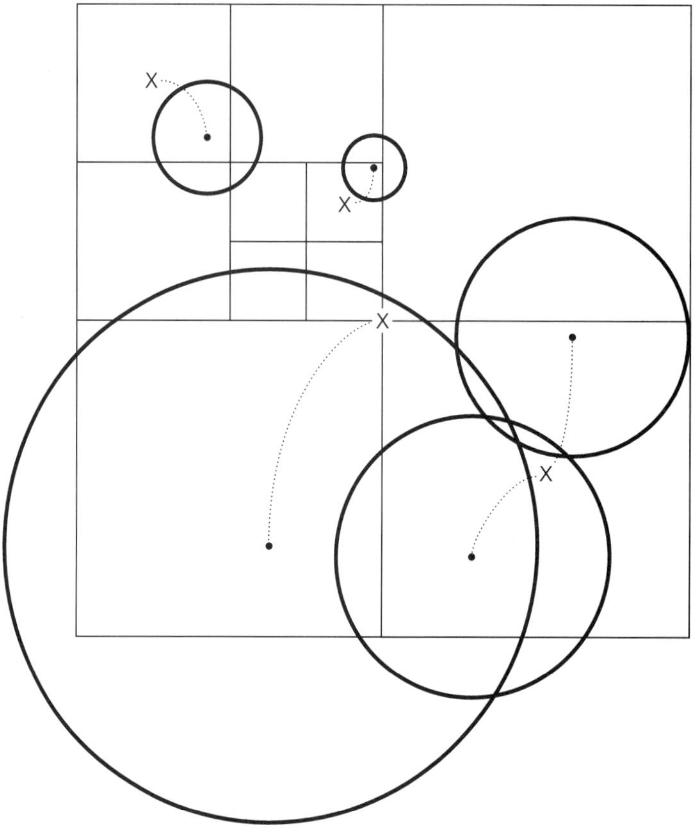

Figure 12.15 Five indirect values are shown with their respective domains (circles) linked by dotted lines to their respective octree nodes (squares).

This algorithm searches not only the octree nodes containing the point *P*, but any octree node with a boundary within half its side length of *P*. This guarantees that all relevant cached irradiances will be examined. Because of the loose fit of the octree and the fact that $w_i(\mathbf{P})$ depends on other things besides the distance to a value, many irrelevant cached values will also be examined. The ratio between octree node size and valid domain may be reduced and fewer irrelevant values will be examined, but more nodes will be empty and therefore the amount of searching will be roughly the same.

Besides caching these values in memory, it is often a good idea to store them on disk so they can be reused for later renderings. The **-af** rendering option provides this facility. In fact, the same file and values may be used simultaneously by multiple rendering processes. Consistency is maintained by the network lock manager.[33]

33. The network lock manager is not available or working on all operating systems. If you have trouble sharing ambient files between multiple processes or using **rpiece**, the operating system is probably at fault.

(This is discussed in some detail in Chapter 15.) Using the AMBFILE variable in rad also allows what is called an *overture calculation*, which populates a scene with indirect values prior to rendering by making a low-resolution first pass over the image and throwing away the results. This increases interpolation accuracy and smoothness significantly at a very modest expense, and is highly recommended.

Multiple Diffuse Reflections

What about multiple reflections between surfaces? How does indirect irradiance caching affect this? Do we have to do anything special?

Diffuse interreflections in *Radiance* are limited to a maximum depth, set by the **-ab** option. Since diffuse interreflections are expensive to calculate and in many cases do not affect the distribution of illumination after one or two bounces, it makes sense to limit them separately. This also provides a simple means of turning the interreflection calculation off when it is not needed or desired, by setting -ab to 0.

While indirect irradiance caching results in big savings for a single-bounce calculation, it results in huge savings for multiple-bounce calculations. Without caching, our initial hemisphere samples would each go out and spawn many additional samples, proportional to the number of initial samples *to the power of the number of bounces*. Caching avoids such geometric growth in the calculation by storing and reusing values at each level, keeping the number of higher-order samples to a minimum.

The only special modification we must make to our algorithm is to keep track of what recursion level a value corresponds to. We can do this either by keeping separate lists for each level or by storing a number corresponding to the recursion level in our data structure and testing against it as part of determining whether or not to use a particular value. We chose the latter approach because it minimizes storage and permits us to easily use lower levels for higher values when the opportunity arises. (It usually does not, because we must calculate our higher levels first in order to get our lower-level values.)

Figure 12.16 illustrates what happens when *Radiance* computes multiple interreflections. Deeper levels in the ray tree end up spawning new indirect calculations only when there are no nearby values cached. This happens relatively less frequently as the calculation goes on and the deeper levels become sated. Additional optimizations in the calculations reduce the number of hemisphere samples by 50% at

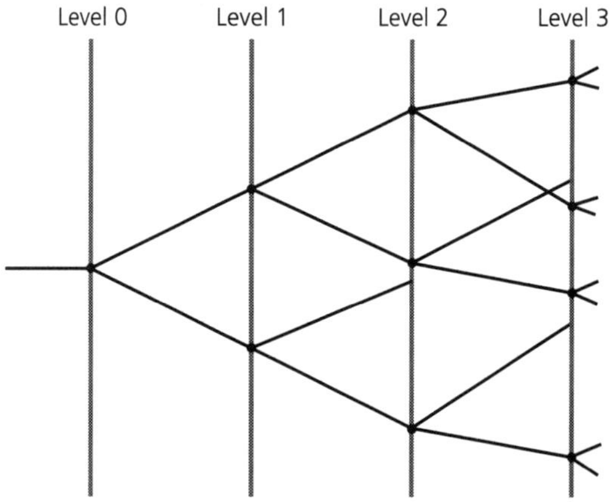

Figure 12.16 The lines represent rays, and the points represent indirect evaluations. The rays that reuse cached values do not propagate.

each higher level and increase the effective value of the target interpolation accuracy by 40%, because the effect on the final error decreases by the average surface reflectance each time. (We assume the average reflectance to be about 50%.)

Figure 12.17 shows how this works in a three-bounce calculation. When the calculation starts out, the deepest level is being filled. As level 3 reaches saturation, level 2 begins to fill. Eventually, the initial level starts to fill up, though it never constitutes the bulk of the calculation because only as many values as are needed for the particular view are computed.

Constant Ambient Approximation

Obviously, we cannot calculate an infinite number of interreflections no matter how efficiently we go about it. In most cases, the light being reflected is more or less uniform after one or two bounces anyway. That is why, in *Radiance*, we apply a constant approximation to interreflection after the requested number of bounces has been computed. This ambient value is set by the **-av** option, given in units of watts/steradian/m^2. It corresponds to the average radiance measured in all directions over the visible scene (excluding light sources) and is used in place of a locally computed average from hemisphere samples.

The actual ambient approximation used in the calculation may not be a constant, but may instead be a moving geometric average computed from the user-specified ambient value and the accumulation of all indirect irradiances computed so far. As the calculation progresses, the ambient approximation gradually becomes more accurate and the initial -av value becomes less important. However, if the

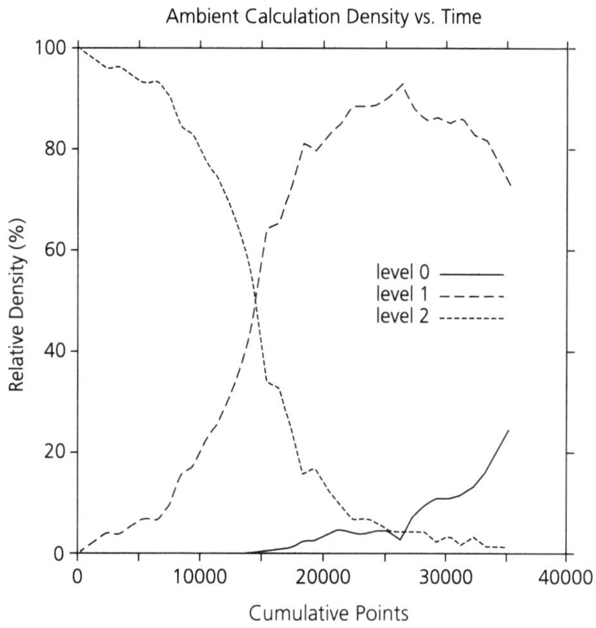

Figure 12.17 This plot shows the relative computation time spent on each level of the interreflection tree as the calculation progresses.

initial value contained large errors, some of the indirect values cached early on may be too high or too low, resulting in a few lighter or darker areas. The **-aw** option controls this moving-average process. The initial value carries the integer weight given by this parameter, and all indirect irradiance values are given unit weight in a weighted geometric average (moving as new indirect values are added). If this value is set to 0, the initial value is always used. This is preferable in scenes where some areas are very much brighter than the area of interest, since indirect irradiance computed in those brighter areas might otherwise "leak" into the darker regions. Using a geometric mean rather than an arithmetic mean reduces the likelihood of this, but it still happens in some circumstances.

12.2.2 Diffuse Illumination

Another use for the indirect irradiance calculation is to handle very large light sources, especially distant sources such as the sky. Even though we know the sky to be a significant source of illumination, and do not need an interreflection calculation to determine its brightness, it is difficult to treat it properly as part of the direct component. This is because it is so widespread that determining the associated (very weak) shadow is both expensive and wasteful if undertaken at each pixel. If we use the glow material type instead of light in our sky definition, we can avoid sending large numbers of shadow rays and take advantage of the more thorough, but less frequent, hemisphere sampling and value caching of the indirect calculation.

Another example of putting light sources into the indirect calculation is when they are very large and uniform, as with a luminous ceiling system. Rather than describing the ceiling as one big light source, use the glow material type with an active distance of zero. The illumination will then be considered as part of the interreflection calculation, with a significant reduction in computation time and most probably an improvement in appearance as well.

12.2.3 Limitations

As with any optimization, there are times when the indirect irradiance caching algorithm runs into trouble. Most radiosity calculations have a serious problem with "light leaks." These are places where the illumination sneaks under an obstructing surface during interpolation. A floor polygon near an outside wall in a scene with daylight may, for example, look too bright near the corner because values are being interpolated from the other side of the wall, where it is much brighter. This tends to happen less often in *Radiance* than in radiosity programs, because interreflection values are adaptively spaced closer and closer together on inside corners and in cramped places. It can still happen, though, under certain conditions.

Figure 12.18 shows a classic case in which light leaks can happen in *Radiance*. Because the two indicated points are so far away from the structure, they have very large valid domains, and may accidentally be used for the floor inside the building, whereas the nearby values have smaller domains that would prevent it. The solution is to set the **-ar** (ambient resolution) value correctly. The ambient resolution controls the minimum distance under which the interpolation accuracy is allowed to gradually degrade. When you use this option, the minimum spacing between cached values is the maximum scene dimension divided by the ambient resolution times the ambient accuracy. The -ar parameter limits not only the minimum distance between cached values, but also the *maximum distance*, which is set to 64 times the scene size over the ambient resolution (except when -ar is 0). Placing a limit on the maximum distance avoids the problem we have just illustrated by forcing additional calculations over the exterior ground plane.

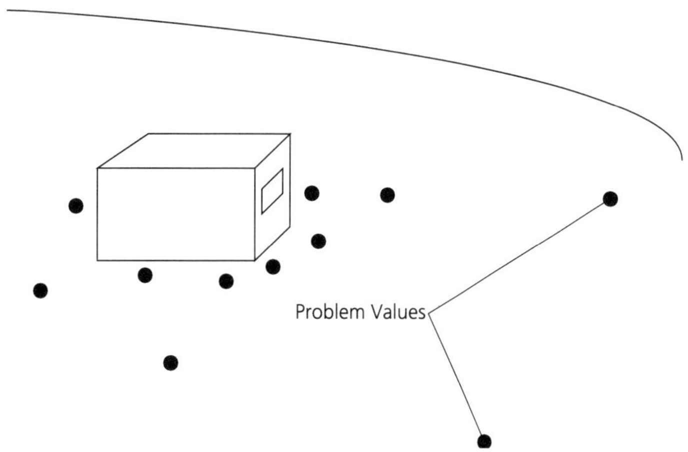

Figure 12.18 A typical scene with potential light leaks in *Radiance*. The points show cached indirect irradiance values. The ones farthest from the building geometry are most likely to cause problems, since they see no nearby surfaces.

Another, more common problem arises in scenes with very high detail, such as a forest or a library full of bookshelves. Such a scene would require hundreds of thousands, if not millions, of indirect irradiance values to accurately portray the illumination on all the surfaces. In many cases, the indirect illumination of these small surfaces is of minor consequence in the overall calculation, and a constant ambient approximation would suffice in these areas. So that interreflection may still be considered on more important surfaces, *Radiance* offers the **-ai**, **-aI**, **-ae**, and **-aE** options to specify materials to include in, or exclude from, the indirect calculation. Surfaces made of the named materials will be included or excluded from indirect irradiance computation and caching, depending on the setting.

Sometimes interreflection is desired even on these detailed areas. In these cases, the -ar option can be used to limit the number of values cached, or caching and interpolation may be turned off entirely by setting -aa to 0. This generally necessitates a small setting for the number of initial samples (-ad) to keep the problem tractable. The drawback here is greater noise, but in a scene with many thousands or millions of tiny surfaces, the noise may not be noticeable.

12.2.4 Relation to Rendering Parameters

Several parameters control the "ambient" calculation in *Radiance:*

-av Sets the constant *ambient value* approximation to the given RGB radiance. This corresponds to the average radiance in all directions in the visible scene, in watts/steradian/m^2. If irradiance caching is taking place, the given constant will be moderated by a moving average with the cached values. As more values are computed, the original setting will have less and less influence.

-aw Sets the *ambient weight* for the given ambient value to the specified integer. The initial value set with the -av option will dominate the internal calculation until this number of new indirect irradiances has been computed, at which point the computed values will begin to dominate. A value of 0 turns the moving average computation off, so that the initial value is always used. This is often necessary in scenes with wildly varying indirect contributions, which might give splotchy results if a true global average were employed.

-ab Sets the number of *ambient bounces* to the specified integer. This many diffuse interreflections will be calculated before the constant ambient value will replace a hemispherical sampling and/or interpolation. A setting of 0 turns the interreflection calculation off.

-ad Sets the number of *ambient divisions*, which is how many initial samples will be sent out over the divided (stratified) hemisphere. Increasing this value improves the accuracy of the calculated indirect irradiances and is necessary in a scene with a lot of brightness variation.

-as Sets the number of *ambient supersamples*. This is the number of extra rays that will be used to sample areas in the divided hemisphere that appear to have high variance. Supersampling improves accuracy significantly in scenes with large bright and dark regions by carefully sampling the shadow boundaries. It is rarely useful to specify more supersamples than initial ambient divisions. In scenes with a lot of small detail, it is better to put the extra samples into the divisions and leave the supersamples at 0.

-aa Sets the *ambient accuracy* to the specified fraction. This is the maximum error permitted in the indirect irradiance interpolation, and is generally less than 0.3. (Note that this would allow up to 30% error in the indirect calculation, not in the overall calculation, which depends heavily on direct contributions.) Smaller values result in closer spacing of indirect calculations, at a commensurate cost. A setting of 0 turns indirect irradiance caching off.

-ar Sets the *ambient resolution* to the given integer. This setting is akin to a universal grid resolution in a more conventional radiosity calculation. The accuracy of the indirect interpolation will start to relax at distances less than the maximum scene size divided by this number. This setting places a lower bound on the variable R_i (see Equation 12.12) to avoid overkill on unimportant geometric detail. (It also places an upper limit on R_i—see the section entitled Limitations, above, for a discussion.) A setting of 0 allows R_i to take on any value.

-af Stores cached values to the named *ambient file*. This provides a convenient mechanism for sharing indirect irradiances in multiple invocations of rpict, rtrace, and rview. On systems with a working network lock manager, values may even be shared between simultaneously active processes over the network. The *Radiance* program **lookamb** can be used to examine or translate the contents of this portable binary file.

-ae Adds the named material to the *ambient exclude* list. Any surfaces modified by this material are excluded from the indirect irradiance caching and receive the constant ambient value approximation instead. This is an effective way to avoid wasting time on minor geometric detail. Additional materials may be given by additional -ae and -aE options. See the **rpict** or **rtrace** manual pages for descriptions of these and the complimentary -ai and -aI options.

Recommended Settings

Setting these parameters correctly is very important, because they affect both rendering quality and time dramatically. Unfortunately, finding the optimal values is not easy and requires some understanding of the underlying algorithms, as well as knowledge of the scene being rendered and the desired output quality. Fortunately, this is the sort of intelligence built into the rad program, with the required scene information distilled into its more intuitive input variables.

The rad input variables that influence the ambient parameter settings are `QUALITY`, `INDIRECT`, `VARIABILITY`, `DETAIL`, `ZONE`, and `EXPOSURE`. In addition, the `AMBFILE` variable is used to indicate an ambient file for the -af option.

The EXPOSURE setting determines the -av parameter, which is set to 0.5/EXPOSURE. If EXPOSURE is not set, a -av value of 0.01 is used for interior zones and 10.0 is used for exterior zones.

Because of the interrelated nature of the variables and parameters, we show the rad settings in a slightly different format in Table 12.1.

	QUALITY = Low	QUALITY = Med	QUALITY = High
	-ab 0	-ab *I*	-ab *I*+*1*
DET = Lo	-ar 4*d*	-ar 8*d*	-ar 16*d*
DET = Med	-ar 8*d*	-ar 16*d*	-ar 32*d*
DET = Hi	-ar 16*d*	-ar 32*d*	-ar 64*d*
VAR = Lo	-aa .4 -ad 64	-aa .3 -ad 128	-aa .25 -ad 256
VAR = Med	-aa .25 -ad 196 -as 0	-aa .2 -ad 400 -as 64	-aa .15 -ad 768 -as 196
VAR = Hi	-aa .15 -ad 256 -as 0	-aa .125 -ad 512 -as 256	-aa .08 -ad 1024 -as 512

Table 12.1 Parameter settings corresponding to rad input variables where *I* represents the integer setting of the INDIRECT variable and *d* represents the maximum scene size divided by the average ZONE dimension.

In certain pathological scenes, even setting VARIABILITY to High is not enough to sample the indirect component adequately. In such scenes, the render variable can be used to override the rad parameter settings. The render variable is also convenient for setting -ae and -aE options, which are not controlled by rad.

An example of a problem scene might be a forest, where any kind of irradiance caching will get out of hand. To avoid interreflection calculations on the trees, we can use the render option to name some excluded materials, like this:

```
render= -ae tree_bark -ae leaf_mat
```

If, instead, we want interreflection to be done everywhere but without caching, we can use the following settings instead:

```
render= -aa 0 -ad 16 -as 0
```

Setting -aa to 0 turns off caching, which requires that we reduce the number of hemisphere samples so that the calculation will finish in a reasonable time.

12.2.5 Algorithm Details and Source Code

There are two main modules that implement the diffuse indirect calculation in *Radiance*, *src/rt/ambient.c* and *src/rt/ambcomp.c*. A header file, *src/rt/ambient.h*, and an additional input/output module, *src/rt/ambio.c*, are also shared with the lookamb program. The *src/rt/ambient.c* module contains routines for caching and interpolating indirect irradiances. The *src/rt/ambcomp.c* module contains routines for sampling the hemisphere and computing the indirect irradiance gradients.

Most material functions see only a single call interface, `ambient(acol,r)`, which returns the ambient color for an intersected ray. It does this either by using the irradiance caching method we have discussed, or by using a modified `ambient_value`, which is computed from the sum of the `nav` indirect values computed so far (`avsum`) and the -av and -aw settings as follows:

```
if aw == 0 then
       ambient_value = av
else
       ambient_value = exp ((aw * Log(av) + avsum)/(aw + nav)
```

The `ambient` routine is defined in *src/rt/ambient.c*, and given in pseudocode here:

```
ambient(acol, r) begin
       if -ad is zero or #bounces >= -ab or \
                            material is excluded then
              set acol = ambient_value
              return
       end if
       if -aa is zero then
              call doambient(acol,r,..)
              return
       end if
       call sortambvals(0)
       call sumambient(acol,r,..)
       if successful then return
```

```
        call makeambval(acol,r,..)
        if successful then return
        set acol = ambient_value
end ambient
```

Obviously, most of the actual work is carried out in other routines. The procedure `doambient` computes the indirect irradiance and (optionally) the irradiance gradients. It is also called by `makeambval`, which stores the results in the cache octree. The `sumambient` function attempts to interpolate indirect irradiance from cached values, returning nonzero if successful. Finally, the `sortambvals` procedure periodically re-sorts the cache to optimize virtual-memory performance when the number of stored values is large.

Two principal data structures are employed by the indirect caching routines:

- `AMBTREE atrunk;`
  This is the base of the octree holding all the cached indirect irradiance values. Each node contains a list of cached values at this cube and/or a pointer to eight child nodes (an array of eight `AMBTREE` structures). The location and size of the global octree cube are identical to those of the scene octree, which is stored in the global variable `thescene`.
- `typedef struct ambrec AMBVAL;`
  This is the basic structure in which indirect irradiances are stored. As well as the indirect value itself (a *Radiance* color), there are fields for the 3D position and surface normal vectors associated with the sample point. Also stored here is the harmonic mean distance to other surfaces determined during hemisphere sampling, the associated recursion level and sample weight, and the translation and rotation gradient vectors.

Let's start with a brief introduction of the routines in *src/rt/ambcomp.c*, which sample the hemisphere and compute the actual indirect irradiance value and its gradients:

- `double doambient(COLOR acol, RAY *r, double wt, FVECT pg, FVECT dg);`
  This function computes the indirect irradiance for the ray intersection stored in `r` and returns the harmonic mean distance to other surfaces, or zero if the calculation fails for some reason. If the vector pointers `pg` and `dg` are non-NULL, `doambient` also computes the translation and rotation gradients. The routine `inithemi` is called to compute the number of samples to use over the hemisphere based on the sample weight, `wt`, and `divsample` is called to compute each ray sample. If supersampling is done, `comperrs` is called to estimate the error at each hemisphere division. If gradients are requested, `posgradient` and `dirgradient` are called to compute the translation and rotation gradients.

- `void inithemi(AMBHEMI *hp, RAY *r, double wt);`
  Computes the number of divisions to use over polar and azimuthal directions based on the sample weight and the user's -ad setting. Sets up the coordinate axes needed for vector generation in `divsample`.
- `int divsample(AMBSAMP *dp, AMBHEMI *h, RAY *r);`
  Computes a ray sample for the given `dp` structure on the given hemisphere `h` from the given parent ray, `r`. Returns 0 on success, or −1 if `rayorigin` indicates some limit has been reached.
- `void comperrs(AMBSAMP da[], AMBHEMI *hp);`
  Estimates variance for each ambient sample in the array `da` corresponding to the sampling hemisphere `hp`. It does this by computing the average difference between each value and its neighbors.
- `void dirgradient(FVECT gv, AMBSAMP da[], AMBHEMI *hp);`
  Computes the rotation gradient vector `gv` for the ambient samples `da` over the hemisphere `hp`. This is a straightforward implementation of Equation 12.8, given earlier in this chapter.
- `void posgradient(FVECT gv, AMBSAMP da[], AMBHEMI *hp);`
  Computes the translation gradient vector `gv` for the ambient samples `da` over the hemisphere `hp`. This is a straightforward implementation of Equation 12.9, also given earlier in this chapter.

The following procedures are contained in *src/rt/ambient.c*, and are called by the `ambient` routine to cache and interpolate indirect irradiance values:

- `double makeambient(COLOR acol, RAY *r, int al);`
  Computes and caches an indirect irradiance value at the ray intersection point of `r` and ambient bounce level `al`. Calls `doambient`, to sample the hemisphere and compute the associated gradients, and `avsave`, to store the resulting `AMBVAL` structure in the octree `atrunk`. Returns the harmonic mean distance to visible surfaces, or zero if unsuccessful.
- `void avsave(AMBVAL *av);`
  Calls `avstore` to store the passed ambient value in its own allocated memory and inserts the result into the octree `atrunk` with a call to `avinsert`. If an ambient file has been opened (-af option), `writeambval` is called. If `AMBFLUSH` calls have been made since the last file sync, `ambsync` is then called to update the ambient file.
- `void avinsert(AMBVAL *av);`
  Insert the ambient value `av` into the octree `atrunk`. To do this, we simply descend the tree looking for the cube that contains the sample point associated with `av` and has the correct size relative to the associated value radius. (This routine is given in pseudocode in the Irradiance Cache section of this chapter.) New nodes are created as necessary along the way.

- `int ambsync();`
  If the target operating system does not support network file locking, this is merely a call to the `flush` library routine and a resetting of the `nunflshed` variable. For systems with file locking, `ambsync` permits the sharing of ambient files and values among multiple, simultaneous invocations of the rendering programs. It accomplishes this by first checking to see if the ambient file has grown in size. If it has, `ambsync` reads in the new indirect values (which must have come from other running processes) before writing out its own buffer. A write lock is put on the file during this operation to avoid contention and race conditions.
- `double sumambient(COLOR acol, RAY *r, int al, AMBTREE *at, FVECT c0, double s);`
  This recursive function searches the octree node `at` and its children, looking for usable indirect irradiance values. Such values are modified by their gradients by `extambient`, multiplied by their respective weights, and added into `acol`. `Sumambient` returns the sum of all these weights plus the sum of all recursive calls to itself. Zero is returned if no suitable values are found in the cache.
- `void sortambvals(int always);`
  The purpose of this routine is to sort cached `AMBVAL` structures by most recent access, so as to minimize thrashing in virtual memory environments. The Boolean parameter `always` indicates whether rebuilding the octree is mandatory or not. If not, sorting takes place only if the `ambclock` variable has been incremented `sortintvl` times since the last sort. The variable `sortintvl` itself doubles on each successive sort, to reduce the frequency of sorting as the process continues. Each `AMBVAL` structure contains a `latick` member that is set to the `ambclock` value at the time of its last use by `sumambient`. This is used as the key for the sort.

12.3 Conclusion

In this chapter, we have described the accounting of indirect specular and diffuse light components in *Radiance*. It is especially important to understand the indirect diffuse component calculation in order to set sensible values for the associated rendering parameters. Although these are controlled to some extent by the rad program, there are always circumstances under which it is beneficial to override these settings to arrive at a more efficient, quicker, or more accurate result.

In cases where the assumptions of the diffuse irradiance computation are not met, specifically where there are bright, concentrated sources of indirect illumination, the performance of these algorithms will never be satisfactory. In such cases, it is usually necessary to reclassify these sources back into the direct component calculation. The next chapter, on secondary light sources, explains how this is done.

CHAPTER 13

Secondary Light Sources

In the last two chapters we have discussed the direct calculation, which handles concentrated sources of illumination that are identified a priori, and the indirect calculation, which handles large, diffuse, and unknown illumination sources. What happens, though, when there is a concentrated source of illumination that *Radiance* does not know about ahead of time? Perhaps there is a window with translucent curtains, or a skylight that is not itself the source of illumination but is relatively smaller and brighter than the rest of the environment. If we treat this as part of the indirect calculation, we violate one of that algorithm's key assumptions, which is that concentrated sources are accounted for elsewhere (in the direct calculation).

Figure 13.1 shows an interior space illuminated via a window and a reflecting skylight. Daylight enters the skylight and, after being reflected internally, exits through a diffuser mounted in the ceiling. The only explicit light source in this scene is the sun (since we treat the sky as a *glow* source).

In order to understand this calculation, we must think the way *Radiance* does—in terms of view rays going out in search of light sources. Looking at the surfaces of this room, *Radiance* will first send shadow rays to the sun to check for obstructions, which will in most cases be blocked by the walls and ceiling. Next, we will send out hemisphere (diffuse indirect) samples, hoping to hit something bright. A few of

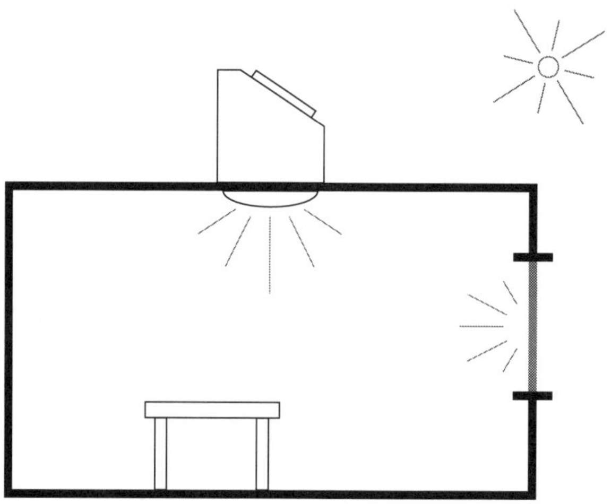

Figure 13.1 A room with a reflecting skylight. The illumination of the interior depends critically on the way light reflects inside the roof enclosure, and the relatively small opening in the ceiling is difficult to integrate in the standard indirect calculation.

these samples will hit the window and the skylight diffuser, which are the main sources of indirect illumination. Rays that hit the window will mostly pass through to collect illumination from the sky, but rays hitting the diffuser will require additional bounces to compute the interactions inside the skylight box.

The reason this calculation is so expensive is that the number of hemisphere samples must be large in order to properly find and integrate the two concentrated sources, the window and the skylight diffuser. Multiple bounces are also required to account for interreflection inside the skylight. Furthermore, intervening surfaces (such as the table) will cast shadows that will not be resolved very well by the caching algorithm unless the tolerance (**-aa**) setting is reduced. Together with the increased **-ad** setting, this adds up to a very expensive, time-consuming calculation.

Life would be so much easier if we could treat the skylight and the window as ordinary light sources. After all, they are concentrated sources of illumination, which is what we said characterizes a light source back in Chapter 11. The fact that they are not self-luminous makes little difference. When you think about it, the exit points of most light fixtures are not self-luminous either, yet we treat them as if they were, and with good reason. When a shadow ray strikes a light source, we want it to return a good average value for the whole source, not a local value corresponding to that point on the luminaire. By presampling and integrating our source output in this way, we avoid unnecessary sampling and filtering on the image plane.

Let us start by considering the simpler of the two objects in our room: the window. If we were to replace the window with an ordinary light source, we would have two problems. First, we would have to somehow include the highly directional (and extremely bright) beam component from the sun in our output distribution. Second, we would not be able to see out through the window, since our view would be of a light source with an averaged output, not a pane of glass.

Fortunately, both of these problems have a common solution, which is embodied in the *Radiance illum* material type, given by example here:

```
# Our sky distribution (skyfunc):
!gensky 7 12 14:30PDT

# What our window used to be made of:
void glass original_glass
0
0
3 .92 .92 .92

# Our illum material, with the glass as alternate:
skyfunc illum window_material
1 original_glass
0
3 .88 .88 .88
```

The trick is to treat the window as a light source only when we are computing its contribution to the illumination of some point. When any other ray happens to hit the window, we go back to treating it as glass. This includes view rays looking out the window, and shadow rays sent to compute the contributions from other light sources, such as the sun.[34] The illum type accomplishes this with an alternate (i.e., original) material type, which is used whenever a ray that is not part of its direct calculation hits it. (We will discuss this further in the section called Shadow Testing and Illum Surfaces.)

We still need some way of computing the output distribution of the window. Since we consider the sun separately and we do not have to worry about seeing through the window, we need only compute the light coming indirectly from the sky and the ground. For this, we can use the *Radiance* **gensky** program, which is tailored to this purpose. (See Chapter 6 for a more detailed explanation of how to

---

34. Rays that are sent out as part of the interreflection calculation must receive a zero value when they strike an illum surface. This is because we are now treating the object as part of the direct calculation and we must avoid double-counting.

apply gensky in daylighting calculations.) If there are no external obstructions or shadows to consider, we can apply the output pattern from gensky directly to the illum window. If, on the other hand, there are important external objects, we should use the **mkillum** program to compute the window output distribution. (The mkillum program computes output distributions using **rtrace**; we will discuss it later in detail.)

Whether or not there are any external obstructions, we must use mkillum to compute the output distribution from the skylight, since it involves internal reflections in the roof box. First, we must decide which surface (or surfaces) to treat as the final emitter(s). Depending on how we modeled the diffuser, it may or may not be wise to use the same surfaces for our mkillum source. If we modeled it with many small polygons on a fine mesh, it is probably best to use a simplified representation to avoid overburdening our direct calculation with a lot of little sources.

We start by placing a few polygons around the interior portion of the skylight to completely surround and enclose it. (See Figure 13.2.) We initially set the modifier for these pseudo-objects to *void* so that they do not participate in the normal calculation. We then pass these surfaces (along with the window surface, if we like) to mkillum—or, if we are using **rad**, we set the rad `illum` variable.

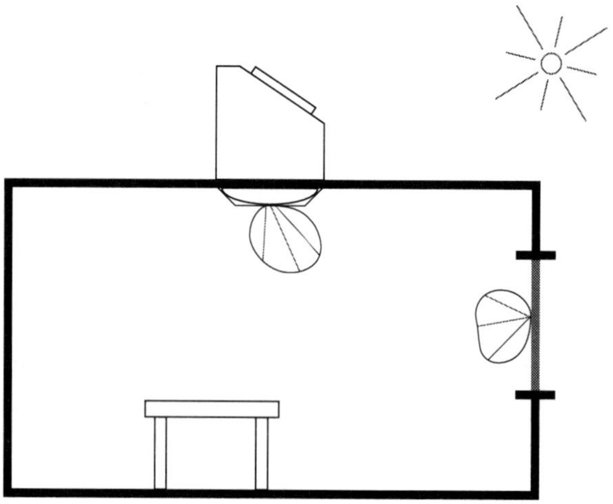

Figure 13.2 The same scene with surfaces placed around the skylight to capture its output distribution for the appropriate illum sources.

The output of mkillum is a modified scene description, with illums or *lights* replacing the original materials of the designated secondary sources, and data files containing the radiance distributions of each affected surface. This modified scene may then be used in a new, more efficient rendering calculation, in which these objects become light sources.

The remainder of this chapter is divided into two main sections. The first discusses the *Radiance* illum material type, its purpose, application, and limitations, how it affects other sampling algorithms, and its source-level implementation. The second section discusses the mkillum program in some depth, including what it does, how it is used, and its parameters, limitations, and implementation.

13.1 The *Illum* Material Type

The essential mechanism for describing secondary sources in *Radiance* is the illum material type. Essentially similar to the light type, illum carries parameters for the radiance output of a surface, but with an alternate material name to direct its behavior for incidental rays not directed to this particular source. Think of this as a mechanism for capturing the average light output of a bright object and including it in the direct calculation. To be valid, an illum radiance must average to the same value at a given point in the space as an image of the object from that same point, minus any direct sources that might be visible through it. In fact, this is exactly how mkillum computes the appropriate value for an illum, as we will discuss in the second half of this chapter.

It is most appropriate to use an illum source when the following two conditions are met:

1. An object contributes significant illumination to the scene, enough to cast visible shadows.
2. Looking at the object directly reveals important detail (such as the view through a window or the structure of a decorative fixture).

Note that the first condition implies not only that the object is relatively bright, but that it is small enough to cast visible shadows. There is little point in using the illum type to describe the ceiling in an indirect lighting system, for example, since the standard interreflection calculation can do an adequate job of determining its smoothly varying contribution.

The second condition is also important, because it distinguishes a source that requires illum treatment from one that can be handled well enough with the regular light type. If there is no important visual detail to capture on the surface (i.e., it looks diffuse), there is no need to describe it as anything but a light source, which will have a uniform appearance. It does not matter whether the object is a primary or secondary emitter in this case, since it will look just like any other light source in the final rendering. Indeed, we may need mkillum to compute the object's output distribution, but the result will still be a light rather than an illum.

13.1.1 *Illum* Examples

Let us look at a few common cases in which the illum type comes in handy: decorative luminaires, clear windows, and complex fenestration. We will examine how each case meets the two conditions described above, and demonstrate the usual approach of applying the illum type.

Decorative Luminaires

Decorative luminaires fit the two conditions outlined in the previous section, almost by definition. Condition 1 is met because luminaires generally cast shadows. Condition 2 is met because "decorative" *means* there is important visual detail.

For luminaires designed to be attractive as well as to illuminate, it is unfortunate when their appearance is lost in a rendering method. If we model a luminaire in full geometric detail, we run into problems with direct ray samples, which strike specific points on the fixture geometry. If a given point happens to be opaque, we get a shadow. Even if we jitter our ray samples, we will generate a lot of shadow noise that we do not need.

Figure 13.3 shows a direct/indirect fluorescent luminaire with louvers on the lower side. If we treat the lamps themselves as the emitters, our shadow rays will have to contend with the detailed fixture geometry, which is a real problem. Sometimes the ray will make it to the lamp and sometimes not. Overall, the average will be correct, but each individual sample will deviate from the mean, resulting in excessive image noise.

What we really want in this case, and indeed in the cases of most light sources, is to have a uniform radiator of the appropriate size to which we can send our shadow rays. That way, wherever the ray hits on the source, we get back a good average value. What makes this even more important in the case of luminaires is that we want to apply the photometric output distribution provided by the manufacturer. This will always provide greater accuracy than attempting to model and compute the output distribution in *Radiance*, which is not optimized for such tasks.[35]

35. Even a program designed to compute luminaire output runs into problems, because an accurate reflectance model of fixture surfaces is difficult to obtain. In general, it is easier and more efficient to measure the finished fixture than it is to simulate it in software, at least if such a fixture exists.

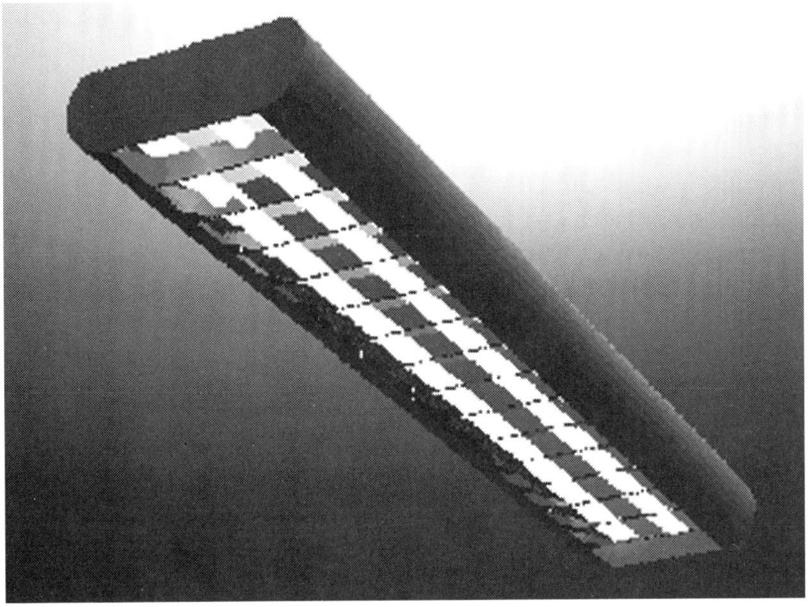

Figure 13.3 A direct/indirect luminaire in need of illum treatment.

We can solve both the problem of output averaging and that of photometric accuracy with the application of illum surfaces. In this case, it makes most sense to place one rectangle on the lower port of the luminaire and one on the upper port. The geometry of the sides will prevent any light from "escaping," so we will be able to assign the glow type to the lamps and still have interior illumination of the fixture for an accurate appearance. (If we did not seal the luminaire with our illum surfaces, random rays from the indirect calculation could sneak in and strike the lamps, producing double-counting errors and noise.)

We place two rectangles over the emitting areas of the fixture, one above and one below. The edges of the rectangles are matched to the boundaries of the emitting regions. The alternate type for our illums will be void in this case, since we want the surfaces to disappear when we look at them directly. Finally, we will apply the measured distribution supplied by the manufacturer using a **brightdata** pattern on each illum. (This is done automatically by the conversion utility **ies2rad**, which was discussed in Chapter 3.)

In our example, we could conveniently fit two rectangles to our fixture geometry as illum surfaces. What happens when the fixture is odd-shaped and we cannot easily attach simple surfaces to it? We may have to enclose the entire fixture in some simple shape, such as a sphere or a box. The surfaces of this simple shape are then defined as illums, with the appropriate output. Penumbra sampling may be less accurate in such cases, but only slightly.

Clear Windows

When does a clear window fit the two conditions for illum modeling? The first condition, that the window cast visible shadows, is met when the exterior is bright and the window is small relative to some points in our space. Unless it is nighttime, or the room has many large windows whose combined illumination is very diffuse, this condition will be met. The second condition, that the object carry important visual detail, is met by any window with a view.

Returning to Figure 13.2, we can replace the *glass* material for our window with an illum material whose alternate is the original glass. (The window surface must, of course, face into the room for it to work as a light source.) We must then set the output of the illum appropriately for the given exterior environment. The view through the window, and the passage of light from exterior sources (such as the sun), will be unaffected.

If accuracy is not critical to our application, or the exterior view is out of a high-rise building with no nearby neighbors, we can apply the **skyfunc** pattern gensky produces directly.[36] This will give the window an output distribution that corresponds to a view of an infinitely distant sky and ground. In most cases, however, we will use mkillum to compute a more accurate window output distribution, considering the effects of exterior geometry.

Complex Fenestration

What happens when a window is covered by venetian blinds or some other shading device? This can dramatically affect the light output, though the window may still be bright enough to warrant treating the combined system as a light source. If the

36. We may want to apply an additional correction for the transmittance of the window. The standard function file, *winxmit.cal* approximates transmission as a function of incident angle closely enough for most glazing types.

visual detail is also important, both the conditions for illum treatment that we outlined earlier are met.

With most shading systems, there is no option but to use mkillum to compute the output distribution. Much as with a decorative fixture, we must seal around the luminous surfaces with an illum whose alternate type is void. In some cases, the system may have large-scale geometry that extends into the interior, such as a horizontal light shelf, in which case the treatment becomes more complicated.[37]

Let us look briefly at the case of interior venetian blinds covering a window. Figure 13.4 shows what we must do. As before, we wish to associate the light output with a simple surface, which must cover the detailed geometry of the blinds. We can create a box around the window system using five rectangles and compute their distributions using mkillum. Since the side surfaces are so small, we may even want to leave them out of the computation by using an illum material with zero radiance. (It is necessary to have something there to block out random indirect sample rays.) The benefit of doing this is that we have fewer light sources in the direct calculation. The disadvantage is that this will leave the areas around the window underlit, which may be objectionable in some environments.

In the latter part of this chapter, we discuss the application and algorithms of mkillum. First let us look at limitations and the interaction of the illum type with other parts of the *Radiance* calculation, along with the source-level implementation.

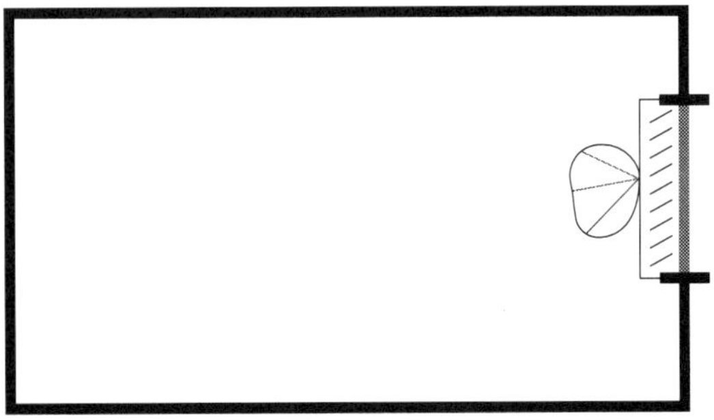

Figure 13.4 A window with venetian blinds whose distribution has been computed on separate illum surfaces by mkillum.

37. A light shelf is a horizontal panel designed to redirect daylight onto the ceiling. An example of this arrangement and of how secondary sources are computed for it is included on the CD-ROM.

13.1.2 Limitations

As we have already discussed, illum surfaces do not interfere with the shadow testing of other, nonillum sources. There is a good reason for this, which has to do with the difficulty of representing sharp peaks in light output distributions. Taking the example of a clear window, we could capture all the light coming through, rather than just the sky component. Although this could work in principle, the solar component is too bright and sharp to be represented well as part of a window's output. Shadows would become unnaturally weak and the boundaries of the window would be lost on the cast beam, because source subsampling and jittering would not be able to resolve the peak if it were made as sharp as it should be. Thus, it is more efficient to leave the solar component as a separate test. It does not add much to the calculation, since samples are sent to bright sources anyway.

13.1.3 Relation of *Illum* Type to Other Radiance Algorithms

Because of its dual nature, the illum type must be applied carefully, with attention to its potential effects on other algorithms in *Radiance*. Specifically, we must understand the impact of an illum surface on the shadow testing of other light sources, the relaying of virtual sources, and the diffuse indirect calculation.

Shadow Testing and Illum Surfaces

In Chapter 11, we presented the major algorithms underlying the direct calculation, but we did not discuss in detail what happens when a shadow ray hits a light source. Because it acts like a light source sometimes and like a nonsource at other times, the illum type complicates the shadow testing process somewhat.

Normally, a shadow ray hits the source it was targeting, and the return value is simply the radiance of the source material in that direction. However, if the ray hits a source other than its designated target, what happens depends on the intercepting source. In the case of an ordinary (nonillum) source, an intercepted shadow ray returns a zero value, because one light source is assumed to shadow another. However, since the behavior of an illum source is derived from another material, that material function will be invoked instead, unless the designated target is a glow or another illum.

We want an illum to block other illums and glows, because allowing rays to pass would usually constitute overcounting. Take as an example the window arrangement shown in Figure 13.5. All three windows are illum sources, whose output distribution has been computed by mkillum or its equivalent. The window surfaces are oriented toward the interior of the space, so that point P1 sees the front side of

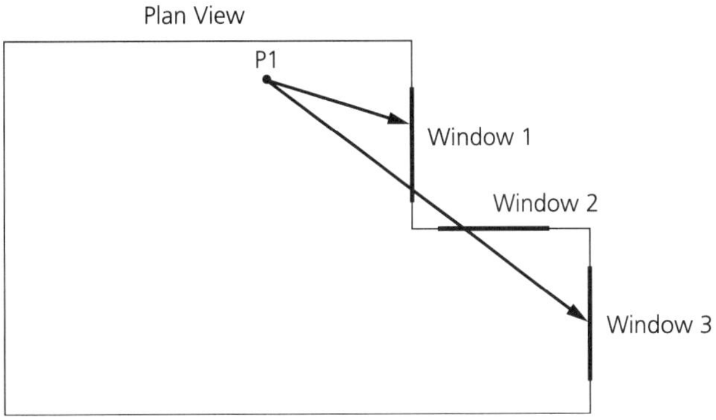

Figure 13.5 Point P1 sees Window 1 and Window 3 as illum sources, but only Window 1 is valid, since it includes contributions from Window 3 in its output.

window 1, the back side of window 2, and the front side of window 3. At this point, we will generate two shadow rays, one targeting window 1 and one targeting window 3. (Window 2 is not a target, since it faces away from us.) The first shadow ray is sent to window 1 and arrives unobstructed, so it gets back the radiance for that sample direction. The second shadow ray could potentially pass through window 1 and window 2 to strike window 3, but we want to prevent this because the output of window 3 is already included in the output of window 1, and counting it twice would be an error.[38]

If the targeted object is an in-range glow, we block it with our illum for a different reason. The glow type is designed for weak light sources, but it is also used for lamps inside a fixture enclosed by illum geometry, as in the first example of the preceding section. Using glow, the lamps can illuminate the local fixture geometry without affecting anything outside the illum enclosure. As a convenience, we therefore block rays headed for a glow surface through an illum. (There is no real instance when this would be useful, anyway.)

Relaying Virtual Light Sources with Illum

What happens when a surface is useful both as an illum and as a relay object for virtual sources? A simple example is a light shelf whose upper surface has strong diffuse and specular components. The diffuse component means that the shelf will

38. The mkillum program, or any sensible program like it, will treat all illum surfaces the same. It is not logical nor necessary to exclude the output of one illum surface from the output of another. There is no advantage in doing so, and it would make the calculation much more difficult owing to additional bookkeeping requirements in rtrace.

serve as a secondary light source, and the specular component means that it may be relaying virtual sources (such as solar reflections).

Since this is an important case that may come up in practice, *Radiance* provides a simple mechanism for handling it. The surface is modified by the illum material, which gives the appropriate virtual source material as its alternate type.[39] When not acting as an illum source, the surface will relay virtual light sources using the specified alternate material. The virtual source material may in turn specify a third alternate for when it is not acting as a virtual relay. (For example, the *mirror* type has such a field.)

Diffuse Interreflection and Illum Surfaces

Like any other light source, an illum source is part of the direct calculation and must therefore be excluded from the interreflected component. It is very important, as we have already mentioned in the introduction to this chapter, to make sure that the illum surface completely covers the indirect contribution it is replacing. We cannot allow light to leak around the sides of the surface or otherwise bring noise back into the indirect component, because this would defeat the whole purpose of using illum in the first place.

It is not absolutely necessary to use computed illum surfaces to seal around a source of indirect illumination being converted into a secondary emitter. If there are only small open areas, they can be sealed by illums with zero radiance, which will be ignored in the direct calculation. There may be a slight loss in illumination, but with fewer sources, the calculation will be considerably faster. (See the complex fenestration example in the preceding section.)

13.1.4 Algorithms and Source Code

The implementation of the illum type is actually quite simple, showing up in only a few places. As with all other source types, the header file *src/common/otypes.h* associates the `T_L` (light) flag with illum, so that surfaces modified by this material type will be added into the direct calculation by the `marksources` routine. This procedure is contained, along with the crucial `m_light` function, in *src/rt/source.c*.

The `m_light` function is designated for shading a ray whenever it strikes a light source. This same function handles the material types light, glow, *spotlight*, and illum. In our opinion, `m_light` is the ugliest instance of special-case programming

39. Similarly, *Radiance* will not search the entire modifier list for a luminous material—it must be the immediate modifier of a surface for it to be identified as a light source.

in all of *Radiance*. The basic steps are few, but the details are twisted. Here are the steps:

```
m_light(m, r) begin
if bad component then return
if wrong source then return
       if pass illum then
              if alternate is void then
                     call raytrans(r)
              else
                     call rayshade(r, alternate)
              end if
       end if
       if ray hit backside then return
       if ignore source then return
       if outside of spotlight then return
       call raytexture(r, modifier)
       assign returned ray color, \
              modified by patterns
end m_light
```

The details of the special-case tests are hidden in the conditions of the `if` statements. For example, the C macro for `pass illum` is defined as

```
(m->otype==MAT_ILLUM && \
       (r->rsrc<0 || source[r->rsrc].so!=r->ro || \
       source[r->rsrc].sflags&SVIRTUAL))
```

Translated into English, the condition might read:

> Our material type is illum and our ray was not aimed toward any source, or at least not this source, or the illum is about to relay a virtual light source.

Nasty as it is, this is the one of the simpler `if` statement conditions in the `m_light` function, which should give you an idea of just how bad the whole thing is. Explaining these conditions in full detail would require a large table and the combined understanding of many of the underlying algorithms in *Radiance*. Unfortunately, such special cases are a necessary part of optimized a priori sampling. (See [VG95] for better insight into sampling strategies.)

13.2 The Mkillum Program

Although the illum type provides the basic mechanism for secondary light sources, it does not make them convenient. We still need to come up with the output distribution of whatever system we are moving into the direct calculation as an illum. This is the purpose of the *Radiance* program mkillum. Input to the program is a scene containing the surface or surfaces we wish to convert to illums, and the output is the converted surfaces and their radiance distributions. These distributions are computed by sending random rays at each designated surface and recording the radiance values computed by rtrace.

In this way, you need only to identify the surfaces in the scene that should be treated as secondary emitters, and mkillum does the rest.

There are two ways of running mkillum: directly from the command line, or using rad. In either case, the result will be the same. The advantage of using rad is that it tracks file changes and keeps the model up to date, so that you can worry about more important things. The basic steps for creating and using illum distributions from mkillum are as follows:

1. Create a scene description, optionally putting the surfaces destined to become illums into one or more separate files.
2. Build an octree using this scene description.
3. Run mkillum using this octree and the scene files containing the surfaces to convert as input.
4. Create a new octree using the converted illum files in place of the originals.
5. Render using the modified octree.

Here is an example sequence:

```
% oconv materials.rad basic.rad secsrc.rad \
        > orig.oct
% mkillum -ab 2 -ad 256 -as 128 orig.oct \
        < secsrc.rad > illums.rad
% oconv materials.rad basic.rad illums.rad \
        > render.oct
```

The rad program makes some small modifications to improve the efficiency of this process, but they are not particularly noteworthy. Control of mkillum is still left up to you, and you must decide which surfaces to convert and how to sample them. Presumably, you know from earlier sections in this chapter how to select surfaces for illum conversion, so all we have left to explain is how mkillum samples and creates secondary sources.

13.2.1 Mkillum Sampling Method

When mkillum comes across a surface designated for conversion in its input, it begins by setting up a sampling pattern over its area. In the case of *rectangles*, *spheres*, and *rings*, the exact pattern is known. In the case of irregular polygons, a bounding rectangle is used and rejection sampling is employed.[40] Both position and direction will be randomly sampled by mkillum, though only sample direction will ever be recorded.

Figure 13.6 shows a polygon and a bounding rectangle as computed by mkillum. For a given segment of the output distribution, rays are randomly sampled over the surface area and within the solid angle for that segment, as shown. Each direction results in a slightly different sampling pattern, but in every case, the rays will be well separated (stratified) to reduce variance in the result.

The output of mkillum is an area-averaged radiance for each direction of the hemisphere. Spherical sources will yield area-averaged radiances for each direction over a sphere. The number of direction segments for the hemisphere or sphere is set by the mkillum **d** control parameter, which sets the number of samples to use per (projected) steradian. For flat surfaces, the division of the hemisphere is the same as that used for the indirect irradiance calculation as explained in Chapter 12. Specifically, azimuth is divided uniformly, and altitude is divided so that every segment has the same projected solid angle. For spheres, azimuth is also divided uniformly,

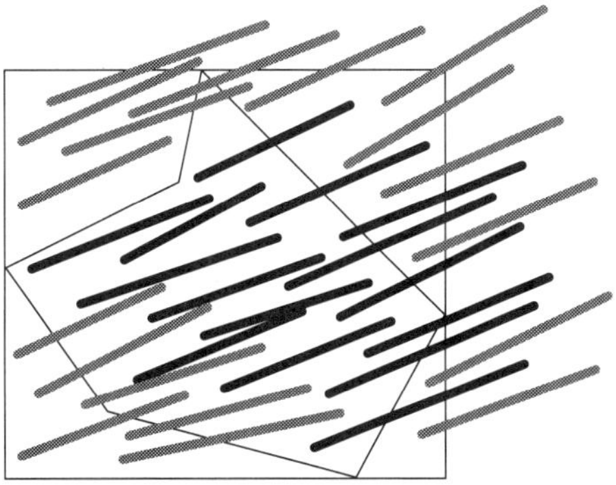

Figure 13.6 A typical sampling pattern for a polygon. The lighter rays were rejected because they did not intersect the target polygon.

40. Rejection sampling is a Monte Carlo method whereby any sample that does not match the given domain is rejected and a new sample is drawn in its place. This tends to slow down the sampling process, but is easier than coming up with an exact pattern for a complicated domain. (The domain in this case is the irregular polygon.)

and altitude is divided so that every segment has the same solid angle. (The projected solid angle is cosine-corrected, whereas the spherical solid angle is not.) These two segmentations are shown in Figure 13.7.

The number of rays used to estimate the illum output in each direction is set by the **s** sampling parameter of mkillum. This number and the complexity of illumination in the environment, being sampled together, determine the accuracy of the computed distributions (along with the parameters given to rtrace, of course). Highly peaked distributions are more difficult to sample, which is one of the reasons direct sources are allowed to pass through illums, since they represent peaks in the distribution functions.

Because mkillum is usually used to create illums, through which other nonillum source rays may travel, it is important to exclude directly visible light sources from the sampled distributions. This is accomplished with the **-dv-** option to rtrace, which mkillum sets automatically. (It is possible to override this option, but it is not advisable except under very unusual circumstances.) This way, rays traveling directly to light sources will return zero values to mkillum, thus avoiding double-counting of their contributions in the resulting illum.

The colors of secondary source distributions computed by mkillum are left partially up to you. Many times, it is best to have neutral-colored light sources and illums so that rendered images do not have a color cast that has to be removed by a postprocess. In such cases, you may instruct mkillum not to color its sources at all. At other times, color may be important, but perhaps the exact distribution of color is either less important or mostly uniform, and an average color value for each sec-

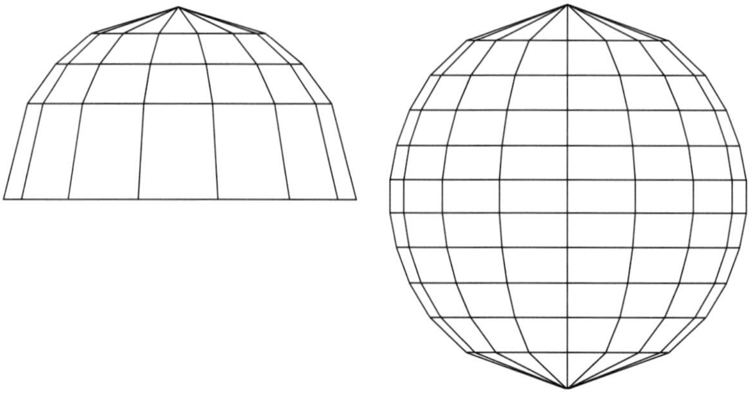

Figure 13.7 Side view of segmentations used by mkillum for hemispherical and spherical direction sampling.

ondary emitter will do. At those times when color accuracy is critical, a full color distribution may be stored; this may take a little extra time and memory during rendering, but gives the highest-fidelity results.

Since mkillum computes an average distribution for an entire surface, it is sometimes desirable to divide a window or other object into smaller surfaces to capture the changing output over its area. Particularly when there is geometry close to a large window, such as large shading features on a building facade, subdividing the window surface is worthwhile. The precalculation and rendering time will increase slightly, but the shading will be more accurate, because it will account for the local effects of the exterior geometry.

13.2.2 Limitations

As much as we would like to claim that mkillum can solve all your rendering problems, there are, unfortunately, some cases that are just too tricky for it. Figure 13.8 shows a double-paned window system with integrated specular louvers. Since the louvers are curved, they will result in a kind of curved reflection of any sunlight striking the window, and this is difficult to compute using a backward ray-tracing methodology.

If the louvers were flat, the specular behavior of the system could be accounted for with the *prism1* or *prism2* type. However, their curvature means that the output distribution will not be specular, and an illum is needed to represent it. However, it is nearly impossible to compute the distribution using a random sampling of rays

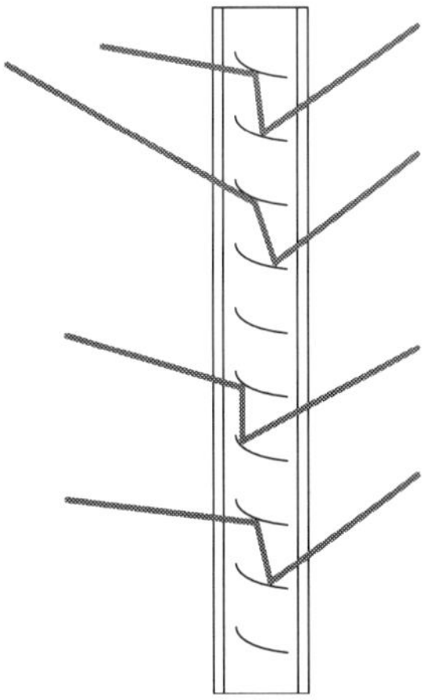

Figure 13.8 A cross section of a double-paned window with specular louvers, with sunlight passing through.

over the window, since the sun represents such a tiny target. The mkillum s parameter would have to be increased to a value of about 100,000 to get a reasonable estimate, which would take a very long time to compute.

Other cases involving curved, specular reflectors pose similar difficulties for mkillum, and the only long-term solution seems to be the creation of a forward ray-tracing module for computing these kinds of illums.

13.2.3 Mkillum Parameters

Mkillum has two sets of parameters. One set is altered on the command line and is passed directly to rtrace to control the ray-tracing calculation. The second set is altered in specially formatted comments in the scene input file(s), which change the functioning of mkillum itself. The reason for giving parameters in the input stream is so that different sections of the scene can be treated differently. In fact, it would be nice to have control over the rtrace calculation as well, but since the same process is used throughout a given invocation, there is no way to give a new command line without rerunning mkillum, which is the recommended procedure if different rtrace parameters are required. (The startup costs are slight.)

Since the options for rtrace are the same as those for the other rendering programs, which are explained in previous chapters covering *Radiance* sampling strategies, we will only go into the mkillum-specific parameters here. The following symbols are used to represent different argument types:

N	Integer
R	Real number
S	String
[*xyz*]	One of the characters *x*, *y*, and *z*

Here are the mkillum control parameters:

d = *N*	Sets the number of directional samples to *N* per (projected) steradians. For flat surfaces, the total number of directional samples will be roughly π times this value. For spherical sources, the total number will be roughly 4π times this value. If this parameter is set to 0, the surfaces are assumed to produce a diffuse output distribution.
s = *N*	Sets the number of samples over the surface to *N* per computed output direction. More complicated geometries should get relatively more samples.

c = [*dan*] Computes full color output distributions (*d* setting), or average colors over all directions (*a* setting), or produces strictly uncolored sources (*n* setting). A full color distribution might be used for a window at sunset to show the orange cast on the floor. An averaged color might be used when the source of color is the alternate material, as for colored glazing. An uncolored setting is appropriate when a color-balanced result is desired, as when a window is the only source of illumination.

l[+ –] Sets light source type on (+ setting) or off (– setting). If on, surfaces are converted to light rather than illum type. This may be desirable for surfaces that have no interesting detail in their original form, and do not permit other source rays to pass for whatever reason. (For example, a *trans* material with no specular component or nonzero roughness will not pass any other source rays or show any interesting detail, so making it into a light will save time during rendering.)

b = *R* Sets the minimum radiance value for producing a source to *R*. The average output of a surface must be above this value before mkillum will replace it with a light or illum source. This provides a convenient, automatic way to determine which surfaces are worthwhile to treat as secondary emitters.

a Following this option, mkillum will consider all subsequent input surfaces for conversion to sources.

i = *S* Following this option, mkillum will consider only input surfaces modified by *S* for conversion to sources.

e = *S* Following this option, mkillum will consider any input surfaces *not* modified by *S* for conversion to sources.

n Following this option, mkillum will pass all input surfaces to the output unmodified.

m = *S* Sets the material name for output illums to *S*. This will also be used as the root filename for output distributions, unless a different **f** parameter is in effect.

f = *S* Sets the root output distribution file name to *S*. This parameter is often used to specify a data file subdirectory as well.

o = *S* Sets the scene output file to S instead of the standard output.

13.2.4 Algorithms and Source Code

There are three source modules for mkillum: *src/gen/mkillum.c*, *src/gen/mkillum2.c*, and *src/gen/mkillum3.c*. They share a common header file, *src/gen/mkillum.h*, which defines data structures and macros. The `main` procedure and initialization code are contained in *src/gen/mkillum.c*, along with basic option and scene parsing routines. The module *src/gen/mkillum2.c* contains ray-sampling code for the supported surface primitives (sphere, polygon, and ring). Finally, *src/gen/mkillum3.c* contains routines for producing output distributions and illum (or light) sources. Unlike most generator programs, mkillum relies heavily on the *Radiance* library in *src/common/*, since it needs to parse and understand scene input files to some extent. For example, it employs the `multisamp` and `urand` routines to select ray sample points and directions, and intersects points with polygons using `inface`.

Probably the only algorithmically interesting code is contained in *src/gen/mkillum2.c*, since the other two modules deal with fairly routine file parsing and output. There are three principal procedures for ray sampling, one for each of the three supported surface primitives. Additionally, there are support routines for computing sample directions and transferring data to and from the rtrace subprocess.

Here is the pseudocode for the `o_face` procedure, which computes the output distribution for a polygon:

```
o_face(ob, il, rt, nm) begin
        compute number of azimuth and \
                altitude samples
        find boundaries of face given in object ob
        foreach azimuth and altitude do
                foreach surface sample do
                        compute random direction \
                                within azimuth and altitude
                        set found = 0
                        while not found do
                                compute random position
                                set found = point is in face
                        end while
                        call raysamp
                end foreach
        end foreach
        call rayflush
        if average radiance is above b level then
```

```
            if d > 0 then call flatout
            call illumout
        else
            call printobj
        end if
end o_face
```

The raysamp routine passes a ray origin and direction to the rtrace process, and the rayflush routine completes any pending ray calculations. The flatout routine puts out the output distribution data, and illumout puts out the illum or light source and its geometry. If the surface radiance is below the b parameter threshold, printobj is called to put out the geometry unmodified.

The other surface handlers, o_ring and o_sphere, are essentially similar, except that the loop to find valid area samples is not necessary because they can be computed directly.

13.3 Conclusion

In this chapter, we have described some of the rationale and algorithms behind secondary light sources, which fall under the general category of *light reclassification* [SWZ96]. In general, it would be nice to automate this process beyond what it is now, so that it did not require you to identify these sources explicitly. Unfortunately, such intelligence is quite beyond what *Radiance* currently offers.

The limitation of mkillum with regard to curved, specular geometries is also something that calls for further development. A forward Monte Carlo ray-tracing process could certainly overcome some of these limitations, but the design and control of such a program is a very challenging and interesting problem. Regrettably, there has not been sufficient time or funding to pursue this to date, but no one knows what the future holds...

CHAPTER 14

Single-Scatter Participating Media (*Mist*)

How can we model phenomena such as beams of light, fog, smoke, and clouds in *Radiance*? One way would be to attempt to model the individual particles themselves. This can work, since instances allow horrendously complicated geometry to be described efficiently, but calculating the ray interactions with this geometry will be very expensive.

The general problem of computing light scattering in participating media is very challenging [Rus88]. Providing a complete calculation of multiple scattering and absorption in anisotropic media with nonuniform density distributions is a tremendous challenge. However, some interesting phenomena can be computed with relative ease and economy, and these we have included in *Radiance*.

We use a *single-scatter* approximation to participating media, with a Heyney-Greenstein eccentricity model for forward scattering preference. *Single-scatter* means that at most one scattering event may be followed from a light source to the ray origin.[41] This model is appropriate for most thin and low-albedo scattering media. Figure 14.1 shows the light paths included in this model.

Even within a single-scatter approximation from light sources, the number of additional rays required can be very large if the number of sources is large, since several rays, on the average, are required for each source. We therefore introduce another optimization which localizes the calculation of scattering from each source.

To accomplish this, we add a new pseudomaterial type to *Radiance*, called *mist*. Mist surfaces are used to enclose volumes within which a given light source or sources show significant scattering. In addition, the mist type offers local control over density and other characteristics of a participating medium. Outside of all mist volumes, extinction is computed for the participating medium whose parameters are set on the rendering command line, but no in-scattering is computed.

In this chapter, we begin with a definition of important properties of participating media, followed by a description of the mist type, then the rendering method and its limitations, parameters, and algorithmic details.

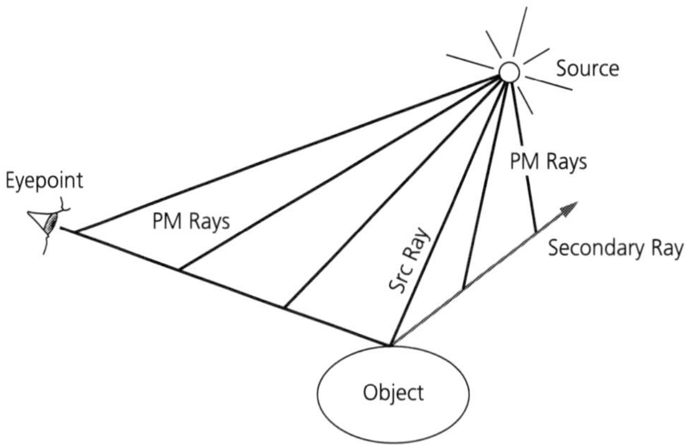

Figure 14.1 Scattering events handled in *Radiance*. Light is scattered into initial ray from source as well as into secondary rays reflected off scene geometry.

41. Technically, a single-scatter approximation should also account for scattered paths from surfaces other than light sources, but this is considerably more difficult and the payoff is negligible under most circumstances.

14.1 Properties of Participating Media

Participating media affect radiation transfer through three related processes, shown in Figure 14.2. These processes are called *in-scattering*, *out-scattering*, and *absorption*.

Absorption occurs when a particulate intercepts a photon and turns the energy into heat. We characterize this phenomenon by the medium's *absorption coefficient*, which is a function of wavelength:

$$\kappa_a(\lambda) = \text{absorbed fraction per unit distance}$$

In-scattering and out-scattering are in fact just different perspectives on the same phenomenon. In the first case, light is being scattered into the view direction by particulates; in the second case, light is being scattered away from the view direction by particulates. Since the particulates do not know one from the other, we characterize both with a single property, called the *scattering function*:

$$\kappa_s(\lambda,\theta) = \text{scattered fraction per unit distance}$$

The scattering function depends in general on wavelength and on the angle between the incident and scattered directions. An *isotropic* medium will scatter light the same in all directions, removing the θ dependency. Even when the medium is not isotropic, the angular dependency is often taken out and characterized by a separate function, using an integrated average for κ_s, like this:

$$\kappa_s(\lambda,\theta) = \kappa_s(\lambda)\, f(\theta) \tag{14.1}$$

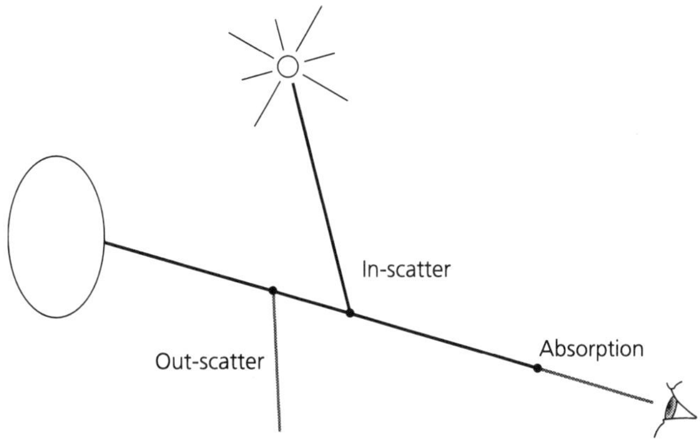

Figure 14.2 The three basic processes in participating media. Along a ray path, radiation may be scattered out of the path, scattered into the path, or absorbed by particulates in the medium.

The averaged scattering for all directions, $\kappa_s(\lambda)$, is called the *scattering coefficient.* Frequently, the absorption and isotropic scattering coefficients are combined into a single, integrated *extinction coefficient,* which indicates the total loss of directed radiation in the medium per unit distance:

$$\kappa_t(\lambda) = \kappa_a(\lambda) + \kappa_s(\lambda) \tag{14.2}$$

The extinction coefficient is the easiest property to measure; thus, it is the value most often found in tables. Sometimes the extinction is given as a fraction per unit distance per unit mass density for a given particulate. In this case, one must know the mass density of the medium in question to arrive at the extinction coefficient as a fraction per unit distance.

For convenience, scattering is often defined using *albedo,* which is the fraction of extinction due to scattering, like this:

$$\Omega(\lambda) = \kappa_s(\lambda)/\kappa_t(\lambda) \tag{14.3}$$

This is a nice parameter, since it is independent of density, unitless, and relatively easy to measure. If we wish to reincorporate directionality into the albedo, we may write it thus:

$$\Omega(\lambda,\theta) = \Omega(\lambda)\, f(\theta) \tag{14.4}$$

Measurements of media anisotropy are often fitted to a function developed by Heyney and Greenstein:

$$f(\theta) \cong P_{HG}(\theta,g) = (1 - g^2)/(1 + g^2 - 2g\cos(\theta))^{1.5} \tag{14.5}$$

The Heyney-Greenstein parameter, *g,* runs from 0, for a perfectly isotropic medium, to near 1 for a medium that scatters strongly in the forward direction.

In *Radiance,* the following properties are used for participating media:

$\kappa_t(\lambda)$	extinction coefficient per unit distance, in RGB
$\Omega(\lambda)$	scattering albedo, in RGB
g	Heyney-Greenstein eccentricity parameter

14.2 The *Mist* Material Type

The mist type is similar to the *dielectric* type in the sense that a surface using it bounds a volume of something, but it is unique insofar as the surface itself is of no true significance. It merely acts as a convenient boundary for what is, in most cases, not well defined in space. There are actually two uses of a mist surface, which can be applied concurrently:

1. Mist can demarcate volumes surrounding light source beams.
2. Mist can increase medium density or change scattering characteristics within a volume.

In the first application, one gives string arguments naming each important light source for a particular region in the scene, then applies the mist material to a surface or surfaces that enclose this volume. In the second application, one gives real arguments specifying the increase in extinction coefficient and applies it to a volume enclosing the denser medium. (New scattering albedo and the eccentricity parameters may also be specified for the volume.)

A common example of the first application is the cone-shaped beam of a spotlight shining through smoke, fog, or dust. The cone is capped and usually made larger than the source at one end and slightly larger than the spot at the other, as shown in Figure 14.3. It is best if the source itself is just outside the mist volume, so that a ray that begins from within the volume will intersect a mist surface before it hits the light source. Without this intersection, *Radiance* is unable to infer the presence of the volume from an interior viewpoint.

An example of the second application, in which one is representing a volume of participating medium, might be the atmosphere in the smoking section of a restaurant. In this case, the room may be divided into multiple sections corresponding to important downlights and changing smoke densities, thus combining both applications together. Figure 14.4 shows a plan view, in which we have diced the room surrounding each downlight and altered the extinction coefficient in each slightly.

Note that the volumes use distinct surfaces as their boundaries (exaggerated in this example), since the mist type does not have a general boundary type analogous to *interface* for dielectric.

In some cases, mist volumes may overlap, as when one spotlight beam crosses another. Extinction coefficients will sum in the intersecting regions, and scattering and eccentricity parameters should agree, or inconsistent rendering could result (similar to coincident surfaces with different materials). In this example, we want the surfaces to be very close together but not touching.

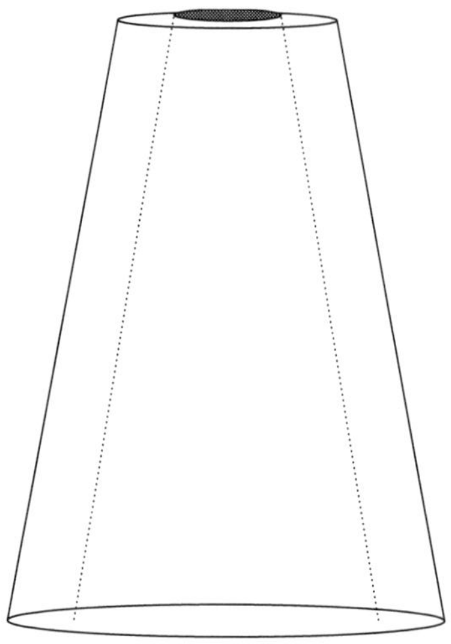

Figure 14.3 A mist volume enclosing the beam of a spotlight. The volume should be large enough to enclose all interesting scattering effects, but not so large that the sampling becomes inefficient.

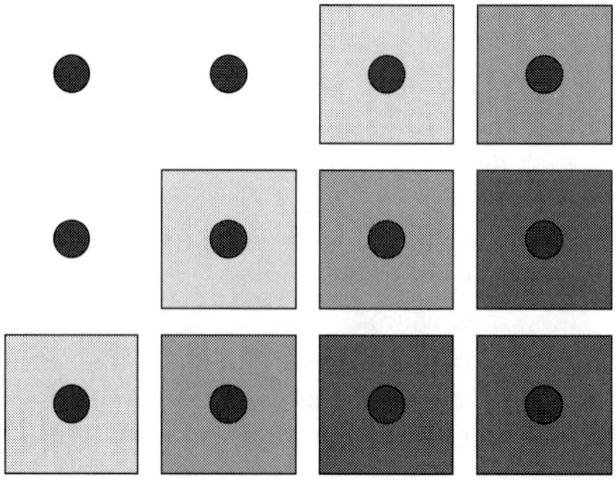

Figure 14.4 Mist volumes used to represent increasing density of smoke surrounding light sources toward the corner of a room (plan view).

14.3 Rendering Participating Media

To compute the effect of medium participation on a returned ray's value, we need to know what media the ray has passed through. In general, a medium can change over a ray's path (especially in density, but possibly in other ways as well). However, because of the difficulty of specifying and computing participating medium properties as a continuous function of position, we restrict changes to occur only at mist pseudosurface boundaries. This way, the actual medium properties remain constant along a ray's path, greatly simplifying our input and our calculation.

Each ray has an associated extinction, albedo, and Heyney-Greenstein parameter. These parameters are controlled globally by the **-me**, **-ma**, and **-mg** rendering options, respectively. When a ray enters a mist volume, these parameters may or may not be affected. Tracking rays entering and leaving such volumes is handled by the mist material function, which will be described later in the section titled Algorithm Details and Source Code.

Radiance calculates the effect of a participating medium after all the ray-surface interactions are computed. In other words, the ray has been sent out into the scene and has intersected whatever object it was destined for, spawning any rays needed for that material, and the ray is returning with its value as though there were no medium between the object and the ray origin. At that point, the following computations take place:

1. The returned color is computed with the extinction formula:

$$L(s) = [L(0) - \Omega a]e^{-\kappa s} + \Omega a \quad (14.6)$$

where

$L(x)$ = radiance at distance x from object

κ = extinction coefficient

Ω = scattering albedo

a = global ambient value (-**av** setting)

s = distance from origin to object

This computes ambient in-scattering, absorption, and out-scattering along the ray. In the special case in which the ray has been sent to a light source as part of the direct calculation, scattering is not considered. The formula then simplifies to a calculation of absorption only:

$$L(s) = L(0)e^{-\kappa(1-\Omega)s}$$

2. If the ray is within one or more mist volumes and specific light sources have been identified, in-scattering is computed for each source using N random samples along the ray' s length. (N is derived from the mist sampling distance, set by the **-ms** option.) This source in-scattering calculation accounts for absorption along the way and adds to the result from the first step, above. Source in-scattering is not computed for rays directed to light sources, since this would complicate shadow testing. The total in-scattering is computed from N samples, i, taken on each source, j:

$$L_{is}(s) = \sum_i \sum_j \kappa\Omega s/(4\pi N)e^{-\kappa t(i)}P_{HG}(\theta_{ij}, g)L_{ij}\omega_{ij} \qquad (14.7)$$

where

$t(i) = s\,(i + X_i)/N$ (random sample distance for random number X_i)

θ_{ij} = angle between ray at $t(i)$ and source j

g = Heyney-Greenstein eccentricity value

L_{ij} = radiance of source j as seen from $t(i)$

ω_{ij} = solid angle of source j as seen from $t(i)$

The extinction formula used in step 1 accounts for light absorbed along the path and ambient light scattered into the path from random directions. (Note that the -av setting should be reduced by a sensible amount for medium absorption.) As the ray distance increases, the radiance value approaches a constant, which is the product of the scattering albedo and the ambient value.

The reason that scattering is not considered for rays sent to light sources as part of the direct calculation is that it is expensive to compute and it affects only the apparent size of the light source, not the total contribution. By pretending that the medium absorbs light only during the direct calculation, we get roughly the correct illumination on surfaces, erring only inasmuch as some of the light would be more diffusely incident than we assume.

In-scattering from sources, computed in step 2, is the most expensive part of the calculation; this is why its application is administered carefully. Only those sources indicated as significant within a specific mist volume are tested for scattering, and the number of samples is controlled by the -ms mist sampling distance option. In addition, there is an upper limit to the number of samples (N), set by the `MAXSSAMP` macro, which is defined as 16 in the current release. This prevents extremely long ray paths from taking a ridiculous number of samples, which would make little difference in the value of the pixel being computed.

The thing to note in this implementation is that calculations for a purely absorbing medium or for places outside of mist volumes are very quick, adding little to the overall rendering time. Only within mist volumes in scattering media do the calculations start to weigh, and the time required is linear with respect to the number of light sources included in the scattering calculations and linear over a short range in the ray travel distance through the mist volume.

The most important thing is to include only those lights that are likely to be important sources of in-scattering within each mist volume.

14.3.1 Limitations

The most obvious limitation of this method is that multiple-scatter phenomena are not modeled. Multiple scatter, aside from being very expensive to calculate, is most important for localized media, such as clouds, which can be approximated in *Radiance* using other methods. For example, a cloud can be modeled as a surface with a fractal noise *mixfunc* that combines a white translucent material (*trans* type) with *void*, yielding variable opacity. This may not be an exact representation, but fidelity is elusive for clouds anyway because atmospheric phenomena are so variable.

Another limitation of mist objects is that it is difficult to vary the density of the medium inside them. A pattern may be applied to the mist material, and this will modify the density along an incident ray's path, but for this to be correct, the pattern must be sensitive to the actual path of the ray through the variable-density volume. In practice, such computations are tedious and difficult, and it would be much nicer if the renderer handled volumetric density directly instead. This would require substantial time during rendering, however, so the idea was abandoned. Instead, we recommend the method illustrated in Figure 14.4 for variable-density situations.

An intentional limit is placed on the number of scattering sources that can be active simultaneously. The macro `MAXSLIST` is set to 32 in the current release, but may be changed with a compile option. Keeping this number small discourages careless inclusion of scattering sources that make little difference in a given region. If many sources are important, smaller regions will yield a more efficient calculation.

14.3.2 Relation to Rendering Parameters

Four command line options are related to participating media:

-me Sets the *medium extinction* coefficient in terms of RGB extinction per unit length. A value of 0 0 0 means that there is no global participating medium. There may still be localized media within the boundaries of mist volumes in the scene.

-ma Sets the *medium* scattering *albedo* to the given RGB value. This quantity is multiplied by the extinction coefficient set with the -me option to arrive at the scattering coefficient per unit length. A value of 0 0 0 means that the global medium is purely absorbing. A value of 1 1 1 means that the global medium is perfectly scattering. The global value may be overridden by localized media defined within specific mist volumes.

-mg Sets the global *medium Greenstein* scattering eccentricity. A value of 0 means a perfectly isotropic medium. As the value approaches 1, the scattering approaches pure forward scattering, which is the same as no scattering at all. Like the other global medium settings, this may be overridden by localized mist volumes. Unlike the other values, the eccentricity has no real effect outside of mist regions, since ambient scattering is omnidirectional.

-ms Sets the *medium sampling* distance, in world units. Source scattering will be computed at this average interval over a ray's travel through a mist volume. If it is set to 0, then just one sample will be taken for any given ray path.

Recommended Settings

Most of the participating medium settings are determined by the properties of the global medium itself. Only the -ms setting is controlled by rad, which is determined by the `QUALITY` and `DETAIL` variables:

	`QUALITY = Lo`	`QUALITY = Med`	`QUALITY = Hi`
DET = Lo	-ms 0	-ms *s/20*	-ms *s/40*
DET = Med	-ms 0	-ms *s/40*	-ms *s/80*
DET = Hi	-ms 0	-ms *s/80*	-ms *s/1600*

where *s* is the average `ZONE` dimension.

If the physical properties of the participating medium are unknown (as is often the case), it helps to have some general idea of typical values for different media. Here is a table with some approximate values to help get started (assume world units in meters):

	-me			**-ma**			**-mg**
Thick smoke	.2	.2	.2	.05	.05	.05	.08
Cigarette smoke	.02	.02	.02	.2	.3	.5	.12
Road dust	1×10^{-5}	1×10^{-5}	1×10^{-5}	.5	.3	.1	.2
Light fog	3×10^{-3}	3×10^{-3}	3×10^{-3}	.999	.999	.999	.84

Feel free to play around with the extinction coefficient to get the desired appearance. Few measurements are available for participating media, so we are forced to base our input on what looks right in many cases. (See [Rus95] for additional information and references.)

14.3.3 Algorithm Details and Source Code

The source code for participating media is contained mainly in three routines. The first routine, `rayparticipate()`, handles the extinction function and ambient scattering, which was step 1 as discussed in the section titled Rendering Participating Media. This function is called after a ray has been traced and shaded by the normal routines. The second routine, `srcscatter()`, is called by `rayparticipate()` to compute source scattering, which corresponds to step 2 as discussed earlier. The third routine, `m_mist()`, tracks rays entering and leaving mist volumes. The `rayparticipate()` function is defined in the source file *src/rt/raytrace.c*. The `srcscatter()` function is defined in *src/rt/source.c*. The `m_mist()` function is defined in *src/rt/m_mist.c*.

The pseudocode for `rayparticipate()` is quite simple, corresponding almost exactly to step 1 as described in the earlier section:

```
rayparticipate(r) begin
        if extinction for r is zero then return
        if albedo is zero or r is shadow ray then
                compute absorption along r using:
                        L(s) = L(0)e^-κ(1-Ω)s
        else
                compute extinction and ambient
                in-scattering along r using:
                        L(s) = [L(0) - Ωa]e^-κs + Ωa
                call srcscatter(r)
        end if
end rayparticipate
```

The pseudocode for `srcscatter()`, corresponding to step 2, is only slightly more complicated, though this is where the most expensive calculation takes place:

```
srcscatter(r) begin
        if no scatter sources then return
        if medium eccentricity is 1 then return
        if ray hit distant object then return
        if ms_setting is 0 then
                set N = 1
        else
                set N = ray_distance/ms_setting
                if (N < 1) then set N = 1
                if (N > MAXSSAMP) then set N = MAXSSAMP
        end if
        foreach scatter source j do
                for i = 0 to N-1 do
                        set t = ray_distance*(i + X_i)/N
                        send ray at position t to source j
                        sum in contribution using:
                        L(s) += kWs/(4pN) exp(-kt PHG(qij,g) Lij wij)
                end for
        end foreach
end srcscatter
```

As we mentioned earlier, the macro MAXSSAMP is designed to prevent excessive source sampling where it would make little difference. In the current release, it is set to 16, but may be changed at compile time.

The code for the m_mist() routine is fairly complicated, despite its simple purpose—tracking rays through mist volumes. Complications arise when a ray that never entered a mist region leaves one and when overlapping regions disagree on parameters. The simplified pseudocode follows:

```
m_mist(m, r) begin
        get scatter source list from arguments
        get extinction coefficient using pattern
        initialize new ray, copying old source list
        if entering mist region then
                if albedo assigned then assign to ray
                if eccentricity assigned then assign ray
                add our sources to ray scatter list
                if number of scatterers > MAXSLIST then
                        call error("too many scatterers")
                end if
        else
                delete our sources from ray scatter list
                if some sources weren't represented then
                        add our sources to parent ray's list
                        assign our mist parameters to parent
                end if
                subtract our extinction value from ray
                assign global albedo and eccentricity
        end if
        evaluate new ray
        copy result to parent ray
        return 1
end m_mist
```

Entering rays are much easier to handle than emerging rays, since we know what is inside our mist volume better than we know what is outside. Specifically, we know that the extinction coefficient increases by the specified amount and that the scattering albedo and eccentricity take on new values (if present). Also, any new sources to test for scattering are given in our mist primitive's string arguments. An emerging ray, on the other hand, takes on new, uncertain scattering albedo and eccentricity parameters. Since it is difficult to determine exactly what they should be, we use the global settings; this points up the danger of intersecting mist volumes whose albedo and/or eccentricity disagree with the command line values. Another difficulty is handling an emerging ray that never entered our volume—that is, from an interior viewpoint. Not only do we need to set the values for the emerging ray, but we also want to correct the parent ray's source list and parameters. Fortunately, this works, because the `rayparticipate()` function is not called until shading is done.

As mentioned earlier in the section titled Limitations, the `MAXSLIST` macro is defined as 32 in the current release. This is to discourage specifying regions with too many scattering sources, which add little to the realism of a rendering but require very long computation times.

14.4 Conclusion

In this chapter, we have offered a brief introduction to the mist type and its uses. Since this is a relatively new feature of *Radiance*, it is difficult to be thorough in our coverage. No doubt many shortcomings, as well as applications that never occurred to us, will become evident as time goes by.

CHAPTER 15

Parallel Rendering Computations

Despite our best efforts to make the ray-tracing calculation efficient, sometimes one CPU is just not enough to get the job done in the time allotted. If more than one processor is available, we may want to run them in parallel to complete the calculation sooner. If we are rendering an animation, the obvious approach is to render different frames on different processors, though, as we will see, this may not give us a linear speedup if we recompute potentially shared information such as interreflections. If we are rendering a single view, we also need to do some work to break up the image into pieces for the different processors.

In this chapter, we will discuss the problems of, and solutions for, parallel rendering on heterogeneous systems with *Radiance*. We begin with a discussion of our target system architecture(s), and of some special challenges posed by the algorithms in *Radiance,* in the Goals section. We then look at useful system functions, and at the way we apply them, in the Approach section. We then talk about the limitations of our methods and the relevant *Radiance* rendering parameters. Finally, we discuss our implementation and give pointers to the source code for further reading enjoyment.

15.1 Goals

One of the first questions to ask in parallel computing is "What is the target architecture?" In our case, we want the widest possible applicability, which means supporting the most common configurations of multiple-processor environments. The two most common configurations are single-processor workstations on a heterogeneous network and multiple-processor workstations with shared memory. We may even combine the two when multiple-processor workstations are connected to a network.

Ideally, our implementation would maximize use of whatever processors were available on a network, however they might be configured. As a practical measure, however, we will limit ourselves to processors with large address spaces running UNIX, since this is the usual platform for *Radiance* and offers the greatest potential for parallel performance.

15.1.1 Challenges

Ray tracing is a natural for parallel implementation because most of the calculations work independently—the computation of one pixel does not depend heavily on the computation of other pixels. However, there are certain optimizations in *Radiance* that result in some pixel interdependency. The most important of these is the diffuse interreflection calculation, which computes and stores hemispherical samplings of irradiance at various points in the scene. (See Chapter 12 for details.) These indirect values are reused many times over many parts of the image, and if the rendering process is divided among different machines that do not share intermediate results, the calculational efficiency will suffer. Therefore, it is crucial that we devise a method to share indirect values among cooperating processes.

Another key feature of *Radiance* is its portability among a wide range of UNIX architectures. We want our parallel implementation to work on as many different machines as possible—not just to minimize coding difficulties, but to maximize parallel potential in heterogeneous environments. Most local networks have workstations from a few different vendors connected, so if our method allows us to share processing among these different machines, we increase our total computing power that much more.

15.2 Approach

For our parallel rendering implementation, we decided to use a least-common-denominator approach. Although there were several parallel computation libraries available at the time, even one or two that worked in heterogeneous environments, we decided that the features they provided were not essential and did not warrant the risk of using a separate package.[42]

We decided early on that very coarse-grain parallelization made the most sense, since the bottlenecks in *Radiance* change from one scene to the next and even from one pixel to the next, so that it is impossible to know on what section of code to focus a fine-grained approach. The only advantage of fine-grain parallelization in ray tracing is superior load balancing, which we may achieve using a coarse-grain approach if we break up our overall rendering problem intelligently.

There are two related issues in the parallel implementation of almost any conventional algorithm:

- Data sharing
- Synchronization

Data sharing is important to avoid duplicate computations in parallel threads, which undermine everything. Synchronization between threads or processes is essential to maintaining data and program integrity. In general, the idea is to minimize the data that must be shared while maximizing the fraction of those data that are shared. (We will address the issue of sharing static data in the section on multiprocessing environments.) Likewise, we want to minimize the degree of synchronization that is necessary while ensuring that contention never corrupts our results.

15.2.1 Indirect Value Sharing

As we have mentioned, the principal challenge to parallelization in *Radiance* is the cache of indirect irradiance values maintained by the diffuse interreflection calculation. We must find some way to share these data between parallel threads or our method is doomed to duplicate a lot of effort and result in little speedup. Fortunately, we already have a convenient means for sharing values, which is the ambient

42. Using a separate library presents a maintenance problem, because that code is updated and its interface is changed over time. Even if the code is relatively bug-free, keeping releases consistent is nearly impossible unless the call interface is frozen or the library is included with the distribution. Including a library usually violates good sense, even when it does not violate copyright laws.

file. This file serves as the ultimate repository of indirect values. Since it is written in a system-independent format, it already provides data translation between heterogeneous systems—and, thanks to the *Network File System* (NFS), we also have a means to share this information over a network.

Data integrity is maintained using the *network lock manager*, which is included with most implementations of NFS. The lock manager provides a simple mechanism for accessing and updating a file shared over the network by asynchronous processes. A process requests either a read or a write lock on a section of the file, and the lock manager handles all such requests at the file server, blocking processes that might clobber data being read by another process. Multiple simultaneous read locks are permitted, but a write lock blocks all other locks on a file section.

During rendering, new indirect values are computed and stored in memory. After 20 or so values have accumulated, they are written to the end of the ambient file. Before this happens, a write lock is obtained on the file, and any new values contributed by other processes are read into memory. This way, all processes share indirect values, plus or minus the few that have accumulated since the last file synchronization. (Resynchronizing the file after every value would slow the processes down as they fought for exclusive access to the ambient file.)

15.2.2 Multiprocessor Platforms

The method we have just described takes care of data sharing over a network, but does not address the issue of memory sharing on machines with multiple processors. It is wasteful to have multiple copies of the same data in virtual memory which may result in unnecessary swapping for large scene descriptions.

Unfortunately, there are as many libraries for sharing memory as there are manufacturers making multiprocessor platforms. Since we want our code to be portable, we always look for some common way to accomplish our goal. Fortunately, the UNIX `fork` call comes to our rescue.

The `fork` system call creates a duplicate process, with an exact image of the calling (parent) process in a new child. A common optimization on virtual memory systems with memory sharing is to use the same VM pages for both the parent and the child, and to create a new page only if one process or the other "touches" it. This memory sharing mode is called *copy-on-write*, and it has the advantage of being completely transparent to the sharing processes.

All we have to do to share memory on a multiprocessor, then, is load our static data structures before we call `fork`. (Static data include geometry, auxiliary files such as images, octrees for instantiation, and so on.) As long as we do not subsequently alter any of this data, it will be shared among our parallel processes. We will not share any new information these processes create, but in most cases the static scene description dominates memory use, anyway.

15.2.3 User Control

Thus far, we have discussed in general terms the way memory and data may be shared between parallel rendering processes on multiprocessors and networked UNIX machines. However, we have not explained how you can take advantage of this capability. As with most aspects of *Radiance*, you are given ultimate control over the way the calculation is done, and for parallel rendering, you bear the responsibility for assigning processors to tasks.

Indirect value sharing is as simple as assigning the same ambient file to different processes using the **-af** option. For memory sharing, we have the **-PP** option, which creates duplicate processes using the `fork` system call as described in the last section. We can attach to these processes transparently using additional, identical **rpict** (or **rtrace**) command lines. We will discuss these options further in the section called Rendering Parameters. First, let's look at the two most common uses for parallel rendering, animation and large-image generation.

Animation

There are many ways to generate animations in *Radiance*, some of which are discussed in Chapter 9. Because animation tends to be a very time-consuming endeavor, we want our interface to be as flexible as possible, even if that makes using it a bit more complicated.

The simplest way to create a walk-through animation of a static environment is to write a list of view points, one per line, to a file. This file is then fed to the standard input of rpict using the **-S** and **-o** options; this results in the creation of one output picture per viewpoint. Generating frames in parallel in this case is simply a matter of having multiple rpict processes on multiple processors. Each rpict process will automatically skip frames in the animation that have already been started by another process, moving on to the next unrendered frame in the sequence. If an interreflection calculation is taking place, the -af option should be used with a networked file so that values will be shared among all the processes. If more than one processor is available on a given host, multiple rpict processes can be started there using the -PP option, so that memory is also shared.

More complicated walk-through animation techniques typically employ the **pinterp** program, which does not affect the use of rpict except that it requires the **-z** option. However, it can affect the rendering sequence, requiring more complicated control methods, especially if disk space is limited. The general animation control program, **ranimate**, uses an input file with variables and settings similar to **rad**, which may be used as a starting point for setting some of the parameters.

Ranimate manages many of the details of creating a large animation by watching disk space use, distributing computations among many processors, and recovering from system crashes. For walk-through animations, ranimate coordinates calls to rpict, pinterp, and **pfilt**, ensuring an efficient calculation on any number of processors and providing additional features such as motion blur (**pmblur**) and smooth transitions from one sequence to another. Scene animation requires additional scripts to create the appropriate scene description for each frame, for which pinterp cannot be used.

Details on how to set up and run animations are provided in Chapter 9, so we will not discuss the subject further here. However, we will touch on some of the algorithms used in ranimate toward the end of this chapter.

Large-Image Generation

Although it is possible to generate a large image in pieces using multiple invocations of rpict and reassembling them with **pcompos**, the details are sufficiently challenging that we felt a new utility to perform this function was a good idea. Thus, **rpiece** was born.

Each rpiece invocation manages a single rpict process, rendering pieces from a subdivided destination picture. Coordination between rpiece processes is managed by a common synchronization file on NFS. This file contains the index of the last piece begun, and each rpiece process locks the synchronization file before getting its next assignment. This way, no process has superiority over any other process and rpiece commands can be started and stopped at will on their respective host computers.

A large image should be divided into five to ten times as many pieces as there are processors to work on them, so that the last piece does not take a significant fraction of the total wall time. Figure 15.1 shows a typical image partitioning during parallel rendering by four rpiece processes, A, B, C, and D. The first piece rendered by process A is A.1, the second piece rendered by process C is C.2, and so on. In this example, we see that processes A and B have completed two pieces each, and process C has finished one and is working on a second. Process D is still working on its first piece, however, either because it is particularly difficult, or because D is a slower processor or is more heavily loaded or got a late start. Whichever process finishes a piece will next work on the one indicated with question marks. (The rendering order used by rpiece is column order, beginning at the upper right of the image.)

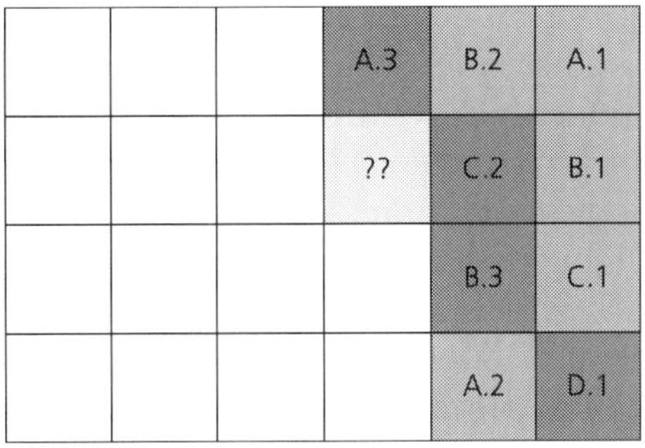

Figure 15.1 A parallel image rendering. The darkest squares are finished, the mid-range squares are in process, and the light square indicates the next piece to be assigned.

At any time, a new rpiece process may be started on a new host, or one may be gracefully terminated using an alarm signal (`kill -ALRM`). Because the processes' coordination is mediated only by the network lock manager, our method is robust even when machines and networks go up and down unpredictably. There is no master process, and therefore no bottleneck other than the file system itself. To avoid the delays associated with I/O completion, rpiece forks a copy of itself to attend to writing each piece.

As with parallel animation, rpiece processes share indirect irradiance values through a common ambient file given with -af, and multiprocessor workstations share memory using the -PP option. A special **-R** recover option may be used to rerender pieces that were left incomplete by rudely killed processes and crashed machines.

15.3 Limitations

As we mentioned in the section titled Multiprocessor Platforms, using the `fork` system call to share memory does not work for new calculated values. If memory growth happens with rpict or rtrace, it is usually because of new indirect values. These values are shared via the ambient file, but memory is shared only for the values read in from this file by the initial invocation before the `fork` call. Therefore, if thrashing becomes a problem on a multiprocessor platform, you can kill the processes and restart them to maximize memory sharing. The alarm signal should be used for rpiece, and the -r option should be used to recover partial animation frames with rpict.

Some UNIX systems do not have reliable network lock managers; this can result in corrupted ambient files, which may cause core dumps or corrupted images. Unfortunately, there is no solution to buggy system software other than complaining to vendors and threatening to take your business elsewhere. If the lock manager does not work, these algorithms will not work either.

At the beginning of this chapter, we said we would focus on the most common parallel processing configuration, which was single- and multiple-processor workstations on a network. We have found our algorithms to work well in environments ranging from a few processors to a few dozen, providing nearly linear speedup under nominal network loads. What happens, though, when we increase the number of processors into the hundreds? We start to run into contention problems over the file system. Depending on how many indirect values are cached before updating and how quickly these values are generated, processes may have to wait for a lock on the ambient file. Using rpiece, there may be contention over the synchronization file as well as the output file, which must be locked in sections to ensure consistent NFS behavior. Also, the network lock manager itself may start to bog down if a large number of processes are accessing the same file.

It is best to avoid applying more than a few dozen processors to any given rendering problem with these algorithms, unless it is separated cleanly so that images and indirect values are shared among smaller groups of processes, preferably on different NFS servers.

15.4 Rendering Parameters

Options that affect parallel rendering are found in both rpiece and rpict, with some overlapping in rtrace. We will start by discussing rpict options, noting when the same option exists for rpiece or rtrace:

-o Sets the *output* picture file specification. In rpict, this specification may contain an integer field for assigning an animation frame number in conjunction with the -S option (described next). If a given frame already exists on the file system, rpict will skip over it to the next one, and so on until it finds a frame that has not been started. This provides a simple and reliable mechanism for parallel rendering of frames in a walk-through animation.

-S Sets the *starting* frame number for an animated sequence. Successive views of a walk-through animation are read from the standard input. Use in conjunction with the -o option to generate a sequence of pictures.

-af Sets the *ambient file* to store and retrieve cached indirect irradiance values. Multiple processes will share values through this file using appropriate network locks, reads, and writes. This option applies to rpict, rpiece, rtrace, and rview.

-PP Executes in the *parallel persistent* mode using the given control file. All of the scene data will be read in and initialized before forking multiple memory-sharing child processes to attach to other invocations with the same -PP option. This option applies to rpict, rpiece, and rtrace. When used with rpict, the -S option must also be in effect, and new views to render are taken from the standard input. All processes must be run on the same machine, and the waiting process may be killed using the process ID stored in the control file.

The following options are specific to rpiece, and control the subdivision of the output picture and synchronization between rpiece processes:

-o Sets the picture *output* file, which must be shared over NFS if different rpiece processes will be run on different machines. This option differs from the rpict equivalent because the file may already exist, and there is no -S option, so animated sequences are not supported.

-X Sets the number of horizontal (x) divisions for the output picture. Use in conjunction with the -Y option.

-Y Sets the number of vertical (y) divisions for the output picture. The total number of pieces is the number of horizontal divisions times the number of vertical divisions, and should be between five and ten times the number of active rpiece processes for best results.

-F Sets the process synchronization *file*. Cooperating rpiece processes will use this file to record what pieces have been rendered and which piece should be rendered next. Like the output picture, this file must be shared over the network via NFS if the different processes are running on different machines.

-R *Recovers* killed pieces from the given synchronization file before proceeding with cooperative rendering. This option is used to rerender incomplete pieces from an unfinished rpiece picture when one or more of the contributing processes has been killed or has crashed.

15.5 Algorithms and Source Code

There are three main components of parallel computation in *Radiance*. The first is indirect value sharing through the ambient file. The second is memory sharing through the `fork` system call. The third is large-image rendering with the rpiece program. We will discuss each component in turn.

15.5.1 Indirect Value Sharing

Indirect value sharing is accomplished by the `ambsync` routine in the *src/rt/ambient.c* module. In pseudocode, this routine works as follows:

```
ambsync() begin
        obtain write lock on ambient file
        if file has grown since last write then
                load values added since last write
        end if
        write new values to file
        record file size for next check
        unlock file
end ambsync
```

The final details add some complexity to the actual C code, but the basic idea is just this simple.

15.5.2 Memory Sharing

On the face of it, the idea behind memory sharing is very simple: load in all the scene data and call `fork` as many times as necessary. The actual implementation is more complicated, because we must somehow connect to these forked child processes. To make this as transparent as possible to the user, we decided to allow subsequent command invocations to find and attach to these processes, thus giving the illusion of a new, independent rpict or rtrace command.

Attaching new invocations to forked children is accomplished in the *rt/src/persist.c* module, whose routines are called from `main` (*rt/src/rmain.c*). Additional help is provided by the *rt/src/preload.c* module, which initializes the scene data structures before calling `fork`, and by the *rt/src/duphead.c* module, which duplicates the output header as needed by the multiple invocations.

We will start with some simplified pseudocode for the `main` routine as it pertains to memory sharing (i.e., we assume that the -PP option is in effect):

```
main(argc, argv) begin
       call persistfile with -PP argument
       duplicate stdout file descriptor for later
       call openheader to record info header
       load octree
       add to info header
       load ambient file
       reconnect original stdout file descriptor
       call preload_objs to initialize scene data
       foreach forked child process do
              call pfhold to await new attach
       end foreach
       call pfdetach to release persist file
       call dupheader if output is to stdout
       call rpict or rtrace procedure
       call ambsync
       call quit
end main
```

It is impossible to understand the above pseudocode without understanding the `persistfile`, `pfhold`, and `pfdetach` routines. These routines are coded in the *src/rt/persist.c* module and are described below:

- `void persistfile(char *pfn);`
  This routine is actually the exit point for an rpict or rtrace process attaching to a waiting child. If the given control file does not exist, `persistfile` creates it and locks it. However, if the file already exists, `persistfile` uses it to attach to the original process, calling `io_process` to handle interprocess communication.
- `void pfhold();`
  This routine is called by `main` to write out the process number and named pipes to the control file, then wait for another invocation to attach to us. The new invocation sends us a `SIGIO` signal from its `io_process` routine after opening our input and output pipes. Upon waking, we attach our ends of the pipes to `stdin` and `stdout` and return to `main`.
- `void pfdetach();`
  This routine releases the control file and header file resources, so that we do not hold up other processes once rendering has begun.

- `void io_process();`
  This routine is called by `persistfile` to attach to an rpict or rtrace process. It reads the control file to get the process ID and named pipes. After calling `pfdetach` to release the control file, it sends a `SIGIO` signal to the waiting process to wake it up, then forks a child process to handle the input side while the original process handles the output side. This routine never returns.

Going back to the pseudocode for the `main` procedure, we can reword the basic algorithm like this:

```
if control file exists then
        attach i/o to other process
else
        create new control file
        load data structures
        fork child process to wait for attach
        run calculation
        clean up and exit
end if
```

The only things left to understand are the subtleties associated with the handling of standard input and standard output. Specifically, it is very important *when* the input and output streams are closed, since this signals to connected processes that we are finished. For example, the first action of the `pfhold` routine is to close the standard input and output descriptors. This signals to any attached I/O processes that we are through with them. It is also important in the original rpict or rtrace parent process that the standard output not be lost while the header information is recorded by `openheader`, since it will be needed later for the parent's output.

15.5.3 Animation

The ranimate program is similar to rad in that it takes an input file with variables and settings, then makes calls to other *Radiance* programs and scripts to do the actual work of generating animations. Input of ranimate control files relies on the same routines used by rad, in fact, since the syntax is identical. These routines are in *src/util/loadvars.c*, which uses definitions from *src/util/vars.h*. Most of the code for ranimate is contained in *src/util/ranimate.c*, and the network process control code is contained in *src/util/netproc.h* and *src/util/netproc.c*. The code details of ranimate are not very interesting or important, but the sequence of *Radiance* program calls is informative, since it gives an idea of what it takes to control an animation effectively.

We can think of the animation process as three processes going on simultaneously. The first process is the initial *rendering* of animation frames by rpict. If we are generating a walk-through animation, we will probably use z-buffer image interpolation (pinterp) to get a smoother sequence from fewer initial frames. Pinterp and pfilt fall into the second process category, which is *filtering*. The third process, which we call *transferring*, is less obvious but equally critical on systems with limited free disk space. Synchronization in the event of a system crash is guaranteed by a status file that keeps track of what has been done so far.

Animation generation is accomplished in batches of *N* frames each, where *N* is determined by the amount of free disk space you have allocated. The main loop is described here:

```
while not done do
       render batch of N pictures with rpict
       update status, marking frames as rendered
       filter views with pinterp and/or pfilt
       archive and delete original frames
       update status, marking frames as filtered
       transfer final frames
       update status, marking frames as transferred
end while
```

Of the above steps, rendering and filtering are carried out in parallel if multiple processors are made available. Parallelism during rendering is accomplished using the property of the rpict -o option, described earlier in this chapter, that prevents more than one process from working on the same frame at the same time. On multiprocessing hosts, the -PP option is also employed to provide memory sharing, and the -af option is used in most cases to share indirect values across all processes. Following the rendering phase, parallel filtering processes are managed using the routines in *src/util/netproc.c*.

If one of the secondary machines goes down, ranimate recovers the failed frame and takes the machine off its list. If the control machine crashes or all of the secondary machines go down, or if some disk error occurs, ranimate must be restarted. In this case, the status file is used to determine where to pick up the processing again. In the worst case, some of the filtering is repeated unnecessarily.

15.5.4 Large-Image Rendering

The rpiece program is implemented in a single module, *src/util/rpiece.c*. It coordinates picture dicing and process coordination, and calls rpict to do the actual rendering work. The program is broken into three major components: initialization, piece selection, and piece output. Initialization is handled by the `init` routine, piece selection is mediated by `nextpiece`, and pieces are output in `putpiece`. We describe each of these routines below.

- `void init(int ac, char **av);`
  If the picture output file does not exist, this routine creates it and writes a new header with the command arguments as given. If the picture file already exists, we open it and check that the resolution agrees with ours. We also open the synchronization file if one is specified, and start the rpict process.
- `int nextpiece(int *xp, int *yp);`
  Gets the indices of the next piece to render from the synchronization file if it exists, otherwise from the standard input. Returns nonzero if there is another piece to render, or 0 if we received a `SIGALRM` signal or finished the picture (if there is a synchronization file; otherwise we hit the end-of-file on our input). This routine handles locking of the synchronization file and recovery of incomplete pieces if the -R option is in effect.
- `int putpiece(int xpos, int ypos);`
  This routine reads the indicated piece from the rpict process and (optionally) forks a process to lock the picture file and write out the piece. If there is a synchronization file, the indices of the finished piece are appended to it following successful I/O completion. This information may be used later by another rpiece process with the -R option to determine that the piece was indeed finished. The parent process immediately returns with the child's process ID. If no forking took place, the function returns a zero value when I/O is completed.

15.6 Conclusion

In this chapter, we have given an overview of parallel computation as it currently stands in *Radiance*. We anticipate, in the near future, developing a new interface that will enable rview-like interactive rendering using parallel processing. This may be based on the existing implementation of rtrace, or some new parallelization. Output may be to a standard display or to a virtual reality (VR) system.

Bibliography

[Arv91] Arvo, James, editor. 1991. *Graphics Gems II.* San Diego: Academic Press.

[Arv95] Arvo, James. 1995. Applications of Irradiance Tensors to the Simulation of Non-Lambertian Phenomena. *Computer Graphics,* Annual Conference Series (July), 335–42.

[Ash94] Ashdown, Ian. 1994. *Radiosity: A Programmer's Perspective.* New York: Wiley.

[BS95] Blanc, Carole, and Christophe Schlick. 1995. A Spline Model Designed for the End-User. *Computer Graphics,* Annual Conference Series (July), 37–86.

[CIE73] CIE. 1973. *Standardization of Luminance Distribution on Clear Skies,* Publication No. 22. Paris: CIE.

[Com93] Compagnon, Raphael. 1993. Design of New Daylighting Systems Using ADELINE Software. *Solar Energy in Architecture and Urban Planning,* proceedings of the 3D European Conference on Architecture. Florence, Italy (May).

[Coo86] Cook, Robert. 1986. Stochastic Sampling in Computer Graphics. *ACM Transactions on Graphics,* 5(1) (January), 51–72.

[CPC84] Cook, Robert, Thomas Porter, and Loren Carpenter. 1984. Distributed Ray Tracing. *Computer Graphics* 18(3) (July), 137–47.

[CR74] Catmull, E., and R. Rom. 1974. A Class of Local Interpolating Splines. *Computer Aided Geometric Design,* Barnhill, R., and R. Riesenfeld, eds. San Diego: Academic Press, 317–26.

[FDFH90] Foley, James D., Andries van Dam, Steven K. Feiner, John F. Hughes. 1990. *Computer Graphics: Principles and Practice.* Reading: Addison-Wesley.

[Fry54] Fry, G. A. 1954. "A Re-evaluation of the Scattering Theory of Glare," Illuminating Engineering, Vol. XLIX, p. 98.

[Gla95] Glassner, Andrew S. 1995. *Principles of Digital Image Synthesis.* San Fransisco: Morgan Kaufmann.

[Hec94] Heckbert, Paul S. 1994. *Graphics Gems IV.* Cambridge: AP Professional.

[Hil76] Hils, B.L. 1976. Visibility Under Night Driving Conditions Part III—Derivation of (Delta-L, A) Characteristics and Factors in Their Application, Australian Road Research, vol. 6, no. 4, Dec. 1976.

[HTSG91] He, Xiao-Dong, Kenneth Torrance, Francois Sillion, and Donald Greenberg. 1991. A Comprehensive Physical Model of Light Reflection. *Computer Graphics,* 25(4) (July), 175–86.

[IES83] *American National Standard: Roadway Lighting (ANSI/IES RP-8).* 1983. New York: Illuminating Engineering Society of North America.

[IES91] *Standard File Format for Electronic Transfer of Photometric Data (LM-63-91).* 1991. New York: Illuminating Engineering Society of North America.

[IES93a] *IESNA Lighting Handbook—8th Edition (HB-93).* 1993. Mark Rea, ed. New York: Illuminating Engineering Society of North America.

[IES93b] *American National Standard: Roadway Lighting (ANSI/IES RP-8).* 1993. New York: Illuminating Engineering Society of North America.

[KA91] Kirk, David, and James Arvo. 1991. Unbiased Sampling Techniques for Image Synthesis. *Computer Graphics,* 25(4) (July), 153–56.

[KV93] Kittler, R., and P. Valko. 1993. Radiance Distribution on Densely Overcast Skies: Comparison with CIE Luminance Standard. *Solar Energy,* 51(5), 349–55

[Lit88] Littlefair, P. J. 1988. Measurements of the Luminous Efficacy of Daylight. *Lighting Res. Technol.,* 20(4), 177–88

[LRP97] Larson, G. W., H. Rushmeier, C. Piatko. 1997. "A Visibility Matching Tone Reproduction Operator for High Dynamic Range Scenes." IEEE Transactions on Visualization and Computer Graphics 3(4), 291-306.

[Mar95] Mardaljevic, J. 1995. Validation of a Lighting Simulation Program under Real Sky Conditions. *Lighting Res. Technol.* 27(4), 181–88.

[MT87] Magnenat-Thalmann, Nadia, and Daniel Thalmann. 1987. *Image Synthesis.* Springer-Verlag.

[NRHGL77] Nicodemus, F. E., J. C. Richmond, J. J. Hsia, I. W. Ginsberg, and T. Limperis. 1977. Geometric Considerations and Nomenclature for Reflectance. National Bureau of Standards (US) Monograph 161.

[Ous94] Ousterhout, John K. 1994. *Tcl and the Tk Toolkit.* Reading: Addison-Wesley.

[Per85] Perlin, Ken. 1985. An Image Synthesizer. *Computer Graphics,* 19(3) (July), 287–96.

[Phi90] Phillips, E. S., et al. 1990. Vision and Visibility in Vehicular Accident Reconstruction. *SAE 1990 Transactions: Journal of Passenger Cars,* Section 6, v 99, paper #900369.

[Phi93] Phillips, E. S. 1993. Computer Visualization of Roadway Lighting. STV vs. Traditional Design Criteria. *Proceedings of the 2nd International Symposium on Visibility and Luminance in Roadway Lighting.* New York: Lighting Research Institute.

[PO83] Petherbridge, P., and D. R. Oughton. 1983. Weather and Solar Data. *Build. Serv. Eng. Res. and Technol.* 4(4), 147–58.

[PSM93] Perez, R., R. Seals, and R. J. Michalsky. 1993. All-Weather Model for Sky Luminance Distribution–Preliminary Configuration and Validation. *Solar Energy*, 50(3), 235–45.

[Rog85] Rogers, David F. 1985. *Procedural Elements for Computer Graphics.* New York: McGraw-Hill.

[Rub81] Rubenstein, R. Y. 1981. *Simulation and the Monte Carlo Method.* New York: Wiley and Sons.

[Rus86] Rushmeier, Holly E. 1986. *Extending the Radiosity Method to Transmitting and Specularly Reflecting Surfaces.* Master's Thesis, Cornell University.

[Rus88] Rushmeier, Holly E. 1988. *Realistic Image Synthesis for Scenes with Radiatively Participating Media.* Ph.D. Thesis, Cornell University.

[Rus95] Rushmeier, Holly E. 1995. Participating Media. *Realistic Input for Realistic Images*, Course 1 Notes, ACM Siggraph Annual Conference.

[RW94] Rushmeier, Holly, and Greg Ward. 1994. Energy-Preserving Non-linear Filters. *Computer Graphics*, Annual Conference Series (July).

[Sch91] Schlick, Christophe. 1991. "An Adaptive Sampling Technique for Multidimensional Integration by Ray-Tracing," Proceedings of the Second Eurographics Workshop on Rendering.

[Shi92] Shirley, Peter. 1992. Nonuniform Random Point Sets via Warping. *Graphics Gems III.* David Kirk, ed. Boston: AP Professional, 80–83.

[SP94] Sillion, Francois, and Claude Puech. 1994. *Radiosity and Global Illumination.* San Francisco: Morgan Kaufmann.

[SW92] Shirley, Peter, and Changyaw Wang. 1992. Distribution Ray Tracing: Theory and Practice. *Third Annual Eurographics Workshop on Rendering*, to be published by Springer-Verlag. Bristol, UK (May), 33–43.

[SWZ96] Shirley, Peter, Changyaw Wang, and Kurt Zimmerman. 1996. Monte Carlo Techniques for Direct Lighting Calculations. *ACM Transactions on Graphics*, 15(1) (January), 1–36.

[VG95] Veach, Eric, and Leonidas Guibas. 1995. Optimally Combining Sampling Techniques for Monte Carlo Rendering. *Computer Graphics*, Annual Conference Series (August), 419–28.

[War91] Ward, G. 1991. Adaptive Shadow Testing for Ray Tracing. *Photorealistic Rendering in Computer Graphics.* P. Brunet and F. W. Jansen, eds. Proceedings of the Second Annual Eurographics Workshop on Rendering. Barcelona: Springer-Verlag.

[War92] Ward, G. 1992. Measuring and Modeling Anisotropic Reflection. *Computer Graphics.* Chicago, IL (July).

[WCG87] Wallace, John, Michael Cohen, and Donald Greenberg. 1987. A Two-pass Solution to the Rendering Equation: A Synthesis of Ray Tracing and Radiosity Methods. *Computer Graphics*, 21(4) (July), 311–20.

[WH92] Ward, G., and P. Heckbert. 1992. Irradiance Gradients. *Third Annual Eurographics Workshop on Rendering,* to be published by Springer-Verlag. Bristol, UK (May).

[Whi80] Whitted, Turner. 1980. An Improved Illumination Model for Shaded Display. *Communications of the ACM,* 23(6) (June), 343–49.

[WR88] Ward, G., and F. Rubinstein. 1988. A New Technique for Computer Simulation of Illuminated Spaces. *Journal of the Illuminating Engineering Society* 17(1) (Winter).

[WRC88] Ward, G., F. Rubinstein, and R. Clear. 1988. A Ray Tracing Solution for Diffuse Interreflection. *Computer Graphics* 22(4).

[WS67] Wyszecki, G., and W. S. Stiles. 1967. *Color Science.* New York: Wiley and Sons.

Glossary

absorption coefficient The fraction of light absorbed per unit distance in a participating medium. In SI units, this is specified as a fraction per meter. In *Radiance*, the absorption is given separately for red, green, and blue.

adaptive sampling The automatic sending of additional samples in cases where the default number of samples is deemed inadequate to achieve the desired accuracy.

albedo The unitless ratio between the *scattering coefficient* and the *extinction coefficient* for a participating medium. An albedo of 0 means that the particles do not scatter light. An albedo of 1 means that the particles do not absorb light.

algorithm A method that is fully described in a procedure or computer program.

alias In a *Radiance* scene description, an alias associates a new identifier (and possibly a new modifier) with a previously defined primitive.

altitude The angle between a vector and the surface horizon, which is equal to 90 degrees minus the *polar angle*.

ambient (value, calculation) An ambient value approximates the global average of radiance over all directions and all points of interest in a scene. It is specified in SI units of watts per steradian per square meter for red, green, and blue. The ambient calculation in *Radiance* replaces this global average with local averages based on indirect irradiance computations. It is more accurately referred to as a *diffuse interreflection calculation*.

ambient file A binary file in which indirect irradiance values and their gradients are stored for reuse in other calculations. (See the CD-ROM section on File Formats for details.)

angular fisheye perspective A perspective view projection in which the angle from the central view direction is proportional to the distance from the center of the image. (Compare to *hemispherical fisheye perspective.*)

animation (walk-through, scene animation) A *walk-through animation* is a sequence of images rendered from the same scene description and lighting but from a changing view point, direction, and so on. *Scene animation* occurs when the actual scene geometry, materials, and/or lighting are changing with each frame.

animation path The sequence of view positions and directions in a walk-through animation. Also called the *camera path.* (See Chapter 9 for details.)

anisotropic A reflection or transmission distribution function (BRTDF) that varies with rotation about the surface normal. Examples of anisotropic reflection include varnished wood with noticeable grain, brushed metal, and combed hair.

antialiasing Any technique that reduces sampling artifacts in the final image, particularly "jaggies" caused by abrupt changes in scene geometry. The usual antialiasing method used in *Radiance* is called *supersampling.*

antimatter A primitive type that provides a rudimentary *CSG subtraction* operation, removing one solid from another.

array transform A type of transform in which an object is repeated at multiple positions. (See the **xform** manual page.)

ASCII The American Standard for Character Information Interchange—the standard encoding of alphanumeric and control characters as integers between 0 and 127.

azimuth The angle about the surface normal relative to some standard direction, such as south.

B-spline A cubic polynomial formulation with the potential for $C^{(2)}$ continuity, which provides a visually smooth curve, even though it does not generally pass through any of its control points.

Bezier curve A cubic polynomial formulation whose parameters specify four points near the desired curve shape. In three dimensions, a Bezier surface is specified by sixteen points near the desired surface patch.

boundary representation (B-rep) A method for representing 3D objects by their surface boundaries, which may be open or closed but do not necessarily have any relationship to one another. (Compare with *Constructive Solid Geometry.*)

BRDF, BRTDF, BSDF The bidirectional reflectance distribution function (BRDF) is a mathematical function that describes the way light is reflected from a point on a locally planar surface. The bidirectional reflectance-transmittance distribution function (BRTDF) is also known as the bidirectional scattering distribution function (BSDF), which describes the way light is transmitted and reflected by a locally planar surface. All are functions of four angles (two incident and two scattered) and return units of 1/*steradian.*

CAD Computer-aided design or Computer-aided drafting. CAD tools are typically used to interactively create and describe geometric entities.

candelas The SI unit for the total visible light leaving a light source in a certain direction, which may be written out as *lumens* per *steradian*.

candlepower distribution The light output distribution for a source, given as a function of direction (two angles in the general case) that returns candelas (in SI units). This is an approximation that assumes the receiver is far from the source.

Cartesian coordinate system A system for locating points based on an origin and two or more perpendicular axes passing through it. In *Radiance*, 3D coordinates are specified via a *right-hand Cartesian coordinate system*, where the z-axis is in the direction of the thumb of the right hand when the fingers are curled in the direction of the x-axis, and then the y-axis.

chromaticity The exact color (but not the luminance) of a light source or reflecting surface, given as two values, for example a *CIE color* (x,y) coordinate. Also sometimes called *chrominance*.

CIE The Commission International de l'Eclairage, which sets international standards for lighting, daylight, and color measurement and estimation.

CIE color Several color systems are put forth by the CIE. The most commonly applied system is the CIE 1931 1-degree standard observer, which specifies a perceived color as a *tristimulus value*, that is, a coordinate triplet indicating the luminance and chromaticity of a stimulus as it is perceived by a 1-degree spot about the foveal center. This may be given equivalently as an *XYZ* or *Yxy* value, where x and y are equal to $X/(X + Y + Z)$ and $Y/(X + Y + Z)$, respectively. (See the section titled Supplemental Information in Chapter 10 for further information.)

CIE standard sky distribution Sky light is a continually varying and unpredictable quantity, so for analysis and comparison purposes, the CIE recommends a specific set of standard sky distributions that approximate average skies. The most commonly applied are the *CIE overcast sky* and the *CIE clear sky*. More recently, the CIE has proposed a third, intermediate sky distribution that better approximates real skies in many countries. (See Chapter 6 for details.)

client A program or process that accesses the resources of a *server* executing locally or on a remote system over a network.

clipping plane An imaginary plane before which or beyond which nothing is visible. The fore clipping plane (-vo option) determines the closest visible surfaces, and the aft clipping plane (-va option) determines the furthest visible surfaces.

color temperature A *black body*, whose radiation is solely the result of thermal activity, emits a characteristic spectrum that is determined exactly by its surface temperature. Light sources that approximate such a spectrum, such as incandescent lamps, are often characterized by their *correlated color temperature*, given in degrees Kelvin.

command expansion In a *Radiance* scene description, an *in-line command* that begins with an exclamation point (!) is executed by the system and the output is read in as more scene input, which may also contain in-line commands that are also executed. (This is called a scene *hierarchy*.)

command line In UNIX, a command line is generally a single line passed to the user's *shell* for command execution. This typically involves searching for an executable binary or shell script corresponding to the first word in the line, and expanding any file-matching wildcards in the remaining (unquoted) arguments. Other substitutions may also take place, such as variable or history substitution; you should consult the manual page for your particular shell for details. Multiple commands may appear on a single command line, joined either by a semicolon (;) indicating sequential execution, or a *pipe* character (|) indicating parallel execution with the standard output of the first command passed to the standard input of the second command. Again, particular shells have additional syntax for other interpretations.

computational complexity The limiting relationship of computation time to the number of objects. It is often given in the form of "big O" notation, which means "on the order of." For example, an algorithm that has $O(N^2)$ computational complexity has time requirements proportional to the square of the number of objects as N goes to infinity. (See also *storage complexity*.)

cone In *Radiance*, the family of cones includes right-angle truncated cones, cylinders, and rings (disks with optional holes).

constructive solid geometry (CSG) A method for representing 3D objects as the union, intersection, and subtraction of solid (volumetric) geometry. In contrast to *boundary representation*, CSG representations are compact and make better use of curved primitives, but place greater requirements on the rendering software.

contrast In lighting, contrast is defined as the difference between the foreground luminance and the background luminance, divided by the background luminance. Contrast is what the human eye relies on to see object detail, and is the most important quantity to reproduce faithfully in any rendering algorithm.

converter See *translator*.

CPU Central processing unit. The *processor* in a computer, usually consisting of registers, an arithmetic logic unit (ALU), memory-addressing logic, and (in most cases) a floating-point unit (FPU).

cylindrical perspective A viewing projection that maps vertical angles the same way as a linear perspective view, but maps horizontal angles such that horizontal distance from the center of the image is proportional to the angle from the center of view. Also called a *panorama*, a cylindrical view can cover a full 360 degrees horizontally, which is needed to generate QuickTime VR movies.

data file A *Radiance* data file describes a scalar function over N-dimensional space as a linearly interpolated table of discrete values. (See the CD-ROM section on File Formats for file syntax and semantics.)

data sharing When multiple rendering or lighting simulation processes are executed simultaneously on the same scene, data sharing permits diffuse interreflection (ambient) values to be used by all processes, avoiding unnecessary duplication of expensive ray-sampling calculations.

daylight factor The ratio of interior illuminance at the workplane to the exterior illuminance at the ground plane. In the common case of the standard *CIE overcast sky* distribution, this value is usually less than 1, and is independent of the time of day or time of year, which makes it very useful for comparison purposes. (See Chapter 6 for further details.)

deterministic Any algorithm that consistently produces exactly the same result for exactly the same input. (Compare to *stochastic* and *Monte Carlo.*)

device driver In **rview**, a device driver is a program or set of subroutines that translates drawing commands and input requests into the appropriate calls for the current display or window system.

dielectric A *participating medium* that refracts, and may absorb, but does not scatter radiation. Examples include water, wine, and glass. A dielectric is generally characterized by an *index of refraction* and an *absorption* or *transmission coefficient.* In the case of the *dielectric* primitive used in *Radiance*, an additional *Hartmann constant* may be used to approximate the change in the index of refraction with *wavelength.*

diffraction The deviation from linear propagation that occurs when light passes a small object or opening. This phenomenon is significant only when the object or opening is on the order of the *wavelength* of light, between 380 and 780 nanometers for human vision. For this reason, diffraction effects are ignored in most rendering algorithms, since most modeled geometry is on a much larger scale.

diffuse Scattering light in all directions, as occurs in *Lambertian* reflection, which is the ideal diffuse case. Diffuse transmission means that light is scattered equally in all transmitted directions, that is, in all directions on the opposite side of the surface.

diffuse interreflection The propagation of light by diffuse reflection and transmission in an environment. The *Radiance diffuse interreflection calculation* computes the diffuse component of light bouncing around a scene. (See Chapter 12 for details.)

direct component The illumination arriving at a surface point directly from *light sources.*

directional-diffuse Non-Lambertian reflection or transmission, in which light is scattered in all directions, but favors some directions over others. (See also *rough specular.*)

dispersion The tendency of light to scatter spatially when refracted through a dielectric medium whose index of refraction varies with wavelength. (See also *Hartmann constant.*)

display Any presentation method, such as a graphics monitor, transparency, or print. The independent color channels available on a display are called the *display primaries.*

emittance The visible light emitted (but not reflected) by a surface, expressed in SI units of lumens per square meter. (Radiant emittance is given in radiometric units of watts per square meter.)

emitter A surface that emits light. See *light source.*

exitance The total visible light leaving a surface, including reflections, expressed in SI units of lumens per square meter. (*Radiant exitance* is given in radiometric units of watts per square meter.)

exposure A scaling factor used to map the computed or measured world radiances or luminances to the appropriate range for display, typically 0 to 1. This assumes a linear range for both input and output. (See *gamma correction.*)

extinction coefficient The fraction of light lost to scattering and absorption per unit distance in a participating medium. A simple sum of the *absorption coefficient* and the *scattering coefficient.* In *Radiance,* the extinction coefficient is divided into separate red, green, and blue components. (See Chapter 14 for details.)

fenestration A window system, including vertical or horizontal blinds, multiple glass panes, and any associated frames or obstructions.

filter Any program that processes a *Radiance* picture and produces a modified picture as its output. Programs that take more than one input picture are sometimes included in this category, but should probably be called something more general, such as *image processors.*

fisheye perspective See *angular fisheye perspective* and *hemispherical fisheye perspective.*

font file A *Radiance* font file describes the polygonal outline of one or more character *glyphs,* which are used to produce text patterns or mixtures (or by **psign** to make pictures directly). (See the CD-ROM section on File Formats for file syntax and semantics.)

fovea The high-resolution central region of the retina, spanning about 1 degree of the visual field in humans.

fractal noise A random function with a frequency spectrum that follows a $1/f$ profile (where f is the frequency). In *Radiance,* the fnoise3(*x,y,z*) function returns fractal noise values between -1 and 1 with an autocorrelation distance of 1, and is defined over all space. (Contrast with *Perlin noise.* See Chapter 4 for examples.)

frozen octree A *Radiance octree* that has been compiled with the **oconv -f** option, so that it contains a binary representation of all the original scene description information. This type of octree is quicker to load, and easier to transport to other locations because the original scene files and their dependencies need not be copied. (Auxiliary files, such as patterns and textures, will still need to be accessible, however.)

function file A file containing function and variable definitions in the *functional language* of *Radiance.* These may be used to define procedural textures, patterns, mixtures, and coordinate mappings for the renderer, or numerous other functions for generators, filters, and other utility programs. (See the CD-ROM section on File Formats for file syntax and semantics.)

functional language A language that replaces programming steps with function definitions in no particular order. Usually, *recursion* replaces looping as the primary construct for iteration, and evaluation sequence is irrelevant because there are no explicit temporary variables or side effects.

gamma correction Most computer and television monitors exhibit a response function that approximates a simple power law, and the exponent is called the monitor's gamma. Typical displays have gamma values between 1.5 and 3.0; 2.2 is a frequently used standard. Some graphics hardware partially compensates for this response function, bringing the effective system gamma down to 1.8 or 1.4. The correct display of images, whether computer-generated or captured, requires proper correction for the system's gamma response. (See Chapter 5 for details.)

Gaussian (distribution, surface) The normal distribution curve for a random variable (i.e., the bell-shaped curve). If the microfacet slope of a surface is normally distributed, it is said to be a *Gaussian surface*. (See also *roughness*.)

generator A generator is a program that produces a *geometric description* on its output for a specified shape, which may be simple but is more often complex. A few generators, such as **gensky**, produce nongeometric descriptions or combinations of materials and geometry.

geometric description A geometric description contains primitives for the *cones, polygons,* and *spheres* that make up a scene's *boundary representation.*

geometric model This is a general term used for any finite model of a scene's geometry. (The complexity of actual geometry is fundamentally infinite in real environments.)

glare (discomfort, disability) The result of bright sources in the field of view. *Discomfort glare* refers to the pain a viewer experiences in trying to see past bright sources; *disability glare* refers to the associated loss of visibility.

glazing The glass associated with a *fenestration* system, which may be single-, double-, or triple-paned with various coatings, films, and thermal barriers.

global illumination The general problem of light propagation in simulated environments, accounting for the many interreflections between scene surfaces.

glyph A bounded 2D graphic typically used to represent some character or other abstraction. A symbol. In a font, a glyph is the name given to one character's geometric description.

ground plane The horizontal surface outside a building corresponding to the approximate ground level.

Hartmann constant A parameter that approximates the change in the *index of refraction* of a particular *dielectric material* as a function of *wavelength.* Usually given in units of nanometers (10^{-9} meters), this constant is divided by the *wavelength* and added to a base index of refraction.

hemispherical fisheye perspective A viewing projection in which the distance from the center of the image is proportional to the cosine of the angle from the central view direction. (Compare to *angular fisheye perspective.*)

hemispherical reflectance The total light reflected by a surface for a given direction of parallel incident radiation.

hermite curve A cubic polynomial formulation whose parameters specify the starting point, ending point, starting tangent vector, and ending tangent vector. In three dimensions, a hermite surface is defined by the four corners with two tangent vectors plus one curl vector at each vertex.

Heyney-Greenstein parameter The main parameter in a formula used to approximate the anisotropic scattering of a participating medium, where a value of 0 indicates perfectly isotropic scattering, and a value approaching 1 indicates a strongly forward-scattering medium. (See Chapter 14 for formula and details.)

hierarchy A tree of objects, such as a *scene description* file that loads in other scene files that load other files in turn via *in-line commands.* Hierarchy allows one to animate a finger attached to a hand attached to an arm attached to a torso, for example.

IES luminaire data Candlepower distribution data together with other miscellaneous information in a standard ASCII format proposed by the IESNA [IES91].

IESNA The Illuminating Engineering Society of North America, a professional organization that sets standard practices for lighting design in the U.S. and Canada.

illum The basic *secondary light source* type in *Radiance*. An illum may also be called an *impostor*, since it is not really an emitter, but plays as one in the direct calculation. (See Chapter 13 for details.)

illuminance The integrated visible light arriving at a surface, expressed in SI units of lumens per square meter, or *lux*. (Compare to *irradiance*.)

illuminance meter A photometric device for measuring *illuminance*.

image plane An imaginary plane on which a picture is projected. The radiances arriving at this imaginary surface are written into a picture as an array of color values.

image processing Operations on images, such as scaling, inversion, summation, warping, and so on. (See *filter*.)

image synthesis The creation of a color or black-and-white image from a mathematical description of a scene. More commonly called *rendering*.

impostor A surface with simplified properties that stands in for a more complete description in the direct component calculation as an efficiency measure. Also called an *illum* in *Radiance*. (See Chapter 13 for details.)

in-line command A command, embedded in a *Radiance* scene description, which is preceded by an initial exclamation point (!). The end of the command is indicated by a new-line character, but if the new-line character is preceded by a backslash (\), then the command continues on the next line. In-line commands may not read from their standard input, and their standard output must contain only valid *Radiance* scene description primitives, aliases, comments, and other in-line commands.

index of refraction The ratio of the speed of light in a vacuum to the speed of light in a particular participating medium. This value determines how light is *refracted* (bent) as it passes from one medium to another. The index of refraction of air is very close to 1, whereas the index of refraction of glass is about 1.52, meaning that light travels over 1.5 times faster through air than it does through glass.

indirect component The component of light arriving at a surface indirectly via bounces off other, nonemitting surfaces. This may include specular and diffuse reflections. (See also *indirect irradiance* and *diffuse interreflection*.)

indirect irradiance A quantity equal to the integrated radiation arriving at a surface point excluding light sources that are counted as part of the direct component. It is expressed in SI units of watts per steradian per square meter.

information header A short section of ASCII text at the beginning of a *Radiance* binary format file, which is terminated by an empty line (i.e., two successive new-line characters). This header usually begins with `#?RADIANCE` and contains the commands that generated the file, along with any pertinent variables indicating the software version, view, exposure, format, and so on. This information may be conveniently read with the **getinfo** command.

instance A single example of an object, which may be repeated many times in many places in a scene. The *Radiance instance* primitive is used to replicate scene information that is compiled in a *Radiance octree.*

intersection point The 3D point at which a ray intersects a surface. In cases where multiple ray intersections are possible, the first is the one that is used. (See *ray tracing.*)

irradiance The integrated radiation arriving at a surface at all wavelengths, expressed in SI units of watts per square meter. In *Radiance*, only visible radiation is considered, but units of radiance and irradiance are still used; they are divided into separate components for the red, green, and blue spectral ranges. (Compare to *illuminance.*)

irradiance gradient The directional derivative of *irradiance* at a surface point. In *Radiance*, this quantity is estimated for changes in *indirect irradiance* as a function of surface rotation and translation, and this is used to improve the accuracy of interpolated indirect irradiance values.

isolux contour A line corresponding to equal *illuminance* values on a surface.

isotropic Equal in all directions. Isotropic scattering occurs when light is scattered equally over 4π steradians. *Isotropic reflection*, in contrast, usually refers to a surface that may have a directional preference, but one that does not depend on the *azimuth* of the incident vector.

jittered sampling A *stochastic* process in which values are sampled uniformly over a rectilinear subspace. For example, a ray may be sampled at a random location on a square pixel by choosing random, independent x and y offsets.

Lambertian Ideal diffuse reflection, in which the luminance (or radiance) reradiated by a surface is identical in all directions. Very few surfaces exhibit this behavior, but some come close and many have a component that is approximately Lambertian, which can be used to accelerate interreflection calculations.

light source A surface that originates light in a scene. In *Radiance*, light sources are identified by their *material* type and geometry. In some cases, *virtual light sources* are created when reflecting geometry is present in a scene, and these sources are used to direct rays back to the original light sources. (See Chapter 11 for details.)

lighting visualization The creation of images, plots, and graphics for the purpose of understanding lighting in a design space. (See *physically based rendering.*)

local illumination The interaction of light with a surface, disregarding the process by which light arrives at the surface.

lumens A *photometric unit* related to the photopic stimulus of the human fovea. It is computed by convolving the *photopic response* function with the *spectral power distribution* function. Normalization is defined so that the conversion from watts to lumens is 1/683 at the peak sensitivity wavelength of 555 nanometers. (See Chapter 10 for details.)

luminaire A light fixture, including any and all lamps, ballasts, reflectors, lenses, baffles, and so on.

luminance The visible light passing through a point in a certain direction, expressed in SI units of lumens per steradian (*candelas*) per square meter, or *nits*. (Compare to *radiance*.)

luminance meter A photometric device for measuring *luminance*.

luminous flux The visible light passing through an area, measured in SI units of *lux*.

lux Shorthand for *lumens* per square meter. (See *illuminance*.)

material The substance from which an object is made. In the context of *Radiance*, the characteristics of a surface that describe its interaction with light.

material description A *Radiance scene description* fragment that defines a particular material's properties, including its type, parameters, and any modifiers such as textures, patterns, and mixtures.

memory overhead The memory (RAM) required for a particular object or operation above what is already in use by a process.

memory sharing On a *multiprocessing* system, memory sharing means that more than one processor is accessing the same RAM in parallel, thereby avoiding duplicate memory requirements.

mesh See *tessellated surface*.

metafile An intermediate, device-independent binary file that contains 2D vector graphics, used for plotting to various supported output devices. (See the *metafile (5)* manual page on the CD-ROM.)

mirror direction A reflected direction that lies in the plane defined by the incident vector and the surface normal, at an equal but opposite angle to the incident direction.

mist A *Radiance primitive* type for *participating media*.

mixture A category of *Radiance primitives* that provides for mixing two different *patterns, textures, materials,* or mixtures.

modifier A *Radiance primitive* whose purpose is to modify another *Radiance* primitive. Specifically, any primitive that does not specify geometry may be used to modify any other primitive.

Monte Carlo Random (i.e., *stochastic*) sampling in the context of an integration or averaging problem. *Monte Carlo inversion* is the process of determining the appropriate random variable for a desired weighting function so that the final sample weights are equal. In the absence of better information or techniques, this results in the most efficient sampling pattern.

multiprocessing The application of multiple processors (CPUs) to the same problem, running in parallel. Ideally, this would result in a linear speedup proportional to the number of processors, but in general, the improvement is somewhat less than this because of overhead, communication delays, and data access contention.

nadir Straight down, usually used for reference in the output of a downward-facing *luminaire*.

nanometer The usual unit of measurement for the wavelength of visible radiation, equal to 10^{-9} meters. Often abbreviated as *nm*.

network A collection of computers connected by wires, optical cables, and/or microwaves. Generally, a small number of machines are connected together on a *local area network* at a single site, which talks via a *gateway machine* to the *global network* (i.e., the *Internet*).

network file system (NFS) A network file access protocol that allows remote disks to appear and act as local disks on a system. File *servers* provide disk access to file *clients.*

network lock manager A service that guarantees file consistency when the same file is accessed by multiple processes over a network. This is a standard part of the *network file system* on most UNIX implementations, but some lock managers do not work efficiently and others do not even operate correctly. The lock manager is a critical part of the parallel processing algorithms in *Radiance.* (See Chapter 15 for details.)

nits Shorthand for candelas per square meter. (See *luminance.*)

normal vector A unit vector. (See *surface normal.*)

NURBS Acronym for Non-Uniform Rational *B-Spline*, a popular class of rational cubic patches used widely for the *geometric modeling* of smooth, curved surfaces.

octree A data structure that subdivides space recursively into eight cubes, each of which may be subdivided into eight subcubes, and so on. An *octree file* is a special *Radiance* binary format that contains this data structure, created by **oconv** to speed ray intersection tests on the scene. A *frozen octree file* contains all of the relevant scene information as well, providing for quick loading and easy portability. (See the CD-ROM section on File Formats for details.)

overture calculation An initial low-resolution pass over an image to collect *indirect irradiance* values into an *ambient file* for later high-resolution rendering. This generally improves the quality of the final results at a modest expense.

panorama See *cylindrical perspective.*

parallel projection A view type in which the distance from the center of the image is proportional to the distance from the ray starting at the view point and continuing in the view direction. Since all imaging rays are parallel, this projection does not exhibit the foreshortening of a normal perspective view.

parallel rendering The simultaneous rendering of a single picture or animated sequence on multiple processors (CPUs). (See *multiprocessing.*)

parallelepiped A right angle, rectangular prism. That is, a closed, convex, six-sided geometric solid, all of whose faces are rectangles.

parametric surface A 3D surface described by a vector function of two independent variables, each typically running from 0 to 1.

participating medium A solid, liquid, gas, or colloid that affects the transport of light through its volume. Examples include glass, water, wine, milk, fog, and smoke. Clear air is also a participating medium, but one that has an effect only over great distances.

pattern A variation in surface color, which can be described in *Radiance* as a procedure, a picture or tabulated data.

penumbra The partial shadow between the unshadowed region and the *umbra*, or fully shadowed region.

Perlin noise A random function with a strong fundamental frequency and few harmonics, first introduced by Ken Perlin [Per85]. In *Radiance*, the noise3(*x*,*y*,*z*) function returns values between −1 and 1 with an autocorrelation distance of 1, and is defined over all space. (Contrast with *fractal noise*. See Chapter 4 for examples.)

perspective projection See *linear perspective projection*, *angular fisheye perspective*, *cylindrical perspective*, and *hemispherical fisheye perspective*.

Phong shading A simple model for *rough specular* reflection (also known as *directional-diffuse*), computed by raising the cosine of the angle between the half-vector and the surface normal to a power. (The half-vector bisects the incident and reflected directions.)

Phong smoothing The interpolation of surface normals on a *tessellated surface* to simulate the appearance of a smoothly curved object during rendering.

photometer A device for measuring visible radiation. Typically divided into two categories: *illuminance meters* and *luminance meters*.

photometric A quantity related to the human *photopic response* to visible radiation. Examples of photometric units are *lumens* and *candelas*. Examples of photometric quantities are *luminance* and *illuminance*.

photometric data The measured *candlepower distribution* of a *luminaire*.

photometry The measurement of visible radiation.

photopic response The average spectral sensitivity of the human cone system to radiation. Sensitivity begins near the far red wavelength of 780 nanometers, growing gradually to peak at about 555 nanometers, then sloping gradually down into the ultraviolet at 350 nanometers. The standard photopic response function is written as $v(\lambda)$. (See the section titled Supplemental Information at the end of Chapter 10 for a plot of this function.)

photorealistic rendering A term used to describe rendering that *appears* as real as a photograph.

physically based rendering A rendering technique that adheres to the physics of light transport, producing images that are accurate predictions of the appearance of a design space.

picture file A *Radiance* floating-point color image, which usually contains physical *radiance* values useful for lighting analysis. (See the CD-ROM section on File Formats for details.)

pipe In UNIX, a "first-in, first-out" (FIFO) interprocess communication channel, typically used to pass the standard output of one command into the standard input of another command running simultaneously. Sometimes, processes may open their own pipes to other commands they start.

pipeline Multiple UNIX commands connected together via *pipes*.

pixel Short for *picture element*. The smallest measured, calculated, or displayed point in an image.

planar Lying in a plane. Completely flat.

polar angle The angle between the *surface normal* and the given vector direction. (Compate to *altitude*.)

polygon An N-sided planar surface with a finite area. A *convex polygon* has no interior angles greater than 180 degrees.

primitive An element in a *Radiance scene description*, which consists of a modifier, type, identifier, and zero or more parameters. (See the *Radiance* reference manual on the CD-ROM for syntax and semantics.)

prism A polygon extruded into the third dimension. If the extrusion vector parallels the surface normal, then the resulting solid is called a *right prism*. (See the **genprism** manual page for details.)

process A running program on a system.

processor A computational unit. See *CPU*.

projected hemisphere A half-sphere, projected in parallel onto the splitting plane along the *surface normal* such that each differential area corresponds to the original area times the cosine of the *polar angle*. A uniform sampling of *luminance* over the projected hemisphere times π (the area of the unit circule) equals *illuminance*. The same relation holds for *radiance* and *irradiance*.

radiance The radiation passing through a point in a specific direction, expressed in SI units of watts per steradian per square meter. In the *Radiance* system, only visible radiation is considered, but units of radiance and irradiance are still used, which are divided into separate components for the red, green, and blue spectral ranges. (Compare to *luminance*.)

radiometric A quantity related to radiation, usually measured in terms of power or power/wavelength. Examples of radiometric units are *watts* and *watts/steradian*. Exapmples of radiometric quantities are *radiance* and *irradiance*.

radiosity A physical quantity equal to the *radiant exitance* of a *Lambertian* surface. (See also *radiosity method*.)

radiosity method A formulation of the *global illumination* problem based on the solution of *radiosity* for a finite number of points in a 3D scene description. Also called *finite element flux transfer*.

RAM Random access memory, usually referred to simply as *memory*.

ray tracing A method based on following one-dimensional rays, where each ray is defined by an origin point and a vector direction. In a rendering algorithm, each ray is followed until it intersects a visible surface, where new rays may be spawned in a *recursive* process. In *light-forwards ray tracing*, light is followed from the light sources to the final measurement areas. In *light-backwards ray tracing* (as in *Radiance*), each view ray is traced from the point of measurement to the contributing light sources. In *bidirectional ray tracing*, light is traced both from the measurement points and from the light sources, meeting somewhere in between.

recursion A function that calls a simpler version of itself to arrive at a solution. For example, the factorial function ($n!$) can be defined recursively as ($n(n-1)!$), where ($0!$) is defined as equal to 1. If a function calls another function that calls back the original function again, it is called *mutual recursion*; most ray-tracing programs fall into this general category.

reflectance The ratio of the light leaving a surface to the light striking a surface. The general reflectance function is called the *BRDF.* The averaged total reflection function is called the *hemispherical reflectance.* This may be a function of wavelength (i.e., the *spectral reflectance*) or may be averaged over the visible spectrum using the *photometric response* function.

refraction The bending of light as it enters a *dielectric* medium at a nonzero *polar angle.* (See also *index of refraction.*)

refractive index See *index of refraction.*

rendering The process of creating a 2D image from a 3D representation. Also, the term given to the resulting *synthetic image.*

resolution The density of discrete samples in a given region, especially the total number of pixels in an image.

RGB color Red, green, blue representation of color. Since there is no defined standard for RGB in computer graphics, *Radiance* defines its own canonical *display primaries,* which can be found in the source header file *src/common/color.h.*

right-hand rule If the right hand points in the direction of the first vector (i.e., the *x*-axis) and the fingers curl in the direction of the second vector (i.e., the *y*-axis), the thumb points in the direction of the third vector (i.e., the *z*-axis). (See also *Cartesian coordinate system.*)

roughness The root mean squared (RMS) microfacet slope of a Gaussian surface. This is equal to the standard deviation of the surface height over the autocorrelation distance of this deviation. In the anisotropic material model used in *Radiance,* this quantity may be given a directional component.

rough specular A *directional-diffuse* component caused by specular (surface interface) reflection or transmission from a rough surface.

run-length encoding A simple data-stream compression method whereby repeated data values (runs) may be given as the value and its count. This technique is used to reduce the size of *Radiance picture files.*

sampling The process of determining an average or integral value by evaluating a function at one or more positions. (See *Monte Carlo.*)

scattering coefficient The fraction of light scattered per unit distance in a participating medium, given in SI units as a fraction per meter.

scene description An ASCII data stream that defines the surfaces, materials, patterns, and textures of a *Radiance* model. (See the *Radiance Reference Manual* and the section on File Formats on the CD-ROM for format specifications.)

scotopic response The average spectral sensitivity of the human rod system, which dominates vision in dark environments. Compared to the cones, with their *photopic response* function, the rods are more sensitive to bluer (shorter) wavelengths. *Scotopic* lumens are defined in a similar fashion to standard photopic *lumens,* with the same conversion to 1/683 lumens/watt at 555 nanometers. However, since 555 is not the peak sensitivity wavelength for rods, the scotopic peak is actually much larger than 1/683. It is closer to 1/329 at 505 nm.

scripting Command-level programming. A sequence of commands in a *shell*-executable file is called a *script*. Sometimes the execution of the commands contained in the script requires other source files, which are considered to be part of the same overall script. (See Chapter 4 for examples.)

secondary light source A surface through which or by which large quantities of light are directed. In *Radiance*, secondary light sources are often made into *impostors* using the *illum* primitive type. (See Chapter 13 for details.)

server A program or process that provides system resources to *clients* executing locally or on remote systems over a network.

shadow ray A ray sent toward a light source to determine whether a point is in shadow. If the ray intersects some other surface between the origin (test) point and the light source, then it is (at least partially) in shadow. To improve shadow and *penumbra* accuracy, the light source may be subdivided and each sample point may be *jittered*. (See Chapter 11 for details.)

shadow testing The process of determining whether points are in shadow or not.

shell A command interpreter, such as the Bourne shell or the C-shell. The job of the shell is to interpret a user's *command line* input or the commands read from a *shell script*. (See also *scripting*.)

SI units Standard International units. A specific recommended set of metric units for physical quantities such as length, volume, temperature, mass, force, power, energy, and *luminous flux*.

sky distribution The *luminance* or *radiance* arriving at a specific point on the earth's surface at a specific date and time as a function of *altitude* and *azimuth*. (See *CIE standard sky distribution*.)

solid A region of 3D space, usually closed. (Compare to *surface*.)

solid angle A solid slice of space starting from a point and extending to infinity in a region of directions that can be indicated by an area on the unit sphere. The size of this area is a measure of the overall solid angle, which is given in *steradians*.

source-γ A *Radiance* primitive describing an infinitely distant light source, described by a *direction vector* and a *solid angle*.

spectral power distribution The density of radiative energy as a function of wavelength, usually over the visible spectrum. Depending on the context, this may be given in watts per nanometer or watts per square meter per nanometer or watts per steradian per square meter per nanometer.

spectrophotometer A reflectance meter that partitions the visible spectrum into sections and measures the reflectance in each section separately.

spectrum A continuum or sequence, such as the spectrum of visible radiation.

specular Pertaining to highly directional reflection or transmission. Specular reflection is usually centered about the *mirror direction*. Specular transmission may be *refracted* in a new direction or unperturbed. Specular interactions usually take place at the surface interface, as opposed to the interior of an object.

specularity The amount of light reflected (or transmitted) by *specular* mechanisms.

sphere A round shell defined by a center point and a surface that lies at a constant distance from this center.

spline A sequence of curves, usually cubic polynomials, joined to ensure $C^{(2)}$ continuity. This term is sometimes loosely applied to any set of cubic curves.

steradian The common unit used to measure *solid angle*, equal to a unit area cut in the surface of the unit sphere. Since the surface area of the unit sphere is 4π, the maximum solid angle is 4π steradians.

stochastic A stochastic method observes random occurrences (samples) generated by some probability distribution function. In practice, digital computers usually do not model ideal stochastic processes, since most random-number generators actually generate a fixed sequence of values, which may even repeat at some point. (Hence, they are dubbed *pseudo–random number* generators.) Nevertheless, they do a sufficient job for most *Monte Carlo* simulation purposes; Monte Carlo is another term for stochastic modeling. (Compare to *deterministic.*)

storage complexity The limiting relationship of storage space (memory and disk) requirements to the number of objects. It is often given in the form of "big O" notation, which means "on the order of." For example, an algorithm that has $O(N^3)$ storage complexity requires storage space proportional to the cube of the number of objects as N goes to infinity. (See also *computational complexity.*)

stratified sampling The subdivision of a sample space into discrete domains for separate (stochastic) sampling. This method improves convergence when there is sufficient coherence in the sampled function.

STV (small target visibility) STV is the weighted average of visibility for a particular arrangement of view targets on a roadway. (See Chapter 7 for details.)

supersampling Sending multiple samples to arrive at an average value for a particular area, such as a *pixel.* The samples may be regularly spaced, *jittered,* or placed by some other *stochastic process.*

surface A 2D region in 3D space. (Technically, a surface may reside in any space with two or more dimensions, but in the context of computer graphics, it is almost always three.) In *Radiance,* surfaces are modeled with *cones, spheres,* and *polygons.*

surface normal A *normal vector* that is perpendicular to the tangent plane of a surface. If the surface is *planar,* the surface normal is constant. If the surface is curved, the normal varies over the surface. A *texture* is a perturbation added to the surface normal. A *tessellated surface* may be smoothed by interpolating normals, which is called *Phong smoothing.*

surface of revolution A surface defined by a 2D curve spun around a coplanar axis. (See the **genrev** manual page on the CD-ROM for details.)

synthetic image A 2D image generated from a computer-modeled environment in a rendering process analogous to photography. See *rendering.*

tessellated surface A surface mesh composed of many connected planar facets, usually used as an approximation to a continuous curved surface. This approximation may be improved during rendering using *Phong smoothing.* (See the **gensurf** manual page on the CD-ROM for details.)

texture A perturbing function added to a *surface normal* to yield the appearance of a macroscopically rough surface. The actual surface still adheres to the original geometry, so silhouettes will not have the correct appearance, self-shadowing is neglected, and some reflections may not intersect the surface properly. Despite these shortcomings, this approximation usually works very well.

transform Short for *transformation.* A sequence of translations (movements), scalings, and rotations applied to an object or set of objects. In *Radiance,* only regular transformations are allowed, since skewing and anisotropic scaling would fundamentally change the nature of certain surface primitives. World coordinate unit changes are implemented as simple scaling transforms.

translator (CAD, image) A program that converts one data representation into another. *Radiance* includes a few different geometric model (i.e., CAD) translators, and quite a few image translators. Image translators usually translate both to and from *Radiance* picture format, but CAD translators usually only import data into *Radiance.* Sometimes also called a converter.

transmission coefficient The fraction of light that is passed per unit length. This coefficient is given as part of a *dielectric* primitive's arguments, and is equal to 1 minus the *absorption coefficient.*

transmissivity The fraction of light that passes through the interior of a glass pane at normal incidence. This does not consider light lost to reflection by the front or back surface, or multiple internal reflections. From the transmissivity and the *index of refraction,* total transmittance and reflectance can be computed for any incident angle via a simple formula. (See the CD-ROM section on materials for details.)

transmittance The total light transmitted by a system, usually given for normal incidence. This is the quantity most easily measured, although it is not the most convenient to work with mathematically. (See Section 4.1.2, Calc and Recalc, in Chapter 4 for information on computing *transmissivity* from transmittance.

umbra The region in complete shadow, where no portion of the light source is visible. (Compare to *penumbra.*)

$\gamma(\lambda)$ See *phototopic response.*

vector A direction and magnitude, specified in Cartesian coordinates as three displacements, one for each axis.

veiling luminance Light scattered in the lens of the eye that makes it difficult to see areas immediately surrounding bright sources. (See *glare,* and the **pcond** manual page on the CD-ROM.)

view ray A primary ray shot from the view point or measurement origin into the scene to determine the value of a pixel or to evaluate radiance.

virtual light source An imaginary light source corresponding to a reflection or redirection of a real light source in a mirror or prism. (See Chapter 11 for details.)

void identifier The word *void* is a special identifier used to indicate no *modifier* for this *primitive.*

walk-through A camera moving through a static scene. See *animation.*

watt The power equal to one joule/second. One horsepower equals 746 watts.

wavelength The longitudinal distance from one peak to another on a wave form. For light, this corresponds to the speed of light $(c \approx 10^8 \text{ meters/second})$ divided by the radiation frequency. The visible spectrum begins in the infrared at 780 nanometers and continues into the ultraviolet at 350 nanometers.

workplane An imaginary horizontal surface situated at the nominal working height in an interior space.

world coordinates The coordinate system used for defining points and distances in a *scene description* file. It is defined by an origin and three perpendicular coordinate axes. (The third is determined automatically by the first two, using the *right-hand rule.*) There is no default unit for world coordinates in *Radiance,* though quantities of illumination are given in SI units. Coordinate conversions are accomplished with the **xform** command.

worm A 3D curve of varying thickness, represented by **genworm** as a sequence of cones joined by spheres. (See the **genworm** maual page on the CD-ROM for details.)

z-buffer file An output file from **rpict** indicating the distance traveled by each *view ray* in a rendered picture. This information is used by **pinterp** to efficiently interpolate frames in *walk-through animations.* (See the CD-ROM section on File Formats for details.)

Index

About the Authors

Greg Ward Larson

Greg Ward Larson is a member of the technical staff in the engineering division of Silicon Graphics. Before that he was a staff scientist at the Lawrence Berkeley National Laboratory. He graduated with an A.B. in physics in 1983 from the University of California at Berkeley and earned his master's in computer science from San Francisco State University in 1985. His professional interests include digital photography and image standards, physically based rendering, global and local illumination, luminaire simulation, electronic data standards, and lighting-related energy and environmental conservation issues. Ward Larson has published numerous papers in computer graphics and illumination engineering. He wrote *Radiance* while at LBNL in California, and PFL in Switzerland.

Rob Shakespeare

Rob Shakespeare is a professional lighting designer, associate professor at the Department of Theatre and Drama of Indiana University, and director of the Indiana University Theatre Computer Visualization Center. He has lighted over 150 stage productions, with recent work including the Utah Shakespearean Festival and *Carmen* at the Lyric Theatre in Hong Kong. His architectural lighting projects have included Times Square; the Jin Jaing Hotel in Shanghai; the Shangri-la Hotel and Convention Center in Dalian, China; the Hong Kong Marriot Atrium; the Harbour-Gateway buildings; and Tsing Ma Bridge in Hong Kong. Shakespeare uses *Radiance* and other lighting visualization software as part of his design process and is developing interface systems to advance the use of these tools. Current projects include linking databases derived from lighting/computer visualization interactions directly to the technology of complex lighting control environments, such as theaters and theme parks. His professional affiliations include the Illuminating Engineering Society of North America, the International Association of Lighting Designers, and the United States Institute for Theatre Technology.

About the CD-ROM

The CD-ROM includes supplemental information that is organized to parallel the book chapters with input files, pictures, animations, and reference material. It is best accessed with a Web browser such as Netscape Navigator and appropriate helper applications such as Adobe Acrobat Reader and an MPEG animation player. The CD-ROM also contains source code and scripts for building *Radiance* 3.1 on nearly any UNIX platform, plus online documentation, notes, technical papers, and contributed models and libraries. Its contents are organized using HTML for convenient access, and it contains the important reference materials listed here:

The *Radiance* Reference Manual is the essential guide to the input language and primitives used in scene description. This document is available on the CD-ROM as HTML and PDF (Acrobat format) and should probably be printed out as a handy compendium. (It is also provided in the main distribution as PostScript and troff input.)

***Radiance* Program Manual Pages** contains the UNIX manual pages for all documented *Radiance* programs, with a summary sheet of program names and applications. It is also available as HTML and PDF.

***Radiance* File Formats** gives detailed descriptions of the binary and ASCII formats used by *Radiance*, with pointers to library functions for reading and writing them, where appropriate. This chapter contains important details on the input formats as well and is valuable to readers creating their own patterns and procedures. It is provided in PDF only.

The Behavior of Materials in *Radiance* describes the mathematical behavior of various materials, for those who need to know. It is provided in PDF on the CD-ROM, and in the main distribution as PostScript and troff input.

Source Tree Roadmap is a guide to the source code, showing how the source tree is organized and where each program is built. It is provided in PDF only.

Accessing the CD-ROM

The CD-ROM should be accessible on any system, including UNIX, PC-compatible and Macintosh operating systems. Simply insert the included disk in your CD-ROM drive, then use your favorite Web browser to open *index.html* or *book/index.html*. The first page is a copy of the main page for the *Radiance* Website, and the second page is an index of supplementary material for this book, arranged to parallel the Table of Contents. These two pages are interlinked, so it does not really matter which one you access first.

Radiance Main Page

From the main CD-ROM page, *index.html*, you can access a short description of *Radiance* by following the "What Is?" link, which is also linked to the book Table of Contents. The "*Radiance* Reference Materials" link takes you to a well-stocked library of technical papers, documents, manual pages, seminar materials, and notes. From the main page, the "*Radiance* Gallery" link takes you to a collection of image files and animations produced by various *Radiance* users, showing some of what the software can do. Finally, the main page links to a list of Web sites featuring *Radiance*, and to a download page for the software itself.

Rendering with Radiance Table of Contents Page

From the TOC page, *book/index.html*, you can quickly access material referred to in this book by looking up the book chapter and section, and scanning for appropriate links. For example, to see screen versions of the color plates referred to in

Chapter 1, click on "CHAPTER 1" in the "Short Contents" section to get to the detailed listing of the first chapter, then click on the "color plates" link for Section 1.1.2.

Some links go directly to HTML or PDF versions of the material, such as the Glossary and the Bibliography. This was done for convenient access and cross-linking. In particular, the *Radiance* Reference Manual is fully indexed HTML, and clicking on any of the Reference Manual links in the TOC brings up that part of the reference manual in a separate browser window. This is an important aid to learning the software, and we recommend that you keep this page handy as you work through the tutorial chapters in Part I. (A printed hardcopy also works.)

Displaying *Radiance* Pictures from a Browser

Some links accessed from the TOC page may point to a *Radiance* picture in *.pic* format. To display such an image, you will need to use the *Radiance* **ximage** program. Assuming you have followed the directions in the next section on Software Installation, you can link your browser to this program by setting it up as a helper application. The figure on page 662 shows an example dialog box, accessed from the "Options->General Preferences" menu, in which we have informed Netscape how to handle a *Radiance* picture file.

Even if you do not set up ximage as a helper application, you can load the linked picture onto your hard disk and run ximage manually, or access the CD-ROM file directly.

Radiance System Requirements

To use *Radiance*, you need a machine running some version of UNIX, though the underlying hardware may be Macintosh or PC-compatible. (For those readers who are unaware, there are inexpensive versions of *Linux* for both platforms.) To build the system, you will also need a working C compiler and the X11 Xlib client libraries and header files. Some systems do not bundle the compiler and library software, so we have provided precompiled executables for Sun and Silicon Graphics computers that should work for these systems.

The memory and disk requirements depend primarily on the complexity of the models you are using. At a minimum, we recommend at least 32MB of RAM and 50MB of free disk space. Processor speed is of course important, but there is no

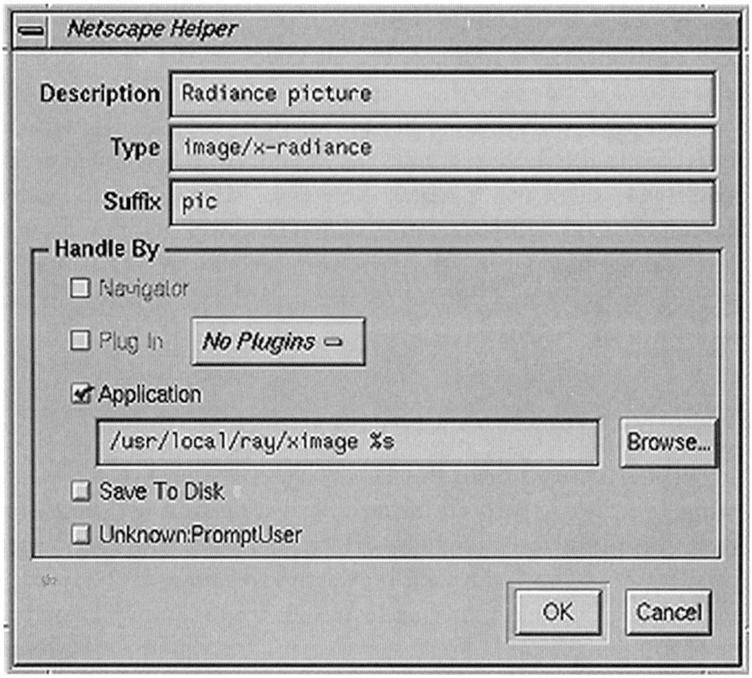

A Netscape helper application dialog window with appropriate settings for passing a *Radiance* picture to the ximage program.

minimum requirement. The graphics hardware should support at least 8 bitplanes (256 colors), with 24 bitplanes preferred. If you have only a grayscale monitor, everything will still work, but the display may be disappointing.

If you wish to model complex environments (25,000 surfaces or more), we recommend at least 64MB of RAM, since memory requirements grow linearly with model size, and virtual memory thrashing can be a problem if there is not enough RAM.

Software Installation

To access the software installation page, simply click on "*Radiance* Software" from the main page, where you will find the LBNL license agreement (reprinted below, under License). Scroll down to the "Main Distribution" heading, and download the software archive as indicated. Save the file on a disk partition with at least 7MB of free space, adding a "*.tar.Z*" suffix. Then, unpack the file using the following UNIX command:

```
% zcat rad3R1p6.tar.Z | tar xf -
```

Be sure that you are in a directory with at least 40MB of free space, and that there is no subdirectory named *ray* there, since that is what this command will create. Once you have unpacked the distribution, change directory to *ray* and execute:

```
% makeall install
```

This script will ask you several questions about your system and preferences, which you should answer to the best of your knowledge. When it is through, it will present you with an **rmake** script, which defines the compiler options and so forth that it needs for your machine. You may modify this script on subsequent runs of **makeall** if you encounter problems or wish to try different compilers or optimization flags. Once you accept the rmake script, makeall runs through each of the source directories, executing `rmake install` in each to build and install the various *Radiance* programs.

Watch the screen carefully for "fatal" compile errors, which will not stop the installation process, but may leave your executable collection incomplete. In general, compiler warnings can be safely ignored, and only fatal errors are significant. If you encounter problems you cannot remedy yourself, first check the official *Radiance* ftp site, *radsite.lbl.gov,* for recent patches, then send email to *radiance@radsite.lbl.gov* for help.

If you have a Sun or Silicon Graphics machine, you can download the precompiled executables from the "*Radiance* Software" page if you lack a C compiler or the installation process fails for some other reason. (It is still a good idea to try running makeall, since it will install the library files you will need in addition to the program binaries.) To unpack the binaries for your machine, simply click on the indicated link, and unpack the resulting file as described above using **zcat** and **tar**. You should then move the unpacked directory to an appropriate location on your system, such as */usr/local/bin* or */usr/local/ray.*

Read the file in the main *ray* directory named *README* for hints on how to set up your UNIX shell environment and how to get started. If you are impatient to try out the software, you can skip to the Scene 0 Tutorial section of Chapter 1, but you might want to read some of the introductory material first.

License